HISTORY OF
MEDIÆVAL
PHILOSOPHY

BY
MAURICE DE WULF
Professor of Philosophy at Louvain and Harvard Universities;
Doctor of Philosophy and Letters; Doctor of Laws; Member of
the Royal Academy of Belgium.

TRANSLATED BY
ERNEST C. MESSENGER, Ph.D.
Lecturer in Logic and Cosmology at St. Edmund's College, Ware.

VOL. I
FROM THE BEGINNINGS TO ALBERT THE GREAT.

7809

LONGMANS, GREEN AND CO. LTD.
39 PATERNOSTER ROW, LONDON, E.C.4
NEW YORK, TORONTO
BOMBAY, CALCUTTA AND MADRAS
1926

Nihil obstat

INNOCENTIUS APAP, S.Th.M., O.P.
Censor deputatus

Imprimatur

EDM. CAN. SURMONT
Vic. Gen

WESTMONASTERII
die 2° Novembris 1925

Made in Great Britain

AUTHOR'S PREFACE TO THE FIFTH FRENCH EDITION

THE researches of the past twenty-five years on the philosophy of the Middle Ages have been followed up with such activity in these latter years that any attempt at co-ordinating the results acquired makes one feel dizzy. So many new personalities have come to light, there are so many cross-currents of ideas, and so many facts are intertwined, that a person bold enough to write a History of Mediæval Philosophy in the West at the present time might well be accused of temerity.

A long time must pass before we shall be in possession of knowledge concerning the productions of the Middle Ages comparable to that for which we are indebted to the historians of Greek philosophy. In the latter case the period of the discovery of texts is closed, but in the former it is in full swing. It is accordingly inevitable that endeavours at a historical synthesis like that which we here attempt, must be of a provisional character. They resemble the planting on new land of a crop which is destined to be sacrificed, but which will fecundate the soil and prepare the way for the harvests of the future.

It will surprise no one that this new edition, separated from the preceding by a number of years by reason of the War, makes use of much new material, and that in many of its parts it has undergone a transformation. It is impossible to enumerate these additions and modifications, for the whole work has been affected.

At the same time, we hasten to point out that these transformations leave intact the general framework of the preceding editions. The two great principles in the light of which we have since 1900 sought a synthetic interpretation of philosophic facts, seem to us to be more necessary than ever, and they dominate the multitude of facts which erudition is unceasingly accumulating as high peaks do a massive mountain.

The first of these principles, namely, that there were in the West in the Middle Ages systems of philosophy distinct from theology, is no longer questioned by anyone who has come into direct contact with mediæval philosophy.

The second, namely, the scholasticism is not the whole of mediæval philosophy, but the best part of it, that it represents the collective inheritance of the majority of the thinkers of the West, and that it had to encounter fierce opposition throughout the centuries,—this second thesis, while gaining numerous adherents, is still disputed, and we do not intend in this place to undertake to justify it.

To those who reject it because their attention is turned to the differential aspects presented by the mediæval systems of philosophy, we would say that in our opinion, the study of these aspects derives its full value and presents all its fruits only when associated with the study of the common doctrines, and is constantly made clearer when viewed in the light of the latter.

On the other hand, we are glad to note that a parallel study of the civilization of the thirteenth century—the culminating point of the Middle Ages—confirms in a remarkable and unexpected way the correctness of our method of interpretation. In all the spheres of mental life—art, religion, customs and politics—the Middle Ages was governed by collective ideals and great cosmopolitan forces which acted in a similar fashion on the various countries of Western Europe.

The study of the philosophic movements in their surroundings, and in their relations of interdependence with other factors of civilization, is destined to throw a new light on the systems of thought the temporal connections of which have not hitherto been thoroughly understood. We have followed this path, not without some hesitation, for to do so with complete assurance the collaboration of the historians of the Middle Ages would be indispensable. In other words, we are aware of the *lacunæ* which might be pointed out in our work from this point of view.

As in the preceding editions, our attention has been devoted above all to theories and systems.

In our exposition of these, as in the study of their developments, we shall take as our basis the internal logic of a man's thought rather than his intentions. Philosophy is full of examples of thinkers who by their express declarations endeavour to escape the consequences to which the dialectical pressure of their ideas would lead them. Thus all the monists of the

Middle Ages wished to safeguard the co-existence of the One and the Many, and the boldest theologians desired to respect Catholic dogma.

But the intention, revealing as it does temperament and personality, is one thing, and doctrine, the more or less vigorous product of thought, is another. The content of a doctrine is independent of the subjective preoccupations which have inspired it. At all times we find men who err in good faith and who are led by the best of motives to the worst of doctrines. We shall have occasion to make numerous applications of this important principle of exegesis.

The reader will permit us to point out some other modifications introduced in the present edition. The historical introduction devoted to Greek philosophy has been suppressed in order to bring out into more complete relief the philosophy of the Middle Ages. But at the same time it would not have been wise to exclude from a work of this nature all references to the great philosophers of Antiquity, for on the one hand the philosophers of the Middle Ages constantly appealed to them, and indeed were the continuers of the ancient tradition, and on the other hand, the divergent expositions which have been given by modern historians of Greek and patristic philosophy on many important doctrines must be dealt with here and now, failing which all comparison with the corresponding doctrines of the Middle Ages would be sterile. Hence the reader will find scattered up and down the work partial data concerning the philosophies of Plato, Aristotle, the Stoics, neo-Platonists, St. Augustine, and pseudo-Dionysius—to quote only the chief inspirers of mediæval thought.

Similar considerations have induced us to reduce to an indispensable minimum the treatment of the oriental philosophical systems of Byzantium, Africa, and Mohammedan Spain. We are concerned with these vast movements of ideas, so little known up to the present, only in so far as they have penetrated into Western philosophy.

Whole departments of the philosophic history of the Middle Ages depend upon learned research, as for instance all that concerns the life and chronological order of the writings of a philosopher. Important work has been done and is still in progress, of which we have endeavoured to make the best use, without pretending that we have been able to acquaint ourselves fully with the productions of these latter years.

The history of the Latin translations of Greek and Arabian works presents a typical example of the difficulties which face any one who in the present state of knowledge undertakes a general exposition of this subject. Our good friend, Mgr. A. Pelzer, one of the admitted authorities on the philosophic history of the Middle Ages, and whose first-class researches have rendered invaluable services to the subject in question, has been good enough to revise the paragraphs relating to this difficult subject. We beg him to accept this expression of our immense gratitude.

A selected bibliography, which does not pretend to be exhaustive, is appended to each of the various chapters or paragraph sections. It should be taken together with the bibliographical indications in the notes, which for the sake of brevity are not repeated. We have above all aimed at mentioning the works which have appeared since 1915, i.e., since the last edition of Ueberweg-Baumgartner (*Grundriss der Geschichte der Philosophie, Die Mittlere oder die patristische und scholastische Zeit*, Berlin), the documentation of which it is unnecessary to repeat.

A synthetic work on the history of mediæval philosophy ought to be accompanied by a collection of texts, following step by step the divisions adopted: we hope to publish this in the near future.

M. DE WULF.

LOUVAIN,
   1st June, 1924.

TRANSLATOR'S NOTE

The second French edition of this work appeared in 1905, and an English translation, by Dr. Coffey, of Maynooth, was published in 1909. Since that date our knowledge of mediæval philosophy has been considerably extended, and accordingly Professor De Wulf has recast the whole work. This new English version is based upon the fifth French edition, which appeared in 1924 and 1925. I have not hesitated to adopt the felicitous renderings of Dr. Coffey wherever possible. An Index will be found at the end of each volume.

WARE,   E. C. MESSENGER.
   1st Oct., 1925.

CONTENTS

CONTENTS

CONTENTS

CONTENTS

ART. III.—THE OLDER SCHOLASTICISM IN THE THIRTEENTH
CENTURY (PRE-THOMIST SCHOLASTICISM).

§ 1.—*Augustinism, or the Older Scholasticism.*

§ 2.—*William of Auvergne and his Contemporaries.*

§ 3.—*Alexander of Hales and John de la Rochelle.*

§ 4.—*Robert Grosseteste and the Franciscan School of Oxford.*

§ 5.—*The anonymous author of the " Summa Philosophiæ."*

§ 6.—*St. Bonaventure.*

§ 7.—*Matthew of Aquasparta and John Peckham.*

CONTENTS

PAGE

ERRATA

Page 144, line 8	-	-	For Doscelin, read Roscelin.
,, 146, line 12	-	-	,, 1910, read 1010.
,, 159, footnote 4		-	,, *ex*, read *et*.
,, 416, 2nd col., line 33			,, NMende, read Mende.
Passim	- - -	-	,, Haureau, read Hauréau.

INTRODUCTION

§ I—*General Notions.*

1. Contempt for mediæval philosophy.—Contempt for the Middle Ages first began with the humanists of the fifteenth century. Fascinated as they were by classical antiquity, they regarded the centuries dividing them from the Greeks and Romans as a period of barbarism. The very term "Middle" Ages, that is, the mean or intermediate period between antiquity and their own time, had a belittling significance.[1] All the features of mediæval civilization were depreciated : its architecture was condemned as *Gothic*, a term which for the Italian classicists of the sixteenth century was synonymous with barbarous.[2] It was repeatedly said that the Middle Ages knew nothing of the love of Nature, and never felt its beauty— indeed, long afterwards the glory of revealing these to the world was attributed to Jean Jacques Rousseau. Others said —and this is repeated even in our own time—that the Middle Ages had no cognizance either of freedom of thought or of respect for personality.

Mediæval philosophy did not escape the sarcasms of the Humanists. Erasmus, Vivès, and Cornelius Agrippa ridiculed it.[3] The Reformers of the sixteenth century encouraged these ideas, and the epithet " scholastic " became one of contempt. According to Thomasius, for instance, Scholasticism was a philosophy which was taught in bad Latin, abused the syllogism, and busied itself with subtleties or foolish trifles. Or, again, it was described as a philosophy which pretended to follow Aristotle but did not understand him. And since all systems of philosophy after the sixteenth century loudly boasted of their independence of dogma, scholasticism was dismissed as a system used in defence of the Catholic religion or of the theology of Popery : *eam esse philosophiam in servi-*

[1] Kurth, *Qu'est ce que le Moyen Age ?* 2nd edn. 1905.
[2] André Michel, *Histoire de l'Art*, I, 934. (Paris, 1905).
[3] See Fourth Period, Chapter II.

tutem theologiæ Papææ (sic) *redactam*.[1] "A Scholastic," wrote Ch. Binder, " is a man who spends the greater part of his life in commenting upon Aristotle and the barbarous commentaries of Albert, Thomas, Holcot, Pricot, Mammatrectus[2], Maffretus, and other obscure persons, concerning whom one might sometimes wonder whether they are using Latin or the language of the Scythians.[3] The chief schools of thought known to this author are the Thomists, Scotists, and the followers of Occam or of Durandus, all of them later than the the thirteenth century. In the same way, Tribbechovius 1641-1687) tells us that the Scholastics are especially the Terminists, Scotists and Thomists of the end of the Middle Ages, and to these he adds the name of Anselm, Abelard, Roscelin, Thomas Aquinas, Albertus Magnus (Hercules Albertus ille magnus), Duns Scotus (tenebrarum magister) and a few others.[4] He adds that the knowledge which the Scholastics possessed came from the Arabs : " Quidquid enim sapuere scholastici, illud omne Arabibus acceptum tulere."[5] It is, however, worthy of note that about the same time Busse carefully distinguished philosophers from theologians, preferring to give the name of " scholastics " rather to the former. He describes them as " Christian doctors who have subjected philosophical and theological science to Aristotle."[6]

It is not surprising that this contempt for scholasticism went hand in hand with ignorance of its teaching, and that the word

---

[1] Preface of Heymannus to the treatise of Tribbechovius, Jena, 1719, p. xxii.

[2] The reference is to a Biblical work edited several times in the fifteenth century, *Mammotrectus super Bibliam*, by John Marchesini, a Minorite who lived about 1300.

[3] "Ab eo tempore nullus fuit ad scholasticum professionem admissus . . . qui non maximam ætatis suæ partem tribuisset in Aristotelis litteris, et post hunc in barbaris commentariis super Aristotelem, Alberti, Thomæ, Holcot Pricot, Mammatrecti, Maffreti et aliorum tenebriorum de quibus interdum dubites an Scythe vel latine loquantur." (p. 15). He continues : " Si Thomas aliquid affirmat, nititur ejus argumenta infirmare Scotus ; quæ labefactare conatur Occam ut sua figat ; at ista quoque Petrus Aliacensis luxat." (p. 17). The Jesuits are described as " loquacissimæ ranæ " (p. 22).—*Scholastica Theologia, in qua disseritur de ejus causis, origine, progressu ac methodo legendi scholasticos*, auctore Christ. Bindero, Tubing. 1614.

[4] Adam Tribbechovius, *De doctoribus scholasticis er corrupta per eos divinarum humanarumque rerum scientia, Giessæ.* 1665 and Jena 1719, pp. 58, 46 *et passim*. This curious and rare little book devoted entirely to Scholasticism constitutes a history of Scholastic Philosophy written a century before the work of Brucker.

[5] p. 126.

[6] " Cum vero duplicem eorum differentiam animadvertamus Theologos alios, alios philosophos, quamquam illis hoc nomen potius tributum sit."— Busse, *De Doctoribus Scholasticis*, Dissert. 1676, Leipzig. a 2 verso.

finally came to stand for vague and childish speculations, "dealing with such questions as that of matter and form, powers and faculties, essence and existence."

The same contempt and the same ignorance are found in the opinions of the modern period concerning scholasticism. Rabelais, Francis Bacon, Locke, Descartes and others had at their disposal a veritable arsenal of cheap sneers. They made full use of these and passed them on to the eighteenth and nineteenth centuries. Thus arose the idea of the " night of a thousand years " during which philosophy was unknown.

2. Beginning of historical study of mediæval philosophy.— Nowadays the Middle Ages are no longer looked upon with contempt. The labours of those who have studied the mediæval period have brought us face to face with a distinct civilization which in the twelfth and thirteenth centuries reached a very remarkable and high degree of perfection. The romance of chivalry, the feudal system, the art of illumination and frescoes, the symbolic poetry, Romanesque churches and Gothic cathedrals, political and social institutions, scientific, philosophical and theological works are not the product of a barbarous age but of the human race in a mature state and capable of great things. We may apply to mediæval civilization as a whole that which Goethe said of Strasburg Cathedral : " Brought up as I was to look upon Gothic architecture with contempt, I despised it, but when I went inside I was struck with wonder, and I felt the attraction of its beauty."[1]

The historic study of mediæval philosophy dates from the middle of the nineteenth century. Victor Cousin was faithful to his eclectical tendencies when in 1836 he examined the twelfth century. Rousselot and De Remusat studied the problem of universals.[2] Prantl wrote a history of mediæval logic. Albert Stöckl (1864-1866), Haureau (1850), and K. Werner (1881-1884) wrote the first general histories.

But the real impulse dates from the time when works in the form of monographs were resolutely undertaken. From this point of view, Denifle, Ehrle and Baeumker are the forerunners. Among the best scholars of to-day we may single our Ehrle, Grabmann, Baumgartner, Pelster, Endres, Baeumker

---

[1] Goethe, *Dichtung und Wahrheit*, IX, **2.**

[2] V. Cousin, *Introduction aux ouvrages inédits d'Abélard*, 1836.—Rousselot *Etudes sur la philosophie dans le moyen âge*, Paris, 1840-1842.—Ch. de Rémusat *Abélard*, 2 vol., Paris, 1845.

and his school, in Germany ; Mandonnet and Gilson in France ; Cl. Webb, Little, and Carlyle in England ; Miguel Asin y Palacios in Spain ; Haskins and Paetow in America ; Pelzer and De Ghellinck in Belgium ; Birkenmajer and Michalski in Poland. We shall come across their principal works in the course of this book.

We may add that in addition to this group of specialists, historians of philosophy and philosophers of every school and of all countries tend more and more to give to mediæval philosophy the attention it deserves.

3. Necessity of the study of mediæval philosophy.—Its necessity is evident :

(i) From the point of view of the history of philosophy. Quite a number of powerful systems of philosophy made their appearance from the ninth to the fifteenth centuries, so that there was no break of continuity between the close of the period of antiquity and the beginnings of modern philosophy. Mediæval philosophy arose out of Greek philosophy, but was at the same time clearly distinct from it, just as in turn it prepared the way for modern philosophy which nevertheless has its own characteristics. The development of human thought was not arrested during the Middle Ages. Is it likely, *a priori*, that during a thousand years the human race in the West should have ceased to philosophize ?

(ii) From the point of view of philosophy proper, it is all the more important to become acquainted with mediæval philosophy inasmuch as some of its systems, as for instance those of St. Anselm of Canterbury, Thomas Aquinas, and Duns Scotus, have an admitted value.

(iii) From the point of view of mediæval history. The civilization of the Middle Ages has become the object of close and detailed study, and it would be impossible to understand this period properly without examining its philosophy. For at no period has philosophy modified more profoundly the spirit of the various elements of society. The study of mediæval philosophy will throw a flood of light upon the art, the economic, political and social life, and the literature of the time.

(iv) From the point of view of modern history. We do not hesitate to add—and we shall return to this point later on— that the twelfth and thirteenth centuries have moulded the philosophic temperament of the Anglo-Celts, the neo-Latins, and the Germans ; and that scholastic philosophy, which was dominant in the Middle Ages, has bequeathed much of its teaching to modern philosophy, and given to the nations of to-day many of their distinctive characteristics.

If these remarks are justified, the study of the philosophical systems of the Middle Ages and especially of the scholastic systems, has an educational value ; it forms a stage in the philosophic training of all those who wish to enter into the thought of the Western Mind. Just as the study of the classics of Greece and Rome is an essential part of literary culture, and mediæval architecture and Renaissance art are valuable for the formation of our sculptors, architects, and painters, so also the study of philosophy ought to include the mediæval conceptions of the world and of life.

4. Methods.—(i) *We must enter into the thought of mediæval philosophy in order to understand it, and must judge it on its merits.* It is impossible to understand the philosophy of the Middle Ages unless we view it from inside, and study the theories its writers put forward as they are in themselves and in their mutual relations, making use for this purpose of the modern methods of historical criticism. In this respect what is true of mediæval philosophy applies to the whole civilization of the period. It has a meaning of its own. Hence in order to understand it, we must think ourselves into its mentality and give up the idea of discovering constant parallels with contemporary civilization—just as a person who wants to speak a foreign tongne must think in that language and not merely translate the words and phrases of his own mother tongue.

If the philosophy and civilization of the Middle Ages are different from those of our time, it follows that they are not necessarily better or worse than ours. This enables us to see what criterion we must use in passing judgment upon them after we have studied them. A civilization is great if it manifests itself in an intense, original, and harmonious expression of the fundamental aspirations of individual and social life. A philosophy is noteworthy if it formulates and solves in a new way the problems connected with a complete explanation of the world and of reality. In our opinion, in order to judge of the value of mediæval philosophy and civilization, these must be compared to one fixed standard : human nature, which remains identical in its profound needs in spite of the diversity of historic conditions.

From this point of view it cannot be denied that the Middle

Ages comprised two great centuries for civilization and philosophy: the twelfth and thirteenth. The centuries which led up to these and ones which followed them are clearly inferior, and this brings us to a second point of method which need only be indicated:

(ii) *The thousand years which formed the middle ages must not be treated in one and the same way.* We ought not to apply to the decadent fifteenth century or to the period of formation that which is true only of the central centuries.

(iii) *We must look for relations of harmony and interdependence between philosophy and the other social factors.* Mediæval philosophy should not be studied merely in itself and in its doctrinal development; it should be viewed in connection with the civilization in which its various systems took their rise. The domestic and political institutions, juridical and economic regime, the moral and religious aspirations, artistic and scientific conceptions, the theological and philosophical systems—all these factors of civilization are interdependent; they act and react upon each other. In addition to the study of the history of mediæval philosophy properly so called, other studies are necessary which will enable us to understand this philosophy in relation to its environment.

5. Classification of the definitions of mediæval philosophy. Extrinsic or relative notions.—Historians define mediæval or scholastic philosophy in very many different ways, and most of these definitions are erroneous or incomplete. They are the echo of the judgments put forth at the time of the Renaissance and perpetuated in the centuries which followed: that means that their origin renders them suspect. The most important group of these definitions has a double defect: they are vague, and purely relative. Being vague they depict the movement of complex ideas in a too simple way. They are extrinsic and do not present us with mediæval philosophy as it is in itself, i.e., in its doctrinal content, but merely in a relative way, by linking up its doctrines with factors which are quite outside them.

Let us endeavour to classify these current definitions, rejecting some and determining the amount of truth and likewise the imperfection, in others. Mediæval philosophy has been characterized by its relations:

(i) with the schools in which it was taught: that is the etymological definition;

(ii) with its methods of exposition and its external apparatus : the pedagogical and didactic definitions ;

(iii) with the Middle Ages, or the time when it flourished : the chronological definition ;

(iv) with religion and theology : the religious definition ;

(v) with other factors of mediæval civilization ;

(vi) with ancient and patristic philosophy.

6. The etymological or verbal definition. Scholasticism and the Schools.—The word " scholastic " had not the same meaning in the Middle Ages and at the time of the Renaissance. In the Middle Ages the *scholasticus* (from *schola*, school) was the master who directed a school, or a man of culture versed in the trivium and quadrivium. In a wider sense the name was applied to any learned man or professor[1] and the title came to have an honorific sense.[2]

The writers of Renaissance and the Reformation period abandoned this professional sense of the word (implying teaching) and adopted instead an ideological sense, according to which it stood for the theologians (" scholastic theology ") or philosophers (" scholastic philosophy ") of the Middle Ages. True, the theologians were distinguished from the philosophers, but at the same time the name implied contempt for both. It was synonymous with sophist.[3]

Because " scholastic " is derived from *schola*, Haureau writes that it is philosophy as taught in the schools of the Middle Ages,[4] and Picavet calls it " the offspring of the schools."[5]

This merely etymological and verbal definition is useless

---

[1] Concerning the historic meaning of the word " scholastic " as used by the Greeks, the Latins, and in the Middle Ages, see Tribbechovius, *op. cit.*, and Manser, *op. cit.*, no. 19, pp. 320 *et seq.*

[2] Abbot Hilduin, about 835, describes a certain Fortunatus as *scholasticissimus. Monum. Germ. Hist. Epp.* T.V., 333, 28.

[3] Tribbechovius, *op. cit.*, pp. 39, 66. Here are some examples, taken at random : " Qui litterarum regnum media in barbarie tenuerunt Scholastici " (p. 37) ; " Scholastici omne punctum tum demum se tulisse arbitrantur, si quando tribus syllogismis instructi de quavis materia litem movere possent " (*ibid.*) ; " abyssos potentionabilitudinalitatum et aptitudinalitatum " (p. 46). He recalls the judgment of Bullinger : " utuntur interpretibus sive expositoribus putidissimis " (p. 49) ; the diatribes of Erasmus : " cum nil nisi meram barbariem evomuerint " (p. 336) ; also those of Vivès, and of Aventin. Speaking of the last period he says: " Habesque post Scotum, Holcot, Tricot, Bricot, Boqinquam et plures alios . . . Et quis sigillatim omnes enumerare, deque operibus eorum commentari posset, cum numerus eorum ad XII M. excreverit " (p. 333).

[4] *Hist. philos. scolastique*, I, 36 ; *Dictionn. sciences philosoph.* by Franck, sub voce *scolastique*.

[5] *Revue Philos.*, 1902, p. 185 ; *Grande Encycl.* s.v. *scolastique.*

from our point of view. In the later Middle Ages, musicians and astronomers are called " scholastics " as well as philosophers and theologians. Even if we admit that *schola* was used to signify the highest teaching, namely, philosophy and theology, the two sciences which complete the edifice of knowledge, still this does not enable us to grasp or to judge the doctrine which was taught. Moreover, if scholasticism is the offspring of the schools, the word could be applied to our own time just as much as to the Middle Ages, for the printing press has not put an end to oral teaching. As a matter of fact, some authors speak of the scholastics " of the time of Kant, Hegel, and Cousin."[1] It is hardly necessary to point out that this wide use of the term is its own condemnation.

7. Definition of scholasticism by its didactic method.—By the " scholastic method " historians mean things which really differ though often confounded.

(i) When used in connection with philosophy the word signifies a particular way of constructing a science (constitutive method) or else the way in which it was taught (didactic method) ;

(ii) When applied to theology, it means the use of dialectics in the service of dogma.

We are concerned here only with the first sense of the term. Some authors define scholastic philosophy, then, by its didactic method. Scholasticism, they say, signifies any pedagogical systemization, the adaptation of knowledge of any kind to the use of a school (*Schulwissenschaft*). They then go on to contrast the disordered state of the scientific material as used by the Fathers of the Church with the cut-and-dried framework which enshrines the teaching of the Middle Ages.[2] Or again, it is defined as such-and-such particular form of systemization : thus the scholastic method is said to be the syllogistic method " deducing consequences *ad infinitum* "[3] ; or again, it is " thought subjected to the constraint of dialectics."[4]

All these ideas are open to criticism on the ground that they

[1] Picavet in *Le Moyen Age*, 1902, p. 34. In this matter he is more logical than Haureau, according to whom the end of scholasticism coincided with the discovery of printing.

[2] For this idea see Willmann, *Gesch. d. Idealismus*, II, 67, nos. 2 and 4.

[3] Fouillée, *Hist. de la Philos.*, p. 198 (Paris, 1883). Cf. Diderot: " Scholasticism is not so much a philosophy as a dry and narrow method of reasoning." (*Œuvres complètes*, t. XIX, p. 362).

[4] Draeseke, in *R. philosophie*, 1909, p. 641.

stop short at the formal arrangement of doctrines and do not penetrate to the doctrines themselves. Pedagogical systemization, and the use of a particular kind of method, may characterize any system of philosophy, and may apply to that of Kant just as much as to that of Thomas Aquinas. Furthermore, the laws of methodology are not peculiar to philosophy, but govern every branch of knowledge.

As for the syllogism, we may add that it is not the only process employed by mediæval philosophers.

It is scarcely necessary to say anything about the ideas—true but superficial—of those who define scholasticism by means of the " peripatetic " phraseology which it employed[1] or else the technical formulæ which it adopted.[2] One might just as well say that Greek philosophy is philosophy taught in Greek, or define Kant's system as one which calls for a special vocabulary in order to understand it.[3] The possession of a technical terminology is common to all philosophies.

8. Identification of scholastic philosophy with that of the Middle Ages. State of the question.—Many historians identify scholastic philosophy with the philosophy of the Middle Ages. All who lived in those times and philosophised were " scholastics " (Cousin, Haureau, Ueberweg-Baumgartner, Erdmann, Picavet, etc.).

The origin of this chronological definition goes back to the Renaissance, when scholasticism was looked upon as a vague and homogeneous philosophy current in the *barbaries medii ævi*. But this homogeneity is one of appearance only. The work already done on this subject tends to show that mediæval philosophy was made up of numerous and divergent systems. Unanimity in the philosophical explanation of things was as impossible in the Middle Ages as at other periods.

Let us examine the results of modern research : we shall then see that they necessitate a more precise use of terminology. These results may be summarized as follows :

(i) *Many divergent systems flourished in the Middle Ages.* On every side the doctrinal horizon was a wide one. In the West a definitely Pantheistic philosophy was in conflict with

---

[1] e.g., Huet, *Recherches hist. et crit. sur la vie, les ouvr. et la doctrine de Henri de Gand* (Gand, 1838), p. 95.

[2] Hogan, *Clerical Studies*, p. 67.

[3] With these notions which characterize scholasticism by its didactic method we may place those which regard it as a vague mentality, or the spirit peculiar to all the intellectual products of the Middle Ages. This is always interpreted in a depreciatory way.

pluralistic systems of thought. The thirteenth century witnessed the commencement of a long struggle between Averrhoism, which had powerful defenders, and the great doctrines to which an Albertus Magnus, Bonaventure, Thomas Aquinas, or a Duns Scotus attached their names. The further we get away from the thirteenth century towards the modern period, the more ardent does the clash of ideas become, until the combined forces of the Renaissance deal a death blow to the reigning system of philosophy.

This is not all. Side by side with Western philosophy we find throughout the Middle Ages currents of Byzantine and Oriental systems of thought, which break up in their turn.

In this way mediæval philosophy consists of Occidental, Byzantine, and Oriental systems, each one with its own peculiar traits.

(ii) *One doctrinal system became dominant in the West.* It took shape gradually and became a sort of patrimony. Anselm of Canterbury, Alexander of Halès, Thomas Aquinas, Bonaventure, Duns Scotus, William of Occam, that is, the chief thinkers, and a hundred others with them, agreed in holding in common quite a number of fundamental theories, and precisely those which determine the structure of a system, inasmuch as they are concerned with the great problems with which all philosophies deal.

This doctrinal system was not the work of a day, nor the product of one man, but the fruit of a long period of time, and the result of progressive additions. The work of building it up lasted from the ninth to the twelfth centuries ; and the majority of philosophers in this first period took part in it : in the twelfth century the common possession—*Gemeingut*[1]— was well marked out in all its fullness, and the great majority of philosophers made use of it ; finally it began to break up little by little after the end of the fourteenth century. The Western Middle Ages were thus at their height in possession of a great doctrinal inheritance which had taken centuries to build up, and this patrimonial factor formed a domestic bond

---

[1] Since our 1905 edition we have found this energetic expression *Gemeingut* in Baeumker, *Die europäische Philosophie des Mittelalters*, p. 366 *et passim.* In the same way Endres acknowledges the reality of a great conception of the world forming " ein Gemeingut aller Schulen und Richtungen." (*Gesch. d. mittelalterlichen Philos. im christlichen Abendlande*, 1908, p. 4.) The existence of a common synthesis has recently been stressed by Bæumker (*Sitzungsberichte d. Kon. Bayerl. Akad. Wiss.*, Munchen, 1913, Abh. 9, p. 5), and by Grabmann, *Die Philos. d. Mittelalters* (Berlin, 1921), p. 27.

between the members sharing it. They defended it against enemies who wished to borrow from it for the use of rival systems, and there was a great struggle. This defence, energetic and triumphant during the period of height, weak and disastrous in the time of decadence, explains how men like Thomas Aquinas, Bonaventure, and Duns Scotus, who engaged in warm controversy amongst themselves on particular questions, nevertheless marched hand-in-hand when they had to repel the attacks of their common enemies.

We find the same progressive development in the history of architecture. The Romanesque church and the Gothic cathedral were likewise the culminating points of progressive changes. Monuments in stone and monuments of ideas developed parallel to each other, and in both cases many generations of architects and workmen were required in order to attain to perfection. The same slow and progressive formation may be seen in the history of the feudal system, the social relations between barons and serfs, the centralizing organization of kingdoms, and other phenomena of civilization.

We shall see later on[1] that the gradual and patrimonial building up of the philosophy of the West, which was one of the most remarkable phenomena in the intellectual life of the Middle Ages, was the result of certain unitive and impersonal tendencies which manifested themselves in every domain and attained their highest expression in the thirteenth century. If we study the civilization of the thirteenth century we shall better understand why the scholastic system was a collective product and why philosophical doctrines were looked upon as an impersonal possession which one generation elaborated and passed on to the next.

(iii) *The unity of the scholastic system did not destroy originality of thought in its various representatives.* Scholastic philosophers agreed concerning the solutions of many organic and essential questions, and in a certain doctrinal minimum which distinguishes the scholastic patrimony from every other. But this fundamental *entente* did not exclude shades of difference, or applications, developments, and interpretations : and it is by these that we can distinguish between the scholasticism of an Alexander of Hales and those of a Bonaventure, Thomas Aquinas, Duns Scotus, or a William of Occam.[2] Those who

---

[1] Second Period, Ch. III., art. I, § 8.
[2] It is in this sense that Descartes writes to Mersenne : " It is easy to upset

utilized the common deposit were not of equal merit. In philosophy, as in art,[3] a comparatively small number know how to impress upon an existing system the mark of their own genius. But there are some such, and these great minds open up new lines of thought in scholasticism.

It is easy to realize now that this common scholasticism is the result of an abstraction ; the living reality was always a particular fixed variety or kind of scholasticism, complete in all its details. A comparison with the Gothic cathedral will help us to see how well founded is this abstraction. The essential characteristics of the Gothic style belong to Amiens and Chartres as well as to Paris and Cologne, and yet each Gothic cathedral is a particular independent monument. In the same way the philosophies of Anselm of Canterbury, Bonaventure, Thomas Aquinas, and Duns Scotus, have each and all their " principle of individuation," to use an expression dear to the philosophers of the Middle Ages.

What exactly is implied in the fact that these systems differ in their developments, applications, or arguments ? Every concrete philosophy is self-contained. The systems of Thomas Aquinas and of Duns Scotus, if regarded as living realities, are just as independent as those of Plotinus and Proclus, or Fichte and Hegel. Still, this does not mean that between Thomas Aquinas and Scotus on the one hand, as between Fichte and Hegel on the other, there may not be affinities which make it impossible to change the arrangement of these couples by bracketing Thomas Aquinas with Fichte, and Scotus with Hegel. The fact is that in both these groups of philosophies we find certain organic theories, or elements of common systemizations which the historian considers apart, or abstractly, and which establish between the ideas of Thomas Aquinas and Duns Scotus a relation differing from that which exists between Fichte and Hegel. This is exactly what we mean when we speak of a *sententia communis*, or a common synthesis in the West. Thus the multiplicity and independence of concrete philosophical systems expressing the whole thought of a man can be reconciled with the existence of an abstract

all the foundations upon which they agree, and when this has been done, all their particular disputes will appear foolish."—*Œuvres*, ed. 1897, III, 232.

[3] *A propos* of Suger, M. Mâle writes : " We readily admit that the great art of the Middle Ages is a collective work . . . But this thought itself took shape in certain superior individuals. It is individuals who create, not the masses." *L'art religieux du XIIe siècle*, p. 151.

system of which every one of these philosophies is a living form. We can study at one and the same time *the* scholastic philosophy—as we can study the type of the Gothic cathedral, the mediæval town, or the fortress of the Middle Ages—and also the great minds which were influenced by this philosophy and interpreted it.

(iv) During the whole period of the Middle Ages, there existed systems which were quite different from the common system dominant in the West.[1] Amongst these, there were some which declared war upon scholasticism, and whose principal doctrines were the very antithesis of it. These opposing systems may be classified in three groups. The monist systems, which were by far the most numerous and important and existed throughout the Middle Ages in more or less complete and coherent forms, were in opposition to the fundamental pluralism of the common synthesis. We shall see later on that Averrhoism, with its theory of the oneness of the intellect, constituted a frontal attack upon the aspirations of the mediæval mind, although " its duration was short and its intensity still less."[2] Materialism and subjectivism are two more doctrines which necessarily involve the systems admitting them in a conflict with the spiritualism and dogmatism (objectivism) of the common philosophy.

Whatever may be the divergence of opinion between Anselm, Thomas Aquinas, or Duns Scotus, they all reject absolutely any community of being in God and His creatures ; they insist upon the value of human personality, the existence of immaterial beings, and the objectivity of human knowledge.

9. The common philosophy dominant in the Middle Ages in the West was Scholasticism.—The outstanding facts just briefly mentioned, the detailed study of which forms the basis of this book, give rise to a new classification, and to a revision of the sense to be attached to the term " scholasticism."

First, to a new classification. If there is one doctrinal system

---

[1] See later on : Second Period, Chapter Three, The Common Synthesis.

[2] Mandonnet, *Siger de Brabant et l'averroïsme latin* (*Philos. Belges*, t. vi, p. 29). We are pleased to find the following in Baeumker : " pantheistische Richtung, *die ausserhalb der scholastischen Philosophie im Mittelalter stets aufs neue antritt.*" (*Die Europaische Philos. d. Mittelalters*, p. 371.) " Wo eine historische Erscheinung nach ihrer *Ideenrichtung* und ihrer formalen Ausgestaltung aus dem Rahmen dieser schulmässigen Ueberlieferung ganz herausfällt, *wie die Mystik und gewisse pantheistische Systeme, wird man sie daher wohl der Philosophie des Mittelalters, aber nicht der Scholastik* zurechnen können." (*ibid.*, p. 342.) In the same way Lappe speaks of the scepticism of Nicholas of Autrecourt as " Kampf gegen die Scholastik." (BGPM., VI, 2, p. 2, 1908).

dominant throughout the period, and together with this, secondary currents of different ideas, and conflicts between the two, then the intellectual Middle Ages themselves provide us with a principle of classification for the study of these complex philosophical doctrines, namely, the grouping of the various systems according to their doctrinal affinities and agreement upon essential theories. That is why we prefer to give the name " scholastic " to one particular group of mediæval philosophies, i.e., that which is pre-eminently Western Philosophy,[1] the dominant system, which unites together as members of one family the best known representatives of thought—and conversely we call "anti-scholastic" all those philosophies which declare war upon the fundamental principles of this system.

Certainly it is still permissible to consider the various mediæval philosophies only in their opposition to each other and in that which characterizes each individual system, and this would enable one to keep a strictly chronological succession. But would this be sufficient ? Can we get to understand differences without considering resemblances ? Anyone who wishes to follow up the filiation of ideas must, in our opinion, pay attention to both. It will not suffice to arrange in a line the philosophies of Thomas Aquinas, Duns Scotus, and Siger of Brabant ; we must also get to know why the two former agree in the main outline of their conception of the universe and join together in an attack upon the third. The principle of classification according to ideas takes precedence of the chronological classification and can be combined with it.

Secondly, the facts mentioned lead to a revision of terminology. We must be more exact and precise in this matter as in other branches of knowledge, and for the same reason : we must not employ terms in contradictory ways or apply the same name to diverse or antagonistic things. Accordingly we must adopt different designations for philosophic systems which are quite separate or which oppose each other.

In the same way the history of Egyptian art and of seventeenth century French literature has developed as situations once looked upon as simple and homogeneous have turned

---

[1] Seth writes correctly in the *Encyclopædia Britannica* (1886) : " Scholasticism is the name usually employed to denote the most typical products of Mediæval thought." He maintains that Scholasticism is not antagonistic to reason, and protests against the statements of Prantl, pp. 417 and 418 (s.v. Scholasticism).

out to be complex. The same thing has happened in biology as the organization of the cell has gradually become known. If in spite of all this anyone continues to use the term "scholastic philosophy " as a label for the whole collection of different mediæval systems (just as the various different systems which flourished in Greece are collectively called " Greek philosophy ") he must obviously be content with unphilosophic, vague, banal and inadequate considerations. (6, 7, 12, 14.) But after all, terminology is a matter of convention, and in fine there is really nothing to say to one who prefers to apply the term " scholastic " to the heterogeneous mass of mediæval systems. The name matters little provided the facts are recognized.

10. Reply to some objections.—(i) "A historian ought to use the term ' scholastic ' in the sense it had in the Middle Ages. But in those days any philosopher was called *scholasticus ;* hence the philosophical systems of the middle ages are scholastic."[1]

What we have already said above concerning terminology suffices to reply to this observation. For the reasons mentioned, we prefer to give to the term the ideological meaning which it was given at the time of the Renaissance and which it has retained ever since.

(ii) " To justify a distinction between scholasticism and anti-scholasticism, the mediæval systems thus classified ought to have nothing in common. But this is not the case, for both were inspired by a particular attitude of mind which separates mediæval philosophy from Greek or Modern philosophy."[2]

To this it may be replied that the opposition which provides a foundation for our classification is so profound that it places scholasticism and anti-scholasticism at the antipodes of thought : pluralism, spiritualism, liberty, personal survival characterize scholasticism on the one hand ; monism, materialism, moral determinism, and impersonal immortality are found in anti-scholasticism on the other. It matters little that these systems happen to agree on certain questions. In spite of this agreement, their spirit is altogether different. There are no philosophic systems which differ so much that they have nothing whatever in common. Moreover, the mentality which is common to mediæval philosophers comes from the civilization

---

[1] " Das Mittelalter selbst soll uns Aufschluss erteilen über Anfang und Begriff seiner Scholastik." Manser, *op. cit.*, p. 321.

[2] Gentile, *Il modernismo e i rapporti tra religione e filosofia* (Bari, 1909), chap. V ; *Il neotomismo, a proposito del libro di M. De Wulf*, pp. 111-148.

of the period and is found in other things as well as in philosophy. Hence it does not affect philosophy as such.

(iii) " There was no real unity in the scholastic systems. The common synthesis is an artificial product ; the philosophers whose names are attached to it, such as St. Thomas and Duns Scotus—disagree on all points, for each scholastic system constitutes an autonomous whole."[1]

The common scholastic synthesis is, as we have pointed out, an abstract conception, and as such is capable of belonging to many individuals, in each of which it takes a concrete form. This is sufficient to justify our conception.

The expression " common possession," " patrimony," *Gemeingut*, corresponds to this idea. Just as a patrimony may consist of diverse things—furniture, lands, credits, etc.—so also the common basis of scholasticism comprises solutions differing in value, source, and significance. Still, it presents a sufficiently organic appearance as a whole to justify us in speaking of it as a coherent and comprehensive type of philosophy. The great doctrines of act and potency, matter and form, the distinction between sensation and thought, etc., all hold together like the flying buttress, the pointed arch, and great bays in Gothic architecture. Thomas and Duns Scotus both accept the same conception of the world and of reality, and in presence of this fundamental agreement Descartes was right in saying that they differed in opinion only in secondary matters.

11. Mediæval philosophy defined by its relation with theology and religion. State of the question.—Of all the current notions about mediæval philosophy, which is loosely designated as " scholasticism," the most widespread is that based upon its relations with the Catholic religion and its dogmas. Stress is laid upon the central place occupied by religion in the civilization of the Middle Ages, and on the religious character of its philosophy (Manser, Picavet). Servant or handmaid for some—*philosophia ancilla theologiæ* (Cousin, Ueberweg-Baumgartner, Freudenthal, Windelband, Dilthey, Paulsen, etc.), companion or helper for other (Gonzales, Erdmann, Willmann, Picavet), mediæval or scholastic philosophy is conceived by all as philosophy subjected to the domination or direction of Catholic theology.

Some authors give to these formulæ a wider sense. Just as

[1] Jacquin, Manser, Gentile.

we might call scholastic any and every product of the schools, (6) so do they apply the name to any philosophy subjected to any kind of dogma. The scholasticity of a philosophy would be measured by the extent of this subjection, and the diversity of the regulating dogma would enable one to distinguish a Hindu scholasticism (Masson-Oursel), a Jewish scholasticism (Zeller), an Arabian scholasticism (Carra de Vaux), and a Protestant scholasticism.

In order to understand the meaning of these formulæ and to discuss their value, it is necessary to outline in its chief features the system of relations which the Middle Ages established between philosophy and theology. The early Middle Ages adumbrated this relationship, and the thirteenth century witnessed its full development. These relations were in some cases non-doctrinal, in others doctrinal.

(i) *Relations not affecting philosophical doctrine.* The Western civilization of the Middle Ages was saturated with the religious spirit ; an atmosphere of religion enveloped all the manifestations of family, social, political, artistic, and scientific life. Everything which the new races received from the past, everything produced by their own natural temperament, was made fruitful by Christianity, and this elaboration was one of the distinctive traits of the period.[1] Hence, regarded as one of the elements of this civilization, philosophy was a function of religion.

This explains why the origin of many philosophic problems must be sought in the sphere of religious and theological discussion, particularly at the commencement of the Middle Ages. (Ch. IV, § 1.)

It also explains how we find philosophic theories side by side with theological doctrines in the same works. But this proximity, due as it is to historical causes, does not deprive philosophy and theology of their respective autonomy.

Again, it explains why from the pedagogic and disciplinary point of view, the Middle Ages regarded theology as the higher branch of knowledge, and organized studies and teaching in such a way as to ensure its full development. That this was so is shown by the programmes drawn up in the monastic and abbatial schools, and later on in the universities. Everyone had the ambition of becoming a theologian after being a philosopher, while still remaining one. (See Second Period.)

[1] Cf. Henry O. Taylor, *The Mediæval Mind* (London, 1914), Vol. I, Ch. 1.

The religious character of the period also explains why theologians scrutinized philosophy for arguments in favour of their faith ; they created an apologetic, and we shall see later on that the apologetic method concerns theology and not philosophy. (Ch. IV, § 1.)

Finally, this same religious character had its influence upon the subjective intentions of philosophers, who, following the example of artists, knights and kings, looked upon the functions of their office as a means of attaining to eternal salvation.

(ii) *Doctrinal relations.* Philosophy, which was first of all confused with theology, was recognized as distinct in the twelfth century. The two branches of knowledge had then each one its constitutive methods and proper principles ; they both followed a parallel course of development, and manifested a solidarity in their evolution. At the same time philosophy was subordinated to theology in certain matters.

It is this subordination, the nature and extent of which we shall discuss later on, and this religious character of philosophy, which inspire the definitions of scholasticism we have in mind. Can this religious character of scholasticism, and the control exercised over its doctrines, provide us with a satisfactory definition of scholastic philosophy ? That is the question.

12. The religious character of scholasticism is not sufficient to define it.—This character is real. It brings out the value of scholasticism as an element of religious civilization, but it will not enable us to distinguish scholasticism from other philosophies, whether they be its imitators or its rivals, which display the same characteristic. Nor will it distinguish philosophy from art or political organization, which were equally illumined by religion. To define a philosophy it is not sufficient to single out a relational element which it possesses in common with other social factors, it is essential to pay attention to its doctrines which alone constitute it and make it what it is. Those who decline to do so are like a man who thinks he can get to know all about an oak tree by describing the composition of the soil in which it grows along with other trees of the forest.

Hence neither the organization of philosophic and theological studies, nor the use of an apologetic method which concerns theology, nor the intentions of philosophers, suffice to define the philosophic doctrines of the Middle Ages.

The proximity of theology and philosophy in one and the same work do not compromise their respective autonomy any more than in the case of a picture and a statue placed side by side in a museum.

13. The primacy of scholastic theology yields an unsatisfactory definition of scholastic philosophy—whether we make the scholasticity of a philosophy a generic notion, differentiated by this or that ruling dogma, or whether we apply the term exclusively to philosophies which are harmonized with Catholicism. And that for the following reasons :

(i) The definition thus inspired neglects that which constitutes scholastic philosophy as such, i.e., its doctrinal content. It limits itself to attributes which are external to a thing to be defined. Moreover, these attributes are quite secondary in importance. For :

(ii) Whatever be the cause, extent and nature of this subordination to theology, it is quite evident that scholastic philosophy had a meaning of its own, apart altogether from the dogma which it had in view, for it offered a rational explanation of the universal order of things.

Even theories connected with dogmas can be studied in themselves, by using criteria of appreciation other than this dependence upon dogma.

(iii) Moreover, quite a number of doctrines have no direct connection with Catholicism.

For instance, there is nothing in theology which obliged the scholastics to explain the constitution and development of bodies by the theory of prime matter and substantial form. Aristotle, who first formulated the theory, did not concern himself about its conformity with Catholicism—and for a very good reason—or with any other religion ; and many mediæval philosophers embraced atomism in spite of their Catholicism. But will anyone say that a theory so fundamental in Aristotle's system as that of matter and form ceases to occupy a similar place in scholasticism because it was introduced into a synthesis in which certain theories are controlled by dogma ?

The fact is that the ground which is common to mediæval philosophy and theology is much less in extent than these philosophies themselves. In order to be of service to anyone or collaborate with him, it is at least necessary to have something in common : and outside the ground which was common to the two branches of knowledge an attitude of subordination of one towards the other would have no sense. Hence such sub-ordination does not suffice to characterize philosophy as such.

(iv) If we take scholasticism to mean " any philosophy subordinated to a dogma," the same difficulties arise in a more general form. The Jewish, Arabian, Protestant, and Catholic scholastics would then be varieties of one genus. The element specifying these different varieties of scholasticism would be a religious and dogmatic factor, i.e., an extra-philosophic element, and so in this case also we should be characterizing a philosophy by something which is not philosophic (i), which is plainly insufficient. Moreover, whatever be the regulating dogma, the philosophic theories subordinated to it have nevertheless their own proper meaning from the philosophic point of view (ii), not to mention that each of these scholastic systems contain a number of solutions over which dogma exercises no control inasmuch as it does not concern itself with the questions which have given rise to them (iii).

(v) Lastly, if scholasticism were simply " a philosophy in harmony with dogma," we should arrive at this strange result : we should be able to distinguish in one and the same scholas-ticism—the Catholic variety, for instance—many contradictory types. In the Middle Ages no one openly opposed dogma, but everyone explained it in his own way. The Pantheists made use of their principle of the allegorical and symbolic inter-pretation of the Scriptures ; the Averrhoists employed their doctrine of the two truths, thinking they thus safeguarded their orthodoxy. All boasted of possessing the true spirit of the Gospels. At the threshold of the Renaissance, Nicholas of Cusa, a Cardinal of the Roman Church, could find the most ingenious connections between his doctrine of the coincidence of opposites and Catholicism. The accommodation is indeed open to question, but the fault lies in the weakness of his philosophy and in any case does not affect our argument. Were Descartes and Malebranche any less Catholic than Thomas Aquinas ? And yet from the philosophic point of view, what a distance there is between these thinkers.

Has not Gothic architecture been defined in the same inade-quate way as the architecture appropriated by Catholicism ? As if the Romanesque style or any other form of art were not capable of inspiring the construction of Catholic churches, or Gothic had not given rise to masterpieces of civic archi-tecture ! Viollet-le-Duc was much nearer the truth when he defined Gothic style according to its forms and its solutions of the problems of gravitation.

To sum up : (i) It is true but inadequate to say that mediæval or scholastic philosophy is a religious philosophy. In the same way the relation existing between this philosophy and scholastic theology is real but does not suffice to define the former. Mediæval philosophic systems must be studied above all in themselves and for their own sakes—and after that they may be considered in their relations with religious civilization and theology.

(ii) It is unscientific to confuse mediæval philosophy and theology. The mediæval philosophic systems, like all philosophies, are synthetic and comprehensive explanations of the world and of the universal order of things in the light of human reason. On the other hand, mediæval theology is a systemization of doctrines proposed to us by a positive revelation from God as found in the Bible. For a long time the existence of mediæval philosophy was denied[1], and it is still confused with theology.

Such a conclusion stultifies the meaning of the historic studies with which this book is concerned, since it makes of the history of philosophy in the Middle Ages a mere department of the history of religions. It was expressly condemned by the great thinkers of the Middle Ages, who clearly established the distinction between philosophy and theology.

It is with philosophy and not with scholastic theology that we are concerned in this history. In particular, when we make use of the term " scholasticism " without any addition, this is to be taken as synonymous with scholastic philosophy.

14. Mediæval philosophies defined by their relations with other factors of civilization.—Since all the factors of a civilization hold together and are interdependent, it is possible to define mediæval philosophy not only by its religious character, but also by other points in which it resembles the various elements of social life ; one might stress, for instance, its unitive tendencies, its intellectualism, optimism, and impersonality. Definitions of this kind will indeed bring out real characteristics, but the study of the latter will not dispense one from examining the philosophical doctrine itself.

---

[1] e.g., Prantl, *Geschichte der Logik*, denies the existence in the Middle Ages of a philosophy properly so-called. According to him there were then only discussions on logic and theology.

In the same way, those who are content to see in the Scholasticism of the West a stage of civilization which may be found in India and the East with analogous characteristics, are on the right path but do not go far enough. Scholasticism is indeed a philosophy which has adapted itself to a formal framework, a system encyclopædic in its beginnings, considering above all the problem of the categories of beings, and attempting an adaptation and a unification of things.[1] But these characteristics tell us nothing of the philosophical doctrine itself.

15. Definition of mediæval philosophies by their relations with ancient philosophy.—Mediæval philosophers did indeed borrow from the philosophic systems of Greece, Rome, and the Fathers, but the elements thus borrowed were thought out again and remoulded according to the mentality of the new races in the West. One would not therefore formulate an adequate definition by saying that scholasticism is a duplicate copy of former philosophies. That which guided the great minds of the Middle Ages was not a blind worship of some personage of bygone days, but the search for the Truth, and this truth they gathered wherever it was to be found. From this point of view they were all eclectics.

Since mediæval philosophers borrowed from almost all the previous systems, it will be useful to outline in brief their relations with the past.

(i) *Aristotle.* It has often been said—and is still said to-day—that mediæval philosophy plagiarizes the Peripatetic system. This prejudice dates back to the Renaissance. The scholastics of the fifteenth and sixteenth centuries were called "Aristotelians," and hence it is easy to understand that they were reproached for their lack of originality, and that no one thought of looking for influences other than that of Aristotle in mediæval philosophy.

It cannot be denied that the scholastics adopted many doctrines from Aristotle, and this quite openly. John of Salisbury calls Aristotle *the* "Philosopher," just as Rome was the urbs κατ᾽ ἐξοχήν[2]. For Albert the Great Aristotle is *archi-doctor philosophiæ*.[3] In addition, throughout the Middle Ages the scholastics studied Aristotle and had an

---

[1] Masson-Oursel, *La scolastique, étude de philosophie comparée* (Revue Philosophique, 1920, pp. 123-141).
[2] *Polycraticus*, vii. 6.   [3] *De propriet. element.* Lib. I. tr. I, c. I.

intimate understanding of his system which many moderns might envy them.

But the Aristotelianism of the scholastics was far from being servile or plagiaristic. Apart from the fact that they looked upon the argument from authority as only of feeble force, they rejected many of the Aristotelian theories. Important groups of scholastics regarded Aristotle with persistent mistrust because of his errors. As for the theories which they did borrow, some of these they completed and widened, others they corrected ; and all were co-ordinated, subjected to an intrinsic control, and introduced into a synthesis much more extensive and more coherent than that of Aristotle himself.

Aristotle was the official patron of the anti-scholastic system which had the greatest vogue in the thirteenth and fourteenth centuries—Averrhoism—but notwithstanding their avowed intention of imitating Aristotle, the Averrhoists combined his philosophy with neo-Platonist and Arabian doctrines.

(ii) *Plato* aroused an admiration no less enthusiastic than that of which Aristotle was the object. The Middle Ages adopted many of his theories. But it never reproduced pure Platonism as such : it tempered the elements borrowed by adding other doctrines. Moreover, Plato was introduced to the Middle Ages much more through the instrumentality of his disciple St. Augustine and the neo-Platonists than by his own Dialogues.

(iii) *Neo-Platonism.* The study of neo-Platonist influences upon mediæval philosophy, neglected for a long time, has recently given rise to extremely interesting researches. By the intermediary of the Fathers of the Church, of Pseudo-Dionysius, Chalcidius, Macrobius, Boethius, and, especially in the thirteenth century, of the *Liber de Causis*, also through the writings of Proclus, and the philosophic systems of Avicenna and other Arabians, many neo-Platonist ideas penetrated into mediæval philosophy.

Scholasticism adopted as its own several special theories from Neo-Platonist sources, for example, those of the good, light, the degrees of being and their hierarchical subordination, also the division of the virtues, and we shall see later on that we can distinguish various stages in the history of this infiltration. But Scholasticism rejected the idea of the becoming of one unique Being, and the procession of beings founded upon this becoming. In other words, it resisted the emanative and monist tendencies which constitute the very nucleus of the neo-Platonic system of Proclus and the *Liber de Causis*. Indeed, the neo-Platonic elements borrowed were incorporated into a pluralistic conception, and lived with a new spirit, constituting so many developments and precisions of a doctrine which was not at all neo-Platonist. Hence it is incorrect to lay down as a principle that Plotinus was " the veritable master of Scholasticism."[1]

On the contrary, the anti-scholastic philosophies which tended towards Monism in some form or other, were based to a great extent on the emanative principles of neo-Platonism, and followed Proclus not indeed in details, but in their fundamental inspiration. Finally, we shall come across in the thirteenth century remarkable but exceptional adaptations of neo-Platonist elements to Western thought.

(iv) *St. Augustine* exercised upon the Middle Ages a fascination which tended to rival that of Aristotle, and all endeavoured to support themselves by his authority. St. Augustine summed up and condensed a goodly portion of the intellectual treasures of the ancient world, and passed them on to the Middle Ages. He was acquainted with Epicureanism and criticized it, he adhered for a time to Scepticism and then refuted it, he was influenced by Stoic and literary eclecticism, and above all he was well versed in neo-Platonism, which he regarded as the philosophy of Plato and never ceased to praise.

Scholasticism is indebted to St. Augustine especially for a number of doctrines concerning God, the Divine Ideas, Creation, the Spirituality of the Soul. All of these helped to modify the naturalistic tendencies of Aristotle in a Platonist sense, and were easily harmonized by Scholasticism with its own tendencies. Let us add that Augustine's was not a didactic mind : his philosophic doctrines are merely incidental, and are embedded in religious preoccupations. Hence it was not from him that the Middle Ages learned how to systematize.

Other philosophies had their influence upon scholasticism

---

[1] Picavet, *Esquisse d'une histoire générale et comparée des philosophies médiévales*, 1907, Ch. V. The principal argument of M. Picavet amounts to this : the union of philosophy and religion is found for the first time in Plotinus, and lasts from thence throughout the Middle Ages. This is confusing civilization with a religious basis, and philosophy as such. Cf. 12. We already pointed this out in 1905 (*Revue d'histoire et de littérature religieuse*, p. 74). We may add that the Middle Ages were not acquainted with the *Enneads* of Plotinus.

besides those already mentioned, namely, the systems of the Pythagoricians, Democritus, Epicureus, the Stoics, pseudo-Dionysius and his commentators. All these influences could with equal reason be introduced into a definition of scholasticism. The latter sought for light in all the philosophies which preceded it, but it followed none in a servile manner.[1]

16. Insufficient intrinsic definitions.—The definitions which we have examined all contain a certain amount of truth, but make the common mistake of defining scholastic philosophy by something which is not philosophic. A sufficient definition can only be based upon its doctrines. Now the doctrinal content of philosophy can be understood in two ways : strictly speaking, a philosophy is a system, that is, a complete and unified collection of theories explaining reality. In a less strict sense philosophy is taken to mean one or a few particular doctrines corresponding to one or a few of the problems which are dealt with in philosophy.

It is this second point of view which is adopted by those who reduce mediæval philosophy to a dispute concerning universals (Haureau, who calls this the scholastic problem *pur excellence ;* Taine). Not only is it insufficient to judge a philosophy by stating the problems which it studies (for these are the same in all philosophies)—one must also pay attention to the solutions given—but as we shall show later on, the Middle Ages dealt with a number of questions which have nothing to do with universals, such as the relations between the intellect and the will, liberty, the existence of God, actuality and potency, etc. A definition based solely upon the problem of universals may be true as far as it goes, but it is decidedly incomplete.

The same objection may be made to those who look for the dominant characteristic of scholasticism " in the conciliation of idealism by means of the immanence of the intelligible ideal in the sensible "[2] or in a predilection for " the problem of the ontological constitution of being."[3] Although wider in scope than the first mentioned, these formulæ deal only with certain doctrines of psychology and metaphysics, and neglect the rest.

---

[1] " Weder die Abhängigkeit von den Autoritäten, noch das Verwiegen der deducktiven Methode ist für die Scholastik besonders charakteristisch."—Harnack, *Lehrbuch der Dogmengeschichte*, III, 313.

[2] Willmann, *op. cit.* I, 322.

[3] Morin, *Dictionnaire de philosophie et de théologie scolastique* (1856), p. 23.

17. Elements of a complete doctrinal definition.—In its mature state, scholasticism was a synthesis wherein were treated all the questions with which philosophy is concerned, and in which the solutions were harmonized, held together (σνν τίθημι) and controlled by one another.

An intrinsic and doctrinal definition ought to be based upon these solutions. It will naturally be complex, like the thing to be defined. Since the problems and solutions were slowly elaborated throughout the history of scholasticism, it will be better to postpone our definition until we have become acquainted with its doctrine as conceived by its ablest exponents at the period of its highest development.

The same applies to the anti-scholastic and other secondary systems which flourished in the Middle Ages : each had its specific doctrinal characteristics, since each had its own proper individuality.

18. Conclusion.—Intrinsic and doctrinal definitions do not exclude notions of a relative character. Moreover, to know a thing in its entirety, we must after analysing it in itself, study its relations with other things. That is why the historian when studying the many forms of mediæval philosophy must pay attention to the reciprocal influences of the various departments of civilization, and the connecting links between mediæval philosophy and the past.

19. Bibliography.—De Wulf, *La notion de la scolastique* (Revue philosophique, June, 1902 ; *Introduction à la philosophie néo-Scolastique*, § 1-10 (Louvain, 1904, translated into English by Dr. Coffey under the title *Scholasticism Old and New* (Longmans, 1907) ; Jacquin and De Wulf, discussion concerning the notion of Scholasticism in the Revue d'Histoire Ecclésiastique, Vol. V (1904), pp. 429, 716 ; Richard, *Etude critique sur le but et la nature de la scolastique* (Revue Thomiste, 1904) ; P. von Holtum (Philos. Jahrbuch, 1906 and 1906) on the relations between philosophy and theology, agrees with our conclusion ; Diego, *Liberalisme philosophique* (Etudes franciscaines, Oct. 1904), confused. Answered by P. Hadelin, Diego, and De Wulf, *ibid.*, 1905. Manser, *Ueber Umfang und Charakter der mittelalterlichen Scholastik* (Histor. Polit. Blätter, Bd. 139, 1907), identifies scholasticism with the philosophy of the Middle Ages, and characterizes it by its religious tendencies. G. Gentile, *II modernismo*, etc. (see note, p. 15) interprets scholasticism from the Hegelian point of view as a historic becoming of the

Absolute Mind. See our reply in *Critica*, 1911, p. 213. B. Nardi, *Scolastica vecchia e nuova* (Riv. fil. neo-scol., Oct. 1911 and 1912), and my reply, *ibid.*, 1912. Cf. De Wulf, *La notion de la scolastique médiævale* (Revue Néo-Scolastique, 1911, pp. 177-196) and 1912 ; Congrès philosophique at Bologna, 1911; Les courants philosophiques du moyen age occidental (3 art. Revue de philosophie, 1912) ; *Western Philosophy and Theology in the Thirteenth Century* (Harvard Theological Review, 1918, p. 409 ; Note in 1923, p. 143). Picavet : see in addition to the studies already cited in notes, the following : *Le Valeur de la scolastique* (in Bibliothèque du Congrès de Philosophie, Vol. IV, 1902) ; *L'origine de la philosophique scolastique en France et en Allemagne* (Biblioth. Ecole hautes études, Vol. I, 1888) ; *La Scolastique* (Revue intern. enseignment, April 1893). Freudenthal, *Zur Beurtheilung der Schol.* (Arch. fur Gesch. Philos. III, 1890), vague. Dewey, *Scholasticism* (Dictionary of Philosophy and Psychology, edited by Baldwin, 1902), weak. Lindsay, *Scholastic and Mediæval Philosophy* (Arch. fur Gesch. der Philos., 1901), weak. Rickaby, *Scholasticism* (London, Constable, 1908), general sketch, borrows our ideas and classifications. J. L. Perrier, *The Revival of Scholastic Philosophy* (New York, 1909, ch. I-VIII), adopts many of our ideas. Grabmann, *Die Geschichte der schol. Methode*, Bd. I. Einfuhrung, pp. 1-36. By " scholastic method " he means the didactic method in theology. This interpretation is too narrow, for there is a scholastic method in philosophy. But it is an excellent work. Henry Osborn Taylor, *The Mediæval Mind* (Macmillan, New York, 1918, two volumes), interesting. Studies the factors of the civilization of the Middle Ages, and the spirit which animates it. Masson-Oursel, *La Scolastique, étude de philosophie comparée* (Revue Philosophique, 1902, pp. 123-141). Ch. Huit, *Brève histoire du mot scolastique*. (L'enseignment chretienne, 1911, p. 444).

Talamo, *L'aristotelismo della scolastica nella storia della filosofia*, 3rd edition (Sienna, 1881. French translation, 1876). Good ; might be more methodical. Schneid, *Aristoteles in der Scholastik* (Eichstadt, 1875). Chollet, *L'aristotelisme de la Scolastique* (Dictionnaire de Théologie Catholique of Vacant), a general view in the light of recent research. C. Sauter, *Der Neuplatonismus, seine Bedeutung für die antike und mittelalt. Philos.* (Philosoph. Jahrbuch, 1910). R. Rubczinski, on the influence of Neo-Platonism in the Middle Ages (Cracow, 1891, and Revue Philos. of Weryho, 1900), written in Polish. Cf. Archiv. fur Gesch. Philos., 1905, p. 566.

Huet, a series of articles on Platonism in the Middle Ages in Annales de la Philosophie Chrétienne, New Series,vols. XX to XXII. M. Picavet endeavours to trace influences from sources other than Aristotelianism in his works (1889-1890). He stresses and exaggerates neo-Platonic influences. Grabmann, *Der Neuplatonismus in d. deutschen Hochschol* (Phil. Jahrb. 1910). Cl. Baeumker, *Der Anteil des Elsasz an d. geistigen Bewegungen d. M. A.* (Strasbourg, 1912), and above all his excellent Festrede : *Der Platonismus im Mittelalter*. Cf. **45**, works on the neo-Platonism of Macrobius, Chalcidius, and under the heading Second Period, works on Grosseteste, Albertus Magnus, and Latin neo-Platonism. For Stoicism see Second Period.

§ 2—DIVISION OF MEDIÆVAL PHILOSOPHY.

20. Chronological limits of mediæval philosophy.—According to the generally received chronology, the Middle Ages began with the death of Theodotius in 395 and ended with the capture of Constantinople by the Turks in 1453. But if we bear in mind the fact that the evolution of scholasticism was the most important event in the period from the point of view of philosophy, then we must make a two-fold reservation in accepting these chronological limits. In the first place, the earliest writings in which we can detect a new mode of thought—and even these are rather precocious and ill-favoured fruits—do not appear before the ninth century.[1] In the second place, mediæval and modern philosophy existed side by side for quite a long time. The modern period was not separated from the Middle Ages by any such violent upheaval as that which marked the destruction of the Roman Empire and the constitution of the Germanic nations. Hence the influence of mediæval philosophy extends well beyond 1453, and right up to the middle of the seventeenth century.

The autonomous evolution of mediæval philosophy, and especially of scholasticism, is the chief criterion which will inspire our delimitation. To this criterion we can add another,

---

[1] Willmann (*op. cit.* II, 342) would have scholasticism commence in the eighth century with the πηγή γνώσεως of St. John Damascene (see page 217) because the parts of this work are preceded by κεφάλαια φιλοσοφικά. In the same way, Taylor (*op. cit.* I, 6) thinks that the civilization proper of the Middle Ages did not commence before Gregory the Great († 604), Boethius († 523) and Cassiodorus († 575).

founded upon the development of the civilization itself in which this philosophy was evolved. Were we to select other criteria we should run the risk of upsetting the fundamental facts of chronology.[1]

Those, for instance, who regard mediæval philosophy as just a philosophy mixed up with religion are obliged to begin with a group of neo-Platonists, eclectic Platonists, and neo-Pythagoreans commencing " about the end of the first century before the Christian era, and lasting up to our own days."[2]

21. Division of mediæval philosophy.—We shall employ the same criteria in determining the internal divisions of mediæval philosophy.

The new civilization which arose in the West was not uniform in its development from the eighth to the fifteenth centuries. During the first period (eighth to eleventh centuries), the dominating period was a passive receptivity. The mediæval temperament became clearly manifest in the twelfth century ; and it produced its characteristic effects in the thirteenth, so that we may look upon these two centuries as the centre of the mediæval age. With the close of the fourteenth century mediæval civilization began to crumble, and the formation of the nations announced the dawn of a new world of ideas.

Western philosophy, with which we are principally concerned, followed precisely the same rhythm of formation, development, and decline. And we already know that scholasticism represents the principal current of ideas in the West. Hence we can establish the divisions of mediæval philosophy *a potiori*, by following the evolution of scholasticism. This evolution was slow, progressive and complex. In this respect mediæval scholasticism resembles the architecture of the period, which underwent a gradual transformation by continuous differentiation. But the divisions usually adopted will not include all the factors of this evolution, and we shall accordingly have to seek for some outstanding feature.

From this point of view, the events which led up to the

---

[1] Brucker fixes on the twelfth century as the commencement of mediæval philosophy. (*Historia critica philos.*, III, 709). But he wrote in the eighteenth century, when practically nothing was known about the early Middle Ages. Tribbechovius (*op. cit.*, p. 312 *et seq.*) begins with the Commentaries of Peter Lombard.

[2] Picavet, *Le moyen âge, caractéristique, théologique et philosophico-scientifique. Limites chronologiques*, in *Entre Camarades (Paris*, 1901), pp. 71 and 74. As for a " terminus ad quem," M. Picavet goes so far as to say that mediæval and modern civilization exist side by side even to-day.

scientific renaissance in the thirteenth century were epoch-making, and the preceding period was one of a long elaboration. In the thirteenth century scholasticism displayed all the wealth of its genius, but its splendour did not last long.   The period of decadence began already in the fourteenth century and was accentuated in the fifteenth.   From the second half of the fifteenth century up to the seventeenth, we may say that scholasticism was in a state of decline, attacked on all sides by new systems which were the forerunners of modern philosophy.   It was in vain that a few distinguished men attempted in the sixteenth century to restore the prestige of the dethroned sovereign : when compared to the glorious past, the reaction which they called forth was only a local and a temporary one. Hence we may distinguish four periods in mediæval philosophy :

  (i)   The Period of Formation (from the ninth to the end of the twelfth century) ;
  (ii) The Period of Full Development (thirteenth century) ;
  (iii) The Period of Decline (fourteenth and first half of fifteenth century) ;
  (iv) The Period of Transition from mediæval to modern philosophy (second half of fifteenth to the seventeenth century).[1]

To these divisions of Western Philosophy we shall attach a brief treatment of Eastern systems which must not altogether be neglected although they do not form the subject matter of this work.   During the first period, they form parallel and independent currents : Paris, Byzantium and Bagdad ignore each other.   These Oriental philosophies will be outlined in an apendix to this part.   From the thirteenth century the various currents of thought unite together : Western philosophy manifests a new and durable vitality in consequence of its contact with Arabian and Byzantine ideas.   On the other hand, the Jewish-Arabian philosophy rapidly disappears, and the Byzantine system falls into a decline.   Hence in the last three periods we shall deal only incidentally with the Byzantine, Arabian and Jewish philosophies, and shall not devote a special section to them.

There will be no need to make use of a geographical principle

---

[1] Tribbechovius, whose work is one of the earliest histories of scholasticism, if not the earliest of all, adopts a division into three periods : (1) from Peter Lombard to Albert the Great ; (2) from Albert the Great to Durandus ; (3) from Durandus to Luther. He does not deal with Byzantine philosophy, and he knows the Arabians only as inspirers of scholasticism.

of classification, for philosophy is cosmopolitan in the West, like civilization itself.

§ 3—ANCIENT AND MODERN SOURCES OF A GENERAL NATURE.

22. Ancient sources.—The philosophic manuscripts of the Middle Ages constitute the primary source for a history of philosophy. They are scattered up and down European libraries. Many are unpublished and even unknown. The history of philosophy will profit by the publication of catalogues of manuscripts : this is being undertaken almost everywhere. In addition, the publication of texts, critical editions, and above all the task of determining the authorship of works—particularly difficult in the case of the Middle Ages—has been going on now for several years. It would be helpful to have a list of the *incipit* of the philosophical manuscripts. Many works are anonymous or of doubtful authorship ; and the application of modern methods of internal and external historical criticism can alone lead to definite results.

In addition to works on philosophy, the general sources for the history of ideas should be consulted. These sources are many, and of unequal value. Among them may be mentioned the works of the ancient chroniclers continuing the *De Viris Illustribus* of St. Jerome (Isidore of Seville, Sigebert of Gembloux, Honorius of Autun, etc.). The information contained in these was utilized and completed by Trithemius in the fifteenth century, Miræus in the seventeenth, and Fabricius in the eighteenth century. Then there are the historical biographies of writers belonging to the religious orders. Each order had its chroniclers ; very often they were tempted to magnify the past, but compilations like that of Quetif-Echard, *Scriptores Ordinis Prædicatorum* (Paris, 1719, two volumes), and Wadding, *Scriptores Ordinis minor.* (with Sbaralea's Supplement, new edition in course of publication at Rome, three parts have appeared from 1906 to 1922) have great historic value. R. Coulon announces a new edition of the Dominican collection : *Scriptores ord. Prædicatorum, etc., emendata, plurimis accessionibus aucta et ad hanc nostram ætatem perducta* (Paris, begun in 1910). The first volumes continue the collection from 1701 up to date. Ossinger, *Bibliotheca augustiniana* (Ingolstadt, 1786) ; Cosmo de Villiers, *Bibliotheca carmelitana* (2 vols., Orleans, 1752) ; Ziegelbauer,

Historia rei literariæ ord. S. Benedicti (4 vols., 1754).   Also the various *Dictionaries of National Biography* such as the *Histoire litteraire de la France* begun by the Benedictines of St. Maur in the eighteenth century, and the English *Dictionary of Nat. Biogr.* Useful documents will be found in the various collections of the *Scriptores Ecclesiæ*, by reason of the close connection between philosophy and theology.

These ancient sources do not deal exclusively with the philosophy of the Middle Ages, and hence modern bibliographies must be consulted. Some of these sources will be referred to in connection with particular questions. The principal modern works of general bibliography concerning the Middle Ages are : Ebert, *Allgemeine Geschichte d. Litteratur d. Mittelalters im Abendlande* (3 vols., 1874-1887) ; Manitius, *Geschichte d. lat. Litteratur d. Mittelalters : Ir. Tiel, von Justinian bis zum Mitte d. 10 Jahr.* (Munich, 1911), an excellent work; *IIr Tiel : von der Mitte d. X Jahrh. bis zum Aushruch d. Kampfes zwischen Kirche und Staat* (1924) ;   H. Oesterley, *Wegweiser durch die Litteratur der Urkundensammlungen* (2 vols., 1885, 1886) ; U. Chevalier, *Répertoire des sources historiques du moyen âge*, I, Bio-Bibliographie (2nd edn.) ;   A. Potthast, *Bibliotheca historica medii ævi* (2nd edn., 1896) ;   E. Bernheim, *Lehrbuch d. historischen Methode und d. Geschichtsphilosophie* (5th edn., 1908). Also the bibliographies relative to particular countries, such as Wattenbach, *Deutschlands Geschichtsquellen in Mittelalter bis zur Mitte d. 13 Jahr.* (7th edn., 1904) ; O. Lorenz, *Deutschlands Geschichtsquellen im Mittelalter seit der Mitte des 13 Jahrh.* (3rd edn., 2 vols., 1886); Molinier, *Les sources de l'histoire de France* (Paris, 1901) ; C. Gross, *The Sources and Literature of English History* (Cambridge, U.S.A., 1915), valuable for English sources and works in English. L. J. Paetow, *Guide to the Study of Mediæval History* (University of California, 1917), a useful work. No history of philosophy was written in the Middle Ages, but information will be found in certain works by the Humanists, Reformers, and Cartesians. The prejudices of the authors must of course be taken into account. L. Vivès, *De causis corruptarum artium* (1555) ; A. Tribbechovius, *op. cit.* ; Ch. Binder, *De Scholastica theologia* (Tübingen, 1614) ; Jac. Thomasius, *De doctoribus scholasticis* (Leipzig, 1676) ; A. Geulinkz, *Discours et questions quodlibetiques*, in his *Opera* (edition of Land, The Hague, 1891-1893).

23. Modern works.—In this bibliography we only mention works concerning the philosophy of the Middle Ages in general. Special books will be mentioned in the course of the work. Also, our list only includes the most important or most recent works. It may be supplemented (down to 1915) by consulting the valuable bibliography of Ueberweg-Heinze, *Grundriss. d. Gesch. d. Philos.*, II. *Die mittlere oder die patritische und scholastische Zeit* (10th edn., 1915, edited by Baumgartner, the last chapter by E. Lasson) ; and the bibliographies published in the Louvain *Revue d'histoire ecclésiastique.* For a comprehensive plan, see F. Ehrle, *Nuove proposte per lo studio dei manoscritti d. scol. med.* (Gregorianum, 1922), pp. 198-218.

(i) *General works on the history of mediæval philosophy.*— Stöckl, *Geschichte der Philosophie des Mittelalters*, Vols. I to III (Mainz, 1864-1866). An excellent work, but now inadequate from the bibliographical point of view. Haureau, *Histoire de la philosophie scolastique* (3 vols., 1872-1881), scholarly, but goes astray concerning many philosophic doctrines ; Windelband, *Zur Wissenschaftsgeschichte der romanischen Völker* (in Gröber's *Grundriss der Geschichte der romanischen Philologie,* II, 1893, pp. 550-578) ; objective, very condensed, follows chronological order. Eusebius Stateczny, *Compendium historiæ Philos.* (Rome, 1898), pp. 234-241 deals with the Middle Ages. Elementary, and not very critical ; the best feature is a parallel exposition of Thomas Aquinas, Bonaventure, and Duns Scotus (pp. 310-388). Willmann, *Geschichte der Idealismus*, Vol. II, Fathers of the Church and the Middle Ages (Brunswick, 2nd edn. 1907), a study of systems ; excellent. Gonzalez, *Histoire de la Philosophie*, Vol. II (1898), good, but inadequate. Erdmann, *Grundriss d. Geschichte d. Philosophie* (4th edn. 1896), sums up modern works. Werner's works deal with practically the whole of the Middle Ages, but are superficial (see later on). B. Adlhoch, *Præfationes ad artis Scholasticæ inter Occidentales fata* (Brunæ, 1898), interesting, the author exaggerates the ideological side and does not pay sufficient attention to chronological order. De Wulf, *Histoire de la philos. scol. dans les Pays-Bas*, etc. (Louvain, 1895), a second edition has appeared under the title *Histoire de la philosophie en Belgique* (1910) ; *Introduction à la philosophie néo-Scolastique* (Louvain, 1904), the first part consists of general studies of scholasticism and the Middle Ages ; English translation under the title *Scholasticism Old and New*, Dublin, 1907). Picavet, *Esquisse d'une historie générale et comparée des philosophies médiévales* (2nd edn. Paris, 1907), many notes and documents ; *Essais sur l'historie générale et comparée des théologies et philosophies médiévoles* (Paris, 1913), collection of separate studies, confuses scholastic philosophy with religion of the Middle Ages, wrongly regards Plotinus as the source of the inspiration of the scholastics. Cl. Baeumker, *Die europäische Philosophie des Mittelalters*, in *Die Kultur der Gegenwart*, Vol. V (Berlin, 2nd edn. 1913, pp. 338-431), excellent general treatment. Endres, *Geschichte der mittelalterl. Philosophie im Abendlande* (Kempten, 1908), elementary, continues to regard as " scholastic " all philosophy in the Middle Ages. J. Rickaby, *Scholasticism* (London, 1908), elementary ; M. Grabmann, *Die Geschichte der Scholastichen Methode, Bd. I : Die schol. Methode von ihren ersten Anfängen in der Väterlitteratur bis zum Beginn des* 12 *Jahrh.* (Freiburg, 1909) ; *Bd. II : Die schol. Methode im* 12 *und beginnen den* 13 *Jahrh.* (1911) ; *Bd. III :* will treat the thirteenth century prior to St. Thomas, an excellent work dealing with and utilizing many unpublished texts ; *Die Philos. des Mittelalters* (Samml. Goschen, 1921), elementary ; E. Gilson, *La Philos. au moyen âge* (Paris, 1922, two small volumes), elementary ; *Etudes de philos. médiévale* (Strasbourg, 1921), good ; J. Verweyen, *Die Philos. d. Mittelalters* (Berlin, 1921), biassed. Fr. Overbeck, *Vorgeschichte u. Jugend d. Mittelalt. Scholastik* (Bale, 1917). The following works are collections of mono-graphs : Jourdain, *Excursions histor. à travers le m. â.* (Paris, 1888), a collection of 21 studies ; R. L. Poole, *Illustrations of the history of mediæval thought and learning* (London, 1920), two good books ; W. J. Townsend, *The Great Schoolmen of the M. A.* (the 1922 edition is a reprint of the 1881 edition), out of date.

(ii) *History of special branches.*—Prantl, *Geschichte der Logik im Abendlande*, Bd. II-IV (Leipzig, 1885, 1867, 1870), quotes many texts, good bibliography, a valuable work. Siebeck, *Geschichte d. Psychologie*, I, 2. ; *Die Psychologie von Aristoteles bis zum Thomas von Aquino* (Gotha, 1884), the mediæval section is cramped. Articles by the same writer in *Archiv. f. Gesch. d. Philos.*, Bd. I-II (1888-90) ; G. Brett, *History of Psychology, Vol. II : Mediæval and Early Modern Period* (London, 1922). Otto Willmann, *Didaktik als Bildungslehre* (3rd edn., Brunswick, 1903). The first volume contains an introduction, followed by a historic study, *Die geschichtlichen Typen des Bildungswesens*. Sections 17 to 20 deal with mediæval didactics and pedagogy. General views, excellent. Werner, *Entwicklungsgang der mittelalterl. Psychol.* (1876). Mabilleau, *Histoire de l'atomisme* (Paris, 1895). K. Lasswitz, *Geschichte d. Atomistik vom Mittelalter bis Newton* (I Band, 1890). Ziegler, *Gesch. d. Ethik* (Strasburg, 1886) ; Klimke, *Der Monismus und seine philosoph. Grundlage* (Freiburg, 1911). T. A. Walker, *A History of the Law of Nations, Vol. I : From the Earliest Times to the Peace of Westphalia* (Cambridge, 1899). R. W. and A. J. Carlyle, *A History of Mediæval Political Theory in the West* (London, Blackwood, 1903-1915), *Vol. I : The Second Century to the Ninth ; Vol. II : The Political Theory of the Roman Lawyers and the Canonists X-XIII c. ; Vol. III : From the Xth to the XIIIth c. ; Vol. IV : The Theories of the Relations of the Empire and the Papacy from the Xth to the XIIth Century* (1923). Very valuable. Otto von Gierke, *Das Deutsche Genossenschaft, etc., Bd. III : Die Staats und Korporationslehre d. Altertums u. d. Mittelalters une ihre Aufnahme in Deutschland* (Berlin, 1881), one chapter translated by Maitland, *Political Theories of the Middle Ages* (Cambridge, 1913). Fr. Pollock, *An Introduction to the History of the Science of Politics* (1914). P. Janet, *Histoire de la science politique dans ses rapports avec la morale*, Vol. I (Paris, 1887). E. Jenks, *Law and Politics in the Middle Ages* (London, 1919). Cl. J. Webb, *Studies in Hist. of Natural Theology* (Oxford 1915). Natural theology in the Middle Ages is dealt with in pp. 137-156.

(iii) *History of the Sciences.*—Berthelot, *La Chimie au moyen âge* (1893). Cantor, *Vorlesungen über d. Gesch. d. Mathematik*, II and III (1894). Rouse Ball, *History of Mathematics*. Poggendorff, *Biographisch-literarisches Handwörtenbuch zur Geschichte d. exakten Wissenschaften* (Leipzig, 1863). Höfer, *Histoire de l'Astronomie* (1873). Jessen, *Botanik d. Gegenwart u. Vorzeit* (1864). Carus, *Geschichte d. Zoologie* (1872). Haser, *Lehrbuch d. Gesch. d. Medizin* (1875). Daremberg, *Histoire des sciences médicales* (Paris, 1870). Pagel, *Einführung in d. Gesch. d. Medizin* (Berlin, 1898). L. Leclerc, *Histoire de la médicine arabe*. E. Gerland, *Geschichte d. Physik* (1892). A. Heller, *Gesch. d. Physik von Aristoteles bis auf d. neueste Zeit* (Stuttgart, 1882). Höfer, *Hist. de la Botanique, de la Minéralogie et de la Géologie*. J. Abert, *Die Musikanschauungen d. Mitt. u. ihre Grundlagen* (Halle, 1905) ; F. Strunz, *Geschichte d. Natur-*

wissenschaften im Mittelalter (Stuttgart, 1910) ; Dannemann, *Die Naturwissenschaften in ihrer Entwicklung und in ihrem Zusammenhange*, Bd. I-IV ; Libby, *Introduction to the History of Science* (1917) ; P. Duhem, *Le système du monde, Histoire des théories cosmologiques de Platon à Copernic* (1913-1917, five volumes), a work of great value, but contains some doctrinal errors in the fifth volume concerning the thirteenth century in the West. *Etudes sur Léonard de vinci : Ceux qu'il a lus et ceux qui l'ont lu*,3 series (Paris, 1906-1913) ; *L'astrologie au moyen âge*, in *R. Quest. scientifiques* (Oct., 1914) ; Ch. Singer, *Studies in the History and Method of Science* (1917 and 1922), two volumes containing a series of monographs ; Lynn Thorndike, *A History of Magic and Experimental Science during the First Thirteen Centuries of our Era* (New York, 1923) ; *Archiv. f. Geschichte der Naturwissenschaften u. der Technik* (Leipzig, commenced in 1902). The reviews *Isis* and *Scientia* are devoted to the history of the sciences.

(iv) *History of Art and Letters.*—J. Bedier, *Les légendes épiques* (Paris, 1909-1913) ; L. Bréhier, *L'art chrétien, Son développement iconogr.*, etc. (Paris, 1918) ; E. Mâle, *L'art religieux du XIIIe s. en France* (Paris, 1923) ; *L'art religieux du XIIIe s. en France* (Paris, 5th edn. 1923) ; *L'art religieux de la fin du m.â. en France* (2nd edn., 1922), important works.—*L'art allemand et l'art français du m.â.* (Paris, 1917). C. Enlart, *Manuel d'archéologie française*, etc., Vols. I-III (Paris, 1902-1906) ; Norden, *Die antike Kunstprosa*, etc. (Vol. II, 1909) ; *Die latein. Litt. im Uebergang v. Altertum zum Mittelalter* (Kultur d. Gegenwart, I, 8, Leipzig, 1905) ; G. Hanoteaux, *Histoire de la nation française*, Vol. XII : *Histoire des Lettres*, par Bédier, Jeanroy et Picavet ; J. Sandys, *A History of Classical Scholarship from the sixth century to the end of the Middle Ages* (1903, 3rd edn. 1921) ; H. O. Taylor, *The Classical Heritage of the Middle Ages* (3rd edn.).

(v) *Civilization and general history of ideas.*—*Beiträge zur Kulturgeschichte d. Mittelalt. u. d. Renaissance*, ed. Goetz (Leipzig : Teubner). Eight parts had appeared in 1910. Reuter, *Geschichte d. religiösen Aufklärung im M. A.*, 2 Bd. (1875-1877) ; Von Eicken, *Geschichte und System d. mittelalt. Weltanschauung* (1887), one sided, see excellent criticism by Von Hertling, *Hist. Jahrb.* 1889, reprinted in *Historische Beitr. z. Philos.* by V. Hertling, published by Endres (Munich, 1914). For the later period see : Alfred von Martin, *Mittelalt, Welt u.*

Lebensanschauung im Spiegel d. Schriften Collucio Salutati
(Histor. Bibl. Bd. 33, 1913), distinguishes between the religious
and the lay ideal in the Middle Ages ; W. Dilthey, *Einleitung
in die Geisteswissenschaften* (1883), I, 338 *et seq.* ; H. O. Taylor,
The Mediæval Mind, 2 vols., 1911, 3rd edn., 1919, general
outlines. Baeumker announces a work, *Die mittelalterliche
Weltanschauung* in the collection of V. Below and Meinecke :
Handbuch der mittelalterlichen und neueren Geschichte (Munich,
Oldenbourg) ; Carlyle, *op. cit.* : Mandonnet, Vol. I of *Siger
de Brabant* (in series *Philosophes Belges*, Louvain) ; E. Troeltsch
Die Sociallehren der christlichen Kirchen und Gruppen, Ch. II :
Der mittelalterliche Katholicismus (Tubingen, 1919), a detailed
study of unitive and particularist tendencies ; F. S. Marvin,
The Living Past (3rd edn. Oxford, 1917) ; *The Unity of Western
Civilization* (Oxford, 1915) ; *Progress and History* (1916).
These two works consist of essays by various writers. M. De
Wulf, *Civilization and Philos. in the Middle Ages* (Princeton,
1922), studies philosophy in its relation to other factors of
civilization ; Rocquain, *La papauté au m. â.* (Paris, 1881) ;
A. L. Smith, *Church and State in the Middle Ages* (Oxford,
1913).

On civilization in various countries.—R. Altamira, *Historia
de Espana y de la civilis espanola*, Vol. I (Madrid, 1913) ; K.
Lamprecht, *Deutsche Geschichte*, Bd. II-III (Berlin, 1892-1893) ;
Steinhausen, *Gesch. d. deutschen Kultur*, Bd. I (Leipzig, 1913) ;
W. J. Ashley, *An Introd. to English Economic History and
Theory*, Part I (London, 1906) ; Traill, *Social England :
A Record of the Progress of the People*, Vols. I-II (London, 1901) ;
T. P. Tout, *France and England, their Relations in the Middle
Ages and Now* (London, 1922) ; A. Luchaire, *Hist. des institut.
monarchiques de la France sous les premiers Capétiens*, Vol. I
(Paris, 1891) ; Vol. III of Lavisse's *Histoire de France* (Paris,
1912) ; C. Langlois, *La vie en France au m. â. d'après quelques
moralistes du temps* ; *La connaissance de la nature et du monde au
m. âge* (Paris, 1911), biassed, regards religion as consisting of
superstitions and legends.

(vi) *History of theology and religion.*—Feret. *La faculté
de théologie de Paris et ses docteurs les plus célèbres. Le moyen
âge* (Paris, 1884-1897), 4 vols., not very critical, biographies
with references, not much place given to the history of ideas.
Hefelé, *Histoires des conciles*, translated into French by Leclerc ;
Schwane, *Dogmengeschichte des mittleren Zeit* (Fribourg, 1882),

from the Catholic standpoint. Harnack, *Lehrbuch d. Dogmenge-schichte*, Bd. III (4th edn., 1910), Protestant standpoint. J. Verweyen, *Philosophie u. Theologie im Mittelalter* (Bonn, Cohen, 1911), biassed ; G. Hanoteaux, *Histoire de la nation française*, Vol. VI : *Histoire religieuse*, by G. Goyau, excellent general view. See the collections by Ehrhard and Kirsch, *Forschungen z. christlichen Litteratur und Dogmengeschichte* (Paderborn) ; Sdralek, *Kirchengeschichtl. Abhandlungen* (Breslau) ; Knöpfler, *Veröffentl. aus d. kirchengesch. Seminar* (Munich) ; Bonwetsch and Seeberg. *Neue Studien z. Geschichte der Theologie u. Kirche* (Berlin) ; Seeberg, *Dogmengeschichte*. Vol. III : *Mittelalter*.

(vii) *Collections of texts and special studies.*—Migne, *Patrologiæ cursus completus*`: (1) *Series Latina*, 221 vols., 1844-1864, goes up to 1216, continued by Horoy in five additional volumes (1879-1885). Cf. A. Noyon, *Inventaire des écrits théolog. du XIIe s. non insérés dans Patrol. latine de Migne*, R. des biblioth., 1912 and 1913). (2) *Series græca*, 161 vols., 1857-1866, containing numerous editions of mediæval works, a well-known and very valuable collection. Sigmund Barach, *Bibliotheca philosophorum mediæ ætatis*, interrupted, two vols. have appeared : I. *De mundi universitate libri duo sive mega-cosmus et microcosmus* (Innsbruck, 1876) ; II. *Excerpta a libro Alfredi anglici " de motu Cordis," Costa Ben Lucæ de differentia animæ et spiritus* (1878) ; *Notices et extraits des manuscrits de la Biblioth. Nationale*. Full of information about the Latin philosophical MSS. Haureau, *Notices et extraits de quelques manuscrits latins de la Biblioth. Nationale*, 6 vols., 1890-1893, collection of notes on various philosophical MSS., in numerical order, valuable. Studies on the same in *Journal des savants*, 1888-1890 ; Ehrle, *Bibliotheca theologiæ et philosophiæ scholasticæ*, interrupted, seven vols. have appeared, very well done : S. Maurus' *Commentary on Aristotle* (1885-87), and the *Summa Philosophiæ* of C. Alamannus (1894), see later concerning these. *Bibliotheca franciscana scholastica medii ævi,* published at Quaracchi, 5 vols., *Bibliotheca franciscana ascetica medii ævi, ibid. Scriptores rerum Britannicarum*, contains poems, archives, and philosophical works by English authors in the Middle Ages. *Beiträge zur Geschichte d. Philosophie d. Mittelalters*, edited at Munster by Cl. Baeumker-Hertling. Very useful and important collection, brought out with the collaboration of von Hertling, F. Ehrle, M. Baumgartner, and M. Grabmann, from

1891 to 1923. The following are the principal volumes
to which reference will be made : Bd. I : 1, P. Correns, *Die d.
Bœthius fälschlich zugeschr. Abhandlung der Dominicus Gundisalvi de unitate;* 2-4, C. Baeumker, *Avencebrolis (Ibn Gebirol)
Fons Vitæ, ex arabico in latinum transl. ab J. Hispano et
Dominico Gundissalino,* Bd. II : 1, M. Baumgartner, *Die
Erkenntnislehre d. Wilhelm von Auvergne;* 3, G. Bulow, *Des
D. Gundissalinus Schrift Von der Unsterblichk. der Seele,
herausgeg. u. philos. untersucht. Anhange enth. die Abhandlung
des Wilhelm von Paris, De immortalitate animæ;* 4, M. Baumgartner, *Die Philos. d. Alanus de Insulis, im Zusammenhange
mit d. Ansch. des 12 Jahrh. darg.;* 6, Cl. Baeumker, *Die Impossi-
bilia des Siger von Brabant, eine philos. Streitschr. aus d. XIII
Jahrh.* Bd. III : 1, B. Domanski, *Die Psychologie des Nemesius;*
2, Cl. Baeumker, *Witelo, ein Philos. u. Naturforscher des XIII
Jahrh.;* 3, M. Wittmann, *Die Stellung des hl. Th. von Aquin
zu Avencebrol;* 4, J. N. Espenberger, *Die Philos. des Petrus
Lombardus und ihre Stellung im 12. Jahrh.;* 5, B. W. Switalski,
Des Chalcidius Kommentar zu Platos Timæus. Bd. IV : 1,
H. Willner, *Des Adelard von Bath Traktat De eodem et diverso;*
2-3, L. Baur, *Gundissalinus De divisione philosophiæ;* 4, Wilh.
Engelkemper, *Die religionsphilos. Lehre Saadja Gaons über
die Hl. Schrift;* 5-6, A. Schneider, *Beitr. zur Psych. Alberts
den Groszen, Ie Teil.* Bd. V : 1, M. Wittmann, *Zur Stellung
Avencebrols im Entwicklungsgang der arabischen Philosophie;*
2, S. Hahn, *Thomas Bradwardinus und seine Lehre von der
Mensch. Willensfreiheit;* 3, P. P. Minges, *Ist Duns Scotus
Indeterminist?;* 6-7, E. Krebs, *Meister Dietrich, sein Leben,
seine Werke, seine Wissenchaft.*—Bd. VI : 1, H. Ostler, *Die
Psychologie des Hugo von St.-Viktor:* 2, J. Lappe, *Nicolaus von
Autrecourt, Sein Leben, seine Philos., seine Schriften;* 3, G.
Grunwald, *Gesch. der Gottesbeweise im Mittelalter bis z. Ausg.
der Hochschol.;* 4-5, E. Lutz, *Die Psychologie Bonaventuras;*
6, P. Rousselot, *Pour l'histoire du problème de l'amour au
moyen âge.* Bd. VII : 1, P. Minges, *Der angebliche exzessive
Realismus des Duns Scotus;* 2-3, B. Geyer, *Die Sententiæ
divinitatis, ein Sentenzenbuch der Gilbertschen Schule.
Herausg. u. historisch untersucht;* 4-5, O. Keicher,
*Raymundus Lullus und seine Stellung zur arabischen
Philosophie;* 6, A. Grünfeld, *Die Lehre vom göttl. Willen bei
den jüdischen Religionsphilosophen des Mittelalters von Saadja
bis Maimûni.* Bd. VIII : 1-2, A. Daniels, *Quellenbeitr. u.*

Untersuch. zur Gesch. der Gottesbeweise im 13 *Jahrh. mit bes.
Berücksicht. d. Arguments im Proslogion des hl. Anselm ;* 3,
J. A. Endres, *Petrus Damiani und die weltliche Wissenschaft ;*
4, Petrus Blanco Soto, *Petri Compostellani de consolatione
rationis libri duo ;* 5. J. Keiners, *Der Nominalismus in der
Frühscholastik ;* 6, E. Vansteenberghe, *Le " De Ignota Littera-
tura " de Jean Wenck de Herrenberg.* Bd. IX : L. Baur, *Die
Philos. Werke des Robert Grosseteste, Bischofs von Lincoln.
Krit. Ausgabe.* Bd. X. : 1-2, O. Renz, *Die Synteresis nach dem
hl. Thomas von Aquin ;* 3, J. Fischer, *Die Erkenntnislehre
Anselms von Canterbury ;* 6, Fr. Baeumker, *Die lehre A. von
Canterbury über den Willen und seine Wahlfreiheit.* Bd. XI : 1,
Th. Steinbüchel, *Der Zweckgedanke in der Philosophie des
Thomas von Aquino ;* 2, M. Meier, *Die Lehre des Thomas von
Aquino " de passionibus animæ " in quellen analytischer
Darstellung ;* 3-4, E. Krebs, *Theologie und Wissenschaft nach
der Lehre der Hochscholastik. An der Hand der Defensa Doctrinæ
D. Thomæ des Hervæus Natalis ;* 5, Anselm Rohner, *Das Schö-
pfungsproblem bei Moses Maimonides, A. Magnus und Th. von
Aquin ;* 6, R. Dreiling, *Der Konzeptualismus in der Univer-
salienlehre des Franziskanererzbisch. P. Aureoli nebst biograph.-
bibliograph. Einleitung.* Supplement : *Studien zur Geschichte
der Philosophie, Festgabe zum* 60. *Geburtstag Cl. Baeumkers.*
Bd. XII : 1, L. Gaul, *Z. der Grossen Verhältnis zu Plato ;* 2-4,
J. Kroll, *Die Lehren des Hermes Trimegistos darg. und im Lichte
griech. Philos. betrachtet ;* 5-6, J. Würschmidt, *Theodoricus
Teutonicus de Vriberg de iride radialibus impressionibus.* Bd.
XIII : 1, M. Schedler, *Die Philos. des Macrobius und ihr Ein-
fluss auf die Wissenschaft des christlichen Mittelalters ;* 2-3,
J. N. Probst, *La Mystique de Raymon Lull et l'Art de Contem-
plació ;* 5, G. Schulemann, *Das Kausalprinzip in der Philos.
d. Th. von Aquino ;* 6, Fr. Baeumker, *Das Inevitabile des
Honorius Augustodunensis.* Bd. XIV : 2-4, E. Vansteenberghe,
*Autour de la " Docte Ignorance," une controverse sur la Théologie
mystique au XVe siècle;* 5-6, G. Von Hertling, *Albertus Magnus,
Beiträge zu seiner Würdigung.* Bd. XV : H. J. Stadler, *Albertus
Magnus de animalibus libri XXVI. Nach der Kölner Urschrift.*
Bd. I (Buch. I-XII). Bd. XVI. Bd. II, Buch XIII-XXVI.
Bd. XVII : 1, Fr. Beemelmans, *Zeil und Ewigkeit nach Thomas
von Aquino ;* 2-3, J. Ant. Endres, *Forschungen zur Geschichte
der frühmittelaltl. Philos. ;* 4, A. Schneider, *Die abendl. Spekul.
des zwölften Jahrh. in ihrem Verhältnis zur aristotel. und*

jüdisch-arab. Philos.; 5-6, M. Grabmann, *Forschungen über die Latein. Aristotelesübersetz. des XIII Jahrh.* Bd. XVIII: 1, K. Michel, *Der " Liber de consonancia nature et gracie" de Raphael de Pornaxio;* 2-3, P. Bliemetzrieder, *Anselms von Laon system. Sentenzen;* 4-6, L. Baur, *Die Philosophie des Robert Grosseteste, Bischofs bon Lincoln,* Bd. XIX: 1, W. Müller *Der Staat in seinen Beziehungen zur sittlichen Ordnung bei Thomas von Aquin;* 3, Cl. Baeumker, *Alfarabi, Ueber den Ursprung der Wissenschaften;* 4, J. Ebner, *Die Erkenntnisl, Richards von St. Viktor;* 5-6, H. Spettmann, *Johannis Pechami Quaestiones.* Bd. XX: 1, J. Würsdörfer, *Erkennen und Wissen nach Gregor von Rimini;* 2, M. Grabmann, *Die Philosophia Pauperum u. ihr. Verfasser Albert v. Orlamünde;* 5, A. Birkenmajer, *Vermischte Untersuchungen zur Geschichte der mittel. Philos.;* 6, H. Spettmann, *Die Psych. des Johannes Pecham.* Bd. XXI: B. Geyer, *Peter Abaelards philosoph. Schriften. I. Die Logica " Ingredientibus."* 1, *Die Glossen zu Porphyrius.* 2, *Die Glossen zu den Kategorien.* Bd. XXII: 1-2, M. Grabmann, *Die echten Schriften des hl. Thomas von Aquin;* 3-4, Georg Heidingsfelder, *Albert von Sachsen, Sein Lebensgang und sein Kommentar zur Nikomachischen Ethik des Aristoteles.* Bd. XXIII: Clem. Baeumker, 1-2, *Des Alfred von Sareshel (Alfredus Anglicus) Schrift. De motu cordis;* 3-4, Luyckx, *Die Erkenntnisslehre Bonaventuras;* Supplt. Bd.: Festgabe 60 Geburststag Cl. Baeumker; 5, A. Daniels, *Eine latein. Rechtfertigungsschrift d. Meister Eckhart.* Bd. XXIV: 1, Cl. Baeumker u. von Waltershausen, *Fruhmittelalterliche Glossen d. angeblichen Jepa z. Isagoge des Porphyrius.*

Les Philosophes Belges (Louvain) : Vol. I, M. De Wulf, *Le traité de unitate formæ de Gilles de Lessines.* Vol. II, M. De Wulf et A. Pelzer, *Les IV prem. Quodlibet de G. de Fontaines.* Vol. III, M. De Wulf et J. Hoffmans, *Le Quodlibeta. V-VII de G. de Fontaines.* Vol. IV, Part One, *Quodlibetum VIII.* Vols. VI. and VII, P. Mandonnet, *Siger de Brabant et l'averroisme latin.* Vol. VIII, G. Wallerand, *Les œuvres de Siger de Courtrai.* Vol. IX, A. de Poorter, *Le traité eruditio regum et principum de Guibert de Tournai.*

Etudes de Philos. médiévale (Gilson). *Bibliotheca de Tomistas Espanoles* (L. Urbano). *Museum Lessianum* (section philosophique) and *Spicilegium Sacrum Lovaniense* (Louvain), will contain studies and documents relative to mediæval philosophy.

(viii.) *Dictionaries, encyclopædias and catalogues.—Dictionn.*

des sciences philosoph. by Franck (2nd edn. 1875), many articles
by M. Haureau, inspired by the general views of the author;
Baldwin's *Dictionary of Philosophy and Psychology* (1901), weak
so far as the Middle Ages are concerned; A. Seth, article on
Scholasticism in the *Encyclopædia Britannica* (9th edition,
1886), general study and historic outline, has the merit of
reacting already against the contemptuous opinions entertained
concerning mediæval philosophy; Fr. Nitzsch, article *Scholastische Theologie* in *Realencyclopadie f. protest. Theol. u. Kirche*
of Herzog-Hauck, Bd. 13 (1884), does not recognise the
autonomous character of mediæval philosophy; articles
concerning mediæval philosophy in the *Grande Encyclopédie*;
good articles in the *Catholic Encyclopædia*; *Dictionary of
Christian Biography*, edited by W. Smith and H. Wace; *Dictionnaire de théologie catholique*, commenced by Vacant in 1899,
continued by Mangenot and Amann, some seven volumes
have so far appeared, containing numerous articles of value;
Hurter, *Nomenclator litterarius theologiæ catholicæ*, Vols. I
and II, 3rd edn., 1903, very useful; new edition of Vol. II
1109-1563); Wetzer u. Welte, *Kirchenlexicon*, 2nd edn. 1882-
1903; Hasting's *Encyclopædia of Religion and Ethics;* Encyclopædia Britannica (11th edn.); *Jewish Encyclopædia;* Basset,
Encycl. de l'Islam (in course of publication).

Lists of *incipit* : A. T. Little, *Initia operum quæ sæculis* XIII,
XIV, XV *attribuuntur, secundus ordinem alphabeticum disposita*
(Manchester, 1904); *Anecdota Oxoniensia, Index Britanniæ
Scriptorum*, John Bale's *Index of British and other Writers*,
edited by R. Lane (Oxford, Clarendon Press, 1902). The
voluminous collection of catalogues of European libraries
must also be consulted. In many important cases the catalogues
of MSS. have not yet been published.

(ix) *Auxiliary sciences.*—Ducange, *Glossarium mediæ et
infimæ latinitatis* (1840. 6 vols). There is not, as far as we know,
any special treatise concerning philosophical paleography.
This is a pity, for many abbreviations in manuscripts are
peculiar to philosophic authors; Ehrle, *Das Studium der
Handschriften d. mittelalterlichen Scholastik mit besond. Berück-
sichtigung d. Schule d. hl. Bonaventure (Zeitschr. f. Kathol. Theol.*,
1883, p. 1-50); Traube, *Quellen und Untersuchungen sur
lateinischen philologie des Mittelalters* (Munich, begun in 1905),
contains amongst other things texts of Johannes Scottus
published by Rand; *Vorlesungen u. Abhandl. II Einleitung*

in d. lateinische Philologie d. Mittelalters, hrgg. von Lehmann, a most important work ; Signoriello, *Lexicon peripateticum philosophico-theologicum in quo Scholasticorum distinctiones et effata præcipua explicantur* (3rd edn. Naples, 1893) ; Reeb, *Thesaurus philosophorum*, edit. Cornoldi. See special lexicons for S. Thomas, Bonaventure, Duns Scotus.

(x) *Reviews.*—There are no special reviews for the history of mediæval philosophy, but many studies will be found in *Archiv für Litteratur und Kirchengeschichte des Mittelalters* by Denifle and Ehrle (interrupted, of great value) ; *Philosophisches Jahrbuch* (Fulda) ; *Annales de philosophie chrétienne* (Paris) ; *Révue de Philosophie* (Paris) ; *Révue Thomiste* (Fribourg) ; *Révue Néo-Scolastique de Philosophie* (Louvain), containing since 1904 our " Bulletins sur la Philosophie du moyen age " analysing and criticizing recent works ; *Archiv. für Geschichte der Philosophie* by Stein ; *Zeitschrift fur katholische Theologie* (Innsbruck) ; *Jahrbuch für Philos, und spekul. Theologie* (Paderborn), replaced by *Divus Thomas* (first at Vienna, and later at Fribourg in Switzerland)[1]; *Révue des sciences philosophiques et théologiques* of Kain (Belgium) ; *Ciencia Tomista* (Madrid, since 1910) ; *Archivum franciscanum historicum* (Quaracchi, since 1908) ; *Franciskan. Studien ; Studi francescani ; Rivista di filosofia neo-scolastica* (Florence, since 1909) ; *Zeitschrift f. wissenschaftliche Theologie ; Theologische Quartalschrift ; Archivo Ibero-Americano* (Madrid, since 1914) ; *Gregorianum, Commentarii de re theologica et philosophica* (since 1921) ; *Quellen u. Forschungen z. Gesch. d. Dominikanerordens im Deutschl.* hrgg. P. von Loë u. H. Wilms (Leipzig, since 1919) ; *Recherches de science religieuse* (Paris) ; *Eludes franciscaines* (Paris).

There are also some reviews devoted to the Middle Ages in general : *Bibliothèque de l'école des chartes ; Le moyen âge* (original and analysed studies).

---

[1] Distinct from the old Plaisance *Divus Thomas* which began to reappear in 1924.

FIRST PERIOD

WESTERN PHILOSOPHY UP TO THE
END OF THE TWELFTH CENTURY

CHAPTER I

General Notions

§1—*The New State of Society and the Formation of the Common Philosophic Heritage*

24. Formation of the new civilization.—The formation of the new societies out of the ruins of the Roman Empire in the West comprised various stages which must be carefully distinguished. It began with a period of tentative efforts, lasting until Charlemagne. The ninth to the twelfth centuries saw the constitution of the most characteristic feature of the mediæval period, namely, the feudal system. It reached its fullest expression in the twelfth century : for it was then that the results of this long period of preparation became manifest, and the new characteristic civilization made its appearance.

(i) Previous to the breaking up of the empire of Charlemagne, the mediæval temperament was in process of development, under the influence of three factors :

(*a*) The passive reception of certain elements from the Roman world (elements of administrative, juridical and political organization, and fragments of scientific and philosophical ideas).

(*b*) The reaction on the part of the new races, which subjected these elements to an assimilative process, and adapted them to their customs and institutions. These new races were the Celts and the German (the latter included different races, Franks, Angles, Teutons, Normans, etc.). The Germans mingled with the Celts who had preceded them in the West, and also with the Latin elements. From this fusion there arose complex nations, chief among them being the neo-Latins of Gaul, Italy, and Spain, the Anglo-Celts after the infusion of Norman blood, and the Teutons or Germans of beyond the Rhine, who all had a part to play in the history of philosophy.

(*c*) Christianity directed the whole process. It had a difficult task in taming the barbarians and turning them into civilized

47

men. The Church extended everywhere by means of bishops, clerics, and Benedictine monks.

(ii) From the breaking up of the empire of Charlemagne to the end of the eleventh century.—The empire of Charlemagne broke up under his successors, and while the kingdoms which resulted from the various divisions became disorganized internally, the new civilization was menaced by invaders from without : the Mohammedans in the South, the Hungarians in the East. In the North the Normans penetrated deeply into Gaul, and were assimilated to the existing population ; and from this fusion there resulted a race endowed with remarkable gifts.

When it became evident that the successors of Charlemagne were not in possession of sufficient power to hold their own, the country of Gaul was parcelled out like a chessboard ; petty nobles usurped the royal prerogatives ; and thence arose a social organization based upon the personal loyalty of the vassal to his suzerain, and a free contract regulating reciprocal rights and duties. This feudal regime appeared first of all in France, and developed rapidly. From France it passed into England, when William the Conqueror and his knights (1066) introduced French ideas into the barbarous society which the Saxon tribes had installed there. Later on, the feudal system with all its accompanying institutions passed into the North of Spain, the South of Italy, and even into Palestine, thanks to the Crusades. As for Germany, it was lifted out of the chaotic state into which it had been plunged at the fall of the Carlovingian Empire, by the Saxon dynasty of the Ottos, which in the tenth century set up a Cæsarian autocracy, thus renewing the Roman Empire. Dukes, bishops, and abbots were bound by a kind of military service and were the servants of the Emperor. The latter had himself crowned by the Pope, whom he himself nominated.

The Church's discipline became relaxed, and the Benedictine monasteries which the Normans had not burnt departed from the primitive rule. The foundation of the Abbey of Cluny in 910 was the starting point of a reform. Modelled as it was upon the feudal hierarchy, the order of Cluny set up hundreds of monasteries, thus forming a vast network all over Europe. Its religious influence was accompanied by a social one. The monks of Cluny worked for the abolition of serfdom ; they organized the Peace of God, the Truce of God, and collective pilgrimages ; they denounced the licentious life of some of the bishops, and protested against their investiture by laymen.

The art of the book was the principal art of the monasteries ; schools like that of St. Martin of Tours attained to a high degree of perfection in caligraphy, illumination, and miniature work. From the eleventh century onwards, Romanesque architecture developed, and the Cluniacs became its propagators.

The economic regime of Europe during this period was above all agricultural. The size of the feudal possessions led to the organization of serfdom. Commerce in the West came into being once more with the rise of the towns at the end of the eleventh century.

(iii) The twelfth century was the springtime of feudal civilization, and the freshness of youth shone out in all the forms of human activity.

France was the centre of this movement. Louis VII inaugurated the new policy, which consisted of increasing the authority and dominion of the king. But he met with only a comparatively small measure of success, and sectionalism remained, though diminished.

Abbeys multiplied in number. In addition to the Order of Cluny, whose great riches hampered its activity, a new Benedictine order was found at Citeaux. The religious and social work of the Cistercians was crystallized in the twelfth century in the ascetic and authoritative figure of St. Bernard. His influence extended everywhere ; he gave directions to kings and popes, to clergy and professors ; he launched the Second Crusade ; he encouraged the foundation of new religious orders, the Templars, Carthusians (1132), Premonstratensians (1120), and the Augustinians of St. Victor, whose monastery in Paris became famous. Side by side with the fighting bishops, a survival of the primitive and rude feudal system, appeared prelates like Stephen of Tournai, William of Champeaux, and Peter of Corbeil, who were renowned for their intellectual worth. Paris possessed a model bishop in the person of Maurice de Sully (1160-1186), who was contemporary with the great educational changes in the French capital. The bishops of Chartres, Laon, and Tournai were patrons of learning. Like the King, they had to reckon with the middle classes of the towns, which had grown rich by commerce, insisted upon having privileges and charters, formed a new

E

class over and above the feudal classes of clerics and serfs, and presented to society as a whole an ideal of individual liberty and independence.

Characteristic customs sprang up ; they were a function of what may be called the feudal and communal sentiment *par excellence*, namely, that of the personal value and dignity of the individual. The feudal man lived as a free man and alienated his activity only by contract. This sentiment was christianized by the Benedictine influence, and the Church extended its benefits to all souls redeemed by Christ. Fidelity to one's spoken word, brotherhood in arms, reciprocal devotion, honour and uprightness, respect for women, kindness towards children —these virtues surrounded knighthood, a quasi-moral institution superposed upon the feudal system, and all its rites received a Christian interpretation. By a sort of contagion the manners of the middle classes also became more gentle, and courtesy presided over the social relations of educated people. Certainly, this picture of feudal virtues is only that of an ideal, and the actual reality was full of faults, but it was an active ideal all the same, and the mediæval man felt its attraction in spite of the excesses of his qualities and failings.

Again, the twelfth century gave rise in France to new forms of art : the *Chanson de geste* (Roland, Ogier, and the Aliscans) created by the Troubadours and full of the ideas of chivalry ; the Latin hymns, written in language breathing the spirit of pure humanism by an Adam of St. Victor ; the poems of an Alan of Lille ; the correspondence between Abelard and Heloise ; and the various particular forms of Romanesque architecture and sculpture, of which the Benedictine abbeys were the promoters.[1]

The Kings of England, who spoke French at their Court, resided in their French possessions, and were buried in the Abbeys of Caen or Fontevrault, were associated with the Kings of France in this expansion of civilization. The two countries were closely connected from the time when Henry II of England acquired considerable feudal possessions (from the Somme to the Gironde) through his marriage with Eleanor of Aquitaine, the divorced wife of Louis VII of France. The wars between the Kings of England and France were the quarrels of a

---

[1] We are not here concerned with the oriental influences which explain the origin of Romanesque iconography and sculpture. See Mâle, *L'Art religieux au XIIe s. en France*, 1922.

suzerain and his vassal, inasmuch as Henry II depended upon Louis VII for his French lands. These quarrels did not prevent prominent Englishmen from sojourning in France, nor French nobles from crossing over to England, nor French clerics from holding English sees, especially that of Canterbury. Romanesque churches were built upon English soil by the Cluniacs, and Gothic ones by the Cistercians. The politics of Henry II were very similar to those of Louis VII : in short, there was a community of civilization in the two countries.

In Germany, the imperial autocracy was broken down step by step ; and by a process which was exactly the contrary of what was taking place in France, the country gradually came to present a feudal and urban appearance. Towards the second half of the eleventh century, the Abbey of Hirschau, an offshoot of that of Cluny, began the reform of the monasteries ; courteous manners were introduced into the Court of the Souabes ; and the new Romanesque and Gothic art passed across the Rhine.

As for Italy, which the German Emperors always wished to subjugate, it was likewise divided up into principalities. The Lombard towns in the North were municipal republics ; the Kingdom of the Two Sicilies, founded in the beginning of the twelfth century by Norman knights and governed by kings of French descent, was a centre of French feudal culture. The Lombard League repulsed Frederick Barbarossa, and the kingdom of the Two Sicilies opposed both the imperial domination and the ever-growing power of the Popes.

Finally there was Spain, at the limits of Western and Arab civilization. The capture of Toledo in 1085 and of Saragossa in 1118 marked the first steps in the " reconquista " of territory from the Unbelievers. The connecting links between the various kingdoms and France multiplied in number, especially in the case of the kingdoms of Navarre, Castille, and Aragon. At the same time the Arab civilization which developed peacefully side by side with Western culture in Mohammedan regions, began to manifest its influence in the scientific, artistic and social spheres.

Lastly, above all the kingdoms which developed an internal organization by compromising between the central power and the feudal and urban elements, the Papacy tended more and more to play a cosmopolitan rôle from the temporal, spiritual and moral points of view. It exercised its ascendancy over the

" three Christian kings " of France, England, and Spain. It assured the unity of faith and of discipline. Certainly there were numerous heretical movements in the twelfth century, but they did not break up the religious unity of the West. They were rather like ripples upon the surface, which did not trouble the depths of a society saturated with Christianity.

On every side the great social forces which go to make up a civilization waxed strong. The feudal monarchy, the great nobles, the clergy, the middle classes of the towns, the country folk—all had their places well marked out ; formulas were sought after which would safeguard the rights of all ; great moral and religious sentiments animated the social body ; art began to grow and was not to die again. Such a civilization was ripe for the works of the mind.

25.—Formation of the philosophic heritage.—Like the civilization of the period, philosophy went through certain stages in its formation. Four characteristics mark its beginnings :

(i) *Passive reception of the knowledge of antiquity*. The first thinkers simply collected together the *débris* of the knowledge of antiquity wherever they could find it. In the realm of knowledge, this passive receptivity ended in an encyclopædic tendency, and in fact the first mediæval writers from the fourth to the eighth century were encyclopædists (§ 3). The *florilegia*, or collections of sentences borrowed from numerous authors and relating to theological and philosophical subjects, were the result of this same desire to form collections.

(ii) *Gradual delimitation of the sphere of philosophy*. Not only was the knowledge of the first centuries encyclopædic in character : in addition, this collection of different kinds of knowledge was called philosophy. Isidore of Seville wrote : " Philosophia est rerum humanarum divinarum cognitio cum studio bene vivendi conjuncta."[1] And Alcuin defined philosophy as "naturarum inquisitio, rerum humanarum divinarumque cognitio quantum homini possibile est æstimare."[2] At first there was no dividing line either between philosophy and theology, or between philosophy and the liberal arts. It was only in the eleventh century that philosophy was separated from the kindred sciences.

---

[1] *Etymol*. II, 24.
[2] *P. L.*, Vol. 101, col. 952, A. Cf. the περὶ φύσεως of the early Greeks, also the definition of jurisprudence given by Ulpianus in the beginning of the Digests, Chap. I : " jurisprudentia est *divinarum atque humanarum rerum notitia*, justi atque unjusti scientia."

(iii) *Gradual formulation of philosophic problems.* Obliged as they were to carry on the traditional line of thought, the new thinkers had to reconstitute the framework of philosophy piece by piece. The first schools had an exaggerated regard for dialectics, and the treatises in use at the time helped to accentuate the predominance. We may indeed infer from this that dialectics alone was *taught* as such, but we ought not to conclude that *it alone constituted the philosophy* of the eighth and ninth centuries. For other pre-occupations manifested themselves very soon. Already in the eighth century metaphysical questions came up in connection with theological discussions; and the newly-risen controversy concerning universals suggested problems relating to Nature, God, and Being in general. In the eleventh century psychological studies multiplied, and that in itself is a clear sign of philosophic progress. Indeed, at the end of the twelfth century, on the eve of the intellectual revolution which was to mark a clear division of the two periods in the history of Western philosophy, all the principal problems were discussed. This gradual elaboration of the philosophic sphere of thought—one of the most interesting features of this period—coincided with the social reaction of the new races and the constitution of a new state of things.

(iv) *Faults of systemization.* Mediæval philosophy gradually delineated the subject-matter of its discussions, by constantly enlarging the sphere of its investigations. How did it develop this framework? We can reply that speaking generally, breadth and doctrinal coherence are lacking in philosophic productions previous to the thirteenth century. The only system which is an exception to this is that of Scotus Eriugena, and later on we shall point out how strange is its appearance here.

The chief cause of this lack of cohesion was the failure of the first thinkers to cope with the disparity of the fragments of ideas which they took over from the past. They cut short some authors, and failed to understand the meaning of others, and did not realize the historic and logical connection between them. In fact, they did not possess that maturity of mind without which one cannot unify heterogeneous elements. This power of unification which was so pronounced in the scholasticism of the thirteenth century, was only in process of formation during this first period.

The disparate influences upon philosophy may be classified into two groups : the Platonic-Augustinian group, which was predominant, and the Aristotelian. In addition, we can also trace the influence of certain Pythagorician, Epicurean, Stoic, neo-Platonist, and Arabian theories.

(A) These doctrinal antinomies manifested themselves even in the *sub-divisions* of philosophy. The majority of the classifications were evidently based upon the Platonic division (logic, ethics, physics), and many authors simply reproduced it. The Aristotelian classification (metaphysics, mathematics, physics) was represented by Boethius, but remained without influence.

(B) In *dialectics*, Aristotle reigned supreme, and the Platonist commentators known to the scholastics unanimously recognized this sovereignty, which was accentuated by external circumstances. St. Augustine himself recommended the study of dialectics, and Aristotle's works benefited by his recommendation. Unfortunately there was an antinomy between the letter and the spirit of Aristotle. Dialectics as studied in the trivium limited itself too often to the study of words and logical forms, and did not find a sufficient counterpoise in metaphysics. Moreover, the deductive or synthetic method was very much in honour up to the end of the twelfth century, and this predominance may be accounted for by the low position assigned to psychology and observation. Scotus Eriugena the anti-Scholastic, and St. Anselm the scholastic, both made use only of deduction. As thought developed and ripened, this excessive use of the synthetic method was corrected, but it was left to the thirteenth century to base philosophy upon the double analytico-synthetic method.

(C) Up to the thirteenth century, *metaphysics* remained fragmentary and incoherent.[1] It displayed a strange mixture of Aristotelian and Platonist ideas. The enunciation of the principle of causality was taken from the *Timæus*, and the scheme of the four causes from Aristotle, but there was no consistent theory of causes.[2] Incoherences were present :

(*a*) In the theory of individuality. The unanimous doctrine of the scholastics from the time of Abelard was that the individual alone is the true substance, and that each human person

[1] Cf. Espenberger, *BGPM*, III, 5, p. 36 : Domet de Vorges, *S. Anselme*, p. 149 *et seq.*

[2] Cf. Espenberger, *op. cit.*, pp. 67 *et seq.* for the idea of causality at the time of Peter Lombard, with sources indicated.

is an independent being. Already in the ninth century the Aristotelian notions of substance, nature and person were interpreted in this sense, but at the same time philosophers were fascinated by the Platonist theory of separated Ideas which is the source of exaggerated Realism, and many centuries were to pass before a satisfactory solution of the problem of universals was found.

(b) In the theory of matter and form. This theory was indeed known through St. Ambrose, Boethius, and the hesitating statements of St. Augustine. But this doctrine, which forms an integral portion of the peripatetic, scholastic, and even numerous anti-scholastic systems, played only an insignificant part and was not properly understood at this time. By some, matter was looked upon as the primitive chaos of the elements (Alcuin); others identified it with the material atom which was thought to be the ultimate residue after division (the Atomists, and William of Conches) ; others again regarded it as a mass endowed with physical qualities and dynamic motion (School of Chartres). A few indeed (Isidore of Seville, Rhaban Maur, Gilbert de la Porree) had an inkling of the character of absolute indetermination and passivity which Aristotle ascribes to matter, but they did not develop this idea. In the same way the form was regarded not as the substantial principle of being, but as the sum of its properties.[1] Hence change was supposed not to affect the fundamental reality of things but only the appearance and disappearance of properties which supervene on this reality. These ideas were due to the transposition of a logical theory into the metaphysical domain. Just as a judgment is made up of a subject and a predicate,[2] so also beings were thought to be composed of matter as a subject, and of form as a property ; so that we find a striking antinomy between the real spirit of the formulæ employed and the erroneous meaning attributed to them.

(D) *Cosmological* doctrines were characterized by the same indefiniteness. We have just seen how a false idea of prime matter served as a basis for atomistic systems of thought. Similarly, under the influence of the neo-Platonist theory of the World-Soul, or of the Stoic idea of fate, Nature as such was commonly looked upon as itself a being *sui generis*, with

---

[1] Baumgartner, *BGPM*, II, 4. This excellent monograph is full of useful information on the history of the scholastic ideas.

[2] *Ibid.*, pp. 57 *et seq.*

an autonomous life. According to Macrobius's Commentary on the Dream of Scipio, there is one world-soul for the heavenly bodies and men. However, the majority of philosophers, and these some of the best (Abelard and John of Salisbury for instance) proclaimed with Aristotle the individuality of every natural substance in the universe. Here we have an instance of two irreconcilable theories. The *Timæus* was a favourite source of philosophical and poetical data concerning the formation of matter and the elements, the rôle of the demiurge, and the function of the Ideas.

(E) We may say that up to the twelfth century, the *psychology* of the scholastics was principally Augustinian and Platonist, with Aristotelian elements introduced. Hence we have a new series of antinomies, which appeared especially :

(*a*) In the theory of ideas. For St. Augustine, as we shall point out later on, the external sensation was the occasion for the re-awakening of the soul to knowledge which it already possessed—an occasionalist doctrine which its holders endeavoured to harmonize with the Aristotelian theory of abstraction.

(*b*) In the doctrine of faculties. The divisions of the faculties and the theory of the absence of any real distinction between them and the soul was taken from St. Augustine. At the same time the *Metalogicus* of John of Salisbury[1] refers to the theory of the real multiplicity of the powers of the soul as held by some in opposition to the Augustinian doctrine.[2]

(*c*) In the doctrine concerning the spirituality of the soul. The Scholastics—and Scotus Eriugena with them—unanimously naintained that the soul is superior in nature to the body. On the other hand, following in the footsteps of Constantine the African (85), some of them adopted physiological observations inspired by Arabian ideas, which tended to confuse the psychical phenomenon with the physiological—a confusion which logically would lead to the ruin of the spirituality of the soul.

(*d*) In the study of the origin and destiny of the soul. There were Traducianists right up to the twelfth century who allowed themselves to be influenced by the hesitation of St. Augustine between creationism and traducianism ; and they

---

[1] IV, 9.
[2] Friedrich, *Geschichte d. Lehre von den Seelenvermögen bis zum Niedergange der Scholastik* (Pädagog. Abhandl. V. A.). He collects the materials but does not elaborate them.

did not realize that their doctrine was destructive of the spirituality of the soul.

(e) In the study of the union of soul and body. The relations between soul and body were still worked out according to the principles of the Platonist psychology, and particularly the ideas of Chalcidius. The soul was said to be united to the body according to the relations between numbers (Pythagoras) or else as a pilot to his ship, or a rider to his steed. Yet in spite of the independence of its component substances, the unity of man was still affirmed. Though the Aristotelian definition of the soul as " the entelechy of the body " was known to the scholastics of the period,[1] they nevertheless refused to regard the soul as the substantial form of the body, for this would mean, according to the ideas of the time, that the soul was a property of matter. There is little doubt that the Platonist doctrine owed its triumph largely to this false interpretation of the theory of matter and form.[2]

(F) *Moral philosophy* was dealt with principally from the theological point of view. Of those who treated the subject from the point of view of philosophy, several confined themselves to a description of the particular virtues, after the manner of the Stoics. It is possible that the *Psychomachia* of Prudentius, which inspired the iconography of the cathedrals[3] may have suggested the representations of the struggle between vice and virtue. Hugh of St. Victor depicted them by means of two trees (the old and the new Adam), the branches symbolizing particular vices and virtues. The most important moral theories were concerned with the subject of liberty. They took over from St. Augustine the idea that the will is free inasmuch as by nature it excludes compulsion.[4]

(G) *Political and social ideas* took definite shape from the eleventh century, and formed a separate department of research, which religious pre-occupations and imperialist pretentions did not fail to influence. (Ch. V. Section VI.)

(H) There remains *Natural Theology*, which was always regarded by the Scholastics as one of the most important

---

[1] Through Chalcidius, who incidentally criticized this definition on the same ground as the Scholastics of the first period.

[2] For the same reason they would not use the theory of matter and form in order to explain the composition of other living beings. Some denied that animals have a soul, others regarded it as a sort of corporeal *spiritus*, etc.

[3] Cf. Mâle, *L'Art religieux du XIIIe s.*, p. 100.

[4] Verweyen, *op. cit.*, p. 77.

chapters of philosophy. Cicero, Augustine, pseudo-Dionysius, and Boethius had left very full dissertations concerning God, exemplarism, creation, and Providence. We may also note the influence of Pythagorean theories concerning harmony and number.

In order to demonstrate the existence of God, two methods were in use : the first, inspired by realist ideas, rested on the postulate that our concepts are themselves a sufficient guarantee of the extramental reality of the thing conceived, and that the idea of a perfect Being demonstrates the existence of this Being. (St. Anselm). The second procedure was based on the principle of causality, and took various forms. The order and government of the world furnished an easy and rudimentary proof (Cicero, Seneca). But we also find arguments based upon the changes of things (St. Augustine, R. Pulleyn, Peter Lombard) ; and the Victorines (Hugh and Richard of St. Victor) appeal very much in this connection to external and internal experience. The Aristotelian argument concerning motion and the prime mover was also taken up (Boethius, Adelard of Bath), but it was not set forth in all its metaphysical fullness. Alan of Lille was the first to show that there must be a starting point in the order of efficient causes.[1]

Aristotle was condemned for having denied the existence of Providence,[2] and in this connection Plato, the *symmystes veri*, was regarded with more favour because, as John of Salisbury explains, he taught the existence of God or the Supreme Good, the distinction between time and eternity, and between Ideas and Matter.[3] All these Platonist doctrines were interpreted in an Augustinian sense. From Augustine, again, was taken the doctrines of transcendence, ideas as exemplary causes of the world, creation, and the eternal law as the foundation of morality and right.

(I) The Middle Ages first of all included under the name " philosophy " not only that which rightly belonged to it, but also the *study of religious dogma* (Augustine), but in practice began to distinguish between the two departments from the eleventh century[4] without, however, succeeding in

---

[1] Baeumker. *Witelo*, pp. 286 *et seq.*
[2] John of Salisbury, *Metalogicus*, IV, 27 : Quod Aristoteles in multis erravit.
[3] Principio docet esse Deum, distinguit ab ævo. Tempus et ideas applicat, aptat hylen.—John of Salisbury, *Entheticus*, lines 941-942.
[4] Cf. Brunhes, *La Foi chrétienne et la Philosophie au temps de la Rénaissance carolingienne*, Paris 1903, pp. 178-180.

formulating the relations between the two sciences in a precise way like that found in the thirteenth century on the first pages of the Summæ of theology.

To sum up, if we leave out Natural Theology, we may say that the philosophy of this period resembled a crucible in which disparate materials were in a state of fusion. John of Salisbury might have applied to all the men of the time that which he wrote of the philosophers of Chartres who endeavoured to harmonize Plato and Aristotle : " They have laboured in vain to reconcile when dead those who were in opposition all their life long."[1]

With the development of thought, contradictory elements were eliminated, and the manifest strivings after unity are an indication of intellectual development. If we compare these early philosophies with the harmonized syntheses of the thirteenth century, we realize that we are in presence of a work of travail, namely, the birth of the scholastic solutions. The lack of systemization had not completely disappeared from the productions of the end of the twelfth century, although they were the most remarkable of the period. Indeed, there were some antinomies which remained and lasted on through the thirteenth century. The language used betrays these hesitations of the mind, and it only acquired its precision and its vigour by stages.

26. Bibliography.—L. Reynaud, *Les origines de l'influence franc. en Allemagne.* Vol. I (Paris, 1913) ; A. Luchaire, *Louis VII, Philippe-Auguste, Louis VIII,* 1137-1226, Vol. III of the *Histoire de France,* published by Lavisse (Paris, 1902) ; Lamprecht, Steinhausen and Taylor **(23)** ; S. R. Maitland, *The Dark Ages : a series of essays intended to illustrate the State of Religion and Literature in the Ninth, Eleventh and Twelfth Centuries* (London) defends the value of the beginnings of the Middle Ages ; Tout, op. cit. **(23)** ; H. Adams, *Mont St. Michel and Chartres* (Boston, 1923), a suggestive book, written by an artist ; D. Berlière, *L'ordre monastique des origines au XIIe siecle* (Paris, 1921), an excellent synthesis ; G. Kurth, *Les origines de la civilis. moderne* (Brussels, 1903). Concerning all the personages of this period see Manitius, *op. cit.* ; John of Salisbury, *Polycraticus* and *Metalogicus.*

Philosophy and Theology : Brunhes, *La Foi chrétienne et la philos. au temps de la Renaissance carolingienne* (Paris, 1903),

[1] *Metal.,* II, 17.

well done ; Heitz, *Essai historique sur les rapports entre la philos. et la foi de Bérenger de Tours à S. Thomas d'Aquin* (Paris, 1909), well done.

Natural Theology : G. Grunwald, *Geschichte der Gottesbeweise in Mitt. bis z. Ausgang d. Hochscholastik (BGPM* VI. 3) ; Baeumker, *Witelo (ibid.* III, 2), pp. 286-338, digression on the history of the proofs of the existence of God, two good studies.

Liberty : J. Verweyen, *Das Problem der Willensfreiheit in d. Scholastik auf Grund d. Quellen dargest. u. krit. gewurdigt* (Heidelberg, 1909), well done ; Carlyle, op. cit. (23) ; A. Schneider, *Die Erkenntnislehre b. Beginn. d. Scholastik*, X, p. 71 (Fulda, 1922) ; Kreutle, *Die Unsterblichheitslehre in d. Schol. von. Alcuin bisTh. v. Aquin*, Dissertat (Fulda, 1918), gives references.

§ 2—*The Organization of the Schools*

27. Types of Schools.—The Middle Ages made a great effort to develop education by utilizing the Christian schools which had taken root under the Roman system, and by erecting new institutions. The schools in which philosophy was taught, in addition to other branches of knowledge, belonged to three types :

(i) *The Monastic schools.* The Benedictines were the great educators of the West. We find them first of all in Ireland, in which country Greco-Latin culture flourished in quite a remarkable way from the seventh to the ninth centuries. Monasteries like those of Clonar, Bangor and Armagh, restored the classical tradition which had been lost. At this time Ireland was the one bright spot in the dark night which covered Europe. In fact it has been called the Lamp of the North. Sedulius, Alcuin, and Scotus Eriugena came from its schools and passed over to the Continent.

Missionary monks who set out from Ireland (St. Columba and his disciple St. Gall, sixth and seventh centuries), and later on from England, (St. Boniface, eighth century), took part in the restoration of the Benedictine schools, the former at Luxeuil and at St. Gall, the latter at Fulda. Other monks who came from Rome (St. Augustine, 596) rendered a similar service to England, and founded the schools of Wearmouth and Jarrow (made famous by Venerable Bede).

The ninth century witnessed a remarkable intellectual restoration, due to Charlemagne and his Benedictine helpers. In the tenth and eleventh centuries the monks of Cluny, and in the twelfth century the Cistercians, carried on the founding of centres of studies, and the twelfth century, the golden age of monasticism, was also the golden age of the schools. The school of Tours founded by Alcuin served as a model for those of Corbie (Paschasius Radbert, Ratramn), Münster (Ludger), Salzburg (Arnulph), Fulda (founded by Rhaban Maur), St. Gall (Notker Labeo, who died in 1022, there translated into German the then known portions of the *Organon*, the *De Consolatione Philosophiæ* of Boethius, and the *De Nuptiis Mercurii et Philol.* of M. Capella). We may also mention in France the schools of Ferrières (Lupus of Ferrières), Cluny (Odo), Citeaux, Fécamp, St. Remi at Rheims, Bec (Lanfranc, St. Anselm), Fleury (Abbo), Auxerre (Remi and Eric), St. Denys, St. Genevieve of Paris, and Aurillac ; in Germany the schools of Reichenau (Walfred Strabo), Corvey (Bovo II), Lobbes (Eracle), and of St. Laurent at Liège (Rupert of Deutz) ; in Italy, that of Monte Cassino (Alfanus, Didier) ; in Hungary the school of Czanad (founded in the eleventh century by Gerard of Czanad, author of a *Deliberatio Gerardi Moresenæ ecclesiæ episc. super hymnum trium puerorum.*[1]

The Benedictine schools comprised two sections, the *schola interior claustri*, reserved for the monks ; and the *schola exterior*, open to seculars.

From the second half of the twelfth century, other branches grew out of the great family of monks in the West, and new religious orders opened schools. One of the most famous was that of the Canons of St. Victor in Paris, who followed the rule of St. Augustine.

(ii) *The episcopal, cathedral, or capitular schools.* In the eighth century, Chrodegang, a Canon of Metz (766) organized for the clergy attached to the episcopal churches a common mode of life modelled upon that of the cloister. In these schools also we find the same division into interior and exterior departments. They were under the authority of the bishop, acting through a chancellor.

The teaching posts (*scholasticum officium*) in these schools were held by persons of distinction. Often, especially in the early time, bishops, chancellors, and monastic abbots fulfilled the functions of the *scholasticus*, Later on this title was extended to the simple *magistri scholæ*.

[1] Endres, *Studien zur Gesch. d. Frühscholastik. Gerard von Czanad. Philos.* Jahrb. 1913, pp. 349-359.

Among the most famous schools we may mention : In England, the school of York (Alcuin) ; in Germany, those of Utrecht (Adalbode), Liège (Ratherus of Verona, Notger, Adelman) ; in France and the countries then connected with it, the schools of Tournai (Odo), Lyons, Rheims (Gerbert), Poitiers, Laon (Anselm, † 1117, and Ralph), Chartres, and Paris. The schools of Chartres, under the direction of Bishop Fulbert (960-1208) and after him, Yves of Chartres († 1115), went through two periods of splendour and rivalled the schools of Paris right up to the middle of the twelfth century. Adalman of Liège and Berengar of Tours followed Fulbert's lectures. In the twelfth century, the chancellors Bernard of Chartres, Gilbert de la Porree, and Theodoric of Chartres were among the most prominent men of their time. In the ninth century Paris already possessed the three schools of St. Genevieve, St. Germain des Près, and the Cathedral school. Their fame went on increasing, and from the second half of the twelfth century the French capital attracted to its professorial chairs all the best intellects and eclipsed the rival academies.

(iii) *The Palace Schools, scholæ palatinæ* or *palatii*, were attached to the Court and probably moved about with it. Their professors were taken from the ecclesiastical world, and they admitted to their lectures clerics and laymen indifferently.

The best known was that of Charlemagne and the French kings who immediately succeeded him.[1] Alcuin was the moving spirit in it ; Elisaeus Fridugise and Wizo assisted him ; the members of the imperial household attended the lessons and took Greek and Roman academic names (Charlemagne became *David*, Alcuin was *Flaccus*, in memory of Horace, and *Eulalia virgo*, to whom Alcuin dedicated one of his treatises, was Charlemagne's cousin). After Alcuin, Scotus Eriguena, Fridugise (ninth century), Agobard, Candidus, and Rhaban Maur taught at the court of the Frankish kings.

Another palatinate school was that of the Othos in the tenth century. In love with French culture, Otho III invited Gerbert of Aurillac to teach at his court, in order that, as he wrote in 997, he might polish off his *rusticitas saxonica* and communicate to him some spark of Greek culture, *Græcorum industriæ aliqua scintilla*.[2] The Ottonian renaissance was brilliant, but

[1] It is probable that the Merovingians already had at Treves a *Schola Gallica Palatii* which Charlemagne merely renewed.—Willmann, *Didaktik*, I. p. 254.
[2] *Lettres de Gerbert* (983-987), edit. Havet, Paris 1889, p. 172.

did not last long. From the eleventh century, the schools of Fulda, St. Gall and Reichenau declined, while that of Liège shone out for the last time in the eleventh century. From thence onwards the schools of Bec, Chartres, and Paris received many Teutons wishing to study.

28. Programme of Studies.—The studies were established according to a hierarchical plan, the stages of which were clearly marked out in the twelfth century : the liberal arts at the base, philosophy in the centre, and theology at the top.

(i) *The liberal arts.* Previous to the Middle Ages,[1] the classification of the seven liberal arts (*artes liberales*) was spread abroad by the manuals of Boethius, Cassiodorus, Martianus Capella, and Alcuin. The expression was derived from *liber*, a book, or better still, a free man, in which sense the liberal arts are those which result from a mental discipline, in contrast with the servile arts which call for bodily work.

They were divided into two groups : the trivium (*artes triviales*, *sermonicales*, *rationales*), which comprised grammar, rhetoric, and dialectic ; and the quadrivium (*artes quadriviales*, *reales*, *physica*, *mathematica*) which comprised arithmetic, geometry, astronomy, and music. Sometimes we come across the expression *sapientia* or *methodus hybernica*, which indicates the part played by the Irish monks in the diffusion of the liberal arts. The number seven was itself looked upon as symbolic.[2]

Grammar included the study of the grammarians and the ancient and mediæval writers. Donatus and Priscian, who had taught grammar, the first at Rome (about 350 A.D.), the second at Constantinople (about 500 A.D.) were the classical grammarians, but a justification of grammatical rules was also sought in the Vulgate.[3] To the grammatical authorities should be added Isidore of Seville, and above all Remi of Auxerre

---

[1] The branches of the Quadrivium are mentioned by Ammonius as a subdivision of mathematics (Zeller, *Die Philos. d. Griechen*, II, p. 177, n. 1). Mariétan claims to have discovered the origin of the complete classification of the liberal arts in St. Augustine (*Problème de la classifica.t des sciences, etc.* pp. 54 *et seq.*).

[2] The seven arts are referred to in these lines : " Lingua, tropus, ratio, numerus, tonus, angulus, ratio—*Gram* loquitur, *Dia* vera docet, *Rhe* verba colorat, *Mus* canit, *Ar* numerat, *Geo* ponderat, *As* colit astra."—Willmann, *op. cit.*, p. 266.

[3] Smaragdus, Abbot of St. Michel about 850 (cf. *Hist. litt. France*, IV, p. 455), writes : " Donatum non sequimur quia fortiorem in divinis Scripturis auctoritatem tenemus." Cf. Thurot, *Notices et extr. de divers man. latins pour servir à l'hist. des doctrines grammaticales au m.â.*, in *Not. et extra. des man. de la Biblioth. Nationale*, XXII, 2e p. (Paris, 1868), p. 81.

(died about 908), author of a commentary on the *Ars minor* of Donatus. Later on, we get versified grammars appearing with the *Doctrinale* of Alexander of Villedieu and the *Græcismus* of Eberhard of Bethune (end of twelfth or beginning of the thirteenth century), and these met with considerable success. In Grammar the Latin classics, Virgil, Seneca, Horace, Terence, Juvenal, etc., and certain Christian writers such as Orosius, Gregory of Tours, and Boethius, were also read. For a long time the study of law was included with that of grammar, inasmuch as the definitions of Justinian supplied dictionary material ; it was not separated from the liberal arts until about the time of Irnerius of Bologna (Chap. VII, § 3).

Rhetoric was less sought after than by the Romans. Cicero, Quintilian and Marius Victorinus are mentioned in the *Heptateuchon* of Theodoric of Chartres (84) as the favourite models in rhetoric.[1]

Dialectics occupied the largest place in the trivium, and its scope became still wider as the parts of the *Organon* became known.

The relative importance attached to the branches of the trivium led to a diversity of tendencies. At Paris the influence of Abelard tended to the exclusion of grammar and rhetoric ; at Chartres, the centre of humanism, on the other hand, the three branches of the trivium received equal treatment[2] ; at Orleans the place of honour was given to the Latin classics.[3] At one time, in certain places dialectics invaded the domain of grammar. The " modists," in their treatises *de modis signi-ficandi*, gave a dialectical analysis of the barbarisms of school Latin, which some even preferred to classical Latin. The movement was given an impetus by Peter Helias, and culminated in the thirteenth century in the appearance of speculative grammar.[4]

[1] Clerval, *Les écoles de Chartres au moyen age du Ve au XVIe siècle, pp.* 221 *et seq.*

[2] See the letter-programme of Peter of Blois in Clerval, *op. cit.*, pp. 309 *et seq.*

[3] A thirteenth century poet, Henry of Andely, in an allegorical poem on the combat between the seven arts, deals with the conflict between the grammarians, represented by the Orleanists, and the dialecticians, represented by the masters of Paris. He depicts the army of the sciences cultivated at Paris marching to the assault of Orleans. This poem has been translated into English with an introduction by L. Paetow : *The Battle of the Seven Arts* (University Press, California, 1914). A. Neckam (*De naturis rerum, de laudibus divinæ sapientiæ*, vv. 607-610) sings the praises of Orleans, and many others do the same.

[4] Cf. Wattenbach, *Deutschlands Geschichtsquellen im Mittelalter bis z. Mitte d.* 13 *Jahrh.* Bd. I, 1904.

The quadrivium was not so successful as the trivium, for the reason that the technical knowledge which it called for was not so easily accessible. The encyclopædic data of ancient authors, the treatises of Boethius, the *Astrolabe* of Gerbert, and, from the time of Adelard of Bath, the theories of Euclid, served as a basis for the teaching of mathematics and astronomy. The study of music was connected with the ceremonies of worship.

(ii) *Philosophy*, the gradual development of which has already been pointed out, must not be looked upon as an extension or an annexe of dialectics, nor must it be included in the trivium (against Ferrère, Mariétan and most historians) ; it forms a new branch of knowledge which was given a place in the scholastic programme between the liberal arts below and theology above (Willmann). This hierarchical arrangement and the preparatory character of the liberal arts which follows from it, were clearly established by the twelfth century. " Sunt tanquam septem viæ," says a codex of Bamberg: they are ways which lead to other sciences, to physics (a part of philosophy), theology, and the science of laws.[1] The same distinction was emphasized by Hugh of St. Victor[2] and the other authors of the first classifications of the twelfth century (103). It was also adopted in the *Hortus deliciarum* of Herrad de Landsberg.[3]

The iconography of the thirteenth century cathedrals and the miniatures of the period provide us with a confirmation of this thesis : philosophy, represented according to the description of Boethius, is distinct from the liberal arts. It is sculptured separately at Laon and at Sens. In the stained glass of Auxerre, as in the manuscript of the *Hortus deliciarum*, it occupies a central lobe, with seven concentric lobes arranged round it[4], and in the mosaic pavement of the Cathedral of Ivrea, the Lady Philosophy is seated in the midst of the seven arts.[5]

This completely upsets the idea that mediæval philosophy was confounded with the liberal arts. It was equally distinct from theology.

(iii) *Theology* was taught simultaneously in the big schools. Its autonomous constitution was also built up gradually, as

---

[1] "Ad istas tres scientias (phisica, theologia, scientia legum) paratæ sunt tanquam viæ septem liberales artes que in trivio et quadrivio continentur." —Cod. Q., VI, 30. Grabmann, *Die Gesch. d. Schol. Methode*, II, p. 39.
[2] *Erud. didasc.*, lib. III.
[3] Willmann, *Didaktik*, I. 278, n. 1.
[4] E. Mâle, *L'Art religieux du XIIIe siècle en France*, p. 112 et seq.
[5] A. K. Porter, *Lombard Architecture* (New Haven, 1907), Vol. I, p. 347.

we shall see later on.   The work had already been accomplished
by the time of St. Anselm, and the writers of the twelfth
century distinguish the *humanæ sapientiæ amatores* (philosophers) and the *divinæ scripturæ doctores* (theologians).

29. The other sciences.—Side by side with this trilogy with
which our history is mainly concerned, other sciences were
cultivated, and it is important to note the place which they
occupied in the studies of the time.   Although the scientific
teaching properly so called was limited to the quadrivium,
other natural sciences were the subject of a somewhat rudimentary research.   *Alchemy* attracted all those who were
interested in the composition of bodies.   *Medicine* was cultivated at Montpellier and in various Italian centres.   There were
two sources for the study of *natural history* in which Gerbert,
the monks of Monte Cassino and the teachers at Chartres were
interested : a collection of facts made by Pliny and transmitted by the first encyclopædists, and the *Physiologus,* a
curious treatise of the Patristic era which contained fantastic
details concerning the habits and the history of animals, and
which was at the same time a source of animal symbolism for
Christian exegesis and art.[1]

History was represented by the various annals.   Those who
cultivated it drew their inspiration from St. Jerome or
Eusebius, and drew up local chronicles.[2]

As for law—canon, Roman and feudal—this underwent a
striking development in the eleventh century.[3]

**30. The organization of the schools as a reflection of the
civilization of the period.**—We find certain reflections of feudal
civilization in the organisation of the schools.

1 Mâle, *L'Art religieux du XIIe siècle en France,* Chap. IX, Le monde et la
nature, also *L'Art religieux du XIIIe siècle en France,* p. 49.
2 Cf. Wattenbach, *Deutschlands Geschichtsquellen im Mittelalter bis z.
Mitte d.* 13 *Jahrh.,* Bd. I, 1904.
3 Ch. Haskins has published an anonymous list of works proposed as manuals
for studies at the end of the twelfth century.   He attributes it to Alexander
Neckam (1157-1217) because of the similarity in its redaction and the *De
naturis rerum* and other works of this author.   Alexander Neckam taught at
Paris between 1175 and 1195, and afterwards became Abbot of Cirencester.
The list recommends the works to be studied by those who wish to be
conversant with the seven arts, medicine, civil and canon law, and theology.
It is one of the few documents of this kind previous to the drawing up of the
university programmes in the thirteenth century.   The list does not mention
Avicenna in medicine, nor the *Almageste* in mathematics, nor the *Doctrinale*
of A. de Villedieu, but it does give the *Metaphysics,* the *De Generatione et
corrupt.* and the *De Anima* of Aristotle, and the works mentioned in the
Heptateuchon of Th. of Chartres.   See *A List of Text-books from the close of
the twelfth century.* (Harvard Studies in Classical Philology, 1909, p. 75-94.)

(i) The sectional spirit which in the eleventh and twelfth centuries led to the dividing up of the West into principalities under lay or ecclesiastical rulers affected all the manifestations of social life and was reflected in the local character of the schools. The maintenance of these schools was a point of honour and pride to abbots and bishops, and they endeavoured to rival each other in attracting professors and students. This educational sectionalism which disappeared with the twelfth century had good effects, for it called forth a host of humanists, dialecticians, jurists, philosophers and theologians.

(ii) Just as the sectional forces of the feudal system were broken down by the unitive policy of the Caputs and the Plantagenets, so also we find, in spite of the local character of the schools, a certain uniformity of programme and methods (28, 32), and the close of the intellectual history of the twelfth century is marked by the preponderance of the schools of Paris.

(iii) The eleventh and twelfth centuries which were predominantly the epoch of French civilization, were also those of French knowledge. If we leave aside Monte Cassino, which had a long tradition behind it, and a few Spanish centres with very special characteristics, it was France which was at the head of the scientific movement, and it was French schools— Le Bec, Laon, Chartres, and Paris—which exercised a decisive attraction upon other countries. They attained to a high degree of prosperity, in spite of the fact that the nobles upon whom they depended were involved in the feudal wars, for war then only absorbed those who were soldiers by profession, and called only for the limited service laid down in the feudal contract.

In the time of Abelard, the influx of foreigners in the French schools was at its zenith. The English came in particularly large numbers, and this is explained by the intimate relations between the two countries, and by the poverty of the educational centres in the British Isles. Adelard of Bath, and Adam du Petit Pont remained in the French episcopal schools, Richard of St. Victor and Isaac of Stella, in the abbatial schools. Others like Alexander Neckam and Walter Map returned to England. John of Salisbury, the most famous of all, remained for some time at Canterbury, and then returned to Chartres. On the other hand, some who were French by origin such as William of Conches, Peter of

Blois and perhaps Alan of Lille, came into England as preceptor of the king, secretary to an archbishop, and monk of a Cistercian abbey respectively.

There was a similar influx of students from Germany. It will suffice to mention Otloh de St. Emmeran, Otto of Freising, Manegold of Lautenbach, and Hugh of St. Victor. An equally numerous contingent came from Italy : Lanfranc in the twelfth century, and, a little later on Peter Lombard, Peter of Capua, and Præpostinus of Cremona, taught at Paris. Roland Bandinelli, before becoming Pope under the title of Alexander III, was a disciple of Abelard, and the future Innocent III studied theology and grammar at Paris.

It is not surprising after all this that we find in the writings of the intellectuals of the twelfth century excessive praises of the French schools. Adelard of Bath speaks of the *Gallicarum sententiarum constantia*[1] ; an anonymous author praises the *Francie magistri*[2] ; Paris is the source of all knowledge, adds Cæsar of Heisterbach ; " the men of science have emigrated to Gaul," writes Otto of Freising, and both are simply echoing the saying of the time : " Italy has the Papacy, Germany the Empire, and France knowledge."[3]

(iv) The delimitation of the frontiers separating the various sciences took place at a time when a similar growth was taking place in all the departments of civilization. It was in the thirteenth century that the feudal society reached a position of equilibrium, the scheme of intellectual work was outlined, and the various sciences vindicated their titles to independence. Phenomena like these are an indication of a mature state of mind.

(v) It is also worthy of note that the local character of the educational establishments was not unconnected with this work of delimitation inasmuch as it favoured the specialization of schools and teachers. Orleans became a school of grammarians ; Paris a centre of philosophy and theology, Chartres specialized in the humanism of the trivium, Bologna, Lyons and Angers in law, Montpellier in medicine, Laon in theology, and the school of St. Victor at Paris in mystical theology.

(vi) Lastly, the argument which we have based upon

---

[1] *De Quibusdam naturalibus quæstionibus.* Cf. De Wulf, *Philosophy and Civilization*, p. 41.
[2] Cf. Haskins, *Mediæval Versions of the Posterior Analytics* (Harvard Studies in Classical Philology, 1904, vol. XXV), p. 94.
[3] Steinhausen, *op. cit.*, p. 355.

iconography in establishing the distinction between philosophy and the liberal arts serves also to show the influence which the latter had upon plastic art itself. They acted similarly upon literature. This phenomenon of interaction between the various mental factors continued to increase and eventually led up to the unity of the spirit of civilization in the thirteenth century. We shall return to it later on.

31. Scholastic customs.—The *scholastici* of the eleventh and twelfth centuries loved to travel from one school to another. Lanfranc and Manegold of Lautenbach wandered through France and Germany like nomads. William of Champeaux, Theodoric of Chartres, and Adelard of Bath taught in various centres, and Abelard, their contemporary, may be taken as a typical knight errant of dialectics.

In the same way the scholastic population moved about and followed well-known masters. Manuscripts were lent from one abbey to another, organizations were formed for the rapid copying of anything new, such as the courses of lectures by contemporary professors or a newly discovered text of some Greek or Arabian author. All this helped to promote the uniformity of the programme of studies, methods of teaching, and the philosophical library, so that right through the sectional life of the twelfth century there was a current of cosmopolitanism which largely helped to bring about the predominance of scholastic philosophy.

32. Methods of Teaching.—(i) Teaching and studies were the monopoly of one social class, namely, the clergy. Those who were destined for this work gave up their life to scientific culture. Not only did they all belong to one and the same ecclesiastical hierarchy : they also spoke and wrote the same language, Latin. Thus there arose side by side with the ordinary tongues differentiating the various national groups, an international learned language the vocabulary of which was understood everywhere. Here, then, was another factor which helped to form a uniform philosophical mental outlook and to assure the cosmopolitan character of scholasticism.

(ii) The commenting on a text (*lectio*) was the first and most natural form of teaching, and glosses of this kind abounded from the ninth to the twelfth centuries.[1] The *disputatio*, a kind of socratic method based upon an exchange of opinion

---

[1] This sense is retained in the English expression *lecture, reading*, and in the German *Vorlesungen*.

between master and pupil, appeared in the twelfth century when the *logica nova* was introduced. There were also quite early on treatises arranged according to plans, and later on we find synthetic compilations (*sententiæ, summæ*).

(iii) The *didactic systemization* of a particular question, rudimentary at first, was perfected at the end of the eleventh century, and the triadic framework became more general (*pro, contra, solutio*). This formal scheme indeed soon became dominant, although it was not adopted in every scholastic work.[1]

(iv) The *liberal arts* and *philosophy* served as a preparation for *theology*, and from this there resulted a phenomenon which is peculiar to the Middle Ages and which became accentuated in the course of time : the mixing up of certain philosophical matters and arguments with others belonging to theology, and the introduction of philosophical arguments into theological spheres (p. 17).

33. Philosophical library.—We may divide the principal works which comprised the philosophical equipment of this period into various groups. They were common to all the schools, and this, again, is yet another factor which helps to explain the uniformity of the current of philosophic thought in the West.

(A) *Greek philosophers.* The Greek authors were rarely read in their original tongue : almost everybody made use of Latin translations.

(i) ARISTOTLE.—(*a*) Logic. In the ninth century the *De Interpretatione* (περὶ ἑρμηνείας) was known in the translations of Marius Victorinus and Boethius ; and from the end of the tenth, the *Categories*, in the translation of Boethius.

Recent researches by B. Geyer have shown that towards 1125 Abelard had read the *Sophistical Arguments*, and that he quotes the *Prior Analytics*.[2] The *Heptateuchon* of Theodoric of Chartres, completed about 1141, contains the two books of the *Prior Analytics*, the *Topics*, and the *Sophistical Arguments*, that is, all the remaining books of the *Organon* except

---

[1] Grabmann, *Gesch. d. Schol. Methode*, 1909, pp. 31 and 32, makes me say that Scholasticism (die Lehrmethode) consisted exclusively in the employment of the scheme " videtur quod sic—sed contra—respondeo dicendum." I have not said that this was the sole procedure of mediæval didactics, but that it was one of the most prominent methods, which Grabmann himself holds. I am the more surprised at Grabmann's criticism because I have always maintained the insufficiency of descriptions of scholasticism based simply upon teaching methods (**7**).

[2] B. Geyer, *Die alten lat. Uebersetzungen d. aristotelischen Analytik. Topik. u. Elenchik*, Philos. Jarhbuch. Bd. 30 (1917), pp. 37-40.

the *Posterior Analytics*.[1] According to a note added to the Chronicle of Robert of Torigny for the year 1128, James of Venice had then already translated from Greek into Latin the *Topics*, the two *Analytics*, and the *Sophistical Arguments*.[2] The *Posterior Analytics* existed in a triple Latin version in a thirteenth century manuscript discovered by Charles Haskins in the Cathedral Library at Toledo.[3] The Latin version contained in this codex accompanied by the commentary of Themistius is certainly the work of Gerard of Cremona († 1187) mentioned in the list of his translations from Arabic into Latin. One of the two Latin translations from the Greek contains a prologue by the translator (some suggest that he was Henricus Aristippus, originally of Santa Severina in Calabria, archdeacon of Catania, who died in 1162). In this prologue the writer says that in his country (*apud nos*) " the version by Boethius " was only partly conserved and in a corrupt text, and that the French teachers did not dare to use that of James because of its obscurity. Towards the middle of the twelfth century, Otto of Freising († 1158) popularized the new works of the *Organon* in Germany.

The second half of the twelfth century was in possession of the whole *Organon* of Aristotle. There was thus in the twelfth century a second partial introduction to the *Organon*, and it served as a basis for a classification of logic into *logica vetus* (the treatises known previous to the twelfth century), and the *logica nova* (treatises known later).[4]

(*b*) Writings other than Logical.—The early Middle Ages possessed neither the *Metaphysics* nor the *Physics* nor the *De Anima*, that is, they were not acquainted with any of the fundamental works of the peripatetic synthesis. Now if one takes the *Organon* by itself, it is easy to get a mistaken idea of the real opinion of the Stagirite, and to reduce his philosophy to a mere collection of logical rules. It was by indirect means (Chalcidius, Boethius) that certain metaphysical, physical and cosmological doctrines became known. Also we find complaints

[1] Clerval, *op. cit.*, pp. 222, 244 *et seq.* ; A. Hofmeister, *Studien über Otto von Freising*, Neues Archiv. d. Gesellschaft für ältere deutsche Geschichtskunde, Bd. 37 (1912), p. 666.

[2] *Monumenta Germaniæ Historica, Scriptores*, Vol. VI, p. 489.

[3] Charles H. Haskins, *Mediæval Versions of the Posterior Analytics*, Harvard Studies in Classical Philology, Vol. XXV (1914) ; C. Baeumker, *Latein. Uebersetzungen des aristotelischen Analytica posteriora*, Philos. Jahrbuch, Bd. 28 (1915), pp. 320-326.

[4] Cf. Mandonnet, *Siger de Brabant*, Vol. II (étude critique), p. 9-11.

made concerning the obscurity of Aristotle, who, in fine, was looked upon simply as a logician.[1]

The thirteenth century indeed made full use of the great works of the Aristotelian synthesis,[2] but this new influence of Aristotle, due to his metaphysics and natural philosophy, must be ascribed to an earlier date than is usually done. " This phenomenon has been universally placed too late," writes Mandonnet, " moreover, this second introduction of Aristotle to the Latin world was spread out over a hundred years beginning with the translation of the fourth book of the *Meteors* by Henricus Aristippus previous to 1162."[3]

The study of this great fact of literary history implies a two-fold line of research : the one is concerned with the translations themselves, their authors, dates, and value ; the other deals with their diffusion and utilization.

Their diffusion can only be studied by looking for the first traces of the new doctrines. Thus Duhem has discovered certain doctrines of Aristotelian physics in the Chartres writers (for instance, in the *De opere sex dierum* of Theodoric of Chartres).[4] But it has not been proved that this knowledge was due to direct contact with some Latin version of the *Physics* or of the *De coelo et mundo*.[5] In the same way, Daniel of Merlai (or Morley) in his *Liber de naturis inferiorum et superiorum*[6] dedicated to John, Bishop of Norwich from 1175 to 1200, mentions various works of Aristotle which his master Gerard of Cremona had translated.

As for the versions themselves, we must distinguish between those from the Arabic and those from the Greek. It was principally by means of the Arabs that the science and philosophy of antiquity was revealed to the West. The translations from the Arabic were more numerous than those from the Greek, and the first to appear. They were also more imperfect, for they often misrepresented the thought of the author, and in many instances contained additions to the original text or glosses on it. If we remember that Aristotle's thought

---

[1] Boethius calls him *turbator verborum ;* an anonymous author of the tenth century speaks of the *aristotelicus labyrinthus* (Baumgartner, *op. cit.* pp. 10-11).
[2] See **144**, p. 237 *et seq.*   [3] *op. cit.*, p. 13-14.
[4] Duhem, *Du temps où la scolastique latin a connu la physique d'Aristote* (Revue de Philos., 1909, pp. 162-178).
[5] A. Schneider, *BGPM*, XVII, pp. 35-40.
[6] Ed. Sudhoff, *Arch. f. Gesch. d. Naturwissenschaft u. d. Technik*, Bd. VIII (1917), pp. 6-40. Cf. Birkenmajer, who mentions another manuscript, Bd. IX (1920), p. 45-51. See also Rose, *Hermes*, Vol. VIII (1874), pp. 329, 349.

underwent successive translations from Greek into Syriac, from Syriac into Arabic, sometimes from Arabic into Hebrew, and finally from Arabic or Hebrew into Latin—often through the medium of some vulgar tongue [1]—we shall not be astonished that once the scholastics of the thirteenth century came into possession of translations from Greek into Latin they preferred these to the misleading versions of Arabian origin.

The true introduction of the West to the works of Aristotle was due to a collective enterprise of translation having its centre at Toledo. In this town, placed on the borders of two civilizations, and in which the Arabian and Jewish population enjoyed a large measure of toleration under the Christian regime, Archbishop Raymond (1126-1151) maintained a college of translators which became famous, thus rendering inestimable services to Western knowledge. Among these translators we may mention the Archdeacon of Segovia, Dominicus Gundissalinus and his Jewish collaborators, especially John Avendehut (= ibn David, son of David), also called Johannes Hispasnus, and above all the Lombard Gerard of Cremona (died 1187). The last-named produced an extraordinary number of works :[2] in addition to the *Posterior Analytics* and Themistius' Commentary on them, he translated from Arabic into Latin the *Physics* (*De naturali auditu*), the *De cœlo et mundi*, the *De generatione et corruptione*, and the three first books of the *Meteorology*.

Under the heading of pseudo-Aristotelian writings, Gerard translated the first part and the end of the second part of the *De causis proprietatum et elementorum*, and the *Liber de causis* (or *Liber Aristotelis de expositione bonitatis pure*.[3] This little treatise is an extract from the Στοιχείωσις θεολογική (*Elementatio theologica*) of Proclus. It was commented upon by many scolastics, amongst others by Thomas Aquinas, who was the first to discover its true origin and to attribute it to Proclus.

To these versions of pseudo-Aristotelian works, John of

---

[1] " The usual method of the translators of the Middle Ages is well known : A converted Jew (or, we may add, an Arab) translated into the vulgar tongue —into Spanish, for example—the Arabic translation of the Greek text, and it was this second translation which was in turn put into Latin by the one who signed the finished product." (Lucquet, *Hermann le Dalmate* (R. hist. relig., Vol. 44, p. 415).

[2] The mediæval catalogue of these versions has been published by many and amongst others by Wüstenfeld.

[3] The Arabic and Latin texts have been published by O. Bardenhewer, *Die pseudoaristot, Schrift über das reine Gute, bekannt unter dem Namen Liber de causis*, Fribourg, 1882.

Spain (Johannes Hispanus) added an extract from the famous *Secretum Secretorum* which was translated into so many languages, for he put into Latin for a Queen Theophina or Tharasia the part concerning dietitics (*De conversanda sanitate*). Later on there appeared the complete version of Philip of Tripoli of this supposed letter to Alexander the Great, which was also known as the *Liber moralium de regimine dominorum*.[1] Alfred of Sareshel (Alfredus Anglicus), who also passed some time in Toledo, added the *De vegetabilibus* wrongly attributed to Aristotle, being in reality the *De plantis* of Nicholas of Damascus. He translated it from the Arabic text of Isaac ben Honein,[2] and dedicated the version to Roger of Hereford (about 1170) ; he also translated the *De mineralibus* or *De congelatis*, three chapters from Avicenna which are often found as an appendix to the fourth book of Aristotle's *Meteorology*.[3]

In the group of twelfth century translations from the Greek, which naturally calls for consideration after those from the Arabic, we may note the translation of the fourth book of the *Meteorology* made by Henricus Aristippus (see above, p. 72). Probably other works of the Stagirite were translated from the Greek during this century, but the authors of these versions are not known. This applies to certain parts of the *Metaphysics* and the *Physics*, the *De Anima*, and the *Ethica vetus*, which consists of Books II and III of the *Nichomachean Ethics*.[4]

---

[1] The version by John of Spain has been published by H. Suchier, *Denkmäler provenzalischer Literatur u. Spracho*, Bd. I (Halle, 1883), pp. 473-480 (Epistola Aristotelis ad Alexandrum cum prologo Joh. Hispaniensis), and by J. Brinkmann, *Die apocryphen Gesundheitsregeln des Aristoteles für Alexander den Grossen in der Uebersetzung dse Johann von Toledo* (Leipzig, 1914). In the fifth fascicle of the *Opera hactenus inedita Rogeri Baconi* (Oxford, 1920), R. Steele gives the text of Philip of Tripoli, translated at the request of Guy of Valencia, with the glosses of Roger Bacon, and a treatise by the latter on this apochryphal work.

[2] Critical edition by H. F. Meyer, *Nicolai Damasceni De Plantis libri duo Aristoteli vulgo adscripti* (Leipzig, 1841).

[3] See concerning this work A. Pelzer, *Une source inconnue de Roger Bacon. Alfred de Sareshel, commentateur des Météorologiques d'Aristote*, Archivium Franciscan. Historic., Vol. XII, 1919, pp. 49-51. There was no mediæval translation into Latin of the *Theology* of Aristotle. This apochryphal work has been published in Arabic together with a German version by F. Dieterici *Die sogenannte Theologie d. Aristoteles aus d. arabischen Handschriften zum erstenmal herausgegeben* (Leipzig, 1882) ; *Die sogenannte Theologie d. Arist aus d. Arabischen übersetzt* (Leipzig, 1883).

[4] M. Grabmann, *Forschungen über die lat. Aristotelesübersetzungen*, p. 137 on the *Metaphysica vetus;* Ch. H. Haskins, *Mediæval Versions of the Posterio Analytics, p.* 88 for the fragment of the *Physics* which he discovered in th MS. Regin. lat. 1855 (not 1885), ff. 88r-94v, in the Vatican Library ; A Pelzer, *Les versions lat. des ouvrages de morale conservés sous le nom d'Aristo en usage au XIIIe siècle* (Rev. néo-scol. de philos., 1921, pp. 324-326), on th *Ethica vetus.*

One or other of these versions might even date back to the time of Boethius.

(ii) As for PLATO, a fragment of the *Timæus* was known in the translation of Cicero and Chalcidius. Already John Scotus Eriguena mentioned this famous dialogue, which entered more and more into literary circulation. But the *Timæus* is obscure : more than one passage gives a misleading idea of the real thought of Plato ; moreover, the eclectic commentaries of Chalcidius helped to make its understanding difficult; in fact we may say that during this first period it was not properly understood at all. Works other than the *Timæus* were known only by their titles (through Chalcidius), or in occasional fragments. It was not till the twelfth century that a few copies of the *Phædo* and the *Meno* found their way into circulation. Henricus Aristippus translated them in Sicily.

(iii) COMMENTARIES ON ARISTOTLE. (*a*) Porphyry's *Isagoge*, also called the *Institutio* or *Introduction*, or *Treatise on the Five Words*,[1] already extensively commented on by the later Grecian philosophers, enjoyed an immense popularity among the earlier mediæval thinkers in the translation of Marius Victorinus, and afterwards in that of Boethius, with the double commentary of the latter. Porphyry was looked upon as a supporter of Aristotle, and his connection with an antagonistic school of philosophy was not even suspected.

The *Isagoge* studies the five predicables or ways in which the predicate of a judgment can be related to a subject (genus, species, specific difference, property, and accident) ; it served as an introduction to the *Categories* of Aristotle. Porphyry in the *Isagoge* did not get beyond this logical aspect of the predicables. He scarcely noticed the problem of the objectivity of universal ideas, and his statement of the question became the starting point of the controversy concerning the Universals. (Chap. II, § 1).

(*b*) Boethius commented on the *Categories* and the *De Interpretatione*. His other commentaries are lost.

(*c*) The commentary of Themistius on the *Posterior Analytics* was translated from the Arabic by Gerard of Cremona, to whom also we owe versions of several works by Alexander of Aphrodisius (*De tempore ; De sensu ; De*

---

[1] Republished by A. Busse, Berlin, 1887 (Vol. IV. of the *Commentaria in Aristotelem græca* published by the Berlin Academy).

eo quod augmentum et incrementum and probably the *De Intellectu*).

(*d*) Priscian of Lydia is represented in the ninth century by a translation not very widely used (possibly made by John Scotus Eriugena) of his replies to nine questions in psychology, physiology, and the natural sciences, addressed to him by Chosroes, King of Persia, about 531 : Prisciani philosophi solutiones eorum de quibus dubitavit Chosroes Persarum rex.[1]

The early Middle Ages did not know any other works of Greek philosophy ; but the Latin writers and the Fathers had handed down the names of a great number of celebrated personalities, and there were extant fragments of the Epicurean, Stoic, and Pythagorian systems.[2] No original work of neo-Platonism was known.

(B) *Latin Philosophers.* The legacy of Latin antiquity, so rich in literature, reduces itself in the case of philosophy to the following :

(i) A series of compilations dating from the period of Latin decadence. Among them : the works of Marius Victorinus, who was a rhetorician under Constantius (about 350), and who translated Porphyry's *Isagoge* and also wrote several treatises and commentaries on Logic ; the works of Claudius Mamertus of Vienne in Gaul (about 450), who wrote the *De statu animæ* in defence of the immortality of the soul against Faustus the Semi-Pelagian ; and the works of Donatus, to whom, with Macrobius, the Middle Ages owed much of their knowledge of the facts of ancient history.

(ii) A number of neo-Platonist commentaries. (*a*) Apuleius of Madaura was made use of in his writings *De dogmate Platonis* (also called *De habitudine Platonis*), and *De deo Socratis*. Another work, *Peri ermeniæ* ($\pi\epsilon\rho\grave{\iota}$ $\epsilon\rho\mu\eta\nu\epsilon\grave{\iota}\omega\nu$) was falsely ascribed to him, and there was also in circulation a " hermetic " or occult work, *Asclepius*, translated from a Greek work by Hermes Trismegistus in which the latter replied to questions by Asclepius. Some scholastics attributed this work to an Egyptian philosopher, Mercurius, to whom also they ascribed a *Liber qui inscribatur Logostileos* ($\lambda\acute{o}\gamma os$ $\tau\acute{\epsilon}\lambda\epsilon\iota os$) *id est*

---

[1] Complete edition by Bywater, *Comm. in Arist. græca, Suppl.* Vol. I, part two, Berlin, 1886.

[2] John of Salisbury also quotes some extracts from a letter by Plutarch. *Polycraticus*, V, 1.

verbum perfectum.[1] In this they were following the author of the pseudo-Augustinian work, *De quinque hæresibus*.

(*b* In the same group may be mentioned the Commentary which Chalcidius appended to his translation of the *Timæus*, and also the Commentary on *Scipio's Dream* by Macrobius. (§ 3).

(iii) Certain works or portions of works of Cicero (the *Topics*, the *De Officiis*, the *De Inventione*, and the *Rhetorica ad Herennium*, two spurious works known respectively as the *Rhetorica Prima* and the *Rhetorica Secunda*) ; Seneca (the *De Beneficiis* for instance) ; and Lucretius.

Cicero was considered an authority on logic and rhetoric. As for Seneca, his stoic maxims, made a ready appeal, because of their puritanism, to the few scholastics who wrote on ethics. From the beginning of the Middle Ages various apochryphal works were in circulation under the name of Seneca, such as his supposed correspondence with St. Paul, and the treatises *Formula honestæ vitæ* (or *De Quatuor Virtutibus Cardinalibus*) really written by Martin of Braga or of Dumio, the *De moribus*, *De paupertate*, writings dating back to the fourth century A.D.[2] On the other hand, Lucretius, the authoritative exponent of Epicureanism, was looked upon with less favour by the scholastics,[3] and appealed to more often by their adversaries. Thus the materialistic psychology of the Cathari borrows his arguments. (Ch. VI.)

(C) *The Fathers of the Church*, the acknowledged founders of mediæval theology, handed down their own philosophical lideas and those of antiquity. They were called *sancti* as contrasted with the *philosophi*.

(i) Among them, St. Augustine occupies the first place. The scholastics were greatly influenced by his psychology, and metaphysical theses were also borrowed from him. (cf. p.24, 115)

(ii) Pseudo-Augustine. The ascendancy of St. Augustine as a philosopher and an interpreter of dogma explains the fact that under his name were circulated a series of apochryphal works, abounding in anti-scholastic and sometimes even anti-Augustinian theories. The principal pseudo-Augustinian

---

[1] Cf. M. Baumgartner, *Die Philosophie des Alanus de Insulis*, pp. 114-116 ; *Die Erkentnisslehre d. Wilhelm von Auvergne*, p. 5 ; Bernays, *Ueber den unter den Werken d. Apuleius stehenden hermetischen Dialog. Asclepius* (in *Monatsber. d. K. Akad. d. Wissensch.* Berlin, 1871, p. 500).

[2] Haureau, *Not. et extr. de qq. man. latins*, II, 202, IV, 15, and 267.

[3] Isidore of Seville, and Rhaban Maur, two compilers, treat him with most favour.

treatises (their apochryphal character is established with the aid of St. Augustine's own *Retractationes*) are the following : (*a*) *Categoriæ decem*, an abridgement of the *Categories* of Aristotle which had a great influence ; (*b*) *Principia dialecticæ*, a grammatical work on the distinction between simple and compound terms ; (*c*) *Contra quinque hæreses*, in which the author quotes " hermetic " texts giving them a Christian meaning ; (*d*) later, in the twelfth century, the *De Spiritu et Anima*, written by the Cistercian Alcher of Clairvaux, a veritable manual of Augustinian psychology in great favour among the scholastics. (Ch. V, § 6).

(iii) The early Middle Ages possessed treatises by Origin in Rufinus's translations, Gregory of Nyssa (see iv, Nemesius), Clement of Alexandria, Lactantius, St. Jerome, and St. Ambrose, whose *Hexaemeron* embodied a number of Aristotelian theories. Cassian, the Semi-Pelagian († 435) against whom St. Augustine wrote his last works, transmitted some philosophical notions to the Middle Ages through the writings of Alcuin and Rhaban Maur. In particular his treatise *De Institutis Cœnobiorum* and the *Collationes Patrum XXIV* were widely read.

(iv) Up to the sixteenth century, a work entitled *De Natura hominis* (περὶ φύσεως ανθρώπου) written by Nemesius, Bishop of Emesa, was attributed to Gregory of Nyssa (*Gregorius Nyssenus*, or *Nicenus*). This work was translated in the first place by Alfanus, Archbishop of Salerno (1058-1085), and later on in 1115 by Burgundius of Pisa the Jurist, who dedicated his work to Frederick Barbarossa.[1] Burgundius, to whom is also due a version of ten medical works by Galen, translated the homilies of St. John Chrysostom, St. Basil, and, about 1150, the *De Fide Orthodoxa* by St. John Damascene, the St. Thomas of the East, who died before 758. This work (ἔκδοσις ἀκριβὴς

---

1 C. Baeumker, *Nemesius* (*Wochenschrift für klass. Philologie*, 1896, 1095-1102) ; B. Domanski, *Die Psychologie d. Nemesius*, p. xii. Alfanus's translation has been published by Holzinger (Leipzig and Prague, 1887), and by C. Burkhard (*Nemesii episcopi Premnon physicon sive* περὶ φύσεως ἀνθρώπου *liber a N. Alfano ... in latinum translatus*, Leipzig 1917), who has also published that by Burgundius (*Gregorii Nysseni Emesini* περὶ φύσεως ἀνθρώπου Progr., Vienne, 1891-1902). Grabmann divides the translations undertaken in the twelfth century from Greek into Latin into two groups : the first was the work of men in contact with the Byzantine world and comprized James of Venice and Burgundius of Pisa. The second group had its centre of activity in South Italy and Sicily, and included Alfanus of Salerno, his friend Constantine the African, and Henricus Aristippus. *Gesch. d. scholast. Methode*, Bd. II, pp. 75 *et seq.* See also Ch. H. Haskins *The Greek Element in the Renaissance of the Twelfth century*, American Historical Review, 1920, pp. 603-615.

τῆς ὀρθοδόξου πιστεως) comprised the third and last part of the πηγὴ γνώσεως of the Doctor of Damascus. There was also in the twelfth century another translation of chapters I to VIII of the third book.[1]

(v) Finally we may mention the writings of pseudo-Dionysius the Areopagite and of Maximus the Confessor. The treatises *De Hierarchia Cœlestia*, *De Hierarchia Ecclesiastica*, *De Divinis Nominibus*, *De Theologia Mystica*, and ten letters which were known in the West in the eighth century[2] were translated between 828 and 835, at the request of Louis the Pious, by Hilduin, Abbot of St. Denis, assisted by several collaborators, and about 858 by J. Scotus Eriugena at the request of Charles the Bald. St. Anselm held them in high esteem. John Sarrasin, a friend of John of Salisbury, translated them towards the middle of the twelfth century, and R. Grossetête in the following century.[3] These works had a great influence upon mediæval mystical theology and æsthetics ; they were commented upon simultaneously in the interests of Neo-Platonist pantheism and of orthodox individualism.

(D) *Arabian works written by Mohammedans or Jews.*—Some products of Arabian science became known to the West in the eleventh century through the Benedictine monks of Monte Cassino. Constantine the African, who was born in Carthage and became a monk under Abbot Didier (about 1060) after long journeys to the East and Egypt and a stay at Salerno, freely translated medical works from the Greek and Arabic, and in particular those of the Jew Isaac ben Salomon Israeli (ninth century), and perhaps also his works on the *Elements* and the *Definitions*. The Lotharingian Walcher who was in England in 1091 employed the astrolabe as used by the Arabs, long before Adelard of Bath. In the twelfth century, the latter translated the Khowaresmian Tables (1126), while Plato of

---

[1] See Haskins, *op. cit.*, pp. 608-610, and J. de Ghellinck, *Le mouvement théologique du XIIe siècle* (Paris, 1914, pp. 245-267.)

[2] Pope Paul I sent a Greek copy of the works to Pepin about 785 ; Michael the First, Emperor of Constantinople, sent another to Louis the Fair in 827.

[3] Cf. M. Grabmann, *Pseudo-Dionysius Areopagita in lat. Uebersetzungen des Mittelälters, in Beiträge zur Gesch. der christl. Altertums u. der byzantin. Litteratur, Festgabe Albert Ehrhard* (Bonn, 1920), pp. 180-199 ; P. Lehmann, *Zur Kenntniss der Schriften des Dionysius Areopagita im Mittelälter*, Revue bénédictine, 1923, pp. 81-97 ; G. Théry, *Hilduin et la première traduction des écrits du ps.-D.* (Revue d'hist. de l'Eglise de France, 1923, pp. 23-39) ; *Existe-il un comment. de J. Sarrasin sur la Hiérarchie céleste du ps.-D?* R. sc. phil. theol. 1922, pp. 72-81. He thinks that Sarrasin commented on Scotus Eriugena's translation before he made his own version). By the same : *Le texte intégral de la traduction du ps.—Denys par Hilduin;* in R. hist. ecclés. 1925.

Tivoli, Robert of Ketene (Retines, or Chester), and Herman the Dalmatian made known other astronomical works.[1]

But it was the translators of the College of Toledo who transmitted the principal works of Arabian and Jewish philosophers to the Latin West in the twelfth century.   John of Spain (Johannes Hispanus) translated not only astronomical works by Albategni (Al-Battani), Alchabitius (Al-Kabi'si), Alfraganus (Al-Fergani), Albumasar (Abu Ma'schar), but also mportant philosophical works. Among them we may mention the *De Intellectu* by Alkindi, the *De Differentia inter Animam et Spiritum* by the Christian doctor and philosopher Costa ben Luca (Constabulus), the *De Scientiis* by Alfarabi, the *Fons Vitæ* by the Jew Avencebrol (Salomon Ibn Gebirol), the philosophy of Algazel (Al-Gazzali), considerable portions of the philosophical encyclopædia of Avicenna (Ibn Sina) called in Arabic the *Kitab al Schifa* or *Book of Healing* and in Latin *Sufficientia* (amongst others, the *Metaphysics* and the *Liber de Anima* or *Sextus Liber Naturalium*). In the case of many of the translations last referred to, the manuscripts mention the collaboration of Dominic Gundisalvi (Gundissalinus).

By means of these works and especially through Avicenna's Encyclopædia, which is a paraphrase of Aristotle, the doctrine of the Stagirite was transmitted in great fullness to the West independently of the later versions of Aristotle due to Gerard of Cremona (see above). Among the translations from Arabic into Latin by the latter we must mention in addition to many books on Greek and Arabian medicine, mathematics and astronomy,[2] the *Canon* of Avicenna and his big work on medicine, the *Optics* of Alhazen (Al-Hasan ibn al-Heitam), the *Liber Definitionum* and the *De Elementis* by Isaac Israeli, the *De Scientiis* of Alfarabi, his *Distinctio super librum Aristotelis de naturali auditu*, the *De Ortu Scientiarum*, translated probably

[1] Cf. Haskins, *The Reception of Arabic Science in England* (Engl. hist. Review, Jan. 1915).

[2] About the same time there appeared in Sicily translations from Greek into Latin of the *Pneumatica* of Hero of Alexandria, three works of Euclid (*Data, Optica, Catoptrica*), and the *Elementatio physica* or *De Motu* of Proclus. These four last versions were the work of an anonymous translator who also rendered into Latin about 1160 the *Almageste* of Claudius Ptolemæus, with the assistance of Eugenius the Admiral, to whom is also due the translation into Latin from Arabic of the *Optics* of the same author. Cf. Ch. H. Haskins, *The Sicilian Translations of the Twelfth Century and the First Latin Version of Ptolemy's Almagest*, Harvard Studies in Classical Philology, 1910, pp. 75-102. *Further Notes on Sicilian Translations of the Twelfth Century*, ibid., 1912, pp. 55-166.

by D. Gundisalvi,[1] and works by Alkindi such as his *De somno et visione, De quinque essentiis,* and *De ratione.*

Thus, by a strange turn of the wheel, the Christians in the West received from the Arabs, thanks to these versions, a considerable number of the philosophical and scientific works of the Greeks which the Syrian Christians had translated from Greek or Syrian into Arabic four or five centuries before at the request of the Caliphs.

(E) *Mediæval Writers.*—We must include in the list of works read widely during the early Middle Ages those first writers referred to in Section 3. Thus at first Gregory the Great was quoted more than St. Augustine. Other mediæval authors such as Hilary of Poitiers soon attained a wide circulation. Later on the works of St. Anselm and books like the *Liber Sex Principiorum* of Gilbert de la Porrée became classics.

34. Bibliography.—L. Maitre, *Les écoles épiscopales et monastiques de l'Occident depuis Charlemagne jusqu'à Philippe-Auguste* (Paris, 1866); A. Ebert, *Die Litterarische Bewegung zur Zeit Karls d. Gr.* (Deutsche Rundschau, II, p. 398-410); Specht, *Geschichte d. Unterrichtswesens in Deutschland* (Stuttgart, 1886), out of date; Willmann, *Didaktik*, Vol. I, § 18, good; Clerval, *Les écoles de Chartres au moyen âge du Ve au XVIe siècle* (Mem. soc. archæol. Eure-et-Loir, 1895), excellent, a general view of the pre-Scholastic schools; Robert, *Les écoles et l'enseignment de la théol. pendant la prem. moitié du XIIe siècle* (Paris, 1909), the first part deals with the general organization of the schools. Mariétan, *Problème de la Classification des sciences d'Aristote à S. Thomas* (Paris, 1901), gives references, but is not methodically arranged; Willmann, *op. cit.,* § 19 (extensive bibliography, especially for each of the liberal arts, pp. 267 *et seq.*); Clerval, *op. cit.* The organization of studies at Chartres gives an idea of what obtained elsewhere; Pfister, *Etudes sur le règne de Robert le Pieux* (Bibl. des Hautes Etudes, Paris 1885), gives programmes of studies; Picavet, *Hist. de l'Enseignment et des écoles du IXe au XIIIe siecle* (R. intern. enseign, 1901); M. Roger, *L'enseignment des lettres classiques d'Ausone à Alcuin* (Paris, 1905); Ferrère, *De la division des septs arts liberaux* (Ann. de philos. chret., June, 1900), not clear; Willmann, *Geschichte d. Ideal. II,* Section 67; De Wulf, *Introd. a la Philos. néo-Scol.,* Sections 4 and 9; (English translation, *Scholasticism Old and New*); G. Kurth, *Notger de Liège et la*

---

[1] Edited by Baeumker, *BGPM, XIX,* 3 (1916).

civilization au Xe siècle (Brussels, 1905), Ch. XIV : L'instruction publique ; Appuhn, *Das Trivium u. Quadriv. im Theorie u. Praxis* (Erlangen, 1900) ; E. Norden, *Die lateinische Litteratur im Uebergang vom Altertum z. Mitt.* (Die Kultur d. Gegenwart, I, VIII, 1912) ; G. Manacorda, *Storia della Scuola in Italia*, Vol. I ; *Il Medio Evo* (Milan, no date) ; L. J. Paetow *The Battle of the Seven Arts, by Henri d'Andeli, edited and translated* (Berkeley, 1914) ; E. K. Rand, *A Vade-mecum of Liberal Culture in a Manuscript of Fleury* (Philol. Quarterly, 1922, p. 158-277) ; *Prudentius and Christian Humanism* (Transactions of the American Philological Association, 1920, p. 72-83); H. O. Taylor, *The Classical Heritage of the Middle Ages*, 3rd edit. J. E. Sandys, *English Scholars of Paris and Franciscans of Oxford*, in the *Cambridge History of Literature*, Vol. I (Cambridge University Press, 1908), pp. 183-216.   Jourdain, *Recherches crit. sur l'âge et l'origine des trad. d'Aristote* (Paris, 1843), served as a starting-point for research work ; Rose, *Die Lücke im Diogenes Lærtius u. der alte Uebersetzer* (Hermes I, 1866, pp. 367-397) ; *Ptolemæus u. die Schule von Toledo* (*ibid*. VIII, 1874, pp. 327-349) ; M. Steinschneider, *Die hebraischen Uebersetz. d. Mittelalters* (Berlin), 1893) ; *Die europaische Uebersetz, aus d. Arabischen bis Mitte des 17 Jahrh.* (Sitz. Kais. Akad. Wiss. Phil.-hist. Kl. Bd. 149 amd 151) ; F. Wustenfeld, *Die Uebersetz. arab. Werke in Latein* (Gottingen, Abhandl. d. Gesellschaft d. Wissenschaften, 1877) ; Leclerc, *Histoire de la médicine arabe* (Paris, 1876) ; Björnbo, *Die mittelalterl. lat. Uebersetz. aus d. Griech, auf. d. Gebeite d. Mathem. Wissensch.* (Archiv. f. d. Gesch. d. naturwissensch. u. d. Technik, I, 1908, pp. 385-394). Cf. also works mentioned in notes in Haskins, Getyer, Grabmann.   For St. John Damascene see De Ghellinck, *op. cit.* For pseudo-Dionysius see works indicated in section dealing with him. A work is in preparation by G. Théry : *Les traductions latines du pseudo-Denis au moyen age : Leur utilisation par les premiers commentateurs dominicains.*   Grabmann, *Die Entwicklung d. mittelalterl. Sprachlogik* (Phil. Jahrb. 1922) ; Steinschneider, *Did arabischen Uebersetzungen*, etc., P. M. Bouyges, *Notes sur les philosophes arabes connas des Latins au moyen âge* (Mélanges Univ. S. Joseph, VII—IX, Beyrout, 1914-24).

§ 3—*The First Mediæval Writers.*

35. Two groups.—The first mediæval writers were, strictly speaking, of Celtic and Germanic stock.   They extended from the fifth to the ninth century, and appeared successively in Rome (Gregory the Great), the kingdom of the Ostrogoths (Boethius, Cassiodorus), and Visigoths (Isidore of Seville), Celtic Ireland, the Palatinate School of Charlemagne, or in the monasteries subject to the influence of the Carlovingian Renaissance (Alcuin, Rhaban Maur). They had the common characteristic of devoting themselves to the work of compilation. The encyclopædias which they brought out made a great impression on their contemporaries who were athirst for knowledge, and they were continually consulted throughout the Middle Ages.

In addition to this group of men who stood for the new aspirations, there were others who were contemporary with or even preceded them, but who were devoted rather to the ideas of antiquity and may therefore be regarded as marking a stage of transition. The most interesting of these were pseudo-Dionysius in the Greek world; Chalcidius, Macrobius, and Martianus Capella in the Roman world. With the exception of pseudo-Dionysius, who was a theorist, the men whom we place in this second group were characterized by the eclectic and encyclopædic tendencies of Greek and Roman philosophy in the period of their decline, and in this respect they resemble the men of the mediæval group.

36. Pseudo-Dionysius the Areopagite.—Of the Greek writers of the early Christian centuries chronologically connected with the Middle Ages, the most characteristic was the author wrongly known under the name of Dionysius the Areopagite, the disciple of St. Paul. Much controversy has centred around his personality. It seems that his works must be put at the end of the fifth or the beginning of the sixth century. They were unknown before the time of the great religious conference at Constantinople in 533, and Hypatius of Ephesus declared that they were apochryphal. On the other hand Pope Martin I maintained their authenticity and introduced them into the West. The treatises of pseudo-Dionysius on the *Divine Names*, *Mystical Theology*, the *Celestial Hierarchy*, and the *Ecclesiastical Hierarchy*, together with his ten letters, contain a systematic conception of the Christian cult, founded on theological and philosophical data.

Numerous parallels have shown that pseudo-Dionysius followed Proclus and Plotinus to a great extent in his terminology, formulas, and in many particular doctrines. But like the other Christian writers inspired by neo-Platonism—St. Augustine being the chief—pseudo-Dionysius rejected the most characteristic feature in this system, namely, Monism.

He starts out with the transcendence of God and the substantial distinction between God and that which is other than Him.[1] God is the centre of Philosophy. Considered in Himself (treatise on the *Divine Names*), He is Goodness, Beauty, Light, Unity, but precisely because of His transcendence and His distinction from the finite world, He may be called Non-Being, Obscure, Ineffable (Plotinus). The methods of positive and negative theology take their rise in the distinction between these two points of view.

God is the principle or beginning of things, and the latter are substantially distinct from Him. All beings are effusions of His goodness, radiations of His light, and just as God is Goodness, Beauty and Light, so also limited beings are good, beautiful, lightsome according to the measure of their being. Evil—explained after the manner of the *De Malorum Subsistentia* of Proclus—has no being in itself : it consists simply of a deficiency in a being which is good. The world is the object of the Providence of God. Between God and man there exists a scale of heavenly beings (treatise on the *Celestial Hierarchy*) of which the ecclesiastical hierarchy is a reflection (treatise on the *Ecclesiastical Hierarchy*).

God, the end of all things, draws them to Himself by the love which He inspires. The good, after having descended into the creature, ascends once more to its source. Deification or divinization, which brings about this return, extends to inorganic as well as organic beings, for all things have within themselves a desire for the Divine. In the case of man, this return towards God involves ecstasy and the delirium of love, in their various forms. Although the mysticism of pseudo-Dionysius[2] takes over from the Alexandrians their allegories, their description of the mystic states, theories of prayer and the divine character of ecstasy " in which like is known by like," it is nevertheless individualistic like all Christian mysticism, for it is based upon grace. (Ch. VII, § 2.)

This does not prevent pseudo-Dionysius from making free use of exaggerated terminology and equivocal expressions,

---

[1] Koch, p. 194, *op. cit.* (**45**).
[2] We do not understand how F. Müller, one of the latest historians, can say that the introduction of Christian elements is a kind of corruption of the true (echte) mysticism of Plotinus. (*op. cit.* **45,** p. 107).

and there are many obscure passages which are capable of either a monistic or a pluralistic interpretation.[1] This explains how it was that his treatises—the influence of which throughout the Middle Ages it is difficult to exaggerate—led some people astray, and that both scholasticism and anti-scholasticism, the pluralistic mysticism of the Catholics and the heterodox monistic mysticism, claimed to be supported by pseudo-Dionysius.

MAXIMUS THE CONFESSOR (580-622) was one of the first admirers and imitators of pseudo-Dionysius.

37. Chalcidius and Macrobius were two personalities of whom not much is known. They appeared in the Roman world at the end of the fourth or the beginning of the fifth century.

The Commentary of Chalcidius on the *Timæus* was principally inspired by that of Posidonius, through the intermediary of Adrastus and Albinus. Chalcidius apparently did nothing more than translate a work of co-ordination on the part of some Greek author who himself made use of Numenius. Thus the work reflects the eclecticism, Platonist in tendency, which flourished in the second century A.D. and lacks originality. It contains extracts of works of Plato other than the *Timæus*, a statement of various Aristotelian theories (it is worthy of note that he rejects the definition of the soul as the form of the body), a few texts of Chrysippus and Cleanthus together with a comparison of their doctrines, also theories of Pythagoras, Philo, Numenius, etc., and likewise extracts from Greek writers on medicine, Ionians, Eleatics and the Atomists of the pre-Socratic period : so that Chalcidius was regarded up to the twelfth century as one of the principal sources for the history of Greek philosophy. This helps to explain the great influence of his Commentary.

His younger contemporary, AMBROSIUS THEODOSIUS MACROBIUS brought up on Roman traditions although not himself a Roman by birth, wrote a Commentary on the *Somnium Scipionis* found in Cicero's *De Republica* (VI, 9). The Middle Ages was provided in this treatise with an exposition of neo-Platonism after the manner of Porphyry and Proclus. It contains in a condensed form (I, 14) the great doctrines of the Monistic emanation theory of the Alexandrian writers : the supreme principle, God, engenders eternally by virtue of a conscious

---

[1] Koch, *op. cit.*, p. 194.

and necessary generation (*superabundanti majestatis faecunditate*) a second principle, the *mens* or *nous*. The latter, which is by nature purely intelligible like its Source, whom it knows, engenders in its turn the world-soul. This is less perfect, carries within itself the germ of multiplicity, and spreads out its universal life into the corporeal things of heaven and earth. By the world-soul which is in a sense divine, all things are bound together in a sort of universal sympathy ; everything is by nature intelligible. The intelligible is projected forth into the manifold appearances of bodies, just as a light may be reflected in numerous mirrors without suffering any alteration in itself.[1]

In addition to this theory of hypostases subordinated to each other, Macrobius reproduces several particular theories of Neo-Platonism. He emphasizes the functions of beauty and light which accompany Being. He holds that the human soul is immaterial and immortal, united to the body by a forced union[2] and ought to aim at deliverance. He assigns to morality the task of freeing the soul from its bondage to the body. He distinguishes with Plotinus between the political virtues of man living in society, the purgative virtues (*purgatoriæ*) of the man seeking to free himself from the demands of sense, the virtue of the free man (*purgati*) who has already attained this end, and finally the contemplative virtues (*quæ in ipsa divina mente consistunt*) introducing man to the mystical contemplation which is the ideal even of life here below. He combines these four Plotinian grades of virtue with the classification of virtues into Wisdom, Justice, Temperance and Fortitude (Plato), which differ in meaning according to the degree of advancement of the soul in the purgative way.

We may add that the Commentary of Macrobius is full of

---

1 Deus, qui prima causa et est et vocatur, unus omnium quæque sunt, quæque videntur esse, princeps et origo est : hic superabundanti majestatis fœcunditate de se mentem creavit. Hæc mens, quæ νοῦς vocatur, qua patrem inspicit, plenam similitudinem servat auctoris : animam vero de se creat posteriora respiciens. Rursus anima patrem qua intuetur, induitur, ac paulatim regrediente respectu in fabricam corporum, incorporea ipsa degenerat. . . . Macrobius, *Comment. ex Cicerone in somnium Scipionis*, I, 14. Secundum hoc ergo cum ex summo Deo mens, ex mente anima sit ; anima vero et condat et vita compleat omnia quæ sequuntur, cunctaque hic unus fulgor illuminet et in universis appareat, ut in multis speculis, per ordinem positis, vultus unus ; cumque omnia continuis successionibus se sequantur . . . invenietur . . . a summo Deo usque ad ultimam rerum fæcem una mutuis se vinculis religans et nusquam interrupta connexio, *ibid.* Julian of Toledo, a contemporary of Isidore, was inspired by him. Cf. H. Beeson, *The Ars Grammatica of Julian of Toledo*, in *Miscellanea Ehrle*, 1924, I, p. 50.
2 Ad hæc terrena corpora deducitur, I, 12.

neo-Pythagorean ideas on the symbolism of numbers and their astronomical applications, and that although the author became a Christian he found a place for polytheism in his system, so that the work is really a syncretic product of neo-Platonist paganism.

Macrobius was also the author of *Saturnalia ;* like M. Victorinus he made use of a commentary on the *Timæus* which connects him with Posidonius ; and he also transmitted a mass of mathematical and astronomical data.

38. Martianus Capella, of Carthage, went to Rome and wrote (about 430) a *Satyricon* and a treatise entitled *De Nuptiis Mercurii et Philologiæ*, which made use of Varron and other grammarians. Martianus popularized the trivium and the quadrivium. The seven arts are represented under the form of young maidens escorting Philologia, Apollo's bride. Grammar, for instance, is a daughter of Memphis, and carries on a tray instruments for loosing the tongues of children. Dialectics is represented by a woman with an emaciated countenance, holding in one hand a serpent, and in the other concealing a fish-hook. The Middle Ages eagerly studied this strange encyclopædia because it was an attempt at a classification of human knowledge and drew up a plan of study. It was commented upon (Remi of Auxerre), translated (Notker Labeo) ; and was a source of inspiration for the arts.

39. Boethius.—Martianus Capella was not a Christian, but Boethius in all probability was. He lived from about 480-525 A.D., and was a much more vigorous thinker than M. Capella. He was one of the principal links between the philosophy of antiquity and that of the Middle Ages. An original civilization was beginning in the kingdom of Theodoric, King of the Italian Ostrogoths. Boethius was the Minister of the latter, and is sometimes referred to as Manlius Consul. Art was beginning to flourish, and the architecture and painting of the period may still be admired at Ravenna. Knowledge was free to develop, and Boethius is a fitting representative. The Lombard invasion (568) put an end to this renaissance so full of promise. Brought up at Rome according to neo-Platonist and Stoic traditions, the patrician Boethius was commanded to present himself at the Court. Later on he was suspected of sympathies towards Rome, put in disgrace, and finally executed by the King's orders. His philosophic work comprised :—

(i) Various translations, notably of the *Isagoge* of Porphyry and of sundry works of Aristotle. He translated the *Categories* and the πepὶ ἑρμενειας. The last three parts of the *Organon* (*Analytics*, *Topics* and the *Sophistical Arguments*) were apparently not found till the end of the twelfth century. He refers to the *Metaphysics* and the *Physics* (in *lib. de interpr.* II), and announces his intention of translating and commenting on the whole of Aristotle.[1]

(ii) Commentaries : a double commentary on the *Isagoge*, and on Aristotle's *Categories*, two on the *De interpretatione* (Aristotle's chief logical work), one on the *Prior* and *Posterior Analytics*, and one on Cicero's *Topics*.

(iii) Original treatises : *De syllogismo categorico* and *De syllogismo hypothetico*, *De divisione*, *De differentiis topicis*, all of them greatly appreciated in the Middle Ages. The Scholastics also eulogistically refer to his works on Mathematics and Music, and above all, to his *De Consolatione Philosophiæ* which he wrote when in prison at Ticinum.[2]

This is written in elegant prose, interspersed with poetry, and bears witness to the wide culture of its author and his knowledge of antiquity. Philosophy visits the prisoner and appears in the form of a majestic lady, the description of whom afterwards inspired the statues of Philosophy belonging to the twelfth and thirteenth centuries. On the lower fringe of her robe she carries the embroidered letters θ and π (initial letters of theoretical and practical philosophy), and a ladder placed against her breast symbolizes the steps which lead to wisdom. Philosophy consoles Boethius in his misfortune and shows that no terrestrial good can confer happiness. For this it is necessary to return to the principle of universal love, the Supreme Good, a personal God, to whom Philosophy prays. The presence of evil in the world and the harmonizing of Divine foreknowledge with human liberty are problems only for our limited intelligences which do not comprehend the Divine simplicity. The same applies to the *fatum*, which is

[1] Ego omne Aristotelis opus quodcumque in manus venerit in Romanum stilum vertens eorum omnium commenta Latina oratione prescribam (*De interpret.*, ed. secunda, lib, II). For the translations of Boethius see a note by P. Mandonnet, *Siger de Brabant*, pp. 7-9. Cf. Grabmann, *op. cit.*, I, 150 *et seq.*; Manitius, *op. cit.*, p. 25 *et seq.*

[2] The following arrangement of the philosophical works of Boethius is given by Brandt (*Philologus*, 62, 141 *et seq.*) : (1) *Commenta in Isagogen Porphyrii* ; (2) *In categorias Aristotelis*, (3) *In libr. Aristotelis De Interpretatione*, (4) *Priora et posteriora analyt. Aristot.*, translation and commentary, (5) *De syllogismo categorico*, (6) *De syllog. hypothetico*, (7) *De divisione*, (8) Works on the *Topics* of Aristotle and Cicero, (9) *De consolatione philosophiæ*.

merely the execution of the providential plan. God alone is eternal, but the world is endowed with perpetuity, since for a philosopher nothing can come from nothing. The *De Consolatione* is an original work which contains the foundations of a system of moral philosophy and of metaphysics.[1] The book was constantly read and translated right up to the fifteenth century.

Boethius also left various theological writings (*De Trinitate, De Hebdomadibus, De Duabus Naturis in Christo*). The *De Fide Catholica* is of doubtful authenticity.

Boethius had a considerable influence upon the philosophy of the period under consideration. Up to the end of the twelfth century, he was the principal source of Aristotelianism, and was looked upon as equal or even as superior to the Stagirite. His translations and commentaries on Aristotle, together with his original abridgements which for a long time took the place of the unknown parts of the *Organon*, became the basis for the study of dialectics. He also made known quite a number of other Aristotelian ideas : thus he mentions various methodological theories, such as the famous tripartite division of theoretical knowledge into metaphysics, mathematics, and physics. He himself prefers and practises the mathematical and deductive method ; we also find scattered up and down his works fragments of ideas concerning the nature and process of knowledge, imperfect concepts of matter, substantial form, and change, substance, person, and causes. The *De Consolatione Philosophiæ* reproduces the argument for the Unmoved Mover, the *De Trinitate* studies the application of grammatical forms to the Divinity, etc. Finally, Boethius was the source of the Latin terminology for very many expressions from Aristotelian philosophy.

Boethius also put into circulation a number of neo-Platonist ideas. Thus the *De Consolatione Philosophiæ* stresses the ineffable character of the First Principle, the Divine Goodness, in which all things share and towards which all return. We likewise come across the theory of reminiscence in terms which recall the Commentary of Proclus on the *Timæus* ; his doctrine concerning the Divine foreknowledge and liberty was evidently influenced by Jamblichus and Proclus, but Boethius in these borrowings avoids everything which might seem to be a concession to Monism. His God is a personal one, and his theory

[1] Cf. Rand, *On the Composition of Boethius' Consolatio Philosophiæ.* The author differs from Usener, who regards the work as a mere encyclopædia.

of Providence respects the rights of human personality which he stresses so much and of which he has given the celebrated definition : *persona est rationalis naturæ individua substantia.* Thus the neo-Platonism of Boethius is free from the neo-Platonist spirit.

We also find in Boethius certain Stoic doctrines, and he speaks of resignation to one's destiny in terms which reminds one of the Philosophy of the Porch. In the same way the Pythagorean theories concerning number and unity play a large part in his theories on the Divine nature, creation, and exemplarism.

Moreover, Boethius is familiar with Augustinism. He links up the Platonist "reminiscence" with the Augustinian doctrine of the *incommutabilia vera.* He lays great stress on the peace which all things desire, on the unity of the world, and the Providence of God.

We may remark in the last place with Rand and Klinger that we already find in Boethius a clear distinction between faith and reason (*fides, ratio*).[1] That is why the *De Consolatione Philosophiæ* does not refer to Christianity but builds up a system of Natural Theology by the unaided efforts of human reason ; while in the *opuscula sacra* it is the theologian who speaks. A distinction of this kind provides a simple solution of the difficulties which have been raised against Boethius' Christianity, and show to what high degree of intellectual maturity this fifth century thinker had attained.

In view of all this it is easy to understand that Boethius handed on to the philosophy of the Middle Ages elements which were very varied. We shall see how the eclectic spirits of the thirteenth century laid them under contribution in their syntheses.

CASSIODORUS (about 470-570) was also a minister under Theodoric. Like Martianus Capella, he was a writer who managed to include in his treatises (*De Orthographia, De Artibus ac Disciplinus Liberalium Litterarum, De Institutione Divinarum Litterarum*), all that he had learnt concerning the trivium and the quadrivium, principally in the school of Boethius. His opusculum *De Anima*, of Augustinian inspiration, was utilized by Rhaban and Hincmar.[2]

---

[1] F. Klinger, *De Boethii Consolatione philosophiæ* (Philol. Untersuchungen hrg. Kiessling, Berlin, 1921). Cf. also Rand, *op. cit.*

[2] Another compiler, Martin of Bracara († 580) makes great use in his moral writings of Seneca : *formula vitæ honestæ, de ira, de paupertate, de moribus, pro repellanda jactantia, de superbia, exhortatio humilitatis.*—Manitius *op. cit.*, p. 110.

40. Gregory the Great (sixth century).—The personality of Gregory the First, known as the Great, who was Pope from 590 to 604, emerges from the chaos caused in Italy by the collapse of the Kingdom of the Ostrogoths. He was a Benedictine monk prior to becoming the founder of the mediæval Papacy, and it was he who sent Augustine the monk to evangelize England. His writings are the work of a practical moralist, attentive to the happenings of the time, but caring not for Greek tradition. In this respect he is a great contrast to Boethius : he is a mediæval personage with all the roughness of the new races, preferring action to speculation, and devoting himself entirely to the spreading of Catholicism and the extirpation of Arianism. His *Moralia* consist of an allegorical and moral interpretation of the Scriptures in which a great number of practical questions without connection with the text are introduced. This work had a wide circulation in the period which followed, and even in the thirteenth century.[1] His *Homilies* and *Dialogues* are also referred to.

41. Isidore of Seville (seventh century).—When the Visigoths penetrated into Spain (414) they amalgamated with the Hispano-Roman race, and from this fusion there resulted a remarkable people. Their King, Chindasvinto, made a codification of laws, known under the name of " Fuero Juzgo " and breathing the spirit of the primitive juridical ideas of the race. Together with the writings of Orosius (417), *Historiarum libri VII*, and the works of Isidore Archbishop of Seville, they constitute the principal intellectual monuments of a civilization which was arrested when at its height by the coming of the Arabs from 711 onwards.

Isidore of Seville, *Hispalensis* (about 570-630), provides us with an excellent illustration of the encyclopædic tendencies of the time in his chief work, *Originum seu Etymologiarum libri XX*. This collection of human knowledge deals not only with the seven liberal arts, but also with all the scientific data which its author had managed to assemble : medicine, jurisprudence, Scripture, languages and literature, etymologies, scraps of anthropology, zoology, geography both universal and local, architecture, agriculture and horticulture, the art of waging war, descriptions of the metals, weights and measures, navigation, clothing, etc. Worthy of note are his treatment of the divine origin of power, the obligation on the part of the

[1] Manitius, *op. cit.*, pp. 98 *et seq.* Cf. Hurter, *Nomenclator*, I, 557.

State of defending the Church, the subjection of all, including the king, to law and justice, the separation of the private patrimony of the monarch and the patrimony of the Crown, and the prestige, inviolability and hereditary character of royalty.[1]

These theories made a great impression on the Middle Ages, which derived much pleasure and profit from the *Etymologies* of Isidore. When the Visigoths had to flee before the Arabs, they took with them into the Pyrenees as a precious possession the writings of the great Archbishop.

42. Venerable Bede (seventh century).—This is another writer who enjoyed a great reputation right up to the end of the Middle Ages. He represents the Celtic culture of the Irish monasteries of the seventh century. The Venerable Bede (672 or 673 to 735), monk at Jarrow in Northumberland, was looked upon as the greatest mind of his time. His chief work, *Historia ecclesiastica gentis Anglorum*, reflecting the exuberant character of similar works by Gregory of Tours, is regarded as the first effort at a serious English history. In addition to treatises on theology, Bede was the author of various scientific and chronological works, in particular of an opusculum *De orthographia liber*, and another entitled *De natura rerum*, evidently inspired by Isidore of Seville.[2]

43. Alcuin and the Carlovingian Renaissance.—With Alcuin the cultivation of knowledge passed into Gaul. In 778, Charlemagne gave to Bangulf, Bishop of Fulda, the famous charter in which he encouraged the foundation of monastic and episcopal schools. This was the signal for a brilliant revival of studies constituting one of the best titles of the Emperor to renown. The renaissance of the eighth and ninth century was not exclusively philosophical in character: it extended to all the branches of learning then known. Furthermore, it was in more direct connection with classical antiquity than with patristic learning. The men of this period reproduced all they were able to save from the Barbarian invasions ; they col-

---

[1] Altamira, *Historia de la Espana*, etc., I, 216. Other works : *De natura rerum*, *De numeris*, *De viris illustribus*, *Historiæ*, and *Chronicles*. See Manitius, *Gesch. d. latein. Litteratur d. Mittel.* (1911), I, p. 52 *et seq.*

[2] Manitius, *op. cit.*, p. 70-87. In the Middle Ages the work *De Mundi cœlestis terrestrisque constitutione liber* was wrongly attributed to Bede, and also a collection of philosophical texts, *Axiomata philosophica venerabilis Bedæ*, taken from a great number of authors, many of whom belong to a later date. For the first-mentioned work see Duhem, *La physique néo-Platonicienne au m. â.*, p. 47. He attributes the work to a disciple of Macrobius.

lected the raw materials of which others after them could make use in more original philosophic works. Alcuin and Rhaban Maur personify this work of compilation. (p. 52.) At the same time this was also the period of the first theological controversies, and thus the Carlovingian Renaissance constitutes the first stage in the formation of the speculative mentality of the early Middle Ages.

Alcuin or Alchvine (about 730-804) was the leading spirit in the emperor's educational reforms. Himself a former pupil of the school of York, Alcuin met Charlemagne at Parma in 781, and taught for eight years at the imperial court. The monarch and his sons and daughters attended his lectures. After a very busy life, Alcuin retired to the Abbey of St. Martin at Tours, founded a school, and died there. He was rather a compiler and a grammarian and does not deserve the great reputation he has enjoyed as a philosopher. There is nothing in his works on logic which is not found in Boethius and Cassiodorus. The liberal arts form the basis of all learning ; they may be likened to the seven columns of wisdom, *nec aliter ad perfectam quemlibet deducit scientiam nisi his septem columnis vel etiam gradibus exaltetur.*[1] The psychological ideas developed in the letter *De animæ ratione ad Eulaliam Virginem*[2] are Augustinian in character. This applies especially to his definition of man (*anima et caro*), his conception of the relation between the soul and body, his notion of sensation and pain, tripartite division of the faculties (which he does not distinguish from the essence of the soul) and the central place given to God and the soul. On the other hand, the moral doctrines developed in this latter are borrowed from Cassian.[3]

If Alcuin lacked originality, he was nevertheless an organizer of learned institutions and a fount of knowledge. He transplanted into Germany the culture and learning of Ireland. He introduced the trivium and the quadrivium into the school of the palace, and his books survived him as manuals. He had one disciple of note, Rhaban Maur, who indeed became more famous than his master. The schools which sprang up as a result of the impulse which he gave to study continued to be

---

[1] *Grammatica*, P. L. 101, 855 c.
[2] Other works by the same author on philosophy are : *De virtutibus et vitiis ad Widonem comitem ; Grammatica; De dialectica; De Rhetorica.* Cf. Manitius *op. cit.*, p. 273-288.
[3] Seydl, *op. cit.*

philosophical centres up to the foundation of the University of Paris.

44.   Rhaban Maur (ninth century).—From the point of view of philosophy, the most significant representative of the encyclopædic literature of the first part of the Middle Ages was Rhaban Maur (Magnetius Hrabanus Maurus, 784-856), the disciple of Alcuin of Tours. He was the founder of the school of Fulda where many followed his lectures, amongst them being Servatus Lupus of Ferrières. Later he became Archbishop of Mayence. His work *De clericorum institutione* gained for him the title of " præceptor Germaniæ ; his treatise *De rerum natura* extended still further the list of subjects treated by Isidore of Seville, and constituted the encyclopædic dictionary of the early Middle Ages. Rhaban Maur gathered up amongst other ancient texts a hundred lines from Lucretius, on which was based the knowledge of Lucretius and Epicureus possessed by the pre-scholastics. Rhaban follows the Latin philosopher in holding that all things save God are by their nature corporeal.[1]

Amongst the early writers of the beginning of the period under consideration, we ought also to mention certain humanists, commentators on works of logic, and teachers of renown, whose principal merit was that they encouraged studies and thus prepared indirectly for the coming of philosophy. Such were in the ninth century SERVATUS LUPUS, a teacher at Ferrières, and ODO of CLUNY; in the tenth century, BOVO II, Abbot of Corvey in Saxony (who wrote a commentary Platonist in tendency on the *De consolatione philosophiæ* of Boethius,[2] POPPO OF FULDA and REINHARD OF ST. BURCHARD (less well known); and in the tenth century, RATHERUS OF VERONA, and especially NOTKER LABEO of St. Gall, who, in addition to translating works into German[3] also wrote on music and rhetoric, and initiated in his school a series of commentaries on the arts and on the works of dialectics then known. The *Hortus deliciarum* of HERRAD OF LANDSBERG, written in the twelfth century for the instruction of religious,

---

[1] Cf. Philippe, *Lucrèce dans la théologie chrétienne du IIIe au XIIIe siècle* p. 58 (Paris, 1896).   Rhaban was at the same time an exegete and commentator on the Bible,—Manitius, *op. cit.*, p. 288.

[2] Endres, *Studien z. Gesch. der Fruhscholastik*, Philos. Jahrb. 1912, p. 364 *et seq.*

[3] He translated the *Categories* and the *De Interpretatione* of Aristotle, the *De Consolatione Philosophiæ* of Boethius, the treatise of M. Capella, etc. See Graff's Berlin edition.

may be mentioned among the last encyclopædic works of this first period. But it already shows signs of the progress of scholasticism. In particular we find therein a division of philosophy into *ethica, logica, physica*, and the seven liberal arts serve as a preparation for philosophy.[1]

45. Bibliography.—H. Koch, *Pseudo-Dionysius Areopagita in s. Bezeihungen zum Neuplatonismus und Mysterienwesen* (Mainz, 1900). For the question of authorship see also J. Stiglmayer, *Das Aufkommen der pseudo-dionysischen Schrifte u. ihr Eindringen in die christl. Litteratur bis zum Laterankoncil* (*Feldkirch*, 1895) ; *Der Neuplatoniker Proklus als Vorlage des sogennanten D. in der Lehre vom Uebel* (Historisches Jahrb. 1895); Otto Siebert, *Die Metaphysik u. Ethik. d. Pseudo-Dionysius Areop.* (Jena, 1894) ; H. Koch, *Proklus als Quelle des Ps. D. in der Lehre v. Bosen* (*Philologus*, 1895) ; H. F. Muller, *Dionysius, Proklus, Plotinos, etc.*, BGPM, XX, 3. For Chalcidius see Switalski, *BGPM*, III, 6. For Macrobius see Schedler, XIII, 1, and Duhem, *Le Système du monde*, II, III. J. Langen, *D. d. Areop. und d. Scholastiker* (R. intern. théologie, 1900).

On Boethius see the following : Usener, *Anecdoton Holderi. ein Beitrag zur Gesch. Roms in ostgoth. Zeit* (Festschr. z. Begrüssung d. 32. Versamml. deutsch. Philol., Bonn 1877), important ; Grabmann, *op. cit.*, p. 148-178; *Boethius : An Essay*, by Hugh F. Stewart (Edinburgh, Blackwood, 1891) ; E. K. Rand, *Der dem Boethius zugeschrieben Traktat de Fide Catholica* (Leipzig, 1901); *On the Composition of Boethius' Consolatio Philosophiæ* (Harvard Studies in Classical Philology, Vol. XV) ; Klinger, *De Boethius Consol. Philos.* (Philol. Unters. hrgg. Kiessling, Berlin 1921) ; the last two are excellent studies on the sources of Boethius. The theological works and the *De Consolatione* of Boethius have been republished by Rand with an English translation of 1609 revised by H. F. Stewart (Loeb Classical Library, 1918). An excellent edition of the Latin text of the De Consolatione with dissertation and notes by Fortescue and Smith has just been published (London, 1925). F. Zimmerman, *Cassiodors Schrift u. die Seele* (Jahrb. Phil. skek. Theol., 1911), p. 414. Marius Michel, *Le livre des origines d'Isidore de Seville* (R. Intern. enseignement, 1891, p. 198), written from the point of view of philology and study of grammar ; A. Schenk, *De Isidori Hispalensis de natura rerum libelli fontibus* (Diss. Jena, 73 p.) ; Schutte, *Studien u.*

---

[1] Willmann, *Didaktik*, I, 278, n. 1.

den Schriftstellerkatalog (de viris illustribus) d. hl. Isidorus von Sevilla (coll. Sdralek, Breslau, 1905) ; A. Schmekel, *Isidor von Sevilla, sein System und Seine Quelle*, Bd. 2 of *Die Positiv. Philos. in ihrer geschicht. Entwickl.* (Berlin, 1914). K. Seydl, *Alkuins Psychologie* (Jahrb. Phil. spek. Theol., 1910, p. 34-55) ; La Foret, *Histoire d' Alcuin*, Paris, 1898, deals with his life and his work of organization ; G. Browne, *Alcuin of York* (London, 1908). Godet, *Bède le Vénérable* (article in *Dict. Theol.* of Vacant, 1903), rather general. For Rhaban Maur see Fr. Kunstmann, *Hrabanus Magnentius Maurus* (Mayence, 1841) ; Hablitzel, *Hrab. Maurus* (Bibl. Stud. 9, 3, Freiburg, 1906, and Histor. Jahrb. 1906); U. Berlière, *Un bibliophile du IXe siècle, Loup de Ferrières* (Mons, 1912).

§ 4—*Division of the First Period.*

46. The doctrinal criterion.—The principal effort of Western philosophy in this period was concerned with the constitution of scholasticism, and consisted in the elaboration of certain important doctrines which were later to form the nucleus of the synthesis of the thirteenth century. These doctrines were : the pluralistic conception of reality, the distinction between corporeal and spiritual beings, and the objectivity of knowledge. The work of elaboration was a slow and tentative process, and in this sense we might describe this period as pre-scholastic, or the infancy of scholasticism.[1] We find everywhere a lack of coherence, due to the introduction of some particular doctrine upsetting the equilibrium of the whole. Or again, some thinkers accept, side by side with the fundamental principles which give a scholastic sense to their interpretation of reality, other doctrines which would lead to different conclusions, if interpreted strictly. But these philosophers took care not to go to these extremes; they did not realize or at any rate refused to accept the consequences of their principles. Thus St. Anselm does not infer from his exaggerated realism consequences which would be inconsistent with his other ideas and ruin his natural theology. That is why we treat all these philosophers as pioneers in one and the same work, although in different ways : *scholastic* is their family name.

There were other philosophers who adopted systems of thought based on principles the very antithesis of scholasticism,

[1] Overbeck, *op. cit.*

and which soon began to manifest their opposition. This applies especially to monism and materialism. Monism penetrates the vital doctrines of a philosophic system to such an extent that there remains nothing common between it and the corresponding solutions of pluralism (**10, ii.**). Similarly the Monism of Scotus Eriugena was completely contrary to the individualistic realism developed in the glosses of Eric of Auxerre or the treatises of Anselm of Canterbury, and this monism did in point of fact give rise to doctrines the antagonistic nature of which was noticed by contemporaries. In the same way the materialism of the Cathari was openly opposed to the spiritualism of an Alan of Lille, and treatises were written *ex professo* to refute it.

Hence it is not possible to judge the scholasticity of pre-scholastic doctrines by tabulating resemblances and differences between them and the scholasticism of the thirteenth century, just as one might treat the contents of the synoptic Gospels. A historic study must treat the doctrines not only from the static, but also from the dynamic point of view, that is, it must study them in their development.[1] Now when we adopt this second point of view, we find ourselves face to face with doctrinal growth of scholasticism which lasted right up to the twelfth century and in fact was only completed in the thirteenth. The problem of universals is a good instance in point. The process of formation must be studied by comparing it with the term in which it ended. In the effort of the early Middle Ages we find the tendencies leading to the stage of maturity, just as in an acorn we have the oak in germ. Hence we have chosen for our criterion for the classification of the systems or fragments of systems in this period into scholastic and non-scholastic, the objective conformity or absence of conformity of the theories formulated with the fundamental tendencies of the scholastic conception of the thirteenth century which completed, unified and solidified the doctrines received from the early Middle Ages.

47. Secondary criteria.—To this ideological principle we can join others based upon the development of various factors of civilization.

---

[1] Père Jacquin objects that prior to the thirteenth century the scholastic synthesis did not exist, and one cannot classify the philosophies of the first period in terms of a non-existent reality. We reply that it did not exist formally as such, but it was present in germ, and that these germs led up to the state of maturity.

We begin with the fact that the twelfth century witnessed not only the first attempt at the scholastic systematization, but also the development of all that was most characteristic in the feudal system ; in addition we bear in mind that this was the golden age of the philosophic schools. In view of this we divide the study of the first period into two sections : the first deals with the period from the ninth to the twelfth centuries, the second treats the twelfth century. In each of these sections the Scholastic systems will be distinguished from the non-Scholastic. We shall also consider the relation between these philosophies with theology and other sciences.

By combining these secondary criteria with the principal we get the following plan :

(A) Western Philosophy from the ninth to the twelfth century.—(i) Scholasticism. (Ch. II). It is in the question of universals that we find the first evidence of the progress of scholastic thought (§ 1). Therein we can follow step by step the gradual widening of the controversy, the coming of psychology, and with it the attempts at a solution which later becomes definitive. In the eleventh century St. Anselm (§ 2) made a first effort at co-ordinating the elements acquired.

(ii) Anti-Scholastic Philosophy (Ch. III).—J. Scotus Eriugena was the Father of the anti-Scholastics. His philosophy contained in germ all those tendencies which opposed scholastic teaching right up to the end of the twelfth century.

(iii) Philosophy in its relation to other sciences (Ch. IV). The theological controversies of this period led to the propounding of more than one philosophical question, and the theologians took up different attitudes towards philosophy. These attitudes became more accentuated as time went on. During the same period philosophy was linked up with law.

(B) Western Philosophy in the twelfth century.—(i) Scholasticism (Ch. V). The twelfth century gave to mediæval civilization its definitive character : it fixed the religious, social and artistic conceptions of the West ; it marked out the ethnical characteristics of the races called to play a preponderating part. An extraordinary activity manifested itself in philosophical ideas, leading to complex and disparate movements. Scholasticism eagerly took up the question of universals, and the discovery of the new logical works of Aristotle added to the ardour of the discussions. It was in the French schools—

particularly at Laon, Chartres, and Paris—that this took place. Chartres was a great centre of culture in the first half of the twelfth century. Its fame then diminished in comparison with the schools of Paris, and the extension of these led up to the creation of the first University of the Middle Ages. Exaggerated realism (§ 1) everywhere met with opponents who in the most diverse ways (§ 2) endeavoured to harmonize the individuality of real being and the general nature of conceptual being. Abelard—a prominent figure in the controversy—triumphed over exaggerated realism and resolved the problem in a way which was at once novel and definitive (§ 3). At the same time didactic methods were perfected, terminology became more exact, and important doctrines were constituted. Although we do not meet with systematizations comparable with those of the thirteenth century, yet we find interesting attempts at a synthesis in Hugh and Richard of St. Victor (§ 4), Alcher of Clairvaux and Alain of Lille (§ 6). The widening of the doctrinal scope of scholasticism led to new work in matters of politics and social law, particularly in John of Salisbury, who was one of the typical representatives of the spirit of the time (§ 5).

(ii) The anti-scholastic philosophies (Ch. VI).—Several pantheistic schools were directly connected with J. Scotus Eriugena. On the other hand materialistic epicureanism appeared in the doctrine of the Cathari and the Albigenses.

(iii) Philosophy and the other sciences (Ch. VII).—We find a powerful theological movement in full swing at this time. The dialectic method predominated, and its adoption heralded the most brilliant era in the history of dogmatic theology (§ 1). There was also an intense outburst of orthodox mysticism (§ 2), and of canon and civil law which exchanged services with philosophy (§ 3).

An appendix deals with oriental philosophies (Ch. VIII).

CHAPTER II

Scholasticism from the Ninth to the Twelfth Century

§ 1—*The Problem of Universals.*

48. How the question of Universals arises in Philosophy.—Although it would be a mistake to look upon Scholasticism as just one long monotonous conflict on the problem of universals (16), still it is true that the problem was one of the first to present itself, and absorbed a great amount of thought. The question itself really belongs to all philosophies. It was the making of Scholasticism, inasmuch as it led to the discussion of the fundamental theories of metaphysics and psychology.

The question of the universals, or universal representations, is concerned with the correspondence which exists between our intellectual concepts, which are abstract and general, and extramental reality. Introspection shows that we have two kinds of knowledge of objects. *Sensation* represents the concrete and individual aspect of material objects (*this* oak tree, *this* gnarled trunk, and so on). Another kind of knowledge, which we term *intellectual*, presents to us the same reality but without implying any note of individuality: reality is in this kind of knowledge *abstract* or detached from its connection with the individual. This kind of knowledge tells us what the thing is *as such*—oak tree *as such*, trunk *as such*, cylindrical form *as such*, and so on. It follows that the content of this kind of knowledge is capable of being *universalized*, that is to say, applied to a quite indefinite number of existing or possible objects, to all oak trees for instance, or to all cylindrical forms.

The question then arises : Are these true conceptions ? Are not the characteristics of the object as intellectually conceived incompatible with those of the object as existing outside us ? Do these concepts give us any information about the extramental world, and if so what kind of information ?

Four answers are possible.

(i) *Exaggerated realism* affirms that there is an adequate correspondence between extramental reality and the real as conceived ; it attributes to the former the selfsame characteristics of abstraction and generality which are found in the latter. *The* oak tree, *the* cylinder exist *as such*, independently of the particular oak trees and cylindrical forms which are perceived by our senses. Exaggerated realism, advocated by Plato and ascribed to him by the Middle Ages, answers the difficulty by this naïve reply.

But does not this do violence to common sense ? Is not every existing thing an individual, and are not individuals independent of each other in their existence ?

If we accept these last statements, which constitute the thesis held by Aristotle and all the opponents of exaggerated realism, there remains the very real difficulty : how then can an abstract and universal concept be in conformity with an extramental world consisting only of particular or individual things ?

(ii) No doubt, reply the *Conceptualists* (for instance, William of Occam, and Kant), the individual is the only existing substance : doubtless also we represent reality to ourselves by means of abstract concepts, distinct in kind from sensation, and of which the content can be universalized ; certainly again in language there correspond to these notions names which are general in form ; but we do not know whether this way of representing things has any foundation in the things themselves, or if, apart from our thought, individuals possess distributively or separately the essence which we conceive in thought : in other words, the universals have an ideal objectivity, but not a real one.

(iii) *Moderate realism*, or Aristotelian realism, also called Thomistic realism, accepts both the ideal and the real value of the concept.

It accepts all the data of the conceptualists : the individuality of everything which exists extramentally, the general form of names, the abstract character of thought, the ideal value of the series of concepts which go to make up our scientific construction of the real : it accepts all these, but completes them. For instead of confining the mind within itself, moderate realism holds that these abstract views of things are derived from the individual things themselves. This kind of representation is doubtless inadequate, since it is obtained by leaving out of consideration the particular way in which the real which is conceived exists outside us, but it is faithful and true as far as it goes, inasmuch as there is nothing in this abstract type which is not entirely verified in the individual thing. As for the universality of the concept, this is an ulterior characteristic which pre-supposes abstraction and is added to it.

(iv) There remains yet another possible solution : by a procedure the opposite of that of Platonist realism, it starts with the thesis that everything real in the external world is individual, and proclaims the adequate correspondence of knowledge with reality. Just as everything real is singular, so also every representation of this real is singular too. " Between sensation and thought there is no distinction in kind. The so-called concept is nothing more than a name understood."[1]

49. The scholastic solutions of the problem.—The fourth solution mentioned above never existed in mediæval scholasticism, for it would upset a fundamental theory : the distinction in kind between sensation and thought. It finds a place only in sensualist or positivist systems like the moderate Nominalism of Taine or Herbert Spencer, and we may set it aside once and for all.

The three other solutions did appear in scholasticism. All three pre-suppose from psychology the suprasensible nature of intellectual knowledge, and also takes for granted the metaphysical postulate that there does exist a reality which is independent of our minds and to which our minds must conform. Here is the historic order in which these solutions appeared in the Middle Ages :

(i) Exaggerated realism flourished from the ninth to the twelfth century.

(ii) Moderate realism only reached its perfect form towards the middle of the twelfth century, but there were

(iii) Numerous solutions combating exaggerated realism in the eleventh and twelfth centuries, and all of them are so many steps towards moderate realism.

(iv) Conceptualism was formulated in the fourteenth century.

50. How the question came to present itself at the beginning of the Middle Ages.—The first scholastics, novices as they were

---

[1] Taine, *De l'Intelligence*, Vol. I, p. 26.

in philosophy, did not perceive the manifold logical, psychological, epistemological and metaphysical aspects of the problem of universals.

In point of fact, the problem did not arise spontaneously in the Middle Ages : it was suggested by certain texts of Porphyry and Boethius, very simple in appearance but obscure, and which many circumstances combined to make the subject of the first speculations.

(i) Porphyry in his *Isagoge* or Introduction to Aristotle's Categories, considers the problem only in relation to the generic and specific notions which we conceive of a reality taken as the subject of a judgment, and he sets out the problem in three stages : (*a*) Do these genera and species exist really in nature, or are they purely mental constructions ? (*b*) If they are realities, are they material or immaterial ? (*c*) Do they exist apart from sensible things or are they realized in these ?[1] The first question alone attracted attention, inasmuch as the other two have no meaning unless we reject the purely subjective character of universals. Now this first question was expressed as follows : are genera and species things in themselves, or are they products of the mind, *sive subsistant, sive in nudis intellectibus posita sint* ? From the point of view of terminology, the question consists of an alternative : does the reality in which our universal notions correspond exist in the generic or specific state or not ? The logical point of view (the function of the predicate in a judgment) or the psychological (abstractive character of thought) are not dealt with, and thus the formula is really very incomplete. Moreover, after enunciating the threefold problem, Porphyry refused to answer it : *dicere recusabo*, and the scholastics never knew that in other works Porphyry solved the question in a Platonist sense.

(ii) Boethius, who wrote two commentaries on the *Isagoge*, sets out the problem in the same way as Porphyry. He also asks the question in connection with the universal predicates which are necessarily connected with a subject inasmuch as they express its essence, or constitution. The objectivity of other types of union (*proprium, accidens commune*) apparently do not interest him. Moreover, in all his examples the subject

---

[1] "Mox de generibus et speciebus illud quidem sive subsistant sive in nudis intellectibus posita sint, sive subsistentia corporalia sint an incorporalia, et utrum separata, a sensibilibus an in sensibilibus posita et circa hæc consistentia, dicere recusabo."

is a substantial being, for instance, man. In other words, he studies the genus and species of the category of substance, the first in position and in importance in the list of the ten categories.[1]

What solution does Boethius offer of the difficulty? In his second commentary, which is the more important of the two, he holds that genera and species are at one and the same time *subsistentia* and *intellecta* (first question), the resemblance between things being the foundation both for their individuality in nature and for their universality in thought. He holds in addition that genera and species are incorporeal, not indeed by nature, but by abstraction (second question), and that they exist both in sensible things and apart from them (third question).[2] Although we thus find in Boethius the elements of the Aristotelian solution of the problem, they were not sufficiently clear for early thinkers: Boethius was not under stood.[3]

We may add that Boethius, who was *the* professor of logic for the first generations of the Middle Ages, insists on the verbal side of logic. When explaining the title of the categories, which he also calls the *decem genera entium*, he writes: *prædicamentorum tractatus, non de rebus sed de vocibus est.*[4] We shall see later on how this opinion helped to formulate the *sententia vocum* and the *secta nominalis*. Not indeed that Boethius went astray concerning the relation existing between these names general in form (*voces*) and the things which they signify (*res*). By studying the former, we attain to a knowledge of the latter

[1] This does not mean that Porphyry's problem does not apply to the nine other categories. As a matter of fact, the problem is a general one: it applies to any abstract concept, and therefore to all the categories of objects of thought, and in each single category to the predicables or various ways in which a predicate may be connected with a subject (genus, species, specific difference, property, accident).

[2] In the twelfth century Godfrey of St. Victor addresses Boethius in these mocking words: "Assidet Boethius stupens de hac lite—Audies quid hic et hic afferat perite—Et quid cui faveat non discernit rite—Nec præsumit solvere litem definite "(quoted by Loewe, *Kampf zwischen Realismus u. Nominalismus im Mittelalter*, p. 30.)

[3] *In Categorias Aristotelis*, I, *P.L.*, Vol. 64, col. 162, A.-D.

[4] Sunt igitur hujusmodi res in corporalibus atque in sensibilibus rebus. Intelliguntur autem præter sensibilia ut eorum natura perspici et proprietas valeat comprehendi. Quo circa cum et genera et species cogitantur, tunc ex singulis in quibus sunt eorum similitudo colligitur, ut ex singulis hominibus inter se dissimilibus humanitatis similitudo, quæ similitudo cogitata animo veraciterque perspecta fit species . . . Cogitantur vero universalia, nihilque aliud species esse putanda est nisi cogitatio collecta ex individuorum dissimilium numero substantiali similitudine.—Migne, *Patrol. Latina*, Vol. 64, col. 84 and 85.

(*assumere*), but a purely logical consideration of the matter concerns itself only with the meaning of the verbal forms.[1]

These then are the historic texts with which the first scholastics were confronted. They considered themselves bound not only by Porphyry's alternative, but also by the very terms in which this was enunciated. Like Porphyry and Boethius, they limited their enquiry to the subject of genera and species of substance—man, animal, Socrates. Hence there are two possible alternatives in terms of the Porphyrian formula : genera and species either exist as such, that is to say, humanity, life, rationality, etc., are subsistent realities (*subsistentia*), or else they are ultimately just mental facts (*nuda intellecta*). Or more simply still, either they are *things*, or they are not.

51. Exaggerated realism.—Those who held the affirmative were the exaggerated realists. We may say that they solved the question *in re ;* hence they were called *reales* or realists. Exaggerated realism was the first solution adopted in point of time : the chronicler Heriman (eleventh century) gave the name of *antiqui doctores*[2] to those who taught the existence *in re ;* Abelard again spoke of it as an *antiqua doctrina*,[3] and up to the end of the twelfth century, its adversaries were known as *moderni*.

This solution owed its credit above all to its simplicity. It all held together without any complication, inasmuch as its fundamental assertion was that there is an adequate correspondence between extramental reality and reality as conceived in thought. Moreover, it seemed to furnish a very simple explanation of the doctrine of the transmission of original sin.

Each genus or species thought of represents a genus or species existing in reality (*subsistentia*), in which individuals share. But in opposition to Plato who separated these essences from the material world, the realists of the early Middle Ages held that they were immanent in particular things. Humanity exists as such, but it exists in the collection of men.

Since there is a multiplicity of genera and species, these first forms of realism remained faithful to a pluralistic concep-

---

[1] Quoniam res semper cum propria significatione conjunctæ sunt . . . quare recte de vocabulis disputans proprietatem significantium vocum de his quæ significabantur, id est de rebus assumpsit. *ibid.*, col. B.

[2] *Liber de restauratione monasterii* S. *Martini Tornacensis*, ed. Waitz (Monum. Germ. historica, SS., t. XIV, p. 275), see the text later on.

[3] Similarly we read in an anonymous manuscript of the twelfth century published by Haureau (*Not. et extr. ms. lat. Bibl. nation.*: Vol. XXXI, 2e p., p. 201) : " Est autem antiqua sententia et quasi antiquis erroribus invet-erata."

tion of the world. It is indeed true that monism lay in wait for them as their logical conclusion, for it is difficult to see why the most abstract and most general of all our notions, namely, that of being, should not likewise have its corresponding reality in the extramental order. But with the exception of J. Scotus Eriugena, the realists of the early Middle Ages did not go to this extreme.

52. The First Realists.—The Athenian sage, ATHENIENSIS SOPHISTA, whom we meet at the court of Charlemagne, attributes reality to death because it has to receive the prize of life. FREDEGIS, the disciple of Alcuin and his successor at the Abbey of Tours, indulges in similar puerilities in his work *De nihilo et tenebris*. Basing himself upon the text of Scripture which says that Egypt was covered with a darkness so thick that it could be felt by the hand, he attributes reality to logical entities such as darkness and even nothing. In a letter to Agobard he develops the same ideas.

At the end of the ninth century, realism enters upon a philosophic phase with REMI of AUXERRE (about 841-908), who succeeded his master Eric in the chair of the Abbey of Auxerre, but abandoned the latter's teaching. Later on Remi taught at Rome (862) and at Paris, where he was the first to introduce dialectics. We possess a commentary by him on the *Ars minor* of Donatus, widely used until the twelfth century, and also commentaries on Priscian, several Latin poets, and on Martianus Capella. In the last-named work Remi makes great use of a similar work by John Scotus Eriugena. Rand has recently discovered commentaries by Remi on the *opuscula sacra* of Eriugena, and Stewart has found commentaries on the *De Consolatione Philosophiæ* of Boethius. According to Remi, the reality of individual things consists simply in the participation in a higher reality, namely, the species (*homo est multorum hominum substantialis unitas*). Species together form the numerical unity of the genus.

53. Gerbert.—The tenth century began with a period of anarchy. The Normans burnt down the monasteries, and the schools passed through a fatal crisis. Learning could not attain once more its normal state until the Cluniac reform and the erection of new abbeys. Gerbert was a shining light in this tenth century darkness. He was one of those who helped to bring about the revival, and was the first of a long line of famous French teachers.

Born towards the middle of the century, Gerbert was brought up in the monastery of Aurillac which Odo of Cluny had re-formed, and he spent three years in study with the Arabs in Spain. At Rheims and at Paris, where he taught in turn, he acquired a European reputation. which led to his being invited to the court of the Ottos. He made several stays there, and exerted a great influence, especially on the mind of Otto III, who wrote him flattering letters. (p. 62). Later on Gerbert became Abbot of Bobbio (982), Archbishop of Rheims, Ravenna, and finally Pope under the name of Sylvester II. One of his contemporaries called him the " philosopher-Pope."

Gerbert commented on more Aristotelian works than any of his contemporaries, and a century later St. Anselm and Roscelin knew no others works of the Stagirite. He was acquainted with the trivium and the quadrivium, he wrote on geometry, arithmetic, and handed on the elements of Arab science. He was at the same time a scholar, a humanist, a writer, an orator, and a savant. His letters show him to have been a superior sort of man, and the monk Richer, a pupil of Gerbert, professes in his History a very legitimate admiration for him. Of Gerbert's philosophical teaching we possess only the account given us by Richer of a dialectical encounter with Otric at Ravenna in the presence of Otto I (970) ; an opusculum *De rationali et ratione uti*, and another of less importance, *De corpore et sanguine Domini*. Should Gerbert be placed among the extreme realists ?[1] Certain texts are explicit ; for instance he takes from J. Scotus Eriugena (Ch. III) the follow-ing declarations and makes them his own : " *Non enim ars illa, quæ dividit genera in species et species in genera resolvit, ab humanis machinationibus est facta : sed in natura rerum ab auctore omnium artium . . . est usitata.*[2] But we must bear in mind that Gerbert was above all a logician ; metaphysics only comes into his writings here and there (we do find the distinction between act and potency), and he does not give a clear and decisive answer to the questions of Porphyry. As a moralist, Gerbert had a liking for certain Stoic doctrines. His moral philosophy is fragmentary and specialized : he defends the political subordination of all Christians to the unity of the Church.

Gerbert's lectures were frequented by the realist FULBERT

---

[1] Haureau, *Hist. de la phil. scolastique*, I, 216 (1880).
[2] *De corp. et sanguine Domini*, Migne, *Patrol. Latina*, 139, 189, B.

who founded the school of Chartres in 990, Bishops GIRARD
and LENTHERIC, the historian Richer, and others, all well known
in the eleventh century.

54. Odo of Tournai flourished at the Cathedral School
of Tournai during the second half of the eleventh century,
and gave a new impetus to realism. For five years (previous to
1092) he was a teacher, and had many pupils. He then founded
in the same town the Abbey of St. Martin, became Bishop of
Cambrai, and died at the Monastery at Anchin (1113). The
chronicler Heriman, his disciple, who has left us a charming description of the professorial career of Odo[1], narrates, that,
following the example of Boethius and the ancient doctors,
he taught dialectics from the realist standpoint, *in re*, and did
not imitate certain moderns who treat it verbally, *in voce*,
" proud spirits with excessive pretensions, having no other
object but to be looked upon as wise men, and to this end invent-
ing new interpretations of Porphyry and Aristotle."[2]   In this
connection he engaged in controversy with Raimbert of Lille,
an upholder of these novelties.

In his principal work, *De peccato originali*[3], Odo defends
the classic thesis of realism and applies it in an interesting way
to the following Catholic doctrines :

(i) *The transmission of original sin.* The human race forms
only one specific reality scattered amongst its many representatives at any given moment of history. When Adam and
Eve sinned, the entire substance in all its ramifications then
existing was infected, and subsequent generations, living an
anticipated life in that vitiated substance, have all suffered
from the consequences.[4] This is obviously a kind of human
monopsychism.

(ii) *The continual creation of souls* when children are born.
Since the substance of a new-born child is simply that of the
species, in what sense is this original substance re-born ? Odo
replies : That which God produces when a child is born is not
a substance, but a new property of one unique substance
already existing. At the surface, as it were, of the permanent
substratum of humanity appear individual properties which

[1] See De Wulf, *Histoire de la Philosophie en Belgique*, Louvain 1910, pp.
24-32.
[2] Dialecticam non juxta quosdam modernos in voce, sed more Boetii
antiquorumque doctorum in re discipulis legebat.—Heriman, *op. cit.*, p. 275.
[3] Heriman also mentions the following works of Odo: *Liber Complexionum,
De Re et ente.*
[4] *De peccato originali*, Lib. II, *P.L.* Vol. 160, col. 1079.

are constantly changing : men differ from each other only by accidents. From this it is easy to understand that Odo appreciates the arguments of the Traducianists.

55. The first adversaries of exaggerated realism.—The realists soon encountered numerous opponents. All agree in defending in the name of Aristotle, Boethius, and common sense this thesis : " Universals are not things realised in the universal state in nature, for the individual alone exists." They are not *subsistentia*, but *nuda intellecta.* We shall see that this phrase designates successive solutions which become more and more precise.

The commentary by a certain JEPA[1] of unknown date repeats without adding anything, the logical doctrine of Boethius that the singular and the universal are the same individual subject.

ERIC OF AUXERRE (841-876), who followed the lecture of Servatus Lupus at Ferrières, Rhaban Maur and the Irishman Dunchad, and himself taught at Auxerre, manifests the same tendencies in the commentaries apparently written by him. Haureau attributes to him commentaries on the *Interpretation*, the *Dialectics* and the *Book of the Ten Categories* of pseudo-Augustine, the *Isagoge*, the Latin text of Apulæus's *Syllogism*, and on various works of Boethius.[2]

An anonymous commentary on Martianus Capella, written by a contemporary of Eric, together with another commentary of the same period on the *Categories* of pseudo-Augustine[3] must be included amongst the anti-realist productions of this time.[4]

It is probable that the commentaries on the *Isagoge* and the *Interpretation* which Cousin attributes to Rhaban Maur[5] and Prantl regards as the work of a pseudo-Rhaban, were written in the beginning of the eleventh century. They reproduce the doctrine of Boethius, and emphasize the reality of the individual substance which is the subject of our universal

---

[1] Cousin, *op. cit.*, pp. LXXXII-LXXXV. Republished by Baeumker, *BGPM*, XXIV, 1.

[2] *Hist. de la philos. scol.* I, 193. According to Baeumker, only a portion of the Commentaries on the *Categories* of pseudo-Augustine should be attributed to Eric. In the opinion of Clerval, (*op. cit.*, p. 105), these Commentaries were written by a disciple of Rhaban Maur. Cf. Rand, *Joh. Scotus*, p. 83. Manitius does not think it likely that Eric was the author of the Commentaries on Boethius, and he attributes the Commentary on Martianus Capella to the Irishman Dunchad. (*op. cit.* 502.)

[3] Known as Barach's anonymous author, after the writer who first made him known.—*ibid.* p. 23, note.

[4] According to Reiners, *Der Nominalismus in der Fruhscholastik*, pp. 8-9, the Commentaries of Eric and his anonymous contemporary had nothing to do with the question of Universals.

[5] *op. cit.*, p. LXXVIII.

predicates. In addition they mention the verbal interpretation
—*sententia vocum*—which a group of logicians upheld in the
eleventh century.[1]

56. Roscelin and the Sententia Vocum.—In the eleventh
century there was an interesting group of anti-realists or
opponents of exaggerated realism : they maintained that
genera and species are *voces*, or words, and they severely criti-
cise those who look upon them as *res*. This is the *sententia
vocum*, or *ars sophistica vocalis*. Roscelin is thought to have
originated it. His contemporary, Otto of Freising, says of him :
" Qui primus nostris temporibus sententiam vocum instituit."[2]
On the other hand, an anonymous chronicle of the eleventh
century[3] gives him a forerunner in a certain John.[4]

Roscelin was born at Compiegne about 1050. He taught at
Compiegne, Loches, and Besançon, and was in ommunication
with Lanfranc, St. Anselm, and Yves of Chartres. He was
accused of Tritheism at a Council of Soissons (1092), where
under the threat of excommunication he denied the doctrines
imputed to him. Later on, however, he returned to them. We
find him successively in England, Rome and Tours, where he
had Abelard for a pupil. We lose sight of him about 1120.

A letter addressed to Abelard is the only writing of Roscelin
we possess.[5] and we are obliged to judge of his teaching from
the writings of St. Anselm, Abelard, an anonymous epigrammist,
John of Salisbury,[6] and from the account in the *De generibus
et speciebus* (90).

[1] Quorundam tamen sententia est Porphyrii intentionem fuisse in hoc
opere non de quinque rebus, sed de quinque vocibus tractare.—Cousin, *ibid.* Cf.
Reiners, *BGPM.*, VIII, 5, p. 21, note.

[2] *Gesta Frederici Imperat.*, I, 47, in *Monum. German.*, SS. XX, 376.

[3] *Recueil des historiens des Gaules et de la France*, ed. Dom. Bouquet,
XII, Paris, 1871, p. 3.

[4] This philosopher, identified by some with J. S. Eriugena (see *Revue
Thomiste*, July, 1897, article by Père Mandonnet) and by others with John the
Deaf or John the Doctor, of Chartres, a pupil of Fulbert (Clerval, *op. cit.*,
pp. 122 *et seq.*), is a person of whom little is so far known. The *Liber miracul-
orum Sanctæ Fidis*, compiled about the beginning of the eleventh century by
Bernard of Angers, mentions a certain Johannes Scottigena, a contemporary
of the author, and whom he very carefully distinguishes from J. Scotus
Eriugena. Possibly he is the same as the unknown John of the anonymous
chronicle.—A. Thomas, *Nos Maîtres, Un Jean Scot inconnu* (Revue internat.
enseignment, 1903, p. 193).

[5] Haureau suggests Roscelin as the author of a text which he has discovered,
Sententia de universalibus sec. mag. R. (*Notices et extr. qq. man. lat.*, Paris, 1892,
V. 224), but this is only a conjecture. Moreover, this document attributes
at least an ideal value to universals, and therefore admits the existence of
universal concepts. Cf. V, 326.

[6] *Polycraticus*, VII, 12. Fuerunt et qui voces ipsas genera dicerent et
species ; sed eorum jam explosa sententia est, et facile cum auctore suo
evanuit. (Ed. Webb, Vol. II, p. 142). Cf. *Metalogicus*, II, 17.

One thing is certain : Roscelin figures in them as above all an opponent of realism : in nature the individual alone exists,[1] genera are not *res* (the *subsistentia* of Porphyry). What, then, are they ? At least they are words in universal form (*voces*), vocal emissions (*flatus vocis*) composed of letters and syllables. The question of universals is thus reduced to a somewhat childish point in elementary phonetics ; it is a question of the *universale in voce* as opposed to the *universale in re* and the *universale in intellectu* with which Roscelin does not concern himself.

But did Roscelin adopt a more advanced position in the controversy ? Was he a sensualist,[2] as has so often been said, that is, did he deny to the understanding the power of forming universal ideas, or again did he exclude all relation between the *voces*, *flatus vocis*, and the universal concept ? There is nothing to justify this interpretation of Roscelin's *sententia vocum*. Certainly, following Boethius and under his influence, Roscelin gives a classification of words (*voces*) rather than of things (*res*) to which the words correspond. But we do not see what foundation there is for the statement that as opposed to Boethius he does not grant to universal words a relation of correspondence (*assumere*) with things.[3] That is a question with which he does not deal.

Roscelin's solution is a weak one, but it is a step in the right direction ; the two theses which it implies, namely, the existence of the individual and the generalized form of the elements of language (which later on came to be known as *universale in voce*), are the first manifestations of the moderate realism of the twelfth century.

The *nuda intellecta* are words of general form, or *voces*— such is the opinion of Roscelin. The interpretation based on this idea was later on described as that of the *nomen*, and thus the word *nominales* came to be used for the first time.[4]

Roscelin was also criticised by St. Anselm and Abelard in

---

[1] Nam cum habeat eorum sententia nihil esse præter individua.—*De generibus et specieb.*, edit. Cousin, *op. cit.*, p. 524. Anselm speaks in the same way, see p. 125.

[2] The accusation of sensualism with which Roscelin is charged by Baumgartner is a gratuitous one (Ueberweg-Baumgartner, *op. cit.*, p. 258). Baumgartner in his account follows the thesis of Reiners. Certainly the universal was a *flatus vocis* for those who held the *sententia vocum* in the eleventh century, but there is nothing to prove that they denied the connection between the vocal term and the abstract concept, or mental operation.

[3] See p. 104.

[4] For Roscelin's nominalism see later, n. 95.

connection with a less clear notion which he set forth of the whole and of a composite substance. According to St. Anselm, he held that colour, for instance, does not exist independently of the horse which serves as a support for it, and that the wisdom of the soul has no being outside the mind which is wise.[1] He did not admit the real existence of parties in a whole such as a house or a man. The word alone would possess these parts : *sicut solis vocibus species, ita et partes ascribebat.*[2] May not these somewhat obscure texts be affirmations in another form of the unique reality of individual substances ?

We shall see later on that Roscelin was vigorously opposed on account of his theological tritheism, and it is to this controversy that he principally owes his celebrity.

John of Salisbury tells us that the *sententia vocum* did not long survive Roscelin.[3] Amongst its adherents was his contemporary Raimbert of Lille. That which the monk Heriman learnt from the latter agreed with the teaching of the master of Compiegne : Universal substances are merely vocal breathings, which means, according to Heriman, " eos de sapientium numero merito esse exsufflandos."[4] Here he is just commenting on Anselm, whose words contain the same raillery : "A spiritualium quæstionum disputatione sunt exsufflandi."[5] He goes on to say that in order to explain the long-winded verbiage (ventosam loquacitatem) of Raimbert of Lille, someome simply breathed into his hand (manuque ori admota exsufflans). This kind of reasoning approaches the sophism, and justifies the appellation *ars sophistica vocalis.*

57. Verbal logic and sophistry.—These verbal sophisms had been in use right from the beginning of the Middle Ages. Fridugisus, according to his rival Agobard of Lille, excelled in extracting unexpected consequences from his syllogisms, and Candidus of Fulda (ninth century), another Master at the Palatine Court, made use of syllogistic extravagances in his

---

1 *De fine Trinit.*, 2.
2 *Liber divisionum*, in Cousin, *Ouvr. inéd. d'Abelara*, p. 471. " Ita divinam paginam . . . pervertit, ut eo loco, quo Dominus partem piscis assi comedisse, partem hujus vocis, quæ est piscis assi, non partem rei intelligere cogatur."— Cousin, *P. Abaelardi opera*, II, p. 151.
3 Alius ergo consistit in vocibus, licet hæc opinio cum Roscelin suo fere omnino jam evanuerit.—*Metal.*, II, 17, *P.L.*, Vol. 199, p. 874, c. Cf. *Policraticus*, VII, 12, quoted on p. 110 n. Robert of Paris and Arnulphus of Laon are also mentioned as holding this view.
4 See p. 108.
5 *Op. cit.*, Migne, *P.L.*, p. 265.

Dicta.[1] These dialectical travesties were multiplied in the eleventh century, and the *sententia vocum* was bound to favour them. Certain lay professors coming from Italy and passing from one school to another after the manner of the time, implanted these tendencies in the centres of studies in the West. They were known as *philosophi, dialectici, sophistæ, peripatetici ;* and the genuine remains of their works shows that they well deserved the severe epithets (*scholaris infantiæ næniæ*) applied to them by P. Damiani. Anselm of Besate (*Anselmus Peripateticus* of Parma, first half of eleventh century) personifies the type, and his *Rhetorimachia* is a model of sophistry. When these dialecticians turned their attentions to theology and proclaimed the absolute rights of their methods, they ended by falling into heresies, and it is easy to understand that they met with opposition from the theologians.

58. Conclusion.—In any case, Roscelin must be given credit for teaching energetically that every reality which is self-sufficient for existence is individual ; he waged war against the Platonist chimera. That gives him his place in the history of ideas. The foundations of the pluralistic philosophy thus laid by Roscelin were built upon by his successors ; they were led to a more exact study of the relation between the general word and the general concept, and between the latter and the existing individual ; and they could only do so by endowing the gradually emerging scholastic system with a theory of ideas. In this way the controversy with exaggerated realism led step by step to the development of psychological studies. The twelfth century was to widen the field of discussion in a very pronounced way.

59. Bibliography.—The works of Fredegis (Migne, Vol. 105); *De Nihilo et Tenebris* in the *Monum. Germani, Epistolæ Karolini Aevi*, III, 615. There is no complete edition of the works of Remi of Auxerre. Cf. Migne, Vols. 131 and 171, among the works of Haymon. The Letters of Gerbert (983-997) have been published by M. Havet. *Collect. pour servir à l'étude et l'enseignment de l'histoire, Paris*, 1889). Richer's History is published in the *Monumenta Germaniæ* (Discussion with Otric, III, LV-LXX). Migne has published the works of Gerbert, Vol. 139 ; of Odo

---

[1] One of these *Dicta* contains a very imperfect proof of the existence of God. Cf. Endres, *Fridugisus u. Candidus*, p. 449.

of Tournai, Vol. 160 ; and a poem of Eric of Auxerre, Vol. 129. On the new mathematical writings of Gerbert see Omont, in *Notices et extr. des man.* (Paris, 1909, Vol. XXXIX). N. Bubnow, *Gerberti opera mathematica* (Berlin, 1899). Edition of the *Rhetorimachia* of Anselmus Peripateticus by Dümmler (1872). The *Dicta Candidi* in *Mon. Hist. Germ., Epistolæ Karol. Aevi*, II, 552 (1895).

Loewe, *Der Kampf zwischen Realismus u. Nominalismus im Mittelalter* (*Abh. d. k. böhmischen Gesellsch. d. Wissensch.*, VI F., Bd. VIII (1876), well done, deals with historical development in antiquity and Middle Ages ; De Wulf, *Le Problème des universaux dans son évolut. histor. du IXe au XIIIe s.* (*Arch. f. Gesch. d. Phil., IX*, 4, 1896) ; Richter, *Wizo und Brunn, zwei Gelehrte im Zeitalter Karl d. Grossen*, etc. (Leipzig *Programm.*, 1890). On Eric and Remi of Auxerre see Manitius, *op. cit.*, p. 499-519. Endres, *Fridugisus und Candidus* (*Philos. Jahrb.*, XIX, 4, 1906), a good monograph. Willmann, *Gesch. d. Idealismus*, II, 69 and 70 ; Picavet, *Gerbert, un pape philosophe, d'après la légende* (Paris, 1897) ; *Roscelin, théologien et philosophe* (Paris, Alcan, 2nd edit., 1911, cf. our analysis in *Rev. Néo-Scolastique*, 1898, p. 75) ; *Quelques documents sur nos vieux maîtres* (*R. intern. enseign.*, 1912). S. Barach, *Zur Geschichte d. Nominalismus vor Roscelin*, 1866. Adlhoch,*Roscelin und S. Anselm* (*Philos. Jahrb.* Bd. XX, h. 4, 1907, completes our interpretation of the pseudo-nominalism of *Roscelin*. G. Canella, *Per lo studio del problema d. universali nella scolastica* (*La scuola cattolica*, 1904-1907), vague and general. Reiners, *Der aristotel. Realismus in der Fruhscholastik* (1907) ; *Der Nominalismus*, etc., by the same (*BGPM.* VIII, 5, 1901), gives the letter of Roscelin to Abelard in an appendix, well done, but see our remarks in the notes to this section, and further on. Buonaiuti, *Un filosofo della contingenza nel sec. XI. Roscelino* (*Riv. storico-crit. d. scienze teol.*, 1908). Endres, *Die Dialektiker und ihre Gegner im. II Jahrh.* (*Philos. Jahrb.* 1906) ; *Zur Fruhscholastik* (*BGPM*, XVII, 1, 2), deals with Alcuin, Fulbert, Anselm the Peripatetic, Gerard of Czanad, P. Damiani, Lanfranc, Roscelin ; *Studien zur Gesch. d. Fruhscholastik* (notes on Bovo II. of Corvey in Saxony, who lived in the beginning of the tenth century, and on Fulbert of Chartres), *Philos. Jahrb.* 1912, p. 364. Stewart, *A Commentary by Remigius Antissiodorensis on the De Consolatione Philosophiæ of Boethius* (*Journal of Theological Studies*, 1915). K. Schulte, *Das Verhält-*

niss von Notkers Nuptiæ Philogiæ et Mercurii zum Kommentar des Remigius Antissiodorensis, Munster.

§2—St. Anselm of Canterbury.

60. The Philosophy of St. Augustine.—Before studying the philosophy of St. Anselm, let us give an outline of certain doctrines of Augustine which he adopted. In view of the fact that the influence of Augustine[1] made itself felt more and more as time went on, we shall consider here, in order to avoid repetitions, not only the doctrines which impressed St. Anselm, but also certain others which were the subject of discussion in the following century.

This is not the place for a detailed examination of the neo-Platonism of St. Augustine. Let it suffice to say that if he derived from that philosophic system his method of investigation by consciousness, his exaggerated distinction between the sensible and the suprasensible, and several isolated doctrines of metaphysics and psychology, on the other hand he denied and opposed the monist and emanative tendencies of the Plotinian system.[2] Moreover, he emphasized the individual character of the Supreme Being. Instead of the decadent triad, the fatalistic emanation of the spiritual and sensible world through the energy of the νοûς, the eternity of the world-soul, the transmigration of souls and the unconscious return of the human soul into the Deity, Augustine taught the Trinity of persons equal in nature, the identity of God with the eternal

---

[1] Principal philosophical works : (1) *Confessionum libri XIII*, an auto-biography, written about 400 A.D., in which he narrates the history of his intellectual and moral development up to the death of his mother in 387 ; (2) *Retractationum libri duo*, written about 427, and containing a critical summary of his works after his conversion ; (3) *Contra Academicos*, written against the neo-Sceptics whose doubts he had shared for a short time ; (4) *Soliloquiorum libri II ;* (5) *Liber de immortalitate animæ;* (6) *De quantitate animæ ;* (7) *De magistro ;* (8) *De libero arbitrio ;* (9) *De anima et ejus origine ;* (10) and (11) the famous works, *De Civitate Dei* and *De Trinitate*, which are principally concerned with theology and apologetics, but are also full of philosophic matter. The language of St. Augustine is rich, but often lacking in precision.

[2] The monistic and emanative character of Plotinism has been denied by Picavet, and recently, in connection with St. Anselm, by M. Koyre (*L'idee de Dieu dans philos. de S. Anselme*, pp. 77-83). But even if the One of Plotinus is an individual, and distinct from the rest of reality—which is open to question, although we cannot deal with it here—all reality other than the One is a development of the Intelligence which has issued from the One: everything is dependent upon the thought of the νοûς and has no being apart from it, so that with the exception of the Intelligence itself which issues from the One and is inferior to it, the monistic tendencies of the Plotinian system cannot be mistaken. See on this subject Inge, *The Philosophy of Plotinus*, 1918, and Arnou, *Le désir de Dieu dans la philosophie de Plotin*.

reasons by which He knows the world, the creation *ex nihilo*, the substantial distinction between God and creatures and of the latter between themselves, and the personal redemption of the soul by grace. Hence it is clear that he belongs to the school of pluralistic philosophers.

(i) The philosophy of St. Augustine has as its centre God in His Holy Trinity ; it aims not only at knowing Him, but also at loving Him[1] so that it is a fusion of intellectualism and mysticism.[2] This being so, it is easy to understand that his philosophy is a religious one, and is set forth in the framework of his dogmatic system. Neo-Platonism, which regarded philosophy and religion as all one, undoubtedly helped to determine his mind on this point.

(ii) Natural Theology.—The existence of God is demonstrated *a posteriori* by the contingence of the world, the order of the universe, the witness of conscience, and by universal consent. But the favourite proof of St. Augustine consists of his interpretation of the characteristics of necessity and immutability found in our ideas and in the primordial judgments which are the foundation of our knowledge and conduct : the object of these ideas possess these characteristics only because they share in the Divine Essence : our judgments concerning truth, goodness, and beauty require the existence of an absolute truth, goodness and beauty which constitutes their norm. Therefore God exists.[3]

There is only one God (against the Manichæans), individual, infinitely perfect, good, simple, eternal, elevated above all the categories, so much so that man cannot comprehend Him (neo-Platonism). The finite is his work, external to Him, and created by Him in time.

(iii) The divine knowledge is the subject of striking developments, and it is in this connection that we come across St. Augustine's theory of exemplarism. The intuition which God has of his own Essence implies the vision of all limited essences He can realize outside Himself and which constitute so many feeble and distant imitations of His Infinity. This objective relation of resemblance which Augustine calls by various names (*exemplar, idea, species, forma, ratio*) varies in the differ-

---

[1] Deum et animam scire cupio. Nihilne plus ? Nihil omnino.—*Soliloq.*, I, 7. Si sapientia Deus est . . . verus philosophus est amator Dei.—*De civit. Dei*, VIII, 1.

[2] O veritas, veritas ! quam intime etiam tum medullæ animi mei suspirabant tibi.—*Conf.*, III, c. 6.

[3] *De lib. arbitrio*, II, 12 and 15.

ent types (the essences of lion and man imitate God in different ways ; *principales formæ quædam vel rationes rerum in divina intelligentia continentur*), and in each single type varies in different individuals (*singula igitur propriis sunt creata rationibus*).

It is from these possibles that God made a selection when He created the actual world. This world therefore existed in God before it was realized, " as the plan of a building is conceived by the architect before it is built "[1] and since things have been created in conformity with the divine types or ideas, these ideas are the ultimate source of all contingent reality and the supreme foundation of the intelligibility of essences. Upon them also rests the certitude of our knowledge.

Exemplarism radically transforms one Platonist theory : the Ideas which for Plato co-exist with God, become God Himself considered in the infinite perfection of his knowledge. Already Philo had effected a similar fusion of doctrines, but it was in its Augustinian form that exemplarism was known to the Middle Ages. We see also at the first glance that Augustine transformed in a no less radical way the neo-Platonist theory which made the Ideas an inferior product of the One, and a scattering of the νοῦς.

When he speaks of God's knowledge, Augustine makes free use of this other neo-Platonist doctrine, that "being is light in the measure in which it exists " (Plotinus). He calls God the uncreated light (a description found in the Bible), and identifies him with the Intelligible Sun of Plato. In the same way he applies the theory of light to the beings which creation has called into existence : these are participated or derived lights, which must be carefully distinguished from the uncreated light.[2]

(iv) The luminous character belongs, therefore, not only to purely spiritual beings (angels, the human soul), but also, although in a less degree, to bodies. This " light " in which they share is that which is most noble in their reality. In order to explain the constitution of bodies, Augustine attributes to them a matter and form, and although in some places his idea of matter suggests a chaotic mass, many passages in the *Confessions* speak of matter as something undetermined, incapable of existing without a form, in terms which recall

[1] See especially L. 83, Q, q. 46.
[2] Aliud est lux quod est Deus, aliud lux quam fecit Deus.—*Contra adv. leg. et propt.*, I, 7, 10. (Migne, *P. L.*, Vol. 42, p. 609).

the doctrine of Aristotle. It is with this idea in his mind that he allows a *quasi materia* in the angels. The connection between matter and the quantitative state of corporeal things is foreign to his physics.   God has implanted in matter a latent treasury of forces, constituted according to the exemplars in the divine mind which correspond to the material essences. They are the seminal reasons, *rationes seminales* (Stoicism, neo-Platonism), the successive germination of which, when suitable circumstances come about, *acceptis opportunitatibus*[1], produces particular beings.   To each natural species of things there corresponds a distinct " reason."   Æsthetic and metaphysical optimism has its foundation in the mind of God, who of course thought out harmonious relations between the essences.

(v) The soul is spiritual. Augustine proves this by the characteristics of intellectual representations, and by the knowledge which the soul possesses of itself. The immortality of the soul follows from its spirituality and its participation in the immutable and eternal truths. When called upon to give his opinion on the origin of the soul, the African philosopher displayed much painful hesitation, which had its effects throughout the early part of the Middle Ages : on the one hand the transmission of original sin inclined him to Traducianism, according to which the soul of the child is detached from that of its generators ; on the other hand, he did not reject Creationism, which teaches the constant creation of souls at the moment of generation.   There is only one soul in us, and this soul which is thus unique and simple (against Plato) is present in the whole body. Together with the body it forms the man.

But soul and body keep their own substantial nature ; the soul makes use of the body[2] and governs it[3].   Augustine explains their union by introducing an intermediary connected with light. He never quite freed himself from these Platonist influences, although we come across formulæ which seem to be inspired by a very different spirit.

The soul manifests itself by manifold activities, and these do not really differ from the substance : Augustine mentions for preference the memory—the permanent storehouse of conscious life, always present to the soul—the understanding,

---

[1] *De Gen. ad litt.*, VII, 28.
[2] Homo anima rationalis est mortali atque terreno utens corpore—*De moribus Ecc. cath.*, I, XXVII.
[3] Regendo corpori accommodata.—*De quant. animæ.* 13.

and the will—one of the numerous tripartite divisions in which he discovers an image of the Trinity.

Three fundamental questions arise in connection with the conscious activities of the soul : the nature and origin of knowledge—its certitude—and the psychic primacy of the will.

(vi) Nature and origin of knowledge. With Plato, Aristotle and Plotinus, the Bishop of Hippo maintains the great doctrine of ideological spiritualism : there is a distinction in nature between sensation, the object of which is the particular, the multiple, the changing, and thought which grasps the abstract, the indivisible, and the stable. The soul, which is a kind of intelligible light, becomes aware of its knowledge in turning back upon itself.[1] Knowledge is a phenomenon of pure activity, as is evident from an examination of consciousness.

The place which Augustine attributes to the bodily senses in the genesis of sensation is in conformity with this innatism. It is not the body that impresses its own image upon the soul by a causal action, but it is the soul that engenders in itself the image of the body.[2]

As for ideas, their presence can be explained either by successive Divine interventions as our intelligence develops, or else by one unique Divine act which deposits in the soul a storehouse of knowledge at the moment of its union with the body.

(vii) Certitude exists, and is necessary for happiness. Consciousness[3] makes us certain of the reality of the thinking ego,[4] the first principles of the logical, metaphysical and moral orders, and also the intellectual representations of the external world (*ratio, intellectus*). If we regard the latter with a confidence which we refuse in the case of sense perception with its fugitive and variable data (Plato), it is because we know the norm of their truth. This norm, however, is not to be found in ourselves, nor in any other finite thing : it can only consist in the conformity of our knowledge with the Divine Ideas, the prototypes of the things with which we come in contact.

If we bear in mind the favour which Augustine shows to the theory of light, we can understand how human knowledge

---

[1] *De quantit. animæ*, 20.

[2] Sensum puto esse non latere animam quod patitur corpus.—*De quantitate animæ*, c. 23, 41. Cf. Ott, *Des hl. Augustinus Lehre über die Sinnesserkenntniss* (*Philos. Jahrb.*, 1900, p. 50).

[3] Noli foras ire, in te redi, in interiori homine habitat veritas.—*De Vera Religione*, 72.

[4] Sicut enim novi me esse, ita novi etiam hoc ipsum, nosse me.—*De Civitate Dei*, XI. c. 26. See the whole of this fine passage.

is related to the Divine knowledge of which it is a reflection, and the various applications of the doctrine of divine illumination in his writings. The truth of our knowledge, he writes, rests upon God,[1] " the sun of the soul (neo-Platonism), the light in which we see the unchangeable truth of things " ; " ea non posse intelligi nisi alio quasi suo sole illustrentur "[2]; " in quadam luce sui generis omnia quæ cognoscit intueatur."[3] The *De magistro* represents God as the interior master of the soul. The *De Trinitate*[4] opposes the *ratio inferior* (quæ intendit temporalibus) to the *ratio superior* (quæ intendit æternis conspiciendis aut consulendis), and knowledge to wisdom.

These formulæ together with others played a considerable part in the philosophic history of the thirteenth century, and the difficulty in their interpretation explains how opposed systems appealed to them for support. It is certain that they are not to be understood in an ontologistic sense, as if our intelligence directly contemplated immutable truths in the Divine essence. It is equally certain that in many passages the illuminative action of God refers to the creative act to which the soul and the understanding owe their reality[5]. But many other formulæ are simply paraphrases of Augustine's favourite doctrine on the nature and foundation of certitude. This is the case with the theory of the *ratio superior*, by which we understand that the essences of all things are in conformity with their increated exemplar the basis of all truth (*incommutabilia vera*), and that the necessity and immutability of our ideas and principles thus repose upon the Divine essence[6]. Lastly, other texts seem to introduce the question of the origin of ideas, which God impresses successively upon us as a seal leaves its imprint upon wax.[7]

[1] Deus intelligibis lux, in quo et per quem intelligibiliter lucent quæ intelligibiliter lucent omnia—*Sol.* I, 1, 3. Migne, *P.L.* 32, p. 807.
[2] *Solil.*, I, 1, c. 8.   [3] *De Trinit.*, XII, 15.
[4] XII, 1-7.   [5] E.g., *De Civit. Dei*, X. 2.
[6] As contrasted with the *ratio inferior*, or the direct knowledge of things by the understanding. Even the knowledge of temporal things " non sunt tamen rationis expertia nec hominibus pecoribusque communia. Sed sublimioris rationis est judicare de istis corporalibus secundum rationes incorporales et sempiternas, quæ nisi supra mentem humanam essent, incommutabiles profecto non essent.—*De Trinit.*, XII, 2. Cf. *ibid.*, XII, 15, where he defines knowledge or science as " temporalium rerum cognitio rationalis " as opposed to *sapientia*, or the knowledge of the foundation of certitude. Cf. *De libero arbitrio*, II.
[7] *De Trinit.*, XVI, 15. Portalie (*op. cit.*, col. 2334 *et seq.*) who studies this question at length, gives an ideogenic sense to all the formulæ. But this is to exaggerate things. Portalie silently passes over the distinction between the *ratio superior* and *inferior* which is very important in this connection, and has to do with the foundations of the essences and of certitude. Cf. Kleutgen, *La philos. scol.*, Vol. II, pp. 411-451.

(viii) The will is preponderant in psychic life, and Augustine affirms its primacy of honour over knowledge. It is not only that the internal sense and intelligence become active under its orders—the purity of the will and its desires is even a condition of wisdom. The pure and holy soul, " quæ sancta et pura fuerit "[1] can alone aspire to a knowledge of truth by the *ratio superior*. Truth is a good which must be loved with all the energies of the soul. Moreover, the adhesion of the mind to certain mysterious truths—such as the union of the soul with the body—only comes about by an intervention of the will. Finally, the will possesses this other prerogative : it is psychologically and morally free.

(ix) The moral system of Augustine closely unites the life of nature with that of grace : it builds up the idea of Christian perfection, and never ceases to oppose the new ideal to happiness and virtue as conceived by the Stoics, Epicureans, and neo-Platonists.[2]

Everything is good in the measure in which it has being (Plato). God, the Supreme Goodness, is our last end, and the union of the soul with God will be its supreme happiness (Eudaimonism). This union will be brought about by the beatific vision, which so far from involving unconsciousness (neo-Platonists), will exalt personality. The justice of God and the necessary relations between essences are the foundation of the absolute distinction between good and evil. The controversies in which he engaged with Manichæism, Pelagianism and semi-Pelagianism led St. Augustine to study the problems of evil, liberty, grace, and predestination. Evil does not share the realm of being with the good (Manichæism) ; it is nothing positive, otherwise the scorpion would die of its own poison ; it is a privation of good, and consequently only affects contingent things endowed with a certain degree of goodness. As for the conciliation of human liberty and the Divine government by grace and predestination, the texts which relate to this matter have been the subject of age-long controversies, chiefly theological in character, and the most divergent systems have based themselves upon the Doctor of Hippo.

To complete our survey of the important elements in the philosophy of St. Augustine, we shall later on refer to some of of his social and political doctrines. (Chapter V, § 6.)

---

[1] Lib. 83, Q. q. 66.
[2] Cf. Mausbach, *op. cit.* (66).

61. Life and Writings of St. Anselm.—Born of a Patrician family at Aosta in 1033, St. Anselm became Abbot of the Norman Abbey of Bec (1078), whither he went at the invitation of Lanfranc. From 1093 up to his death in 1109 he occupied the archiepiscopal throne of Canterbury. His biography was written by the monk Eadmer, whose material has not yet been utilized in a definitive manner.

The most important works of which the authenticity is certain are : the *Monologium* (which reminds one of the Confessions of St. Augustine), and the *Proslogium* (between 1070 and 1078), the *Liber Apologeticus ad Insipientem* (in reply to Gaunilon), *De Fine Trinitatis et de Incarnatione Verbi*, the dialogues *De Grammatico, De Veritate, De Libero Arbitrio*, and the *Cur Deus Homo*.

Anselm was inspired by St. Augustine, for whom he displayed a marked predilection[1]. His attitude of mind was principally that of a metaphysician ; he was secondarily a moralist and a psychologist.

62. Natural Theology.—The metaphysics of St. Anselm constitute one great Natural Theology. God is the exemplary, efficient, and final cause of the intelligible and sensible world : this is the central doctrine of the *Proslogium* and the *Monologium*. The deductive method, which interprets the created by the uncreated, presides over all the Anselmian developments on the existence and nature of God.

The arguments for God's existence are well known, and several are original. The proofs in the *Monologium* may be reduced to three : (i) All good things share in one and the same goodness ; this goodness must be the good-in-itself, which cannot be communicated, and is the sovereign good.[2] (ii) There are degrees in the perfection of beings. Since an infinite number is impossible, there must be a maximum and infinite perfection. (iii) Finite things have not being of themselves, but must receive it from a supreme being which exists of itself. These three proofs start from the fact that finite things exist, and conclude from their hierarchical character that there exists

---

[1] Nihil potui invenire me dixisse quod non catholicorum Patrum et maxime beati Augustini scriptis cohæreat.—*Monolog.* Preface. Anselm was not indebted to Scotus Eriugena or to pseudo-Dionysius, cf. Dræseke, *op. cit.* There is another study by Dræseke on the sources of the *Monologium* and the *Proslogium* in *Neue Kirchl. Zeitschr.*, 1900, p. 243. Cf. Koyré, *op. cit.*, chap. IV-VII, wh.ch, however, contain nothing new.

[2] The same argument is applied to magnitude.

another Being at the summit of the scale.[1] The Platonist and Augustinian inspiration is evident here.[2]

Anselm's name is above all attached to an argument contained in the *Proslogium* known as the Ontological Argument. " We certainly believe," he writes, addressing himself to the Deity, " that Thou art a being such that a greater cannot be conceived . . . Now, such a being cannot exist merely in our understanding which conceives it. For if it were only in our minds, it could be thought of as also existing in reality, which is greater. If, therefore, that than which a greater cannot be thought is in the mind alone, the very thing than which a greater cannot be thought is that than which a greater can be thought. But certainly this cannot be. Therefore it cannot be doubted that there is something than which a greater cannot be thought, both in the mind and in reality.[3]

This argument, remarks Thomas Aquinas[4], passes from the subjective or ideal order to the objective or real order. To conceive a being which is the greatest possible and therefore contains the note of existence does not authorize us to pass to the affirmation of the extramental existence of such a being.

Already a contemporary of Anselm, the Monk Gaunilon, of Marmoutier-les-Tours, attacked the ontological argument, and maintained that it was not convincing for an atheist.[5] The mere idea which we have of a thing is no guarantee of its real existence. If the argument were valid, it would prove too much. We might just as well demonstrate the existence in the ocean of the most beautiful of all islands, in basing ourselves upon the imagination we have of it. Anselm's reply (*Contra insipientem*) points out justly that the existence which we think of is necessary in the case of God—his essence is to exist—but contingent in the case of the perfect island. He does not, however, counter the principal objection, which has to do with the very method

---

[1] Baeumker (*Witelo*, p. 290 *et seq.*) and Grunwald (*op. cit.*, p. 30) give a purely logical and conceptual sense to these arguments, as opposed to Stöckl (*Gesch. d. Philos. d. Mitt.*, I, 163) who endeavours to see in them an appeal to the principle of causality, and Domet de Vorges (*op. cit.*, p. 233) who sees a resemblance between them and the proofs of St. Thomas.

[2] e.g., *De Libero Arbitrio*, II, 1 ; *De Trinitate*, VIII, 3.

[3] *Proslogium*, Ch. II. Et quidem credimus te esse aliquid quo nihil majus cogitari possit . . . Et certe id quo majus cogitari nequit non potest esse in solo intellectu. Si enim vel in solo intellectu est, potest cogitari esse et in re, quod majus est. Si ergo id quo majus cogitari non potest est in solo intellectu, idipsum quo majus cogitari non potest est quo majus cogitari potest. Sed certe hoc esse non potest. Existit ergo procul dubio aliquid, quo majus cogitari non valet, et in intellectu et in re (from Daniel's text, *op. cit.*, p. 5).

[4] *Summa Theol.*, I, q. 1. a. 1.

[5] *Liber pro insipiente adversus Anselmum in Proslogio ratiocinantem.*

of his reasoning.   Incidentally he points out that the idea of
the greatest or most perfect being implies the notion of a
Personal God.

Considered from the logical point of view, the objections
of Gaunilon and St. Thomas are peremptory.   But Anselm's
argument is more than the cold analysis of a concept, and a
dry dialectical decomposition of the idea of God.   He pre-
supposes an intimate and living presence of God in the soul.
The vague and imperfect idea of the Infinite results from a first
mysterious contact which is not subject to the restraints of
syllogistic reasoning and constitutes a sort of primordial fact.
The analysis of the infinitely perfect is a later procedure.
Hence a complete interpretation of the argument ought in our
opinion to deal with it, from the two-fold point of view of
psychology and logic.

The ontological argument had its upholders and its adversaries.   Bruno of Segni († 1123), who used it in Theology,
defended its dialectical value ; William of Auxerre took it up;
William of Auvergne, Alexander of Hales, and Bonaventure
leaned towards it ; Duns Scotus interpreted it (potest colorari
illa ratio Anselmi).   Others such as Albert the Great, Thomas
of Strasburg, and Giles of Rome, allow that the proposition
" God exists " is evident for cultivated minds.   Thomas
Aquinas rejects these opinions, and vigorously combats all the
a priori proofs for the existence of God.[1]

The study of the Divine attributes—simplicity, immutability,
eternity, the creative act, and omnipresence—is simply a chain

[1] Historians do not agree as to the meaning and value of this argument.
Quite recently there have been new and important discussions.   Domet
de Vorges, Baeumker, Grunwald and Fischer interpret it in a purely logical
sense, and see in it a new application of the principle of exaggerated realism.
Ragey, Dom Adlhoch and others defend a psychological interpretation : the
idea of the perfect in our minds can only be explained by the objective existence of the perfect.   Before Adlhoch, van Weddingen saw in the argument
the expression of a higher instinct whose term is the Absolute.   Descartes
reproduced the argument in its logical form.   Leibniz modified it somewhat,
and " coloured " it after the manner of Duns Scotus in basing himself on the
possibility of the Infinite Being.   As for the name " ontological argument "
which has become general especially since Kant, Baeumker (*op. cit.*, p. 297 n.)
justly points out that it is a function of Kantism.   Kant gives the name
" ontological proof " to any proof independent of experience and based upon
a simple analysis of concepts.   This description does not harmonize either with
the spirit of Aristotelianism nor with that of Scholasticism, for Metaphysics
has as its object existing being, and not the *a priori* idea of being and the
subjective conditions of its mental presence.   Furthermore, the ontological
argument has nothing in common with ontologism, or the vision of the Ideas
in God.   For the history of the ontological argument see Grunwald, *op. cit.*,
p. 87 *et seq.*, Baeumker, *op. cit.*, p. 300-317 ; Domet de Vorges, *op. cit.*, p. 280-
298 ; Daniels, *op. cit.*, Folliatre, *op. cit.*, Koyré, *op. cit.*

of deductions in which Anselm brings out what is implied in
the idea of the Infinitely perfect Being whose essence is to
exist. He stresses the Divine knowledge. Before creating
the world, God possessed in His infinite nature—and knew—
the *ratio* of everything which was to exist some day.[1] Here we
have the Exemplarism of St. Augustine.

The metaphysics of truth is simply the extension of this.
" Res sunt veræ quando sunt ut debent "[2] is Anselm's thesis.
In other words, he deals only with ontological truth (the *ut
debent* is the conformity of things with the destiny assigned
them by their essences, which are imitations of the Divine
essence), although in order to arrive at this he sets out from
the truth of the judgment. Truth is the certitude of things,
and can be attained to only by the intelligence—*veritas est
rectitudo sola mente perceptibilis*. It is eternal, superior to the
mind which is subject to change, and its foundation must be
in God who willed things to be what they are—a metaphysical
doctrine which is correct, though incomplete.

63. Exaggerated Realism.—Already in the " ontological
proof " of the *Proslogium* we recognize the principles of exaggerated realism—the transference outside of the mind of the
real as conceived by the mind. Influenced by the same tendencies, Anselm held that justice, truth and goodness exist
as such apart from the just, true and good things which share
in them. In fact, he regarded this doctrine of the diversity
of the essences or ideas of goodness, nobleness and justice, as
a foundation for a proof of the existence of a Supreme Unity
situated at the summit of the hierarchy of reality. We shall
see later on (76) that he based himself upon exaggerated
realism in combating the tritheism of Roscelin. If every
existing thing is individual, said Roscelin, the persons of the
Holy Trinity form three gods. Anselm replies: " How can
one who does not understand that many men are specifically
but one man understand that many persons, each one of which
is perfectly God, are together one God ? "[3]

But it is easy to see that Anselm's realism is more than a

[1] Quoniam priusquam fierent universa, erat in ratione summæ naturæ,
quid aut qualia aut quomodo futura essent.—*Monologium*, cap. 9. Sicut nihil
factum est nisi per creatricem præsentem essentiam, ita nihil viget, nisi per
ejusdem servatricem præsentiam.—Cap. 13.

[2] *De Veritate*, 11.

[3] Qui nondum intelligit quomodo plures homines in specie sint unus homo,
qualiter comprehendit quomodo plures personæ quarum singula perfectus
Deus est, sint unus Deus ?—*De fide Trinitatis*. 2. Cf. Domet de Vorges,
op. cit., p. 153.

mere solution of the problem of universals, as was thought by some of his contemporaries. It was a particular way of uniting individuals to species, species to genera, and genera to God.

The world of sensible things is therefore not the true world, but a kind of participation in the intelligible world. But this is quite different to saying that Anselm was a pantheist.[1] It is true that the individuality of things is weakened in such a hierarchical conception of reality, but it is still there, and not only are individual things distinct from each other, in addition God is distinct from all his creatures.

64. Psychology and Moral Philosophy.—We find traces of St. Augustine in the psychological questions studied by Anselm no less than in his Metaphysics. He sees a reflection of the divine life in the threefold arrangement of the higher activities, *memoria, intelligentia, amor*,[2] but he hesitates when dealing with their relation with the soul. The fundamental principle of ideological spiritualism is clearly laid down : sensation and thought are quite distinct. Sensation is pure activity, so much so that its cognitive contribution is only the development of a deposit within the soul. Intellectual knowledge, which attains to the inmost being of things by means of abstraction, extends to spiritual substances and to God.[3] Anselm speaks of the sensible origin of ideas, but does not deal with the difficulties to which this problem gives rise ; he outlines the theory of intentional species without falling into the erroneous ideas concerning these attributed to him by certain historians ; he dwells with pleasure on the immediate knowledge which the soul possesses of its own existence, *semper sui meminit anima* ;[4] in dealing with intellectual knowledge he assigns to the Divine light an influence which recalls the Augustinian theory of the ultimate foundation of truth.[5]

God dwells in the soul, and the latter experiences His presence (see p. 124). This facilitates the ascent of the mind from sensible things to the ideal essences of genera and species, and from thence to God. Without denying the reality of sensible

---

[1] e.g., Rousselot and De Remusat. St. Anselm's realist solutions as found in the *Monologium* for instance, have nothing in common with the doctrine of the *De Grammatico*, which studies, not what things are, but the value of words and the grammatical forms of language.

[2] *Monol.*, c. 33.

[3] J. Fischer, *Die Erkentnisslehre Anselms von Canterbury*, p. 24 *et seq.*

[4] *Monolog.*, 46.

[5] Quanta namque est lux illa de qua micat omne verum quod rationali menti lucet.—*Proslog.*, c. 14. Cf. Fischer, *op. cit.*, p. 49.

things, Anselm disengages himself from them in order to rise to the suprasensible and the Divine. The body is a weight which the soul drags about, and an independent substance (Augustine). Still, although ignorant of the application of the hylomorphic theory to the human compound, Anselm was deeply convinced of the unity of man in his double nature, material and spiritual, and he never wearied of affirming his individuality. He hesitated when dealing with the origin of the soul.

His moral system is principally theological. He explains the transmission of original sin very much after the manner of Odo of Tournai, and adopts the Augustinian theories concerning evil and predestination.[1] Free will continually preoccupied his mind, and he devoted two treatises to this subject. He defines liberty as the power of conserving the rectitude of the will and of obeying reason.[2] Hence, since reason proclaims the Divine sovereignty, human liberty ultimately becomes conformity with the Divine will and the Divine life.[3] The lower appetites ought to submit themselves to the dictates of reason, for otherwise man would fail to attain to his real good. It is reason, therefore, which directs the will, and this intellectualism is likewise manifest in the notion of beatitude, which consists in the contemplation of God, the Supreme Unity.

65. The Influence of Anselm upon scholastic philosophy.— Anselm appeared in history at a time when Romanesque art was beginning to flourish, the feudal system was coming into being, and the characteristic civilization of the Middle Ages was being prepared for on all sides. He belonged to the past and at the same time was a herald of the future, so that he has been called the last of the Fathers of the Church and the first of the scholastics.[4]

With him the scholastic natural theology was constituted for the first time, with its metaphysical foundation and its pluralistic orientation. God is clearly distinct from his works ;

[1] De concordantia praescientiae, praedestinationis et gratiae cum libero arbitrio.
[2] Libertas arbitrii est potestas servandi rectitudinem voluntatis propter ipsam rectitudinem.—De lib. arb., 1.
[3] " The ideal man, as St. Anselm conceives him, is endowed with a will and liberty modelled on those of God."—Folliatre, op. cit., p. 376.
[4] Grabmann, op. cit., p. 258, calls him the Father of Scholasticism, but for the sole reason that he applied the dialectic method to matters of faith. Dræseke on the other hand writes : " One cannot strictly call Anselm a scholastic," for his thought is not confined to dialectics. (R. de Philos. 1909. p. 641). We regard St. Anselm as a scholastic on philosophical grounds, for his works contain doctrines in metaphysics, psychology and natural philosophy which belong to the scholastic patrimony.

the problems connected with God are linked up with the problems of being, and metaphysics definitely bursts asunder the narrow bonds of the problem of universals. Anselm's psychology, although incomplete, enunciates the fundamental doctrines of spiritualism, and scholasticism is enriched from this new point of view.

At the same time Anselm attempted a first grouping of doctrines.[1] His mind was more systematic than that of Augustine, his favourite master. The synthesis which he built up was far from being complete, but it prepared the way for others, and it was the first which could be compared with the philosophy of John Scotus Eriugena.[2] Anselm reminds one of Gregory VII, who, in the religious and political order of things, organized the Church, defined its relations with the State, and prepared the ground for the work of a Gregory IX or an Innocent III : he was the Gregory VII of Scholasticism. His influence on the development of mediæval philosophy and theology was not immediate. Bruno of Segni (1049-1123), Abbot of Monte Cassino, and Honorius of Autun the hermit of Degensburg, whom we shall consider later on (121), were inspired by his teaching. His name became an authority, chiefly for the representatives of the ancient Franciscan school, who appealed to his teaching as to that of a much-loved master.

66. Bibliography.—L. Bertrand, *S. Augustin* (Paris, no date), a biography ; Willmann (see p. 33), Vol. II, 61-66, general views ; J. Martin, *S. Augustin* (Paris, 1901, in *Grands Philosophes* series), a much discussed work on S. Augustine's system ; Portalié, *S. Augustin*, in Vacant's *Dictionn. de Théol. cathol.* written from the theological and philosophical points of view, an excellent general study ; Grandgeorge, *S. Augustin et le néo-Platonisme* (Paris, 1896), good ; Mausbach, *Die Ethik d. hl. A.* (Freiburg i. Br.,

---

[1] Folliatre, *op. cit.*, p. 4, makes me say that " no philosophical synthesis was attempted before the thirteenth century." Already in 1900 I wrote that the philosophy of Scotus Eriugena was a remarkable synthesis, and that of Anselm less complete because less extensive, but still a real one.

[2] Was St. Anselm a neo-Platonist, as maintained by Koyré ? (*op. cit.*, Ch. III). This can only be upheld by means of an equivocation already pointed out in connection with St. Augustine (p. 115, n. 2). What kind of neo-Platonism is here referred to : that of Plotinus, or that of his successors ? Already in Plotinus one cannot fail to notice monistic and emanative tendencies, and these are absolutely clear in Proclus and Macrobius. On the other hand, Anselm was frankly a pluralist and a creationist. Hence he rejected that which was specifically neo-Platonist. Moreover, he was acquainted neither with Plotinus nor with Proclus, with whom Koyré connects him.

1909), 2 vols. ; H. Weinand, *Dir Gottesidee, der Grundzug der Weltanschauung des hl. A.* (Forsch. z. Christl. Litt. u. Dogmengesch.), Paderborn, 1901 ; M. Grabmann, *Die Grundgedunken d. hl. A. uber Seele u. Gott.* (Köln, 1916). Many works have appeared recently on the evolution of St. Augustine's thought. See especially Ch. Boyer, *Christianisme et néo-Platonisme dans la formation de S. A.* (Paris, 1920) ; *La Vérité dans S. A.* (Paris, 1921) ; M. P. Alfaric, *L'Evolution intellectuelle dans S, Augustin, I. Du Manichéisme au néo-Platonisme* (Paris, Nourry, 1918) ; and above all, the excellent work of De Labriolle, *Histoire de la Littérature latine chrétienne* (Paris, 1920).

Gerberon's edition of St. Anselm, 1675 (containing his life by his secretary, Eadmer) was reprinted in 1721 and again by Migne in Vols. 158 and 159. On works wrongly attributed to St. Anselm see Haureau, *Not. et extr.* IV, p. 192-230. French translation of the *Monologium* and *Proslogium* : Bouchitté, *Le rationalisme chrétien à la fin du XIe siècle ;* English translation : Deane, *Proslogium, Monologium, The Answer of Gaunilon, and the Cur Deus Homo ;* De Remusat, *S. Anselme* (Paris, 1856) ; Van Weddingen, *Essai critique sur la philosophie de S. Anselme* (Memoir crowned by the Belg. Acad., 1875), prolix, and not free from historical errors ; Ragey, *Histoire de S. Anselme* (Paris, 1890, 2 vols.) ; Luigi Vigna, *San Anselmo filosofo* (Milan), incomplete ; Bainvel, *S. Anselme* (in Vacant's *Dictionnaire de Théol. Cath.*, 1901), studies his theology mainly and does not deal sufficiently with his philosophy ; Domet de Vorges, *S. Anselme* (in *Les Grands Philosophes*, 1901), a study of doctrines from the point of view of the development of scholasticism. Many works appeared in 1909 on the occasion of the centenary of the death of St. Anselm (1109). The *Revue de Philosophie* devoted a special number to him (Dec. 1909), with essays on Anselm's times and philosophical surroundings Dufourcq, de Vorges, Porée), on his sources (Dræseke), the ontological argument (Lepidi, Geyser, Adlhoch), his theology and ascetism (Beurlier, Bainvel, Maréchaux). On his proofs or the existence of God and the ontological argument there exists a considerable bibliography. Among modern works see specially the articles by Bertin (Congr. scientif. de Bruxelles, 894), who defends the value of the argument, and Hurtaud Revue Thomiste, 1895) ; Fuzier, *La preuve ontol. de l'exist. de Dieu, par S.Anselme* (Congrès de Fribourg, 1898), who holds that t. Anselm modified his argument in his reply to Gaunilon ;

K

Adlhoch, *Der Gottesbeweis ds. h. Anselm* (*Philos. Jahrb.* VIII, IX, and X) ; by the same : *Roscelin und S. Anselm*, mentioned in No. **59,** also *Glossen zur neuesten Wertung des Anselmischen Gottesbeweises* (*ibid.*, XV, 1903) ; *BGMP* : Grunwald, VI, 3 ; A. Daniels, VIII, 1, collects all relevant texts ; Fischer, X, 3, contains nothing new ; Baeumker, X, 6 ; Reply by Adlhoch to Baeumker's criticisms, in *Philos. Jahrb.* XXIII, 3 (1910); M. Esser, *Finden sich Spuren d. ontol. Gottesbeweises vor dem hl. Anselm* ? (*Jahrb. Phil. spek. Theol.*, XXIV, 3, 1910). On the sources, see the studies mentioned by Dræseke ; Gilson, Grabmann, C. Webb, *op. cit.*, see p. 35 ; Ch. Folliatre, *La Philos. de S. Anselme, ses principes, sa nature, son influence* (Paris, 1920), somewhat confused ; and A. Koyré, *op. cit.* He defends the thesis that Anselm was a neo-Platonist.

CHAPTER III

The Anti-Scholastic Philosophy of Scotus Eriugena

67. John Scotus Eriugena, Father of anti-Scholasticism.— In opposition to the majority of historians, who look upon Scotus Eriugena as the first of the Scholastics, we do not hesitate to call him the Father of the anti-Scholastics and the most prominent of them all during this period. To the pluralistic conception upon which Scholasticism began to build up its theories of reality, he opposed the monist conception,[1] and involved mediæval philosophy in momentous decisive discussions which continued throughout the ages.

The historians who look upon Scotus Eriugena as the first Scholastic base themselves upon reasons which we consider false—either they identify mediæval and scholastic philosophy, and regard Eriugena as the first great thinker of the Middle Ages, or else they think they find in his writings the confusion between philosophy and theology which in their eyes constitutes Scholasticism—or again they refuse to look upon him as an opponent of a philosophy which was not yet constituted.[2] This diversity of opinions proves once more that the rejection or the acceptance of the term " anti-Scholastic " involves a fundamental problem of classification of philosophic ideas.

We have explained above why we do not admit the identification of Scholasticism with mediæval philosophy or with theology. As for the objection that one cannot be opposed to the non-existent, we reply that at the time of Eriugena Scholasticism existed already in an imperfect form[3] but none the less really, just as a fruit exists in the flower.

---

[1] Concerning Monism and its anti-Scholastic character, see Second Period Chapter II, The Scholastic Synthesis, No. **168.**

[2] Ueberweg-Baumgartner, *op. cit.*, p. 224, calls his work " die selbständigste und hervorragendste philosophische Leistung der gesamten Frühscholastik " (the most independent and best-ordered philosophical production of the whole of early Scholasticism).   Saint- René Taillandier says : " Scotus Eriugena is not only the Father of Scholastic Philosophy, but it seems that his system contains all its developments."—*Scot Eriugène et la philosophie scolastique*, Paris 1845.   Delacroix(*R. synth. histor.*, 1902, p. 105), Baeumker (*op. cit.* p. 322), and Glossner (*Jahrb. Phil. spek. Theol.*, 1906, p. 403) admit that he cannot be placed among the scholastics.   Grabmann (*op. cit.*, I, p. 208) gives reasons against it.   [3] Cf. p. 97.

To place Eriugena at the head of a series of anti-Scholastic philosophers is in no way to lessen his historic significance. Rather it emphasizes his personality. This man was in advance of his time. His contemporaries were taking their first faltering steps in philosophy, and for two centuries afterwards his successors dealt with a restricted number of questions, while he himself elaborated in the ninth century a complete synthesis.

68. Scotus Eriugena and neo-Platonism.—This synthesis constitutes a metaphysical and psychological monism which singularly reminds one of neo-Platonism—not indeed in the form given to it by Plotinus (204/5-270), but as it is found in the works of Proclus and others of his contemporaries. Hence we come at once face to face with the question : was Eriugena acquainted with the neo-Platonist system of Proclus, and if so how ?

There is a doubt concerning the more or less absolute character of the monism of Plotinus.[1] But this is not very important in the present matter, for not only Eriugena, but the whole Middle Ages was ignorant of Plotinus. Proclus, more didactic and more thorough-going, installed an integral monism in the heart of his system : everything comes forth from the Prime One in virtue of a necessary and descending procession, and in spite of the complications in which Proclus became entangled by the application of the triadic method to the smallest details,[2] his conception of the universe is character-ized by a striking unity. But Eriugena was ignorant of Proclus as of Plotinus. Hence he could only have been acquainted with neo-Platonism indirectly. Neither Boethius nor Augustine could have been his models, for they purified the neo-Platonist material they borrowed from all monistic elements.[3] On the other hand, he might have been introduced to the older

[1] See p. 115 n. 2.

[2] Every producing principle ($\mu o \nu \dot{\eta}$) at no matter what stage in the hier-archy, engenders ($\pi \rho \delta o \delta o s$) a product, which ends by returning ($\dot{\epsilon} \pi \iota \sigma \tau \rho o \phi \dot{\eta}$) to the bosom of its generator, for the term produced is but the prolongation of the producer, and is endowed with a necessary tendency to become reabsorbed in it. From the undetermined One comes forth the $\nu o \hat{\nu} s$, but this emanation is only possible because of intermediate units ($\alpha \dot{\nu} \tau o \tau \epsilon \lambda \epsilon \hat{\iota} s \ \dot{\epsilon} \nu \dot{\alpha} \delta \epsilon s$), which Proclus looks upon as personal gods (Jamblichus). The $\nu o \hat{\nu} s$ divides itself into three spheres, which in their turn are subdivided into triads and heb-domads in such a way that they constitute a framework adapted to pagan Pantheism. Matter is a direct product of one of the triads of the $\nu o \hat{\nu} s$, and not at all a final emanation of the world-soul as Plotinus held. Upon this metaphysics Proclus builds up a mystical psychology, having as its basis the ecstatical illumination, and the deification of the soul by means of poly-theistic practices (Plotinus and Jamblichus).

[3] See p. 89 and 115.

neo-Platonism by pseudo-Dionysius and Maximus, interpreting their equivocal passages in a monist sense (see p. 84). He may even have discovered the main principles of substantial monism in a small collection of suggestive passages from Macrobius, and it is possible that not sufficient importance has been attached to this Commentary on Scipio's Dream which Eriugena must have known although he does not quote it (see p. 85).

In any case, the utilization of these sources does not detract in any way from the originality of Eriugena, nor from his power. The plan of his philosophy, and the way in which he executed it, are entirely his own. The appearance of monism in the early Middle Ages is an important fact which is due to him.

69. Life and writings.—Little is known of the life of John Scotus Eriugena.[1] He was born in Ireland between 800 and 815, studied first of all in some Irish monastery, and belonged to the group of distinguished foreigners who passed on their learning to the Continent. Charles the Bald invited him to his court, and he became the favourite philosopher of the Palatine School. After the King's death in 877, we lose all trace of him in history. We shall see later on how he was involved in the theological controversies of his time.

There were two periods in his literary formation. Up to 851 he devoted himself almost exclusively to the study of the Latin authors, above all, of S. Augustine, Boethius, Cassiodorus, M. Capella, Isidore; and wrote the *De Prædestinatione* and the commentaries on Martianus Capella. After 858 he came into contact with Greek authors; he possessed the rare attainment of a knowledge of Greek, of which Alcuin hardly knew the alphabet. In 858 he translated and commented on the works of pseudo-Dionysius (except the *Mystical Theology*),[2] which had been presented to Louis the Fair in 827 by an embassy from Constantinople in the name of the Emperor Michael the Stammerer.[3] He also translated the *Ambigua* of Maximus

[1] The early manuscripts have the name Johannes Scotus Eriugena—Baeumker, *Jahrb. Phil. sp. Th.*, 1893, p. 346, n. 2. The Irish were known as *Scoti*, and *Eriugena* signifies one belonging to the land of Erin. The contemporary texts referring to Scotus are collected by Traube, *Monumenta Germ. Hist., Poetæ Ævi Carolini*, III, 518 (1896).

[2] The commentary on this which is attributed to him belongs to the thirteenth century.

[3] Jacquin, *Le néo-Platonisme de J. Scot*, in *R, sc. phil. et th.*, 1907. p. 678. Cf H. Omont, *Manuscrit des œuvres de S. Denys l'Aréopagite envoyé de Constantinople à Louis le Débonnaire en 827 (Revue des études grecques*, XVII, 1904, p. 230-236). Already Pope Paul I had sent a copy of the works of pseudo-Dionysius to Pepin in 757, but no one at the Court was able to translate them.

the Confessor and a treatise by Gregory of Nyssa. His chief
work from the point of view of philosophy is the *De divisione
naturæ*, in which, following a didactic method in vogue in the
Carlovingian period, the subject is developed in the form of a
dialogue between the master and his disciples. At the end of
his life—between 867 and 901—he wrote commentaries on the
opuscula theologica of Boethius, which were widely used up to
the twelfth century.[1]

70. Metaphysics.—Here the fundamental principle is that
there exists only one reality—God—who, by a series of substantial and descending emanations gives birth to all things,
and to Whom all things return. Thus Eriugena studies the
Divine Being (natura, φύσις) in four stages or forms which
he calls the fourfold division of nature (*De divisione naturæ*).
In the beginning we have the Uncreated Being which creates,
thus giving rise to the Being which is created and in its turn
creates. The latter gives rise ultimately to being which is
created but does not create, and ultimately to the simple
uncreated.[2] In this very original conception, the first and fourth
stages give us the Infinite Being as starting-point and terminus,
the second and third constitute the evolution or devolution of
the Divine Being. Let us consider them in detail.

(i) Nature uncreated and creating, or God in His primordial
reality. Being Infinite, He possesses all perfections, but precisely because of His Infinity He is impenetrable so far as we
are concerned. He is above all the categories, for these cannot
be applied to the being which can neither be conceived nor
expressed.[3] Not only is God unknowable by us—He is impenetrable to Himself for knowledge involves the duality of
knower and known, and all duality is repugnant to the Infinite

[1] There are extant revisions and developments of the text in the form of
marginal notes. See E. K. Rand, *Autographa des J. Scotus* (Palæographisch
Forschungen de Traube. V. Akad. Wiss. Munchen 1912), with photograph
of the manuscript *De Divisione* at Rheims. This manuscript contains marginal
notes which later were incorporated in the text of the Bamberg manuscript
together with new additions, and in a Paris codex Rand traces five revisions.
He holds that these notes are not the work of Eriugena, but additions by scribes
writing under his direction (see *Supposed autographa of John the Scot* (in Univ.
of California *Publicat. Classical Philol.*, Oct. 1920). Manitius, *op. cit.*, p. 338
mentions as also written by Eriugena a translation of Priscianus Lydus, an
extract from Macrobius, and some poems.
[2] Videtur mihi divisio naturæ per quatuor differentias quatuor species
recipere : quarum prima est in eam quæ creat et non creatur, secunda in eam
quæ creatur et creat, tertia in eam quæ creatur et non creat, quarta quæ nec
creat nec creatur (*De divisione naturæ*, I, 3).
[3] Nam in ipsis naturis a Deo conditis, motibusque earum, categoriæ quali-
cunque sit potentia, prævalet. In ea vero natura quæ nec dici nec intelligi
potest, per omnia in omnibus deficit.—*ibid.*, I, 15, Migne, *P.L.*, Vol. 122, c. 463

Deus itaque nescit se quid est, quia non est quid.[1] Thus following in the footsteps of pseudo-Dionysius, Eriugena's God is simply the Inexpressible (cf. Plotinus and the Negative Theology).

(ii) Nature created and creating. God Who is thus elevated above all things is the essence of all beings derived from Him— *ipse namque omnium essentia est, qui solus verus est.*[2] Participations[4] or emanations scatter forth the Infinite One into the Limited Many. In the first place in virtue of a fatalistic *progressio,* God engenders within Himself the *primordiales causæ* or *primordialia exempla* of all things. He knows them as reflections of the perfection contained in His abysmal being (*abyssus*). These "*species vel formæ in quibus omnium rerum faciendarum priusquam essent, incommutabiles rationes conditæ sunt*" constitute an internal self-determination of God, which is eternal but created. By reason of the plurality of these species they are a lowering of His being (in opposition to St. Augustine). The Divine λόγος (God the Son) maintains them in unity.

In the third stage the Divine ideas are externalized.[3] They become creatures under the impulse of the Divine Love (Holy Spirit).

(iii) Nature created but not creating, or beings realized in time. Whether they be corporeal or spiritual, all are manifestations of the Divine Substance, or " Theophanies " as John Scotus energetically describes them. Thus the Godhead flows or runs in the entrails of the Universe. He derives Θεός from θέω to run[4]. Again, he compares the manifold Divine appearances to indefinitely varied reflections of light on the feathers of a peacock.[5] God takes the form of particular things without movement (*motus*), and without losing anything of His immutability ; He realises Himself in particular being and emerges from the depths of His Infinity ; He becomes in some category of the knowable. Thus underlying everything there is the one substance, God.

[1] II, 28.   [2] I, 13.

[3] Est igitur participatio . . . divinarum dationum et donationum a summo usque deorsum per superiores ordines inferioribus distributio.—III, 3, Migne, c. 630.

[4] Et creari et creare conspicitur divina natura. Creatur enim a seipsa in primordialibus causis, ac per hoc seipsam creat, hoc est, in suis theophaniis incipit apparere, ex occultissimis naturæ suæ finibus volens emergere, in quibus et sibi ipsi incognita, hoc est, in nullo se cognoscit, quia infinita est, et supernaturalis . . . descendens vero in principiis rerum ac veluti seipsam creans in aliquo inchoat esse . . . Creatur ergo et creat in primordialibus causis ; in earum vero effectibus creatur et non creat.—III, 23, Migne, c. 689. Cf. III, 4, c. 633 ; III, 17, c. 678.

[5] Ipse enim in omnia currit, et nullo modo stat, sed omnia currendo implet. —I, 12.

This resolution of the theophanies into God involves in particular the final disappearance of evil and the impersonal absorption of man, body and soul, in the Infinite ; for it is evident that life after death must be of the same nature as our present life, in which we are but a Divine becoming.

It is indeed true that following the example of all pantheists, Eriugena endeavours to harmonize this thorough-going monism with a distinction between God and other things. The One does not exclude the Many. Thus he writes : " *Totum vero quod creavit et creat, intra seipsam continere ; ita tamen ut aliud sit ipsa quia superessentialis est, et aliud quod in se creat.*"[2] But this *aliud* does not necessarily imply a real distinction, for the superessential state of God (first stage) might be called other than the product of His becoming without going beyond the bounds of monism, especially as it is in Himself (*in se*) that God creates this *aliud*. Such nuances seem to us to be inspired by the desire to seem orthodox which is often evident in the works of Eriugena. They throw light upon the intentions of the writer, but do not change the logic of his doctrine.[3]

Let us point out some peculiarities of the monistic system under consideration. Since all that is real in the sensible world is only a blossoming forth of the Logos and the *causæ primordiales*, reality is intellectual in nature, and depends upon mind (cf. Plotinus) ; the corporeal state of beings is not their true state, but an illusion, a non-being. The world-soul which lives with a Divine life, unites all the parts of that which we call the sensible universe by bonds of cosmic sympathy. Moreover, it is quite clear that it is the very substance of God, His Being, and not only His activity, which spreads itself out in the spiritual and sensible universe, and this constitutes a difference between Eriugena and the dynamistic conception of Plotinus.[4] Again, the descending hierarchy of the *rationes* in the universe has gradations which correspond to our conception of the world, so that the degrees of the real and of the known coincide :

---

[1] IV, 5.   [2] III, 17, Migne, c. 675 ; cf. V. 25, c. 911.

[3] It is in basing themselves on the intentions of Eriugena that Poole, *op. cit.*, and Koyre, *op. cit.*, p. 160 deny his pantheism.   Cf. Gilson, *La philos. du m. â.*, I, 25.   At this rate there would not be any pantheists at all, for all wish to explain diversity.   The question is whether they succeed in doing so without sacrificing their own theories or becoming involved in contradictions.

[4] Since God develops himself really, independently of the human mind, we cannot hold with M. Delacroix that the pantheism of Eriugena is subjectivist. " He teaches," writes Delacroix, " the possibility of attaining to the most obscure aspects of the Divine by the mere effort of consciousness."—*Essai sur le mysticisme spécul.*, etc., p. 2.

the higher genus evolves before the inferior, the latter before the species, and the species or type before the individual.[1] This is exaggerated realism.

(iv) Nature neither creating nor created, or God as term of the Universe. Everything which arises from a principle tends to return to it ; the terminus of a movement is the return to its starting-point. *Finis enim totius motus est principium sui . . . quod appetit et quo reperto cessabit, non ut substantia ejus pereat, sed ut in suas rationes, ex quibus profectus est, revertatur.*[2] Of necessity God returns within Himself : this is the deification of things, θέωσις the absorbing of the cosmos in the bosom of the Great Whole (cf. Plotinus and pseudo-Dionysius). The universal cause draws towards it all things which have arisen from it, without in any way changing, and by the pure efficacy of its beauty.[3]

71. Psychology.—John Scotus applies the fundamental principles of his monism to man. Here are the essential points of his teaching :

By means of the external senses (*sensus exterior*) man knows sensible things ; by the internal sense (*sensus interior*) he attains to the essence through these phenomenal manifestations ; by reason (*ratio*) he grasps the primordial causes of things ; by intellect (*intellectus*) he discovers God in His immutable reality. (cf. Plotinus, the three aspects of the soul.)

But in addition to this ascending way which starts from sense knowledge, there is a descending way (*gnosticus intuitus*) by which the human soul, in acquiring knowledge, travels along a path parallel to that of the Divine substance in its self-development. First of all, unconscious of itself (*intellectus*), the cognitive faculty knows itself by the representation of primordial essences (*ratio*). This representation grasps the realized essence (*sensus interior*) and its sensible attributes (*sensus exterior*). Thus human thought, divine in its foundation, follows the movements of the Divine Being. Moreover, human knowledge is unlimited, since it is God Himself who thinks in us.

Man is a *microcosmos*, uniting in himself the perfections of spiritual and material creatures. Certainly each man has his

---

[1] Intelligitur quod ars illa, quæ dividit genera in species et species in genera resolvit . . . non ab humanis machinationibus sit facta, sed in natura rerum ab auctore omnium artium condita.—IV, 4, Migne, c. 748 and 749.

[2] V, 3, Migne, c. 866.

[3] Ita rerum omnium causa omnia, quæ ex se sunt, ad seipsam reducit, ine ullo sui motu, sed sola suæ pulchritudinis virtute.—I, 75. He likens this attraction to that of a magnet.

own soul which is simple and unique.[1] But in the last analysis "all our souls are but a single soul." The individual is absorbed into Humanity, and Humanity in its turn is one with the rest of nature, and a projection of the Deity.

The original corporeal being, " as conceived in the second state of nature " was free from imperfections. Thus we are in a violent and fallen condition (Plato, Plotinus). The return of man to his original state in the bosom of God is effected through the Redemption by Christ, and as the whole universe shares in the same substance with man, it is through Christ that the final cosmic evolution will be brought about.

72. Influence of John Scotus Eriugena.—Although Eriugena's philosophy would seem to have been misunderstood by his immediate contemporaries, it had a considerable and enduring influence on the development of Western thought in the Middle Ages. Remi of Auxerre and Gerbert made use of it in the tenth century. Berengerius appealed to Eriugena, and in the twelfth century, Abelard, Isaac of Stella, Garnerius of Rochefort, and Alan of Lille were acquainted with his doctrines. Hugh of St. Victor utilized his work on pseudo-Dionysius. Anselm of Laon quoted the *Perifision*. His commentaries on the *opuscula sacra* of Boethius were highly thought of.

The *De divisione naturæ* greatly influenced the *Clavis physicæ* of Honorius of Autun.[2] The work was known at Chartres, and many teachers of that school adopted a kind of pantheism evidently inspired by Eriugena.[3] At the end of the twelfth century, Amalric of Bene found therein his pantheistic theories ;[4] the Albigenses appealed to him, and this explains why on the 25th January, 1225, Honorius III condemned the *De divisione naturæ*, which had already been forbidden by a Council of Sens.[5] Although the Pope ordered that the works of the Palatine philosopher which were still being read *in nonnullis monasteriis et aliis locis*[6] should be committed to the flames, they did not altogether disappear from literary circulation. In the fourteenth and fifteenth centuries we come

[1] IV, 5, Migne, c. 754.
[2] Endres, *Honorius Augustodunensis* (Kempten, 1906, pp. 241-145). Endres quotes long extracts from the *De divisione naturæ*.
[3] Clerval, *op. cit.*, p. 245.
[4] See No. **118**.
[5] Chartul. Univ. Paris, I, 106-107.
[6] Jacquin, *L'influence doctrin. de J. Scot. au début du XIII s.*, pp.104-106. The writer thinks that the Pope may have referred to Cistercian abbeys, inasmuch as Isaac of Stella, Garnier of Rochefort and also Alan of Lille belonged to this order.

across them in two catalogues,[1] and several manuscripts have come down to us.

The principal tendencies due to John Scotus Eriugena are :

(i) Pantheism and Monism. John Scotus affirms the community of being of God and creatures ; he gives an evolutionistic sense to the Divine ideas, since they are a stage in the formation of God's essence ; he denies the individuality of substances. It is because of his pantheism that Eriugena is an anti-Scholastic philosopher : the substantial distinction between God and contingent things, the distinction between the Divine ideas and creatures existing outside God, and the individuality of every substance are fundamental principles of Scholasticism. Indeed, all the pantheists combated by the scholastics up to the thirteenth century appealed to John Scotus Eriugena. Being a pantheist, *a fortiori* he was an exaggerated realist.

(ii) The second tendency is that of heterodox or pantheistic mysticism, which regards the disappearance of personality and the substantial identity of the soul with God as the terminus of the mystical life. We find the influence of Scotus in all the popular corruptions of mysticism.[2]

73. Human monopsychism.—The *De Constitutione Mundi* of pseudo-Bede refutes the opinion of certain philosophers who believed in the world-soul, and held that this unique soul confers racial unity and impersonal immortality upon mankind. "According to this doctrine, no one man is worse than another, since one and the same good and immaculate soul resides in all bodies ; but we may say that it is more degenerate in one body than in another. . . . Again, according to this doctrine, no man dies, for he is not separated from the soul, although he may be separated from the four elements."[3] Is this a sort of pre-Averrhoism ?[4] The name is not well chosen. We have here only a partial monism, a simple application to

---

[1] Manitius, *op. cit.*, p. 329.

[2] Chap. VII, § 2.

[3] Sicut unus vultus in pluribus speculis et in uno speculo plures vultus apparent, ita una anima in pluribus rebus, et ubique omnes vires suas habet licet in diversis habeat exercitium pro habilitate corporum.—Migne, P.L., Vol. 90, c. 902. Nullus homo videtur esse pejor alio, quia una eademque anima bona et immaculata in sui natura est in omnibus corporibus, sed dicitur magis degenerare in uno quam in alio . . . secundum hanc quoque sententiam nullus homo moritur, ita quod patiatur separationem animæ, quanquam separatur a quatuor elementis . . . Præterea dicunt quidam eamdem mondanam animam pariter cum humana anima esse in homine . . . sicque hominem duas animas asserunt habere—*ibid.* col. 903.

[4] Renan, *Averroes et l'averroisme.* Cf. Duhem, *La physique néo-platonic*, p. 45.

man of the doctrine of the unity of the cosmic soul and a logical commentary on the doctrines of Macrobius.

Possibly the treatise of pseudo-Bede refers to the teaching of Macarius Scotus. Ratramn of Corbie, in his work *De quantitate animæ*, attributes to the latter a similar psychology and sets out to refute it.[1]

74. Bibliography.—Works of J. Scotus Eriugena in Migne, Vol. 122 (Floss's edition). His commentaries on Martianus Capella have been edited by Haureau, *Not. et extr. ms.*, Vol. XX, Part II (1862). Traube, *Monum. Germ. hist. Poetæ alt. ævi Carolini*, Vol. III, 1896 ; A. Schmitt, *Zwei noch unbenutzte Hss. des Joh. Scotus Eriguena*, Bamberg, 1900. Manuscripts of the *De Divisione Naturæ* at Bamberg and Avranches show that Floss's edition is unsatisfactory. Rand has published the commentaries of John Scotus and Remi of Auxerre on the *opuscula* of Boethius (see p. 134). See also Rand, *Johannes Scotus* (Quellen u. Untersuchungen z. latein. Philol. des Mittelalters, I, 2, Munchen, 1906) ; Huber, *Joh. Scotus Eriugena* (Munich, 1862) ; Astier, *Mémoire sur Scot. Eriugène au Congrès des sociétés savantes* (Biblioth. *école Chartres*, Vol. 62) ; Dræseke, *J. Scotus u. dessen Gewährsmänner in Divisione naturæ* (Bonwetsch-Seebergs Studien, IX, 2, Leipzig, 1902) ; cf. *Zeitschr. f. wissenschaft. Theologie*, XLVII, N. F. XII, 1, in which Dræseke utilizes and completes similar conclusions by Brilliantoff (*Influence de la théologie orient. sur la théol. occidentale dans les œuvres de J. Scot. E.* (St. Petersburg, 1898). On the sources of the *De Prædestinatione*, an earlier work in which pseudo-Dionysius was not referred to, see Jacquin, *Le néo-platonisme de J. Scot.* (R. sc. philos. et theolog., 1907, p.p 745-685) ; *L'influence doctrinale de J. S. au début du XIIIe s.*, by the same, (*ibid.*, 1901, pp. 130-106), also *Le rationalisme de J. Scot.* (*ibid.* 1907, pp. 745-746) ; Manitius *op cit.*, pp. 322-339 ; Buchwald, *Logos Begriff d. J. Scotus Eriugena* (Leipzig, 1884). On the theory of the stars, see Duhem, *La phys. néo-platonic* (R.Quest. scient., 1910, p. 8). A Schneider *Die Erkenntnisslehre des Joh. Scotus E.*, in two parts. (Berlin, 1921 and 1923).

[1] All that remains of this treatise is the letter to Odo of Beauvais. " Dicit namque quod omnis homo unus homo sit per substantiam. Quod si ita est, sequitur ut non sit nisi unus homo et una anima."—*Mon. Germ. Hist.*, Ep. 6, 151, n. 11.

CHAPTER IV

Philosophy and other Branches of Knowledge

75. The Theological Controversies.—The historian of mediæval philosophy cannot overlook the theological controversies, for it was in connection with these that more than one philosophical problem arose. In the ninth and tenth centuries, the controversy on predestination led to the discussion of human liberty and its relations with Divine Providence and Justice ; the Paschasian controversy concerning the Real Presence of Christ in the Eucharist called forth dissertations on substance and accident, and substantial transformation ; the dogma of the Holy Trinity suggested discussions on the notions of nature, individual and person.

The confusion between philosophy and theology in early times gave those controversies a mixed complexion. But this confusion gradually passed away, and we observe the progressive constitution of philosophy and theology as two distinct sciences. The study of philosophy in its relation to the first theological controversies provides us with a useful means of dissipating the old-established prejudice that mediæval philosophy had no existence of its own.

We may distinguish three groups of theologians according to the attitude they adopted towards philosophy : the rationalists recognized dogmas only in so far as they were demonstrated ; the reactionaries accused dialectics itself of the abuses into which its first disciples fell, and persuaded ecclesiastical authority to interfere in ways sometimes excessive ; the moderates endeavoured to harmonize the respective rights of reason and authority and clarified the relations between theology and philosophy.

76. First Group : the rationalistic theologians.
(i) *Eriugena and the confusion between philosophy and theology.*—John Scotus Eriugena starts out from the neo-Platonist and Augustinian principle that there is no distinction at all

between philosophy and religion, and hence they cannot contradict each other.[1] He adds that Scripture is the principal source of our knowledge of God.[2] Reason does not excel Scripture ; it establishes its data, illumined as it is by God. Hence so far from revolting from dogma, Scotus wishes to remain faithful to it ; he displays a constant anxiety to respect it, and the glosses which he writes with his own hand in the margins of *De Divisione Naturæ* tend to mitigate the effect of too daring expressions concerning God.[3]

But as soon as he passes on to applications, John Scotus ceases to be orthodox. Fortified by the principle that reason itself is the judge of the interpretation of Scripture, he adapts dogma to his monistic conceptions, having recourse to allegory, sacrificing sometimes the logic of his system and at other times dogma itself. Thus it seems very difficult to recognize the Divine persons in the stages of development of the One Nature, or to apply to the evolution of the Infinite Substance into the finite the name of creation *ex nihilo* in the sense in which this is understood by the Scholastics. In the same way the whole history of the fall is transformed after the manner of gnostic symbolism. The transmission of original sin is explained in his pantheistic system in the same simple way as in the works of Odo of Tournai.

Already in his lifetime John Scotus was suspected of heresy, and it is interesting to note that in 860-2 Pope Nicholas I. complained of the bold opinions which he had developed in the *De Divisione Naturæ* without submitting them to a previous censure. We may call John Scotus the father of mediæval rationalism ; but in opposition to modern religious rationalism, which would reject Christian dogma in the name of reason, the religious rationalism of the Middle Ages endeavours to

[1] *De div. prædest.*, I, 1. " Quid est aliud de philosophia tractare nisi veræ religionis, qua summa et principalis omnium rerum causa Deus et humiliter colitur et rationabiliter investigatur, regulas exponere ? "

[2] *De div. naturæ*, I. 64 ; " Sacræ siquidem scripturæ in omnibus sequenda est auctoritas." I, 66 : " Vera enim auctoritas rectæ rationi non obsistit, neque recta ratio veræ auctoritati. Ambo siquidem ex uno fonte, divina scilicet sapientia, manare dubium non est." There is an often quoted passage : " Omnis enim auctoritas quæ vera ratione non approbatur, infirma videtur esse. Vera autem ratio, quoniam suis virtutibus rata atque immutabilis munitur, nullius auctoritatis astipulatione roborari indiget " (*De div. nat.*, I, 69). Here Scotus places reason above the authority of the Fathers, but not above all authority. Cf. Jacquin, *La rationalisme de J. Scot*, p. 748 ; Ueberweg, *op. cit.*, p. 226.

[3] Rand, p. 6 and 7, of *Autographa*. See also what Eriugena wrote in commenting on the Gospel of St. John : In omnibus quæ scribo suspendor virorum ac Piorum Patrum judicio. Interim dico quæ sentio.—*Ibid.*, p. 6, note.

establish this very dogma in the name of reason. Others followed in the path opened up by John Scotus and ended in heresy.

(ii) *Controversy on predestination and liberty.*—Gottschalk, a monk of Orbais, contemporary with Rhaban Maur, adopted St. Augustine's doubts as to the possibility of harmonizing human liberty and Divine grace. From the absolute pre-destination of the good and bad, he concludes that man is the plaything of God, and there is neither liberty nor responsibility.

If we bear in mind the disturbances which the similar statements of Jansenius led to in modern times, we shall understand the commotion which Gottschalk caused. Rhaban Maur and above all Hincmar of Rheims (806-882) and in a less measure the deacon Florus of Lyons, defended human liberty. Ratramn of Corbie and Servatus Lupus took the side of Gottschalk ; while both opponents and partisans of the latter joined together against John Scotus Eriugena, who had intervened in the debate in order to formulate an equally bold theory. Gottschalk's doctrine was condemned at the synods of Mayence (848) and Quiercy (849).

(iii) *Controversy on transubstantiation.*—Berengarius of Tours (998-1088) was a disciple of the school of Chartres, and his ideas on universals seem to belong to those of the anti-realists. He took as his motto : *per omnia ad dialecticam confugere.* He held that the accidental qualities of the eucharistic bread and wine (colour, figure, taste, etc.) cannot remain without the underlying support which upholds them and which Aristotle calls substance.[1] He concludes that the Gospels cannot have meant to teach a real transubstantiation, and that the body and blood of Christ are present in the sacramental species in a hidden manner. Berengarius was a restless and fiery spirit, and caused trouble in the schools. Lanfranc (about 1010-1089) attacked him, and Adelman of Liege (1048), Durandus of Troarn, Hugh of Breteuil and other former fellow students of Berengarius at Chartres[2] opposed his theories, but it required twenty years of controversy and four synods to stamp them out.

---

[1] Berengarius had predecessors in Ratramn of Corbie († 868) in his *De Quantitate Animæ*, and Heriger Abbot of Lobbes, who were opposed by Paschasius Radbertus or Radbertus of Corbie (died about 860), author of the *De Corpore et Sanguine Domini*.

[2] Clerval, *op. cit.*, pp. 64 and 131-141.

(iv) In the eleventh century, the development of the sophistical method led to the introduction of a false and purely verbal dialectic into theology(57). We learn from Otloh of St. Emmeram and others that a group of dialecticians, exaggerating still more the verbalistic tendencies of Anselm of Besate, took no notice of any authority in their exposition of dogma, and preferred Boethius to the Scriptures.[1]

(v) *Tritheism of Roscelin.*—Doscelin owes his reputation very much more to the tritheism he supported than to his doctrine on universals. He held that the three Divine persons are three independent beings, after the manner of three angels ; if usage permitted, one might say that there are three Gods. In order to safeguard dogma, Roscelin adds that the three Divine persons have only one will and one and the same power.[2]

This very marked tritheism[3] which St. Anselm and Abelard continued to refute even after the retractations on its author, seems to us to be an evident application of anti-realism : in Roscelin's mind a Divine person is an individual and independent substance.

77. Second group : the reactionary theologians.—The rationalism of certain theologians and the heresies in which their way of treating dogma ended led to the formation of a reactionary party who were more or less hostile to all philosophy, and desired the only theological method to be the literal study of the Scriptures. This opposition movement was closely connected with an attempt at the reform of the monastic life of which we find traces in the Benedictine monasteries in France and Germany. The most prominent personalities of this group belong to the eleventh century : in Italy St. Peter Damian, in Germany Manegold of Lautenbach and Otloh of St. Emmeram.

PETER DAMIANI, a hermit monk, was born at Ravenna in 1007, and died in 1072. He despised earthly knowledge. The liberal arts are useless, according to him, and dialectics a *superfluum.* Damiani protests against the religious who make light of St. Benedict's rule and take pleasure in the rules of Donatus (*parvipendentes siquidem regulam Benedicti, regulis*

---

[1] Magisque Boetio quam sanctis scriptoribus in plurimis dictis crederent—Migne, Vol. 146, c. 60.

[2] Audio . . . quod Roscelinus clericus dicit in Deo tres personæ esse tres res ab invicem separatas, sicut sunt tres angeli, ita tamen ut una sit voluntas et potestas, aut Patrem et Spiritum sanctum esse incarnatum ; et tres deos vere posse dici si usus admitteret.—Letter of St. Anselm to Fulco.

[3] Against Picavet, *Roscelin,* etc., p. 25.

gaudent vacare Donati.[1] All the same, he himself makes use of reasoning in his *De Divina Omnipotentia*, dedicated to Didier of Monte Cassino, in which he endeavours to show that the rules of human knowledge cannot be applied to God. Commenting on the words of the psalmist *Omnia quæcumque voluit fecit*, Damian claims an absolute omnipotence for God. The Almighty has not subjected nature to invariable laws; and if He wished he could bring about that that which happened in the past did not happen. Certainly such an assertion seems to violate the principle of contradiction; but this principle is valid only for our poor human reasoning (*ordo disserendi*) and does not apply to the Majesty of God and sacred knowledge.[2] If it sometimes happens (*quando*) by way of exception that dialectics deals with these theological matters, and particularly of the mysteries of the Divine foreknowledge (*mysteria divinæ virtutis*), it ought not to dominate but rather to consider itself inferior to the dogma in question. The servitude of philosophy is a corollary of its lack of value and its impotence. " Quæ tamen artis humanæ peritia, si quando tractandis sacris eloquiis adhibetur, non debet jus magisterii sibimet arroganter arripere, sed velut ancilla dominæ quodam famulatus obsequio subservire ne si præcedit oberret."[3]

Here we get for the first time this celebrated phrase often misunderstood, which has been quoted as a proof that the whole Middle Ages despised reason. In point of fact it represents the view of a restricted group of theologians who were disowned by the great Scholastics of the thirteenth century.

We find the same opinions in MANEGOLD OF LAUTENBACH (died after 1103). His *Opusculum Manegoldi contra Wolfelmum Coloniensem* endeavours to show that the philosophy of Macrobius, Plato, and the Logic of Aristotle are tissues of errors, irreconcilable with dogma, and dangerous for those who study them. Hence philosophy is a *superfluum*, which ought to rank below theology. But Manegold, like Damian, succumbs to its attractions. By way of exception it is good. He uses it in moral subjects, and especially in political matters, in which it occupies a foremost place (109).

As for OTLOH OF ST. EMMERAM, who lived at Regensburg

---

[1] *De perfectione monachorum*, c. 11, Migne, P. L., Vol. 145, c. 306.
[2] Hæc porro impossibilitas recte quidem dicitur, si ad naturæ referatur nopiam, absit autem ut ad majestatem sit applicanda divinam.—Migne Vol. 145, c. 612.
[3] Migne. *ibid*. c. 603.

(about 1010-1070), and wrote *Dialogus de Tribus Questionibus*, and *Liber de Tentationibus Suis et Scriptis*, the doubts which haunted him and of which he gives a striking account in his *Liber de Tentationibus*, lead him to declare that profane science contains much *superflua*, that its usage ought to be forbidden to monks since the latter have renounced the world in order to devote themselves to divine knowledge (*res divinæ*) ; and that dialectics is inferior to the Scriptures. But he does not condemn dialectics in itself, and he himself makes use of certain arguments, which incidentally are as superficial as those of Damian.

78. Third group: The Moderate Theologians.—(i) LANFRANC Born at Pavia about 1910, first a Jurist at Bologna, then a wandering dialectician, Lanfranc travelled through France from one school to another. Later he retired to the Abbey of Bec, which acquired a great reputation under his direction (*magnum et famosum litteraturæ gymnasium*),[1] then became Archbishop of Canterbury (1070 up to his death in 1089). With Lanfranc a new notion makes its appearance : The liberal arts and philosophy are good in themselves ; their abusive employment in theology is alone reprehensible (*non artem disputandi vituperat, sed perversum dispulanlium usum*).[2] Lanfranc makes use of philosophical reasoning, but he never[3] gives it a value above that of the Scriptures. Since he recognizes the respective rights of philosophy and theology, he admits their distinction.

(ii) ST. ANSELM : Faith and Reason. Anselm, his most celebrated disciple, was like him Abbot of Bec and Archbishop of Canterbury. He goes one step further and sums up the theory of the relations between the two branches of knowledge in formulæ which breathe the spirit of St. Augustine. The first lays down the primacy of faith over reason : "*neque enim quæro intelligere ut credam, sed credo ut intelligam.*"[4] The second establishes that faith is perfected by a rational study, and that *rationes necessariæ* ought to confirm the content of a dogma once the latter has been settled : *negligentia mihi videtur,*

[1] William of Malmesbury, *De gestis Pont. Angl.*, Lib. I., Migne, *P.L.* Vol. 179, c. 1459.
[2] Migne, *P. L.*, Vol. 150, col. 323.
[3] Endres, *Die Dialectiker, etc.*, p. 33.
[4] *Prolog.* 1 ; Migne, Vol. 158, c. 227. The *crede ut intelligas*, then, applies literally only to theology. Domet de Vorges things that this aphorism had in St. Anselm's thought a wider scope, and concerned the dispositions required in anyone who wishes to arrive at the truth : " To believe in the true is a necessary disposition in order to discover it," *op. cit.*, p. 135. This is going too far.

si postquam confirmati sumus in fide, non studemus, quod credidimus, intelligere.[1] But if a Christian does not succeed in understanding a point of doctrine, he must still believe it, because of the primacy of faith.[2]

Such are the Anselmian principles. We see that they concern the believer and not the philosopher, and that the method to which they led in the following century in the schools of Abelard, Gilbert de la Porrée, and Hugh of St. Victor, belongs to theology and not to philosophy (Ch. VII, § 1).

Passing on to the application of his principles, Anselm undertakes the rational justification of certain doctrines such as the Trinity and the Redemption by Christ. Perhaps he goes beyond the rules he himself laid down.[3]

79. Canon and Civil Law.—With the eleventh century we get the first collections of canon law: Burchard of Worms, Deusdedit, Yves of Chartres († 1117) were the first represent-atives of the Rhenish, Gregorian (Gregory VII) and French groups. These early condifications were primarily practical in character, and inspired by the political and religious situ-ation. Thus the questions of the Pontifical supremacy and of the value of the sacraments conferred by schismatics were intro-duced by the canonists of the Gregorian group, and Yves of Chartres dealt with the Berengarian controversy. Theologians made great use of these condifications, and took from thence many literary and patristic quotations. But with the *Decretum* and the *Polycarpus* of Yves of Chartres unitive tendencies made their appearance, and canonists as well as theologians began to undertake the delicate task of harmonizing contra-dictory texts of the Fathers or of the *authentici doctores*. While Isidore of Seville sided with the earliest authority in a case of disagreement, the preface of the *Decretum* of Yves of Chartres distinguishes between what is obligatory and what is optional, strict justice and mere equity, precept and counsel. The question of harmony entered upon a new phase when Abelard introduced the principles of philosophical order into canon law. We shall indicate later on the progress accomplished by Civil, Roman and Feudal law from the middle of the eleventh century

[1] *Cur Deus Homo*, c. 2, Migne, Vol. 158, c. 362.
[2] Christianus per fidem debet ad intellectum proficere, non per intellectum fidem accedere, aut si intelligere non valet, a fide recedere (*ibid.*, c. 1192).
[3] " He unconsciously approximates to rationalism without falling into it." Heitz, *Essai historique sur les rapports entre la philosophie et la foi de Béranger Tours à Thomas d'Aquin* (Paris, 1900), p. 63. Grabmann (*op. cit.*, I, p. 265 *seq.*) does not allow this suggestion of rationalism.

onwards, and the influence which they exercised upon philosophy.

80. Bibliography.—The literature of the controversy on
predestination was collected by Gilbert Mauguin in 1650
(2 vols. in 4to). The works of Lanfranc are found in Migne,
P. L., Vol. 150. The authorship of the *Elucidarium sive
dialogus de summa totius christianæ theologiæ* is doubtful.

Endres, *Lanfranc's Verhaltniss zur Dialektik* (*Der Katholik*,
1902, pp. 215-231), good, corrects the erroneous view that
Lanfranc was hostile to speculation ; W. Burger, *Rhabanus
Maurus, der Begrunder d. theolog. Studien in Deutschland* (*ibid.*,
pp. 51 and 122). On Hincmar see : Schrors, *Hincmar, Erzbischof
von Reims* (Freiburg, 1884) ; Manitius, *op. cit.*. On Berengarius
see : Schnitzer, *Berengar von Tours, sein Leben u. seine Lehre*,
Grabmann, *op. cit.*, 218-224 ; Vernet, *Bérenger de Tours*
(Vacant, *Diction. Théol. Cathol.*, fasc. XII, p. 729) ; Picavet
*Les discussions sur la liberté au temps de Gottschalc, de Rhaban
Maur, d'Hincmar et de J. Scot* (Paris, 1876) ; Gabriel Brunhes
*La foi chrétienne et la philosophie au temps de la renaissanc
carolingienne*, 1903, good ; Endres, *Die Dialektiker und ihr
Gegner in XI. Jahrh.* (*Philos. Jahrb.*, 1906). On Otloh see
Dümller, *Ueber d. Monch Otloh v. Emmeram* (Sitz. d. k. p
Akad. Wiss. Berlin, 1895, II, p. 1070) ; Endres, *Otloh's von St
Emmeram Verhaltniss zu den freien Kunsten* (*Philos. Jahrb
1904*, pp. 44-72), also 1906, H. 1 ; *Petrus Damiani, etc., BGPM*
VIII, 3, well done, and *Forschungen*, etc., *ibid.* XVII, 2, 3
Manegold von Lautenbach (*Hist. polit. Blatter*, 1901, pp. 12
389, 486) ; Grabmann, *op. cit.*, pp. 178-246. General accoun
in De Ghellinck, *Dialectique et dogme aux X-XIIe s.* (*BGPM*
Suppl. 1913, p. 79-100), and especially *Le mouvement théologiq
du XIIe s.* (Paris, 1914), excellent.   For John Scotus Eriuger
and St. Anselm see Nos. **54** and **62**.   Cf. Gilson, *Etudes*, etc
Ch. i., and Koyré, *op. cit.*, ch. I, VI ; C. Webb, *Studies N
Theology*.   For condemned propositions see Denzinger, *Enchir
dion Symbolorum et Definitionum* (Herder, 1921).

CHAPTER V

Scholasticism in the Twelfth Century

§ 1—*Exaggerated Realism (First Half of Twelfth Century).*

The first half of the twelfth century witnessed a revival of Exaggerated Realism, which attributed universality to the objects of our specific and generic concepts, without, however, subscribing to the monistic view of being or substance. These realist theories may be classed in two groups : (i) The theory of William of Champeaux; (ii) the realism of the School of Chartres.

81. William of Champeaux was born in 1070 and died as Bishop of Châlons in 1120. During his youth he followed the lectures of Manegold of Lautenbach and Anselm of Laon. In 1103 he held a chair in the cathedral school of Paris, and there opposed the teaching of Roscelin, under whom he had studied at Compiègne. He himself was in turn bitterly attacked by one of his own pupils, Peter Abelard.

The principal sources of information concerning the teaching of William of Champeaux are the works of Abelard, and the *De Generibus et Speciebus*. His dialectical treatises are lost. He also wrote a book of *Sentences*, extracts of which have been published[1]. According to Abelard and the work *De Generibus*, William of Champeaux changed his opinions from time to time, and successively held the following views :

(i) *The " Identity " Theory.* The universal essence of substance is unique and identical in all its subordinate members ; its whole reality is contained in each of them ; the individual is merely an accidental modification of the specific substance, and the species an accident of the generic essence.[2]

[1] G. Lefèvre, *Les variations de Guillaume de Champeaux et la question des universaux, Etude suivie de documents originaux* (Lille, 1898).
[2] Erat autem (Willelmus) in ea sententia de communitate universalium, ut eamdem essentialiter rem totam simul singulis suis inesse adstrueret individuis : quorum quidem nulla esset in essentia diversitas, sed sola multitudine accidentium varietas.—*Abelardi opera*, Amboise's edition, p. 5. We find the same formula in the *De Generibus et Speciebus*, published by Cousin in his *Ouvr. edit. d'Abélard*, p. 513.

149

Abelard found it a simple matter to ridicule this doctrine : if each man is the whole human species, then the latter is whole and entire in Socrates at Rome, and in Plato at Athens. Consequently, Socrates is present wherever the human essence is found ; at the same moment he is in Rome and in Athens, which is evidently absurd.[1]   The satires of Abelard drove William from the school of Notre Dame in 1108, and he retired to the Abbey of St. Victor, where he opened a new school and changed his theory.

(ii) *The "Indifference" Theory*.   " Sic autem istam tunc suam correxit sententiam ut deinceps rem eamdem non essen-tialiter, sed indifferenter diceret."[2] William, then, had given in to the arguments of his opponents, and had forsaken Exag-gerated Realism, for here he subscribes to the "Indifference" theory, one destined to have great success (**90**).   Abelard adds that William was beaten again in his new position, and finally gave up the fight,[3] but here we must make allowances for the well-known boastfulness of Abelard.   William's Sentences certainly contain a third formula, but this is, like the "Indif-ference" theory, anti-Realist in character, and as a matter of fact merely completes the former view.

(iii) *Theory of the similitude of essences*.   These are really multiplied in individuals, although similar in each of them. Roscelin and Abelard themselves speak in the same way.[5]

[1] *De Gener. et Speciebus*, p. 514. We come across the same refutation of the " elegant inexactitudes " (*pulchra mentientes*) of realism in an anonymous work on genera and species published by Haureau (*Not. et extr. de qqes man lat.*, V, 306) : " Sed quotiescumque homo qui est in Socrate agit vel patitur et homo quo est in Platone agit vel patitur, cum sit eadem essentia, et si (Platone) agente aliquid, agit Socrates et quælibet alia substantia, et flagellat Socrate flagellatur quælibet alia substantia, quod est inconveniens et etiam hæresis " (No. 17813, *Bibl. Nat.* fol. 16).

[2] Cousin, *op. cit.*, p. 6. In this text Haureau reads *individualiter* instead of *indifferenter* (*Not. et extr. de qqs. man. lat.*, V, 324, and *Hist. phil. sco* I, 338). In this case William of Champeaux would not be an upholder of the " Indifference " Theory.   But we prefer with Cousin to read *indifferenter* for what possible meaning can be attached to the formula as given by Haureau " the same reality existing according to its individuality in all individuals *ut eamden individualiter rem totam simul singulis suis inesse adstrueret* " ?

[3] Cum hanc ille correxisset, immo coactus dimisit sententiam, etc.—Cousin *ibid*.

[4] Ubicumque personæ sunt plures, plures sunt et substantiæ . . . Non es eadem utriusque (scil. Petri et Pauli) humanitas, sed similis, cum sint du homines.—*Guillelmi Campellensis Sententiæ vel Quæstiones XLVII*, Lefèvre edition, p. 24.

[5] This is not the opinion of Lefèvre.   The second and third formulas bein opposed to exaggerated realism, we may say with Dehove (*op. cit.*, n.86, p. 156 that William of Champeaux held successively two doctrines only : exag gerated realism, which he afterwards repudiated in favour of anti-reali formulæ.

82. The School of Chartres.—Founded by Fulbert, the School of Chartres became a stronghold of Platonism and Exaggerated Realism in the twelfth century.[1] But while men like William of Champeaux confined their attentions to one particular aspect of the problem of universals, the teachers of Chartres incorporated it into more comprehensive theories. Although these theories were impregnated with Platonism and neo-Platonism, they were purified from all trace of monism. Bernard of Tours alone went to extremes.

Another remarkable feature of the School of Chartres was that the *trivium* was held in high honour there. Rhetoric and the study of the Latin classics was considered an indispensable preliminary to all culture. Philosophy benefited by this taste for literature, for the philosophical works of the School are full of classical allusions, and are written in a very pure Latin which has won for the best of them an honourable place in the history of mediæval Latin literature. Their language was not merely technical, it was also elegant.

We may add that the *quadrivium* (particularly astronomy and mathematics), and the physiological and medical sciences were likewise closely studied, so that Chartres was a centre of general culture.

About the same time the Cathedral was built and the innumerable statues which ornament the edifice were carved in the workshops of the town. The liberal arts occupy their own place in the Virgin's Porch.

83. Bernard of Chartres (not to be confused with Bernard of Tours (*Silvestris*) or with Bernard of Moćlan[2] was the first of an interesting line of masters at Chartres. He was teaching prior to 1117, and in that year had Gilbert de la Porrée among his hearers. Later on (before 1120) William of Conches and Richard the Bishop attended his lectures. Bernard became Chancellor of the Church of Chartres in 1119 and died before 1130. He left a treatise *De Expositione Porphyrii*. John of Salisbury, who calls him *perfectissimus inter Platonicos sæculi nostri*[3] has in addition preserved for us some fragments of other works which are lost. Bernard is the metaphysician of the group.

There are three kinds of beings : God, the supreme and

---

[1] There were also anti-realists at Chartres. See Clerval, *op. cit.*, p. 266, also later on, under *Gilbert de la Porrée*.
[2] *Ibid.*, pp. 158 *et seq.*
[3] *Metalog.*, IV, 35, in Migne. *P. L.*, Vol. 199, c. 938.

eternal reality ; matter, derived from nothingness by the creative act of God, and forming by its union with the Ideas the world of sense ; and the Ideas or prototypic forms by which the world of existences and possibilities is present to the Infinite intelligence from all eternity. How are these three principles related to each other in the mind of this philosopher ? According to John of Salisbury, Bernard taught that God created what he calls the " formæ nativæ " upon the model of these Immutable Ideas. The former are distinct from the latter, as a copy is distinct from the original ; hence all suggestion of pantheism is avoided. These *formæ nativæ* or " reasons " of things, when united to matter form perishable beings.[1] Divine ideas and *formæ nativæ* constitute two aspects of reality (in God and outside God) which Bernard brings together in a synthetic view. The *formæ nativæ* being an imitation of God's ideas, we can see why according to John of Salisbury Bernard intended to harmonize Plato and Aristotle.

After the general metaphysical framework, we must examine more closely Bernard's conception of the constitution of perishable beings composed of matter and a " native form."

In the first place, these *formæ nativæ* have a universal mode of existence, so much so that the Exaggerated Realism of Bernard is expressed in a way similar to the original Platonism : substantial essences (generic and specific) are endowed with unity and fixity throughout the series of evolutions which correspond to sensible things ; in fact, they alone are corporeal being, and the rest is but a fleeting shadow. Bernard even seems to have extended this doctrine to accidental realities, and he is one of the few who developed the Realist solution in this way.

As for the *materia primordialis* with which the *formæ nativæ* unite, it is an already constituted but chaotic mass (*Timæus*) which undergoes a series of transformations under the influence of these forms. This dynamism, which distorts the Aristotelian theory of hylomorphism (p. 55) constitutes one of the favourite conceptions of the School of Chartres. We find it side by side with this other Platonist thesis : Nature is personified, and constitutes a peculiar kind of organism superior to the individual things which it contains, and hence it has a soul. Numerical

---

[1] Ideas tamen quas post Deum primas essentias, negat in seipsis materiæ admisceri, aut aliquem sortiri motum, sed ex his formæ prodeunt nativæ, scilicet imagines exemplarium.—*ibid.*

relations (Pythagoras) regulate the information of Nature by the world-soul, as well as that of material things by the Ideas.

Bernard of Chartres had numerous disciples,[1] and a still greater number flocked to the lectures of his successors, and especially those of Theodoric, his younger brother, under whom the Schools of Chartres reached the highest point of their development.

84. Theodoric of Chartres.—Thierry, or Theodoric, as he is more usually called, was *magister scholæ* at Chartres in 1121. He taught at Paris in 1140, having John of Salisbury as one of his pupils ; returned to Chartres in 1141, where he succeeded Gilbert de la Porrée as chancellor, and died before 1155. Of his works we have extant the *De sex dierum operibus*, the *Eptateuchon*, and a commentary on the *De inventione rhetorica ad Herenium*.

Theodoric personifies for us the Humanist, Platonist, and scientific tendencies of the School of Chartres. About 1130 he put himself at the head of a campaign against the Cornificians, who wished to reduce the programme of study and proscribed the cultivation of literary form. Hence his designation by John of Salisbury as *artium studiosissimus investigator*.

We have already referred to the progress realised by Theodoric in Logic : his *Eptateuchon*, a manual on the seven liberal arts in use at Chartres, mentions important parts of the *Organon*, and it was probably Theodoric who thus popularised them. He was equally interested in mathematical, natural, and medical science ; he introduced astronomical treatises into Chartres, and in 1144 received from Hermann the Dalmatian the translation which the latter had made of Ptolemy's *Planisphere* from Arabic into Latin. In fact, he was one of the most learned men of his time.

Theodoric soon adopted a metaphysic impregnated with Platonist, neo-Platonist, and Pythagorean doctrines, and of which Exaggerated Realism is simply one feature. God is the supreme Unity, whose existence is proved by means of *probationes arithmeticæ* in the sense that all multiplicity— and therefore the world of creatures—pre-supposes unity. Creation is the production of the multiple within the bosom of

---

[1] John of Salisbury mentions, besides William of Conches, Richard of Coutances, professor at Paris in 1122, and afterwards Bishop of Avranches till his death in 1182. He wrote commentaries on Aristotle, no longer extant.

the One. We do not admit with Haureau and Clerval that Theodoric subscribed to pantheism. His favourite dissertations on the superessence of God, the essential dependence of creatures upon the Creator must be interpreted with care, and we must not be led astray by his use of Pythagorean elements. When he says that God is the eternal, the Supreme One, anterior to duality, and that other things exist by virtue of the Infinite (*divinitas singulis rebus forma essendi est*,)[1] he adds in formal terms that each of these beings which have their origin in God, as " the light is the origin or principle of that which is illumined," possesses an essence which is distinct from God, and is the work of His creative hands.[2] His system is not founded on a radical distinction between essence and existence, as is that of Eckhart in later times.

In Cosmology, Theodoric accepts the ideas of his brother, and establishes their conformity with the Biblical account of creation. The *De sextum dierum operibus* contains definitely Aristotelian ideas in the physics of place, the necessarily circular motion of the heavens, and the presence of an immobile earth in the centre of the world.[3]

John of Salisbury, Hermann the Dalmatian, and Robert of Retines were some of the best known disciples of the Chartrain philosopher.

85. William of Conches.—William of Conches (about 1080-1154) may be linked up with the School of Chartres through his master, Bernard of Chartres (1110-1120), his humanism, his opposition to the Cornificians, his devotion to the physical sciences, and his first philosophical doctrines. After teaching in Paris about 1122, he became tutor to Henry Plantaganet. Besides various notes on the *Timæus* and the *De Consolatione Philosophiæ*,[4] William wrote a treatise *De*

[1] At æternum nihil aliud est quam divinitas ; unitas igitur ipsa divinitas est. At divinitas singulis rebus forma essendi est ; nam, sicut aliquid ex luce lucidum est, vel ex calore calidum, ita singulæ res esse suum ex divinitate sortiuntur. Unde deus totus et essentialiter ubique esse vere perhibetur. Unde vere dicitur : Omne quod est ideo est quia unum est.—Haureau, *Not. et extr.*, I, 63. Baeumker has shown that the latter phrase should read *ideo est.*, and not *in deo est* (*Arch. f. Gesch. d. Phil.*, X, 138, n. 37). This Pythagorean formula is common enough among Theodoric's contemporaries. Thus one of the main arguments for the latter's pantheism falls to the ground.

[2] Sed cum dicimus singulis rebus divinitatem esse formam essendi, non hoc dicimus quod divinitas sit aliqua forma, quæ in materia, habeat consistere—Haureau, *ibid.*

[3] Cf. Aristotle, *Physics*, Book IV ; *De Coelo et Mundo*, Books I and II.

[4] According to Jourdain, (*Excursions*, etc.), William of Conches was regarded as *the* interpreter of the *De Consolatione* up to the fourteenth century. His commentary was plagiarized by Nicholas Trivet (see Second Period).

Philosophia Mundi, often attributed to Venerable Bede or to Honorius of Autun,[1] another entitled *Dragmaticon Philosophiæ*, and a *Summa Moralium Philosophorum*, known under many names and ascribed to a great number of philosophers, generally to Hildebert of Lavardin.[2]

At the commencement of his career, William leaned towards Exaggerated Realism. Led astray by a transposition of Pythagoreanism into theology, he maintained a doctrine which Bernard and Theodoric also seem to have accepted, namely, the identification of the Holy Spirit with the world-soul. He was attacked by William of St. Theodoric, retracted, and gave up metaphysics in order to devote himself to the study of the sciences.

Medical studies occupied the place of honour in the Schools of Chartres.[3] William of Conches familiarized himself with the physiological theories of Galen and Hippocrates through the translations of Constantine the African, and linked them up with the process of sense knowledge. It was Constantine who introduced into the Western Schools the study of the physiological concomitant of knowledge, and indeed he stressed too much the organic side of things, for he came dangerously near to confusing the psychic and physiological aspects of sensation. Adelard of Bath, William of St. Theodoric, William of Hirschau, and many others were influenced thereby, and we shall come across traces of it again in the thirteenth century.

The two great masters of Chartres gave a dynamic explanation of the universe, but William had recourse in cosmology to the atomic hypothesis : the four elements consist of combinations of homogeneous and invisible particles.[4] All the works of nature, including the human body with its highest vital perfections, originate in the plasticity of the atoms : hence the soul is in no sense the constituent form of the body. We need not be surprised to find in William of Conches the

---

[1] Haureau, *Not. et extr. de qqes. man.*, V, 195.

[2] Duhem, *La Physique néo-platon, au moyen âge* (*R. quest. histor.*, 1910, p. 393) questions the existence of a *Magna de Naturis Philosophia*, of which there is no exemplar extant, according to him.

[3] They had there the *De Arte Medica* of the doctor Alexander, the *Isagoge Johannitii*, the *Aphorisms* of Hippocratus, the *De Pulsibus* of Philaretus, the *De Urinis* of Theophilus, the *Theorica* of Constantine the African, and Galen's *Commentaries*.—Clerval, *op. cit.*, p. 240.

[4] Elementa sunt simplæ et minimæ particulæ, quibus hæc quatuor constant quæ videmus. Hæc elementa nunquam videntur, sed ratione divisionis intelliguntur (*Elementa philos.*, I, Migne, Vol. 90, col. 1132).

doctrine of the world-soul—this co-exists in every man with his own soul.

The *Summa Moralium Philosophorum* of William of Conches is one of the few moral treatises of the early Middle Ages. It is a collection of precepts, devoid of originality, and borrowed principally from Seneca (*De Beneficiis*) and Cicero (*De Officiis*). Following their example, the author devotes his attention to questions of detail, such as the distinction between that which is useful and that which is upright, and the minute description of virtues. We must not expect to find therein the economy of the scholastic moral system, and in particular the last end and the essence of morality are not dealt with. The scientific study of moral philosophy was not developed fully until the thirteenth century.

86. Bibliography.—Fragments of William of Champeaux in Migne (Vol. 163), and Lefèvre, *Les variations de G. de Champeaux et la question des universaux* (Lille, 1898), good ; Michaud, *G. de Ch. et les écoles de Paris au XIIe s.* (Paris, 1867) ; H. Dehove, *Qui præcipui fuerint labente XIIe s. ante introductam arabum philosophiam temperati realismi antecessores* (Lille, 1908), good and clear ; Hurtault, *Théologie de G. de Champeaux* (*R. sc. ecclésiast. et sc. cath.*, 1908 and 1909) ; Adlhoch, *War Wilhelm von Champeaux Ultrarealist?* (*Philos. Jarhb.*, 1909) ; Picavet, *Note sur l'enseignement de G. de Champeaux d'après l'Historia Calamitatum d'Abelard* (*R. intern. enseign.*, Oct. 1910), contains nothing new. Fragments of Bernard of Chartres in John of Salisbury (Migne, Vol. 199, col. 666 and 938) ; E. Gilson, *Le platonisme de Bernard de Ch.* (*R. Néo.-Scol.*, 1923, p. 1-19). For Theodoric's *De sex dierum operibus* see Haureau (*Not. extr. ms.*, Vol. 32, pp. 2 and 167) ; P. Thomas, *Melanges*, 1884, gives extracts from the commentary on the *De inventione rhetorica*. William of Conches : the *De philosophia mundi*, Migne, Vol. 172, col. 39 ; *Dragmaticon*, Vol. 90, under the title *Elementorum philosophiæ*, 1, IV ; fragments of the notes and commentaries in Cousin, *Ouvr. inédits d'Abélard*, p. 669 ; Jourdain, *Not. et extr.*, etc., Vol. 20, p. 2. Article by Baeumker in *Wetzer u. Weltes Kirchenlexicon*, II, 1885. On the School of Chartres, see the important work of Clerval mentioned above. Werner, *Die Kosmologie u. Naturlehre d. scholast. Mittelalters mit specieller Beziehung auf Wilhelm von Conches* (Sitzungsb. K. Akad. Wiss. Philos. Kl. Wien, 1873, Bd. 75, p. 309, good references, and well done. Steinschneider, *Constantinus*

Africanus und seine arabischen Quellen (*Arch. f. pathol. Anatomie u. Physiol.*, Bd. 37, p. 315), a study of his writings. Reiners, *op. cit.*, Duhem, *op. cit.*

§ 2—*The opponents of exaggerated realism.*

87. The anti-Realist formulæ.—Under this heading we group together numerous solutions which carried on the war against Exaggerated Realism. Faithful to the mind of Boethius, they start out with the thesis that genera and species are nothing but the individual being regarded from different points of view. We shall see that these solutions are so many steps towards moderate Realism. They were known to John of Salisbury, and are also found in a series of recently published manuscripts. All consist of :

(i) Anti-Realist declarations to the effect that reality exists only as individuals, and that in consequence, as Boethius says, the ideas of humanity, life, and reason do not refer to universal realities, but to the individual substance, e.g., *this* man, looked at from different points of view.

(ii) The theory that all men are *unum et idem*, but this *unum* is a product of thought.

To this group of anti-Realist solutions at the first half of the twelfth century belong the doctrines of Adelard of Bath and of Walter of Mortagne, i.e., indifferentism, and the theory of the *collectio*.

88. Adelard of Bath and the theory of the " respectus."— Adelard of Bath, professor at Paris and at Laon, was one of the first to complete his scientific education by a voyage to Greece and to Spain. The *Quæstiones Naturales* resulted from this contact with a new world.[1] In addition to a translation of Euclid made from the Arabic in 1116, an *Astrolabe* dedicated to Henry Plantaganet,[2] and mathematical works, Adelard left a work *De eodem et diverso*, written in 1105-06, and dedicated to Bishop William of Syracuse. It consists of a dialogue between Philosophy (the unchangeable, *de eodem*), and Philocosmy (changeable knowledge, *de diverso*), full of Platonism as found in early sources (Chalcidius, Augustine, Boethius), and especially in the contemporary productions of the School of Chartres.[3]

[1] In the prologue, he praises the *Gallicarum sententiarum constantia* and the *Gallica studia*. See De Wulf, *Philosophy and Civilization*, p. 41.
[2] Ch. Haskins, in *English Historical Review*, July, 1913.
[3] The treatise contains a description of the liberal arts, and it is evident from what Adelard says concerning dialectics, that he knew all the parts of the Organon.—Willner, *op. cit.*, p. 97.

The *De eodem et diverso* opposes Exaggerated Realism: the same concrete being is genus, species and individual all at once, but according to different aspects (*respectus*).[1] Genus and species are ways of regarding the individual; they are the terminus of a more profound intuition, *altius intuentes, acutius considerata*.[2] Hence, the unity of the generic element in different individuals belongs to the conceptual and not to the real order, and the theory of the *respectus* is a stage in the development of anti-Realism. Adelard does not examine the question further. The logical point of view is uppermost in the work, and this leads to difficulties in the interpretation of the text.[3]

Adelard was more than an opponent of Exaggerated Realism. The *De eodem et diverso* and the *Quæstiones naturales* reveal him as a psychologist and a man of science, cultivating observation and experience. His psychology is inspired by Platonism and Augustinism. Intellectual knowledge, which is the only source of certitude is innate, and the senses do not exert any causal influence upon its production. The immaterial soul created by God is a substance independent of the body, to which it is violently united. The faculties are identical with the soul. From Constantine the African Adelard adopted a theory concerning the localization of the functions of the soul, and various physiological ideas coming from Galen and Hippocrates. His cosmology, like that of William of Conches, consists of an atomism resembling that of Democritus; he stresses the Pythagorean idea of unity and harmony, and looks upon the universe as one great organism.

89. Walter of Mortagne and the theory of the " status."—Born at Mortagne in Flanders, Walter[4] was educated in the school of Tournai. From 1126 to 1144 he taught rhetoric and philosophy at Ste. Geneviève (Paris), and died as Bishop of Laon in 1174. Of his works we possess a *Tractatus de Sancta Trinitate*, and six *opuscula* of little philosophical interest. Walter adopts the Platonist attitude in a letter to Abelard, and regards the

---

[1] Si res consideres, eidem essentiæ et generis et speciei et individui nomina imposita sunt, sed respectu diverso.—*ibid.* p. 11.

[2] Eosdem autem acutius intuentes videlicet non secundum quod sensualiter diversi sunt, sed in eo quod notantur ab hoc voce " homo " speciem vocaverunt —p. 11. Quoniam igitur illud idem quod vides, et genus et species et individuum sit, merito ea Aristoteles non nisi in sensibilibus esse proposuit. Sunt enim ipsa sensibilis, quamvis acutius considerata.—p. 12.

[3] Willner, following upon Haureau (*Notices et extraits qqes ms. lat.*, V, pp. 293-296) publishes in an appendix an anonymous commentary on the *Isagoge* written from the same point of view as the *De eodem et diverso*.

[4] Cf. De Wulf, *Histoire de la Philosophie en Belgique* (2nd edit., 1910) p. 34.

body as an obstacle to the exercise of the higher faculties of the soul.

It is through John of Salisbury that we know the formula of the *status* defended by Walter of Mortagne[1]. According to different states (*status*), Plato is an individual (Plato), a species (man), and subaltern *or supreme* genus (animal, substance). The text of John of Salisbury is laconic, and gives rise to exegetical difficulties.[2] It seems to us that the *status* of Walter of Mortagne is simply another way of describing the *respectus* of Adelard of Bath, for both express themselves in similar terms when treating of the real identity of the individual, genus, and species.[3]

According to a hypothesis of Haureau, Walter would be the author of a text contained in No. 17813 of the Latin Section of the *Bibliothèque Nationale*,[4] in which we come across a new formula : indifferentism.

90. Indifferentism.—Besides the document just mentioned, we possess an account and a refutation of indifferentism in the *De generibus et speciebus*, in which we find the expression : *Sententia de indifferentia.*[5] Every existing thing is an individual, but in every individual there are determinations which belong to it alone and which differentiate it from all others (*differens*), and also specific and generic realities which are found without any difference (*indifferentes*) in the other individuals of the species and genus. In so far as they are endowed with life and reason, men form an *unum et idem*.[6] Although the text does

---

[1] *Metalog.* II, 17 : Eorum vero *qui rebus inhærent* (the Realists), multæ sunt et diversæ opiniones, siquidem hic, *ideo quod omne quod est, unum numero est* (Migne wrongly gives : *omne quod unum est, numero est*) aut rem universalem, aut unam numero esse, aut omnino non esse concludit . . . Partiuntur itaque status duce Gautero de Mauritania, et Platonem, in eo quod Plato est, dicunt individuum ; in eo quod homo, speciem ; in eo quod animal, genus, sed subalternum, in eo quod substantia, generalissimum.—Migne, *P. L.*, Vol. 199, pp. 874 and 875.

[2] John of Salisbury mentions yet another theory of the *status*.

[3] This text of the *Polycraticus*, VII, 12 (Webb's edition, I, 14), attributes a conceptual function to the *status*, and affirms the existence of individuals alone : Inde est quod sensibilibus aliisque singularibus apprehensis *quoniam hæc sola veraciter esse dicuntur*, ea in diversos status subvehit, pro quorum *ratione* in ipsis singularibus specialissima generalissimaque constituit.

[4] *Not. ex extr. qques man. latins*, V, 313 *et seq.*

[5] The theory is also referred to in the *Glossulæ super Porphyrium* of Abelard (Cousin's edition, pp. 552 *et seq.*)

[6] Sed simpliciter attendatur Socrates, non ut Socrates, id est in omni proprietate Socratis, sed in quadam, scilicet in eo quod est animal rationale mortale, jam secundum hunc statum est differens et indifferens : *differens* a qualibet alia re existente hoc modo quod, ipse Socrates nec secundum statum hominis, nec secundum aliquem alium, est essentialiter aliquod aliorum ; item *indifferens* est, id est consimilis cum quibusdam, scilicet cum Platone et cum aliis individuis hominis in eo quod in unoquoque eorum est animal

not state the nature of this unity which is found in Socrates and the rest of men, it can only be a product of thought, for nothing exists outside the individual, *nihil omnino est præter individuum*.[1] Indifferentism is an anti-Realist formula.

91. The theory of the " collectio."—The same applies to the theory of the *collectio*, defended by the author of the *De generibus et speciebus* after expounding and refuting successively the theories of identity, indifferentism, and that of the *voces* (Roscelin). Every essence exists in the individual state. We call species the collection (*collectio*) of beings possessing this same essence, the unity thus attributed being based on the similarity of nature belonging to each one.[2] In other words, while the preceding formulæ approach the question from the point of view of comprehension, the formula of the *collectio* looks at the species from the point of view of its extension. But why restrict the collection to the beings existing at a given moment ? Why not include the possible beings ? From his peculiar way of regarding the *collectio* the author derives certain consequences from the point of view of logical predication, but this does not prevent him from subscribing to the fundamental theses of anti-Realism.[3]

John of Salisbury attributes to Jocelin of Soissons a theory of the *collectio* which agrees fairly well with the account in the treatise *De generibus et speciebus* : " Est et alius qui, cum Gausleno Suessionensi episcopo, universalitatem rebus in unum collectis attribuit, et singulis eamdem denuit."[4]

92.   Conclusion.—Whatever the term employed—whether it be the *respectus* of Adelard of Bath, the *status* of Walter of Mortagne, the *non differens* of the indifferentists, or the *collectio* of Jocelin of Soissons—all these theories are rejections of Exaggerated Realism, and constitute so many steps to-

---

rationale mortale. Et attende quod Socrates et unumquodque individuum hominis, in eo quod unumquodque est animal rationale mortale sunt *unum et idem* . . .—Haureau, *op. cit.*, V, 313 (Paris, 1892).

[1] *De gen. et spec.*, Cousin's edition, p. 518.

[2] " Et sicut Socratitas quæ formaliter constituit Socratem, nusquam est extra Socratem, sic illa hominis essentia quæ Socratitatem sustinet in Socrate, nusquam est nisi in Socrate. Speciem igitur dico esse non illam essentiam hominis solum quæ est in Socrate, vel quæ est in aliquo alio individuorum, sed totam illam collectionem ex singulis aliis hujus naturæ conjunctam," pp. 524 and 525. "Neque enim diversum judicaverunt unam essentiam illius concollectionis a tota collectione, sed idem, non quod hoc esset illud, sed quia similis creationis in materia et forma hoc erat cum illo."—p. 526.

[3] We cannot agree with Reiners, who considers this theory a form of realism grosser than indifferentism.—Reiners, *Der aristotelische Realismus*, etc., 1907 p. 34.

[4] *Metal.*, II., 17.

wards the definitive solution.[1] The decisive step was taken by Abelard.

93. Bibliography.—John of Salisbury, *Metalogicus*, II, 17. The *Quæstiones naturales* of Adelard of Bath are among the Munich *incunabula*, the *De eodem et diverso* is edited by Willner (*BGPM*, IV. 1, Munster, 1903), with a good study. The *Tractatus de S. Trinitate* of Walter of Mortagne is in Pez, *Thssaurus anecd. nov.*, II, 2, the letter in d'Achery, *Spicileg.* III (1723). The *De generibus et speciebus* is in Cousin's edition of unpublished works of Abelard. Reiners, *op. cit.*, p. 173, interesting and well done, but exaggerates the differences between the various Realist systems. Dehove, *op. cit.*

§ 3—*Abelard and Gilbert de la Porrée.*

94. Peter Abelard, born at Le Pallet in 1079 of a military family, may be called the champion in the field of dialectics. From the School of Roscelin he passed to that of William of Champeaux. He taught dialectics in turn at Melun, Corbeil, and at Paris, where he quarrelled with his old master. He occupied chairs at the School of Notre Dame and at Mont St. Genèvieve. He was initiated in theology by Anselm of Laon, and later on (1113) he himself taught the sacred science in the French metropolis, but allowed his head to be turned by the praises of his enthusiastic hearers. He was obliged to leave Paris in consequence of his romantic relations with Heloise, and he retired to the cloister. Later on he again took up teaching in his retreat at Le Paraclet. After his condemnation in 1121 he became Abbot of another monastery, then returned to Le Paraclet, and, from 1136 to 1140, yielded to the attractions of the School of St. Genèvieve at Paris, where he once more became famous. After a fresh condemnation in 1141, he retired to Cluny, where he was welcomed by Peter the Venerable, and died in 1142 at the Cluniac priory of St. Marcel-les-Châlons.

Abelard's writings are numerous. In theology : *De Unitate et Trinitate Divina* (about 1120, condemned in 1121) ; *Sic et Non ; Theologia Christiana* (1123-24) in which he defends

---

[1] John of Salisbury also mentions an author who replaced *status* by *maneries rerum*—*Metal.* II, 17. (Migne wrongly has *materies rerum*), and the English writer looks upon this as an ultra-realist solution. After referring to this theory, he concludes : Longum erit, et a proposito penitus alienum, si singulorum opiniones posuero, vel errores ; ut, cum, ut verbo comici utar : Fere quot homines, tot sententiæ.—II, 18.

himself against his condemnation, and especially his *Theologia*, of which we possess the first part under the title *Introductio ad Theologiam*. In Philosophy : *Scito Te Ipsum seu Ethica ; Dialogus inter Philosophum, Judæum et Christianum*, the *Glossulæ super Porphyrium*[1] in two parts, which together with the *Dialectica* edited in part by Cousin form the three divisions of his dialectics. Here we are concerned only with Abelard the philosopher ; as theologian he will be considered elsewhere.

Abelard's temperament was that of a feudal knight, excelling both in defects and qualities. His *Historia Calamitatum* (1133-36) and his letters to Heloise, to which he partly owes his fame, are some of the few autobiographical writings of the time, and manifest the sentimentality of their author. He is boastful and bitter in his criticisms of his contemporaries, and his judgments must be received with reserve. On the other hand, his is a mind of a strength not very common in philosophy and theology.

95. His Philosophy.—(i) The problem of universals and " nominalism." Abelard's reputation has gained much by Geyer's recent publication of his works. To him belongs the honour of having considered the problem of universals under all its aspects (metaphysical, logical, psychological and epistemological), and of having gathered together the solutions into one whole, to which the centuries which followed could add nothing.

First of all he criticises the exclusivism of Roscelin, and deals the death-blow to Exaggerated Realism by ridiculing William of Champeaux. Then after demolishing he builds up, and makes use of the theses enunciated before his time by other opponents of realism, namely :

(*a*) The individual being is alone capable of existence ; the existing substance is individual, it is *this* man, *this* horse.[2]

(*b*) Human language consists of conventional words general in form : *nativitas sermonum vel vocum hominum institutio* (Roscelin). He adds :

(*c*) The word (*vox*) stands for an abstract and general idea, and hence it is a *nomen* or *sermo*, i.e., conforming to the ter-

---

[1] The *Glossulæ super Porphyrium* discovered by Ravaisson and summarized by Remusat (*Abélard*, Paris, 1845, Vol. II, p. 93) were lost. Geyer has found them in two forms at Lunel, and Grabmann has found another manuscript at Milan very similar to that of Lunel. Geyer has published definitive texts in *BGPM*, XXXI, 1. He compares the tripartite division of Dialectics with that of Theology which also comprises three works.

[2] Singuli homines discreti ab invicem, cum in propriis differant tam essentiis quam formis.—Ed. Geyer, p. 19.

minology of Boethius, it is speech related to a signified content, a reality which is thought of : *nomen est vox significativa*.

(*d*) This *nomen* has a logical function : it is capable of being predicated of many subjects in a judgment, *natum prædicari de pluribus*. The unity of the logical order which belongs to the name " man " when we say " Peter is a man, and Paul is also "—only affects the predicate in the judgment. So that from this point of view the universal *nomen* is not a *res*. For a *res*, being an individual substance, can only be predicated of one subject, *rem de re prædicari monstrum ducunt*.[1]

So far Abelard has considered only the logical function of the universal. It is in this sense that John of Salisbury attributes to him the theory of the *sermones*,[2] and that on two occasions he compares his theory to that of Roscelin. It is likewise in this sense that he calls him the founder of the *nominalis secta*. Following the English historian we can describe as " nominalism " or " twelfth century nominalism " the position, principally in logic, which adopts the various theories just quoted, but it must be borne in mind that nominalism thus understood is quite different from the nominalism of the fourteenth century, and still more from modern nominalism. In point of fact, Abelard's nominalism really belongs to Aristotelian or Moderate Realism, which the Middle Ages found once again, thanks to him.

This is the way in which the philosopher sets out the real problem : does the *nomen*, the idea " man " for instance, attain to something similar in each man, *quod pluribus commune est rebus* ? That is the great question, *quam rem in ipsam intelligam quæro*. Abelard answers by a psychological and a criteriological theory.

(*d*) Although each human individual is one substance

---

[1] See following note.

[2] Shortly after the text concerning Roscelin, the *Metalogicus* adds : Alius sermones intuetur et ad illos detorquet quidquid alicubi de universalibus meminit scriptum. In hac opinione deprehensus est peripateticus palatinus Abælardus noster qui multos reliquit, et adhuc quidem aliquos habet professionis hujus sectatores et testes. Amici mei sunt, licet ita plerumque captivatam detorqueant litteram, ut vel durior animus, miseratione illius movetur. Rem de re prædicari monstrum ducunt, licet Aristoteles monstruositatis hujus auctor sit.'—II, 17, Migne, *P. L.*, Vol. 199, p. 874. Again, after the text concerning Roscelin quoted above, p. 000, the *Polycraticus* says : Sunt tamen adhuc qui deprehenduntur in vestigiis eorum (i.e., of those who look upon universals as *voces*) licet erubescant auctorem vel sententiis profiteri, solis nominibus inherentes, quod rebus et intellectibus substrahunt sermonibus asscribunt,—VII, 12 (Webb's edition, I, 142). Remusat, *op. cit.*, II, 104, gives an epitaph on Abelard which says : *et genus et species sermones esse notavit*.

independent of every other, I grasp something which is similar in all men, namely, the *natura rei*.[1] This content of thought leaves aside the individualising envelope which clothes every element of reality outside the mind, and it is this characteristic stripping off by the mind which constitutes the abstractive process. Genera and species are therefore immanent in individuals, and conversely, the *natura rei* is reflected in the terms which are combined by logic.[2]

(e) A concept of this kind is faithful, though inadequate ; for there is nothing in my idea of man which does not as a matter of fact belong to every man, although I do not and cannot grasp the complete reality of which each man is constituted : *nihil nisi quod in ea est intelligo, sed non omnia quæ habet attendo.* If I were to deny the existence in the individualized state (*status*) of any element of reality which I conceive, then my concept would be erroneous, *cassus*. But this is not the case, *non est ita*. My mind operates *divisim*, but does not affirm the *divisa*.[3] The thing could not be better expressed, and Abelard is justified in concluding that the triple question of Porphyry is easy to answer (*facile*).[4] It is not surprising that John of Salisbury, a partisan of the Aristotelian solutions, referred to Abelard and his followers as his friends, *amici mei sunt*.

(ii) The widening out of the problem of universals led Abelard to consider the question of ideology. He developed two important scholastic theses in great detail :

[1] Cum autem rerum natura percepta fuerit, vocum significatio secundum rerum proprietates distinguenda est.—*Ouvr. inédits*, p. 351.

[2] Neque enim substantia specierum diversa est ab essentia individuorum, nec res ita sicut vocabula diversas esse contingit . . . Cum videlicet nec ipsæ, species habeant nisi per individua subsistere, etc."—*Dialect.*, in *Ouvr. inédits*, p. 204. Cf. : nunquam etenim genus nisi per aliquam speciem suam esse contingit.—*Abelardi opera*, II, 98.

[3] " Nunc . . . diligenter perquiramus, scilicet quæ sit illa communia causa secundum quam universale nomen impositum est . . ." (p. 19). " Intellectus scilicet universalium fieri per abstractionem et quomodo eos solos, nudos, puros, nec tamen cassos appellamus, definiendum est " (p. 24). One might think that abstraction deforms reality : " hujusmodi autem intellectus per abstractionem inde forsitan falsi vel vani videbantur, quod rem aliter quam subsistat, percipiant . . . rem aliter quam sit, videntur concipere atque ideo cassi esse. Sed non est ita. Si quis enim hoc modo aliter quam se habeat res intelligat . . . iste profecto cassus est intellectus." He replies by this decisive text : " Sed hoc quidem non fit in abstractione. Cum enim hunc hominem tantum attendo in natura substantiæ vel corporis, non etiam animalis vel hominis vel grammatici, *profecto nihil nisi quod in ea est, intelligo, sed non omnia quæ habet attendo* . . . Aliter tamen quodam modo quam sit dicitur intelligi, non alio quidem statu quam sit . . . sed in eo aliter quod alius est modus intelligendi quam subsistendi. Separatim namque hæc res ab alia non separata intelligitur . . . Intellectus per abstractionem divisim attendit non divisa, alioquin cassus esset.—p. 25-6.

[4] p. 27.

(*a*) Between the sensible and imaginative perception which is confined to the particular and which we possess in common with animals—and the abstractive perception " which perceives the same reality in another way," and which is peculiar to man, there is a difference of nature. Anselm was aware of this doctrine, but he did not develop it.

(*b*) The content of the abstract perception is found in the data of the senses,[1] just as in a picture the design is grasped through the colours.[2]

(iii) Abelard gathered together and handed on the principal theses of pluralistic metaphysics. He believed in the world-soul ; he lent his support to an erroneous theory of matter and form ; he developed at length the thesis concerning the Divine ideas, which he attributed to Plato, but interpreted with St. Augustine as concepts of the Divine Intelligence.[3]

(iv) Abelard was also one of the principal moralists of his time, and he has indeed been called the founder of the moral system of the Middle Ages.[4] His moral doctrines are incorporated into a theological framework, but we see the beginnings of purely rational solutions in the constant endeavour, revealed in the *Scito te ipsum*, to refer all ethical problems to the subjective conscience—a notion which occupies a central place in his doctrine. Intention is more important than the act, and an error in judgment lessens the fault. Studies on sin, grace and freedom count among his favourite subjects, and he looks upon Christian morality as a *reformatio* of natural ethics.

(v) Abelard in expounding his philosophy makes use of a formal scheme which was destined to have a tremendous success. He collects together in his *Dialectica* a great number of texts from profane and sacred authors, with the intention of harmonizing them. The *Sic et Non*—which will be dealt with later on—is an example of the same dialectical method. It goes back to the canonists of the eleventh century,[5] and will be taken up and perfected by the writers of *Summæ* in the twelfth, and the scholastics of the thirteenth centuries.

96. Conclusion.—With Abelard the anti-realist solutions

[1] Intellectus humanus sine imaginatione non haberi.—p. 124-5.
[2] p. 123.
[3] *Introd. ad theolog.*, I, 9 (Migne, Vol. 178, p. 991, A).
[4] Endres, *Gesch. d. mitt. Phil.*, p. 68.
[5] Bernold of Constance († 1100), Deusdedit, Yves of Chartres († 1116)—Grabmann, *op. cit.*, I, 234-246 ; II, 216. The same is found in Adelard of Bath, see Willner, *op. cit.*, p. 40. The *Florileges* of the early Middle Ages (Prosper of Aquitaine, Tajus), were collections of quotations, not classifications of different opinions.

were completed, and Moderate Realism definitely established. The great doctors of the thirteenth century had nothing to add to his formulæ. For the first time, the Aristotelian ideology was clearly enunciated, although Abelard did not know the treatise *De Anima*, and had at his disposition only the texts of Boethius. The theories of the active intellect and the passive understanding which appear in the thirteenth century are merely the logical extension of his doctrine. In solving the apparent difficulties which his theory suggested, Abelard confirmed metaphysical pluralism. He stressed the value of human personality, and it is interesting to note that he found a philosophical basis for the sense of personal dignity which was the animating spirit of the feudal civilization of his time, and which was destined to become, through scholasticism, the soul of modern civilization.[1]

97. Gilbert de la Porree.—The impression produced by Abelard was a profound one. After his time, Alberic was the chief opponent of the school which he had founded.[2] Gilbert de la Porrée (Porretanus) was influenced by him, and upheld his Moderate Realism. Born at Poitiers (1076), Gilbert attended the lectures of Hilary of Poitiers and Anselm of Laon, became a friend of Bernard of Chartres, and himself taught at Chartres for more than twelve years. Later he became a master at Paris (1141), and John of Salisbury, who attended his lectures there, assures us of the great reputation which he enjoyed in the metropolis of letters. In 1142, Gilbert became Bishop of Poitiers and continued to hold this office up to his death in 1154, but he did not give up his professorial functions when he assumed the charges of the episcopate. His most important philosophical works are the *Liber Sex Principiorum*, two commentaries on the supposed Boethian treatises *De Trinitate* and *De Duabus Naturis in Christo*.[3]

Gilbert was greatly influenced by Boethius and his deductive method. He also worked on the new books commentated upon by Theodoric of Chartres. But especially he undertook in the *Liber Sex Principiorum*, to complete the *Categories* of Aristotle. To the four predicaments studied by Aristotle (substance, quantity, quality, relation) and which Gilbert calls

[1] De Wulf, *Philosophy and Civilization*, p. 55.
[2] John of Salisbury writes : Post discessum ejus (Abelard) . . . adhæsi magistro Alberico, qui erat nominalis sectæ acerrimus impugnator.—II, 10, p. 867.
[3] The *De causis* which Berthaud and Clerval attribute to him does not belong to him.

formæ inhærentes, he adds the *formæ adjacentes*, or accidents which characterize the substance in relation to other substances (*actio, passio, ubi, quando, situs, habere*). It is easy to see that the proposed classification will not do, for it is difficult to place relation among the absolute accidents. But it is the endeavour to complete Aristotle which is noteworthy, and it assured the fame of the author. Included in the list of classical manuals (p. 81), the *Liber Sex Principiorum* was commented on by Albert the Great and Robert Kilwardby, was quoted by St. Thomas, and studied right up to the end of the Middle Ages.

Gilbert was a resolute opponent of excessive realism : essences exist only in individuals, and are really multiplied in each one of them.[1] The " native forms" or *subsistentiæ* inherent in sensible things are copies of the Divine ideas, from which they differ essentially : Gilbert adopts the thesis of his master Bernard and thus succeeds in harmonizing his solution of universals with the theory of exemplarism.[2] But what then is the origin and value of universals ? Gilbert replies : the mind compares (*colligit*) the essential determinations (*diversæ subsistentiæ*) realized in various beings, and brings about a mental union of their similar realities : it is this similar or conformable element (*cum-forma*, with the same form) which is called the genus or species.[3] Or again : the genus and species are the collection of beings in which are found these similar realities, although the latter belong properly to each one of them,[4] *quamvis conformes, tamen diversas*.[5] The *ratio* abstracts them, *quodammodo abstrahit, ut earum naturam perspicere et proprietatem comprehendere possit*.[6]

---

[1] Unus enim homo una singulari humanitate . . . ut pluribus humanitatibus plures homines et substantiæ.—In *Bœth. de duab. nat.*, Migne, *P. L.*, Vol. 64, 1378.

[2] Non ideæ sed idearum εἴκονες i.e., imagines.—In *Bœth. de Trinit.*, *ibid.*, 1267.

[3] Universalia quæ intellectus ex particularibus colligit etc.—*ibid.*, 1374.

[4] Genus vero nihil aliud putandum est, nisi subsistentiarum secundum totam earum proprietatem ex rebus secundum species suas differentibus similitudine comparata collectio, etc.—*ibid.*, 1389.

[5] *ibid.*, 1262.

[6] *ibid.*, 1374. Prantl calls him an ontologistic realist (?) (*op. cit.*, II, 221) ; Stöckl a conceptualist (*op. cit.*, I, 227) ; Clerval an exaggerated realist (*op. cit*,. 262). The following is the laconic judgment of John of Salisbury on Gilbert : Universalitatem formis nativis attribuit . . . Est autem forma nativa, originalis exemplum, et quæ non in mente Dei consistit, sed rebus creatis inhæret. Hæc græco eloquio dicitur εἶδος habens se ad ideam ut exemplum ad exemplar ; sensibilis quidem in re sensibili, sed mente concipitur insensibilis, singularis quoque in singularibus, sed in omnibus universalis.—*Metal.*, II, 17. The " in omnibus universalis " must evidently be harmonized with " singularis quoque in singularibus " which leaves no doubt as to Gilbert's anti-realism.

Still, there are weak places in the metaphysics of the Bishop of Poitiers. He distinguishes in an actual being the essential realities which it possesses and which are found similarly in other things (*subsistentia, id quo est*), and individual determination which places the thing in the realm of real existence (*substantia, id quod est*).[1] Indeed, Gilbert tends to exaggerate the distinction between the common and the individualized essence, and he seems to regard the latter as a part really distinct from the former. The same unfortunate tendency leads him to look upon certain transcendental attributes of individuals—such as unity—as proper *subsistentia*, whereas of course they are not really distinct from the being itself.[2] But none of these doctrines contradict Moderate Realism, for these metaphysical elements of a being are endowed not with a universal existence, but with one which is proper to each individual.

When he opposes form to matter, Gilbert makes the former a property of the being, thus perpetuating an erroneous conception peculiar to this period. It is not surprising, in consequence, that he admits a plurality of forms.

Gilbert's mind was not a thorough one ; side by side with doctrines of pure scholasticism, we find illogical features and failings. But even the best philosophers in the middle of the twelfth century were affected by the lack of systemization which is one of the characteristics of scholasticism during this period. We shall see later on that Gilbert's metaphysical doctrines had their repercussion on his theology (Ch. VII).

Among Gilbert's contemporaries who endeavoured to follow in his footsteps, we must mention, besides the anonymous author of the *Liber de Vera Philosophia*, the historian Otto of Freising (1114/15–1158), educated at Paris and Bishop of Freising. His two great works, in which one is pleased to find a philosophy of history, the *Chronicle* and the *Gesta Frederici*, contain in connection with some historical episodes digressions dealing with the Greek philosophers, universals, logic, and the Divine nature.[3] Gilbert's theories concerning native forms, the similitude of the specific essence, and other metaphysical

---

[1] Genera et species, i.e., generales et speciales subsistentiæ, subsistunt tantum, non substant vere.—*ibid.*, 1318.

[2] *ibid.*, 1148. Quod est unum, res est unitati subjecta, cui scilicet vel ipsa unitas inest, ut albo, vel adest ut albedini . . . Ideoque non unitas ipsa sed quod ei subjectum est, unum est. Cf. Prantl, p. 221.

[3] *Chron.*, II ; *Gesta*, I, 5 and 60.

notions are faithfully adhered to.[1] We have already mentioned the rôle of Otto as a propagator of the *Logica nova* in Germany (p. 71).

98. The Verbalists.

—The middle of the twelfth century witnessed a recrudescence of the sophistic logic which since the preceding century had not ceased to develop in the schools as a sort of parasitical movement (p 112.). The putting into circulation of the *logica nova* furnished a new field for subtleties. John of Salisbury wrote in scathing language about these *nugiloquos ventilatores*, word tricksters, who argue for the sake of arguing, and who imagine that dialectics consists of verbosity, *qui sapientiam verba putant.*[2] His *Cornificius* is one of their number.[3] In their school they discuss whether a pig led to market is held by a rope or by the one leading it.[4] Alexander Neckam, who was at Paris about 1180, mentions other arguments of the same kind,[5] and his *De Naturis Rerum* contains a thorough-going attack on these abuses of Logic. The best known of these dialecticians was a certain Adam of Petit-Pont,[6] whose *Ars Dialectica* (1132) was a triumph of sophistry. These sterile discussions, which undiscerning historians have identified with scholasticism, are simply its counterfeit.

99. Appearance of Moderate Realism.

—Abelard marks a turning point in the history of the twelfth century. After his time, Exaggerated Realism declines and disappears; Moderate Realism triumphs and becomes one of the constituent doctrines

---

[1] The texts are collected by Schmidlin, *Die Philos. Otto's v. F.*, p. 321 *et seq.* and given side by side with corresponding texts of Gilbert. Universalem dico on ex eo quod una in pluribus sit, quod est impossibile, sed ex hoc, quod ura in similitudine uniendo ab assimilandi unione universalis, quasi in unum ersalis dicitur.—*Gesta*, I, 53. Quamvis Socrates ct Plato ratione partiendi a numerum veniant, ut duo dicantur homines, tamen ratione assimilandi nus possunt dici homo.—I, 5. In the formula of Otho : Quidquid est, aut nuinum (i.e., *a se*) est, aut nativum (*i.e., ab alio*). Schmidlin sees resemlances here with the *natura naturans* and the *natura naturata* of John Scotus riugena.

[2] *Polycrat.* VII, 12. Again : Fiunt itaque in puerilibus Academici senes, nnem dictorum aut scriptorum excutiunt syllabam, imo et litteram ; dubintes ad omnia, quærentes semper, sed nunquam ad scientiam pervenientes. -*Metalog.*, II, 7. Debuerat Aristoteles hanc compescuisse intemperiem rum, qui indiscretam loquacitatem dialecticæ exercitium putant.—*ibid.*, II, 8.

[3] See p. 177.

[4] An porcus qui ad Venalitium ducitur, ab homine an a funiculo teneatur. em an capucium emerit qui cappam integram comparavit.—I, 3.

[5] *De naturis rerum*, in the chapter *De septem artibus* (Wright's edition in olls Series, 1863, p. 303) : Docuere idem enuntiabile omni tempore fuisse rum et omni tempore fuisse falsum . . . Docuere infinitam esse lineam, et illam lineam esse infinitam, salve pace Aristotelis.

[6] Born at Balsham near Cambridge. Called " du Petit Pont " (Parvintanus) because he taught the *trivium* in a school situated near the little idge over the Seine.

of scholasticism. This realism is clearly developed in an anonymous work *De Intellectibus*,[1] which at the same time expounds with a precision hitherto unknown the sensible origin of ideas,[2] the immateriality of the concept, and the function of abstraction. The intelligence conceives the real " absque suorum scilicet individuorum discretione "[3]; the universal is the product of a mental abstraction, "ab individuis universale abstrahitur," but the content of the universal idea belongs to real or possible beings.

We find the same theses in the writings of Simon of Tournai (between 1176 and 1192), who has been unjustly accused of rationalism and Averrhoism,[4] and they also appear clearly in the works of John of Salisbury.[5]

100. Bibliography.—The collected edition of the works of Abelard of 1616 has been added to by the researches of Durand, Pez, Cousin and Stölzle. Stölzle has discovered and published : *Abælards* 1121 *zu Soissons verurtheilter Tractatus de Unitate et Trinitate Divina*, 1891 ; the *Theologia Christiana* was published by Martène in 1717 (*Thesaurus novus anecdot. V.* 1139) ; the *Introd. ad Theol.* by Amboise in 1616 ; the *Epitome* and the *Dialogus* by Reinwald in 1835 ; *Sic et Non* by Henke (1851) the glosses and the *Dialectica* in Cousin, *Ouvr. inédits d' Abélard pour servir à l'hist. de la philos. scolast. en France*, 1836, with an introduction by Cousin. He gives the *Sic et Non*, *Dialectica* the treatise *De Generibus et Speciebus* (which is not by Abelard) glosses on Porphyry the *Categories*, the *De Interpretatione* and the *Topica* of Boethius. Cf. Migne, Vol. 178. Cousin, *Petri Abælardi opera hactenus inedita*, 2 vols., Paris, 1849 and 1850 Geyer publishes some texts of the Lunel MS. in *BGPM* Baeumker Festschr. Important texts in *BGPM*, XXI, 1 Grabmann, *Mitteilungen über schol. Funde in der Bibliothec Ambrosiana zu Mailand* (*Theolog. Quartalschr.*, 1911, p. 536 550). De Rémusat, *Abélard, sa vie, sa philosophie et sa théologie* 2 vols., 1855 ; Deutsch, *Peter Abaelard*, 1883 ; MacCabe *Abelard*, 1901. For Biography see Poole ; Portalié, *Abélar*

---

[1] Printed by Cousin in *P. Abælardi opera hactenus inedita*, II, 733.
[2] Totam humanam notitiam a sensibus adeo urgere, p. 747.
[3] p. 745.
[4] Author of a commentary on the Athanasian Creed (published), also Disputationes, and a *Summa* (unpublished) in which he often quotes Joh Scotus Eriugena, but which contains nothing which is anti-scholastic. Simo was one of the first to be acquainted with the Physics of Aristotle. Cf. I Wulf, Hist. philos. en Belgique, p. 56.
[5] There is no trace of exaggerated realism in Nicholas of Amiens, author a *Summa* against the Mahometans (*De Arce Fidei*), or in Robert Pulleyn.

(*Dict. Théol. Cath.*, Vol. I) ; E. Kaiser, *Abélard critique* (Fribourg, 1901), very good : Heitz, *op. cit.*, pp. 7-30 ; Picavet, *Abélard et Alexandre de Hales, créateurs de la méthode scolastique* (*Bibl. E. Hautes Etudes. Sciences religieuses*, Vol. VII, 1) ; G. Robert, *Abélard créateur de la methode de la théologie scolast.* (*R. sc. philos. et théolog.*, 1901).

Migne has edited the *De Sex Principiis* of Gilbert in Vol. 184 and his *Commentary on Boethius* in Vol. 64. A. Berthaud *Gilbert de la Porrée et sa Philosophie*, 1892. De Hove, *op. cit.*

§ 4—*Hugh and Richard of St. Victor.*

101. Hugh of St. Victor, born at Hartingam in Saxony (1096), was educated at Paris, whither he went at the age of 19 years. He entered the Monastery of St. Victor in Paris, and about 1125 he took over the direction of the teaching and continued to supervise it till his death in 1141. His chief works are the *De Sacramentis Christianæ Fidei*, and the *Didascalion*, a kind of encyclopædia of profane and sacred knowledge. Besides works on Holy Scripture, he wrote a commentary on the *Celestial Hierarchy* of pseudo-Dionysius, making use of the translation by John Scotus Eriugena. He also wrote an *opusculum, De Unione Corporis et Spiritus*,[1] and numerous works on mysticism (*De Arca Noe Morali, De Arca Noe Mystica, De Vanitate Mundi, De Arrha Animæ, De Amore Sponsi ad Sponsam*, etc.).

Hugh was a complex personality—a philosopher and a humanist, a dogmatic theologian and a mystic—qualities which fitted together in him in a very harmonious way, and made him one of the most cultivated men of his time.

It is not true that he looked upon philosophy with the same proud disdain as some of his successors at St. Victor. The contrary is the case. While Peter Damian considered profane knowledge as a *superfluum*, Hugh wrote these striking words: *Omnia disce, videbis postea nihil esse superfluum.*[2] He not only wished to know all things, but he also co-ordinated what he knew, and from this standpoint he well represents the synthetic tendencies which manifested themselves more or less everywhere, and prepared the way for the great thirteenth century. The following points in his philosophy are worthy of note :

[1] Unpublished works : *Epitome in Philosophiam*, and *De Contemplatione et ejus speciebus*.
[2] *Didasc.*, VI, 3, Migne, Vol. 176, p. 800, c.

(i) The classification of the sciences found in his *Didascalion*, which with other similar efforts inspired the classifications of the thirteenth century. Hugh writes at length on the three conditions for the acquisition of knowledge : natural talent (*natura*), scholarly practice (*exercitium*, including *lectio* and *meditatio*), and zeal (*disciplina*).

The Aristotelian scheme replaced the Platonist divisions (p. 54) and this widening of Aristotelianism introduced the *quadrivium* into Mathematics, while logic was given a place apart.[1]

(ii) The proofs for the existence of God open a new phase in the history of natural theology. For Hugh abandons *a priori* arguments, and bases himself exclusively on experience. On internal experience above all : from the existence of an ego which is not always known, he concludes that it has begun to be, and thence he infers the existence of a Being to whom all else owes its existence. He argues also from external experience, which bears witness to the mutability of things, and leads us to infer the fact that they have begun to be, and thence to the existence of the Creator.[2]

(iii) IIis affirmation of pluralism. In his exegesis of pseudo-Dionysius, he clearly manifests his antipathy for pantheism, and corrects in an individualistic sense the suspected formulæ of John Scotus Eriugena.[3] He adopts Abelard's solution of the problem of universals. In connection with the composition of bodies, pluralism leads him to a rather confused atomist theory : bodies are constituted of atoms the motion of which explains the change of corporeal forms, but these simple elements instead of being fixed and unchangeable are capable of multiplication and growth.[4]

(iv) Psychology was his favourite study, as we should expect in a mystic. His system was inspired by Augustine and pseu-Augustinian theories. Consciousness of self bears witness not only to the existence of the soul, but the wise man also discovers

---

[1] Division of profane knowledge : (1) *Theorica* (theology, mathematics, physics ; mathematics including the sciences of the quadrivium) ; (2) *practica* (ethics, economics, politics) ; (3) Mechanics, *scientiæ adulterinæ* ; (4) Logic.

[2] See the texts in Grunwald, *op. cit.*, p. 69 *et seq.*

[3] Ostler, *Die Psychol. des H. v. St. Victor*, p. 9, n. 3, gives many examples. Speaking of the unity of beings in God, he says : " ut unum sint in illo, qui unam trahunt similitudinem ex illo."

[4] Qualia sunt corpora simplicia, quæ atomos dicunt, quæ quidem ex materia non sunt quia simplicia sunt, sed tamen materia fiunt, qua in semetipsis multiplicantur et in augmentum excrescunt.—*Sacram.*, I, vi, 37 (Migne, *P. L.*, Vol. 176, col. 286).

thereby the substantiality of the soul, its spirituality, and its presence in the whole body and in each one of its parts. The soul is not other than the ego; it is one, spiritual, immortal; it alone constitutes the human person, and the body shares in personality only because it is united to the soul.[1] The faculties of the soul are manifestations of its being.

Intelligence has a threefold object: by the *oculus carnis* it knows the external world, by the *oculus rationis* it penetrates itself, by the *oculus contemplationis* it attains to God. The external world is known by abstraction, and, under the influence of sense images, the intelligence engenders within itself a resemblance to the nature of sensible things (*oculus carnis*). The knowledge of self is the fruit of introspection (*oculus rationis*). As for the knowledge of God, to which introspection leads us, this is perfected in mystical illumination. Just as the threefold eye of the soul corresponds to a triple object of knowledge,[2] so also a threefold mode of vision marks the degree of penetration with which we grasp an object: *cogitatio* is a superficial and scattered regard; *meditatio* is sustained and deliberate reflection on a given point; *contemplatio* is a profound intuition, leisurely and comprehensive.[3] Like St. Augustine, Hugh finds the inmost being of the soul in the will.

According to the *Didascalion*, philosophy is the gateway to a higher science, theology, which the celebrated Victorine studies from the dogmatic and mystic standpoints (Ch. VII, § 2).

102. Richard of St. Victor.—Scotch by birth, Richard entered the Victorine Monastery at Paris when quite young, and remained there until his death (probably 1173). A disciple and successor of Hugh, he possessed the same complex mentality of philosopher, theologian and mystic. The *Liber Exceptionum* (taken from the *Didascalion*) and his important works *De Præparatione Animi ad Contemplationem*, and *De Contemplatione* are the most interesting from the philosophical point of view. They are full of repetitions, and display an abundance of terminology and comparisons which often makes him obscure.

---

[1] In quantum ergo corpus cum anima unitum est, una persona cum anima est; sed tamen personam esse anima ex se habet, in quantum est rationalis spiritus; corpus vero ex anima habet, in quantum unitum est rationali spiritui.—*ibid.*, col. 408.

[2] Tria sunt animæ rationalis visiones: cogitatio, meditatio, contemplatio.— *Hom.* I (Migne, Vol. 175, c. 116).

[3] Contemplatio est perspicax et liber animi contuitus in res perspiciendas usquequaque diffusus.—Cf. Ostler, p. 145.

Richard bases his proofs for the existence of God on observation and on the principle of causality ; he also makes use of
the grades of being, but he will have nothing to do with the
a priori method of St. Anselm. Hence it has been said that for
the period between St. Anselm and Thomas Aquinas, the proofs
of Richard are the most philosophical.[1]

His metaphysics is pluralistic ; his solution of the problem of
universals is that of Moderate Realism ; but like his master,
and for the same reasons, Richard applies himself principally
to psychological questions.[2]

Sensation has corporeal reality for its domain, reason (*ratio*)
knows the essence of the corporeal by the intermediary of
sensation, and without the aid of the latter it attains to the
incorporeal (*intelligentia pura*). Richard speaks of an interior
Divine light which assists the *ratio* in all its operations, but does
not explain its nature. The abstract concepts which we have
of corporeal reality are the fruit of a spontaneous activity
(Augustine). Just as a metal which receives an impression
becomes representative by its internal power, so the soul clothes
itself with resemblances of the external world.[3]

The knowledge of the incorporeal includes the first principles of speculative thought (principles of contradiction and
of causality) and also the practical ones ; the nature of the
soul itself (*nihil recte æstimat quæ seipsum ignorat*) ; and the
essence of God, to which the knowledge of the soul leads us.[4]

Attracted above all to mystical theology, Richard treats
psychology as a preliminary study to the description of the
direct ways leading to God. Although he does not deny the
autonomy of philosophy, he does not ascribe to it the same value
as Hugh of St. Victor, and the Victorines who succeeded him
went still further in this direction (**128**).

103. Classifications of the Sciences.—The classifications of
Hugh and Richard of St. Victor were not the only ones : similar
endeavours were numerous in the twelfth century, and this
fact is yet another sign of the mental development of the time.
Grabmann has made known several of these classifications
from unpublished documents. They are not homogeneous,

---

[1] Grunwald, *op. cit.*, p. 87. Cf. Baeumker, *Witelo*, p. 312.
[2] Cf. J. Ebner, *op. cit.*, (**104**).
[3] Cum vero impressor metallo figuram imprimit, ipsum quidem non extrin-
secus, sed ex propria virtute et naturali habilitate aliud jam aliquid repræ-
sentare incipit.—*Didasc.*, I, 2.
[4] Ebner, p. 46, 66, 67.

and constitute progressive steps towards the *Wissenschaftlehren* of the thirteenth century. We notice neo-Platonist influences in the classification adopted by Randulfus de Longo Campo (Commentary on the *Anticlaudianus*)|; and others perpetuate the Platonist division. One of the most remarkable classifications, contained in a Bamberg manuscript, distinguishes very clearly between philosophy and theology, and divides theoretical philosophy according to Aristotelian principles.[1]   Another establishes the preparatory character of the liberal arts, and the hierarchical arrangement of the arts, philosophy, and theology[2] (28).

104. Bibliography.—Works of Hugh of St. Victor in Migne, Vols. 175-177. Many works were wrongly attributed to Hugh in the Middle Ages. See Haureau, *Les œuvres de H. de S. Victor* (1886), and *Notices et extr., passim.* De Ghellinck, *La table des matières de la 1re édit. des œuvres de H. de S. V. (Recherches de science relig.,* 1910, p. 270). Works of Richard of St. Victor in Migne, Vol. 194. A Mignon, *Les origines de la scolast, de H. de S. Victor* (2 vols., Paris, 1895), good ; J. Kilgenstein, *Die Gotteslehre des H. von S. V. nebst einer einleitenden Untersuchung uber H's. Leben u. scine hervorragendsten Werke* (Wurzburg, 1898) ; H. Ostler, *Die Psychol. des H. von S. Viktor, BGPM,* VI, 1, good, but rather diffuse ; J. Ebner, *Die Erkenntnisl. d. Richard v. S. V, BGPM,* XIX, 4, good ; Grabmann, *op. cit.*

§ 5—*John of Salisbury.*

105. John of Salisbury (Johannes Parvus) was born between 1115 and 1120. He went to Paris when quite young (1136), and the autobiography which he has given us in his *Metalogicus* (II, 10, 17) tells us that he followed the lectures of all the best-known professors in dialectics and in theology

---

[1] Cod. Q. VI, 30.   Philosophia, Sapientia : (1) Theoretica (theologia, phisica, mathematica) ; (2) Practica (ethica, echonomica, politica) ; (3) Mecanica.   The higher sacred science is distinct from philosopy.   Certain subjects are proper either to philosophy or to theology, others are common to both : Tribus autem modis anime occulta dei innotescunt, vel ratione tantum, vel divina tantum revelatione, vel utroque modo.—Grabmann, *op. cit.,* II, p. 39.

[2] Codex, Paris, lat. 6570 : Ad istas tres scientias (phisica, theologia, scientia legum) parate sunt tamquam vie septem liberales artes, qui in trivio et quadrivio continentur.—p. 46, n.   The same clear distinction between philosophy and theology and treatment of the liberal arts is found in the following text of Cod. 14401 of Regensburg (XIIth century) : " Non solum enim *philosophi* humane videlicet sapiencie amatores rite discendo docendoque hos prædictos (namely, the liberal arts) sequebantur gradus, sed et s. divine scripture doctores . . ."—*ibid.,* I, 191.

at Chartres as well as at Paris : Abelard, Alberic, William of Conches, Gilbert de la Porrée, Adam of Petit Pont, Robert Pulleyn, and others. From 1148 onward he led an active public life : he was in turn secretary to Theobald, Archbishop of Canterbury, to whom he was introduced by St. Bernard at the Council of Rheims ; secretary to St. Thomas à Becket (1162), whom he supported in his quarrel with the King, whose exile he shared, and whose assassination he witnessed in Canterbury Cathedral ; then finally he was elected Bishop of Chartres (1176), and remained there until his death (1180).

He was the first of the line of English intellectuals who were at one and the same time statesmen, humanists, writers, and philosophers. Besides the Letters, which are of great interest, two lives of St. Anselm and of St. Thomas of Canterbury, and several religious *opuscula*, he has left a philosophical poem, *Entheticus de Dogmate Philosophorum*, the first part of which is devoted to a history of Greek and Roman philosophy ; and, most important of all, two works written about 1159, when he was in disgrace with the King of England, the *Polycraticus* and the *Metalogicus*. Of these two books, which constitute a unique monument of the history of ideas, the first contains a theory of the State and a description of humanist culture as seen by the author ; while the second develops a complete programme of logic. Let us glance rapidly at the principal features of this complex personality.

(i) John of Salisbury the Humanist energetically defended the cultivation of the liberal arts : the *trivium* and the *quadrivium* are the seven ways which conduct the mind into the sanctuary of science.[1] He did not despise grammar, but he protested against those who would shut themselves up in the dry-as-dust analyses of Priscian. John was, in fact, a typical representative of the literary humanism, which made the name of the Schools of Chartres, and which arose from a wise and discerning extension of rhetorical studies. Familiarity with the great Latin classics, and especially with Cicero, made him the most elegant and the most concise Latin writer of the twelfth century ; his prose and verse are saturated with classical reminiscences. It was doubtless his love of literary form which led him to join in the vigorous campaign of the masters of Chartres against a party of know-nothings, the " Cornificians," who systematically vilified not only the *trivium*, but all branches

[1] De septem septenis, ii.

of study, as being simply the means of attaining rapidly to lucrative posts. The *Metalogicus* opens with a sweeping attack against these detractors of learning, whom John of Salisbury typifies by a strange being, Cornificius, of whom he gives a by no means flattering portrait.[1] After showing the importance of dialectics, *cum itaque logicæ tanta sit vis*, he again turns angrily upon this *logicæ criminator, philosophantium scurra.*[2]

(ii) As a dialectician, he defends dialectic against its own excesses, and chastises the wordy disputants who confuse it with a pretentious phraseology.[3] Dialectics is the queen of the *trivium* ; it is a science which forms the mind, and by its means beginners learn the art of thinking and speaking, without which philosophy is impossible.[4] And so John of Salisbury dwells with pleasure on the notion of logic, its divisions, and the way in which Aristotle and Porphyry should be read.[5] But he stresses no less the insufficiency of dialectics when cultivated to the exclusion of the other philosophical sciences : abandoned to itself it is bloodless and sterile. "*Sicut dialectica alias expedit disciplinas, sic, si sola fuerit, jacet exsanguis et sterilis, nec ad fructum philosophiæ fecundat animam, si aliunde non concipit.*"[6] Alan of Lille speaks in the same sense : the despotism of logic is at an end.

(iii) As a historian of philosophy he is extremely reserved. He would examine everything before accepting anything as true. He goes back to the great sceptics of antiquity,[7] and praises the " academic temperament,"[8] not in order to take refuge in doubt, but in order the more surely to arrive at the truth. Many have pointed out his long list of doubtful matters (*dubitabilia*) but forget that he is enumerating questions which are difficult, but not insoluble. Some have been surprised to see that he includes among them the questions of substance, universals, Providence, and many others, in view of the fact that he gives his own answers to these questions. But his sole

---

[1] According to Clerval, *op. cit.*, 227, the Cornifician party rose under the direction of a monk named Reginald about 1130. Mandonnet identifies him with a certain Gualon—*op. cit.*, p. 122, note.

[2] *Metal.*, IV, 25.

[3] *ibid.*, II, 8, 9.

[4] Inchoantibus enim philosophiam, prælegenda est, eo quod vocum et intellectuum interpres est sine quibus nullus philosophiæ articulus recte procedit in lucem."—*ibid.*, II, 3.

[5] *ibid.*, II, 11 ; III and IV, 1-7, etc.

[6] *ibid.*, II. 10. Cf. II, 9 : Quod inefficax est dialectica si aliarum disciplinarum destituatur subsidio.

[7] *Polycrat*, VII, 1-6.

[8] VII, 2.

aim is to insist on the limits of our knowledge, and its insufficiency. The wise man (*sapiens*) ought to be satisfied with it, and be modest. And in this no thirteenth century scholastic will oppose him.

Again, he made a point of hearing those of his contemporaries who were well known, and discusses their opinions. The curriculum of his student life constitutes a very complete picture of the schools of the twelfth century.[1] His inquiries concerning the opinions of others make him the chief philosophical historian for this period. In particular, he is a very useful source for the study of the progressive solutions of the problem of universals.

(iv) As a philosopher, the English writer does not allow himself to be limited by didactic divisions. His works treat of the most varied questions without much sequence, and many of his doctrines are found in incidental digressions.

The *Metalogicus* adopts the Platonist division of philosophy,[2] but the doctrinal influence of Aristotle is preponderant. The question of universals occupies a prominent place. This was natural, since in discussing it " the world had grown old, and it had taken up more time than the Cæsars had occupied in conquering and governing the world."[3] John of Salisbury is an opponent of Exaggerated Realism : " *qui autem ea esse statuit, Aristoteli adversatur.*"[4] Again : " he who seeks for the object of genera and species outside the things of sense is wasting his time." His solution is that of Moderate Realism, which he presents in a formula very similar to that of the treatise *De Intellectibus* : the mind operates upon the data of sense and brings about a segregation of the elements which are common to various beings and those which differentiate them, in order to gather up in one concept of genus and species that in which many individuals resemble each other.[5] Moreover, he adds, there is no

---

[1] Webb (*Polycraticus*, Vol. I, p. 21, *et seq.*) gives the list of authors quoted in the *Polycraticus*.

[2] II, 2 and 5.

[3] In qua laborans mundus jam senuit, in qua plus temporis consumptum est quam in acquirendo et regendo orbis imperio consumpserit Cæsarea domus. —*Polycrat.*, VII, 12.

[4] *Metal.*, II, 20.

[5] Diffinit ergo ratio quod concipit intellectus . . . Dum itaque rerum similitudines colligit, etc.—*Polycrat.*, II, 18. Per abstrahantem intellectum genera concipiantur et species quæ tamen, si quis in rerum natura, diligentius a sensibilibus remota, quærat, nihil aget et frustra laborabit . . . Ratio autem ea deprehendit, substantialem similitudinem rerum differentium pertractans. —*Metal.*, II, 20.

sense in letting one's hair turn grey in the schools over this eternal question. Many other subjects demand the attention of the thinker.

These subjects are found in psychology, to which the question of universals itself belongs, and comprise especially the study of our faculties, and our mental acts. Sensation is an organic excitation which affects the mind provided it is sufficiently intense.[1] It is followed by sense judgments, and acts of imagination, which all lead to opinion, and do not exclude error. Truth belongs to a higher faculty, the exercise of which follows on that of the senses. But here a new subdivision comes in between the *ratio* and the *intellectus*.

By the *ratio*, which deals with the data of the senses,[2] we subject corporeal reality to a threefold abstraction, physical, mathematical, and metaphysical ; in addition we penetrate into the domain of the spiritual ;[3] lastly we attain to the *rationes æternæ*, the foundation of all certitude.[4] By the *intellectus*, we accomplish the work of abstraction which provides the *ratio* with its abstract concepts.[5] Hence from this point of view the *ratio* is inferior to the *intellectus*. It is inferior also from another point of view, for the *intellectus* has in addition the function of co-ordinating the data of knowledge into a synthesis having God as its basis, and thus attains to wisdom. With the exception of the fundamental distinction between sensation and thought, these classifications are rather confusing. The English philosopher is careful to attribute the characteristic activities of the soul to distinct faculties or powers, but his applications of this correct principle are not very happy. He tempers the psychology of St. Augustine by that of Aristotle, without obtaining a coherent result. The soul is simple and immortal.[6] Volumes would be required, he says, for a complete study of its activities and its nature.

In moral philosophy, John of Salisbury discusses and condemns Epicureus and gives a detailed description of the vices.[7] He studies Providence and the Divine foreknowledge, which

[1] Nisi enim eadem aliquid violentiæ habeat, nec ad animam pervenit nec cadit in sensus forma.—*Metal.*, IV, 9. Cf. anima pulsata sensibus, IV, 15.
[2] Ars, sive scientia originem trahit a sensu.—*Metal.*, IV, 20.
[3] Ratio transcendit omnem sensum et judicium suum, etiam in corporalibus et spiritualibus rebus immergit.—*Metal.*, IV, 16.
[4] IV, 32 *et seq.*
[5] See note, p. 178. There is no trace of a passive understanding. The abstractive process of the *intellectus* is pure activity.
[6] IV, 20.
[7] *Polycr.*, VII.

he endeavours to harmonize with human liberty.[1] On the subject of political theory, he is the author of a philosophy of the State which is the most complete of the whole of this first period, and which in certain respects is the culminating point of the preparatory work of the two previous centuries.

106. Bibliography. — Works of John of Salisbury in Migne, Vol. 199. Webb has published a critical edition, *J. Sarisburensis ep. Carnotensis Policratici* . . . l. VIII (Oxford, 2 vols., 1909, with a preface on the manuscripts, editions and authors cited by John of Salisbury). Schaarschmidt, *J. Sarisburensis nach Leben u. Studien, Schriften u. Philos.* (1862), out of date. Articles by Siebeck (*Arch. f. Gesch. Phil.*, I, 520), R. L. Poole in *Dictionary of National Biography*, XXIX, p. 439, and a study by C. Webb in *Proceedings of Aristotelian Society*, 1894, p. 91. Buonajuti, *G. de Salisbury e le Scuole filosofiche del suo tempo* (*Riv. stor. crit. delle scienze teolog.* 1908). A good study is found in Poole, *Illustr.*, etc., Ch. VII ; A. Schneider, *Die Erkenntnisslehre d. J. v. S.* (Festgabe von Hertling) ; Deminuid, *J. de Salisbury* (Paris, 1893), a biography.

§ 6—Political and Social Philosophy.

107. The beginnings of political and social philosophy date from the second half of the eleventh century. The theories which then appeared were indeed scattered and fragmentary, but still they constituted the basis of the thirteenth century systems of social rights.

Various causes explain their rise : the development of civil, Roman, feudal, and canon law, elevated the discussion of positive questions to the level of philosophy ; the political writings to which the quarrel between the Papacy and the Empire gave rise in great abundance led to the discussion of the relations between Church and State ; lastly, the study of the *Civitas Dei* and other works suggested many isolated questions.

108. Sources.—Bearing in mind these facts, we may tabulate the doctrinal sources of the new discussions as follows :

(i) Certain texts in Cicero : there is a natural law, unwritten indeed, but impressed upon the soul of man, and the existence of which is revealed by an interior *vox* ; men are equal by

[1] *ibid.*, II, 20, 21.

nature (against Aristotle) ; justice is essential to the State, and where it does not reign the State disappears.[1]

(ii) Certain passages in Seneca concerning the natural equality of men, and a state of innocence in which the State and private property were absent and unnecessary.

(iii) Texts in the Roman jurists of the third century A.D. (*Ulpianus and Florentinus*) gathered together by Isidore of Seville. Here we get doctrines of Stoic origin on the popular origin of political authority—*Res publica, res populi*[2]—and on the distinction of law into *jus naturale, jus gentium, jus civile.*

(iv) The *Civitas Dei*, an apologia for Christianity the City of God—as against Paganism the terrestrial city. Amongst many other subjects, St. Augustine studies peace, the reign of which constitutes the essence of the State (justice, on the other hand, is not necessary) ; the unity of Christians (*omnium christianorum una respublica est*) ; the unity of the human race and the resulting equality of all men ; the unity of history ; the benefits of civil life ; the natural character of family and social life ; the Divine origin of power and the Providential government of the world ; the qualities of a ruler (V, 24) ; the conventional nature of property and slavery, and the despotism of the *dominium* as understood by the Roman law.[3]

(v) Certain doctrines of Mediæval Roman law which the mediæval jurists, especially Irnernius and the other masters of Bologna, took over from the jurists of the Justinian epoch— especially the following doctrines : (*a*) the law is not the expression of the will of a sovereign, but the echo of justice ; (*b*) the source of authority is to be sought in the *populus* : according to some, the *populus* have given it up to the emperor ; others, and these the most important, look upon the people as the permanent subject of governmental power ; (*c*) the doctrine of the co-existence of two legal systems equally sacred, that of the State and that of the Church.

(vi) Certain doctrines of feudal law, formulated by the feudal jurists, e.g., that the object of authority is to maintain justice and not to serve the caprice of the prince ; that law is chiefly the result of custom, and that through custom it rests on the natural and the Divine law ; that the relations between the

---

[1] Cicero, *De Legibus*, I, 6, 19.
[2] Even the saying : " Quod principi placuit, legis habet vigorem " is not absolute, for the text continues : " utpote cum lege regia, quæ de imperio ejus lata est populus ei et in eum omne suum imperium et potestatem conferat," see Carlyle, *op. cit.*, I, 64.
[3] Figgis, *op. cit.*, 111.

king as supreme suzerain and his vassals or subjects are governed by a pact. All these are ideas arising out of the feudal system, and agreeing with the conceptions of the mediæval Roman jurists.

(vii) Certain doctrines of Canon Law (79), especially the theory that the natural law is restricted to mankind ;[1] that it is immutable, contained in the Gospel, and comprises *mandata, prohibitiones* and *demonstrationes* or counsels ;[2] the notion of the *jus gentium* originating in custom ; the theory that authority is of Divine origin although only a remedy rendered necessary by sin ; the doctrine of the superiority of the Church over the State, and the Pope's right to supervise temporal rulers and depose them if necessary.

(viii) The Christian moral code, which proclaims the equality of all men from the standpoint of redemption and grace, and which supplements justice by charity.

109. Manegold of Lautenbach.—Peter Damian, Gregory VII, Otto of Verceuil, Otloh of St. Emmeram, and Honorius of Autun, took part in the controversy between the Pope and the Empire, and touched incidentally on several political questions. Similarly Otto of Freising in his *Chronicle* and *Gesta Frederici* did not get beyond the quarrel. He speaks of the opposition between the earthly and Divine cities, and makes the interesting remark that from the time of Christ there is but one city—the Catholic Church (*ecclesia*) with two functions, the priesthood and the monarchy.[3] But does he not study the organization either of civil or ecclesiastical society.

The two most interesting writers from the standpoint of pure theory are Manegold of Lautenbach and John of Salisbury.

MANEGOLD, author of a *Liber ad Gebehardum* and an *Opusculum contra Wolfelmum*, combines discussions on the rights of the Empire and the Papacy with incidental reflections on the office of authority in the State. Divine in its origin, the monarchy is a function, *officium*[4] which must be exercised for the good

---

[1] Rufinus, *Summa Decretorum*, D. 1. Dict. Grat. ad cap. 1 : Vis quædam humanæ creaturæ a natura insita ad bonum faciendum cavendumque contrarium.—See Carlyle, *op. cit.*, II, 103.

[2] *ibid.* Thus slavery and property, which the natural law neither imposes nor forbids, are recognised as good and advisable, according to Rufinus.

[3] Quia omnis non solum populus, sed et principes exceptis paucis catholici fuerunt, videor mihi non de duabus civitatibus, sed pene de una tantum, quam ecclesiam dico, hystoriam texuisse.—*Chron*. IV, Prol. in *Mon. Germ. Histor*. SS. Vol. XX.

[4] Quod rex non sit nomen naturæ sed vocabulum officii, cap. XXX. *Manegoldi ad Gebehardum liber. Libelli de Lite* I, p. 365.

of the community and conformably with justice. Thus the prince ought to manifest moral qualifications, which the German writer describes after the manner of St. Augustine. If he becomes a tyrant and forfeits his office, like Henry IV who had just been deposed, he breaks the pact made with his people when the latter placed him in power. He may be dismissed, writes Manegold in his rough German tongue, like the swineherd who allows the flock confided to his care to be dispersed.[1] The theory of the *pactum* outlined in these passages is certainly the most remarkable feature in Manegold.

110. John of Salisbury.—The *Polycraticus* of John of Salisbury is the most comprehensive work of this period, and the first complete attempt at a philosophy of the State, *in usum civitates regentium*.[2] The *De Officiis* of St. Ambrose, the *Civitas Dei*, and the doctrines of the Stoics and the Roman lawyers are made great use of,[3] not to mention a great number of ancient writers with whom the author was familiar. The fourth book opens with a distinction between a prince and a tyrant. The prince is subject to *æquitas*, which John defines with the lawyers as *rerum convenientia, tribuens unicuique quod suum est*.[4] The law is but the interpreter of this equity or justice (*lex vero ejus interpres est*), and the prince is the servant of the law.[5] Then comes a picture of the qualities which the prince ought to manifest, and which makes him a sort of moral superman.[6] Here the Augustinian influence is manifest. The authority of the prince comes from God, but there is no suggestion of a *pactum* with the people. Still, the people's rights come out in the case of an abuse of power : a tyrant is opposed to the common good, and may be killed or suppressed by any possible means save poison. Tyrannicide is not only lawful and praiseworthy, but even obligatory.[6] Passing on to the organization of the State, the English writer has recourse to a comparison with the human organism which he takes from the *Institutio Trajani* of pseudo-Plutarch, and which was in great favour in the Middle Ages. He adds that

[1] Neque enim populus ideo eum super se exaltat ut liberam in se exercendæ tyrannidis facultatem concedat, sed ut a tyrannide ceterorum et improbitate defendat.—*Mon. Germ. hist., Libelli de Lite*, I. p. 365.
[2] Webb's edition, Vol. I, Proleg. p. xlviii.
[3] *ibid.*
[4] Cap. 2.
[5] Cap. 2.
[6] Cap. 4. Quod divinæ legis auctoritate constat principem legi justitiæ esse subjectum.
[7] Lib. VIII, cap. 20.

kings are subject to the Church, and that the latter is the dispenser of the power which they possess.[1]

These materials for a social philosophy were made great use of in the thirteenth century, which built them up into a system by means of metaphysical and psychological principles.

The *De Bono Regimine Principis* of Helinandus of Frigidimonte is merely a compilation of tests from John of Salisbury.

111. Bibliography.—J. N. Figgis, *The Political Aspect of St. Augustine's City of God* (London, 1921), good, traces its influence in the Middle Ages. An excellent List of Authorities in chronological order is given by Maitland (*op. cit.*, see p. 000), pp. lxiii-lxxvii. Carlyle, *op. cit.*, Vols. I-IV, *The theories of the relation of the Empire and the Papacy from the Xth Century to the XIIth* (1923). John of Salisbury, No. 106 ; Poole, *op. cit.*, ch. viii. For Otto of Freising see Hashagen, *Otto von Freising als Geschichtsphilosoph und Kirchenpolitiker* (1900) ; Schmidlin, *Die Philosophie Ottos von Freising* (*Phil. Jahrb.*, 1905, pp. 154, 313, 407), gives bibliography, good ; *Die Geschichtsphil. u. Kirchenpolit. Weltanschauung, O. v. F.* (1906) ; Hofmeister, *Studien über Otto von Freising* (*Neues Archiv.*, 1911, p. 37) ; H. Hublocher, *H. von Froidmont und s. Verhältn. zu. J. v. Salisbury* (Progr. Regensburg, 1923).

§ 7—*Alcher of Clairvaux and Alan of Lille*

112. Isaac of Stella and Alcher of Clairvaux—There are two small works on psychology dating from the middle of the twelfth century which may be regarded as the product and the summing up of the Augustinian psychology. The first, entitled *De Anima*, is a letter written by an Englishman, ISAAC OF STELLA,[2] containing a number of somewhat disconnected considerations, drawn up at the request of Alcher of Clairvaux.[3] The other work, *Liber de Spiritu et Anima*, written probably by Alcher in reply,[4] is a well-arranged treatise full of erudition. Alcher

---

[1] Hunc ergo gladium de manu Ecclesiæ accipit princeps.—L. IV, c. 3.

[2] Isaac of Stella was a Cistercian Monk at Clairvaux, where he knew St. Bernard ; he became Abbot of the Cistercian monastery of l'Etoile in Poitou (1147 till his death in 1169) ; and discussed philosophy with his compatriot John Beaumains, Bishop of Poitiers.

[3] "Cogis me, dilectissime, scire quod nescio et quod nondum didici docere." —Migne, Vol. 194, col. 1875.

[4] This identification has been suggested by Stöckl (*Gesch. d. Phil. d. Mittel.* I, 384 *et seq.*), and Haureau (*op. cit.*, V. 113, Paris, 1892). Albert the Great (in *Lib. Sent.* I. d. 8, art. 25) rejects the ascription of the treatise to St. Augustine, and puts forward a certain Cistercian named William. Thomas

incorporates Alcuin's letter *Ad Eulaliam virginem*, and fragments of Augustine, Boethius, Isidore, Cassiodorus, Hugh of St. Victor and others. He compares the soul to the City of God. His definitions are of Augustinian inspiration ; some indeed reproduce Aristotelian formulæ but these are misunderstood. The soul governs the body ; it is bound to it by bonds of friendship, although the body interferes with the exercise of its activities ; it cherishes its prison.[5] The powers of the soul are manifold, but none is really distinct from the substance. In various threefold divisions which do not harmonize very well with each other, the author discovers vestiges of the Holy Trinity.[6] Alcher describes our faculties at length, from the *vis vitalis et animalis* up to intelligence. Sensation is an activity of the soul, *anima per corpus videt* ;[7] intelligence is an abstractive faculty. The soul knows itself, and by a Divine *illustratio* it knows God. Alcher sums up the solution of universals in this concise and significant formula : *"Abstrahit a corporibus quæ fundantur in corporibus."*[8]

113. Alan of Lille.—Little is known of his life. He was born about 1128, seems to have taught at Paris, and was present at the third Council of Lateran. He became a Cistercian, took part in the propaganda of the Order against the Albigenses, and died at the Abbey of Citeaux (1202). Later generations awarded him the title of *Doctor Universalis*.

His principal works are the *Tractatus contra Hæreticos*,[9] the *Theologicæ Regulæ*, the *Anticlaudianus*,[10] and the *De Planctu Nauræ*. Their standpoint is at once theological and philosophical.

While he brought together a considerable number of ideas, he philosopher of Lille did not build up a personal synthesis ; ae limited himself to collecting and harmonizing theories of

Aquinas in many places (e.g., *In Lib. Sent.* IV. d. 44, q. 4, a. 3), ascribes the work to " quidam Cisterciencis qui eum ex dictis Augustini compilavit et quæam de suo addidit." (*ibid.*). See note by G. Théry, *L'authenticité du De piritu et Anima dans S. Thomas et A. le Grand* (R. sc. phil. theol., 1921, . 373-377).

[5] Sociata namque illi, licet ejus societate prægravetur, ineffabili tamen onditione diligit illud ; amat carcerem suam.—*De Spiritu et Anima*, in ligne, Vol. 40, col. 789.

[6] Cap. 6.

[7] Cap. 2.

[8] *ibid.*, col. 787.

[9] The *Ars Catholicæ Fidei* is ascribed to Nicholas of Amiens by Haureau, on Hertling, and recently by Grabmann (*op. cit.*, II, 459 *et seq.*). Baeumker hinks that it was written by Alan (*Handschriftliches zu den Werken des lanus*, Philos. Jahrb., 1894).

[10] Adam de la Bassée published a work under the same title—Haureau, ot. et extr. V, 548, 549, 559.

different origin and tendencies advanced during the period then coming to a close. Alan's mind was quick, he was a consummate dialectician, and excelled in controversy. In addition, he possessed the rather rare talent of clothing his ideas in poetic language, which makes his work, like that of John of Salisbury, a noteworthy example of the humanism of the twelfth century. For this reason he has attracted the attention of those who are endeavouring to reconstitute the golden chain of Christian writers of the Middle Ages. His style is picturesque and elegant, but often allegorical and obscure. Alan ought not to be placed among the mystics (Haureau) ; he is a speculative writer, joining together Platonism with Aristotelian and neo-Pythagorean elements, and colouring the whole with Christian thought. He was not influenced by contact with Arabian literature, although he seems to have known the *De Unitate* of Gundissalinus, and to have been one of the first to quote the *Liber de Causis*.

Logic is no longer the despotic goddess of thought. It appears in the form of a pale young girl, exhausted by excessive vigils. Of the logical theories of Alan, the most interesting is his conception of philosophic method : he proclaims the absolute rights of the mathematical and deductive method. The argument based on reason ought to be preferred to that based on authority, which is too easily invoked on behalf of contradictory opinions.[1] Mysteries themselves are subject to the syllogism of the philosopher ; at the same time, while the mind can find out the motives of credibility, it is incapable of demonstrating them scientifically.

But it is psychology and metaphysics which are preferred by the doctor of Lille. His metaphysics is inspired by Boethius. Through the latter, Alan knows the Aristotelian doctrine on the categories, personality, and the four causes of being. Prime matter is not indeterminate or potential, but a kind of *chaos antiquum*, a mass which exists and is therefore already informed : a theory which has nothing in common with that of Aristotle. As for the form, instead of being the constitutive principle of things, it is a property, or the sum of the properties of a being (p. 55). In the question of universals, Alan is an anti-Realist after the manner of John of Salisbury.

In psychology he passes over the problem of the genesis

[1] Quia auctoritas cereum habet nasum, i.e., in diversum potest flecti sensum, rationibus roborandum est.—*Contra Hæreticos*, I, 30. Cf. Baumgartner, *Die Philos. d. Alanus*, pp. 27-38.

of our knowledge. His attention is concentrated on the nature of the soul, for his work is controversial, defending against the Cathari its immateriality, simplicity and immortality (Ch. VI). In consequence of his erroneous conception of form, he will not allow that the soul is the form or " property " of the body ; it is an independent substance, united to the body in consequence of a *connubium*, or *copula maritalis*. A *spiritus physicus* serves as a connecting link, and relations between soul and body are governed by number and harmony. The Augustinian conception mingled with Pythagoreanism dominates Alan's doctrine concerning the nature of the soul : Aristotelianism here has no place.

The Pythagorean idea of number is put forward as the principle of unity of the cosmic elements, and Alan invokes in his support the hermetic texts of Asclepius. His natural theology is Augustinian ; and his proofs for the existence of God, although they make use of the principle of causality, reflect his ultra-deductive method. Between the Creator and individual beings there is an intermediary, Nature, the Servant of God, *Dei auctoris vicaria*, a sort of world-soul governing the universe[1]. Is this a distinct reality, a real being, or rather a poetical personification of the forces of nature ? It is difficult to decide.[2]

Alan enjoyed a fair reputation among his immediate successors: Radulfus de Longo Campo commented on his *Anti-claudianus* (1216) and utilized his *Regulæ*, and the same is true of William of Auxerre and Alexander of Hales.

Alan was one of the last personages in the twelfth century. He appeared at a moment when decisive events were happening, destined to hasten the full development of Scholasticism. One may wonder what Scholasticism would have become without the concourse of these favourable external circumstances, but it would be unjust to overlook the work accomplished during the period which we have just been studying. Whole groups

[1] Baumgartner, *op. cit.*, pp. 77 *et seq.*
[2] Allegory is also prominent in another work of the middle of the twelfth century, the *De Consolatione Rationis* of Petrus Compostellanus. This treatise in prose and verse is a discussion between *mundus, caro, ratio*, the seven liberal arts, etc., and Petrus Compostellanus who sees them in a dream in the form of young girls. The work is devoted to philosophical and moral questions. Blanco, who has studied the treatise after a manuscript in the Escurial (*BGPM*, VIII, 4, 1912), thinks it was composed after 1120 and sees in it a possible work by Petrus Micha. The treatise is dedicated to the Archbishop of Compostella, Berengarius of Santiago. It still breathes the spirit of Western Gothic culture, and manifests the influence of Boethius, Isidore of Seville, and St. Augustine, although appearing at the dawn of the Renaissance which began in Spain with Dominic Gundisalvi.

of doctrines concerning God, the plurality of beings, and the activities of the soul are ready to be incorporated in more comprehensive philosophic systems. On the other hand, the construction and development of the thirteenth century syntheses would not have been so rapid if the intellectual milieu had not been made ready to receive them.

114. Bibliography.—Works of Alan of Lille in Migne, Vol. 210. New edition of the *Anticlaud.* and *De Planctu Naturæ* by Wright (*Rer. Britannic. Script. M. Aevi.* London, 1872, Vol. II). Works of Isaac de Stella in Migne, Vol. 194; of Alcher of Clairvaux in Vol. 40. Concerning apochryphal works of Alan, see Haureau *Not. et extr. de qqes. ms., BGPM*, II, 4, excellent, and full of material for the history of particular theories; Haureau *Mémoire sur la vie et qques œuvres d'Alain de Lille* (*Mém. Acad. Inscript. et B. Lettres, Vol.* 32); P. Braun, *Essai sur la philos. d'Alain de Lille* (*R. Sc. eccles.*, 1898 and 1899). P. Bliemetzrieder, *Isaac von Stella, Beitrage zur Lebensbeschreibung* (*Jahrb. f. Philos. u. spekul. Theol.* XVIII, 1); also *Ein unbekannte Schrift I. von Stella* (*Studien u. Mittheil. aus d. Benediktin u. Cistercienserorden*, 1908, p. 433), by the same concerning an *Expositio* on the Book of Ruth, dedicated to John, Bishop of Poitiers.

CHAPTER VI

The Anti-Scholastic Philosophies of the Twelfth Century

115. Various forms.—The twelfth century witnessed the rise of philosophical doctrines opposed to and contradicting fundamental principles of scholasticism : psychological and moral materialism, denying the distinction between sensation and thought, and the spirituality and immortality of the soul ; the Manichæan dualism of Good and Evil, which destroys the Divine Infinity ; and lastly, Monism, which compromises human personality, and the substantial distinction between God and the world.

These three forms of anti-scholasticism did not appear as merely speculative theories : they were closely allied to religious and social movements.

116. Materialism.—Alan of Lille tells us that some of his contemporaries taught that the human *spiritus* ceases to exist at the moment of death, and that a resurrection is impossible. " Hi autem volunt dicere ideo resurrectionem non futuram, quia anima perit cum corpore, sicut nostri temporis multi falsi christiani, imo hæretici."[1]

In the works in which he directly combats these ideas, he mentions several of the arguments advanced by those who held them. Thus they invoked in favour of their thesis the opinion of certain scholastics (Adelard and William of Conches for instance) who held that every vital principle is incorporeal, and then proceeded to argue as follows : " Si incorporalis est (spiritus animalis) sicut spiritus humanus, qua ratione perit cum corpore et non spiritus hominis ? Qua enim ratione aut vi conservabitur potius anima humana in corpore quam anima bruti ? "[2]

But they appealed above all to Epicureus and Lucretius, whose Atomism and utilitarianism especially was bound to lead astray anyone who did not believe in the future life with its rewards and punishments. For then the only thing to do

[1] *Contra hæret.*, I, 27 (col. 238).   [2] *ibid.*, et I, 63.

is to seek the maximum of enjoyment in the present life ; and
as a matter of fact chronicles tell us that people holding these
easy-going ideas were found both in the towns and in the
country.[1]

117. The Dualism of the Cathari and the Albigenses.—The
Cathari and Albigenses, two sister sects exceedingly widespread
in the twelfth century in France and Italy, founded their
strange religious and social doctrines on a metaphysical and
moral dualism which is the negation of the fundamental
theories of scholasticism.   Through Byzantium they received
a group of oriental ideas, and borrowed from Manichæism the
dualistic thesis of the co-existence of God, the principle of
Good, and of a Principle of Evil.   Both of these have formed
man : the soul is the work of the former, and the body that
of the latter.   Since the body is evil and corrupt, it is our duty
to destroy sensibility ; hence purifications and austeries are
commanded and the propagation of the race is condemned.
Alan of Lille[2] mentions that according to Albigensian theory
the souls of some privileged and superior men are really
fallen angels, condemned to be united to human bodies a
certain number of times (Pythagorean doctrine).

The " perfect " aimed at leading an ascetical life and
at suppressing their evil nature.   Their followers praised
their efforts at reform, together with their criticisms of the
religious life of the twelfth century.   Since only a few were
expected to be " perfect," and others were allowed to lead
an ordinary life provided they received the blessing of a
" perfect " one before death (consolamentum), the sect rapidly
grew in numbers.

The metaphysics of the Cathari compromised the infinity
and unicity of God ; while their psychology and moral system
went astray on the question of the nature of the union between
soul and body.   If we add that the Cathari forbade not only
marriage but also oaths and war, even a just war, we shall
realize that they were undermining the foundations of the
existing social order.   This helps to explain the intervention

1 Marbodius thus describes this materialism : " Inter quos habitus non
ultimus est Epicurus—Ex atomis perhibens mundi consistere molem.—Iste
voluptatem summum determinat esse—Perfectumque bonum, quo quisque
fruendo beatus—Congaudensque sibi sine sollicitudine vivat ;—Scilicet aut
animas cum corporibus perituras—Aut nullum credens meritum post fata
manere—. . . Quis numerare queat regiones, oppida, vicos—Urbes atque
domos Epicuri dogma sequentes ? "—*Liber decem capitulorum*, c. 7.   Quoted
by Philippe, *Lucrèce dans la théol. chrétienne*, etc., p. 67.

2 *Anticlaud.* I, 1, 12, 318 CD.

of the Church, the guardian of mediæval civilization, and the Inquisition which she organized in concert with the civil power.

118. Pantheism, or the negation of pluralism and the distinction between God and other beings, is destructive of the scholastic system. Its twelfth century manifestation coincided with a revival in popularity of Scotus Eriugena's *De divisione naturæ.*

(i) *The Pantheism of Chartres.* We come across Pantheism at Chartres first of all in an intimate friend of the Chartres teachers, BERNARD OF TOURS, or *Silvestris.* Between 1145 and 1153 he wrote at Tours a treatise *De mundi universitate,* dedicated to Theodoric of Chartres. This work is full of neo-Platonist and Pythagorean doctrines, and teaches Monism and Emanationism. " Ea igitur νοῦς summi et exsuperantissimi Dei est intellectus et ex ejus divinitate nata natura."[1] All reality flows from the Divine *monas.* The world-soul is an efflux of the Divinity (velut emanatione defluxit) and it permeates the whole universe (naturam informavit)[2]. The *formæ exemplares* which the author introduces sustain and penetrate the particular things in which they appear. Thus the material world is a Divine manifestation (ex ejus divinitate nata natura) in which everything is arranged hierarchically according to genera and species. This is exaggerated realism and monism. The *De mundi universitate* is an allegorical poem, partly prose, partly verse, in which metaphysical concepts are anthropomorphised and transformed into stage actors—which makes it very difficult to follow and understand it.

(ii) *Amalric* (or Amaury) *of Bène and the Amauritian Sect.*—AMALRIC OF BENE, born in the neighbourhood of Chartres († 1206-7) was undoubtedly influenced by the Chartres theories. He taught a substantial Pantheism at Paris, both in dialectics and in theology.

The Pythagorean formula that everything which is, is one (omne quod est, ideo est, quia unum est) is interpreted in a Monist sense. God is immanent in everything : " Omnia unum, quia quidquid est, est Deus." According to the laconic judgment of Thomas Aquinas on Amalric, the latter maintained that God is the formal principle of everything[3]—an

---

[1] *De mundi univers.,* I., 1, 2, Barach's edition, p. 150.
[2] P. 168 and 123.
[3] S. Thomas, *Summa Theol.,* I, q. 3, a, 8, in corpore.—Alii enim dixerunt eum esse principium formale omnium rerum, et hæc dicitur fuisse opinio Amalricianorum.

Aristotelian expression which signifies that God permeates everything and is the one existing being. Or again : " Dixit enim deum esse essentiam omnium creaturarum et esse omnium " according to a chronicler.[1] Since God is the *esse formale omnium*, the changing world is really God. Everything, man included, becomes God.

Thus humanity is deified, and every man is a Divine member just as Christ was. " Nemo potest esse salvus nisi credat se esse membrum Christi."[2] The Scripture texts which refer to the Deity may be applied literally to each one of us. There can be no doubt about the kinship of these ideas with those of Scotus Eriugena.[3] It was noticed by his contemporaries, and both master and disciple were associated in a common condemnation. Amalric's theories were being exploited by many heretics, and Amalric was himself proceeded against, but he retracted before his death in 1204.

From 1200 onwards, these ideas made progress, and various sects put Amalric's theories on deification into practice. They preached to the people that at the end of five years (after 1210) every man would be the Holy Ghost, and that man, being a Divine member, is above sin, and hence Nature should not be refused anything—*qui cognoscit Deum esse in se, lugere non debet, sed ridere*. An act is devoid of moral value in itself, it is the intention alone that counts. A certain GODINUS, and a goldsmith named WILLIAM spread abroad these ideas in the first years of the thirteenth century. They had some points in common with the extravagant theories put forth independently by JOACHIM OF FLORIS († 1202) ; and they were naturally welcomed by the followers of the *Evangelium æternum*, who identified the succession of the great periods of the history of humanity with the generation of the three Divine persons, and justified moral disorders in the name of the Divinity immanent in our being.

Philosophers and theologians rose up against the Amauritian doctrines. An anonymous treatise *Contra Amaurianos* (1208-10

1 Martini Poloni Chronic. M. G. SS XXII, 438, 28. Note the distinction between *essentia* and *esse*.

2 Baeumker, *Ein Traktat gegen de Amalricianer*, etc., 386.

3 Henry of Ostia points this out in *Super quinque lib. decret.* 1. Cf. Huber *op. cit.*, p. 436. Alberic of Trois Fontaines writes in his chronicle under the year 1225 : " Hoc anno damnationem incurrit (J. Scotus) propter nova Albigenses et falsos theologos qui verba bene forsitan suo tempore prolata et antiquis simpliciter intellecta male intelligendo pervertebant et ex eo suam heresim confirmabant.—*Monum. Germ. Hist.* SS. XXIII, 914, 42 *et seq.*

which Baeumker[1] attributes to GARNERIUS OF ROCHEFORT[2] refutes the principal theses of the Amauritians : Is it not absurd to say that God becomes stone in a stone, and Godin in Godin ? In 1210 the doctrines in question were condemned by the Synod of Paris, and these censures were renewed five years later, by Robert de Courçon at Paris, and by the Lateran Council.

(iii) *David of Dinant.*—According to the anonymous chronicler of Laon, Amalric of Bènes derived his doctrines from DAVID OF DINANT[3]—a person of whose life practically nothing is known[4], but whose works have at times been famous. It was he who in the last years of the twelfth century formulated a most thorough-going system of materialistic pantheism. The title of his work *De Tomis id est De Divisionibus* (also referred to under the name of *Quaternuli*) at once shows the influence of Scotus Eriugena. Possibly David was also acquainted with the *Fons Vitæ* of Avencebrol, but his pantheism has nothing in common with the *De Unitate* of Gundissalinus (see below) as has been often suggested, for the latter work is conceived in the spirit of scholastic individualism.

The materialistic pantheism of David of Dinant is a sort of fusion of Parmenides' doctrine with Aristotelian elements : the world of diversity manifested to our senses, and which is connected with forms, is a world of appearance, without reality. It pre-supposes the real, or substance, which is one, immutable and indivisible. This substance—the real being— is a trinity of indivisibles identical with each other : God,

---

[1] Baeumker, *op. cit.*, p. 346.

[2] Garnerius of Rochefort was a Cistercian monk who became Bishop of Langres in 1192 and died at Clairvaux after 1215. He composed sermons, and drew from the writings of Peter of Poitiers and John Beleth. He did not escape the influence of Scotus Eriugena, although he has never been suspected of pantheism. Baeumker's attribution of the *Contra Amaurianos* is rejected by Mandonnet (*R. Thomiste*, I, p. 261) who thinks the author was Rudolph of Namur. Baeumker replies in *Jahrb. f. spekul. Theol.*, 1894.

[3] See A. Boghært-Vache, *David de Dinant liégeois ou breton ?* (*Wallonia*, 1904, 266-272).

[4] The chronicler says that he was in communication with Pope Innocent III. He mentions, together with Amalric and David, another " robber of souls," Walter of Muissi: "A. 1212. Nota superiori anno hibernis temporibus quidam presbyteri et alii clerici Parisiensis diocesis convicti fuerunt errorem magistri Almarici innovasse, quam etiam defendere presumpserunt ... Magister vero David, alter hereticus de Dinaunt, hujus novitatis inventor, circa Papam Innocentium conversabatur, eo quod idem papa subtilitatibus studiose incumbebat. Erat enim idem David subtilis ultra quam deceret ; ex cujus quaternis, ut creditur, magister Almaricus et ceteri heretici hujus temporis suum hauserunt errorem. Tertius trux et animarum lanista fidei et honestatis fuit magister Galterus de Muissi."—*Chonicum universale anonymi Laudunensis von 1154 bis zum Schluss 1219*, herausg. A. Cartellieri, bearbeitet von Wolf Stechele, Leipzig, Paris 1906, pp. 69-70.

the νοῦς and prime matter. God, the foundation of all things, is a finished substance ; he is identical with the transformable element in the domain of bodies (prime matter) and of spirit (νοῦς). According to the Amauricians, corporeal things possess reality inasmuch as God permeates them, but in David of Dinant's conception they are devoid of reality.[1] The Walloon sophist establishes his thesis of the identity of being by logical subtleties, specimens of which have been conserved for us by Albert the Great and Thomas Aquinas : " In order that two things may differ, we must find in them a common element and a differential element. Now, if mind were different to matter, there would have to be another matter in prime matter, and so on to infinity."[2]

The *Quaternuli* were condemned in 1210 in a Council at Paris held by Peter of Corbeil, Archbishop of Sens. Five years later, Cardinal Robert de Courçon forbade the reading of David's works in the Faculties of Theology and Arts. The same proscription applied to AMALRIC and MAURICE OF SPAIN.[3]

Why did Albert the Great and Thomas Aquinas devote so much attention to this gross Monism—" most foolish " is the epithet applied to it by the latter—in the service of which David used all his sophistry, and which the Council of Paris in 1210 banned from the schools at the same time as the philosophy of Aristotle ? G. Théry ingeniously suggests that it was in order to separate the two names which the Council had connected, and to show that the cause of Aristotle was not compromised by the vagaries of the sophist of Dinant.[4]

Amalric of Bènes and David of Dinant appeared at the dawn of the thirteenth century, but both really belong to the period then coming to a close. In the thirteenth century antischolasticism continued to wage war in other forms against the triumphant scholastic system.

119.—Bibliography.—Barach and Wrobel have edited the *De mundi universitate libri duo sive Megacosmus et Microcosmus* of Bernard of Tours (*Silvestris*) in *Bibl. philos. mediæ ætatis,* 1876.

Baeumker, *Ein Traktat gegen die Amalricianer aus den Anfang d. XIII Jahrh.* (*Jahrb. f. Phil. u. spekul. Theol.* 1893

---

[1] G. Théry, *Essai sur David de Dinant d'après A. le Grand et St. Thomas* in *Mélanges Thomistes,* 1923, p. 402.
[2] Albertus Magnus, *S. Theolog.,* p. 1a, tr. 4, q. 20, m. 2.
[3] *Chartul. Univ. Paris,* published by Denifle and Chatelain, I, 70.
[4] *op. cit.,* p. 408.

p. 346). This treatise which Baeumker has published is a first-class source of information on Amauritian theories. The other sources are Cæsarius of Heisterbach, William the Breton, and an account of the acts of the council at which Amalric was condemned, published by Martène and Durand, *Thesaurus Anecdotorum*, IV, 163. On Amalric, see Delacroix, *op. cit.*, ch. II. Jourdain, *Mémoires sur les sources philosophiques des hérésies d'Amaury de Chartres et David de Dinant (Excursions*, etc., 1888, p. 101), conclusions need to be revised. On the Cathari, Waldenses and Amauricians, see P. Alphandéry, *Les idées morales chez les hétérodoxes latins au début du XIIIe s.* (*Biblioth. Ec. Htes. Etudes sc. relig.*, xvi., 1, Paris, 1903), studies the moral ideas, principally in their popular form. The moral system of the Cathari was based on the principle that since sin consists on subjection to matter, perfection is attained by detachment from all that binds us to the body. The author regards the theories mentioned by Alan of Lille as " deviations from the genuine teaching of the Cathari." (p. 107). On Joachim of Floris, see Denifle, *Das Evangelium æternum u. d. Kommission v. Agnani (Arch. Litt. Kirchengesch. Mitt.* I, 1885) ; Fournier, *Joachim de Flore et le livre de vera philosophia (R. Hist. et litter. relig.* 1899, p. 37, et *R. Quest. histor.* 1900, p. 457). G. Théry, *op. cit.* on David of Dinant.

CHAPTER VII

Philosophy and other Sciences

§ 1—*Schools of Theology in the Twelfth Century*

120. Development of Scholastic Theology.—Having become quite detached from philosophy, theology underwent a considerable development in the twelfth century in its twofold form of dogma and mysticism.

Dogmatic or "scholastic" theology, which was the more closely related to philosophy of the two, was cultivated in great schools and made considerable progress, in the following directions :

(i) *The systematic codification of materials.* This work underwent a progressive development, from the Sentences (*sententiæ, flores, excepta*) or collections of texts and explanations from the Fathers, *Libri Sententiarum* and *Sententiæ* which gradually arranged these texts in groups and made them the subject of dialectical treatment, to the *Summæ*, which were the result of an elaboration and ordering of these materials.[1] The work of codification already evident in the *Sententiæ* of Anselm of Laon and William of Champeaux, was perfected in the work of Peter Lombard.[2]

It is interesting to note with De Ghellinck that this theological codification was elaborated principally in the French centres of learning (cf. p. 67) either by Frenchmen or by foreigners educated in the part of France north of the Loire.[3]

(ii) *The method of exposition* known as *triadic*, the use of

[1] Sententiæ : "Aussprüche, Thesen, Quæstionem, Abhandlungen, welche man aus den hl. Vatern, den kirchlichen Lehrern u. Canonensammlunger nahm." Sometimes the name of *Sentences* was given to the works themselves of those who compiled these extracts.—Denifle, in *Arch. f. Litt. u. Kirchen gesch. d. Mitt.*, I, 588. In a collection of sentences dating from between 1121 and 1141, mentioned by De Ghellinck (*R. hist. eccles.*, X, 2, p. 200), we read " ut ex diversis præceptis et doctrinis Patrum excerperem et in unum colli gerem eos flores quos solemus, quasi singulari nomine, Sententias appellari." Again, we read in Robert of Melun : " Quis enim summa est ? Non nis singulorum brevis comprehensio " (cod. Brug. 191, fol. 1, quoted by Grabmann)

[2] Grabmann, *op. cit.*, II, 141.

[3] *op. cit.*, p. 87-93.

which became general from the time of Abelard, and which was practised also by the philosophers. This consisted of an exposition of the *pros* and *cons* and then the solution.

(iii) *The method of constructive apologetics.* Theology was distinct from philosophy and had its own autonomous methods. The principal one was always the literal interpretation of the Scripture and the Fathers, practised by all from the time of Rhaban Maur, " the founder of theology in Germany."[1] But quite early there appeared a subsidiary method, the beginnings of which may be seen in Lanfranc and St. Anselm (78), and which is therefore posterior to Abelard[2], to whom it has too long been ascribed. We refer to the apologetic method which consists in demonstrating by reason a doctrine once defined, or at least in developing its rational side.

The apologetic method of the twelfth century appears in a twofold form, dialectical and metaphysical. The former is the more prominent : theologians make use of it in order to put the data of the Scriptures in a syllogistic form, or else they subject dogmatic concepts and the formulæ expressing them to the action of dialectical categories, or again they classify arguments as probable and necessary.[3] The dialectic method owes its rapid success to the development of logic and the utilization of the newly discovered works of the *Organon*. From this time the *disputatio* is introduced into theology : " Quæ omnia Deo annuente loco suo secundum doctrinam Aristotelis explicabimus."[4] But these dialectical exercises led up to a metaphysics of dogma such as that applied to certain questions by Anselm of Canterbury, an isolated forerunner who was not understood. Abelard, Hugh of St. Victor, Alan of Lille and others were led to make incursions into speculative problems, and their work heralded the organic codifications of the thirteenth century. Thus the authority of the Scriptures, *auctoritates*, was supported by a veritable apologetic, *rationes* : the distinction of the two terms appears in Peter of Poitiers[5] as later on in Thomas Aquinas, and it is not an idle one.

[1] Burger, *op. cit.* (*Der Katholik*, Aug. 1902, p. 135).
[2] Cf. Ueberweg, p. 180.
[3] De Ghellinck, *Dialectique et dogme au X-XII siècle* (Baeumker Festgabe, 1913).
[4] Taken from an anonymous work of the middle of the twelfth century mentioned by Grabmann, *op. cit.*, II, p. 20. As a type of theological teaching in the middle of the twelfth century, Grabmann refers to the *Quæstiones* of Odo of Ourscamp edited by Pittra : *Quæst. mag. Odonis Suesssionensis*, in *Analecta novissima Spicilegii Solesmensis*, II, Paris 1888.
[5] An unpublished commentary mentioned by Grabman, *op. cit.*, I, 33.

The apologetic method, then, or the utilization of philosophy by the theologians, is a method of *theology*[1] the use or abuse of which cannot be imputed to *philosophy*. The application of the dialectical method gave rise to lively controversies between theologians, and serves as a basis for a division into three classes. We may distinguish between :

(*a*) The *reactionaries*, opposing the introduction of dialectics into theology ;

(*b*) The *moderates*, who allowed it, but subordinated it to the method of Scriptural interpretation. Moreover, they recognized the independent value of philosophy, which the majority cultivated for its own sake. These argumentative theologians are the true representatives of scholastic theology.

(*c*) The *rationalists*, who regarded the dialectical method as supreme, and placed reason above dogma.

121. First group : the moderate theologians.—(i) Between St. Anselm of Canterbury and the theological schools properly so called, there are a few isolated names such as those of BRUNO OF SEGNI, Abbot of Monte Cassino (1049-1123), and HONORIUS OF AUTUN. The latter was a complex and enigmatic personality of the first half of the twelfth century who, after having been *scholasticus* at Autun, led the life of a hermit near Regensburg. He was a popular writer rather than a *savant*, and at times a poet. He wrote numerous works, the most important being the *Elucidarium sive Dialogus de Summa Totius Christianæ Theologiæ*, which had a great success.[2] It is an attempt at utilizing theological material, in which we discern the didactic method of St. Anselm and the style of the collections of sentences which began to appear everywhere at this time. Similarly, we notice the influence of St. Anselm and St. Augustine very clearly in the *Inevitabile*, a dialogue dealing with the reconciliation of freedom and grace. This work exists in two forms, the one stressing the doctrine of absolute predestination, the other adding the thesis that the decisions of free will, known by the Divine foreknowledge, are one of the factors which

[1] This is precisely what Grabmann refers to as the " scholastische Methode " *op. cit.*, I, p. 36. To avoid all misunderstanding and safeguard the rights of the methods of scholastic philosophy the author would have done better to entitle his important work : " Geschichte d. *theologischen* scholastischen Methode."

[2] De Ghellinck, *op. cit.*, p. 81. His *Speculum Ecclesiæ*, a collection of sermons, is one of the sources of inspiration of the symbolism of Cathedral sculpture. See Mâle, *L'art religieux du XIIIe siècle*.

decide the character of predestination.[1] The *Clavis Physicæ*
of Honorius is strangely enough taken bodily from the *De
divisione naturæ* of Scotus Eriugena, which may be explained
by the encyclopædic tendencies of the writer. In any case,
in the *De cognitione vitæ*, in which Honorius closely follows
the *Monologium* of St. Anselm, he clearly teaches the pluralism
of creatures and their distinction from God.

(ii) ANSELM OF LAON, *magister Anselmus*, the *magister divinitatis* of the beginning of this century, was for a time famous.
His *Sententiæ*, and another collection, *Sententie divine pagine*
attributed to him by Bliemetzrieder, display the first systematic
arrangement of theological questions (God in Himself; the
Trinity; God as Creator; God as Redeemer). The questions
are clearly enunciated, but the solutions are brief, often incomplete, and occasionally omitted. These two works are full of
philosophical theories of considerable interest. Anselm starts
from the idea of God, Ineffable because of His perfection. The
Divine Essence is *essentialiter tota in singulis creaturis (Scotus
Eriugena)* in the sense that everything pre-exists in the wisdom
of God, and that everything comes from Him (*ex ipso omnia*)[2].
An analogical knowledge of the Trinity seems to be implanted
in human reason[3]. It was fitting (*decuit*) that God should
create beings outside of Himself[4]. The human soul, comprises
rationalitas and *sensualitas*, but Anselm hesitates when discussing the question whether these *vires* or *proprietates* are
really other than the soul itself.[5] Then come dissertations on
freedom of the will, in which he adopts the definition of St.
Augustine instead of that of St. Anselm of Canterbury, on
Providence and free will, on the *lex naturalis omnibus communis*[6]
and on Predestination. In one of the appendices to the *Sententie*,
devoted to the return of all things to God, Anselm writes some
high-flown pages in which the influence of Scotus Eriugena
is evident, but which are free from Monism. So long as we are
on this earth, the body is an obstacle which prevents us from
understanding the Divinity. Our *senses* grasp corporeal
properties, *ratio* rises above the individual and grasps the

---

[1] Baeumker, *Das Inevitabile*, etc. Honorius was also the author of a *Summa
totius*, an encyclopædia of natural sciences, and of many other works.
[2] Bliemetzrieder's edition, pp. 4-5 : Mutabilia enim et variabilia non sunt
in deo essentialiter, cum hoc sit constans : quicquid est in deo, deus est.
And again : Cum . . . ita deus reperiatur essentialiter in omnibus sanctis
suis creaturis, ut impossibile esset aliquam quomodocumque parvam sine
essentia sui creatoris, que in eo non esset, subsistere,—p. 151. This is to be
understood in the sense that everything derives its being from God.
[3] p. 7.   [4] p. 10.   [5] p. 24..   [6] p. 79.

essence in the abstract state, but intuition or *intellectio* is lacking to us. After the resurrection, the blessed will experience a change in knowledge : the senses will take the place of the reason, and the reason will have an intuitive power. We shall see God in His works, and the presence of creatures will not affect the vision of the Divinity, " just as in the case of white hot iron in a fire we behold the splendour of the state of heat and do not avert to the iron itself."[1]

Anselm of Laon prepared the way for the great schools of Abelard and Hugh of St. Victor.[2]

(iii) *The School of Abelard.* Abelard's *Introducio ad theologiam* is a rational systemization of dogma, and his division of theology into three parts is distinctive (*fides, caritas, sacramentum*). Theology ought to make use of philosophy. True, the human mind can neither demonstrate (*comprehendere*) a mystery, nor have experimental knowledge of it as we have of present things (*cognoscere seu manifestare*), but we can attain to an approximate notion by means of analogies and similitudes (*intelligere vel credere*).[3]

The principles of Abelard are therefore far from rationalistic. But he goes beyond them when he passes to applications. In his anxiety to combat Roscelin's Tritheism, he destroys the Mystery of the Trinity, which he declares accessible to reason. The Greeks had glimpses of it, for the three persons may be seen in the trinity of God, the νοῦς and the world-soul (neo-Platonism). Furthermore, Abelard subscribes to a sort of Sabellianism : a Divine person does not of itself constitute the whole Divine essence, but represents a modality of the one essence, and the three persons correspond respectively to the Divine power, wisdom, and goodness. Again, he teaches *quod Christus secundum quod homo non sit aliquid*—which De Ghellinck calls Christological nihilism.[4]

St. Bernard did all he could to destroy the heresy of Abelard, just as he did in the case of Gilbert de la Porrée. The *De*

---

[1] Similiter de ferro candente in igne licet dicere in quo nimia exustione caloris fulgorem et formam ignis discernamus, ut ferrum non attendamus,— p. 153. Pages 150-155 are worth reading.

[2] De Ghellinck, *The Sentences of Anselm of Laon*, etc., p. 435, does not attach so much importance to Anselm. During the interval separating Anselm from Abelard, Grabmann mentions in addition to William of Champeaux, a series of secondary personalities : Otho of Cambrai ; the Sentences of Irnerius ; Alcher of Liege († 1131 or 1132), Ralph of Laon, Alberic of Rheims, a theologian († 1141), and a long series of unknown writers.

[3] On this terminology see Kaiser, *Pierre Abélard critique ;* Heitz, *op. cit.,* p. 16 *et seq.* and Grabmann, *op. cit.,* II, 1, 8.

[4] *op cit.,* p. 153.

Unitate et Trinitate Divina were condemned at the Council of Soissons in 1121 ; the *Theologia* at the Council of Sens in 1140 or 1141. These condemnations, to which Abelard submitted himself, led many to adopt an attitude of excessive mistrust towards philosophy.

In a more masterly way than in the *Dialecta*, in the *Sic et Non* Abelard employed a pedagogic method the success of which is greatly due to him. In connection wtih a hundred and fifty theological questions, he collects together a number of divergent texts, taken chiefly from Yves of Chartres. This exposition of the *pros* and *cons* precedes a work of reconciliation, for in the prologue he appeals to dialectics as a means of harmonizing opposed texts : the same word has different meanings in different authors and at different times ; if we bear this in mind, oppositions disappear and the mind discovers unity.[1]

Abelard was the founder of a school. Père Denifle has discovered four *Summæ* directly inspired by the *Introductio ad Theologiam* in the threefold division of their matter, their method of exposition, and their teaching. These are : the *Epitome Theologiæ*, attributed hitherto to Abelard, but really the work of a disciple who faithfully follows his master's teaching ; *Sententiæ Rodlandi Bononiensis magistri auctoritatibus rationibus fortes* of ROLAND BANDINELLI (Alexander III), posterior to 1141, published by Gietl ; a *Summa* by OMNIBENE, a contemporary of Roland ; and another anonymous *Summa* in the Library of St. Florian.

(iv) *The School of St. Victor* was more prudent than the other two : it confined itself within the limits of the strictest orthodoxy. HUGH OF ST. VICTOR, its best-known representative, was the author of a treatise *De Sacramentis* in which the dogmatic synthesis is more perfect than in the *Introductio ad theologiam* of Abelard, but in any case it is a later work. In it, the theological subject-matter is arranged according to a different plan (Creation or *conditio*, and Reparation or *restauratio*).

[1] Robert, *Les écoles et l'enseignement de la Théologie*, etc., pp. 170-178 attributes to the Sic et Non a preponderating influence on the methods of teaching and exposition in theological works subsequent to Abelard. Grabmann, *op. cit.*, II (217-221) without denying this influence, makes this two-fold reservation : the *disputatio* was not fully established as a scholastic exercise before the end of the thirteenth century, and the Logica Nova, especially Aristotle's Topics, had at least as much influence as Abelard. He recalls the words of John of Salisbury : " Sine eo (i.e. libro Topicorum octavo) non disputatur arte sed casu." (*Metal.*, 3, 10).

To the theological work of Hugh we may compare that of RICHARD OF ST. VICTOR, whose *De Trinitate* establishes a system of relations between Faith and Reason after the style of St. Anselm. Faith precedes reason ; it possesses a certitude which is *supra opinionem et infra rationem*, but reason must explain it. In his exegesis of the *Fides quærens intellectum*, Richard admits in order to justify the contents of faith, not only *rationes probabiles*, but also *rationes necessariæ*. This might seem excessive,[1] but the expression must not be taken literally, and Richard does not always use the phrase in the same sense.[2]

Among the other composers of Sentences who belonged to the School of Hugh of St. Victor we may mention HUGH OF ROUEN, and especially ROBERT OF MELUN.[3]

(v) *The School of Gilbert de la Porrée.* We may say of GILBERT DE LA PORREE, as of Abelard, that after establishing between faith and reason certain theoretical relations which safeguard the superiority of the former and the dialectical function of the latter, he arrives at heterodox conclusions on some points. He extends to God the distinction between the universal and the singular, and " regards God (*Deus*) and the Divinity (*Divinitas*), the Father and Paternity, and even Nature and Persons as different things."[4] This is a denial of the Divine unity. These propositions were condemned in the Synod of Rheims (1148), and the Bishop of Poitiers withdrew them.

The existence of a school of Gilbert de la Porrée is proved by the *Sententiæ divinitatis* (written between 1141 and 1148) which reproduces the characteristic errors of Gilbert condemned by the Synod of Rheims in 1148, and at the same time was greatly influenced by the *Summa Sententiarum*.[5] Among the disciples of Gilbert de la Porrée (Porrectani) we come across RADULFUS ARDENS, writer of homilies, a *Liber epistolarum*, and especially of a *Speculum universale*. This great work, written between 1179 and 1215,[6] opens with a classification of the sciences, makes an endeavour to systemize the date of

---

[1] Heitz, *op. cit.*, pp. 72 *et seq.*

[2] This is discussed in Ebner, p. 87-91.

[3] Grabmann also mentions among the productions of St. Victor the *Fons philosophiæ* of Godfrey of St. Victor and an anonymous treatise *De Trinitate*— II, 318-328.

[4] Clerval, *op. cit.*, p. 263.

[5] According to Geyer, *op. cit.*, no. 125.

[6] Grabmann, *op. cit.*, I, puts Radulfus Ardens in the eleventh century ; Geyer, *Radulfus Ardens u. das Speculum Universale* (*Theolog. Quartalschrift* 1911, p. 63) shows that his work is a twelfth century one, for it mentions Gilbert de la Porrée, and also makes use of Peter Lombard and John Damascene.

theology, deals with the transposition of philosophical terminology into theological matters (*qua necessitate quave intentione nomina sunt translata a naturali facultate ad theologiam*),[1] and at the same time is a noteworthy exposition of moral teaching.

(vi) As for the *Summa Sententiarum*, in which the tendencies of Abelard and the Victorines converge,[2] and which is of uncertain origin,[3] this was a work manifesting still further development in the clearness of its exposition. In its turn it influenced several collections of *Sentences* in the period immediately following.

(vii) *Robert of Melun*. The Englishman ROBERT OF MELUN deserves a place apart. He succeeded Abelard in the teaching of dialectics at St. Genèvieve, and then opened a school of theology at Melun. John of Salisbury, who followed his lectures, described him as *in responsionibus perspicax, brevis et commodus*. He became Bishop of Hereford in 1163, and held the post till his death in 1167. His two books of *Sentences*,[4] which were subsequently abridged, show the influence of Hugh of St. Victor, but are nevertheless the work of a vigorous mind. They contain a noteworthy systemization in which the two theological methods (authority and apologetics) are well balanced.

The Prologue affirms the intellectualist character of faith ; it contains valuable information on the superficial didactic methods employed by certain contemporary commentators, which the author would replace by a more critical technique. Robert left no disciples, and by the end of the twelfth century he fell into an obscurity from which " he deserves to be rescued."[5]

---

[1] Grabmann, *op. cit.*, I, 255. R. Martin mentions other disciples of Gilbert : Jourdain Fantasme, Yves of Chartres († 1165), and John Beleth. See *Le Péché originel d'après G. de la Porrée* (*Rev. histoire ecclés.*, 1912, p. 676).

[2] De Ghellinck, *op. cit.*, 121.

[3] The ascription of this work to Hugh, questioned by Denifle (*Arch. Litt. u. Kirchengesch. Mitt.*, III, 1887, p. 634) is defended by Fournier and Ostler. Gietl attributes it to " a disciple of Hugh greatly influenced by the school of Abelard " (*op. cit.*, p. 57). Portalié (*Ecole théolog. d'Abelard*, in *Dict. théol. cath.*) and others draw attention to errors which in their opinion shows that it was not written by Hugh. Grabmann (*op. cit.*, II, 297), regards the ascription to Hugh as probable, adding that there are no conclusive arguments either for or against. The latest historian, M. Chossat, ascribes the work to Hugh of Mortagne, and dates it about 1155. In this case it would be posterior to Peter Lombard. See *La Somme des Sentences, œuvre de H. de Mortagne vers 1155*, with Introd. by De Ghellinck, Spicileg. Lovaniense, fasc. 5, 1923.

[4] In addition he has left *Quæstiones de Divina Pagina*, and some exegetical works. See Grabmann, *op. cit.*, p. 323 *et seq.* for numerous unpublished extracts from the *Sentences*. Robert defended Abelard after the Council of Sens. See Martin, *Pro P. Abælardo*, in *R. sc. phil. theol.* 1923, p. 308.

[5] R. Martin, *L'œuvre théologique de R. de Melun* (*R. hist. ecclés.* 1920, p. 456). For his ideas on original sin, see *R. sc. phil. et théol.*, 1914-19, 1922.

(viii) *Peter Lombard.* The best-known composer of Sentences was PETER LOMBARD, author of *Libri quattuor sententiarum.*[1] Born about 1100 in Novara in Lombardy, he received his theological education at Paris, where he taught (1139 or 1140) and whither, after a stay in Rome (1148-50) he returned as Bishop (1159). His work is the natural culmination of the arranging of materials which began at the commencement of the century. He is a moderate man, for he places the arguments of authority first, and has recourse to philosophical notions only in so far as they may be of service to dogma. This utilitarian pre-occupation explains why Peter Lombard is not a philosopher, except in appearance,[2] and why his philosophical considerations are incidental, and devoid of originality. We may describe him as " an eclectic, who adopts ideas from almost every source, sometimes in a very superficial way, sometimes with profound reflection, in order to explain the Church's doctrine."[3] In theology Peter Lombard is equally devoid of originality. He imitates and often copies Abelard, Hugh of St. Victor, Alcher of Liège, and many others ; he takes his patristic and conciliar texts from Gratian ; he makes use of the classifications and certain of the ideas of the *De Fide Orthodoxa* of St. John Damascene (**134**), a Latin translation of which, from the pen of Burgundius of Pisa[4] he had found at Rome. In spite of these borrowed elements, his work forms an excellent systemization inspired by a division of the material into *res* and *signa ;* it provides schemes and subjects for lectures, excludes all imprudent curiosity and deals with all the questions at issue without succeeding in harmonizing completely the divergent authorities. All this explains the astonishing celebrity of the work, and the title " Master of the Sentences " given to its author. For in spite of opposition on the part of Walter of St. Victor, John of Cornouailles, Gerhoch of Reichersberg and others to Lombard's method and the " Christological nihilism," which he adopted from Abelard,

[1] Completed in 1150 according to Denifle, 1152, according to F.Pelster (*Wann hat Petrus Lombardus die Libri IV Sententiarum vollendet ?* in *Gregorianum*, 1921, p. 387-392).
[2] Espenberger, *Die Philosophie des Petrus Lombardus und ihre Stellung im zwölften Jahrh.*
[3] *ibid.*, p. 11. Dehove (*op. cit.*, p. 119) shows that in spite of his hesitations Peter Lombard must be included amongst the partisans of moderate realism.
[4] De Ghellinck (*op. cit.*, p. 141-144). It served as a model for the *Summa Sententiarum*, or else he made use of the data of the latter, according to whether he is prior to or later than this codification, the authorship of which is disputed.

and the attacks in the *Liber de Vera et Falsa Philosophia* and Joachim of Floris, the fame of Peter Lombard lasted for four centuries.[1]

Among the first imitators of Peter Lombard must be mentioned Master BANDINUS, GANDULPHUS OF BOLOGNA who wrote about 1150 and summarized him in several chapters[2]; and especially PETER OF POITIERS († 1205), Professor of Theology, afterwards Chancellor of Paris, his most faithful disciple[3], whose *Sententiarum libri quinque* and important commentaries (*Glossæ super sententias*, written before 1175) greatly helped to spread the work of the master. Abridgments[4] and Commentaries[5] on the Master of the Sentences appeared as early as the second half of the twelfth century. The Lateran Council (1215) confirmed his magistral authority, and in the thirteenth century the commentaries on his work were numbered by hundreds. Up to the middle of the sixteenth century his plan of treatment remained classic, and the *Sentences* were explained side by side with the Bible in the theological faculties of the European universities.

(ix) *The utilitarian theologians.* Some writers, such as PETER THE EATER (Comestor, Chancellor of Paris, died about 1178, author of a *Historia Scholastica*) and PETER THE SINGER or of Rheims (*Cantor, died* 1179) endeavoured to give a practical and positive direction to theology. Without going so far as to condemn philosophy, they themselves had no use for it. We find the same tendency in LIEBHARD OF PRUFENING, GUIDO

---

[1] Grabmann, *op. cit.*, II, p. 398, and De Ghellinck, *op. cit.*, p. 150-169. In view of the place in history occupied by the *Sentences* of Peter Lombard, we give an outline of the contents of the work. The author treats successively the *res*, or things which are not symbols of anything else, and then *signa*, or symbols. The *res* comprise : (*a*) the object of our beatitude, namely, God (Book One); (*b*) the means of attaining thereto, i.e., creatures (Book Two); (*c*) the virtues, which are at one and the same time objects of happiness and means of attaining to beatitude (Book Three). The *signa* or symbols are the sacraments (Book Four).

[2] De Ghellinck, *op. cit.*, Ch. III.

[3] Grunwald, *op. cit.*, p. 53, points out that the proofs for the existence of God invoked by Peter of Poitiers are clearer than those of Lombard, and are not without originality, particularly in respect of one founded on the division of beings into substances and accidents, and the insufficiency of either for self-existence (*a se*). Another proof is founded on the insufficiency for self-existence (*per se*) of any being composed of parts.

[4] One of the last abridgments properly so-called has been pointed out by Martin in an anonymous manuscript, *Filia Magistri*, about 1232-45. (See *Bulletin* of the John Rylands Library, 1915).

[5] Grabmann, *op. cit.*, p. 394-398, says that the Lombard was commented on chiefly in two ways. First of all commentators confined themselves to the exposition of the text. Later with the Dominican Hugh of St. Cher, we find a freer and more personal method.

OF ORCHELLES, and a group of English writers : RICHARD OF LEICESTER, WILLIAM DE MONTIBUS, PETER OF LONDON, STEPHEN LANGTON, Archbishop of Canterbury, and especially ROBERT DE COURCON, whose *Summa* is worthy of note, and who was one of the first organizers of the University of Paris.[1]

122. Second Group : The rigorist theologians.—Amongst those who were led by the abuse of the dialectic method into extremes in the opposite direction must be mentioned in the first place certain exalted mystics, as for instance WALTER and ABSALOM OF ST. VICTOR, who condemned all knowledge, but were not listened to.[2] Walter of St. Victor in his treatise *Contra quatuor labyrinthos Franciæ* (about 1179) included in a common condemnation the author of the *Sententiæ divinitatis*, Abelard, Gilbert de la Porrée, Peter Lombard, and Peter of Poitiers.   Citeaux and Fonteavellana were the centres of similar reactions.   There was also an influential group of seculars who with PETER OF BLOIS[3] and STEPHEN OF TOURNAI († 1203) " were angry with the makers of new *Summæ* "[4] and complained to the Pope of the dialectical malady which had affected the body of teachers. ST. BERNARD, ERNAUD OF BONNEVAL, HUGH OF AMIENS, GODFREY OF AUXERRE, JOHN OF CORNOUAILLES, PHILIP OF HARVENGT († 1182), MICHAEL OF CORBEIL († 1199), wrote of the " Inutilis inquisitio studium philosophiæ ", and RUPERT OF DEUTZ attributed to the dialectical method the theological errors of Roscelin, Abelard, and Gilbert de la Porrée. Indirectly they condemned philosophy

---

[1] Studies questions of moral theology and canon law. One of the most interesting parts, dealing with usury, is published by G. Lefèvre, *Le traité de usura de R. de Courçon* (Lille, 1902). The author does not invoke the texts of the Ethics and the Politics in order to condemn gain from usury, as was done later on. This leads Lefèvre to conclude that up till the thirteenth century the attacks upon loaning money for interest were conducted independently of the authority of Aristotle.

[2] Hildebert of Lavardin, Bishop of Tours (1057 till about 1133) must not be grouped with the writers of *summæ* and philosophers, for the *Tractatus theologicus* ascribed to him was really by Hugh of St. Victor (see Haureau, *Not. et extr.*, etc., V, 251), and the *Philosophia moralis* bearing his name was by William of Conches. Grabmann classifies the *summæ* and similar writings of the twelfth century into four groups : (1) the dialectico-theological works of Anselm of Laon and William of Champeaux ; (2) the ascetical and moral works of Hugh of St. Victor, Abelard, R. Bandinelli, Gandinus, and Omnibene ; (3) the Biblical and moral works of Peter Comester, Peter the Singer, Robert de Courçon and Cardinal Laborantis : (4) the dialectico-theological works of Peter Lombard and his school. See *Forsch.*, etc., p. 36, *BGPM.*, XVII, 5-6. We prefer to adopt the historical order instead because of the difficulties which such a classification presents.

[3] Author of the *Letters* imitated by John of Salisbury. One of the numerous Frenchmen who came over to England (*Cambridge History of Literature*, I, 188).

[4] *Epist. ad R. Pont.*, quoted by Portalié, *op. cit.*, col. 55ʳ

itself. That was going too far. Philosophy was not responsible for theological errors, and in any case the abuse of the dialectical method could not render its proper use illegitimate.

123. Third group : the rationalistic theologians.—There were also theologians who, paying no attention to the letter of the Scriptures and the interpretations given by the Fathers, put forth explanations of Catholic dogma which ended in destroying it. The CATHARI, ALBIGENSES, AMAURICIANS, followers of DAVID OF DINANT and JOACHIM OF FLORIS were of the number.

It is in view of their principles that we have included Abelard and Gilbert de la Porrée amongst the moderates.

In the measure in which they were led on to teach doctrines incompatible with dogma, Abelard[1] and Gilbert de la Porrée may be included amongst the rationalists. But they erred in good faith : such is the opinion of the majority of historians. Moreover, if we remember that they submitted to the decrees which condemned them, their intentions admit of no doubt. But the intentions of a man do not alter his doctrines, and cannot prevent these from developing into their logical consequences.

124. Conclusion.—The personalities which chiefly interest us in the history of theology in the twelfth century.—Abelard, Gilbert de la Porrée, and Hugh of St. Victor, to mention only the heads of schools—were both philosophers and theologians. As philosophers they aimed at constituting a doctrine explaining reality by the light of reason. As dogmatic theologians they made a systematic exposition of Catholic belief. In this exposition the argument based on authority played the principal part, but they also had recourse to philosophical arguments, the value of which was stressed by the majority. This shows yet again that philosophy had a double function in the Middle Ages : it had an autonomous value, and it inspired the apologetic method in theology. For a long time the Church was accused of condemning philosophy as such in the person of Roscelin, Abelard, and Gilbert de la Porrée. Nothing is more inexact. What the Church condemned was neither the so-called nominalism,[2] nor realism, nor philosophy in gen-

---

[1] Portalié writes of the good faith of Abelard thus : "Abelard was never a freethinker or an unbeliever . . . he was and wished to be a sincere believer."—*op. cit.*, col. 41. Cf. De Ghellinck, *op. cit.*, p. 103.

[2] " Nominalism was the old enemy, and it is in fact the doctrine which is farthest removed from the axioms of the faith precisely because it agrees

eral, nor the method of argumentation in theology, but *applications* of this method.[1] It was with theological doctrines alone that she concerned herself. In the thirteenth century a host of teachers adopted the philosophical theories of Roscelin and Abelard, and no councils were called in order to condemn them. We may add that heresies, in exaggerating some point of doctrine, helped to determine its real meaning, inasmuch as their condemnation involved the clear statement of the doctrine concerned.

125. Bibliography.—G. Robert, *Les écoles et l'enseignment de la théologie pendant la première moitié du XIIe s.* (Paris, 1909) ; Simmler, *Des Sommes de Théologie* (Paris, 1871) ; Grabmann, *Die Gesch. d. scholas. Methode*, Vol. II ; the second part is particularly important, it contains studies on the schools of William of Champeaux and Anselm of Laon, Abelard, Hugh of St. Victor, Robert of Melun, Peter Lombard, the School of Chartres up to Prapositinus ; De Ghellinck, *Le mouvement théologique du XIIe s.* (Paris, 1914), excellent general work, reproduces numerous articles published in various reviews ; A. Palmieri, *Theologia Dogmatica orthodoxa* (i.e., the Russian Church) *ad lumen cath. doctrinæ examinata et discussa, Cap.* 6 : *De Theologia scolastica ac de usu rationis in rebus fidei* (Florence, 1911).

Theological works of Abelard and Hugh of St. Victor are mentioned in **100** and **104**. Critical edition of the *Libri quatuor Sententiarum* of Peter Lombard in the Quaracchi edition of the Works of St. Bonaventure, Vols. I-IV. New critical edition, *P. Lombardi l. IV Sentent.*, with prolegomena on his life and works, Quaracchi, 2nd edition, 1916, 2 vols.

Migne has published the *Sentences* of R. Pullus in Vol. 186, Peter of Poitiers in Vol. 211, and fragments of Walter of St. Victor in Vol. 199. B. Geyer, *Die Sententiæ divinitatis* (*BGPM*, VII, 2-3) publishes the text of two MSS. of Munich, and extracts from the treatise *Contra quatuor labyrinthos Franciæ* of W. of St. Victor, as well as a study. Bliemetzrieder, *BGPM*, XVIII, 2 and 3, publishes the *Sententie* and the *Sententie divine pagine* of Anselm of Laon, with four dissertations which he calls *Notanda*. A. Endres, *Honorius Augustodunensis, Beitrag zur Geschichte des geistigen Lebens im* 12. *Jahrh.* (Munich, 1906),

with reason best of all. Brought up before many councils, nominalism was condemned in the person of Abelard, as it had been in the person of Roscelin." —Haureau, *Hist. philos. scol.*, I, 292.

[1] Cf. Willmann, *Gesch. d. Ideal.* II, 360.

collects together the historic elements concerning this little known personage. On his particular works, there are numerous monographs by J. Kelle, 1901-1906, in *Sitzungsb. der k. Akad. d. Wissenschaft. in Wien. Philos-histor. Klasse;* Daux, *Un scolastique du XIIe siècle trop oublié, H. d'Autun (Rev. sc. eccles. et science catholique,* 1907); Fr. Baeumker, *Das Inevitabile,* etc., *BGPM*, XIII, 6. On Abelard see work cited in note; H. Ligeard, *Le rationalisme de P. A. (Rech. science religieuse,* 1911), reconstitutes a controverted text in Book II of the *Intro. ad theolog.,* and holds that Abelard is not a rationalist pure and simple. *Studien z. Gesch. der Theologie und Kirche,* Bd. VIII, h. 5, *Die Sentenzen d. Petrus Lombardus, Ihre Quellen und dogmengeschichtliche Bedeutung* by O. Baltzer. Denifle, *Abaelard's Sentenzen u. die Bearbeitung seiner Theologia (Arch. f. Litt. u. Kirchengesch. d. Mittelalt.,* 1885, Vol. I), a masterly treatment; Gietl, *Die Sentenzen Rolands nachmals Papstes Alexander III,* 1891, gives text, and a first class study; Portalié, *Ecole théolog. d'Abelard,* in *Dict. Theol. Cath.,* Vol. I, col. 49 *et seq.,* an excellent study. By the same: *Alexandre III;* Claeys-Bougaert, *La Summa Sent. appartient-elle à H. de St. Victor?* (*R. hist. eccles.* 1909); Delatour, *Pierre le Chantre (Bibl. ec. Chartres,* 1897); Gutjahr, *P. Cantor parisiensis* (Graz, 1899); G. Lefèvre, *Le traite de usura de Robert de Courçon,* text and translation, with Introduction, (*Trav. et mem. Univ. Lille,* X, 30).

Protois, *P. Lombard, son époque, sa vie, ses écrits, son influence,* (Paris, 1881); Espenberger, *Die Philos. d. Petrus Lombardus* (*BGPM*, III, 5, 1901), traces the sources of Peter Lombard's philosophical ideas: studies by Père Martin (mentioned in note, p. 203), on Robert of Melun, Gilbert de la Porrée, and Honorius of Autun. For Decrees of councils condemning various theories, see Denzinger, *op. cit.*

Mag. Gandulphi Bononiensis Sententiarum l. IV, ed. J. de Walter, Breslau. 1925.

§ 2—*Speculative Mysticism*

126. Practical and Speculative Mysticism.—It is not easy to define Mysticism. The word comes from the root μυ, which means to shut up or close, and in general signifies a tendency leading man to seek union with the Infinite in an intimate and hidden way. Understood in this sense, mysticism is closely connected to religion. It flourishes more and more according as the religious sentiment is more universal. Inversely, religious unbelief excludes mysticism.

The twelfth century, which lived with an ardent Catholic faith, witnessed all the forms of mysticism. There were in the first place *practical* mystics, who lived their lives in this state of union with God but did not trouble to write books. The monastic rules favoured the life of prayer and silence, and tended to make one despise earthly things. Indeed, the enemies of human knowledge (122) and those who wished to banish art from the Churches were found among the more fanatical of these mystics.

There were also the *mystical writers*, who under the influence of the mystical life enshrined their religious experiences in ardent prayers (e.g., certain hymns in the Benedictine Breviary, and the prayers of St. Bernard).

Lastly there were others, less in number, who developed the theory of mysticism. These are the *speculative mystics*, who alone concern us here. They practised the method of introspection, described the states which bring about in varying degrees the direct communication between the soul and God, and explained the world of reality in terms of such union. They imply :

(i) That the communication with God is the fruit of love. Certainly it necessitates contemplation, which reveals to the soul the majesty and greatness of the Infinite, but it is completed in an affective movement of our being, and in a peaceful possession of God, which may take very different forms (apathy, quietism, loss of consciousness, etc.).

(ii) The communion is direct, that is to say, it is not based on ordinary or analogical knowledge of God derived through creatures, but on an immediate intuition. That is why, in addition to the senses and reason, the mystics admit internal visions, or other modes of knowledge. They also admit corresponding affective movements. God seeks the soul, and takes possession of it in such a way that the soul is drawn outside itself, and loves itself no longer, but God alone.

(iii) This union is the culminating point of psychic activity, and indeed the end of our earthly life. Other studies, and especially philosophic researches, are subordinated to it.

The nature of speculative mysticism explains certain other features in the work and temperament of those devoting themselves to it. The exalted realms of mysticism, being hidden, lend themselves easily to poetry, allegory, and personification, and the titles of mystic works themselves reflect this tendency. The mystics readily adopted the symbolic method, which consists in interpreting the visible world as a sign and symbol of the supernatural world, and they applied it not only to the Bible, but also to nature, which they explained in detail. Lastly, it is natural that those among them who occupied themselves at the same time with philosophy singled out for preference problems in psychology and ethics. They concentrated their attention upon the interior man, stressed the dualism of soul and body, and taught how the soul could be freed from the bonds of sense.

127. Division of speculative mysticism—There are two kinds of speculative mysticism, according to the nature of the union between the soul and God : *Pluralistic* or individualistic mysticism bases this union on an exalted activity of the knowing and loving soul, which, however, remains distinct from the Divine Being in its substantial entity. *Monistic* mysticism makes the Divine communion more intimate still, and in some way or other identifies the soul with God Himself.

From this classification we derive another which completed the former in the Middle Ages : the division into *natural* and *supernatural* mysticism. Those who maintain a substantial distinction between the finite soul and the Infinite God do not allow that the soul has the power of attaining to God in a sufficiently intimate and direct way when left to its own resources, but require in addition, on the part of God Himself, an indispensable supernatural help, a grace which is not due to the soul, but which God gives to whom He pleases. On the contrary, those who deify the soul in order to identify it with the Infinite have no need to invoke this addition, and look upon mystic intuitions as the highest but still a natural manifestation of psychic life.

Those who subscribe to metaphysical pluralism in philosophy cannot without being illogical admit a natural or philosophic mysticism. For according to their ideology, the human mind can know and consequently love God only through creatures. Obviously, knowledge of this kind attains to God indirectly. Hence the direct communication, which is the central phenomenon of the mystical life, and which Hugh of St. Victor and St. Bonaventure describe with such ardent enthusiasm, is essentially distinct from the philosophic knowledge of God.

Even in the Augustinian ideology, according to which the ideas of God and creation are innate, and God is present to us by the very analysis of the content of our minds, He is perceived as distinct from our knowing minds.

The mystic ways form therefore steps on a higher path which man cannot mount without grace[1]. That is why scholastic philosophers treat mysticism as a department of theology.[2]

In the Middle Ages we come across the two types, theological or pluralistic mysticism, and philosophical or pantheistic mysticism. Their representatives make use of the same sources: the *Confessions* of St. Augustine, the *Stromata* and the *Pædagogus* of Clement of Alexandria, the *De Institutione cœnobiorum* of Cassian, the *De Vita Contemplativa* attributed to Prosper of Aquitaine, and above all, the works of pseudo-Dionysius. At the end of the twelfth century we also notice the influence of Arabian mysticism.

128. Theological or pluralistic mysticism.—In the twelfth century there arose a group of mystical writers basing the ascent of the soul towards God on a supernatural grace granted even in the present life. PAULINUS OF AQUILEIA, ODO OF CLUNY, ST. ANSELM OF CANTERBURY, and HILDEBERT OF LAVARDIN wrote on the stages of ordinary asceticism rather than on mysticism proper. We come across some mystical theories in RUPERT OF DEUTZ (died 1135), ODO OF TOURNAI, WALTER OF LILLE, and HONORIUS OF AUTUN.

The first great name in the methodic study of the high realms of contemplation is ST. BERNARD (*Doctor Mellifluus*, 1091-1153), who combined in himself the personality of a practical mystic, a mystical writer, and a theorist.

But for the complete code of the laws which govern the soul's journey towards God we must go to the great sanctuary of mysticism, the School of St. Victor. HUGH OF ST. VICTOR was at once the initiator and the chief representative of this school.

---

[1] According to some (Père Pacheu for instance), mysticism includes the whole domain of the supernatural life of the soul ; according to others (Père Poulain for instance) it comprises only one category of supernatural phenomena, namely, those which result from an experimental possession of God which He grants to a few privileged persons without the intervention of their own wills.

[2] We may say that it is Christianity which, by its religious theories on grace and the supernatural, has given rise to the distinction into natural and supernatural mysticism. This is confirmed by the fact that the historic forms of mysticism previous to Christianity (the Vedanta, Buddhism, neo-Platonism are pantheistic in character.

His writings on mystical theology[1] deal with faith in its object-ive aspect (*fides quæ creditur, materia fidei*) and particularly in the affective sentiment to which it gives rise (*affectus, fides qua creditur*). He describes the stages in the ascent towards God after the manner of St. Augustine. The soul attains to God by the eye of contemplation (p. 173)[2] All knowledge is brought about by a resemblance, and the soul finds in this possession of God a completion of its being, and the love of God, to which contemplation leads, gives to the soul its most perfect form. Although this union with God does not require the intervention of a faculty distinct from intelligence, Hugh invokes the supernatural help of grace in order to lead the soul to these heights. By contemplation the soul gazes without effort and in a free and penetrating way upon the infinite being of its Creator. Hugh gives a keen psychological analysis of the act of faith, which he defines as " voluntaria certitudo absentium supra opinionem et infra scientiam constituta "[3] and of the relations between believing and knowing.[4]

RICHARD OF ST. VICTOR, prior of the Abbey from 1162 to 1175 and the immediate disciple of Hugh, is almost as well known as his master.[5] He describes the " degrees of contemplation," and contrasts the knowledge of God reached by philosophers by the discursive use of reason and the study of the sensible world, with the states of knowledge and love which are superior to the powers of reason.[6] The " philosophical arks " or systems collapse ; the Ark of Moses, or the free contemplation of God remains unshaken when He visits our soul by grace.

---

[1] *Commentary on the Celestial Hierarchy of pseudo-Dionysius ; De Arca Noe Mystica, De Vanitate Mundi, De Arca Noe Morali, De Arrha Animæ, De Laude Charitatis, De Modo Orandi, De Amore Sponsi ad Sponsam, De Meditando, De Contemplatione et ejus Speciebus.*

[2] Qui autem Spiritum Dei in se habent, et Deum habent ; hi Deum vident, quia oculum illuminatum habent, quo Deus videri potest, et sentiunt non in alio vel secundum aliud, quid ipse non est, sed ipsum et in ipso, quod est, quod præsens est.—*Hier.* III (Migne, Vol. 175, c. 967. Cf. Ostler, *op. cit.*, p. 139.

[3] Ostler, *op. cit.*, p. 148 ; Grabmann, *op. cit.*, II, p. 279.

[4] Heitz sees neo-Platonist or Augustinian influences in this system, and writes in this connection : " The neo-Platonism of the Victorines may be said to consist in the following : all that we know of God is known by revel-ation, or, in other words, by illumination . . . Rational knowledge is con-ditioned by illumination to such an extent that a modern theologian would not be quite sure whether rational knowledge is supernatural, or whether revelation is lowered to the level of reason."—*op. cit.*, p. 83.

[5] *De Exterminatione mali et promotione boni ; De Statu interioris hominis ; De Eruditione hominis interioris ; De Præparatione animi ad Contemplationem ; Libri quinque de Gratia Contemplationis ; De Arca Mystica.*

[6] Constat itaque supra hominem esse et humanæ rationis modum vel capacitatem excedere quæ ad hæc novissima contemplationum genera videntur permanere.—Migne, Vol. 196, col. 79 A. and 135 A.

After these two masters, mysticism flourished exuberantly at St. Victor. The act of faith was more and more looked upon as a purely affective sentiment independent of the motives of credibility. Philosophy was regarded as a needless study. Contempt for all speculation is manifest in ACHARD and GODFREY OF ST. VICTOR, and attains its highest degree in WALTER, Richard's successor, for whom dialectics is the Devil's art. He wrote a book, *In quatuor labyrinthos Franciæ* (p. 206). We find the same tendencies elsewhere, in ADAM THE PREMONSTRATENSIAN, and ADAM OF PERSEIGNE. Later on, THOMAS GALLUS, Abbot of Verceil (died 1246) combined the mysticism of the Victorines with that of pseudo-Dionysius, and marks the transition from the school of St. Victor to that of St. Bonaventure.

129. Heterodox or pantheistic mysticism.—Pantheism is the contradictory of Catholic theology, just as it is the antithesis of scholastic philosophy.

We have seen that pantheistic mysticism appeared already in the ninth century with Scotus Eriugena, and its history runs parallel with that of the system of Eriugena. After an eclipse, it reappears in the twelfth century in the theories of deification maintained in the writings and practised by the sects favouring the monism of man and God (118).

One of its most curious manifestations is the mystical work of ST. HILDEGARD OF BINGEN (1098-1180), whose life, at once contemplative and active, was passed in various Benedictine convents in the Rhine country. The treatises which she wrote (principally *Scivias, Liber Divinorum Operum simplicis hominis*) are noteworthy in many respects : fascinated by the monism of the *De Mundi Universitate* of Bernard Sylvestris, she describes the evolution of the Divine Spirit which permeates the universe, gives rise to the beings of the *microcosmos*, and absorbs the human soul. This description of the world is intimately combined with her own affective experiences and mystical transports towards God. Furthermore, she herself commented on her mystic visions, and had them depicted in wonderful miniatures in which she is represented as seated in contemplation. She enlists in the service of these visions all the cosmological and astronomical data found in the writings of Galen, Ptolomy, and other men of science known in the School of Chartres.[1]

---

[1] Ch. Singer, *Studies in the History and Method of Science*, Vol. I, The *Scientific Views and Visions of St. Hildegard* (Oxford, 1917) reproduces th

130. Bibliography.—Works on mysticism in general : Denifle, *Eine Geschichte d. christ. Mystik.* (*Histor. Polit.* B.I, 1875) ; Pacheu, *Introduction à la psychologie des mystiques* (Paris, 1901) ; *Psychologie des mystiques, Les Faits. Dante et les mystiques* (Paris, 1909) ; Sharpe, *Mysticism : Its True Nature and Value* (London, 1910), clear notions and classifications ; Père Pourrat, *La spiritualité chrétienne*, Vol. II : *Le moyen age* (Paris, 1921), studies the mysticism of the Benedictine, Victorine, Dominican and Franciscan schools ; J. Maréchal, *Quelque traits distinctifs de la mystique chrétienne* (*R. de Philos.*, 1912). Works of St. Bernard, in Mabillon's edition, 1696 and 1719. Vacandard, *Vie de S. Bernard, abbé de Clairvaux* (Paris, fourth edition, 1910, in two volumes), good, studies his doctrinal rôle, cf. 125. Buonamici, *Riccardo da S. Vittore, saggi di studio sulla filosofia mistica del sec. XII.* (Alatri, 1898), *Dict. Theol. Cath.* : *Ste. Hildegarde* (Vernet). For Scotus Eriugena see **74**.

§ 3—*The Development of Law*

131. Gratian and Canon Law.—GRATIAN did for Canon Law what Peter Lombard accomplished for theology : so much so that their works have been described as " two eggs from the same nest." The *Decretum* is an ordered arrangement and completion of the collections of the eleventh century which Gratian's successors, as for instance Stephen of Tournai and Rufinus, developed and commented in their turn.

As in the preceding century, Canon Law provided theology with many subjects for discussion and an abundant collection of patristic quotations, but it was itself influenced by theology in return, and derived therefrom some important questions such as the study of the sacraments. Moreover, the same person often combined the offices of theologian and canonist.

The relations between Canon Law and philosophy were equally close. Gratian owed to dialectics and to Abelard (**121**) the method found principally in his *Introduction*, namely, the distinction between the various senses which the same word has in different authors, in view of which they cease to be *adversi* but are simply *diversi*. Peter of Blois and the other successors of Gratian made use of this principle, but sometimes carried its application too far.

miniatures from the Wiesbaden MS. See also E. Wasmann, *Die hl. Hildegard von Bingen als Naturforscherin* (Festchr. von Hertling, II, 1913).

Inversely, Canon Law was one of the sources inspiring the social and political philosophy of the twelfth century (**108**).

132. Roman and Feudal Law.—Up to the eleventh century, Roman civil law had been studied in a very narrow way by commentators, and the only works which appeared were compilations of the *Breviary* of Alaric or of one of its epitomes. But after this time the school of Bologna became a great centre for juridical studies. IRNERIUS (about 1100) and after him, PLACENTINUS († 1192) and many others took up and developed the study of the great Roman jurists, at the same time giving a Christian complexion to their conceptions. We find in these writers a noteworthy theory of *æquitas* (*rerum convenientia quæ in paribus causis paria juria desiderat*) which is said to have its foundation in God, becoming *justitia* when it is the object of the human will, and *jus* when expressed in terms of law. Based upon this notion we get the idea of the natural law as a body of inviolable moral principles, dictated by reason of which the law of nations or civil law are merely the prolongation. In the same way the mediæval jurists tended to mitigate slavery, and touched on political doctrines which, as we have already seen, served as materials for the first philosophies of the State.

The same is true of the works of the feudal jurists, who did not constitute themselves into a school, but appeared in different parts of Europe, especially in France (BEAUMANOIR, *Les coutumes de Beauvoisis*), England (BRACTON, author of a treatise *De legibus et consuetidinibus*, and a little later on, GLANVIL, *De Laudibus et consuetudinibus regni Angliæ*), Italy RATHERUS OF VERONA) and Germany (the author of *Sachsenspiegel*).

133. Bibliography.—De Ghellinck, *Le Mouvement théol.*, etc.; Gratian in *Dict. Théol. Cath.*; Carlyle, *op cit.*, Vol. II and III. For Canon Law see works of Père Fournier. He has in preparation a comprehensive work on Canon Law from Charlemagne to Gratian.

CHAPTER VIII

Appendix : Byzantine and Arab Philosophy

134. Byzantine Philosophy.—Banished from Athens by a decree of Justinian (529), and driven out of Alexandria by the invasion of the Arabs (640), Greek philosophy took refuge at Byzantium, the rallying point of the last upholders of neo-Platonism, Themistius and Proclus. There it maintained itself throughout the Middle Ages. The intellectual relations between Byzantium and the West were sporadic in character during the first period of this history. At the time when the revival of studies began to make itself felt in France and the neighbouring countries, the Greek Schism (858) gave rise to serious misunderstandings and separated the West from the Byzantine world. It was not until the Crusades and the Capture of Constantinople in 1204 that there was any great intellectual exchange of ideas between the two civilizations.

Already in the sixth century the *Isagoge* of PORPHYRY and the works of PSEUDO-DIONYSIUS enjoyed a great reputation in Byzantine circles, and it was through Byzantium that these apochryphal writings were introduced into France (p. 79).

Another writer to whom we have already referred is JOHN DAMASCENE (died 750), who lived in the midst of the troubles created by the rulers of the Isaurian dynasty. His chief work, $Πηγὴ$ $γνώσεως$ was one of the first systematic collections of theological and philosophical material. The work opens with a sort of philosophical introduction ($κεφάλαια$ $φιλοσοφικά$) founded on Aristotelian logic and metaphysics, with elements borrowed from Porphyry and Ammonius. The apologetic tendency of the work is clearly set forth, and explains why philosophy and profane science are represented therein as servants of theology. After a second part, devoted to a catalogue of heresies, the author proceeds to give in a systematic treatise an ordered arrangement of patristic texts and an exposition of Christian doctrine (God, creation, the Incarnation ; the glorification of the Man-God, the sacraments, etc.). This last part, known later on under the title *De fide orthodoxa*, and used as a source by Peter Lombard and others, was divided into four books. It was translated in 1151 by Burgondius of Pisa and it profited by the unexampled success of Peter Lombard,[1] so much so that it had, not only in the twelfth but also in the thirteenth century, an ever-increasing attraction for theologians and philosophers. Alexander of Hales made use of the second book of the *De Fide Orthodoxa*, and Albert the Great and Thomas Aquinas mention it frequently.

MICHAEL PSELLUS THE ELDER and the Patriarch PHOTIUS are the striking figures of the ninth century. In the eleventh century Michael Psellus the Younger (1018—after 1096), Prime Minister of Michael Parapinakes and Professor at the Academy of Constantinople was the initiator of an Eclectic Platonism which culminated, without any break of continuity, in the Platonism of the Italian Renaissance. But he was not known in the Middle Ages, and we may say the same, with some exceptions, of a group of commentators of the twelfth century such as JOHANNUS ITALUS, the successor of Psellus at the Academy, and EUSTRATIUS OF NICÆA.

135. Origin of philosophy among the Arabs.—It was through the intermediary of the Syrian Christians that the Arabs came into contact with Greek thought, and the Syrians had themselves received it at first hand thanks to the Grecian influence in their country resulting from the expeditions of Alexander the Great.

Certain works of Aristotle, chiefly the *Organon*, Porphyry's *Isagoge*, and the works of pseudo-Dionysius, were translated from Greek into Syriac and commented on by savants of the Nestorian School in the fifth century (Theodore of Mopsuesta, Theodoret of Cyr and others), in the sixth by the Monophysites of Resaina (Sergius) and Chalcis; in the seventh by James of Edessa, and in the eighth by other Nestorians. When the Arabs conquered Persia and Syria, they in their turn received the philosophic deposit from those they had vanquished, and this gave rise to a great development of Arabian philosophy, which the cultivation of the sciences of observation and religious discussions had already endowed with a tendency toward autonomy. The Abassides, who in 750 replaced the Ommaiades invited to the Court of Bagdad certain Syrians who translated from Syriac into Arabic the great works of Greek philosophy. This work of translation began under the Khalifate of El

---

[1] De Ghellinck, *op. cit.*, p. 273.

Mansour (753-774), and was vigorously promoted by El-Mamoun. The latter established at Bagdad, about the year 832, a school of translators under the direction of HONAIN BEN ISAAC, the *Johannitius* of the Scholastics († 873), a contemporary of Scotus Eriugena at the Palatine court and of Photius of Byzantium. The work of translation was continued in the tenth century by the Syrian Christians, among whom we may mention COSTA BEN LUCA. They translated not only works of Greek philosophy,[1] but also treatises on medicine and mathematics. They translated the principal works of Aristotle, and the Commentaries of Alexander of Aphrodisias, Porphyry, Themistius, and Ammonius. Plato was not so well known, but the Arabian world was soon introduced to neo-Platonism, for one of the first works translated (840 A.D. at the latest) was the famous *Theology* of Aristotle, wrongly attributed to the Stagirite, being in reality a compilation from the *Enneades* of Plotinus (iv-vi) made in the third or fourth century.[2] As for Arabian commentaries on the *Isagoge*, more than five hundred of these have been counted.

The Arabian philosophy flourished for three centuries and a half, and developed successively in the Eastern kingdom, and then in Spain.

136. Characteristics of Arabian philosophy.—(i) Respect for Aristotle, whom the Arabians looked on as the philosopher κατ᾽ ἐξοχήν, and whose doctrine they excelled in condensing. They derived from Aristotle their conception of science, the value of the observation of facts, and a number of particular doctrines which the Scholastics afterwards adopted in their turn. But it would be a mistake to think that Arabian philosophy was a slavish imitation of the Peripatetic system. The Arabians made use of texts of Aristotle which were defective obscure and inaccurate by reason of the processes of translation, and moreover they interpreted him chiefly through the Greek commentators. They transformed his doctrines by forcing texts which were obscure in the original, particularly in respect to the human intellect. Above all, they adulterated their Aristotelianism with neo-Platonist elements

---

[1] There were also some translations made of Persian and Indian works, but these did not exert the same influence. See Carra de Vaux, *Avicenne*, p. 37.

[2] A Latin paraphrase appeared at Rome in 1519 under the title : *Sapientissimi Aristotelis Stagiritæ Theologia sive mistica philosophia secundum Ægyptios noviter reperta et in latinum castigatissime redacta.* See Carra de Vaux, *op. cit.*, p. 74.

such as the doctrine of emanation and ecstasy, so that when later on Scholasticism began to study Arabian philosophy, it received fresh neo-Platonist infiltrations from this source. These neo-Platonist elements were wrongly attributed to Plato, and efforts were vainly made to harmonize these with Aristotle in the name of the unity of the philosophic tradition. Lastly,[1] we find in the Arabians some traces of Greek science. The psychologists especially adopted the physiological theories of Galen and other Greek physicians with all their materialistic tendencies. Thus the Arabians finally arrived at a sort of philosophic syncretism *sui generis*.

(ii) Three doctrines give a distinctive character to their explanation of reality, namely, those concerning the emanation of the spheres, the human intellect, and matter.

The *theory of emanation*, clearly set out in the *Theology* of Aristotle, establishes a bond of origin between the Supreme Being and the Intelligences which emanate either directly from it (Averrhoes) or else by a series of intermediaries (Avicenna). These Intelligences are extrinsically united to the heavenly spheres (stellar or planetary) and are the source of their local motion. An artificial but close connection exists between the metaphysics of the Intelligences and astronomical data.

The *human intellect* is the last and most imperfect of pure intelligences. This theory is based on an obscure text in Aristotle where he says that the acting intellect is a divine principle coming from outside ($\Theta\dot\eta\rho\alpha\theta\epsilon\nu$), and that it alone is immortal, while the passive understanding begins with the body and disappears with it. The Arabians inferred from this that the human intellect is impersonal, separated from human individuals, and unique for the whole race, and they linked it up to the system of intelligences, in which it occupies the lowest rank and acts as moving power to the moon. The Aristotelian doctrine was thus mixed up with a mass of neo-Platonist ideas.

Matter is eternal (as in Greek philosophy). Those who look upon it as an emanation from the Supreme principle are frankly Pantheists (Avencebrol) but the best writers maintain the existence of a matter distinct from God and co-eternal (Avicenna, Averrhoes).

(iii) The conciliation of philosophic thought with Moham-

[1] Carra de Vaux, *op. cit.*, pp. 79, 272.

medan doctrines was one of the chief preoccupations of the Arabian philosophers. At the same time, the majority distinguished between the religion of cultivated people, based on the literal exegesis of the *Koran*, and the religion of the common people founded on its philosophic study. In this connection we may mention the discussions between the orthodox *Mutakallimun*[1] and several heretical sects the details of whose history do not concern us here. Carra de Vaux and others call this attempt to harmonize philosophy with the *Koran* " Mohammedan scholasticism." But it must not be forgotten that Arabian philosophy had an autonomous existence as an explanation of the world, independently of its subordination to the *Koran*. We must apply to the Arabian philosophy in the matter of its relations with the *Koran* what has already been said of the relations between Western Scholasticism and Christian doctrine (13).

137. Eastern Branch. Alfarabi, Avicenna.—The first great name is that of ALKINDI (died about 873), a contemporary of Scotus Eriugena. He was a logician, a translator, and an encyclopædist, and his works were translated into Latin (see p. 80). He probably revised a primitive Arabian translation of the *Theology* of Aristotle.

The Scholastics were better acquainted with ALFARABI (died 949-50), another savant of the Bagdad School, an interpreter and commentator on Aristotle. Among his many works may be singled out his Commentaries on the *Posterior Analytics*, a treatise *De Ortu Scientiarum*, and another *De intellectu et intelligibili*, greatly used in the Middle Ages.[2] Alfarabi proves the existence of God by the Aristotelian argument for an immovable mover. God creates all things by the intermediary of the acting intellect. The system is completed by mystical tendencies. There is nothing in Avicenna and Averrhoes, according to O'Leary, which is not found in germ in Alfarabi.[3]

[1] " Mutakallimun " signifies all those who treated philosophico-religious problems. See Pollak, *Entwicklung d. arab. u. judischen Philos. im Mittelalter*, in *Arch. f. Gesch. d. Philos.* XVII, p. 214.

[2] He was also the author of a *Tehafot*, which Asin translates as " The *unreflecting precipitation* of the Peripatetics towards reason. Despising revelation they burnt themselves like the moth in the flame." (Asin y Palacios, *Revue Africaine*, 1906.)

[3] De Lacy O'Leary, *Arabic Thought and its Place in History*, p. 155. Similarly Carra de Vaux writes the following tribute : " Farabi was a truly powerful and singular character. In my opinion he is more attractive than Avicenna, having more interior fire, capable of more sudden outbursts and unexpected developments. His thought runs on like that of a lyric ; his dialectics are acute, ingenious, and full of contrasts ; his style has the merit of concision combined with a rare profundity." (*op. cit.*, pp. 102-116.)

Alfarabi's successor, IBN-SINA (AVICENNA, 980-1037)[1] was at the same time a philosopher, theologian, and a physician. In spite of the vicissitudes of an eventful life, he managed to write a great many works—indeed, they are said to have numbered over a hundred. Avicenna was one of the most faithful interpreters of Aristotle among the Arabian theologians. Starting with the synthesis of Alfarabi, he freed it from many neo-Platonist ideas in order to bring it nearer to Peripatetic pluralism.

His chief work, *Kitâb assifâ*, or Book of Healing, is a philosophic encyclopædia dealing with Logic, Physics, Mathematics, and Metaphysics. It was known to the Scholastics under the title *Sufficientiæ*. The *liber sextus naturalium*, deals with Psychology ; the *Metaphysica Avicennæ, sive ejus Prima Philosophia*, published at Venice in 1499, is another part ; while the *Nadjât* is an abridgment of the whole work. The *Book of Theorems* ; the *Guide to Wisdom* ; the *Philosophy of Aroudi* ; the *Philosophy of Alâ*, and other special treatises deal with a number of important questions. In addition, Avicenna also wrote many mystical works and treatises on medicine and astronomy.

His Logic is clear and concise. It consists of a free commentary on Aristotle, giving an important place to definition and reasoning. Logic is the instrument which enables one to acquire philosophic knowledge, it is not philosophy itself. Avicenna's classification of the philosophical sciences was widely adopted in the Middle Ages, and the Scholastics of the thirteenth century preferred it to any other. Physics, mathematics, and theology together form speculative philosophy, each branch having a pure and an applied part ; ethics, economics and politics constitute practical philosophy.

To metaphysics Avicenna gives the place of honour. He explains the emanative procession of beings or the generation of the multiple from the One in the following way : At the highest point of the metaphysical empyrean is situated the First Being, God, the Perfect Intelligence and the Absolute Good. From the First Being proceeds the first caused being. " The knowledge which the first caused being has of the first being gives rise to an intelligence which is next in order to the latter. This intelligence is that of the sphere of Saturn.

[1] The " Brothers of Purity " who appeared about this time were encyclopædists and popularizers ; they also formed a mystic sect. Dieterici has published extracts from their writings.

Again, the first caused being knows itself as necessary by reason of the first being, and this gives rise to a soul, which is that of the limiting sphere. Again, it knows itself as possible in itself, and this explains the existence of the body of this limiting sphere. This procession continues in the same way following the astronomical scale. From the intelligence of Saturn, inasmuch as it knows God, comes the intelligence of the sphere of Jupiter ; from the same intelligence inasmuch as it knows itself comes the soul and body of the sphere of Saturn. The derivation continues until we arrive at the acting intellect, and there it stops, for as Avicenna remarks, there is no need for it to go on indefinitely."[1]

The theory of the procession of the spheres is completed by that of their motion ; and both are co-ordinated with astronomical data : the circular motion of the spheres has its ultimate ground in the finality exercised by God, inasmuch as the intelligent soul of each sphere seeks the Supreme Good. The acting intellect, the last to be generated, governs our world, and from it also come, under the influence of the motion of the heavens, all the substantial forms destined to actuate " sublunar " matter. It is clear from this that the acting intellect is not merely a psychological factor, but is also a metaphysical principle giving rise to human souls in the emanative process, as well as to other terrestrial forms. As for matter, this is not an outflow of the intelligence according to Alfarabi, but an eternal element, co-existent with God, and characterized by a complete indifference to being or non-being.

The theory of causes, the Aristotelian solution of the problem of universals, and particularly the thesis of the individuality of substances and the three states of essences (*ante multiplicitatem, in multiplicitate, post multiplicitatem*)[2] gave his other metaphysical doctrines a frankly Aristotelian spirit which won for them the attention of the Western Scholastics.

Avicenna was an Aristotelian in psychology. Although he reduced the number of the faculties of the soul, which the Brothers of Purity had multiplied excessively, he nevertheless allowed himself to drift into exaggerated developments. Thus he recognises in the speculative understanding (i.e., the passive intelligence proper to each man) a fivefold stage corresponding to successive actuations, to say nothing of the intervention

---

[1] Carra de Vaux, *op. cit.*, p. 247.
[2] Logic, Venice edn., 1508, fol. 12, V.A.

of the acting intellect, a separated form the illumination of which is necessary for all intellectual activity.   These five stages are : the material intelligence, or mere possibility of knowing ; the possible intelligence, furnished with the prime truths ; the intelligence in act, or perfectly prepared to receive other knowledge ; the acquired intellect, which is in possession of this knowledge ; and the holy spirit, or mystical intuition reserved to certain privileged souls.   Other faculties form the subject of similar interesting developments.   Pre-existence and metempsychosis are rejected, but the spirituality and personal immortality of the human soul are affirmed—another example of the individualism by which Avicenna endeavours to counterbalance the monist tendencies of his theory of emanation.   The philosophy of Avicenna, like that of Alfarabi, culminates in mysticism ; and finds room for many degrees of ecstasy and prophecy (neo-Platonism).[1]

ALGAZEL or ALGAZZALI (1058-1111) is the most important of the theologians who opposed the philosophers properly so called in the name of Mohammedan orthodoxy.   In his chief works, *The Destruction of the Philosophers*, and *The Renovation of the Religious Sciences*, he rejects as heretical many solutions defended by the philosophers, particularly the eternity of the world[2] and the procession of the spheres.   In place of their rationalistic science he would substitute an orthodox theology ; he does not reject the services of speculation provided it be humble, submissive, and that in any case it does not claim to suffice as a foundation for the truths of faith.   His moral teaching though based on the *Koran* manifests infiltrations of Greek and Christian ideas.   It is indissolubly linked up with mysticism

Sufism, or the orthodox mysticism of the Mohammedans was not the product of the *Koran* ; it resulted from three great influences, Indian, neo-Platonist, and Christian thought, the last-named giving it its characteristic features.   Endowed with a profoundly mystical temperament, Algazel studied all the degrees of that intuitive science which is the work of asceticism and faith, while ordinary knowledge is the work of the sense and the reason.[3]   The mysticism of Algazel and of the Sufi

---

[1] We may also mention Alhazen, a psychologist and physician, whose treatise on light was translated by Witelo.

[2] The question of the eternity or non-eternity of the world served as a part shibboleth between believers and non-believers.   See Worms, *op. cit.*, no. 140 p. 231.

[3] Cf. Asin, *La Mystique d'Al-Gazzali* (*Mélanges de la faculté orientale*, 1914 p. 67-104).

is not pantheistic, any more than is the Christian system. This is all the more remarkable since, in contrast with Christian mysticism, ecstasy seems to be brought within the reach of the natural powers of man.[1]

Side by side with orthodox mysticism, there was from the time of Avicenna a neo-Platonist form known as the " illuminative philosophy."

After Avicenna, Arabian philosophy declined in the East, but its renown was continued in Spain.

138. Western branch : Averrhoes.—The Spain of the tenth century was the meeting-place of the most diverse races. In the Mohammedan kingdoms, Jews and Christians lived side by side with the Arabs, and for the most part enjoyed the same liberty of thought which later on the Christians of Toledo conceded to the Jewish and Arab populations occupying the cities at the time of the *reconquista*[2] (p. 51). This helped to make Spain the centre of an intense philosophic movement up to the thirteenth century.

The origins of the Arabo-Spanish philosophy date back to the ninth century with ABENMASARRA, who reproduced the theories of pseudo-Empedocles. In the eleventh century we find the names of ABEN-HAZAM of Cordova, AVEMPACE (end of eleventh century to 1138), and ABU-BACER (Ibn Thofail, 1100-1185). The last two leaned rather towards mysticism.

AVERRHOES (Ibn Roschd) was immeasurably greater than any of the foregoing. He was born at Cordova in 1126. He was in turn held in honour in the courts of the great, and then disgraced. He died in 1198. He was a physician and a man of science, and a great commentator on Aristotle. His admiration for the Stagirite became a sort of worship. He was known in the Middle Ages as the *Commentator*. In spite of this, his commentaries, like those of Avicenna, and for the same reasons, do not give the authentic doctrine of Aristotle on all points. Averrhoes was also the author of original treatises in philosophy. Among them many may be mentioned : the *Destruction of destruction*, in reply to Gazali ; *Quæsita in libros logicæ Aristotelis ;* four treatises on the unity of the intellect ;[3] *De*

---

[1] Carra de Vaux, *Gazali*, p. 207.   [2] Cf. Altamira, *op. cit.*, p. 410 *et seq.*
[3] *De animæ beatitudine ; Libellus seu Epistola Averroes de Connexione intellectus abstracti cum homine* (Vol. X in Venice edition) ; a treatise on the material intellect exists in a Hebrew version translated into German and published by L. Hannes (Halle, 1892) ; *Tractatus Averroys qualiter intellectus materialis conjungitur intelligentiæ abstractæ.* (Renan has published extracts from the last-named in *Averroes et l'Averroisme*).

substantia orbis ; and various works on the harmony between religion and philosophy. The following are his principal theories :

(i) The Supreme Being brings forth from all eternity, but all at once, all the *Intelligences.* These, then, do not emanate from one another as in Avicenna ; all come forth directly from God. Their plurality results from the fact that they are unequal in perfection and simplicity.[1]   They are extrinsically united to spheres. The heavens are composed of several spheres, each with an intelligence which is its form. The first mover puts in motion the first sphere, and the latter passes on the motion to the planetary spheres as far as the moon, which is moved by the human intellect (*intelligentia vel motor lunæ*). This intellect, which intervenes in our acts of understanding, has a metaphysical rôle as in Avicenna's system.

(ii) *The eternity and potentiality of matter.*   While the Eastern Arabians followed the neo-Platonists in consigning matter or the principle of corporeal imperfection to the region of non-being, Averrhoes on the contrary conceives of it as no mere void, but a universal potency containing in itself the germ of all forms. In presence of eternal matter, the first motor (*extractor*) draws forth (*extractio*) the active forces of the latter : the material world results from the uninterrupted sequence of these developments. The series of generations is necessary *a parte ante* and *a parte post.*

(iii) *The monism of the human intellect and the denial of personal immortality.*   The human intelligence, the last of the planetary series, is an immaterial, eternal form, separated from individuals, and endowed with numerical unity. This intelligence is both the active intellect and the material or possible intellect.   The whole human mind is impersonal and objective ; it is the torch which illumines individual souls, and thus secures for humanity an unchangeable participation in the eternal truths.[2]

In the individual man, the act of intelligence takes place in the following manner : by its action on the sense images

---

[1] *Destructio Destructionis,* Disp. III, Cf. the commentaries of Shem Tob Ibn Falaquera on the *Guide to the Perplexed* of Maimonides, Part II, Introd., Propositio XVI.
[2] Cum ex hoc dicto nos possumus opinari intellectum materialem esse unicum in cunctis individuis, possumusque adhuc ex hoc existimare humanam speciem esse æternam. . . ideo opportebit intellectum materialem non posse denudari a principiis universalibus natura notis universæ humanæ speciei.— *De anima,* III, ed. Juntes, Venice, 1550, p. 165, R.B.

which are proper to each man, the separated intelligence contracts an accidental union with the individual according to the dispositions of each one, and without suffering any detriment to its numerical unity from these manifold unions.[1] This first degree of possession engenders in the individual the acquired intellect wich one may call " the impersonal reason participated by the personal being."[2] But there are still more intimate unions of man with the universal intellect—that which results from the actual possession of the abstract essences; and, at the highest point in the scale, that which is brought about by the mystical knowledge and prophetic illumination.[3]

From this doctrine follows the extinction of individual consciousness and the impersonality of life after death. Happiness consists in an ever closer union with the intelligence of the race; individual souls die, but humanity is immortal in the eternity of the objective reason.

(iv) *Philosophy and the allegorical interpretation of the Koran.* Many of Averrhoes' doctrines ran counter to the Mohammedan religion. It was indeed because the caliphs suspected his philosophy that he was banished. Nevertheless, Averrhoes was not irreligious, nor an adversary of the religion of the *Koran*; but the system of relations which he established between faith and science led him to rationalism. For he distinguished between the literal interpretation of the *Koran*, suitable for the illiterate, and the allegorical interpretation to which philosophers have access and which alone leads one to the higher truths. It belongs to philosophy to decide what is traditional in religion, what doctrines need to be interpreted, and in what way. These principles enable Averrhoes to reconcile the thesis of the temporal origin of the world defended by Gazali, with the Peripatetic thesis of its eternity. He

---

[1] Et, cum declaratum est ... quod impossibile est ut intellectus copuletur cum unoquoque hominum, et numeretur per numerationem eorum per partem, quæ est eo quasi materia, secundum intellectum materialem, remanet ut continuatio intellectorum cum nobis hominibus sit per continuationem intentionis intellectæ cum nobis et sunt intentiones imaginatæ, etc.—*ibid.*, p. 164, V. A. Cf. the whole commentary on Book III of *De Anima*, and the *opuscula* on the separated intellect. So, too, the great scholastics of the Middle Ages, e.g., St. Thomas in his treatise *De Unitate intellectus*, Dante in the *Purgatory*, XXV, 64, and the Averrhoists of the thirteenth century (Siger of Brabant for instance), who were careful and exact commentators on Averrhoes, attribute to him the thesis of the unity of the acting and the possible intellect, or the unity of the human intelligence in general. In certain places, Averrhoes enumerates five intellects : active, passive, material, speculative, and acquired. Cf. Avicenna's theory (p. 223).

[2] Renan, *Averroes et l'Averroisme*, 5th edn. p. 140.

[3] Ita ut ipse idem recipiat seipsum—*De animæ beatit.*, c. 4.

devotes a special treatise to this attempt at reconciliation.[1] Here we find the first suggestion of the doctrine of the two truths so extensively used by the latin Averrhoists.

The line of Arabian philosophers came to an end with Averrhoes, but their influence survived in the person of the Jewish philosophers.[2]

139. Philosophy among the Jews : Avencebrol, Maimonides. —If we exclude mysticism which centred round the Cabala, we may say that Jewish philosophy is an adaptation of the doctrine of Judaism to Greek philosophy as transmitted by the Arabs. This feature is already noticeable in PHILO (30 B.C.–50 A.D.) and is more prominent still in the Middle Ages. Among the philosophic writers prior to the eleventh century we may mention the physician and logician ISAAC ISRAELI († 940). DAVID BEN MERWAN the caraïte, and especially his contemporary and opponent, SAADJA (892-942), who has been called the first Jewish philosopher. His chief work, "Amânât," or *Book of Faith and Science*, written in 933 at Sura in Babylonia, is at once exegetical and apologetical, inasmuch as it endeavours to show the harmony existing between Judaism and reason. Saadja was an eclectic : he took his philosophic arguments from the Greeks and the Arabian rationalists as well as from the Orthodox Arabs. The work was written in Arabic, but was twice translated into Hebrew, one version being made in 1186 by Jehuda ben Saul ibn Tibbon.

Jewish philosophy developed principally in Spain, where also their science and literature flourished, thanks to the freedom they enjoyed under the Arab domination.

SALOMON IBN GEBIROL (AVENCEBROL, about 1020-1050 /70), of Saragossa, was the first Jewish philosopher in Spain, and with him began a period of brilliant thought. His chief work, *Fons Vitæ*, the only one known to the West in the thirteenth century, and which made a great impression, develops a powerful and original system in which the Aristotelian and neo-Platonist influences of Arabian philosophy are closely combined.

The first fundamental idea is that of emanative and degenerate monism. God, the supreme Being, One and Unknowable

[1] Published by Worms, *op. cit.* In connection with the temporal creation of the world, Averrhoes writes for instance : Omnia ista sunt existimationes vulgares, valde sufficientes secundum cursum quem nutriuntur homines in eis, non secundum sermonem sufficientes.—*Comment. Physics* of Aristotle, Vol. IV, in Venice edition of the *Opera* (1560), Book VIII, c. 1, p. 271 v.

[2] Renan, *op. cit.*, p. 173, says that " Arabian philosophy was never taken seriously except by the Jews."

(Plotinus) is the only reality, whence is derived the series of limited beings as from an inexhaustible source. God produces the Cosmic Spirit, inferior to Himself, and composed of matter and form (Aristotle), two universal principles which permeate all finite reality, and which God brings together in an indissoluble union by His Will. The potentiality and finite nature of all the stages of the Cosmos are explained by the presence in all things of *materia universalis*, just as their plasticity and all the determinations connected therewith are derived from the *forma universalis*. When the Cosmic Spirit spreads itself out by the process of degenerating emanation, its development at once divides into two lines, in which it recognizes its own being, namely, the line of pure spirits, and that of corporeal things. This division is explained by a new state of potentiality (matter) and actuality (form). In pure spirits, there is a spiritual matter and form existing in the cosmic matter and form. In the same way, in corporeal things, to the various perfections of intellectual life in man and to those of sensitive and vegetable life and corporeal extension, there correspond new forms, according to the degrees of the hierarchical scale, united to matter or corporeal potentiality. Thus each individual substance possesses within itself a plurality of matters and forms determining its place in the system of emanations ; and all things derive their being from the Divine source in the Cosmic Spirit.

Man is a *microcosmos* since he is an image of the universe or *macrocosmos*. His body, a *résumé* of the corporeal world, results from cosmic matter and corporeal matter, which are actualized by the inferior forms of corporeity (extension), figure, colour, etc. At the same time it is the seat of vegetative, sensible and rational souls, which are so many derivatives of the universal Soul or cosmic form. He also possesses intelligence, which can rise to the intuition of the Infinite. The Cosmic Spirit, together with everything which comes forth from it, tends towards God, the Absolute and Unique Good.

That which is peculiar to Avencebrol is not his emanative monism, but his theory of the plurality of matters and forms in one and the same individual, and the cognate thesis that the composition of matter and form is found also in spiritual substances. The discussion of these two doctrines played a great part in the scholastic metaphysics of the thirteenth century.

To the name of Avencebrol we may join that of JOSEPH BEN ZADDIK († 1149). His *Microcosmos* marks the transition from the religious science with which the Motakallimîn opposed philosophy, to the Jewish Aristotelianism represented by Moses Maimonides.

MOSES MAIMONIDES was born at Cordova in 1135, and died in Egypt in 1204. In his *Book of Precepts*, and *Guide for the Do ʒting* (which the Scholastics called *Dux neutrorum sive dusiorum*), he builds up on an Aristotelian foundation a philosophic justification of the doctrines of Judaism. The perplexed ones whose doubts he wishes to remove are the Jews who do not question the existence of God, but represent Him in anthropomorphic ways.

The highest object of metaphysics is God. Maimonides proves his existence after the manner of the "philosophers" of Alfarabi and Avicenna, by the argument for the first mover, and the distinction between the possible and the necessary, two proofs which he derives from his predecessors, and which he supports by "twenty-six propositions of philosophers" drawn from Aristotle's *Physics* and *Metaphysics*. A third proof deduces the existence of a necessary and infinite Being from that of contingent and limited beings, and this is peculiar to Maimonides. A last argument, very similar to the first, leads to the existence of a first and unique cause. The similarity between these arguments and the "five ways" of Thomas Aquinas has often been pointed out.

Maimonides stresses the unity and spirituality of God. We attain to God only by negative ideas, by excluding all potentiality and resemblance with limited being. We are able to say what He is not, not what He is. God created the world in time, and above man there are pure spirits constituting a hierarchy of perfection. Of all corporeal beings, man alone is the object of a Providence extending to each single individual. The knowledge of God is the end towards which tend both philosophy and religion, by convergent efforts. In order to harmonize belief and reason, Maimonides admits side by side with the literal exegesis of the Bible, a philosophic and allegorical interpretation by means of which the texts take a sense which does not contradict certain scientific truths.[1] This method is tinged with rationalism, and led to controversy and opposition in the Jewish schools of the thirteenth and fourteenth centuries.

[1] Husik, *op. cit.*, p. 240 *et seq.*

Maimonides was the last great representative of Jewish Philosophy in Spain. He exercised a considerable influence on the Jews of Provence and on the Scholastics.

140. Bibliography.—Ludwig Stein, *Die Continuität der griechischen Philosophie in der Gedankewelt der Byzantiner* (*Arch. f. Gesch. d. Philos.*, Bd. II, h. 2, 1896) ; K. Krumbacher, *Gesch. der byzant. Litteratur*, 2 Aufl. Munchen, 1897 ; articles by M. Huit in *Annales Philos. Chrét.*, 1895 ; Minges, *Zum Gebrauch der Schrift de fide orthodoxa des J. Damascenus in d. Scholastik*, in *Theol. Quartsch.*, 1914, pp. 225-247.

The following are some general works relative to the history of Arabian and Jewish philosophy. For other works see those mentioned in notes : Munck, *Mélanges de philos. juive er arabe* (Paris, 1859) ; Boer, *Gesch. d .philos. in Islam* (Stuttgart, 1901), good ; De Lacy O'Leary, *Arabic Thought and its Place in History* (London, 1922) ; Carra de Vaux, *Avicenne* (Paris, 1900) ; *Gazali*, by the same (1902), both good. The *De ortu scientiarum* of Alfarabi is published by Baeumker, *BGPM*, XIX, 3. Many good studies by Miguel Asin y Palacios, Professor at Madrid. See also Worms, *BGPM*, III, 4 ; E. Renan, *Averroes et l'Averroisme*, 3rd edit., Prem. partie. Neumark, *Gesch. d. judischer Litter. d. Mittelalter nach Problemen dargestellt* (*Berlin*, 1908 and 1910), three volumes ; I. Husik, *A History of Mediæval Jewish Philosophy* (New York, 1916), good. The *Fons Vitæ* of Avencebrol is published in *BGPM*, I, 2-4. See studies by Wittmann, Grunfeld, and Guttmann in the same collection, V, 1 ; VII, 6 ; X, 4. The *Guide of the Doubting* has been edited by Munck (Paris, 3 vols.) in Arabic and French.

Latin translations of Alfarabi, Algazel, Avicenna and Averrhoes were published in the fifteenth and sixteenth centuries. The editions of Averrhoes were particularly numerous, and his commentaries were included in editions of Aristotle. All these works are rare, and a critical edition is required. In 1515-16 the works of Isaac Israeli were published in Latin. The *Amânât* of Saadja has been published in Arabic by Landauer, in Hebrew in 1562 and 1789, and has been partially translated into German by Bloch (1879), Horten, who in 1906 announced a critical edition of Avicenna's *Metaphysics* and *Psychology*, has translated several works into German : *Metaphysik* (Halle, 1907), *Das Buch der Genesung d. Seele* (Leipzig, 1907-1909). Dieterici, *Die Sogenannte Theologie d. Aristoteles*, 2 vols., Leipzig, 1882-83, text and German translation. Dr. A. Nagy has edited the *opuscula* of Alkindi, *Die philosophischen Abhandl. des Al-Kindis*, *BGPM*, II, 5. Max Horten, *Die Philosophie des Islam*, Munchen, 1924, in collection *Gesch. der Philos. in Einzeldarstellungen*, good.

SECOND PERIOD

MEDIÆVAL PHILOSOPHY IN THE THIRTEENTH CENTURY

CHAPTER I

The Philosophical Renaissance in the Thirteenth Century

141. Western, Arabian, Jewish and Byzantine Philosophy.—
The thirteenth century was the golden age of mediæval philosophy, and the West was the seat of its greatest triumph. Western philosophy came into contact with the Arabian, Jewish and Byzantine thought, to its own exclusive advantage. Indeed the historic rôle of the Arabs and Jew may be looked on as terminated.[1] As for the Byzantine genius, this slumbered on until the Renaissance.

An Arabian School of Christian theologians was founded by JAHJA IBN ADI († 1285), a translator of Aristotle and author of theological works in which he defends the Christian doctrines.[2] The Jews produced nothing original. On the one hand, the discussions on the system of Maimonides were limited to a few synagogues in Provence, Catalonia and Aragon, whither the Jews had been driven by the fanaticism of the Almahades, and although the rationalistic philosophers triumphed over the theological party, they did not depart from the teaching of the *Guide for the Doubting*. On the other hand, the ascendancy of Averrhoes over the Jewish writers became still more marked. SAMUEL ABEN TIBBON in *The Opinions of the Philosophers* (written at the beginning of the thirteenth century), JUDA BEN SALOMO COHEN, a protégé of Frederick II, in *The Search for Wisdom* (1247), the Spaniard FALAQUERA (born about 1226), and GERSON BEN SALOMON, in his *Gate of Heaven* (second half of thirteenth century), produced what are little more than encyclopædias of the teaching of Averrhoes. Similarly, there were numerous translations of Averrhoes from Arabic into Hebrew in the thirteenth century.

As for Byzantium, its philosophic output is represented by the work of two or three encyclopædists. NICEPHORUS BLEMMIDES (1197 or 1198-1272) gained the title of "The Philosopher" (ὁ φιλόσοφος) by reason of the breadth of his knowledge.

---

[1] De Lacy O'Leary, *op. cit.*, p. 260.
[2] G. Graf, *Die Philosophie und Gotteslehre des Jahjâ ibn Adî und späteren Autoren*. Skizzen meist nach ungedrukten Quellen. *BGPM*, VIII, 7.

In particular he wrote a summary of logic and physics.[1] GEORGE PACHYMERES (1242-1310) made a résumé of the Aristotelian philosophy, and a well known paraphrase of the works of pseudo-Dionysius. SOPHONIAS and LEO MAGENTINOS were two other commentators on Aristotle.

Our attention during this period will be concentrated on the masters of Western thought, and chiefly on the Scholastics.

142. Division.—Scholasticism did not triumph without a struggle : it had to wage a philosophic crusade against rival theories. Hence two chapters will deal respectively with :

(i) The Scholastic Group (Chapter II).

(ii) The anti-Scholastic group (Chapter III), this comprising all those philosophers who subscribed to materialism or else to monism—the two sworn enemies of Scholasticism—in some form or other.

(iii) In a third group (Chapter IV) we shall place those philosophies which do not enter into this classification : they are distinct from Scholasticism, but do not declare war on its vital theories of pluralism and psychological spiritualism. The most important of these is Latin neo-Platonism. A second school, represented above all by Roger Bacon, developed the natural sciences. Another, with Raymond Lully, revived the rationalism of Scotus Eriugena. It is worthy of note that the philosophers of this group opposed the Averrhoists when they came to deal with problems which the latter discussed with the Scholastics.

The variety of these systems is the best proof of the intellectual vitality of the thirteenth century. Before considering them in detail, we must briefly recall the causes of the renaissance in science and philosophy.

143. The philosophic renaissance.—The sudden and widespread philosophic renaissance which characterized the first years of the thirteenth century in the West was due to the converging action of three causes :

(i) The introduction of the West to a great number of philosophical works up till then unknown.

(ii) The erection of the Universities, especially those of Pari and Oxford.

(iii) The rise of the mendicant orders.

To these external causes may be added the vitality of the philosophical movements of the twelfth century (cf. p. 187).

[1] C. Mercati, *Blemmidea*, in *Bessarion*, 1915.

§ 1—*The New Philosophical Revival in the West*

144. The new Latin translations.[1]—For the second or even the third time, the West rediscovered a portion of the philosophical treasures of ancient Greece. Also, new texts were discovered of those works known already, and at the same time the Arabic works by Mohammedan and Jewish writers became better known.

If we leave out of account the part played by Humanism at the end of the Middle Ages, we may say that this introduction of the Latin West to the works of ancient Greece was completed during the thirteenth century, and comprised two periods. In the first, the translations were made from the Arabic just as much, if not more than, from the Greek. Translations direct from the Greek mark the second period. Chronologically then, we shall deal first with the translations from Arabic into Latin. Works of speculative philosophy were translated before works on ethics, economics, politics and rhetoric, of which no complete version existed before 1240.

If we arrange them in geographical order, almost all the translations were produced in a few particular centres. In Spain, a country well known to the West by reason of the pilgrimages to St. James of Compostella, Toledo was the centre. To Toledo came strangers from afar, attracted by the traditions of Dominic Gundisalvi, John of Spain, and Gerard of Cremona. In England there was the circle of Robert Grosseteste, Bishop of Lincoln from 1235 to 1253 ; in Italy the centre was the court of the two Kings of Naples and Sicily, Frederick II (1198-1250) and his natural son, Manfred (1258-1266), and the Pontifical Court, especially under the pontificate of Urban IV (1261-1264).[2] The influence of these centres is explained not only by the protection which the sovereigns and prelates

---

[1] This section, together with pp. 70-82 have been read through and brought up-to-date so far as the Latin translations are concerned, by A. Pelzer, of Rome.

[2] See Haskins, *Science at the Court of the Emperor Frederick II*, in *American Historical Review*, 1922, pp. 669-694 ; Grauert, *Magister Heinrich der Poet in Würzburg u. die römische Curie* (Abhandlungen d. k. Bayer, Akad. d. Wissenschafte philos.-philol. u. hist. Klasse, Bd. 17, 1 and 2 Abhandlg), Munich, 1912. The poem here edited and studied at length (*Liber de statu curiæ Romanæ*) was probably composed between 1261 and 1265. It gives a picture of the Pontifical Court under Urban IV. The author not only praises the scientific discussions which the Pope had with those around him, but also speaks of a someone of all-round excellence, present at the Court, and capable of rediscovering philosophy if it were to disappear. This would be St. Thomas Aquinas according to Grauert ; Albert the Great according to Grabmann (*Histor. Jahrbuch*, 1917, pp. 315-320).

accorded to science, but also by the relations which were there kept up with the Byzantine and Mohammedan worlds.

(i) *Translations from Arabic into Latin, of Greek, Arabian or Jewish authors.*—MICHAEL SCOT begins the series of translators.[1] A Scotsman by birth, he finished his version of the *Sphere* of Al Bitrogi (*Alpetragius*) in 1217, and the *De Animalibus* of Aristotle before 1220. The latter was a work of nineteen books in which the Arabs combined the *History of the Animals* (ten books), and the *Generation of Animals* (five books). The translation of this big work met with great success, and Albert the Great incorporated it in his *De animalibus*. To the period of Michael Scot's stay in Spain doubtless belong also a *Divisio philosophiæ*, after Gundisalvi, of which Vincent of Beauvais has preserved some fragments,[2] the *Quæstiones Nicolai peripatetici*, attributed to Scot by Albert the Great, and translations of several works of Aristotle accompanied by the *Middle (Minor) Commentary* of Averrhoes. These works are respectively the *De Cælo et Mundo* (dedicated to Stephen of Provence), the *De Anima*, and probably the *Physics* and *Metaphysics*, if it was really he who translated these two last-named works. From 1220 Michael Scot was in Italy, and while there the Popes Honorius III and Gregory IX conferred upon him ecclesiastical benefices in England and Scotland. But he definitely threw in his lot with Frederick II, and became his official astrologer. Towards 1230 he dedicated to the Emperor his version of the *De Animalibus* of Avicenna, and an astrological work in three parts (*Liber introductorius, Liber particularis, Physionomia* or *De Secretis Naturæ*), recently studied by Haskins.[3] He died some time before 1236.

In Toledo again appeared the first translation by another writer, HERMANN THE GERMAN,[4] Bishop of Astorga in Spain from 1266 to 1272 the year of his death (not to be confused with Hermann the Dalmatian). This work, dating from 1240, was the *Minor Commentary* of Averrhoes on the *Nicomæan Ethics* (*liber Nicomachiæ*). Hermann also translated an Alexandrian *Summary* of the same work of Aristotle[5] in 1243 or

[1] C. H. Haskins, *Michael Scot and Frederick II, Isis,* Vol. 4, 1921, pp 250-275 ; *Science at the Court of the Emperor Frederick II (passim)*.
[2] Reprinted by L. Baur, *Dominicus Gundissalinus de divisione philosophiæ BGPM,* IV, 2-3, pp. 398-400.
[3] *Op cit.,* pp. 260-275.
[4] G. H. Lucquet, *Hermann l'Allemand* (in *Revue de l'hist. des réligions* Vol. 44, 1901, pp. 407-422.
[5] Cf. Pelzer, *Les versions lat. des ouvrages de morale,* etc., pp. 339-341. The

1244 ; and about 1250 a work by Averrhoes on the *Rhetoric*, after translating the commencement of the glosses of Alfarabi on this same work. Some time after he wrote an original treatise on the *Rhetoric*, and in 1256 a translation of the minor commentary of Averrhoes on the *Poetics*.

Pelzer has discovered an unknown translator, PETER GALLEGO, a Franciscan, and first Bishop of Cathagena (1250 to 1267, the year of his death).[6] Of his works we only possess an abridged version of the *Book of Animals* (from various authors) and an opusculum on *The Government of the House*.[7]

Lastly we may call attention to a translation into Latin from the Hebrew version of the great philosophical work of the Jew Maimonides (Moses ben Maimuni ; known to the Middle Ages as Rabbi Moses). This was the *Guide for those in perplexity*, or, as it was commonly called, the *Guide for those astray* (139). It was written originally in Arabic, and translated into Hebrew (*more Nebuchim*) first during the author's lifetime by SAMUEL TIBBON, and shortly afterwards by JEDHUA CHARISI. It was Charisi's text which was translated into Latin in the early part of the thirteenth century (*dux neutrorum seu dubiorum*).[8]

(ii) *Translations of Greek writers into Latin*. Already in the first decade of the thirteenth century the works of Aristotle dealing with natural philosophy and metaphysics were " read " and " explained " at Paris. This is evident from the condemnations of Aristotle which will be referred to later on, and also from certain statements made in the *Chronicles* of Robert of Auxerre for the year 1210,[9] and of William the Breton. The latter tells us that " certain metaphysical works attributed to Aristotle " had just been brought from Constantinople and translated from Greek into Latin.[10]

text of the summary is given in C. Marchesi, *L'Etica Nicomachea nella tradizione latina Medievale*, Messina, 1904, pp. 41-86.

[6] Study, with texts in the *Miscellanea Fr. Ehrle* (*Studi e Testi* of the Vatican library), in the press.

[7] The West also acquired a knowledge of the Arab religion. Already in the twelfth century Peter the Venerable, Abbot of Cluny, caused to be translated into Latin the *Koran*, a short apologetical treatise against Islam, and three short works concerning Mahomet. He himself wrote a work against the Saracens. See Mandonnet, *Pierre le Venerable et son activité litteraire entre l'Islam*, in *Revue Thomiste*, 1st year, pp. 328-341.

[8] This Latin version was edited at Paris in 1520 by Giustiniani (Augustinus Justinianus).

[9] *Monum. Germaniæ Hist.*, S.S., Vol. XXVI, p. 276.

[10] F. Delaborde, *Œuvres de Rigord et de Guillaume le Breton*, Vol. I, Paris, 1882, p. 233. In 1204 the Crusades captured Constantinople, and Baldwin became Emperor. The following year, at his request, Innocent III invited

On the other hand, Baeumker has pointed out in the *De motu cordis* of Alfred of Sareshel, composed about 1215 if not earlier, quotations from Latin translations of the *De anima*, the *De somno et vigilia*, and the *De exspiratione et respiratione*, the *Metaphysics*, and the *Ethica vetus*[11]. RADULFUS DE LONGO CAMPO utilized the *De anima* and the *De sommo et vigilia* about 1216 in his glosses on the *Anticlaudianus* of Alan of Lille.[1] According to V. Rose,[13] ARNOLD OF SAXONY incorporated into his *De finibus* (or rather *De virtutibus*) *rerum naturalium*, written between 1220 and 1230, certain passages from the *De cæl et mundo* of Avicenna, and from Gerard's translation of Aristotle's *De cælo et mundo*. These he calls respectively " *D cælo et mundo secundum veterem* and *secundum novam transla tionem*. Of the translation made by Michael Scot, Arnold knows only the nineteen books of the *De Animalibus*. Never theless, he has recourse to Latin versions of the *Metaphysics*, the *Physics*, the *De generatione et corruptione*, the *De Anima*, the *Parva Naturalia*, and the *Ethica vetus* which he contrast with the *Ethica nova* or first book of the Nichomachean Ethics These last two works he calls the *Liber Ethicorum secundu veterem* and *secundum novam translationem*.

Who were the authors of all these Latin translations in us at Paris, in England, and Germany during the first part of th thirteenth century, and when were they made ? We do no know. Some of them must belong to the twelfth century, a we have already seen (p. 74) ; others belong to the beginnin of the thirteenth century. But in any case we do not know th name of any one who translated philosophical works directl from Greek into Latin between 1162, the year of the death o

the French bishops to send religious to Greece as missionaries, and also invite the University of Paris to send many of its masters there in order to promo studies. Does the " College of Constantinople " at Paris date from this time Certainly from 1248 onwards, if not earlier, the Popes arranged for at lea ten " Eastern " clerics of Arabic and other tongues to attend the Universit Cf. Ch. Jourdain, *Un collège oriental à Paris au XIIIe siècle, Excursio historiques et philosophiques à travers le moyen age*, Paris, 1888, pp. 221-229.
[11] *Die stellung des Alfred von Sareshel* (Alfredus Anglicus) *u. seiner Schr De motu cordis in d. Wissenschaft d. beginnenden XIII. Jh.*, Sitzungsberich d. k. Bayer. Akad. d. Wissensch., philos.-philol. u. hist. Klasse, Munich, 191
[12] Cf. Haureau, *Notices et extraits de quelques mss.*, Vol. I, Paris, 1890, p 351-356.
[13] *Aristoteles de lapidibus u. Arnoldus Saxo, Zeitschrift für Deutsches Alterthu* XVIII, 1875, pp. 341-344, 447-454. Cf. Stange, *Die Encyclopadie d. Arnold Saxo zum ersten Mal nach einem Erfurter Codex herausg.*, Progr., Erfurt 190 1906, 1907. For Alexander Neckam see above (p. 66 note 3) ; for oth authors see chapter entitled *Die Aristotelesrezeption in d. ersten Hälfte d. Jahrh.*, in Grabmann, *Forschungen* etc. (pp. 16-55). See also *ibid.*, pp. 74- concerning the *Compilatio de libris naturalibus* which begins : *Cum om desiderii compos*.

Henricus Aristippus, and 1240 or thereabouts. About the year 1240 we have the activity of Robert Grosseteste, with whom the undertaking of Latin translations from the Greek enters upon a new stage.

ROBERT GROSSETESTE, the *Lincolniensis* of mediæval writers, was a friend and professor of the Friars Minor at Oxford, the first Chancellor of the University there, and Bishop of Lincoln from 1235 until his death in 1253. He was a great prelate and scholar, and the recent researches of Baur, De Ghellinck and Pelzer have shown the great part he played as a translator. He had translated into Latin the *Testament of the Twelve Patriarchs*,[1] the *Letter*s of St. Ignatius of Antioch in their second recension, the works of pseudo-Dionysius on *Mystical Theology*, the *Celestial Hierarchy*, the *Ecclesiastical Hierarchy*, and the *Divine Names*,[2] the *De Orthodoxa Fide* of St. John Damascene,[3] extracts from the *Lexicon* of Suidas, the *opusculum* on Virtues and Vices (*De Virtute* or *De laudabilibus bonis*), and probably the work of pseudo-Andronicus of Rhodes on the Passions (i.e., the first part of the Περί παθῶν).[4]

He also undertook towards 1240-1243 the first Latin translation of the whole of the *Nichomachean Ethics*, wrongly ascribed to William of Moerbeke or else to an imaginary personage, Henry Krosbein or Kosbien.[5] To his translation of this work, the bishop added the commentaries of Eustratius,

[1] According to Matthew of Paris, Robert caused to be brought from Greece the Greek text to which John of Basingstoke had called his attention, and translated it in 1242 assisted by Master Nicholas the Greek, one of his collaborators in the work of translation.

[2] Cf. L. Baur, *Die philos. Werke d. Robert Grosseteste*, BGPM, IX, Munster, 1902, pp. 31*-43*.

[3] Cf. J. de Ghellinck, *Le mouvement théologique du XIIIe s.*, Paris, 1914, pp. 255-262 ; E. Hocedez, *La diffusion de la " translatio Lincolniensis " du " De Orthodoxa Fide,"* Bulletin d'ancienne litter. et archæol. chrét., Vol. III, 1913, pp. 189-198.

[4] Pelzer, *Les versions latines*, etc., pp. 393, 321-323.

[5] *ibid.*, pp. 401-408. Henry of Brabant and Aurelius (confused with Alfredus) are other imaginary personages who must be removed from the list of translators, in addition to the Dominican, Thomas of Cantimpré, the author of *Bonum universale de apibus* and *De natura rerum*. In the Preface to his Latin translation of the *Nichomachean Ethics* (1417 or 1418), Leonard Bruni d'Arezzo violently criticizes Grosseteste's translation, which he attributes to a Dominican. In special apologias, Alphonsus Garcia of Carthagena, Bishop of Burgos, and Baptiste de Giudici, Bishop of Ventimiglia defend the old translation against the humanist's attack, the former writing in Leonard's own lifetime, and the latter between 1481 and 1484. See Grabmann, *Eine ungedruckte Verteidigungsschrift von Wilhelms von Mœrbeke Uebersetzung d. Nikom. Ethik* (in *Abhandlungen aus d. Gebiete d. Philos. u. ihrer Geschichte*, Festgabe G. von Hertling, Fribourg, 1913, pp. 133-142) ; Birkenmajer, *Vermischte Untersuchungen zur Gesch. d. Mittelalterl. Philosophie*, BGPM, XX, 5, Munster, 1922, pp. 129-210, 226-235 (gives Leonard's Preface, the treatise by Alphonsus, and several letters concerning the controversy).

R

Metropolitan of Nicea (eleventh and twelfth centuries) on Books I and VI, those of an anonymous writer on Books II—V and VII, those of Michael, Metropolitan of Ephesus (eleventh century) on Books V, IX, and X, and that of Aspasius (second century) on Book VIII. The notes which the Bishop appended to his version are full of information on Greek lexicography and syntax, and are intended to explain and justify his translation.[1]

Albert the Great and Thomas Aquinas owed a great deal of the knowledge of Greek displayed in their writings to these notes and to other versions by Robert Grosseteste similarly annotated. Lastly, many libraries possess copies, not indeed of a real commentary or a collection of questions, but an *Abridgment*, in which Grosseteste gives a summary of the ten books of the *Nichomachean Ethics*[2] (Cf. 232).

BARTHOLOMEW OF MESSINA, who lived at the Court of Manfred, King of Naples and Sicily, has left a version of the *Magna Moralia* of Aristotle. In addition, a Paduan codex[3] of the fourteenth century contains translations by him of five pseudo-Aristotelian *opuscula : Problemata, De Principiis, De mirabilibus auscultationibus, Physionomia, De signis*. The same codex informs us that these translations were made by order of the King, and proceeds to give anonymous translations of other *opuscula*, among them the following : *De eupragia,*[4]

---

[1] Cf. V. Rose, *Ueber die griech. Commentare zur Ethik d. Aristoteles, Hermes* V, 1871, pp. 61-113. The study of the manuscripts of this translation (cf. Pelzer, *ibid.*, p. 378-401) confirms the information given by Hermann the German about 1250 in the Prologue to his translation concerning the *Rhetoric :* " Hunc librum (i.e., the *Nichomachean Ethics*) prout potui in latinum verti eloquium ex arabico. Et postmodum reverendus pater magister Robertus Grossi Capitas, sed subtilis intellectus, Lincolniensis episcopus, ex primo fonte unde emanaverat, græco videlicet, ipsum est completius interpretatus et græcorum commentis proprias (not *præcipuas*) annectens notulas commentatus."—Pelzer has shown that outside the *Ethica vetus* (i.e. Books II and III) and the *Ethica nova* (i.e. Book I) published by C. Marchesi (*L'Etica Nicomachea nella tradizione latina Medievale*, pp. 1-26, 27-40), other partial translations from the Greek into Latin were known during the first half of the thirteenth century, in particular : (1) " Another translation of the end of the *Ethica nova* " (Borghesi MS: 108, f. 262 r-v) ; (2) extracts from Book VII (*ibid.*, ff. 283-285), utilized by Albert the Great. Grabmann, *Ein griech. Homerzitat bei Albertus Magnus, Hist. Jahrb.*, 1921, pp. 278-281 ; (3) the first part of Book VIII (*ibid.*, ff. 285r-289r) referred to by Albertus as the *Liber de amicitia*.

[2] Already printed at Venice in 1483 in the edition of Aristotle and Averrhoes. Cf. Pelzer, *op. cit.*, pp. 336-338, 339.

[3] Described by C. Marchesi, *L'Etica Nicomachea*, etc., pp. 9-11.

[4] This is Chap. XIV (supplemented by the two first sentences of Chap. XV) of the VII (sometimes known as the VIII) Book of the *Eudemian Ethics*, or the second part of the opusculum *De bona fortuna*, the first part of which reproduces Chap. VIII of Book II of the *Magna Moralia*. Cf. Pelzer, *ibid.*, 317-321.

De inundatione Nili, De respiratione et exspiratione, De juventute et senectute, De causis mortis et vitæ, De mundo.[1] Many translators are referred to in the letter which the King Manfred (and not apparently, the Emperor Frederick) sent to several universities together with the new versions due to his initiative.[2]

Special mention must be made of the Flemish Dominican, WILLIAM OF MOERBEKE, the author of a geomancy. He exchanged ideas with Thomas Aquinas the philosopher and theologian, Campanus of Novare the mathematician, Witelo the physician, Henry Bate of Malines the astronomer, and Rosello of Arezzo the doctor. All these were interested in the Latin translations of works in connection with their respective studies. Some of the versions were made in Nicæa in Asia Minor, Thebes, or Corinth in Greece, and in Viterbo or Orvieto in Italy, where William lived under Urban IV as a member of the Pontifical Court. He was penitentiary and chaplain to many Popes, and was present at the Council of Lyons in 1274. From 1278 till his death in 1286 he held the archiepisopal see of Corinth. At the request of St. Thomas, he undertook a partial translation of Aristotle's works, and in the case of some of these a revision of existing versions.[3] To the category of translations belong the *Politics*, which neither the Latin West nor the Arabian

[1] This version of the *De Mundo*, made for Manfred, must be distinguished from another translation made at Paris and due to Nicholas of Sicily (. . . *a Nicolao Siculo ex greco in latinum translatus parisius*, according to the *explicit*). Perhaps he is to be identified with Nicholas of Reggio, who translated from the Greek for Robert of Anjou, King of Naples (1309-1343). A critical edition of the two versions will be found in W. L. Lorimer, *The Text Tradition of pseudo-Aristotle " De Mundo " together with an appendix containing the text of the mediæval latin versions*, St. Andrew's University Publications, No. xviii, Oxford, 1924, pp. 42-96.

[2] Text sent to Paris is in Denifle and Chatelain, *Chartul.*, Vol. I, pp. 435 *et seq.*

[3] William of Tocco, in his Life of St. Thomas, writes as follows : " Scripsit tiam super philosophiam naturalem et moralem et super metaphysicam, quorum librorum procuravit ut fieret nova translatio quae sententiae Aristotelis ontineret clarios veritatem."—*Acta sanctorum*, Vol. I, martii, p. 665. Mandonnet, in *Siger de Brabant, Etude Critique*, p. 40, has collected together the earliest witnesses to the nature and extent of William's work ; these must be compared with each other and tested above all by an examination of the MSS. of the translations. Roger Bacon, who is rather unjust towards William, distinguishes carefully between translations and revisions : " Willielmus Flemingus . . . omnes translationes factas promisit immutare et novas cudere varias. . . ." (*Compendium studii philosophiae*, in Brewer's edition, London 1859, p. 472). The Catalogue of Stams relative to the Dominican writers (1312) is too general in its statement : " Fr. Wilhelmus Brabantinus, Corinthiensis, transtulit omnes libros naturalis et moralis philosophie de greco in latinum ad instantiam fratris Thome " (Denifle's edition, in *Archiv. f. Litt. u. Kirchengesch. d. Mittelalters*, Vol. II. pp. 226 *et seq.*)

world had known up till then, the *Rhetoric*,[1] the biological works of Aristotle (about 1260),[2] the eleventh book (K) of the *Metaphysics*, the Fourth Book of the *Meteors*, and probably the *Economics*.[3]   The second category, the revisions of already existing translations, comprises especially the other books of the *Metaphysics*.[4] and the *Meteors*[5] as well as the *De Anima*. Future research will decide concerning other works of the Stagirite.[6]   To this list of works must be added the translations of various commentaries : those of Alexander of

[1] Latin texts edited by Susemihl (*Aristot. Politicorum libri octo cum vetusta translatione Guilelmi de Moerbeke*, Leipzig, 1872) and by Spengel (*Aristot. Ars rhetorica, Leipzig*, 1867, Vol. I, pp. 178–342).

[2] L. Dittmeyer has edited a part (Book One and Chapters I to III of Book Two) of the *De Generatione Animalium* translated by William (Progr. Dilligen, 1915); G. Rudberg, the translations into Latin from the Arabic and Greek of the tenth book of the *Historia Animalium*, which in point of fact is not authentic (*Zum sogenannten Zehnten Buche d. Ar. Tiergesch.*, Skrifter utgifna af K. Humanistika Vetenskaps Samfundet i. Uppsala, XIII, 6, Upsala 1911, pp. 109–120, 121–137 respectively).   According to Rudberg this thirteenth century translation from the Greek was not made by William.

[3] To the second half of the thirteenth century belong at least two Latin translations from the Greek of the *Economics* of Aristotle, the one prior to 1270, the other to 1295.   The latter is attributed to Durandus of Auvergne in the *Explicit* of several manuscripts : " Explicit economica ar. translata de greco in latinum per unum archiepiscopum et unum episcopum de grecia et magistrum durandum de alvernia latinum procuratorem universitatis parisiensis tunc temporis in curia Romana. actum anagnie in mense augusti pontificatus domini bonifacii pape VIII anno primo."   See the Preface of F. Susemihl (*Ar. quae feruntur Oeconomica recensuit*, Leipzig, 1887), who published after the Greek text the third book (which is the second in Rose, *Ar. pseudepigraphus*, Leipzig, 1863, p. 647 ; *Ar. fragmenta, ibid.* 1886, p. 140) in a double Latin translation.   He had edited a Latin translation of the First Book in 1870 (Progr., Griefswald).

[4] The researches of Grabmann (*Forschungen über die lat. Aristotelesübersetzungen*, pp. 104–169) of Geyer (*Die Uebersetzungen d. Arist. Metaphysik bei Albertus Magnus u. Thomas v. Aquin, Philos. Jahrbuch*, 1917, pp. 392–415, and of Pelster (*Die griech. lat. Metaphysikübersetzungen d. Mittelalters*, Festgabe C. Baeumker, Munster 1923, pp. 89–118) show that the *Metaphysic* was utilized in the thirteenth century in the following Latin translations made from the Greek : (*a*) *Metaphysica vetus*, in three different redactions, stopping at the fourth chapter of Book Four (or Book *Γ*); (*b*) *Littera* or *translatio Boethii*, as St. Thomas calls it, comprising Books I to X (*I*) and XII (*Λ*) (*c*) *Metaphysica media* (Pelster's terminology) consisting of Books I–X and XII–XIV, represented by the Borghesi MS. 304 and paraphrased toward 1270 by Albert the Great ; (*d*) *Metaphysica nova* (Pelster's terminology) in fourteen books, this is the *Metaphysica Media* revised by William of Moerbek and supplemented by Book XI (K) which he translated.   We may add that Books XI, XIII (M) and XIV (N) are lacking in the Latin translation from the Arabic, in which Book I comprises Book *à* (the Second Book of the Latins) and a part of Book A (Bekker's edition, Chap. V, p. 987*a*6, Chap. VII, p. 989*b*5), while Book II simply consists of the rest of Book A.

[5] Cf. F. H. Forbes, *Mediæval Versions of Aristotle's Meteorology* (*Classic. Review*, Vol. X, 1915, pp. 297–314) and Pelster's *Die griech. lat. Metaphysik übersetzungen*, p. 110.

[6] There is room for a general work dealing with William's method of translation, and his collaborators.   Observations concerning certain translations will be found in Ch. Thurot (*De partibus animalium* and Alexander Commentary on the *De Sensu*), Rudberg (*Historia animalium*), Forbes

Aphrodisius on the *Meteors* (1260) and the *De sensu et sensibili*,[7] those of Simplicius on the *Categories* (1266) and the *De cælo et mundo* (1271), those of John the Grammarian or Philopon on the chapter concerning the intelligence (taken from the commentary on the *De Anima*[8], those of Themistius on the *De Anima* and probably those of Ammonius on the *De Interpretatione*. That is not all. William translated also the *Elementatio theologica* of Proclus (1268) and three of his *opuscula*[9] the Greek text of which is now lost : *De providentia et fato et eo quod in nobis, De decem dubitationibus circa Providentiam, De malorum subsistentia* (all in February 1280).

Birkenmajer was the first to study the partial translations of the Commentary of Proclus on the *Timæus* and the *Pneumatics* of Hero,[10] which he attributes to the Flemish dominican, wrongly according to Pelster. The list of William de Moerbeke's translations also comprises medical works by Hippocrates and Galen, and the autograph of the Vatican (MS. Ottoboni lat. 1850, ff. 11-64) mentions a number of writings chiefly mathematical (1269, the last 1270), many treatises by Archimedes, two commentaries by Eutocius, the Catoptrics of Hero and the Analemma of Ptolemy.[11]

William of Moerbeke's translations were strictly literal, but we find some mistakes therein. They were depreciated by Roger Bacon[12] and certain humanists, but they are thought more of in our own time, even by philologists : some lost works of Greek writers, or Greek MSS. which have now disappeared, superior to those which we possess, can be recon-

---

(*Meteorology*), Pelster (*Metaphysics*), and above all, in W. L. Newman (*The Politics of Aristotle*, Vols. II–IV, Oxford, 1887 and 1902).

[7] Latin translation of the second commentary edited by Ch. Thurot (*Notices et Extraits des mss. de la Bibliothèque Nat. et autres bibliothèques*, Vol. 25, 2nd part, Paris, 1875).

[8] Not the same as the corresponding chapter from ps.-Philopon in the *Commentaria in Arist. graeca* (Vol. XV) published by the Berlin Academy (1897).

[9] Edited by V. Cousin, *Procli philos. platonici opp.*, Vol. I, Paris 1820.

[10] These are the two treatises referred to in the touching letter of condolence sent by the University of Paris after the death of St. Thomas to the General Chapter of the Friars Preachers at Lyons, re-edited and explained by Birkenmajer (*Vermischte Untersuchungen*, p. 4). For the dates of the translations see *ibid.*, pp. 31 *et seq.* ; Forbes, *op. cit.*, pp. 299 *et seq.* ; Grabmann, *op. cit.*, pp. 146–150.

[11] Cf. V. Rose, *Archimedes im Jahre* 1269, *Deutsche Literaturzeitung*, 1884, coll. 211 *et seq.* (first detailed description of the MS. Ottob. lat. 1850) and H. Bosmans, *Guill. de Moerbeke et le traité des corps flottants d' Archimède, Revue des Quest. scientif.*, April, 1922.

[12] Cf. Grabmann, *Forschungen, op. cit.* He collects together and discusses the opinions and statements of Roger Bacon concerning translations of Aristotle.

stituted in their original form by making use of William's literal translations, in which he employed them.[1]

As we have seen, many Latin versions of Aristotle were the work of unknown authors. This is also the case with a translation made from the Greek, probably in the thirteenth century, of the *Hypotyposes pyrrhonienses* of Sextus Empiricus (*pirronie informationes*.)[2] It was not much used.

The Scholastics of the thirteenth century knew only a few philosophical works produced in Byzantium—such as the commentaries of Michael of Ephesus and Eustratius of Nicæa already mentioned, which were known to Albert the Great and St. Thomas Aquinas. On the other hand, the Byzantines were exchanging ideas with the West to an increasing extent, and translated several Latin works into Greek. The first Byzantine translator was MAXIMUS PLANUDES (1260-1310), whom Andronicus II sent on a scientific mission to Venice in 1296. He translated the works of Cicero, Macrobius and Boethius. His version of the *De Consolatione Philosophiæ* of Boethius is still used in teaching the humanities.

The thirteenth century also witnessed the appearance of numerous translations from Arabic into Hebrew which do not directly concern this history. " When the civilization of the Jews migrated from Mohammedan Spain into Provence and the country adjacent to the Pyrenees, Arabic which up till then had been their common as well as learned tongue ceased to be familiar to them, and they felt the need of putting all the important writings in science and philosophy into Hebrew."[3] This work of translation was undertaken chiefly by the family of the Tibbonides established at Lunel, and it was concerned almost exclusively with the works of Averrhoes, and above all his commentaries on Aristotle, as well as the text itself of Aristotle to which these commentaries were joined. Some of these commentaries exist in more than one version.

145. Influence of the new translations.—It is useful to

[1] For an example of what textual criticism reveals, even in the case of certain Latin translations from the Arabic, see A. Mansion, *Etude crit. su le texte de la Physique d'Aristote*, L. I–IV (*Revue de Philologie, de Litter. e d'Hist. anciennes*, 1923, pp. 5–41). This article contains many useful genera remarks concerning the translations of Aristotle (pp. 5–14).

[2] Ch. Jourdain, *Sextus Empiricus et la philos. scolastique*, *Excursion historiques*, pp. 201–217 ; Baeumker, *Archiv. f. Gesch. d. Philos.*, 1891 pp. 574–577 ; and the edition of Sextus Empiricus by Mutschmann, Vol. I Leipzig, 1912.

[3] Renan, *op. cit.* p. 185.

distinguish between the works of Aristotle, the Arabian and Jewish works, and the neo-Platonist texts.

(i) The great works of Aristotle called attention to new problems ; and furnished a rich doctrinal storehouse to all philosophies. In particular, the Scholastics derived therefrom a number of solutions which they sorted out, completed and corrected before incorporating them into their syntheses.

(ii) The Arabian and Jewish philosophers bequeathed to the Western world a number of neo-Platonist ideas and scientific and psychological data ; in addition they served as guides in the interpretation of more than one doctrine of Aristotle. Avicenna above all helped to determine many Scholastic theories.

What is to be said of the philosophic syntheses of the Arabs ? Were they reproduced and adopted in the West in the thirteenth century? We may reply that in general the Scholastics rejected these products of the Eastern mind so foreign to their genius. To show this it suffices to consider their attitude towards the most prominent Arabian personalities. They declared war without ceasing upon the philosophy of Averrhoes. Avicenna, whose fame was never equal to that of Averrhoes, was opposed in his own special theories and his false interpretations of Aristotle. Avencebrol, whom the West regarded as an Arabian, transmitted some very important doctrines to certain Scholastic centres and Duns Scotus boasted of having taken him as his guide. But these doctrines were from the outset purified of their monistic meaning and hence a new spirit animated them. Maimonides attracted attention chiefly by his endeavours to reconcile Aristotle and the Bible, inasmuch as the Scholastics were engaged in a similar task, that of reconciling their philosophy with Catholic doctrine. His influence on the Western world was real, but it has been exaggerated by many historians.

On the other hand, the synthesis of Averrhoes was revived in an important group of philosophers who adopted an aggressive attitude towards Scholasticism. He was the Doctor of Anti-scholasticism. No other Arabian or Jewish philosopher had his system adopted in its entirety.

(iii) The neo-Platonist writings, which, in conjunction with the Metaphysics of Avicenna, led to a better knowledge of the Alexandrian theories in the West, were surprisingly popular in the thirteenth century. In particular, the little *Liber de Causis* circulated everywhere and was abundantly quoted.

The influence exerted by these writings varied, and acted in at least three directions : during the first decades of the thirteenth century, the neo-Platonist theories appealed to philosophers as a novelty which they juxtaposed to other theories, in a rather naïve and clumsy way. In St. Thomas, Duns Scotus and other scholastics we find the ideas of the *Liber de Causis*, pseudo-Dionysius, etc., reflected upon, re-cast, and assimilated into higher systemizations.   Lastly, they occupy a prominent place in the system of a less influential group of thinkers who towards the middle of the century inaugurated a movement called Latin neo-Platonism.   We shall see later on why their action was only of secondary importance, and why, in spite of the attraction which monism had for some of them, they must not be looked upon as enemies of Scholasticism in the same way as the Averrhoists.

146. Prohibition of Aristotle's Works at Paris.—Early in the thirteenth century, the works of Aristotle were repeatedly condemned by the ecclesiastical authorities. A Council of the Ecclesiastical Province of Sens held at Paris in 1210 forbade the public or private teaching of the natural philosophy of Aristotle and of the commentaries (*nec libri Aristotelis de naturali philosophia nec commenta legantur Parisius publice vel secrete*).[1] At the same time it condemned the teaching of Amalric of Bène and ordered the *Quaternuli* of David of Dinant to be publicly burnt. It is probable that the *libri de naturali philosophia* comprised not only the *Physics* of Aristotle but also the *Metaphysics*. The commentaries in question are those of Averrhoes and Avicenna. Five years later, the legate Robert of Courçon[2] renewed the same prohibitions at the young university ; he sanctioned the ancient and modern logic in the programme, allowed the *Ethics*, but expressly forbade the *Philosophia naturalis*, the *Metaphysics*, the *Summæ de eisdem*, and also the teaching of David of Dinant, Amalric the heretic, and Maurice of Spain.[3] These interdictions were renewed by the Popes in 1231, 1245 and 1263 but with modifications which, as we shall see, changed their scope.

[1] *Chartul. Univ. Paris.*, I, 70. Mandonnet justly points out : " Aristotle's works on natural science and the metaphysics were not only utilized towards the end of the thirteenth century ; they were *read*, that is to say, taught at Paris at the commencement of the same century, otherwise the prohibition of these works in 1210 and 1215 would have no meaning." *op. cit.*, p. 15, note.

[2] Robert of Courçon, Cardinal and Professor at Paris († 1218).

[3] *Chart.*, I, 78.   Mandonnet thinks that Mauricius Hyspanus signifies Averrhoes, the Moor of Spain. (*op. cit.*, VI, 18).

Various causes led up to these severe ecclesiastical censures. In the first place, the theologians were alarmed at certain Aristotelian doctrines which contradict Catholic doctrine, such as the eternity of the world. Hence their opposition to certain Arabian commentaries which emphasized these theories under cover of interpreting Aristotle. They also noticed the tendency to attach all kinds of new doctrines to badly translated texts, or others capable of divergent interpretations. The Papacy upheld this opposition to Aristotle on the part of the theologians, and changed its attitude but slowly, as Aristotle's philosophy became better known and was put to the service of apologetics.

Indeed, when the first panic had passed away and the scholastics, more familiar with the new peripatetic theories, were able to discriminate between what was compatible with dogma and what was not, the Church modified the severity of its prohibitions. If they were not expressly withdrawn[1] they certainly fell into desuetude, and the competent authorities shut their eyes : and so usage abrogated the law. Here are some stages : in 1231, Gregory IX, a patron of learning, while maintaining the prohibitions, gave them a provisional character, and entrusted three theologians (William of Auxerre, Simon of Authie and Stephen of Provence) with the task of correcting the forbidden books, with the manifest intention of including the amended work in the programme of the Faculty of Arts at Paris, *ne utile per inutile vitietur*. The Pope conferred upon the Abbot of St. Victor and the Prior of the Dominican convent the necessary powers for absolving those who had infringed the ecclesiastical prohibitions.[2] These first steps seem to have remained ineffectual, but from 1252 the Faculty of Arts (English nation) authorised the teaching of logic and the *De Anima*,[3] and in 1255 it officially organized the public teaching of all the known works of Aristotle, including the *Physics* and the *Metaphysics*.[4] The Papacy took no notice ; the decree of Urban IV in 1263[5] recalling the prohibitions of Gregory IX was perhaps provoked by the menace of Averrhoism, but it remained a dead letter and did not affect the peripatetic movement at Paris.[6] Moreover, it has been pointed

[1] *Chart.*, p. 427.   [2] *ibid.*, pp. 138 and 143.   [3] *ibid.*, p. 228.
[4] *ibid.*, p. 278, and see later on.   [5] *ibid.*, p. 427.
[6] In 1229 the professors of Toulouse boasted of this. See *ibid.*, p. 131. In 1245 Innocent IV extended the prohibition to Toulouse under the form fixed by Gregory IX in 1331.

out that William of Moerbeke and Thomas Aquinas met at the Court of Urban IV, and that the Pope must have known and perhaps encouraged the projected new translation and commenting on Aristotle.

It is also important to remember the restricted scope of the censures of 1210 and 1215 : they were obligatory only in the schools of Paris, and they did not apply to the personal studies of the professors, but only their public and private teaching. We may add that the reputation which Aristotle afterwards enjoyed, amply made up for these early suspicions. In 1366 the legates of Urban V required that candidates for the licentiate in arts should understand all the works of Aristotle.[1]

§ 2—*The Rise of the Universities*

147. The Beginnings of the University of Paris.—The circulation of the new Aristotelian literature coincided with the founding of the University of Paris. It originated in the last years of the twelfth century or the beginning of the thirteenth, from the grouping together of the professors and pupils belonging to the Cathedral schools of Notre Dame under the jurisdiction of its chancellor (*universitas magistrorum et scolarium*). Little by little common interests grouped the masters into four "faculties" : the theologians, the artists or philosophers, the canonists and the physicians. In the course of the thirteenth century there appeared scholars' unions known under the name of "nations" (Picards, Gauls, Normans, and English).[2] They comprised only the masters and pupils of the faculty of arts, but as these were the most numerous, and both masters and pupils remained incorporated in their respective "nations" after they had finished their courses, they came to represent the whole University. They were a turbulent crowd. The masters were dispersed in 1229, and from 1252 to 1259 a group of seculars carried on a campaign against the regulars. Again, in 1266 quarrels broke out between the "nations" in connection with the nomination of the rector, and the French "nation" nominated one on its own account. After 1270 the sections of the university were divided by the great doctrinal disputes against the mendicants and those between the Scholastics and the Averrhoists.

At the head of the "nations" was the rector, and from the

[1] *Chart.*, III, 145.
[2] This last was replaced by the *Allemanni* after the Hundred Years War.

beginning he was in conflict with the chancellor who represented the bishop, conferred degrees, controlled the *facultas
docendi* and was the general director of the teaching system.
This conflict lasted for a century and a half, but gradually
the chancellor was supplanted by the rector, who became the
head of the University.

The institution of the University of Paris put an end to the
regional character of the schools. It coincided in time with the
first attempts at the centralization of the royal power. The
University became the metropolis of theology and philosophy
in the West, a nursery of theologians and philosophers who came
together from all countries and spread out everywhere from
Paris. This European influence helped to a large extent to
endow scholastic philosophy with its cosmopolitan character
and its unity (204).

The University owed its rapid expansion to the many
privileges granted to it by the Kings of France and by the
Papacy. The Popes wanted to make it a stronghold of theological studies for the service of the Catholic faith. This
" University policy "[1] which consisted of encouraging the
University in order to make use of it, explains why the Popes
looked upon philosophy chiefly as an auxiliary or servant of
dogma[2] and why they favoured the introduction of the Dominicans and Franciscans, the official defenders of Catholic orthodoxy. But it must be added that the University theologians
of the thirteenth century did not lend themselves to the part
which the Papacy wanted them to play. While making use
of philosophy for utilitarian ends, they raised it above this
simple apologetic function and accorded to it an independent
scientific value. Thus they united in their persons the qualities
of theologians and philosophers.

**148. The organization of the philosophic and theological
teaching.**—(i) Just as philosophy was subordinated to theology,
so also the Mastership in Arts was a preparation for degrees in
theology[3]. Students did not allow their hair to grow grey in

---

[1] The phrase is taken from E. Gilson, *Etudes de philos. médiévale*, p. 44.
[2] They recall in pompous terms the metaphor of St. John Damascene and
Peter Damian. De Ghellinck, *Le mouvement théologique*, p. 69, mentions in
this connection a ludicrous mistake by Luchaire, who understands literally
a text in which Pope Gregory IX complains that the Paris theologians give
up too much of their time *ad pedissequas amplectandas*, that is to say, to the
study of philosophy (Luchaire, *La Société franc. au temps de Ph.-Auguste*,
Paris 1908, p. 200).
[3] And also for the study of law and medicine. But in point of fact the
study of philosophy and theology dominated all the others.

the Arts : *non est consenescendum in artibus, sed a liminibus sunt salutandæ*. Thus the organization of the University of Paris was a reflection of the intellectual mentality of the Middle Ages. But when a master of arts (*magister artium*) became a theologian, he still remained a philosopher. The extension of the apologetic method in theology, and the insufficiency of the philosophic preparation in a certain number of auditors—*propter imperitos*, says Henry of Ghent[1]—explains the incursions of the professors of theology into philosophic subjects. Hence philosophical teaching is found in the lectures of the theologians as well as in those of the artists.

(ii) Two principles governed the teaching : the corporate organization and the freedom which followed therefrom. The University was a corporation, and so was each faculty within it. There was no matriculation, the student attached himself to a master—*nullus sit scolaris qui certum magistrum non habeat*.[2] His studies were a preparation for teaching work ; he was a candidate for a professorship. When he became a Master, he officially accomplished the scholastic acts and exercises previously performed as an apprentice. From this there resulted a great extension of the mastership, and a complete freedom in teaching. By hard work and the obtaining of a series of degrees, anyone with the necessary talent could become a professor and open a school by the side of his old masters. Freedom of teaching also manifested itself in the independent language used by certain masters in their *quodlibeta* or public debates.[3]

(iii) Robert of Courçon in 1215 laid down as the minimum age for teaching twenty years for the arts, thirty-four for theology. In each case a minimum of preparatory studies was required : six years for the arts, eight for theology.

The series of academic acts so accomplished by the student under the direction of his master in preparation for the university degrees varied according to the epoch, especially after 1350.

To obtain the mastership in arts one had to pass the " determination " and the " baccalaureate " (*determinantia, baccalaureatus*). In the thirteenth century the candidate

---

[1] *Quodl.*, X, 7.
[2] Organic articles given by Robert of Courçon in 1215. *Chart.*, I, 79.
[3] The *Quodlibeta* of Godfrey of Fontaines are a case in point. See De Wulf, *Un preux de la parole au XIIIe s.*, in *Revue néo-Scolastique*, 1904, p. 416. Cf.n. 3, p. 256.

underwent an examination before three, and later before four masters of the faculty. If he satisfied the conditions of age and attendance at the schools, and his preparation was judged sufficient, he was licensed for the " determination," *determinatio :* under the presidency of the master he had chosen, he commenced solemnly to " determine " at the beginning of Lent and continued during forty days, unless replaced by a " subdeterminator " for the second half of the period. The " determination " was so called because the " determinator " did not content himself with arguing for and against, but solved and " determined " the questions at issue.[1] Bachelors had to " read " or explain the text books assigned for two years. Then they were admitted to the mastership (*magister*). Of the masters of arts, the majority did not continue to profess after their inaugural lecture (*magistri non regentes*) ; they left Paris or else took up other studies. On the other hand, titular professors (*magistri actu regentes*) designated by the " nation," gave the regular annual courses in the halls of the nation, or else in their own schools.[2]

The Faculty of Theology was organized in a similar way, save that the stages of the baccalaureate were longer and more numerous. There were three degrees : the student became successively *biblicus, sententiarius* and *baccalareus formatus*. The first was improperly called *baccalarius*, for the baccalaureate only really began with the reading of the Sentences. In the fourteenth century, " each formed bachelor undertook four defences of theses against his colleagues : one ' aulica ' (*in aula episcopi*), a second ' vesperalis,' a third in the halls of the Sorbonne during the vacation, and a fourth in Advent (*de quolibet*)."[3] Then alone had he the right to be presented to the Chancellor for the licentiate. After a merely formal examination, the chancellor with great pomp gave to the bachelor his licence to teach and preach. Having gone through all these stages, the *licentiatus* was admitted to the full and official exercise of the duties he had hitherto been discharging as an apprentice. As for the mastership, or incorporation in the group of masters, the acts which this comprised (*vesperiæ, aulica* and *resumptum*) were rather of an honorary character.

[1] *Chart.*, I, 563 and II, 673. *Auctarium*, I, p. 29.

[2] *Auctarium*, I, p. 28 *et seq.* Cf. *Chart.*, I, 530 for the *ordinatio facultatis artium de determinantibus, de baccalaureis et de magistris*, of 1275, also the indexes of the *Chartul.*, and Thurot.

[3] Thurot, *De l'Organisation de l'enseignement dans l'Université de Paris*, Paris 1850, pp. 149 and 150.

According to Thurot, " the mastership was to the licence what the nuptial festivities are to the marriage blessing." The masters *actu regentes*, or those who continued to teach after obtaining their mastership and were not content with the mere honorary title (*actu non regentes*) were on giving their public lectures and conducting discussions.

(iv) In the various grades of teaching—baccalaureate, licentiate and mastership—we find a twofold method in use : the lecture (*lectio*) and the disputation (*disputatio*).[1]

The professor read (*legere*),[2] that is, he took as the basis of his instruction some text which he explained according to the letter (*legere cursorie*) or else made the subject of development (*legere ordinarie*) by discussing questions arising therefrom.

In theology, masters read first of all the Bible, from the literal point of view (*lectores biblici*), and later on the *Sentences* of Peter Lombard (*baccalarei sententiarii*). Finally, the *magistri* took up a deeper study of the Bible so that, as Denifle says, " the Bible was the *alpha* and *omega* of theological studies."[3] The programme for the *lectiones* in the faculty of arts is sketched out by the constitution of Robert of Courçon in 1215. We know it in detail from two sources dating from the middle of the thirteenth century : the statutes of the English " nation " (1252) regulating the conditions for the admission of bachelors to the Lenten *determinatio* ;[4] and especially a statute of the Faculty of Arts (1255) " de modo docendi et regendi in artibus deque libris qui legendi essent."[5] We learn from this latter document that the following books were read : the *Vetus logica* (*videlicet librum Porfirii, predicamentorum, periarmenias divisionum et thopicorum Bœcii*), Priscian (*major* and *minor*), the *Logica nova* (the *topica, elenchi, priora* and *posteriora*), the *Nicomachean Ethics* (the four first books), the *Liber Sex Principiorum* of Gilbert de la Porrée, the treatise on Barbarism by Donatus (the third book of his *Ars Major*), that of Priscian on Accentuation ; Aristotle's *Physics, Metaphysics, De Animalibus, Liber Cœli et Mundi, Meteors* Lib. I, *De Anima, De Generatione, De Causis, On Senses and Sensations,*

---

[1] *Chart.*, I, 178.
[2] In English we have kept the word *lecture*, cf. the German *Vorlesungen*.
[3] Denifle, *Quel livre servait de base à l'enseignement des maîtres en théologie dans l'Université de Paris ?* (R. Thomiste, 1894, pp. 149–161.)
[4] *Chart.*, I, 288.
[5] *ibid.*, pp. 277 *et seq*. This statute dates from the 19th March, and put an end to certain difficulties : " magistris aliquibus lectiones suas terminare festinantibus antequam librorum quantitas et difficultas requireret."

Sleep and Vigil, Plants, De Memoria et Reminiscentia, Costa Ben Luca's *De Differentia Spiritus et Animæ,*[1] and the book *De morte et vita.* If this programme is compared with the classification of philosophical science (156-159), it is easy to see the parallelism between them.

The *disputatio* was a co-operative form of teaching. It was a sort of living lesson, to which each one contributed according to his ability. The disputations in the faculty of arts took place in the hall in the Rue du Fouarre, *in vico Straminis,* but it was above all in the Faculty of Theology that the most important discussions took place, and especially those which interest the history of philosophy. These disputations were of two kinds : the *disputationes ordinariæ,* in wihch the master himself propounded and solved technical questions directly concerned with teaching ; and the *disputationes generales de quolibet,* extraordinary and solemn discussions in which those who assisted themselves submitted questions to the master in charge. The quodlibetic disputations took place twice a year (at least, at the University), namely, at the approach of Easter, and Christmas (*quolibet de pascha, de natali*). In these, most varied subjects were debated concerning not only theology, but also pure philosophy, applied ethics, canon law, and even burning questions of the day. All Paris used to attend them, and it was not unusual to see great personages mingling with the masters and students on these occasions.

The character of these two types of academic discussions, and particularly the nature of the disputations *de quolibet* can only be established when a particular study of the numerous *disputationes* which have come down to us[2] has been made. The *disputatio ordinaria,* like the *disputatio de quolibet,* consisted of two acts : first there was a passage at arms between one or many objectors (*opponens*) and a person replying (*respondens*) different from the one charged with the final

[1] Edited by Barach, *Biblioth. philosoph. med. aetatis,* 1878, II.

[2] See the materials in R. Janssen, *Die Quodlibeta des hl. Th. v. Aquin* (Bonn, 1912); Mandonnet, *Chronol. des quest. disputées de St. Th.* (*R. Thomiste,* 1918); Destrez, *Les disputes Quodlib. de St. Thomas* (*Mélanges thomistes,* 1923) Pelzer, *Livres de philos. et de théol. de l'abbaye de Ter Doest,* etc. (Bruges, 1913), pp. 24–26 ; Pelster, *Thomas von Sutton,* etc, pp. 368 *et seq.*; Ehrle, J. *Trivet,* pp. 45 *et seq.* ; Grabmann, *Jean Quidort,* etc. (See later on for the full titles of these works). The statutes of the faculty of theology of Bologna, which Cardinal Ehrle will shortly publish, will also throw light on what happened at Paris. In a recent work, *La Littérature quodlibétique de* 1260 à 1320 (Bibliothèque Thomiste, Vol. V), the Abbé Glorieux gives a long study (p. 9-96) of the structure and value of the *quodlibets,* and then (pp. 97-307) gives a list of the questions discussed by over thirty scholastics.

defence.[1] When the discussion had gone on sufficiently long, the master entered upon the scene, and in another part of the function (Pelster), or on another day (Mandonnet) he took up again in a methodic way each question propounded, grouped the opinions and arguments, summed up the objections and replies, dealt with certain difficulties which the person replying had intentionally left in suspense,[2] and finally presented a definitive solution or *determinatio*, introduced by the words : " respondeo dicendum " or a similar formula. In the *disputatio de quolibet*, the master not only solved one by one each question propounded, but also grouped together the numerous and varied questions submitted to him to the best of his power so as to form an ordered arrangement in his *Quodlibet*. This word then designates the whole collection of questions discussed and solved at one of the two dates, Easter or Christmas, and we must be careful not to confuse a *quodlibet* with a " quodlibetic question."[3] What were the rules determining the choice of objectors and the *respondens*, the secondary personages who prepared the way for the solution by the principal champion ? Was the latter free to set aside questions which he did not like, and who had the right to ask questions ? What were the common and differentiating elements in the ceremonial of the ordinary disputations and the disputations *de quolibet* ? These are points which have not yet been sufficiently elucidated.[4]

Side by side with the *disputationes ordinariæ* and the

---

[1] On the functions of the *opponens* and *defendens* see Grabmann, Neue aufgefundene Werke des Siger v. Brabant und Boethius v. Dacien, in Sitzungs-berichte Akad. Wissensh. Philos.-philol. kl. 1924, 2.

[2] Pelster, *op. cit.*, pp. 366–370.

[3] The " quodlibetic disputations " were chiefly in vogue from 1258 to 1350 or thereabouts. They took place even in the general chapters of religious orders. Giles of Rome organized a " quodlibetic disputation " in 1295 on the occasion of the general chapter of the Augustinians, held at Sienna (Mandonnet, *op. cit.*, p. 87), Here are some figures taken from Pelzer, *Livres de philos.* etc., p. 26 : Gerard of Abbeville left 18 quodlibet, St. Thomas 12 (or 11), Henry of Ghent 15, Richard of Middleton 3, Godfrey of Fontaines 14, Peter of Auvergne 6, John of Viterbo 2, Giles of Rome 6.

[4] John Quidort, speaking of the *opponens*, writes : " ex verbis arguenti non apparebit ejus intentio. Sed, ut dictum fuit mihi, intendit quaerere . . . (Grabmann, *op. cit.*, p. 39.) " In order not to be obliged to pronounce," writes Pelzer, " the master sometimes refused to receive a question "(*op. cit.*, p. 25). On the other hand, Godfrey of Fontaines, after sharply criticizing his superior, the Bishop of Paris, for his inactivity in the matter of the censure against Thomism (see later on), discusses the following question : " Utrum liceat doctori praecipue theologiae recusare quæstionem sibi positam cujus veritas manifestata per determinationem doctoris offenderet aliquos divites et potentes." (*Quodl.*, XII, 6.) He replies in the negative, for the master in theology is a *doctor veritatis habens officium publicum docendi*. He ought to tell the truth to the great as well as to the lowly, *ex debito justitiæ distributivæ*

disputationes de quolibet there were others, as for example the *disputatio magistralis*, which took place between two masters.[1]

Under this same form of teaching may be included the *disputationes magistrorum in studio solemni* and the *sophismata* which concern the Faculty of Arts. The *sophismata*, which the bachelors of the English " nation " had to frequent for two years[2] were exercises in intellectual gymnastics in which they learnt how to demolish the paralogisms advanced by objectors ; but sometimes the *sophisma* also became a teaching method properly so called.[3] While the subject matter of certain *sophismata* was connected with Aristotle's treatise on sophisms, that of many others concerned questions taken either from grammar, or the various sections of philosophy.[4]

(v) The philosophic works and treatises which were the fruits of teaching correspond to the twofold form of the commentary (*lectio*) and the disputation (*quæstio*).

The commentaries on the *Sentences* were strictly speaking paraphrases of the text of the Lombard. But side by side with this traditional type, there arose *Quæstiones in IV libros Sententiarum*, the various subjects of which were suggested by some text of the Lombard, but outgrew its limits and came to have an independent value.[5] The commentaries on Aristotle

[1] See Pelzer, *Thomas von Sutton*, etc., pp. 368–371.
[2] Statute of 1252 : " Per duos annos . . . disputationes magistrorum in studio solemni frequentaverit, et per idem tempus de sophismatibus in scolis requisitus responderit."—*Chart.*, I. 228.
[3] Siger of Courtrai, for instance, makes great use of this pedagogic method. See the *Sophisma* " O Magister," Wallerand, *Les œuvres de Siger de Courtrai* (Vol. VIII of *Les Philosophes Belges*, p. 145). Siger several times states that he passes over certain points because they have been dealt with in the *Sophismata*, e.g. *ibid.*, pp. 107, 135, 138, 140. Again, Siger of Brabant in the question in logic which Pelzer is publishing makes use of the expression : *determinare in sophismate.*
[4] There exist numerous *sophismata* in MSS. Cf. *Chart.*, II, 65, Mandonnet (*Siger*, Vol. VI of *Philosophes Belges*, 124), quotes a certain number of them from Peter of Auvergne, Boethius of Dacia, Nicholas of Normandy. See also MS. Bibl. Bruges, 435, 500. Cf. the *Sophismata* of Siger of Brabant (edited by Mandonnet) and of Siger of Courtrai (edited by Wallerand). Cf. Prantl, *op. cit.*, III, *passim*. Wallerand in a special chapter devoted to the matter establishes a distinction between the *insolubilia*, the *impossibilia*, and the *sophismata* properly so called, as well as the various kinds of the latter. The three classes are moreover together called *sophisma* in a broad sense. A *sophisma* was a statement taken as a basis for discussion and there were certain stereotyped questions which went the rounds, as for instance : *Utrum homo sit animal, nullo homine existente.* But the replies to the questions differed.
[5] Grabmann, *op. cit.*, etc., p. 42. Many Commentaries on the Sentences are found in two or even more forms. Being obliged as a Bachelor to comment on the Sentences, one might adopt a current opinion on a difficult question, and then later on in a second edition put forth a personal view. In this connection Michalski draws attention to the interesting texts in William Alnwick, one of the first disciples of Scotus. Thus he says, referring to the

which have come down to us consist either of an *expositio litteræ* of the text, or else make it the subject of a free interpretation developing the ideas contained therein.[6]

Similarly, the *quæstio* which appeared towards 1230-40[7] in theological teaching existed in two forms, the *quæstiones disputatæ* (*ordinariæ*) and *quolibet*. The numerous works which have come down to us under the name of *Quodlibeta* were usually edited by the master himself. A few were " reported," i.e., consist of materials put together by an auditor present at the discussion.[8] This method (*reportatio, reportare ab aliquo, sub aliquo, post aliquem*) was also applied to the other forms of teaching and to the sermons of the Middle Ages. We must distinguish between these various types of summaries and the original redactions made by the professors themselves.[9]

There also exist monographs of all kinds which were not the results of teaching but dealt *ex professo* with some question of theology or philosophy (an example is the *De Ente et Essentia* of St. Thomas). Again, there were pamphlets and topical writings inspired by polemical considerations.

We may add that it is not unusual to find philosophic dissertations in sermons.[10]

Divine ideas, " Loquebatur [Scotus] enim in hoc secundum communem opinionem, quæ tunc currebat in ore hominum. . . . Et hoc quidem expertus sum in ipso, quia sequendo communem sententiam loquentium, solebam cum eis dicere, etc." (*Quæst. de esse intelligibili*, I, 4). Again : " Et hanc opinionem ad præsens tenui gratia illorum qui in Scoto student. Forte alias viam tenebo quæ hic non ponetur." (*Determinat.*, q. xvi.). See C. Michalski, *Die vielfachen Redaktionem einiger kommentare zu Petrus Lombardus*, in *Miscellanea Ehrle*, I, p. 220 ; Pelzer, in Louvain *Annales*, Vol. V, p. 455.

6 We find the two methods in the unpublished lecture of Albert the Great on the *Nichomachean Ethics*, reported and edited by St. Thomas. See Pelzer, *Le Cours inédit*, etc. *Revue néo-Scolastique*, 1922, pp. 14–16. See also *Les versions lat.*, etc., p. 411.

7 Cf. Ehrle, *St. Domenico*, etc., p. 28. He relies especially on a text of Roger Bacon.

8 N. Trivet notes that the *reportatores* who assisted at the disputation did not correctly inform him on the theories of his opponent, and that he himself had not been understood properly by his own *reportator*. Ehrle, *N. Trivet* p. 47, n. 6.

9 Already in the thirteenth century the author or his agents sent to the booksellers and stationers a manuscript-type, or exemplar, which was a basis for the reproduction by the copyists. Thus the University drew up catalogues of books, and fixed the prices. Cf. Pelzer, *ibid.*, J. Destrez, *Le Pecia*, R. sc. phil. théol. 1924, pp. 182-197. On the nature and value of the reporting method see A. Pelzer, *Le premier Livre des Reportata Parisiensie de Jean Duns Scot*. The *reportatores* were not all equally attentive or impartial Hence the different versions of those following one and the same course See Michalski, *ibid.*

10 See for instance the sermons of James of Vitry and Stephen of Bourbon also that of St. Bonaventure, *De humanae cognit. ratione*, etc., p. 1 (see later on). Ch. Langlois (*Sermons parisiens de la Ire moitié du XIII s* etc. *Journal des Savants*, 1916, p. 488 and 548) points out interesting incur

(vi) The Latin of the thirteenth century philosophers had no literary pretensions. All sacrificed the form to the idea; but their technical terminology was precise, and the language of the great scholastics clear and vigorous.

The didactic methods were fully perfected. The subjects treated were developed according to a triadic process (exposition of the *pros* and *cons*, solution, and replies to the objections) which was logically connected with the aristotelian doctrine of the ἀπορία and continued the traditions of the twelfth century. This method, however, though dominant, was not adopted in certain treatises in which the subject was freely expounded as in our modern works.

149. Foundation of the Universities of Oxford and Cambridge. —The University of Paris served as a model for the Universities of Oxford and Cambridge, and later on for the numerous Universities instituted practically all over Europe. The University of Oxford, founded in the thirteenth century, itself recognized the supremacy of its rival, to whom it owed its organization[11] and its best professors. Less important than that of Oxford, the University of Cambridge was not completely organized until the fourteenth century.[12] ROBERT GROSSETESTE, and his Chancellor, WILLIAM OF SHYRESWOOD, went to Paris; the Franciscans ADAM OF MARISCO, RICHARD CORNUBIENSIS and many others taught at Paris before teaching at Oxford. As for the University of Bologna, which was as ancient as that of Paris, it was chiefly celebrated for its schools of law, but it also possessed several theologians and philosophers of merit.

§ 3—*The Mendicant Orders*

150. Conflicts between Regulars and Seculars.—Immediately upon establishing themselves at Paris (1217 and 1219-20), the

---

ons into philosophy. He also mentions criticisms of theologians who manifested a too great predilection for philosophy (p. 555). The *Liber de Virtutibus Vitiis* of Servasanctus, a Franciscan of Faenza who lived at Florence about 1277-1285, is a moral repertory for the use of preachers, and is brimful of philosophy. See P. L. Oliger, *Servasanto da Faenza e il suo liber De Virtutibus Vitiis*, in *Miscellanea Ehrle*, 1924, I, p. 176. Cf. Grabmann, *Der liber De xemplis Naturalibus d. Franciskaner theologen Servasanctus*, in *Franc. ud.* 1920, p. 85. The freer forms of philosophic teaching, such as poetic xpositions, sermons, and writings in the vulgar tongue, appeared later on. a the thirteenth century, Dante and Eckhart were exceptions to the rule.
[11] About 1240, Robert Grosseteste invited the professors of theology at xford to follow in their lectures the order adopted at Paris (*Chart.*, I, 169). a 1246, Innocent IV made the same recommendation to Robert Grosseteste *hart.*, I, 189).
[12] Denifle, *Die Univers. d. Mittel.*, p. 371.

Dominicans[1] and Franciscans sought to occupy chairs of theology in the University. They succeeded, too, but not without some difficulty. After a general strike of the masters, resulting from a disagreement between the Bishop of Paris and the Chancellor of Notre Dame, the Dominicans obtained a chair of theology in 1229.[2] They secured a second chair in 1231, and about this date also the Franciscans obtained a chair in the faculty. The first Dominican masters were Roland of Cremona and John of St. Giles ; the first Franciscan, Alexander of Hales.[3]

The rights of the mendicant orders (so called because they were bound by the rule of St. Dominic or of St. Francis) rested upon legitimate grounds. Nevertheless, the secular doctors who had unsuccessfully opposed the incorporation of these " regulars," were consistently hostile to them and showed their animosity in various ways. First of all, from 1252 to 1259 there was trouble about their presence in the faculty of theology. The seculars, led by Nicholas of Lisieux, Gerard of Abbeville (died 1271) and especially by the turbulent William of St. Amour (died 1272) wanted to carry a rule to the effect that a religious order could not hold more than one chair. At the same time, the seculars contested the excellence of the religious state, and in this connection there arose interminable controversies the echoes of which are found in theological disputes. William of St. Amour published in 1255 a pamphlet, *De periculis novissimorum temporum*, to which St. Thomas replied by the opusculum *Contra impugnantes Dei cultum*.[4] The trouble

---

[1] The official title of the Dominicans is the " Order of Friars Preachers." Those of Paris were popularly known as the " Brothers of St. James," and those of Bologna as the " Brothers of St. Nicholas." These were the two principal centres of the order. But Humbert of Romans (1277) protested against these designations. See Mandonnet, in *Note de symbolique médiévale Domini Canes*, p. 4 (*Revue de Fribourg*, Dec. 1912).

[2] Mandonnet, *De l'incorporation des Dominicains dans l'ancienne Universi de Paris* (*R. Thomiste*, 1896, p. 138), and Ehrle, *S. Domenico*, etc., p. 8.

[3] According to the hypothesis of H. Felder, O.C. (*Geschichte d. Wissen schaftl. Studien im Franziskanerorden bis in d. Mitte d. 13. Jahrh.*, 190. pp. 216–231), the Franciscans held a second chair between 1233 and 123' namely, that instituted by John de la Rochelle. This thesis has been strongly contested. See the critical study by Seppelt, quoted on p. 267. Felder ha since recognized the erroneous character of his hypothesis, and has shown tha John de la Rochelle succeeded Alexander of Hales as *magister regens*, an that there were not two masters who were regents simultaneously. L *franciscains ont-ils eu deux écoles universit. à Paris* (from 1238 to 1253), *Etudes francisc.*, June 1911.

[4] In 1256–57, a Franciscan, whom Bierbaum identifies with Bertrand Bayonne, but who, according to Pelster (*Thomas v. York, als Verfasser Traktats manus*, etc. *Archiv. franc. hist.* 1922, pp. 3-22) may have been Thom of York, wrote against William of St. Amour in a treatise *Manus que cont*

ended in the condemnation of the *De periculis* and the banishment of its author. In 1257 the Bishop of Paris communicated to the students and masters of the Faculty of Arts pontifical letters forbidding the publication of pamphlets against the regulars, and recognizing their incorporation in the University.[5] Hostilities broke out again from 1268 to 1272, when Gerard of Abbeville, the leader of the opposition after the departure of William of St. Amour, published (about 1268) his treatise *Contra adversarium perfectionis christianæ*. This work was the beginning of a war of pamphlets. Thomas Aquinas, St. Bonaventure, and John Peckham wrote refutations ; Nicholas of Lisieux intervened to defend the thesis of the seculars, and hostilities lasted more or less until the General Council of Lyons.

Still more bitter were the discussions aroused by the Bull *Ad Uberes Fructus*, in which Martin IV conferred on the mendicant orders the important privileges in regard to faculties for hearing confessions. The campaign of the seculars ended in a new condemnation of their attitude (Council of Paris, 1290). No matter to what philosophical school they belonged—and usually they belonged to different ones—the regulars stood shoulder to shoulder in the defence of their canonical rights.[6]

151. The Mendicant Orders and Philosophy.—Dominicans and Franciscans exercised a preponderating influence on the destinies of thirteenth century philosophy. These great religious corporations insisted on the education of their members in order to foster in the latter a taste for learning : they thus produced the most illustrious representatives of philosophy in the thirteenth century.

The regulations of the Dominican Order, minute and complete from the end of the thirteenth century, do not tell us much about the initial organization of studies. Opposition had to be

---

omnipotentem tenditur. This treatise is published by Bierbaum in a collection of unpublished documents, which also contains a reply by Gerard of Abbeville consisting of 110 objections against the treatise referred to (about 1270); a sermon by the same, a small treatise by Nicholas of Lisieux, *Liber de ordine preceptorum ad consilia*, and extracts from the *De Periculis* of William of St. Amour. Max Bierbaum, *Bettelorden und Weltgeistlichkeit an d. Univ. Paris, Texte u. Untersuch, zum Literarischen Armuts u. Exemtionstreit d.* 13 *Jahr., Franzisk. Stud.*, Beiheft 2, Munster 1920. Cf. A. van Denwyngaert, *Querelles du clergé séculier et des ordres mendiants à l'Univ. de Paris.* in *La France Francisc.* 1922 and 1923.

[5] *Chart.* I, 402.

[6] In 1397 another quarrel broke out between the Dominicans and the University, this time over the too bold theological theses maintained by the Dominican John of Montesono. It ended in a temporary exclusion of the Dominicans from the faculty of theology.

overcome, and Albert the Great compares the opponents of philosophy to stupid animals, blaspheming that of which they are ignorant.[1] The study of the arts (philosophy) was first of all allowed only by dispensation,[2] but very soon the exception became the rule. The early hostility gave way to an irresistible attraction under the influence of Albert the Great and Thomas Aquinas. It suffices to glance at the catalogue of Dominican works known as the Catalogue of Stams[3] to be convinced of the wonderful fecundity of the Friars Preachers in the thirteenth and fourteenth centuries. Indeed, in 1271 a General Chapter endeavoured to temper this enthusiasm for philosophy. Quite early on, in addition to the *studia solemnia* proper to each province[4] it was decided to found *studia generalia*, reserved for the study of philosophy and theology for the whole order. " Paris, to which each province was allowed to send three students, became at once and always remained the most important."[5] From 1232, the Franciscans took an active part in the intellectual movement, but their share was less extensive. They also had their *studia particularia* proper to each province, and *studia generalia* (chiefly at Paris, Oxford and Toulouse) devoted to theological studies, in the university centres.[6] The *studia generalia* of the mendicant orders were not autonomous universities, but part of the university organization in so far as the faculties of theology allowed the incorporation of the regular chairs. Where this was the case, the *magistri regentes* wearing the religious habit also shared in the privileges so jealously defended by the faculties. The rivalry between Franciscans and Dominicans stimulated the zeal of all;[7] and other religious orders fell in with the intellectual movement and obtained theological chairs.[8] In 1271 Roger Bacon could say—

[1] " Quidam qui nesciunt, omnibus modis, volunt impugnare usum philosophiæ, et maxime in Prædicatoribus ubi nullus eis resistit, tanquam bruta animalia blasphemantes in iis quae ignorant." In *Epist. B. Dionysii Areopag.* Ep. VIII, n. 2.
[2] Constitution of 1228.
[3] Published by Denifle, see No. **153**, §3, *Quellen*, etc.
[4] The regulars studied logic and the liberal arts inside their convents.
[5] Douais, *Essai sur l'organisation des études dans l'ordre des Frères Prêcheurs*, p. 130. The general Chapter of 1248 decided to create four new *studia generalia :* that of Cologne, which was organized by Albert the Great after his departure from Paris, and those of Bologna, Montpellier, and Oxford.
[6] At Oxford the master was only chosen from the order after 1247. See Little, *The Grey Friars in Oxford*, p. 30.
[7] It was often said in the thirteenth century that like Esau and Jacob, the Franciscans and Dominicans quarrelled in their mother's womb.
[8] The Cistercians were allowed to teach in 1256, the Hermits of St. Augustine about 1287 (Giles of Rome), the Carmelites in 1295. According to Thurot

with some exaggeration—that for forty years the seculars had not composed a single treatise on philosophy or theology.[9]

To the Dominicans chiefly, by reason of the gigantic labours of Albert the Great and Thomas Aquinas—and in a lesser degree to the Franciscans also—belongs the honour of having carried out the project of Gregory IX, namely, the correction of the works of Aristotle. The two orders both helped to build up the peripatetic elements of the scholastic system. The secular masters, on the contrary, continued to regard the Stagirite with great suspicion up to the end of the thirteenth century.

In philosophical matters, Dominicans and Franciscans pursued different paths, and even in each order the traditions were not always the same. Not to mention that according to the testimony of St. Bonaventure, the Friars Minor tended chiefly to unction, and secondarily to speculation,[10] in contrast to the Friars Preachers, the Franciscan school manifested two very marked tendencies : (i) the early philosophical line, traced out by Alexander of Hales and carried on by St. Bonaventure, resulting from a compromise between the Aristotelian doctrines and theories inspired by other sources ; (ii) the later philosophical tendency, due to the influence of Scotus, and which is in many respects the continuation of the former line of thought. As secondary tendencies we have the ideas of Roger Bacon and Raymond Lully. The " terminist " movement which began with William of Occam appeared only in the following period, and spread rapidly outside the Order of Minors. As for the " spiritual " party, this adopted a hostile attitude towards philosophy. The first Dominicans rallied to the prevailing doctrines of the older scholasticism, and were thus in agreement with the first Franciscans and the seculars, but from the time of St. Thomas, with some exceptions they more uniformly supported the scholasticism of the Thomist School. There were also among the Dominicans some isolated thinkers who differed from their brethren, like Eckhart, and the disciples of Albert the Great who originated the movement afterwards known as Latin neo-Platonism.

152. Secular colleges. The Sorbonne.—It was probably the necessity of counterbalancing the influence of the regulars that first led to the institution of great colleges, open to the

(*op. cit.*, p. 112) " In 1253, out of the twelve chairs required by the numbe of students in theology, nine were in convents."

[9] *Opera inedita*, Brewer's edition, p. 428.

[10] *Opera*, in Quaracchi edition, V, p. 440.

seculars, and organized after the manner of the convent schools. The most famous was that of the Sorbonne, founded in 1253 by Robert of Sorbon (1201-1274), chaplain to Louis IX. It admitted a certain number of theological students for the purpose of training them for disputations and preaching. They were bound to live in common, and under the direction of a provisor. The masters called themselves—after the fashion of the mendicant orders—*pauperes magistri de Sorbona*. Among the writings left by Robert of Sorbon, the most remarkable were the *De conscientia* and the *De tribus dietis*. The first deals with the Last Judgment, which the author compares to the examination for the licentiate, and this leads him to give valuable and interesting information on matters pedagogical. The second work has for its subject the ways that lead to Paradise.

The courses at the Sorbonne were closely connected with the teaching in the Faculty of Theology, for the disputations were not private exercises confined to the internal students, but public debates.

153. Bibliography.—(i) TRANSLATIONS.—See the works previously mentioned (pp. 70-82 and especially p. 82) and others mentioned above. Mandonnet, *Siger de Brabant*, etc., Vol. II, ch. 1 and 2, a very good general account of the translations of Aristotle's Works and the condemnations; Grabmann, *BGPM*, XVII, 5-6, the best general work, giving a list of *incipits* at the end. Jourdain, *Recherches sur l'origine des trad. latines d'Aristote* (referred to on p. 000) is always indispensable, and gives specimens of the translations (pp. 402-450). Wood Brown, *An Enquiry into the Life and Legend of Michael Scot* (Edinburgh, 1897), must be corrected by the excellent articles by Haskins mentioned in No. **33**. Under the title *Studies in the History of Mediæval Science* (Cambridge, U.S.A., 1924) Haskins has collected together in one volume a number of studies on the translations from Arabic and Greek into Latin, and the general scientific culture at the Court of Frederick II. Several chapters are new: Translators from the Arabic in Spain (I); Adelard of Bath (II), Hermann of Carinthia (III); Some twelfth century writers on Astronomy (V); Translators in Syria during the Crusades (VII); North American Translators of the Twelfth Century (X). G. Turlani, *Le Antiche versioni araba, latina ed ebraica del De partibus animalium de Aristotile*, in *Riv. d. studi* *orientali*, IX, 1922, pp. 237-257, with specimens. Luquet, *Hermann l'Allemand* (quoted on p. 238) corrects biographical errors and mistakes in literary attribution. M. Steinschneider, in addition to works mentioned on p. 82 : *Die arabischen Uebersetzungen aus d. Griechischen*, Leipzig, 1889 and 1893 (Beiheft V, 2 u. XII zum Centralblatt für Bibliothekswesen) ; Rose, *Die Lücke im Diogenes Lærtius u. der alte Uebersetzer, Hermes*, I, 1876, pp. 367-397 ; *Ptolemæus u. die Schule von Toledo, ibid.*, VIII, 1874, pp. 327-349. Concerning Maimonides, see Steinschneider, *Die hebr. Uebersetzungen* (mentioned on p. 82), pp. 413-434 deal with the *Guide for the Perplexed* ; Munck, *Le Guide des Egarés* (Paris, 1856, 1861, 1866), publishes the Hebrew text and a French translation ; J. Perles, *Die in einer Münchener Handschrift aufgefundene erste lat. Uebersetzung d. Maimonidischen " Fuhrers " (Monatsschrift fur Gesch. u. Wissenschaft d. Judensthums*, 24e Jhg., 1875), with a specimen. C. Baeumker, *Die Stellung d. Alfred v. Sareschel* (mentioned on p. 240); critical edition of the *De motu cordis* (220), with many fresh details on the translations of Aristotle known at the beginning of the thirteenth century. F. Seymour Stevenson, *Robert Grosseteste* (London, 1899), must be corrected by L. Baur, *Die philos. Werke d. R. Gr. (BGPM*, IX), a critical edition with a valuable introduction.

Pelzer, *Les versions lat. des ouvrages de morale* (mentioned on p. 74) corrects and completes the works of A. Vacant, *Les versions lat. de la Morale à Nicomaque anterieures au XVe s.*, Revue des Sc. ecclésiastiques, 1885 (a good study) ; C. Marchesi, L'Etica Nicomachea (mentioned on p. 242, describes many Italian MSS. relative to the Latin translations of Aristotle, gives the *Eth. vetus, Eth. nova*, the Alexandrine abridgment, and the *Ethica de Aristotele traducta in volgare da mæstro Nicolao Anglico*) ; and of Grabmann, *op. cit.*, pp. 204-238. Translations of the biological works of Aristotle have been dealt with by Ch. Thurot (*De Partibus Animalium*, Révue archeologique, 1867 and 1868), Dittmeyer, Rudberg (mentioned p. 244 ; the latter has produced *Textstudien zur Tiergeschichte d. Arist.*, Upsala, 1908, and articles in the Review *Eranos*, VIII, IX, XII, 1908, 1909, 1912) ; for the *Economics*, see Rose, Susemihl (mentioned on p. 244), Egger (*Mémoires Acad. Inscript. et Belles-Lettres*, Vol. 30, Ire *partie*, 1881), and Haureau (*ibid.* 1881) ; on the *Metaphysics*, studies by Grabmann, Geyer, Pelster (mentioned on p. 244). P. Minges has studied the use made of some translations (biological works, *Nichomachean Ethics*) in *Philos. Jahrbuch*, 1914, pp. 551 *et seq.* ; 1919, pp. 230-243. On the translations of Proclus published by Birkenmajer, see his *Vermischte Untersuchungen* (*BGPM*, XX, 5). Lucquet, *Aristote et l'Université de Paris pendant le XIIIe s.* (*Bibl. Hautes Etudes sc. rélig.*, XVI, 2, Paris, 1904), examine the effect of the Council of 1210. See also works by Talamo, Schneid, Chollet, referred to on p. 27. Renan, *Averroes et l'Averroisme*, Paris, 1869 ; Mandonnet, *Siger de Brabant*, Vol. II. J. Guttmann, *Die Scholastikd. XIIIe Jh. in ihren Beziehungen zum Judenthum u. zur jud. Litteratur*, Breslau 1902 ; *Der Einfluss d. maimonid. Philos. auf d. christl. Abendland* (in the commemorative work by Bacher, Braun and Simonsen, *Moses ben Maimon, Sein Leben, seine Werke u. sein Einfluss*, Vol. I, Leipzig, 1908, pp. 135-230 ; works by Rohner, *BGPM*, XI, 5 ; Schneider, XVII, 4 ; Wittmann, III, 3.

(ii) UNIVERSITIES.—One of the principal sources is Denifle and Chatelain, *Chartularium Universitatis Parisiensis*, first two vols. Paris 1889-1891, a first-class work for the history of the organization of the University from 1200 to 1350, with important introductions. By the same : *Auctarium Chartul. Univ. Paris*, Vol. I : *Liber Procuratorum nationis anglicanæ* (*Alemanniæ*) *ab anno* 1333-1406, Paris, 1894 ; Vol. II : *ab anno* 1406-1466 (1897). Denifle, *Die Universitaten d. Mittelalters bis* 1400 (Berlin 1885), an excellent history of their origins ; Ch. Thurot, *op. cit.*, insufficient, but some portions are excellent. The following are also worth mentioning : Douais and Felder, work referred to later on : Luchaire, *L'Université de Paris sous Philippe-Auguste*, Paris, 1899, a short monograph. On the teaching of grammar and rhetoric, see : Pætow, *The Art Course at Mediæval Universities with special reference to Grammar and Rhetoric* (University of Illinois, Bull. VII, 19, 1910), with very full references. Maxwell, *History of the Univ. of Oxford ;* Hastings Rashdall, *The Universities of Europe in the Middle Ages*, Oxford, 1895, clear and complete; E. Coppi, *Le univers. ital.*, 2nd edn. ; Mauri Sarti and Mauri Fattorini, *De claris Archigymnasii Bononiensis professor. a sæc. XI u. a. s. XIV*, Bononiæ, 1888-1896 ; *Chartul. studii Bononiensis*, Vol. I, Bologna, 1909 ; *Studi e memorie per la storia dell' Universita di Bologna*, Bologna, Vol. I, 1909, Vol. II, 1911 ; Ehrle, *op. cit.*, p. 243, note. Dr. Liessen, *Die quodlibetischen Disputationen an d. Universität Köln* (Progr. d. K. Wilhelm. Gymnasium zu

Köln, 1886), pp. 58-70 ; Ch. Langlois, *Les Universités du moyen age* (*Révue de Paris*, 1896, pp. 788-820).

(iii) MENDICANT ORDERS.—Quétif and Echard (referred to on p. 31, Denifle, *Quellen zur Gelehrtengeschichte d. Predigerordens im 13 u. 13 Jahrh.* (Arch. Litt. u. Kirchengesch. Mitt., II, pp. 165 *et seq.*) ; Mandonnet (see notes on previous pages) ; Douais, *op. cit.*, well done, clear and complete ; Reichert, *Acta capitulorum generalium Ordinis fratrum Prædicatorum*, Romæ, 1898, Vol. I ; Mortier, *Hist. des maîtres generaux de l'ordre des Frères Prêcheurs*, Paris, 1905 ; Douais, *Acta capitulorum provincialium*, Toulouse, 1894 ; Lucchini, *Il beato Rolando da Cremona* (Cremona, 1886) ; Mandonnet, *La Crise scolaire au début du XIIIe s.* (*R. hist. écc.*, 1914, pp. 4-39) ; Ehrle, *San Domenico, le origini del primo studio generale del suo Ordine a Parigi e la Somma teologica del primo Mæstro Rolando de Cremona* (Miscell. Dominicana in memoriam VII anni sæcul. ab obitu S. Dominici, Romæ, 1923). Wadding and Sbaralea (mentioned p. 31) ; Franciscan reviews (see p. 43) ; Franciscan articles in *Kirchliches Handlexicon* by Buchberger (Munich, 1907) ; Ehrle, *Die Spiritualen, ihr Verhältniss z. Franciskanerorden u. zu. d. Fraticellen*, in *Arch. Litt. Kirchengesch. Mitt.* I-IV ; *Die ältersten Redaktionen d. General-constitutionen d. Franciskanerordens, ibid,* VI, 1 and 86 ; V. Döllinger has published the *De Septem tribulationibus Ord. Min.* by Angelo da Clareno in *Beitrage zur Sektengeschichte d. Mittelalters*, Munchen, 1890, Vol. II ; Sabatier, *Collect. de documents pour l'hist. rélig. et litt. du moyen age*, Paris, 1898-1902, 4 vols. ; De Martigne, *La Scolastique et les tradit. franciscaines*, 1888, studies the two doctrinal tendencies in the order. Sandys, *op. cit.* Dr. H. Felder, *op. cit.*, utilizes all the documents, many of his theses are disputed. French translation by Eusèbe of Bar-le-Duc, *Histoire des Etudes dans l'ordre de S. Francois dépuis sa fondation jusque vers la moitié du XIIIe siècle*, Paris, 1908. V. Seppelt, *Der Kampf d. Bettelorden a. d. Universität Paris in d. Mitte d. 13 Jahrh.* (Kirchengeschicht. Abhandl., Breslau, Vol. III, 1905) ; *Wissenschaft und Franciskanerorden, ihr Verhältnis im ersten Jahrzehnt des letzteren, ibid.* Vol. IV, pp. 149-179. Little, *The Grey Friars in Oxford* (Oxford, 1893), in publications of Oxford Historical Society. Denifle, *Quellen z. Gelehrtengesch. d. Carmelitenordens im 13 u. 14. Jahrh.*, in *Archiv.* etc., V, 329. Perrod, *Etude sur la vie et sur les œuvres de G. de Saint-Amour* (*Mem. de la Soc. d'émulation du Jura*, 1902).

On the colleges much ill-assorted information will be found in
Feret, *op. cit.*, p. 37. There is in MS. a treatise by Claude
Héméré, *Sorbonæ origines, disciplina et viri illustres* (Bibl.
Nation. lat. No. 5493) and an anonymous manuscript work :
Domus Sorboniæ historica (Bibl. Arsenal, Paris, Nos. 1020 and
1021). Franklin, *La Sorbonne, ses origines*, etc., 1875 ; F. Cham-
bon, *R. de Sorbon* (1903) ; gives a full bibliography, a summary
of his life, and publishes with notes the *De Conscientia* and the
De Tribus Dietis ; Mgr. E. Méric, *La Sorbonne et son fondateur*,
Paris, 1888.

The *Scholia* published in the edition of St. Bonaventure
(Quaracchi, 1882-1902) contain a mass of documentary material
in which the theories of St. Bonaventure are compared with
those of the principal philosophers of the thirteenth century.
As a general study of the doctrinal movement of the thirteenth
century, scholastic and anti-scholastic, we may mention the
splendid work by Mandonnet, *Siger de Brabant et l'averroisme
au XIIIe siècle*, Deuxieme Partie, 2nd edn. Louvain, 1908-
1910, in *Philosophes Belges* series). Hurter, *Nomenclator
Litterarius* (1109-1563), Innspruck, 1906. Von Hertling,
*Wissenschaftliche Richtungen u. philosoph. Probleme im XIII
Jahrh*. Festrede Akad. *Wissensch*. (Munchen, 1910), vague
and general.

CHAPTER II

The Group of Scholastic Philosophical Systems

154. The common patrimony.—Scholasticism, the progressive formation of which we have now studied, attained its most perfect expression in the thirteenth century. It dealt with all the problems which a complete system of philosophy implies, and gave coherent solutions to them. The collection of these solutions forms a specific body of doctrine with its own place in history, a conception of reality which corresponded to the intellectual requirements of the Western mind, and which opposed any movement calculated to interfere with its expansion. It was, as it were, an attractive ideal, a force acting everywhere and from which no one could altogether isolate himself. The majority of philosophers of the thirteenth century —those whom we call " scholastics "—accepted what is essential in this system of ideas by a sort of silent assent ; and it was precisely this assent that made discussions possible and fruitful. " No one has ever seriously denied that there was an agreement on fundamental principles which authorizes us to regard scholasticism as a system, a school of philosophy."[1] Following in the footsteps of others, we shall endeavour to outline this body of doctrine, this *sententia communis*, in its abstract form.[2]

Our brief summary of the scholastic synthesis (Art. I) does not pretend to exhaust all the points of view. After glancing at the classification of the sciences (§ I), we shall study in turn its metaphysics (§ 2), natural theology (§ 3), physics, and more especially psychology (§ 4), moral philosophy (§ 5), and social philosophy (§ 6), logic (§ 7) and æsthetics (§ 8). In a conclusion we shall set out the doctrinal

[1] Ehrle, in *Stimmen aus Maria Laach*, 1880, p. 28.
[2] See for instance the excellent work of Kleutgen, too much neglected nowadays. *Die Philosophie der Vorzeit*. We shall follow here a deductive plan. In our *Mediæval Philosophy illustrated from the system of Thomas Aquinas* (Oxford Univ. Press, 1923) destined for beginners, we have adopted an analytical arrangement.

characteristics of scholasticism (§ 9) and its relations with the civilization of the thirteenth century (§ 10).

155. Division.—The living forms in which the scholastic system expressed itself were many ; for the thirteenth century was, like all periods of full development, filled with prominent personalities. Each of the great scholastics expressed the abstract synthesis in a concrete way, and marked it with the seal of his own individuality (p. 11). But in spite of the variety of scholastic philosophical systems in the thirteenth century, we can arrange them in certain groups :

(i) The first group combined Aristotelian, Arabian and neo-Platonist theories with the doctrines handed on by the twelfth century, and thus gave rise to philosophies of the transition stage, appearing during the first two decades (Art. II).

(ii) Very soon we notice a more uniform and consistent tendency, namely, that of the older or pre-Thomist scholasticism, commonly called the Augustinian school (Art. III).

(iii) Albert the Great occupies a place by himself, for he commented on and introduced into the world of thought a considerable number of new doctrines from neo-Platonist, Arabian and Aristotelian sources (Art. IV).

(iv) Thomas Aquinas, his disciple, elaborated these materials and constructed on foundations mainly Aristotelian in character a new philosophical system differing from the scholasticism of his predecessors on many points (Art. V).

(v) A conflict between Thomism and the older scholasticism inevitably arose. Those engaging in it were either out-and-out opponents who defended the traditional ideas against the Thomistic innovations, or else faithful and enthusiastic disciples of the new philosophy (Art. VI).

(vi) A group of personalities appearing shortly after the death of Thomas Aquinas formulated other philosophical systems, in which we find a continuation of the older scholasticism on certain points, together with an adhesion to Thomism on others, the whole being accompanied by the introduction of solutions of a personal character. The list of these eclectics, in which the names of Henry of Ghent, Geoffrey of Fontaines, and Robert of Middleton stand out in the first rank, is constantly being lengthened (Art. VII—IX and XI).

(vii) Duns Scotus closed the series. In the last years of the thirteenth century he formulated a unique variety of scholasticism (Art. X.)

(viii) A group of scholastics applied themselves to special questions in logic and grammar (Art. XII).

Art. I—The Scholastic Synthesis

§ 1—*The classification of the sciences*

156. The gradation of the sciences.—The thirteenth century was in possession of a vast classification of the sciences which may be compared to a three-story building, with the particular sciences below, philosophy in the middle, and theology at the top. Philosophy is divided up into different sections according to peripatetic principles ; and its divisions, indicated but not employed by Boethius, taken up again by Hugh of St. Victor and his contemporaries in the twelfth century (**101-103**), given the place of honour and completed by Gundissalinus and Robert Kilwardby (**215, 259**), are henceforth accepted by all. They enlarge the Aristotelian scheme ; they absorb and extend the Platonist divisions hitherto in use ; and these new divisions will be our guide in our exposition of the scholastic synthesis. Theology in its turn utilizes and completes the divisions introduced in the twelfth century.

157. The particular sciences.—In the lowest place, and in conformity with the Scholastic ideology which constructs knowledge upon sense data (**179**) we find the particular or experimental sciences. They deal with particular classes of corporeal things (material object) each from its own special point of view (formal object) which is proper to itself and gives to each science its autonomous character. The thirteenth century witnessed the first remarkable outburst of experimental research (Albert the Great, Roger Bacon, Witelo), and it suffices to examine the regulations of the faculty of arts of Paris in 1255 (p. 254) to realize that the programme of courses comprised a complete scientific training : astronomy, botany, physiology, zoology, chemistry and physics (in the modern sense). Side by side with the natural sciences we ought to mention the remarkable group of juridical sciences (canon law and Roman civil law). The medical sciences were, as all the world knows, still in their infancy.

But this piecemeal exploration of the world did not satisfy the mind. According to the Greek and Scholastic conception, the science *par excellence, sapientia* or philosophy, is a synthetic knowledge of reality, a means of knowing all.

158. Divisions of philosophy.—Philosophy has as its domain all that exists or can exist (material object), but it considers all reality, not after the manner of a particular science or an encyclopædia of particular data, but in order to discover aspects of reality which are found everywhere (formal object).

If these aspects of reality are studied for their own sakes, and our attention does not turn to the relations which we can contract with reality, we have a general view of the universe as it exists outside of us and apart from us. This is theoretical philosophy ($\theta\epsilon\omega\rho\epsilon\iota\nu$).

If we study the universe in relation to the conscious activities which bring us into contact with it, then philosophy takes a practical form ($\pi\rho\acute{a}\tau\tau\epsilon\iota\nu$). Both theoretical and practical philosophy admit of further subdivision.

Theoretical philosophy comprises Physics, Mathematics, and Metaphysics, which respectively study three aspects of reality found in the corporeal world directly present to our minds : corporeal change, quantity and being. It is important to note that these aspects of reality are the result of abstractions of increasing profundity. Intelligible quantity, which is the subject-matter of Mathematics, is not bound up with the corporeal states studied by Physics. Metaphysics grasps aspects of reality which change and quantity both pre-suppose. Questions of metaphysics and psychology (which is a part of Physics) are dominant in the scholasticism of the thirteenth century, and here again we find a progressive widening of the horizon. The generations contemporary with William of Auvergne applied themselves above all to the problem of knowledge, the origin and duration of the world, the nature of immaterial substances, and the human soul.[1] With Albert the Great we find all the doctrines of psychology and all the great problems in metaphysics.

Practical philosophy deals with the functions of knowing, willing, and producing, functions which man can apply to all that exists ; it comprises Logic, Ethics, and Aesthetics.

The order in which these subjects were taught respected these subdivisions ; physics came before metaphysics, and logic before ethics ; but the two series, speculative and practical were studied together.[2]

[1] Cf. Baumgartner, *Die Erkenntnislehre d. Wilhelm v. Auvergne*, 10.
[2] In the commentary on the *Liber de Causis*, lect. 1, Thomas Aquinas suggests the following order : logic, mathematics, " cujus etiam pueri possun esse capaces," physics or philosophia naturalis, ethics, " cujus juvenis ess

159. Philosophy and the natural sciences.—In a conception like this, the experimental sciences serve as a preparation for the philosophical study of the sense world[3] and of man. To ethics are attached the juridical and historical sciences, the science of education, and a part of what we call to-day the social sciences. Logic was linked up with grammar and the logical study of grammatical forms. This led to the following consequences :

(i) The particular sciences were cultivated not so much for their own sake as for their value as a preparation for philosophic work

(ii) Scholasticism was essentially scientific. The synthetic interpretation of the material world rested at each stage on analysis, and remained in permanent contact with reality.

(iii) Between the philosophic sciences and the particular sciences there was no distinction in nature, inasmuch as both categories resulted from the same intellectual process, namely abstraction. But they differed in degree, according to the degree of abstraction involved.

(iv) Science and philosophy necessarily shared the same characteristics. The Middle Ages knew no distinction between that which we nowadays call the knowledge of the man in the street, and scientific knowledge. Ordinary everyday but careful observations were sufficient to lead to legitimate syntheses : imaginary facts naturally led to wrong generalizations.

160. Theology and philosophy.—Theology appeared in the thirteenth century in its twofold form, speculative and mystical.

(i) Speculative theology is the systematic and coherent codification of dogma, studied both from the standpoint of Scriptural data (*auctoritates*) and from that of apologetics (*rationes*). It attained to its maximum perfection in the works of the great masters of theory at the end of the century. This systematic study of Christian doctrine was looked upon as the natural finishing-off of knowledge.

We find in the majority of the *Summæ* of the thirteenth century a methodic study of the distinction between philosophy and theology, and of the subordination of the former to the latter.

conveniens auditor non potest," metaphysics. Boethius of Dacia mentions the following arrangement : logic, ethics, physics, mathematics, metaphysics. (Quoted by Grabmann, *Der Metaph, d. Thomas v. York*, p. 192 (see later). Grabmann sees a difficulty to this arrangement in the division adopted by Thomas of York.

[3] The philosophic study of nature was thus distinct from the scientific encyclopædias such as the *De proprietatibus rerum* of Bartholomæus Anglicus, and the *Speculum* of Vincent of Beauvais.

The distinction between the two sciences so clearly taught implies their mutual independence and the autonomy of their constructive methods. It was agreed by all that the criterion of the diversity of sciences rests not on the difference of subject matter (material object), but on the use made of these materials (formal object). Now, the formal objects of theology and philosophy differ : the one studies the supernatural order as revealed by God, the other subjects the natural order to investigation by the reason ; the one rests on authority, the other on scientific demonstration.

The distinction between philosophy and theology did not prevent the former from being subordinated to the latter. Convinced as they were that Catholic doctrine is the infallible expression of the truth, and that on the other hand, truth cannot be opposed to truth, the scholastics drew the conclusion that if philosophy should deal with matters which are also studied by theology, it must never oppose dogma. The subordination in question here had a *prohibitive* force, and never an *imperative* one ; that is to say, the scholastics never *imposed* upon philosophy the duty of establishing a dogma.[1]

A whole series of works which can be regarded as treatises both of dogmatic theology and philosophy, had an apologetic aim, the demonstration of Catholic doctrine. The opponents in view were the Arabians (unbelievers), and the Cathari and Albigenses (heretics). Among the best known, let us mention the *De fide catholica contra hæreticos* of Alan of Lille, the *Magisterium divinale* of William of Auvergne, the *Pugio fidei adversus Mauros et Judæos* of R. Martin, the *Ars catholica fidei* of Nicholas of Amiens, and the *Summa contra Gentiles* of St. Thomas.[2]

(ii) Mysticism was a development of theology, the mystical union being the work of grace. St. Bonaventure points this out clearly in his *Itinerarium mentis ad Deum*, and when Dante arrived at the mystic spheres he changed his guide. It was no longer Virgil, the representative of human knowledge, who accompanied him, but St. Bernard, symbolizing the contemplative life.

---

[1] Such is, in our opinion, the meaning of the state of 1272 of the Faculty of Arts which enjoined that students should not *determinare contra fidem* if they should deal with a question *qui fidem videatur attingere simulque philosophiam. Chart.* I, 499.

[2] For the works specially directed against the Cathari and the Albigenses see Kramp, *Gregorianum*, 1921, p. 43.

§ 2—*Metaphysics.*

161. Central position of metaphysics.—Scholasticism not only made the study of being and its profound and general characteristics one of the most favoured objects of its researches, it also considered all other philosophic problems in the light of metaphysics. Hence its eminently synthetic character. The idea of metaphysics was taken from Aristotle, but it was at the same time broadened : its starting-point was still the being of the things of sense experience, which anchors it to the living rock of reality, but in addition it considers being apart from that which ties it down to the corporeal state, so that what it studies in corporeal reality is *being as such,* " immaterial by abstraction."

162. Pluralism.—The universe of the scholastics is made up of individual realities : the individual alone exists and can exist. *Nihil est præter individuum.* The primordial elements of the inorganic world and compound bodies,[1] plants and animals, men and pure spirits, God Himself : all that exists or can exist is individual (*indivisum in se*) i.e., a being centred upon itself, incommunicable in that which constitutes it. The notion of individuality is the subject of developments unknown to the Greeks and the early Middle Ages.

We may group the questions concerning the individual in the realm of material things which it is above all accessible to us, by considering it successively from the static and the dynamic points of view.

163. Problems of the static order.—(i) *Substance and accidents.* Any being, an oak tree for instance, has quantity and qualities, performs certain actions and is affected by those of others, and is in time and space. These are manifestations, attributes, or phenomena, which scholasticism calls supervening or *accidental* realities (*accidentia*) because they suppose a more profound reality, a manifested subject, the substance. Without the substance we could not conceive of an accident, and without it an accident cannot exist. The substance is the inmost reality, the constituent and primordial foundation which exists in itself and is self-sufficient ; accident is a reality which is added to the substance and simply determines it. Thus the existence of substances is the sufficient but indispensable reason for the existence of the accident. To explain the possibility of a

---

[1] The idea of the compound or *mixtum* is applied on p. 290.

phenomenon, we have to go to a non-phenomenon. It does not follow from this that we know the inmost nature of the substantial basis of things. Reason alone shows its necessity.

Scholasticism starts, then, from the Aristotelian division of the categories, and takes up the study of the nine accidental predicaments, developing them considerably, especially quality, quantity, relation, time and space. In particular, the study of quality (*accidens modificativum substantiæ in seipsa*) gave rise to new controversies : what distinction is there between a substance and its powers of operation, which are included among the qualities ? What is the nature of the bond which unites them ? Can action be substantial in a contingent being ? or does the latter necessarily act through the intermediary of its faculties ? This was a much discussed problem in the thirteenth century, and the solution affected other matters too. Augustine had treated the problem as a psychological one, but it was left to the thirteenth century to absorb the psychological point of view in the wider one of metaphysics.

(ii) *Hierarchical arrangement of the multiple*. Although each corporeal substance is identical with itself, it has within itself a specific principle (we shall see later on that this is the *substantial form*) : the substance of an oak tree is altogether other than that of a man, and all existing or possible substances are arranged hierarchically according to the degrees of a scale of perfection (neo-Platonism). Hence the perfection of any one kind of substance—that of man, for instance—does not admit of degrees. One is either man, or something else, one cannot be more or less man. *Essentia* (i.e. *substantia*) *non suscipit plus vel minus*.

On the other hand, in any one type of corporeal substance, such as humanity, this fixity does not exclude the wonderful diversity found in individuals, such as particular men. Each of the latter is endowed with an essence which is the same in nature, but accompanied by indefinitely varied attributes. Equality in substance and inequality in accidents is the law which presides over the hierarchy of individuation in the corporeal world and also, according to some scholastics, in the incorporeal world.

(iii) *The transcendental aspects of being*. This is a new chapter, hardly touched upon by Aristotle, first studied by Plato and the neo-Platonists, and which the scholasticism of the thirteenth century introduced into its pluralistic meta physics. Each thing, being itself, has an internal unity which ensures the coherence of all its parts (*ens et unum convertuntur*). Hence also, each being is distinct from others. It is *good* for itself, inasmuch as it seeks its perfection : it is *true*, for it can become the object of mind.

164. Problems of the dynamical order: Act and Potency.— In order to grasp the meaning of metaphysics, we must study substantial being in its change or becoming. Here scholasticism adopts the central theory of Aristotelianism : there is no other way of explaining change than by regarding reality as consisting of act and potency.

Consider for instance any real change : a being E passing from a state a to a state b. The reality of the change requires that E should possess already in state a that without which the state b could never exist, namely, the real principle of its change into b. Before it was, it could be ; it was capable of receiving the being which it now has, it had *in potency* that which it now has *in act*. *Actuality* is therefore any present perfection, any degree of being which really exists ; *potency* is the aptitude for receiving another degree. It is itself non-being and imperfection, but still it is not nothing, for this non-being holds in germ that which will be its future actualization. The passage from the potential to the actual state is movement (*motus*). A corporeal being is entirely subject to change, each of its categories can be studied in its actual or in its potential state ; everything is able to be before it actually is. Observation alone reveals to us the potentialities belonging to each being, or the states through which a being can pass, and which are in it like a treasure stored up. It is actuality that measures potency.

It is important to note that the scholastics extend the theory of act and potency far beyond the limits in which Aristotle confined it. They apply it to all contingent beings, corporeal or incorporeal, and in corporeal being itself, to realms undreamt of by the Stagirite. Act and potency become synonymous with determinant and determinable, and affect all the compositions of changing being.[1]

The couple of potency and act are found in the fundamental compositions of substance and accident, matter and form,

[1] It is even introduced into logic and ethics ; and everywhere it signifies the same primordial relation of the determinable to the determinant : for instance, genus is to species, or a free act is to its subjective end, as potency is to act.

essence and existence. The theory of causes is also linked up with it.

165. The change of substance. Matter and Form.—(i) Corporeal substance in clothing itself with the unceasing and always changing determinations which form the series of its accidents, is only actualizing its potentialities : the oak tree is capable of growth before it grows. But the potentiality of growth is not indefinite, and it limits the actual growth. Substance is to its accidents as potency is to act. Hence, taken in its dynamic sense, which is the only true one, substance is not an inert mass to which the accidents are fixed—as the gross imagination of Locke represented it—but a subject in a state of flux, affected constantly by changing attributes.

(ii) It is not only the attributes of corporeal substance which pass from potency to act ; the corporeal substance itself evolves, since it changes into other substantial beings, and itself results from substances which have ceased to be. This is the profound kind of change, which puts us in presence of a *terminus a quo* and a *terminus ad quem* specifically different the one from the other. Wine does not change into wine, but into vinegar; an oak tree does not become an oak tree, but numerous heterogeneous beings very different in nature to an oak tree. In order to explain these facts, and in virtue of the principle of sufficient reason, scholastics hold with Aristotle that :

(*a*) In the two substantial beings, there must be a common element which passes from one to the other, an element belonging to the substantial order, but undetermined. This is *materia prima*.

(*b*) In each of the two terms of the process, this indeterminate principle or common substratum receives the impress of a proper, specific element which determines the formless subject : this is the *forma substantialis*.

From this it follows that corporeal substance is composite in its inner nature ; *prime matter* is in potency to becoming such or such a form ; and *form* functions as an actuality.

Let us examine the respective office which matter and form play in the constitution of corporeal being. The two elements are correlatives. Matter is a passive and homogeneous principle, an incomplete substance, betwixt being and non-being. The form on the other hand is the principle of perfection, the source of activities,[1] and the seat of the natural inclinations directing

[1] The substance considered as internal principle of activities was called *natura* ; it is by the form (*id quo*) that the complete essence (*id quod*) fulfils this function.

these activities towards an end. It is the form that gives to a substantial being its fixity and its immutability. Unlike accidental forms, which endow a substance already constituted with a mode of being, the substantial form—and therefore the substance—is not capable of increase or of diminution (*forma substantialis non suscipit plus vel minus*), so that Scholastic Metaphysics condemns the quidditative evolution of forms. The form is also the principle of unity, and in a corporeal being it holds together the extended elements in one substantial state. Finally, it is also the principle of the intelligibility of a being.

The scholastics agreed concerning the composition of corporeal substances, which are all constituted by matter (principle of indetermination, potency) and form (principle of determination, act). But in the matter of applications, they differed on four principal questions, which led to keen discussions unknown to Aristotle.

The first point was whether this substantial composition applies to all contingent beings and therefore also to immaterial beings such as the human soul, and the angels who constitute an intermediary stage in the hierarchy of reality, between man and God. These discussions led up to a new chapter of metaphysics, an angelology having nothing in common with the vague indications of Aristotle on the intelligences which move the spheres.

A second divergence of view manifested itself in connection with the unity or plurality of forms. Is one substance capable of receiving the intrinsic determination of several forms ?

Again, there was discussion on the point whether prime matter, being real, is capable of existing as such without the help of a substantial form.

Lastly, the scholastics sought to discover the ultimate reason for the possibility of many individuals in one and the same species, and how fixity and similarity go together with the wonderful diversity of " individuations." All held that the foundation of individuation must be essential and intrinsic to a being ; but there was discussion on the point whether it is matter or form or the union of these two principles that renders possible or requires this individuation.[1]

---

[1] *Individuation* is accordingly different from *individuality* which was previously touched upon. It has to do with the multiplication of individualities with the same specific type, for instance, the indefinite multiplicity of human beings.

These questions divided the followers of the pre-Thomist, Thomist and post-Thomist schools. But they imply the agreement of all on the fundamental doctrines of the hylomorphic theory. It must be added that the concepts of matter and form which in their original sense were merely explanations of extramental reality, were extended by the scholastics as were those of act and potency : in the logical order, *formalis et actualis*, *materialis et potentialis* are synonymous terms.[1]

To sum up, according to the scholastics, two types of change suffice to explain the corporeal world : the one accidental, and the other substantial. Reality is a combination of the fixed and the moving. Beings evolve, but not everything in them changes. Something of the past remains in the present and will persist in the future (moderate dynamism).

166. Essence and existence.—We have analysed the rich reality found in each one of the myriads of individual things to the extent of distinguishing in them substance and accident, and, in the domain of substance, matter and form. These principles, whether considered from the potential point of view or as actualities, reveal to us *what the thing is*, its *quiddity* or essence. Now this essence has or receives *existence*. Existence is the supreme determination, in relation to which essence is potentiality and non-being : existence is the actuation *par excellence* (*actus secundus*)[2] which cannot be reduced to any other kind of actuation.

That the *concept* of essence differs really from that of existence, and a *possible* essence from an *existing* one, no one will deny. But it is open to discussion whether, *in an existing thing*, its fundamental and constituent reality (*essentia, id quod est*) is really different from the actuality by which this reality exists (*esse, id quo est*). This is the sense of a famous question scarcely dealt with by Aristotle : is there a real distinction between essence and existence ? From the beginning of the thirteenth century there were scholastics who answered in the affirmative, but a no less important group decided in the negative. For both parties, created existence is a limited actuality or perfection ; it increases or decreases with the

---

[1] In the logical order, the correlation of the two ideas is absolute, and signifies the determinable and the determinant. For instance, the concepts of genus and species represent objective aspects of one and the same reality.

[2] The expression *actus secundus*, actuation *par excellence*, is used in two senses : existence in relation to essence, and operation compared to the simple power of action. Essence and the simple power to act are then called *actus primus*.

complete essence (substantial and accidental) to which it is proportioned. Existence is unique for one complete being according to some ; it is multiple like the essential parts to which it refers, according to others. The limitation of the perfection of existence is the ultimate foundation for the finite character of the world. Anti-scholastic Averrhoism was the only system which inferred from the absence of a real distinction between essence and existence that the world and the natural species constituting it are eternal.[1]

All these compositions in limited and changing being, which we have regarded as aspects of potentiality and actuality are, like potency and act themselves, introduced into metaphysics in virtue of the principle of sufficient reason. Without them there can be no complete explanation of the facts. They are not the object of sense intuition, but the term of a reasoning process. From that which is, the scholastics infer that which must be in order to render that which is intelligible. They do not claim that we are able to penetrate into the inner and adequate nature of the elements in which we seek the explanation of reality. These elements are there, in the being, even if we do not know everything about their nature.

167. Causes of being.—The theory of causes, which is a chapter of Aristotle enlarged and corrected, is the complement of the theory of act and potency; for it explains how and why the actuation of a potency takes place. Scholasticism understands by " cause " anything which exerts a real and positive influence upon any state of a being, and distinguishes four types of causality which complete each other :

(i) The *efficient* cause produces the movement or passage from the potential state to actuality. As for the action which constitutes this passage, this complement of reality constituting movement (*motus*) or change, no being can acquire it of itself ; otherwise it would have to possess it before acquiring it, and be already that which it is not yet, which is contradictory. The action which brings about the change comes from another being. *Quidquid movetur ab alio movetur.* The network of actions and reactions establishes close bonds of union between substances independent of each other in their inner nature.

(ii) *Material* and *formal* causes. The constituent elements

[1] Table of the compositions of contingent being :

| Essence, *essentia* | { Substance, *substantia* | { Prime matter Substantial form. |
| Existence, *esse* | { Accidents, *accidentia* | |

of a being, matter and form, are involved in causality from another point of view. By their intimate compenetration, in giving themselves to each other, the receptive matter and the determining form act as constituent causes of a compound or of a new state. They are constituent causes either of the substance itself (prime material cause, substantial formal cause) or else of some mode of being following upon substantiality (second material cause, accidental formal cause).

(iii) The *final* cause is the attraction exerted on every efficient cause by some good towards which it tends. This attraction manifests itself in the inclinations of which substantial forms are the seat, and which lead them to expend their energies not anyhow or indifferently, but in a particular direction. It is finality that accounts for the recurrence of the specific activities of a being, and in particular, for the initial tendency of the intelligence towards the true, and of the will towards the good. It is always present, even when obstacles arise, and in spite of the superficial disorders such as physical and moral evil.

In addition to this internal finality there is an external or collective finality resulting from the co-ordination of particular finalities. Solicitation by finalities can alone explain the order and beauty of the universe. If order were an exception, it might result from a chance encounter of causes. But its permanence and universality are unaccountable without the convergence of particular finalities. Dante concludes the *Divine Comedy* by singing the attraction of the universe in progress towards an end.[1]

This end can only be God, for the creature must tend towards the glory of the Creator. Now this glory consists not only in the contemplation of the spectacle of the *cosmos* by the Infinite Intelligence, but also in the knowledge which intelligent beings other than God obtain of Him by beholding the wonderful order of the universe. As God is a spirit, the acquisition of this knowledge suggests the idea of intellectual possession. This is the reply to a question which Aristotle asked but did not answer : how is God the final cause of the world ?

Finality, internal and external, is superposed upon the determinism governing the corporeal world. It harmonizes with and completes it, for it explains change from a different point of view.

168. Scholasticism and Monism.—From this system of

---

[1] *L'Amor che muove il sole e l'altre stelle.*

doctrines explanatory of pluralism, it follows that scholasticism is the sworn enemy of monism, according to which all or some beings compenetrate and form but one being. The theories of the numerical unity of the world-soul, and Averrhoistic monopsychism (see later on) were mitigated forms of monism ; the pantheism of Avencebrol or of David of Dinant, according to whom God the Supreme Being is also the Unique Being, was an extreme form, and it is easy to see that pantheism affects all the constituent theories of a philosophical system. Whether mitigated or absolute, monism suppresses diversity or else declares it to be an illusion.

Scholasticism, which looks upon every existing thing as one and independent of every other, claims that monism involves a contradiction in the very notion of being.

§ 3—*Natural Theology*

169. The Existence of God.—The proofs commonly accepted in the thirteenth century rest on the imperfect and contingent nature of the world : the existence of a perfect and infinite being is the sole sufficient reason for the existence of that which is imperfect and finite (*a posteriori* proofs). Among these proofs, the most widespread is that based on an analysis of change. Nothing can pass of itself from potency to act, and hence the fact of change calls for the existence of a being which is the cause of it, is not itself subject to becoming, and is unique. It would not help matters to postulate the existence of many efficient causes constituting a series without a starting-point, for this would involve the denial of the actual existence of the change or fact that has to be explained. Actuality always precedes potency ; the former is ultimately the perfect being without which no actuation can be realized. To this proof others were joined, equally based on observation, particularly the teleological argument, which infers the existence of a unique governor of things from the order and unity of the world.

Besides these *a posteriori* proofs, some scholastics accept those called *a priori*, such as the argument of St. Anselm, which they endeavour to modify or to colour (*colorari*)[1] ;

---

[1] Daniels, *op. cit.*, p. 122, gives the following summary of the attitude of the thirteenth century scholastics towards the argument of St. Anselm : (*a*) Thomas Aquinas and Richard of Middleton reject it; (*b*) William of Auxerre, Richard Fitzacre, Alexander of Hales, St. Bonaventure, Matthew of Aquasparta, John Peckham, Giles of Rome, and Duns Scotus accept it; (*c*) Albert the Great, Peter of Tarentaise and Henry of Ghent are undecided.

or again they adopt the favourite argument of St. Augustine based on the immutability and universality of first principles ; or else they take as their basis the data of conscience.

The existence of God requires demonstration for the former group, but for the latter it is an evident fact. There is in the thirteenth century no trace of any mistrust of the ability of reason to discover God.

170. The Divine attributes.—As corporeal reality alone is proportioned to the knowing faculties of man (p. 294), the nature of God can only be known by means of creatures : we attribute to God all perfections, at the same time excluding from them anything which might limit them.

Does this procedure enable us to obtain a *proper* knowledge of some aspect of the Divinity ? Does the notion of being, at any rate, apply to God and creatures in a *univocal* way (Duns Scotus) ? Or is all our knowledge of God *analogical* ? (Thomas Aquinas). Whatever be the answer, we may say that our knowledge of God is anthropomorphic in some ways, and not in others. It is anthropomorphic in the sense that unless we are going to say nothing at all, we must speak of God in the way human beings speak. It is not anthropomorphic, inasmuch as we are aware of the restricted meaning of the " names " that we give to the Divinity.

To banish from the idea of God all potentiality and limit is to represent Him as Pure Existence. Limited beings have only a certain degree of existence, proportionate to their essence, but the Perfect Being is Existence limited by nothing, that is to say, Infinite. He is " He who is." This is the reasoning stressed by those who would grant no common measure between the Infinite and the finite. To study the Divine attributes is to seek by a vigorous effort of thought to seek out the manifold aspects of the Infinite, without ever forgetting that such multiplicity does not affect the unity of God.

God is a conscious being who knows and wills Himself (Aristotle did not ascribe will to the *Actus Purus*). He is Goodness and Beauty (Plato and the neo-Platonists). No doubt attaches to His individuality : in God, as in every other being, existence is individual. Hence the transcendent individuality of God cannot be confounded with that of any limited being which comes into existence by a decree of His will. Finite beings, whether regarded from the point of view of their existence, or of their essence, are *other* than the Infinite. If their existence were the very existence of God, as Eckhart said later on, then God's existence could not communicate itself to the finite without limiting itself, and ceasing to be infinite. If the essence of finite things were a part of the Divinity, then the latter would consist of a sum of limited essences, and would therefore be itself limited. The finite is therefore something apart from the Infinite, but absolutely dependent upon the latter. The scholastics are unanimous in condemning pantheism.

171. God and the world.—Three principal theories sum up the relations between God and the world:

(i) *Exemplarism* and the *rationes æternæ* (Augustine). God has an adequate knowledge of Himself, and in knowing Himself He knows finite and possible essences, which, while not equal to His own being, are objectively and necessarily related to His being as imitations. From this it follows that God knows all realities before and independently of their actual existence (*universalia ante rem*). The *rationes æternæ* are the ultimate foundation of essences, and also the source of the intelligibility and truth of things, and of the certitude of our knowledge : not because we know things in God (Ontologism), but because reasoning shows us that the attributes of all things reproduce their uncreated exemplar. Harmonized with the initial tendency of the intelligence towards the truth, these synthetic views constituted the favourite point of view of thirteenth century epistemology.[1]

(ii) *Creation.* From these Divine ideas which are the exemplary cause of the world, God draws forth from nothing by IIis creative act the particular contingent realities which it pleases Him to call to existence. Scholasticism went beyond Aristotle not only by the theory of exemplary causality which is incompatible with the immobility of the peripatetic Divinity, but still more by that of efficient causality. According to Aristotle, efficient causality does not apply to the production of the first subjects of movement ; matter and form are pre-supposed and are eternal, and movement necessarily results from their coming together. Hence the world is necessarily eternal, and natural species have always been and will always be. For scholasticism, on the other hand, the very substance of things

---

[1] The scholastics accordingly treat the problem of certitude from the metaphysical rather than the psychological point of view.

in its most profound constituents comes under the influence of the Divine efficient causality.

Creation is the direct work of God. The neo-Platonist thesis of the production of the world by intermediaries is rejected by scholasticism. God does not create in virtue of a necessity of nature, but by His knowledge and free will.

(iii) *Providence.* The Creator possesses sovereign power over the creature which He has called into existence by an all-powerful act. He produces the *esse* (existence) of the concrete being, and conserves the created essence ; He co-operates in the activity of things, while respecting the nature proper to each one (*concursus congruens naturæ creaturæ*).[1] He is Providence, and takes care of each and all. He is also, but in a more profound sense than for Plato and Aristotle, the final cause of the universe. Towards God tend all things. The confusion which we find in the Stagirite between motion properly so-called (efficient causality) and motion by attraction disappears, thanks to the theory of creation.

172. Conclusion.—The scholastic natural theology is a powerful synthesis of theistic doctrines, a combination and modification of Aristotelian and Augustinian theories which supplement each other and bring into relief the Divine Infinity. It is much wider in conception than Aristotle's theory of the *Actus Purus*, and substitutes the notion of the Necessary Existence (*a se*) for the immobile mover ; it explains the co-existence of the finite and the Infinite, and furnishes a solution of problems which neither Aristotle nor Plato had unravelled ;[2] it links up the Augustinian theories with an original metaphysical theory, that of essence and existence.

We can also see how the natural theology of the scholastics is a development of their metaphysics (**161**). The latter deals with being apart from that which concerns its corporeal nature; hence it is a study of being as such, corporeal or incorporeal, and provides us with a considerable number of ideas which are applicable by analogical extension to immaterial beings if it can be shown that such exist. Thus the name " theology " (rational) found in Aristotle, the Arabians, and

---

[1] Applied to the act of understanding, the Divine concourse is often called *illuminatio ;* applied to liberty, the question of the Divine concourse later on led to the famous controversy on premotion or physical predetermination, and simultaneous concourse.

[2] This, as Ritter remarks (*Gesch. d. Philos.*, VIII, 251) constitutes a remarkable progress : " darin muss man einen bedeutenden Fortschritt erkennen." Cf. Willmann, *op. cit.*, II, 340.

sometimes in the scholastics as a synonym for metaphysics, is justified.

§ 4—*Physics and Psychology*

173. Problems in General Physics.—Metaphysics deals with the changes of things in so far as they reveal their contingent nature and their inmost essence. Physics studies corporeal change and its kinds. Following Aristotle, scholasticism reduces these kinds to four general types : the commencement and disappearance of substantial compounds, qualitative and quantitative changes, and local motion, which is pre-supposed by the three others.

The following general aspects revealed by the world of bodies subject to these various types of passage from potency to act deserve a brief treatment : the rhythmic evolution of forms, the specific character, finiteness and unity of things.

(i) *The rhythmic evolution of forms.* Matter is a storehouse of potentialities. But the plasticity, thanks to which it successively takes on various forms, follows certain directions. Nature does not change a stone into a lion ; it observes in its evolution a law of progress the detailed study of which belongs to the particular sciences. In scholastic language, prime matter does not give up a form in order to take *any* other, but one which corresponds to the type immediately next to it in the natural hierarchy. It thus goes through a series of progressive stages. Privatio (στέρησις) is the absence of an ulterior form towards which nature inclines the substantial compound, and which the matter requires by reason of the dispositions found in this particular compound. It explains the imminence of a transformation at a given moment.[1] Such is the meaning of the formula : "Corruptio unius est generatio alterius." To ask where the vanished forms have gone to, or where are the others that will appear, betrays a misunderstanding of the theory of act and potency. One might as well ask "whereabouts in the acorn is the oak tree ? "

In this genetic process of forms (*eductio formarum e potentiis materiæ*) the great doctors are unanimous in recognizing the intervention of three factors, each with its own part to play : the First Cause exercising its *concursus generalis*, pre-existing

---

[1] According to many, the human body, before its union with the spiritual soul, goes through several intermediary forms until the activity of nature gives to the embryo a perfection calling for the final determination conferred by the spiritual soul.

matter ready to unite itself to the new form in order to give rise to the new compound, and the natural agents which are the efficient principles of actualization.

We have already seen that finality governs the series of these transformations. The doctors of the thirteenth century never regarded nature as an organism with a real and physical unity as did the ancients and certain earlier scholastics.

(ii) Every natural body is endowed with an unalienable *specific character*. This is evident from the theory of substantial form. Prime matter, in all the scholastic systems, is fundamentally connected with quantity, spatial diffusion being the primary attribute of bodies, but the form reduces the multiple quantified parts to unity. This is equivalent to a rejection of atomism in the modern sense.

(iii) *Finite character and unity* of the corporeal world. In the domain of abstract quantity conceived by the mind, the mathematician can exceed any magnitude by way of addition, and obtain a quantity smaller than any other by subtraction. But when we come to the real magnitudes found in bodies, there are limits to divisibility beyond which one cannot go without destroying the body in question. On the other hand, since each body is finite and occupies a finite internal space, the sum total of bodies in the universe is finite, although the limits of this multitude may be indefinitely extended. The question of the plurality of worlds is answered in different ways. By its nature, the world is not eternal (against Aristotle). Many refuse to allow even the possibility of creation *ab æterno*, while others do not find any contradiction in the idea itself.

We find in the scholastics the favourite theory of antiquity that there is a distinction of nature between heavenly and terrestrial substances, and the scholastics, like their predecessors, combine together their astronomy, mechanics, and philosophy.

174. Celestial and terrestrial substances.—Physical and mechanical astronomy, the theory of sublunar bodies and of the action of the heavens on terrestrial bodies, are based on the postulate that astral substances are more perfect than terrestrial ones (Aristotle). This leads to a somewhat artificial system, inspired by the need of unification and of satisfying the mind, and which brings out very clearly the desire to treat the world as an ordered whole.

(i) The superiority of the stars consists in their *constitution* and in their *motion*.

A heavenly body is formed of an element which is superior to the four terrestrial elements : it is unchangeable. The heavens are not subject to generation or corruption. Some explain these cosmological properties by saying that the heavenly bodies are doubtless composed of matter and form, but that these two elements are indissolubly united. Hence, as matter cannot give up its form in order to take on another (*corruptio unius est generatio alterius*), it follows that a heavenly body can neither begin nor cease to be. Other scholastics, less numerous, have recourse to a more radical hypothesis, and attribute to the stars a simple essence, excluding matter. From the immutability of the stars the scholastics did not, like Aristotle, infer their eternity, for their system in this respect was in harmony with their doctrine on creation. But they affirmed the unique character of each sidereal type, the form either existing alone, or determining all the matter which it is capable of informing.

For the philosophers of the Middle Ages, motion is a necessary manifestation of the essence of bodies, and every specific substance must possess a specific or natural motion. Now the heavenly bodies move with circular motion, and this was looked upon as the most perfect form, inasmuch as it is the most regular, and has neither commencement nor end. The displacement of the stars was explained by the rotation of concentric spheres ; that of the planets by various hypotheses : homocentric cycles, excentrics, and epicycles.

Intelligences may be united to the heavenly bodies ; but they are there as movers causing rotation, and do not contract a substantial union with the star they inhabit.

(ii) *Terrestrial or sublunar bodies.* From Aristotle is derived the theory of the four elements, their qualities, and the rectilinear movement which indicates their inferior nature. The earth or absolutely heavy element is at the centre ; water surrounds the earth, air surrounds the water ; and fire, the absolutely light element, occupies the upper regions. Each of these elements moves in a straight line, in a direction depending on its nature (from above to below for the first two, from below to above for the last two). They tend towards a natural place, which determines their direction when displaced by an efficient cause. Any other movement impressed on the elements is

violent and unnatural.   These theories which the majority
accepted (for as we shall see already in the thirteenth century
some began to break away from them) are the antithesis of
modern mechanics.   Elements differ by their sensible qualities
as well as by their movements : the active pair of hot and cold,
and the passive pair of the dry and humid are disjunctively
united according to a quadruple conjunction.

Albert the Great and many other scholastics of the thirteenth century speak of the *qualitates primæ* (hot and cold,
dry and humid) and *qualitates secundæ* which result from the
former.   Both kinds were regarded as having real objectivity.
All qualities pre-suppose quantity, which is a *proprium* of
corporeal substance, its fundamental attribute, and the normal
manifestation of its perfection.

In virtue of their transformations into each other, their
association, and more intimate combination (*mixtum*) the four
elements explain the evolution of inorganic substances.   In
living beings we find a higher perfection which the scholastics
explain by the presence of one or several souls, and they define
the soul, with Aristotle, as " the form of a body called by nature
to exercise immanent activity."

(iii) *The action of the heavenly bodies on the development of
terrestrial beings.*   The heavenly bodies intervene as immediate
efficient causes, but not the only ones, of all terrestrial generation, for " it is fitting that the superior should act upon the
inferior."   The movements taking place on our globe are
initiated by heat, which is engendered by the friction between
the spheres and the layers of air surrounding the water and the
earth.   This friction changes air into fire.   The inclination of
the sun according to the ecliptic and its consequent periodical
variations of distance from certain parts of the earth, explains
the alternating rhythm of the generation and corruption of
beings (Aristotle).

The greater or less importance accorded to astral and
planetary influences varies from one philosopher to another.
But the belief in their action is universal.   This explains the
exaggerated regard of the Middle Ages for the occult sciences
investigating the hidden powers of the heavens; astrology
which studies the governing authority of the stars, and alchemy,
which seeks to substitute for the ordinary series of terrestrial
transformations an artificial mode of which man should be
the master, and also tries to direct the mysterious power

which the heavens possess of making matter pass through all sublunar forms.

175. Notion of psychology.—According to the spirit of the scholastic classifications, psychology forms a chapter of physics. It has for its object not only consciousness, but all the activities of man, and also the substance from which they emanate. The study of activities constitutes the inductive part of psychology, for it starts from the facts ; the study of human nature forms the metaphysical part, for it applies to man the doctrines concerning the constitution of beings.

176.   Activities of the soul.   Spiritualism.—The inferior functions of the vegetative life such as nutrition and reproduction, the cognitive, and the appetitive functions are the three groups to which all the activities of the soul can be reduced. The last two are chiefly studied, for they constitute the psychic life of man.

Knowledge implies the duality of something present to us (*objectum ; id quod objicitur*) and a knowing subject. There is formed in the knowing subject a kind of resemblance of the known object (*omnis cognitio fit secundum similitudinem cogniti in cognoscente*), and it is clear that this present of the object in us differs from its extramental presence when endowed with real existence.

On the other hand, knowledge, a vital act, is a mode of being of the knowing person (*cognitum est in cognoscente secundum modum cognoscenti*).   This is simply an application of this general principle, that change takes place in conformity with the nature of the changing being (*receptum est in recipiente secundum modum recipientis*).   Hence all knowledge is the product of two factors, the known object and the knowing subject. The intervention of the subject explains why scholasticism rejects naïf realism, according to which the object is projected in us as in a lifeless mirror, and explains how the subject transforms the known object in *living it*.   The intervention of the object guarantees the veridical character of knowledge.

Scholasticism establishes a fundamental distinction between two types of knowledge which are altogether distinct—sensation, and thought. These belong to different orders, the sensible, and the suprasensible or spiritual.   Thought is both different from sensation and higher than it.   Sensation belongs to certain animals as well as to man but thought is proper to the latter, and denotes his superiority over the other beings in the world. It is by the doctrine of the " spirituality " of thought that scholasticism is linked up to the line of Greek and patristic spiritualism. As the distinction between the sensible and the suprasensible orders affects the theory of appetition as well as that of knowledge, we must introduce this dichotomic division into the study of both faculties.

177. Sense knowledge.—(i) *Nature*. Everything which we grasp by our senses is particular, and linked up with a concrete being depending on time and space, and this is so whatever form sensation may take.

(ii) These *forms of sensation* are studied after Aristotle. In addition to the external senses (sight, hearing, touch, smell, taste) there are internal senses : the common sense (*sensus communis*) which perceives the acts of the external senses and co-ordinates their data, the sensible memory, and the constructive imagination. To these are added the *vis æstimativa* of the animal or the *vis cogitativa* in man. By the *vis æstimativa* an animal instinctively appreciates the useful or harmful character of concrete objects, and by the *vis cogitativa* man attains to the same knowledge under the direction of intelligence. This function is but vaguely referred to by Aristotle. It was, however, made the subject of long commentaries by the Arabians, and it was they who chiefly inspired the doctors of the thirteenth century.

(iii) The *seat of sensation* is the organism, that is to say, the body informed by the soul. Influenced by a twofold current of Arabian thought, the first coming from Monte Cassino (p. 155) and the second from the Arabian schools in Spain (**217**), the Western philosophers were accustomed to study rather the physiological side of sensation ; and indeed a few allowed themselves to be led astray into conclusions bordering upon materialism. The scholastics of the thirteenth century corrected this tendency : beside the physiological aspect of sensation, they emphasized its psychic aspect. They maintained the complete distinction between the two phenomena, and at the same time treated their interdependence as a fundamental law of sense life, and consequently of all perceptive and appetitive activity.

(iv) *Genesis of sensation*. Certain Augustinians continued to look upon sensation as a psychic phenomenon which the soul produces within itself on the occasion of a sense impression

(p. 119). But the majority of the scholastics of the thirteenth century, Albert the Great, Thomas Aquinas, Bonaventure, Henry of Ghent, Duns Scotus, etc., explained the origin of sensations in a peripatetic way. Here is their theory : Left to itself, a sense does not suffice for knowledge ; it is devoid of actual knowledge, it is a passive power.[1] The solicitation by the object constitutes the initial impulse without which it would remain inactive. Thanks to this intrinsic determination, the sense reacts, and this reaction completes the knowing process. " Impressed and expressed species " (*species sensibilis impressa, expressa*), or representation impressed from without and exhibited within, are the usual terms employed to indicate the two stages of the phenomenon.

The psychic event the double aspect of which is denoted by these two expressions, takes place in us. This has nothing to do with the question of the *medium*, which explains how the corporeal object manages to affect the organism. Certain scholastics confused these two questions. They regarded the impressed species not as an action produced in us, but as a material image which starts from the object, passes across the medium, and penetrates into the sense organ. The great scholastics rejected this gross interpretation.

After it has disappeared from the sphere of consciousness, sensation still leaves a trace, or an image (*phantasma*). This lives on in the imagination, and its principal office is to contribute to the production of thought when the object is absent.

178. Intellectual knowledge.—(i) *Nature and object*. Besides sense knowledge, which grasps the concrete and particular, we possess another way of knowing, in which the object is abstract and universal, and to make clear the distinction between these two kinds of knowledge, scholasticism attributes this second kind to a faculty distinct from the senses, namely, reason or intelligence (*ratio, intellectus*), We represent to ourselves the elements of reality, substantial or accidental, without the features which belong to their state of particularity, and confine ourselves to apprehending what they are, *quod quid est*, pure and simple (for instance, what it is that con-

[1] A passive faculty is not an inactive faculty, but one which is receptive before it is operative, and which must undergo determination by something other than itself before it can exercise its activity. This is in contrast to an active power, which has no need of this external stimulus from outside, but acts as soon as the necessary conditions are present.

stitutes a plant, height, movement). The notion thus obtained is abstract (*abstrahere, separatim considerare*).

It is precisely because this content of representation, or *objectum* is no longer viewed in connection with a particular being, as it is in sense perception, that it is characterized by an indefinite elasticity ; we can conceive this object of thought in relation with an unlimited multitude of realizations or beings in which it may be found. This elasticity of the concept constitutes its universality.

Abstraction and universalization, the peculiar privilege of man, are the central acts of the life of the mind, and are found not only in apprehension, but also in judgment and reasoning ; the intellectualism of the scholastics which appears here in its fundamental form is present throughout the whole system.

The scholastics agree in saying that abstraction is the law of the mind, and that our intelligence is " a reasoning reason." Does it follow from this that the mind does not directly seize the individual, or is there side by side with this abstract knowledge an intuition of the existing thing ? On this point there is disagreement, and we shall indicate the opinions as we proceed.

Thanks to the process of abstraction, the intellect can know everything. At any rate, the aspect of being can be attained in all reality, existing or possible. *Intellectus humanus potest quodammodo omnia fieri*. Still, the quiddity of sensible things is the appropriate and natural object of human knowledge. Some add that we attain to the nature of the soul and of God in the same way, while others establish this knowledge on analogical and negative processes.

The existence of the *ego* is an intuitive *datum*, implied in all conscious activity. As St. Augustine puts it : *ipsa (anima) est memoria sui*.

(ii) *Genesis*. The origin of abstract ideas which are forthwith universalized by the understanding was a favourite subject of discussion in the thirteenth century.

It was recognized by all that the content of abstract ideas depends upon the content of our sensations (*nihil est in intellectu quod prius non fuerit in sensu*) ; and it is precisely for this reason that the proper object of the understanding is the corporeal and sensible world. It is admitted no less generally that there are no ideas which are altogether innate. The dependence of the ideas upon sensation is explained in different ways :

(a) The vast majority of the scholastics of the thirteenth century regard the human understanding as a *tabula rasa*,[1] an empty slate, and hence the phenomenon of knowledge is explained by the initial reception of an influx which does not come from the understanding but from the object to be known (*species intelligibilis impressa*), an influx followed by a characteristic reaction (*species intelligibilis expressa*). That is why the human reason or understanding is called a passive faculty, which means that before it can operate, it needs an intrinsic complement which it does not possess of itself ;[2] it is acted upon before it reacts. From this point of view the human understanding and the sense faculty resemble each other.

But the problem is more complicated than in the case of sensation, and for the following reason : the real which must act upon the mind does not exist in an abstract state outside the mind. Hence the initial determination is not produced entirely by the corporeal object sensed or imagined but by this object together with a spiritual or abstractive force within ourselves, called the " active " or " acting intellect " (Aristotle). It is by means of this concourse that the object present in sensation is able to stimulate the understanding, which in consequence is called the " passive intellect."

How does this concourse take place ? There are many explanations offered. Some have recourse to the theory of the " spiritualized phantasm," as if the sensible image could be transformed by the action of the active intellect. But this explanation is criticized and rejected by the great scholastics, who solve the problem in terms of the general theory of double causality in which agents which are diverse and distinct in nature produce one effect, and both contribute in their own way to the common result : the active intellect makes use of the sensible image as a principal cause uses an instrument.

It is important to note that in any case the theory of the active intellect is not concerned with an object found in consciousness, but, as in the case of matter and form, with something which is the result of a reasoning process.

(b) In the explanation briefly sketched out above, the object presented by the senses exerts an efficient causality on the production of thought. A small group of thinkers, however, remained faithful to the Augustinian ideology : they belittled

---

[1] The expression itself was used in the thirteenth century.
[2] Cf. note p. 293.

the function of sensation which for them was simply the occasion or condition of thought, and they stressed the activity of the mind. Those who began with this interpretation and ended by excluding the active intellect from their psychology were after all consistent and logical, for the mechanism is no longer required.

This way of regarding thought as a psychic phenomenon which the soul arouses within itself is found accompanied by a similar explanation of sensation indicated above. But certain scholastics, St. Bonaventure for instance, retained the Augustinian doctrine only in order to explain the origin of sensation, whilst others, as for instance his disciple, Matthew of Aquasparta, adopted it also in their ideology.

All groups of scholastics were unanimous on this other important point : the faculties which explain the act of abstraction are all within the soul. Each man has his own intellect (active and possible). The Arabian thesis of the impersonal and separate human intellect was the subject of indignant refutations.

(iii) *Value*. What is the value of an abstract and universalized notion ? Here we touch upon the problem of universals. The unanimous answer of the thirteenth century scholastics was the same as that of Abelard : since every real existing thing is endowed with individuality, the common or universal state is the product or work of the mind ; it is subjective. The quiddity is individual in each existing thing, and is general only in the being as conceived by the mind. But since the characteristic of universality follows upon a previous process of segregative abstraction, and abstraction does really grasp extramental reality although imperfectly, it follows that the universality of the concept has its foundation outside the mind. Synthetic formulæ, derived from Avicenna,[1] were current in the schools, which summed up the relations of the individual and the universal from the metaphysical (162) and psychological points of view. The chief formula deals with the reality of essences viewed from three standpoints, *ante rem, in re, post rem*. Universals *ante rem* were defined by the theory of exemplarism (St. Augustine). Universals *in re* were explained by

---

[1] Cf. Proclus, *In Euclidi element*. prol. II, p. 51, Friedlein's edn. (Lipsiae, 1873) : κατὰ γὰρ ταύτας ὅιμαι τὰς τριπλᾶς ὑποστάσεις εὑρήσομεν τὰ μὲν πρὸ τῶν πολλῶν, τὰ δὲ ἐν τοῖς πολλοῖς, τὰ δὲ κατὰ τὴν πρὸς αὐτὰ σχέσιν καὶ κατηγορίαν ὑφιστάμενα. And before that : ἐν τοῖς καθ . . . ἕκαστα . . . πρὸ τῶν πολλῶν . . . ἀπὸ τῶν πολλῶν.

the theory that individual things alone exist; universals *post rem* have to do with the subjective elaboration of essences in the mind which considers them apart from their individual conditions.

Although superior to sensation, the abstractive mode of knowledge is poor and limited : in the first place the hall mark which fixes each essence in its individuality escapes us (even if one holds the theory of an intuition of existing reality) ; then again, we do not see how generic elements (such as life) are diversified in the essences which specify them (i.e., the specifying element in a particular kind of life). We know only the surface of things. But although our modes of knowledge are limited, we are able to determine their limits and the reason for their imperfection. And to be conscious of the precise degree of one's weakness is itself a strength.

179. The sensible and rational appetite.—In addition to the perceptive side of life there is another, the appetitive, which inclines us to seek that which will perfect or is good for us (*appetere*). This may consist in the exercise of a faculty, or it may be something external, the possession of which is desirable and constitutes a source of satisfaction. For us as for all other beings, the mainspring of appetition is our good—*bonum est quod omnia appetunt.*

A general law governs the conscious appetitions directed towards a particular object : *nihil volitum nisi cognitum.* There is no appetition without previous and concomitant knowledge ; and just as there are two separate forms of knowledge, so also there are two corresponding and equally distinct forms of appetition.

The sensible appetite is the tendency of the organism towards a corporeal object presented by the senses as good. The intensity of the appetition gives rise to the sensible passions, movements or reactions of an organic nature. These provide a fruitful subject of observations and classifications by the scholastics.

The rational appetite or will is consecutive to the presentation of the good as such. For in any concrete good thing the intelligence attains to the good, and this aspect of goodness attracts us in a way which is always present and efficacious. Nevertheless, reflection soon makes us realize that the particular object from which we have derived this abstract and general aspect of goodness, has only a limited degree of suitability, and hence is to that extent deficient—so that in virtue of the general tendency towards *all* good, and the consequent solicitation by *something* good, the reflecting reason finds itself in presence of two contradictory judgments : to will such a thing is good under one aspect ; not to will it is good under another aspect. It belongs to the will to decide freely, that is to say, to choose one of the two alternatives. We see from this that the decision depends both on the judgment and on the will.

Is this permanent tendency towards the good different in nature to the choice of a concrete good thing freely chosen ? Is this latter choice itself always dependent upon the greatest good (psychological determinism) ? The reply to these questions furnishes us with divergent interpretations of liberty. They were the subject of interesting discussions in the thirteenth century, and we may say that all the possible solutions were suggested. According to some, the general tendency towards the good and the concrete volition of a particular good thing always necessarily follow upon the presentation by the intellect (Godfrey of Fontaines for instance). For others, they remain independent of this presentation in a sense which we shall explain later on (Henry of Ghent). For Thomas Aquinas and Duns Scotus, we must distinguish between the presentation of the good as such, and that of the concrete good things presented to our choice and involving two contradictory judgments.[1]

180. The primacy of knowledge or of the will.—Equally keen was the discussion of the question which of the two higher faculties of man is the nobler and more excellent. Is it the intellect or the will ? In each case, the pre-eminence of each is founded on the way in which it grasps its object. By analogy, the reasoning concerning human intelligence and will are applied to the life of angels and to that of God.

These discussions arose out of opposition to the doctrine of St. Augustine, who attributes to the will a preponderating function in psychic life. They have nothing to do with epistemology. Recently there have been applied to the solutions offered names borrowed from modern philosophy : voluntarism and intellectualism. If this terminology is not to be misleading, we must remember that neither the voluntarists who stress the

[1] Pleasure and pain are consecutive to appetition, of which they are modalities, but they may have their source in any conscious activity.

primacy of the will, nor the intellectualists who stand up for the primacy of knowledge, intend to upset the hierarchy of psychic functions. All maintain that the intellect alone apprehends being : the will is void of any cognoscitive function, and the adage, " nihil volitum nisi cognitum " is paramount. In this sense, all are intellectualists. This exclusive competence of the intellect explains that no will, not even that of God, can change the nature of the true ; and that the theory of the two truths is absurd (against the Averrhoists).

181. The substance of the individual ego.—The human activities which as we have seen are separate and distinct from each other, are connected to as many principles of operation or faculties. But the latter are not juxtaposed like the squares on a chessboard ; they compenetrate each other in a certain sense, and are all rooted in one unique *substratum*, the ego. How is this ? Are they realities distinct from this one foundation, or are they simply diverse modalities of one and the same activity applied to different objects ? This question which was so much discussed in the thirteenth century belongs in our opinion to metaphysics. It involves the application to man of the theories interpreting contingent being (**163** (i)), and the same is true of all the doctrines concerning the nature of the human ego.

The ego belongs to the order of real beings self-sufficient for existence, in the sense that it does not need to inhere in any other being : it is a substance. Moreover, it is a complete substance, undivided in itself, or an " individual." It is called a " person " in order to denote that in the human type, the individual being is endowed with the prerogative of reason : *persona est rationalis naturæ individua substantia.* Consciousness reveals the ego as acting and existing : it also bears witness to its permanence.

Since the true and unique human reality is the particular human individual, or the particular person, to speak of a " collective person " would be to fabricate a concept out of contradictory notions and violate the universal law of intelligibility. Any compenetration of human persons is repugnant to our consciousness, and psychological individualism is simply an application of metaphysical individualism.

Like all other limited beings, and particularly the corporeal substances occupying adjacent places in the hierarchical scale of being, man is the subject of two kinds of becoming.

182. The development of personality.—Human personality, and in particular the soul, which as we shall see, is one of its constituent elements, is not an inert mass upon which are superposed accidents and activities (Locke) but a substance subject to an accidental " becoming." That is to say, each person is endowed with potentialities, and becomes richer by their development. Moreover, liberty, education, and environment may have various effects upon this development.

183. Soul and body.—On the other hand, the human being is characterized by the profound " becoming " which leads to the appearance and disappearance of the corporeal substances and the transformation from one kind of being to another **(165)**.

The substantial ego, then, is not a simple substance, but one composed of matter and form. The soul fulfils the function of form, and the body that of prime matter. Thus is established both the solidarity of the two elements which together make up the substantial ego, and the unity of the latter. Like every other living being, man is a body extended in space and organised from within by a soul. The soul by retaining the body under its compenetrating influence, makes it *its* body ; it makes it exist as a *human* body ; it gives it cohesion and unity ; it is the source or formal principle (*id quo agit*) of the activities of the human being (*id quod agit*). Soul and body give themselves to each other and are mutually adapted to each other. The thirteenth century abandoned once for all the Augustinian theory which regarded the soul and body as substances complete in themselves, heterogeneous, and violently united together.

It is true that the partisans of the plurality of forms and of souls aimed at assuring for the body and soul a sort of semi-independence, which those maintaining the unity of forms regarded as useless, illogical and compromising. But this sort of plurality is not incompatible with the unity of the compound provided each form accomplishes its function of organizing the body. Here again we are on metaphysical ground, but it is in connection with man that the partisans of the unity or plurality of forms have their warmest discussions, and this is easy to understand.

Man occupies a unique place by reason of the fact that he is capable of operations which no other corporeal being can produce. In his acts of abstract knowledge, the soul captures reality by depriving it of that which imprisons it in the corporeal and multiple. Hence it exercises an immaterial activity, that is to say, one independent of corporeal conditions. From this the scholastics conclude that the soul itself is immaterial and spiritual.[1] Unlike inorganic forms and the souls of animals which are plunged (*immersæ*) in their bodies, the human soul is of a superior nature. Being spiritual, it is simple. Being simple, it is beyond the reach of death, for corruption cannot dissolve it. Short of an annihilation willed by God, it naturally survives after death. And since immateriality belongs not only to the active intellect (Aristotle) but to the whole soul, that which survives the death of the body is not an intellect sterile in its isolation, but the soul enjoying a conscious life and still capable of abstract concepts and volitions. Since it is naturally destined to survive after death, and on the other hand naturally made to inform a body and to find in sensations the materials for its concepts (p. 295) a second union with a body— which it would again make *its* body—does not present any contradiction. The chain of deductions goes on, and the great doctrines of the spiritualism of Plato, Aristotle, Augustine are all given a place. The arguments of the *Phædo* and of the *De Anima* are joined to those of the *Confessions* and the *Elementa Theologica*. Materialism, which confuses sensation with thought, and looks upon death as the end of all things so far as man is concerned, has an implacable enemy in scholasticism.

Augustine's hesitation between traducianism, which holds that the soul of the child is detached from that of its parents, and creationism according to which it is directly created by God as each child is born, had its repercussions right up to the twelfth century. But from the thirteenth, the scholastics are unanimous in holding that only the direct and daily intervention of the Creator can call into existence the souls destined to animate the bodies of children. Is it necessary to point out that creationism has nothing in common with the Platonist doctrine of the pre-existence of souls, nor with the system of Aristotle who subjects the possible intellect to the laws of generation ?

Being a spirit destined to live in a bodily substance, man is mid-way between pure bodies and pure spirits, a *microcosmos* in which are reflected all the perfections scattered throughout reality.

[1] This proof of the spirituality of the soul is the chief one appealed to by the scholastics. The organic activity accompanying the exercise of the act of reason is only an extrinsic condition, *sine qua non*.

§ 5—*Moral Philosophy*

184.   Notion.—The study of human conduct in so far as it is directed towards ends, is the subject of ethics.   The scholastics of the thirteenth century treated from the philosophical point of view moral questions which up till then had only been treated from that of theology ; and they discussed many other questions.   They based themselves upon Aristotle, but went beyond him in all their theories, so that ethics was one of the most original sections of their philosophy.

We may group the scholastic discussions around three questions : (i) the problem of ends and of morality ; (ii) obligation and the moral law ; (iii) conscience and the virtues.

185.   The problem of ends and morality.—Like the other beings of nature, man acts in view of an end, and as he is endowed with consciousness, reason and liberty, he can control the end which he pursues.   This end can only be his good. To will the good, and all good, is the purpose of all men.   This good is in its ultimate analysis, personal to the one seeking it It is *my* good, because I am an individual being. Observation again teaches us that the goods pursued are systematically arranged, some are subordinated to others as means ; lastly it bears witness that we have within us manifold tendencies which are necessarily conflicting : pleasure, riches, honours, friendship, health, etc., attract us, and these various goods are not always approved by the reason.

Such are the facts.   The scholastics infer from them that there must be a supreme end, and that a scale of values is necessary.   The true and ultimate human good must be that which satisfies specifically human aspirations, and answer to the most elevated tendencies, the intellect and will.   Other goods are such only in a complementary sense and if controlled by reason.   None of them is to be neglected, not even pleasure provided it is sought in a reasonable way.   To know in perfect way that which is accessible to reason, that is to say to build up into an ordered assembly of abstract notions the universality of the corporeal world around us, and then to know God the author of the Great Wonder ; to desire and love knowledge for its own sake, to delight in it, and through knowledge to love God the Creator : such would have been the essence of philosophic beatitude or happiness.   In this state we should n doubt have understood that a higher knowledge and love, a vision of the Godhead face to face and a direct love were conceivable but at the same time we should have understood that they were unattainable, and the reason why.

At this point Catholic theology intervenes and completes philosophy : it teaches us that a grace or gratuitous favour calls man to this intimate union with God to which he has no right, and that the " beatitude of abstractions " will disappear in the beatitude of vision, " as a shadow is absorbed in a ray of light."[1] The passage from the philosophical to the theological point of view is effected by all the scholastics of the thirteenth century in a spontaneous way, and the one aspect is not treated without the other. This is the part of their philosophy—and perhaps the only one—in which the connection with the Catholic religion is an essential one.

The end of man is therefore primarily intellectualist, although the scholastics discuss at length whether knowledge (*visio*) or the love which follows in the will (*delectatio*) is the " formal " or precise act by which we take possession of God.

We tend towards our ends or away from them by acts of the will, and especially by free volitions.

Given the end and an act tending towards it, morality consists simply in the relation between the two. In the first place the profound and permanent tendency towards the good possesses a moral quality, and we have seen that it is impossible to stifle this insatiable desire. But it is above all to the free acts of the will by which this tendency manifests itself and by which man has the power to choose his ways, to turn towards his real good or to turn away from it, that moral goodness applies. The free act alone entails responsibility. The morality of an act is based upon the nature of man, and ultimately on the objective and fixed relation of resemblance between human nature and the Divine essence.

From all this it follows that goodness and moral goodness are not synonymous. It also follows that there is an objective distinction between a voluntary act in harmony with man's end (moral goodness) and one which is not (moral evil). God Himself could not change this relationship. Similarly, the factors which complete the morality of an act (proper object of the act, the circumstances, and subjective end intended by the agent) are also those which fix the perfection of the act.

[1] Comparison already employed by Anselm of Laon. See p. 200.

Everywhere we come across the metaphysical foundations upon which ethics rests.

186. Obligation and the moral law.—Not every morally good act is obligatory. Only the " spirituals " treated heroism as a duty. The scholastics made a detailed study of the extension and nature of moral obligation, and here again they innovated upon the Greek philosophers who did not distinguish between an upright act and one which is obligatory.

Man is bound to will his true end : the law prescribing this obligation is simply an application to man of the eternal law (*lex æterna*) which orders all things to their natural end and inclines them to conform to the relations uniting them to God (exemplarism, finality). Being morally obliged to attain our end, we are also obliged by way of corollary to perform those acts which are the necessary means for obtaining it. Moral obligation stops there, so that a vast field of our moral actions is outside its province.

Thus the obligatory force of the moral law does not consist in the coercive character revealed to us by our conscience nor the interior voice which warns us of it ; it rests upon human nature, and ultimately, upon God's command.

Obligation dictates orders, but admits of the power to accomplish them freely : for the law which governs man must respect his own nature.

187. Moral conscience and the virtues.—We are inclined to the knowledge of the ways leading to our end by a *habitus principiorum rationis practicæ* which the scholastics called *synderesis*. Under its influence, the intellect formulates the general principles which are the standards of our moral life. Moral conscience is but the application of these universal principles to a particular case. The obligation in a given case is imposed through the intermediary of an act of knowledge. This is required by the intellectualist data of psychology and ethics.

The practice of morally good acts engenders moral virtue in the will ; their repetition impresses certain permanent tendencies which incline us to act well in the various circumstances of life. Following Aristotle, the scholastics distinguished four fundamental virtues : prudence, justice, fortitude and temperance, and each writer treated them according to his own ideas and preferences.

[1] The doctrine of the *synderesis* appears already in Alexander Neckam and Alexander of Hales.

§ 6—*Social Philosophy*

188. Principles of social philosophy.—After determining morality, obligation and virtue in general conduct, the scholastics take up questions concerning family and political life, social institutions, and the relations between Church and State.

The fundamental principles of the group-life which some formulate with remarkable clarity, are part of the spirit of the whole school, for they are in logical harmony with the system. We may enunciate them as follows :

(i) Man is called by nature to life in community (Aristotle) in order the better to attain his end. Hence :

(ii) The community exists for the good of its members, and the member is not subordinated to the good of the community.

(iii) Men are naturally equal in their essential perfection. The community cannot restrict the exercise of those activities without which man cannot attain its end.

This is in accordance with the requirements of metaphysics, which teaches that the individual alone possesses reality, and of ethics, which assigns to each one his own end.

189. The family and the State.—The family, the social cell or unit, comprises the husband, wife, children, and servants (*servi*). Marriage is monogamous and indissoluble by natural law. The father, the head of the family, derives his authority from God. The subjection of children and *servi* is stricter than that of the wife. With reference to the *servi* employed on the land, the thirteenth century had not yet given them complete freedom, but canonical and civil legislation continually ameliorated their situation, and their rights as human beings were sacred.

Like the family, the political group is a natural one. But only a few scholastics deal with the philosophy of the State *ex professo*. We shall study it in connection with Thomas Aquinas, who simply crystallizes the ideas of his time.

In the same way, when he professes the subordination of the temporal power to the Church, while justifying the co-existence of both, Thomas Aquinas is the mouthpiece of the scholastic philosophers who see in this subordination of the Christian State to the Church the means of realizing the ideal of the *Civitas Dei* of St. Augustine.

190. Social questions.—The thirteenth century discussed only a few of what are known as social questions. They dealt with that of individual property, which they held to be a natural right ; that of work, and of the salary to which a man has a right and which should be sufficient for his upkeep ; and that of the morality of gain in the case of the artisan, contracts, and commercial exchange.   The domain of social questions became wider in the fourteenth century.

We find in the social ideas of the thirteenth century a reflection of the communal and feudal life of the time.

§ 7—*Logic*

191.   Pedagogic and Scientific Logic.—The Universities of the thirteenth century retained the scholastic practice of logical exercises which taught one how to analyse syllogisms and refute sophisms (p. 257).   This kind of logic, corresponding more or less to dialectics, the queen of the *trivium* (p. 64) and serving as a training for the mind, is distinct from scientific or philosophic logic, which is the study of the architecture of knowledge or of the methods which the mind employs in order to co-ordinate and piece together its judgments and build them up into scientific systems.   This second kind of logic is the *scientia scientiarum*.   It arose out of commentaries and discussions on the Aristotelian treatises of Aristotle, especially the *Analytics*.   We may say that scholastic logic is a development of that of Aristotle.

192.   Judgment and reasoning.—A human science or branch of knowledge is composed of arguments linked together. Reasoning itself is a nexus of judgments, so that the judgment is the unit in logical construction, from which all knowledge starts and in which it all ends.   Judgment consists in the realization that a content of representation (white, for instance) agrees or does not agree with another (snow, for instance) it unites or separates two contents or concepts of objects Reasoning consists in passing from known judgments to a third less known or not previously known at all.

The judgment which is capable of forming a part of a human science is the necessary and universal judgment or law " Scientia non est de particularibus."   Hence it follows that reasoning, of which the syllogism is the typical expression starts with the enunciation of a necessary connection or relation based on the nature of the things in question (for instance it is of the nature of a spiritual being to be simple), with a view to realizing that this law applies to all or certain beings included under the extension of the law (for instance, that the human soul, belonging to the class of spiritual beings, has the privilege of simplicity).

The logical law or judgment upon which the syllogism rests, is obtained either from or independently of experience. In the latter case, the proposition is *per se nota*, or knowable by the simple analysis and bringing together of the terms. In the former case, it is *per aliud nota*, the *aliud* being something other than the mere bringing together of the terms, namely, experience. The scholastics did not study the experimental methods with the same care as moderns have done, for they go hand-in-hand to some extent with the development of the experimental sciences. Still, we find in some, particularly in Duns Scotus, a keen analysis of the inductive methods or ways which enable us to pass from the observation of certain cases to the law which governs all.

193. Scientific systemization and its methods.—Arguments or reasonings are joined together like the links of a chain ; each one is demonstrated by a previous reasoning, and it is evident that in virtue of this dependence the order cannot be reversed. Moreover, there must be a starting-point in this series, just as there must be a fixed point for the first link of a chain. To go back to infinity would render all knowledge impossible.

There is, then, at the basis of each science certain judgments which do not admit of demonstration, called the " first principles " of the science in question. They express certain very simple, and therefore evident relationships found in the object studied by the science. In addition, there are the *axiomata* or simple judgments which direct and underlie all knowledge, inasmuch as they express the simple relations between being and itself and its relevant notions. All science studies being under some or other aspect. Reasoning, definitions, and prime judgments all form a coherent whole. The unity which determines their order and arrangement and which characterizes them all according to their importance, comes from the formal object (*objectum formale*) of each science. By that is meant, not the things themselves studied by the science (*objectum materiale*), but the point of view from which it studies them. These notions provided the basis for the classification of the particular and philosophic sciences to which we have already referred, the autonomy of each, and the diversity of human sciences and theology.

The laws of scientific construction apply to metaphysics, physics and ethics just as much as to the particular sciences. Certain scholastics, inspired by the Arabians, called logic the *vestibulum* of philosophy, to which it serves as a preliminary study, or is related as a design to a picture.

194. Speculative grammar.—The great reputation enjoyed by logic explains its invasion of the teaching of grammar in the faculty of arts. Donatus and Priscian were still the classical authorities. But instead of commenting upon their arid formulæ, the grammarians of the end of the thirteenth century and the beginning of the fourteenth created a veritable philosophy of language and borrowed largely not only from dialectics, but also from metaphysics and psychology.

§ 8—*Æsthetics*

195. Æsthetical questions.—Theories on æsthetics are not found in treatises dealing with the subject *ex professo*, but are scattered up and down works on other subjects, or else in commentaries, particularly those on the treatise on the *Divine Names* of pseudo-Dionysius.

Æsthetics studies the laws which govern the production of external things. It owes its philosophic or general character to the fact that all exterior production by man is capable of possessing beauty. The thirteenth century made no difference between the work of an artisan and that of an artist. If he works upon matter, man is a creator, and as Dante says, by reason of this he is " God's nephew."[1] Again, Nature is in itself beautiful, it is like a magnificent symphony (Bonaventure) or a noble tree (Duns Scotus), for it realizes order by the convergence of particular finalities. In short, the whole domain of reality is covered with the mantle of beauty.

But beauty is studied above all in its general aspects, as depending upon metaphysics and psychology. Beauty is a complicated thing, and comprises :

(i) On the part of the exterior object, a realization of order (Plato, Aristotle), and hence an unfolding of the perfection of the object, its unity, and its form (pseudo-Dionysius). By attaching order to the unity and form of the being, scholasticism

---

[1] *Che vestra arte a Dio quasi nepote. Inferno*, XI, 103.

unites together an Aristotelian doctrine and a neo-Platonist theory.

(ii) On the part of the subject in contact with the object, beauty implies a psychic impression which begins with a sensation, comprises an act of contemplation by the intelligence (intellectualism), and culminates in the enjoyment of contemplation.

(iii) It also comprises an adaptation of the order to the impression, i.e., between subject and object, a clear manifestation of order, *claritas pulchri*. By thus shining forth, the objective element of beauty is proportioned to man, manifests itself in a powerful way, and produces a facile and adequate impression.

Beauty, therefore, does not belong exclusively either to things (theory of the Greeks), or to the subject, nor is it merely an attitude of the subject (modern theory) ; it is mid-way between the object and subject and consists in the correspondence of the one to the other.

§ 9—*Doctrinal characteristics*

196. Elements of a doctrinal definition.—After this brief exposition of the body of doctrine common to the scholastics and differentiated by each one, we can take up a question which we left undecided, that of the definition of scholastic philosophy (7). Its real and intrinsic characteristics, that is to say, those derived from its inmost nature or from its organic solutions, will tell us what it is.

These solutions may be considered in two ways, either separately, or in their relations with each other.

197. The scholastic solutions and their characteristics.—If we glance at the doctrines just expounded one by one, we shall see that they present certain salient characteristics.

To begin with, scholasticism is a *pluralistic* and not a monistic metaphysic. The substantial distinction between God, Pure Act, and His creatures which are combinations of act and potency, makes scholasticism the sworn enemy of pantheism. The compositions of matter and form, the individual and the universal, and the distinctions between the knowing subject and the object known, the souls of the blessed and God how atisfies their powers, are doctrines which are incompatible with monism and frank affirmations of individualism. We cannot insist too much upon the care with which the scholastics deprived the doctrinal elements borrowed from the Arabians of any emanative or pantheistic sense. It is in connection with man, whose supremacy in the *cosmos* they endeavour to establish by every possible means, that scholastic individualism comes into conflict with the monopsychism of the Averrhoists. Each being is itself, distinct from every other, and it is not essential that it should be known by us. In virtue of another group of doctrines, scholastic metaphysics is *substantialist*, and very far removed from exaggerated relativism. The metaphysics of contingent being is also a form of *dynamism* (act and potency, matter and form, essence and existence), and this dynamism governs the appearance and disappearance of natural substances. From another point of view, the material world is interpreted in an evolutionist and *finalist* sense. The natural theology of the scholastics is *creationist*. God whose existence it demonstrates is an infinite being, the beginning and end of all things, providence, judge, and principal cause of all, and in particular, He collaborates in our acts of thoughts.

In psychology, the finalist conception explains the optimism and dogmatism of scholastic criteriology : the intellect is made for the truth, and attains to things as they are, although in an imperfect way. Sensation is equally infallible when concerned with its proper object. The whole ideology of the scholastics *is objectivist*, and if we pass from the critical to the genetic point of view, it is experimental and opposed to innate ideas and *a priori* conceptions. Above all it is *intellectualist* for it proclaims the radical distinction between sensation and thought ; *spiritualist* inasmuch as it bases the suprasensible character of intellectual representations upon abstraction. On the other hand, its moderate realism harmonizes the individuality of extramental things with the universality of the concept which correspond to them. The spiritualism of the scholastic ideology has its repercussions in the theories on the nature of the soul, its origin and its immortality, and in this connection scholasticism rejects all materialist ideas.

Based as it is on the data of psychology and metaphysics scholastic logic is *intellectualist*, and gives the place of honour to the analytico-synthetic method.

As for ethics, this is *anti-determinist*, and its optimism is evident in this eudaimonistic formula that the end of man is attained by the use of the highest of his superior faculties.

If we were to multiply points of view, and consider scholasticism in other ways, we should find fresh characteristics, all of them clear and precise. It may be that one or other of these characteristics or doctrines belong in common to scholasticism and other historic solutions, but in any case the sum-total belongs to scholasticism alone. Moreover, they all stand together. For if we consider the characteristics found not in any particular doctrine but in the relations of each one with the whole, we cannot but be struck by their coherence and interpenetration, their moderation and measure.

198. The interdependence of doctrines.—Scholasticism is a system in which everything hangs together. Not many philosophies have such a care for unity. It is by its unity, corresponding to a mental need, that it has exercised such an attraction for thinkers in the West. We may say of each scholastic doctrine that it overflows its own borders and invades the field of others. In this way all the problems of physics, psychology, and natural theology are impregnated with the theories of act and potency, causality, form, essence and existence : metaphysics sustains all, and is the framework of the whole. Ethics and social philosophy are saturated with metaphysics, and can only be understood in the light of its principles. Logic is linked up with ideology, and ethics with psychology.

There are three doctrines the unifying functions of which are above all easily recognized, and which are found everywhere, as the pointed arch is found in all the corners of a Gothic cathedral. These doctrines are : intellectualism, the value of personality, and the idea of God.

Intellectualism, which proclaims the supremacy of abstractive reason, affects all the doctrines of scholasticism. If we suppress the abstract nature of the concept, judgment becomes inexplicable, logic collapses, science is impossible, the spirituality of the soul is compromised, liberty is unaccountable, life is without an ideal, happiness must be sought in material things, and social life changes its meaning. Dante merely voices the sentiment of all when he writes : " Reason is to the individual what the father is to the family, and the ruler to the city : it is the master."[1]

The value of *personality*, which follows from the pluralistic metaphysics, makes the human individual an autonomous being possessing his own body, soul, and faculties, and master

[1] *De Monarchia,* l. I.

of his activities, equal in nature to his fellows, with a right to personal happiness, safeguarded against the encroachments of the State, and assured of personal immortality. The abhorrence of scholasticism for monism is strengthened by its repugnance for anything suggesting an abdication of personal dignity.

Lastly, *God* is found everywhere in the scholastic system, and the other doctrines converge towards Him as the radii of a circle towards its centre. Without God the real cannot be explained, and human life would lack its end.

199. The sense of measure.—There is a second characteristic which explains the tremendous expansion of scholasticism in the West : its moderation or sense of measure. It completes Aristotle by Plato, and Plotinus by St. Augustine. All its solutions are temperate. Abstraction is based upon sensation, whence it follows that scholastic ideology is a combination of spiritualism and sensualism. Scholastic realism is moderate, a middle course between naïve realism and phenomenalism. The theory of the union of the soul and body constitutes man an intermediary between pure spirit and mere matter. We find the same moderation in ethics, for intellectual happiness does not exclude the reasonable satisfaction of the body ; and duty is harmonized with pleasure. Again, in social philosophy the good of the individual harmonizes with the collective good, in logic the deductive and inductive methods aid each other, in æsthetics beauty is at once an objective attribute and a conscious state. The limitation of act by potency, and form by matter constitute a moderate form of dynamism, for the expansion of a principle of activity (form)in passive and quantified extension is a corrective of the doctrine of pure energy.

Lastly, this sense of measure appears in a characteristic conciliation of the fixed and the changing, a sort of moderate evolutionism, which is primarily a metaphysical doctrine, but which also permeates the whole system. In the types of corporeal beings and also in the human type there is a reality which does not change in the course of ages (the substance) while other elements accommodate themselves to circumstances (powers of operation and accidental determinations). Thanks to this, the human species, while not ceasing to be fixed, is declared capable of perfection ; the moral law is constant in some of its prescriptions and variable in others ; human laws accommodate themselves to different times and circumstances while still depending upon the decrees of the eternal law ; human civilization in its entirety, constituted as it is by human activities, is capable of progress, and at the same time the great manifestations of the mind, when they reach a certain stage of development, present certain common characteristics in spite of variety of climate and period. Humanity is not pursuing a path of indefinite progress ; it travels rather in circles and periods. In virtue of its sense of measure, scholasticism is an eminently human philosophy.

The scholasticism of the thirteenth century, which completed the efforts of the early Middle Ages, inspired the philosophies of later ages, and represents the zenith of mediæval thought, corresponds best of all to the scheme of ideas and doctrinal characteristics outlined above. Hence it deserves to be known as scholasticism pure and simple.

§ 10—*Civilization and Philosophy*

200. Relations of harmony.—The zenith of scholasticism coincided with the full development of mediæval civilization, of which it was one of the most characteristic manifestations. Between the other factors of this civilization and scholasticism we observe relations both of *harmony* and of *interdependence*.

By relations of harmony we mean the unitive, cosmopolitan, optimistic, impersonal, and religious tendencies found everywhere at this time, in virtue of which the aspirations of philosophy coincided with those of the age as a whole.[1]

201. Universal and unitive tendencies.—The desire to include all the questions to which philosophy gives rise, to explore the complete cycle of the natural, moral and juridical sciences in order to give an account of facts and documents, and the constant endeavour to study this vast mass of detail in the light of principles of a rigorous unity, are the essential characteristics of thirteenth century scholasticism.

These same characteristics are manifest in the works of the theologians—the very title of *Summæ* is an indication of this. They are also found in the writings of the jurists ; in Accursius († 1252), the author of the *Glossa ordinaria*, the lawyers of Philip Augustus, Edward I, and James I of Aragon, or again in the supplementary matter added to the Canon Law of

[1] See De Wulf, *Civilization and Philosophy in the Middle Ages* (Princeton Univ. Press, 1922).

Gratian. The same spirit inspired the great encyclopædic works which all aimed at universality—the *Golden Legend* of Jacobus de Voragine, and the *Rationale Divinorum* of William de Mende, which gathered together all that was known of the legends of the lives of the saints and the various interpretations of the liturgy, the works of general information written by Bartholomæus Anglicus (*De Proprietatibus*),[1] the *Speculum Quadruplex* of Vincent of Beauvais († 1268),[2] the *Great Treasure* by Brunetto Latini, the *Catena Aurea* of Henry of Hereford (fourteenth century), and even the *Romance of the Rose*, which contained in a free form all that an educated layman was supposed to know. The men of the thirteenth century not only wished to know everything : they also wanted to put everything in order, and carried out thoroughly the Aristotelean dictum, *sapientis est ordinare*. When there was a question of putting ideas into order, Aristotle was looked upon as the authority, or, in the words of Dante, as the "master of them that know."

Art aspired to a similar greatness and universality. The Gothic cathedrals are mirrors reflecting the whole character of the material and moral world, as well as history-books and pictorial catechisms. They were built in order to teach the multitude, and they astonish one by their faultless logical arrangement and proportions.

This same passion for unity and universality characterized the Catholic Church : the whole of the West was covered by the network of one united Hierarchy ; the mendicant orders spread throughout all Christendom, and the ever-increasing sovereignty of the Popes extended to all parts of the civilized world. The Papal theocracy reached the zenith of its power in the person of Innocent III, reaching to the most intimate details of the internal life of dioceses and monasteries.

The political world was subject to analogous movement towards unification, for it was at this time that the rulers developed the organization of the great European States on a more or less uniform plan, based upon the happy combination of two principles of order, the central authority of the kings, and respect for particular social tendencies. Philip Augustus and Louis IX, Edward I and Frederick II, Ferdinand III and Alphonso X were the builders of States and organizers of civil

[1] No. 219.
[2] Written at the request of Louis IX, who entrusted him with the instruction of his son. It comprises the *speculum historiale, naturale, doctrinale, morale*. The *Speculum Morale* is not, however, by Vincent of Beauvais.

society. At the same time the autonomy of the towns, the result of the spread of commerce, and the gathering together of the clergy and nobles in the beginnings of Parliaments, helped to counterbalance the central power : thus the West seems to have been inspired throughout in the thirteenth century by the desire for a unified type of civilization.

202. The exaggerations of philosophic speculation.—This strongly-marked passion for systemization explains the exaggerations found in philosophers, theologians, jurists and publicists, and the fact that imagination had sometimes to supplement weakness of certain arguments. So imperious was the passion for ordered arrangements that in the absence of convincing arguments recourse was had to pleasing fictions.

The artificial union brought about by the scholastics between their metaphysics and the doctrine of the perfection of the heavenly bodies, together with all the corollaries derived therefrom, furnishes us with an interesting example of this curious turn of mind. Thus St. Thomas Aquinas, writes that it is fitting that the superior (the heavens) should rule the inferior (the earth). It is fitting that the world should be unique, for unity is more perfect that multiplicity.

Another example of these exaggerations to which the best minds were led by the passion for unity and order is found in the dream of a universal monarchy or *respublica humana*, indulged in by publicists, lawyers and canonists. The need for one unique government for the whole world which would respect the autonomy of the various kingdoms, was not seriously contested by anyone. Such a government seemed to the intellectual spirits of the thirteenth century to be the natural realization of the ideal outlined by St. Augustine in the *De Civitate Dei*. The differences between lawyers and canonists concerned only the relations between the Papacy and the Emperor or universal monarch. According to the lawyers, the latter would be independent of the Papacy in temporal matters, while the canonists upheld his dependence.

203. Cosmopolitan tendencies.—The scientific and philosophical classifications were accepted by all the thinkers of the thirteenth century ; they inspired the programmes of studies at Paris and Oxford (p. 254) ; they also governed private teaching ;[1] and were pre-supposed in philosophic treatises.

[1] They form the plan of the *Speculum divinorum et quorundam naturalium* written by Henry Bate of Malines for the education of Guy of Hainault.

The scholastic synthesis was itself a cosmopolitan production. It was given its definitive form at Paris, the metropolis of speculation, the rendezvous of philosophers of all countries, and the point from which they spread out everywhere. This conferred upon the thought of the time a uniformity which had not existed since the Alexandrian period, and which has not existed again since the Middle Ages. A philosopher enjoyed not a local but an international reputation, and at the end of the century we come across the titles by which authors were known throughout the West. The universality of the learned language, Latin, and the attractions of Paris, favoured the expansion of scholasticism.

This cosmopolitan character of philosophy is not an exceptional feature in the history of the period ; it is closely bound up with the characteristics of the other departments of social activity. For although France remained the chief centre of the philosophic, scientific, moral and artistic movements and the centre of mental culture in Western civilization, still we find throughout the West the same fundamental criteria in the appreciation of values. Everywhere the same feudal customs prevailed, there was a tendency to institute the same type of royalty, art displayed the same features ; and everywhere we find the same methods of building and sculpture. Gothic architecture and sculpture arose indeed in France, but were adopted by other countries with wonderful rapidity.

Lastly, and above all, the West professed the same faith, obeyed the same ecclesiastical hierarchy, and was inspired by the same desire to combat heresy. In matters of belief and morals, the Pope was the agent of cosmopolitan unity ; he was the arbiter of the public and private conduct of sovereigns, reminding them of the precepts of Christian morality, and at one time Innocent III thought he would be able to bring back the Oriental schismatics to the unity of the Church. In spite of heresies, revolts and disorders among the clergy, the catholicity of the West remained intact ; the time for apostasy had not yet come.

204. Optimism.—The scholasticism of the thirteenth century is an optimistic philosophy. It accepts reason, and holds that it is capable of leading us to the truth, *in cujus natura est ut rebus conformetur*.[1] For is not human reason a spark derived from the flame of eternal truth ?

[1] Thomas Aquinas, *De Veritate*, q. 9, art. 9.

This optimism, which is found also in ethics and social philosophy, and which passes from theory to practice, is another characteristic of the century. The men of this period looked upon life as worth living. The *Chansons de Geste*, the *Divina Commedia*, the *Fioretti* of St. Francis of Assisi, the frescoes of Giotto, and the cathedrals breathe a serenity and joy which make each work of art a poetical expression of optimism. Under the feudal regime, the populace was relatively happy, and the thirteenth century knew neither pauperism nor the great plagues which later on desolated Europe. For the rest, there was the promise of happiness in the faith and moral conduct enshrined in Christian dogma.

205. Impersonality and its consequences.—Above all, scholasticism is a monument of ideas resulting from the impersonal collaboration of many. Truth was not regarded as the property of the one discovering it, but as a patrimony which one generation bequeathed to another, and which grew rich by an uninterrupted process of development.[1] This explains better than anything else why scholasticism was not a system invented by some man of genius, but was gradually and slowly formed in the course of time.

From this impersonal and patrimonial character the scholastics infer the perpetuity of philosophic doctrine. The latter ever retains a constant value. It is not, as many modern writers think, a provisional thing which each generation constructs and employs, leaving the next generation free to recommence the work all over again ; for the truth which it aims at attaining is fixed and immutable, like the essences of things themselves, and God upon whom the order of essences rests. In spite of the part which scholasticism attributes to change in nature, science, ethics, politics and social government, in spite of the place it gives to progress, rise and fall, and the diversity of civilizations, it loudly proclaims the permanence of those underlying factors which are indispensable to change itself. It consciously takes up and completes the truths bequeathed by the Greeks, the Fathers of the Church, and the Arabians, adapting them to the Western mind. Indeed, its whole work consists in this adaptation. The philosophers of the thirteenth century thought in the Greek way, but their thought was transformed by Christianity, and by the intellec-

---

[1] See the declarations of Roger Bacon, *Opus majus*, par. I, cap. 6 (edited by Bridges, III, p. 14) ; and of Thomas Aquinas, in *Lib. II Metaph.* lectio I.

tual and moral contribution of the new races to which they belonged.

The impersonal character of scholasticism, and its progressive and collective constitution explains why the work alone counts, and why the thirteenth century troubled little about the name of the workman. Outside a small number of authorities[1] known by all and quoted (*allegari*) in the schools, little importance was attached to persons, and contemporaries were designated by anonymous appellations (*unus dicit*).[2] Even the style of the scholastics is impersonal, and only exceptionally does it manifest the emotions of the writer.

It is easy to see that impersonality and the idea of permanence are found not only in scholasticism, but also in the other products of civilization. We find them in theology, and again in canon law, which was already in process of constitution in the works of Yves of Chartres and Gratian by successive additions.

The hymns of the Catholic liturgy, the style of the *chansons de geste*, the technique of sculpture and of architecture, all manifest the same impersonality, and delight to hide themselves behind the veil of anonymity : the treasury of art is, like that of speculative thought, a well from which all think they have a right to draw, a common possession for the use of all, acquired by the labours of a multitude of unknown men. On the other hand, the builders of the cathedrals had the same ambition as the builders of scholasticism, namely, that of working for eternity. The religious and political organization of the West was looked upon by all as definitive. Humanity seemed to have arrived at a decisive stage, and the beautiful definition of peace left by St. Augustine : *Pax est tranquillitas ordinis*, seemed to have a striking application in the actual state of things.

206. The history of philosophy.—The impersonality of philosophy led the scholastics to treat the history of ideas and doctrines in a peculiar way. Although this aspect occupies a large space in their exposition of the *pros* and *cons*, they intro-

[1] Albert the Great and later on Thomas Aquinas ranked among the *auctoritates* in the same way as Aristotle, Augustine, Avicenna, etc. After denying that the *De Spiritu et anima* was by Augustine, Thomas Aquinas writes ; " Unde quod ibi scribitur, pro auctoritate habendum non est." *In IV Sent.* Dist. 44, q. 4, a. 3.

[2] Ehrle (*A. de Villenova, etc.*, p. 494), points out that this custom did not disappear until the middle of the fourteenth century. Alfonso Toletano (1344), Petrus de Tornaparte (1337) and Johannes Canonicus are the first to mention their contemporaries by name.

duce it merely in order to lead up to the solution which they consider the true one, so that the history of philosophy has no value in itself.

This attitude helps us to understand to some extent the absence of a critical attitude in the determination of a fact or point of doctrine ; the habit of explaining away difficult texts (*in melius interpretari ; pium dare intellectum*) and of reproducing other stereotyped quotations. It also explains the methods of literary transmission such as the *deflorationes* or plagiarisms, second-hand copies, interpolations and modifications which copyists made in the original text, the ready fashion in which apochryphal works were put into circulation under the patronage of illustrious names, and the whole mass of pseudo-epigrapha resulting from this. Lastly, it explains the little value attached to the argument of authority. Adelard of Bath compared authority to a muzzle (*capistrum*)[1] and Alan of Lille to a wax nose capable of being turned in different directions.[2] The argument of authority, wrote St. Thomas, is the weakest of arguments, " locus ab auctoritate quæ fundatur super ratione humana est infirmissimus."[3] So if the thirteenth century sinned against the critical spirit, it was by excessive freedom rather than by the lack of it.

207. The religious spirit of scholasticism.—We saw above that scholastic philosophy is clearly distinct from scholastic theology, that apologetics was a dependance of the latter, and that scholastic philosophy was forbidden to contradict theology. We have also pointed out why these relations of distinction, collaboration and subordination between the two sciences do not upset their autonomy (**13, 121, 160**).

In addition to these doctrinal relations, there were others outside doctrine, all based upon the social superiority of the theologian (cf. p. 17). In academic functions, the philosopher gave place to the theologian, i.e., to the " doctor of truth," and the interpreter of Catholic dogma. Towards theology all profane knowledge converged, philosophy included. Was it not to some extent in virtue of this privileged position that the theologian dealt with everything—philosophy, civil and canon law, and the leading questions of the day ?

What is there astonishing in the fact that philosophy was

[1] *De quibusdam naturalibus quæstionibus*, man. lat. Escorial O. III, 2 fol. 76 vb.
[2] See p. 186.
[3] *Summa theol.* la, q. 8.

affected by the religious spirit in a civilization of which religion was the soul? The social ascendancy of Catholicism was evident everywhere. Teaching in all its grades was in the hands of the clergy : schools for the people and schools of chivalry, as well as the universities, owed their origin to the Church or were sanctioned by its authority. Religion permeated the family, and the corporate organization of work ; it disciplined the system of exchange, and condemned usury and simony.

Art manifested the same close alliance between religion and beauty. The Gothic cathedrals are at once masterpieces and symbols ; the sculptures, windows and frescoes realize a complete iconographic programme. The poems of St. Francis of Assisi, while singing the beauties of Nature, lift up the soul towards God. The social primacy of Catholicism explains the central position of the Papacy ; it is the reason why political authority was looked upon as a delegation from God ; it forced all statesmen to recognize the function of the Church, even those who quarrelled with the Popes. The religious spirit continually inspired Crusades, and called forth into existence the new monastic orders of the Dominicans, Franciscans, Carmelites, and the Augustinian Canons. In spite of the immorality portrayed in the satires and the chronicles, in spite of certain superstitions, the exaggerated cultus of relics, and the abuse of pilgrimages, the masses were profoundly impregnated with Catholicism and lived according to the Gospel; and the heresies themselves arose out of an unbridled zeal for religion.

208. The influence of scholasticism.—In addition to the relations just pointed out, which reveal a sort of static harmony between scholasticism and civilization, there are also dynamic relations, namely, the influences exerted by scholasticism on various factors of this civilization.

(i) Scholasticism permeated the other sciences, and especially theology, civil and canon law, by the didactic methods which it imposed upon them. The application of its arguments to dogma led to the full development of apologetic. The sermons of the thirteenth century abound in philosophic material.

(ii) Scholasticism also influenced works of art. The *Roman de la Rose*, the *Images du Monde* and other French didactic poems, the tales of Chaucer, and the *canzone* of Guido Cavalcanti, are full of doctrines derived from various scholastic philosophers, and show how great was their influence upon the general culture of the time.[1] The painting by Traini conserved at Pisa, and the numerous repetitions of this theme symbolize the triumph of St. Thomas and Scholasticism over Averrhoism ; the representations of the seven arts and the virtues in the sculptures of the Cathedrals are another witness to the action of philosophic ideas upon the plastic arts. We find similar influences in the miniatures and mosaics.

(iii) Scholasticism also acted upon language. According to Saintsbury and Brunetière,[2] the clearness and precision of scholastic Latin had a beneficent effect upon modern languages, which were then in process of formation and derived from it a portion of their vocabulary. The methods of distinction and division, together with the syllogism, disciplined the mind and prepared the way for modern prose. Many popular sayings arose out of scholastic theories.[3]

(iv) Scholasticism reacted upon the temperament of the races which constituted it.

209. Scholasticism and the philosophic temperament.—The constructors of the scholastic synthesis were all in the sphere of French influence, and the majority were educated or taught at Paris. Scholasticism was a product of neo-Latin and anglo-Celtic genius. It helped to a large extent to form certain ways of thinking in the French and English, Flemish and Walloon, Italian and Spanish peoples—and this chiefly by the influence of three doctrines : the love of clear ideas, individualism, and moderation.

We shall see later on that other special tendencies were developed in the Teutonic group of peoples.

210. Dante.—Dante[4] is the personification of all the tendencies which we have endeavoured to indicate. He is not only a great poet and writer admired by all—he is also an excellent representative of the civilization of his time.

[1] See De Wulf, *Philosophy and Civilization*, pp. 174-178. Cf. also : P. Sandauer, *L'élément scolastique dans l'oeuvre de Raoul de Houdenc* (Lwów, 1922, in *Trav. Semin. philol. romanae*).
[2] G. Saintsbury, *Periods of European Literature*, Vol. II : The Flourishing of Romance and the Rise of Allegory, pp. 16, 20, 21 ; F. Brunetière, *Manuel de l'Histoire de la Littérature française*, Paris 1898, pp. 24, 25.
[3] See for instance Willmann, *Gesch. d. Idealismus*, II, 330. He points out in Zingerle, *Deutsche Sprichwörter d. Mittelalters* (Wien, 1864), sayings which reflect the Scholastic ideology. e.g., " Erfahren macht Klug ; Erfahrung ist der Narren Vernunft."
[4] Born at Florence in 1265, Dante belonged to the party of the white Guelfs, and when Charles of Anjou entered his native town as ruler in 1301, he was exiled because of his political opinions. From that time he wandered everywhere, and died at Ravenna in 1321. After his exile he leaned towards the Ghibbelines but did not join the Imperial party.

The poet of the *Divina Commedia* puts in the mouth of his characters a compact mass of scholastic theories in which we can recognize the thought of Thomas Aquinas, Albert the Great, or of their predecessors, together with neo-Platonist and Arabian doctrines. He is acquainted with the controversies in the University of Paris, and in the burning questions dividing scholastics from anti-scholastics he frankly sides with the former.[1] The *De Monarchia* makes use of polysyllogisms " in the second figure," deals with the speculative and the practical intellects, reproduces the sayings of the school, and manifests a constant endeavour on the part of the author to deal with political matters in the light of philosophy.

Not only does Dante give a large place to philosophy : the latter also takes on the many varied aspects just pointed out. The unitive and universalist aspirations of the *Divina Commedia* make the masterpiece of Dante a complete explanation " of the heavens and the earth."[2] The *Banquet* begins with an invitation to all who thirst for knowledge. The *De Monarchia* looks forward to the coming of a " respublica humana " in which all political and religious life will be brought together in the closest unity. In spite of the troubles of the poet and his country, the poems of Dante breathe a serene optimism, and his ambition is to produce works which will endure " for the good of posterity."[3] The religious spirit is manifest everywhere. Everything is illumined by Christianity, for Dante wishes to save himself, and " to conduct the living from this state of misery to the state of happiness."[4]

211. Bibliography.—Kleutgen, *op. cit.*, p. 269, also *Beiträge z. d. Werken über d. Theologie u. Philos. d. Vorzeit*, by the same, Munster, 1875 ; Willmann, *op. cit.*, II, pp. 67-73 ; De Wulf, *Scholasticism Old and New*, pp. 12-17. Baur. *D. Gundissalinus*, etc. (**214**), contains in Ch. III a good history of the classification of the sciences in the Middle Ages, clear and more methodic than

[1] B. Nardi holds that the wholehearted Thomism of Dante is a legend, and that in his theories concerning prime matter, the origin of organic forms and the relations between the world and the first cause, Dante does not follow Thomism, but the Arabian philosophy, especially that of Avicenna. B. Nardi *Siger di Brabante e le fonti della filosofia di Dante* (*Riv filos. neo-scol.* 1912) The Thomism of Dante has been recently defended against this thesis by G. Busnelli, *Cosmogonia e Antropogenesi sec. D. Alighieri e le sue fonti* (Rome 1922).
[2] *Paradiso*, XXV.   [3] Beginning of the *De Monarchia*.
[4] Dicendum est breviter quod finis totius et partis est removere vivente in hac vita de statu miseriae et perducere ad statum felicitatis.—Epistola X (*Opere Latine di Dante*, ed. G. Giuliani, Firenze 1882, Vol. II, p. 46).

Mariétan¹ (p. 81). Philosophy and theology: Grabmann, Heitz, *op. cit.*, Scheeben, *Handbuch d. kathol. Dogmatik.* Schindele, *Zur Gesch. d. Unterscheidung v. Wesenheit u. Dasein in der Scholastik* (Munchen 1900), notes on the principal scholastics of the thirteenth century; Mandonnet, *Les premières disputes sur la distinction réelle entre l'essence et l'existence* (1276-1287), in *Revue Thomiste*, 1910, p. 741; Henry, *Contrib. à l'hist. de la distinction de l'essence et de l'existence dans la scolastique, ibid.* 1911, p. 445. Natural Theology: works by Grunwald, Baeumker, *op. cit.*, Daniels. Physics: Tedeschini, *Dissertatio historica de corpore simplici quoad essentiam* (in *Institut, philosophicæ* of Dalmieri, III, 321 *et seq.*), contains errors. On the history of the occult qualities: Glossner, in *Jahrb. Phil. spekul. Theol.* 1906, p. 307; Duhem, *Le mouvement absolu et le mouvement relatif* (Extr. from *Revue de philos.* 1909), studies the theories concerning the movement of the heavens and the notion of the place in the principal scholastics; A Lalande, *Histoire des sciences, La Physique du moyen age* (in *R. de Synth. histor.*, Oct., 1903), a review of the experimental sciences; J. Laminne, *Les quatre elements, le feu, l'air, l'eau, la terre,* Bruxelles, 1904; *Studies in the history and method of science,* edited by Singer, Vol. II, Oxford, 1921 (II: *Mediæval Astronomy,* by J. Dreyer); L. Thorndike, *A History of Magic and Experimental Science during the first thirteen centuries* (New York, 1923). Psychology: Gutbertlet, *Der Voluntarismus* (*Philos. Jahrb.* 1903 and 1904), an exposition of the intellectualist and voluntarist arguments; Verweyen, see p. 38. Ethics: Stockums, *Die Unveränderlichkeit d. natürl. Sittengesetzes in d. scholast. Ethik,* Freiburg in Breslau, 1911; Rousselot, *Pour l'histoire du problème de l'amour au moyen age* (*BGPM,* VI, 6; cf. *Revue néo-Scolastique,* Feb. 1909); R. Bedel, *La notion de la loi chez théol. et canonistes du XIIIe s.,* Paris, 1914); Grabmann, *Das Naturrecht d. Schol. von Gratian bis Thomas v. Aquin* (*Arch. f. Rechts. u. Wirtschaftsphil.* XVI, 1); Leiber, *Name und Begriff der Synderesis in d. mittelalt. Scholastik* (*Philos. Jahrb.* 1912, p. 372); A. Dyroff, *Ueber Name u. Begriff der Synderesis* (*ibid.,* p. 487). Social and political philosophy: works by Von Gierke and Walker, p. 35; I. de Pange, *Les théories politiques du m. age* (Paris, 1914); A. C. Krey, *The International State of the Middle Ages* (*American Hist. Review,* 1922, pp. 1-12); Brants, *Esquisse des théories economiques professées par les écrivains des XIIIe et XIVe s.* (Louvain,

1895), good ; G. O'Brien, *An Essay on Mediæval Economic Teaching* (Longmans, 1920) ; Kantorowicz, *Albertus Candinus u. das Strafrecht d. Scholastik, I. Die Praxis* (Berlin, 1908) ; Amberg, *Die Steuer in der Rechtsphilosophie des Scholastiker* (Beiheft zu Bd. II, Heft 3 *Archiv. fur Rechts. u. Wirtschafts-philos.*) ; Hans Prutz, *Die Friedensidee im Mittelalter* (Sitz. Ber. Ak. Wien, 1915) ; Vanderpol, *Le droit de guerre d'après les théologiens et les canonistes du m. âge* (Paris, 1911). Ehrle, *Grundsätzliches zur Charakteristik der neueren und neuesten Scholastik* (Friburg in Breslau, 1918) ; *Die Ehrentitel der scol. Lehrer im Mittelalter* (Sitzungsb. der Bayerischen Akad. wissensch. Philos. phil. u. hist. Klasse, 1919, IX Abh.) ; Pelster, same title, in *Theol. Quartalschrift*, 1922, p. 37-55.

Civilization: works mentioned on pp. 36-7. F. Harrison, *The Meaning of History*, Ch. V : A Survey of the Thirteenth Century, New York, 1904 ; J. Walsh, *The Thirteenth Greatest of Centuries* (New York, 1912) ; J. Bryce, *The Holy Roman Empire* (New York, 1911), a classical work ; L. Gillet, *Histoire artistique des ordres mendiants* (Paris, 1912) ; W. Ganzenmüller, *Das Naturgefuhl im Mittelalter* (Beitr. z. Gesch. d. Mitt. u. d. Renais., Vol. 18, 1914). Liturgy : *Rationale divinorum officiorum* by G. Durand. History : *Speculum Quadruplex* of Vincent de Beauvais ; *Golden Legend* of Jacobus de Voragine. Sermons : Honorius of Autun, *Speculum Ecclesiæ*. Roman Law : P. Vinogradoff, *Il diretto romano nella Europa mediævale* (Palermo, 1914).

Dante : Hauvette, *Dante, Introd. à la Divine Comédie* (Paris, 1911) ; A. Leclere, *Le Mysticisme catholique de l'âme de Dante* (Paris, 1906) ; Carboni, *La sintesi filosofica del pensiero dantesco* (Pitigliano, 1899) ; V. Berthier, *La Divina Commedia con commenti secondo la Scolastica* (Turin, 1893). Works cited by B. Nardi and Busnelli ; *Scritti vari* on Dante published by *Riv. fil. neo-Scol.*, Milan, 1921 ; various translations of the *Divina Commedia*.

Art. II—The Forerunners

212. Different groups.—The appellation "forerunners of the great systemizers, or persons of an epoch of transition" may be applied to a group of theologians and philosophers who carried on the traditions of Peter Lombard, but were at the same time influenced by the new spirit at the beginning of the thirteenth century.

The title applies in another way to certain men who came into contact with the school of Toledo, such as Dominicus Gundissalinus, who acted as a link between the Arabian world and the Latin West, and Alfredus Anglicus, who was one of the first to be influenced by the Arabian philosophy.

Finally, the title applies to a group of writers, such as Alexander Neckam and Bartholomæus Anglicus, who collected together the early materials of Arabian science.

213. Writers of Summæ and Sententiæ.—A compact group of theologians and philosophers marks the transition from the scholastic theology and philosophy of the twelfth century to the more comprehensive doctrines of Alexander of Hales, St. Bonaventure, Albert the Great, and Thomas Aquinas. They belonged to the past by their methods of work. At the same time they were influenced by the rich and abundant literature then in circulation, which they utilized together with the *Organon*, the works of Boethius and those of St. Augustine. But they used it only in a superficial manner, and contented themselves with vague citations, which seem to have been made at second-hand.[1] Their poverty helps to bring out by way of contrast the immense services rendered to the West by the popularization of Aristotle by Avicenna and still more by Albert the Great.

These early thirteenth century writers were principally theologians, and only secondarily philosophers. They have left us commentaries or *Summæ* on the books of the *Sentences*, which they explained in their capacity as " bachelors," commentaries on the Scripture, which they expounded as " masters," and in some cases works dealing with these matters in a freer form.

We may mention in the first place SIMON OF TOURNAI (about 1184-1219), a master at Paris whose work manifests the influence of Aristotle's Physics and Scotus Eriugena. He wrote a *Summa theologica* or *Sententiæ*, also an *Expositio symboli S. Athanasii*, and in his *Quæstiones de quolibet* we have one of the first specimens of a type of dissertation which arose out of teaching, and was destined to have a great success.[2]

Then there was PRÆPOSITINUS or PREVOSTINE OF CREMONA, theologian of Paris, and Chancellor of the University

---

[1] Ehrle, (*S. Domenico* etc., p. 28, 32 *et seq.*), remarks that this was the case p till about 1230. Richard Fitzacre mentions the work from which he takes is Aristotelian citations.

[2] Grabmann, *Gesch. d. Schol. Meth.*, II, p. 550 *et seq.*

from 1206 to 1209. He was the author of *Quæstiones*, and a *Summa contra hereticos catharos* which, like that of PETER OF CAPUA[1] (about 1219-1241) was largely based on Peter of Poitiers. Another contemporary summist was PHILIP OF GREVE († 1236), a Chancellor of the University, who wrote a *Summa theologica* or *Summa de bono* (unpublished). This work, the interest of which is primarily theological, also touches upon philosophical problems. The author sets out to strengthen (*firmare*) the faith by philosophic arguments, particularly the doctrines concerning the super-eminent goodness of God, the natural goodness of different creatures, and the moral and supernatural goodness of man in the state of grace. He makes abundant use of the great treatises of Aristotle, especially the *Ethics ;* he mentions Averrhoes, and seems to be acquainted with Avicenna. Thus the *Summa de bono*, written by Philip after 1228,[2] manifests the influence of the new Greek and Arabian works to a greater extent than the writings of his contemporaries. We see the influence of Arabian philosophy again in certain philosophical theories upheld by the Parisian Chancellor. In particular, he teaches that incorporeal substances and also the human soul are composed of matter and form, for we must distinguish in them between the *quod est* and the *quo est.* Alexander of Hales and the *Summa de virtutibus* borrowed largely from the *Summa de bono*, the philosophic study of which has not yet been undertaken.

About the same time, WILLIAM OF AUXERRE († 1231), another theologian of Paris, and a member of the Commission which Gregory IX charged with the purification of the works of Aristotle (p. 249), composed a commentary on the *Anticlaudianus* of Alan of Lille, and a more important work, *Summa super IV. lib. Sententiarum* (*Summa aurea*), which enjoyed a great reputation during the first half of the thirteenth century, and of which we have many summaries and compilations. In the former work he utilized the *Metaphysics* of Aristotle and the commentary by Averrhoes.

To the same group belong GODFREY OF POITIERS, a master at Paris about 1231, and ROLAND OF CREMONA. The latter was a master at Bologna (*excellens in philosophicis habebatur*). Later he became a Dominican, and carried on his scientific work at

---

[1] Grabmann, *ibid.*

[2] M. P. Minges, *Philosophie-geschichtliche Bemerkungen ü. Philipp von Grève*, (*Philos. Jahrb.* 1914. pp. 21–32), also *additamentum etc. Archiv. franc. histor.*, 1913, pp. 433–438.

Paris and Toulouse. He died at Bologna subsequent to 1244 (perhaps after 1258). He seems to have written his sole work, *Summa theologica*, only one manuscript of which is extant, at Paris. In it he frequently discusses the opinions of his compatriot and colleague at Paris, Præpositinus. The *Summa* of Roland belongs to the past ; it presents all the characteristics of the group of dialectico-theological works composed after the style of Peter Lombard and his successors. The subjects are treated according to the method of *auctoritates* and *rationes*. Roland would put all the liberal arts at the service of theology. He bases himself upon the *Organon*, but on the other hand makes abundant but vague mention of the other works of Aristotle and the Arabian treatises on philosophy and science. Thus he may be said to be on the first stage of the way leading to the full development of scholasticism.[1]

Ehrle says of the *Summa* that it displays no trace of the struggle between Augustinianism and Aristotelianism. Indeed, he considers that the current of ideas coming from Peter Lombard is continued in a group of commentators well on in the thirteenth century. An instance would be HUGH OF ST. CHER (died 1263), who taught about 1230-1244, and became a *magister* under Roland of Cremona. He followed in the path of Peter Lombard, but commented on him in a free way and in sober terms. Others are ODO RIGAUD, Archbishop of Rouen in 1248, RICHARD FITSACRE, master of theology at the Dominican College in the University of Oxford about 1240-48, and ROBERT KILWARDBY at the time when he wrote his commentaries and was engaged in teaching (1248-1261). It was only later that Kilwardby came under the influence of the ideas to which the Thomist movement gave rise.[2] Hence we see that intellectual periods cannot be divided off as by a knife, but admit considerable compenetration.

It is the second group of writers which directly concerns the history of philosophy.

214. The Toledo group.—DOMINICUS GUNDISALVI (GUNDISSALINUS), Archdeacon of Sevogia, was not only one of the most noteworthy of the Toledo school of translators (p. 73), but also a philosophical writer of considerable importance. Five works by him are extant : *De divisione philosophiæ*, *De immortalitate animæ*, *De processione mundi*, *De unitate*, and *De anima*.

---

[1] Ehrle, *San Domenico*, etc., p. 33.
[2] *ibid.*, pp. 28 and 29.

The last three were written after 1140, for they utilized the *Fons vitæ* of Avencebrol which Gundisalvi helped to translate.

Gundisalvi was an eclectic compiler, open to all influences. Aristotelian in metaphysics and psychology, he did not go to the original sources, but had recourse to Arabian commentaries and texts. Hence his Aristotelianism was tinctured by neo-Platonist doctrines of Arabian origin. But these doctrines had lost their monistic signification : Gundisalvi was an individualist, as were his favourite authors Boethius and St. Augustine.

The most important philosophic ideas of Gundisalvi are concerned with the classification of the sciences, metaphysics, and psychology.

The *De Divisione philosophiæ*, written about 1150, is a didactic work freely compiled from the *De scientiis* of Alfarabi (utilized in its entirety), numerous writings by Ammonius, Isaac Israeli, Avicenna, Boethius, Isidore of Seville, and Bede. After emphasizing the distinction between theology, " divina scientia " (*Deo auctore, hominibus tradita*) and philosophy, " humana scientia " (*quæ humanis rationibus adinventa esse probatur*), the author lays down this principle, which is so dear to all scholastics after him : *nulla est scientia quæ philosophiæ non sit aliqua pars.* He collects together six definitions of philosophy, and accepts them all ;[1] then he outlines the following general scheme, a triumph of the peripatetic spirit :

(i) The philosophical sciences properly so called (*scientiæ sapientiæ*) comprise a theoretical and a practical group. The former includes (*a*) Physics (*scientia naturalis, de his quæ non sunt separata a suis materiis*) and its subdivisions : *medicina, indicia, nigromantia, ymagines, agricultura, navigatio, specula, alquemia ;* (*b*) Mathematics (*de his quæ sunt separata a materia in intellectu non in esse*) and its subdivisions : *arithmetica, geometrica* (including optics), *musica, astrologia, scientia de aspectibus, de ponderibus, de ingeniis ;* (*c*) Metaphysics (*scientia divina, de his quæ sunt separata a materia in esse et in intellectu*). Practical philosophy in its turn comprises politics, economics, and ethics.[2]

[1] " Assimilatio hominis operibus creatoris secundum virtutem humanitatis —tedium et cura et studium et sollicitudo mortis—rerum humanarum divinarumque cognitio cum studio bene vivendi conjuncta—ars artium et disciplina disciplinarum—integra cognitio hominis de seipso—amor sapientiae." We quote them from Baur's edition.

[2] A. Levi, *La partizione della filosofia practica in un trattato medievale,* (Atti d. r. Istituto Veneto di scienze, 1908, t. LXVII, parte 2). The author

(ii) Logic, in conformity with the Arabian conception, is an *instrumentum* preliminary to philosophy, since all acquisition of knowledge pre-supposes it ; but from another point of view it is a *pars philosophiæ*. In its turn, it ought to be preceded by the next group.

(iii) Two groups of propedeutic sciences : (*a*) *scientia litteralis* or grammar; (*b*) the *scientiæ civiles*, i.e., poetics (including history), and rhetoric.

Having established this general classification, the Archdeacon of Toledo treats each science in detail. His work constitutes a decisive step forward in the history of scientific classifications. Hesitations and tentative essays disappear (cf. **103**). His influence is manifest in the similar works of the thirteenth century. The contemporary treatise by Michael Scot, *Divisio philosophiæ*, is simply a compilation from the work of Gundisalvi ;[3] Albert the Great was influenced by it ;[4] and Robert Kilwardby, who made further progress in the classification of the sciences, derived a great number of his ideas from Gundisalvi and acknowledged this.

In metaphysics, Gundisalvi is an Aristotelian, but at the same time appeals to Avicenna and Alfarabi. The *scientia prima* has as its object being and the *consequentia entis* (substance and accident, universal and particular, cause and effect, act and potency). At the same time the *De unitate* adopts the theory of emanation and the metaphysical hierarchy of beings. God is unity, *creatrix unitas*, whence is derived the *creata unitas*. The derivation of the creature is not an emanation in the sense of Avencebrol, but a general participation, the nature of which is not explained. There are three stages in the appearance and hierarchical development of unity in creation : the intelligence, the soul, and the world. Moreover, all beings other than the First One are compounded of matter and form, two opposed principles maintained in compenetration by unity, a cohesive force. The influence of the *Fons vitæ* is evident here.

The *De immortalitate animæ* is a short treatise on rational psychology, the plan of which is due to Gundisalvi, and which constitutes a curious mixture of Aristotelian and neo-Platonist (Arabian) ideas. He holds the theory of abstraction (which he

udies this classification of practical philosophy in Gundisalvi, and gives s history.

[3] Fragments of this are reproduced in the *Speculum doctrinale* of Vincent f Beauvais : edited by Baur in an appendix.

[4] Baur, *Dominicus Gundissalinus, de divis. philos.*, pp. 365, 375.

describes after the manner of Avicenna), the complete distinction between sense perception and intellectual knowledge, and the individuality of the things of nature to which our universal concepts apply. Gundisalvi demonstrates the immortality of the soul by the famous Aristotelian argument based upon the characteristics of thought. But at the same time he has recourse to the Arabian and neo-Platonist theory of ecstasy (*raptus*) : when the body is enfeebled, and its resistance to the impulses of the soul is lessened, the latter succeeds in freeing itself entirely, and takes flight by ecstasy towards the intelligible world. From this the philosopher concludes (with Plato, against Aristotle), that death, by breaking the corporeal bonds of the soul, secures for it the plenitude of its perfection. This proof of the immortality of the soul was exceedingly popular in the thirteenth century.[1] Man is a microcosmos. The soul is represented sometimes as the vital principle of the body (Aristotle), sometimes as its associate (Plato). It is created from spiritual matter by the angels, at the command of God. We may add that Gundisalvi's close contact with Arabian science explains his predilection for psycho-physiological theories.

The influence of Gundisalvi's psychology may be recognized in Helinand of Frémont, John de la Rochelle, and to a less degree in Albert the Great and St. Bonaventure. It is most apparent, however, in William of Auvergne, who plagiarized the *De immortalitate animæ*.

215. Alfredus Anglicus was also a translator of Arabian texts and a philosophic writer. Like Gundisalvi, he endeavoured to profit by some of the new doctrines of which he had learnt in Spain. His *De motu cordis*, dedicated to Alexander Neckam († 1217), and which Baeumker dates about 1210, betrays a very extensive acquaintance with the new materials which were later on to form part of more complete systemizations. We find therein a singular mixture of Platonism in the form it took at Chartres, Aristotelianism inspired directly by the *De Anima*, and neo-Platonism, derived from the *Liber de Causis*, the whole being combined with medical theories from Galen and the physicians of Salerno and Montpellier.

Baeumker, to whom we owe a recent edition of the *De motu cordis*, has corrected the erroneous judgments of Barach, who thought he saw in this work an affirmation of pantheism, and

[1] Bülow, p. 115 *et seq.* (No. 220).

has likewise shown that there can be no question of materialism either in this connection.[1]

From God, the supreme principle of all things, there flows forth (*effluens*) and emanates a series of beings which are arranged according to the descending scale of neo-Platonism : the intelligence (*intelligentia*), the intellect (*intellectus*), the universal reason (*ratio*) or the sum-total of relations of imitation which exist between God and limited essences ; the universal imagination which distributes these essences in genera and species ; and finally the sensible reality in which they are manifested and subjected to the process of change.[2] To these various stages there correspond beings distinct from God, not necessary but free productions of his creative work (*creator omnium Deus arbitrii sua potestate*), objectively related to a *norma* which is the Divine essence (*hæc [norma] in ipso ab ipso non discrepat*). In all this Alfred is faithful to the scholastic tradition. The theory of emanation (*effluens*) which later on became an essential feature in the Latin neo-Platonists, had for Alfred only the value of an explanatory image.

The human soul is one of these spirits which have " emanated " from God. It is an incorporeal substance, capable of higher kinds of knowledge and of illuminations which ultimately come from God.[3] But inasmuch as it is united to a body, it also possesses a sensible and imaginative knowledge of the particular, which the author calls *ratio particularis*, and which in the case of the majority of mankind, does not lead to more than probable knowledge. It is important to note that to explain the union of the soul with the body, Alfred adopts the Aristotelian definition : *perfectio est corporis physici organici*.[4] This definition made from the outset a great impression on the philosophers of the middle of the century, but it is clear that Alfred did not realize all that it involved, since he had recourse to the hypothesis of a *spiritus vitæ* or fiery breath infused from the first moment of conception,[5] which serves as a link (*medium*) between soul and body.[6] The heart is the place in which the vital spirit and the soul come together.[7] The soul presides over all organic functions,

---

[1] *Die Stellung*, etc., pp. 55–64.
[2] See the characteristic text of Cap. XV reproduced by Baeumker.
[3] In se enim considerata substantia est incorporea, intellectiva, illuminationum quae a primo sunt ultima relatione perceptiva. Ed. Baeumker, p. 2.
[4] p. 3.   [5] Cap. XII.   [6] Cap. XVI.
[7] Cor domicilium est vitae, p. 12 : cor igitur animae domicilium est, p. 33.

which Alfred describes after the manner of a naturalist and a physician.

Pelzer has shown that Alfred was also the author of commentaries on the four books of the *Meteors*, and on the pseudo-Aristotelian work *De vegetabilibus*—a commentary which was utilized by Roger Bacon.[1]

216. The new neo-Platonist influences.—Gundisalvi and Alfred of Sereshel were both attracted by the neo-Platonism underlying Oriental philosophy, and they gave a ready welcome to the doctrines of the *Liber de Causis*.

The neo-Platonist current of thought issuing from Arabian philosophy was thus present in the early years of the thirteenth century, and lasted till its end. It strengthened the neo-Platonist tendency which had already penetrated into the West through St. Augustine, Boethius, Macrobius and Chalcidius, and it is important to note that in each case it was purged of all pantheistic tendencies. It underwent a similar purification in pseudo-Dionysius. All this helped to counteract the monistic influence of the *Liber de Causis*, and to keep in the path of pluralism and spiritualism the early Latin philosophers who were attracted by the originality of the Arabian work in question.

As a matter of fact, Gundisalvi and Alfred of Sereshel did not succeed in harmonising the elements borrowed from neo-Platonism with their Aristotelianism, and they had to be satisfied with incoherent and sterile compromises. It was reserved for the later scholastics, principally St. Bonaventure, Thomas Aquinas, and Duns Scotus, to assimilate thoroughly the ideas of the *Liber de Causis* and pseudo-Dionysius as well as the Aristotelian and Augustinian theories and to build them up into more perfect syntheses.

Neo-Platonist ideas were also prominent in another but less important group of philosophers, some of whom were attracted towards Monism in spite of themselves.

217. The early influences of Arabian science.—The astronomy, alchemy, physiology and medicine of the Arabs made an impression no less deep than their philosophy, and Arabian science was the starting-point of scientific investigations which were likewise continued throughout the thirteenth century.

ALEXANDER NECKAM was a master at Paris about 1180, and

---

[1] A. Pelzer, *Une source inconnue de R. Bacon, Alfred de Sareshel, commentateur des Météorol. d'Aristote* (*Arch. franc. hist.* 1919, pp. 44–67.)

afterwards became Abbot of Cirencester († 1217). He wrote a treatise *De natura rerum* and a poem *De laudibus divinæ sapientiæ*.[1] He was acquainted with Aristotle's *De Cœlo*, and the writings of Algazel and Israeli. Roger Bacon referred to him, but added that he was not an authority on the point in question.[2] His compatriot and friend Alfred of Sereshel was also a man of science, and the same is true of Michael Scot, author of treatises on alchemy and astronomy, and Bartholomæus Anglicus.

218. Bartholomæus Anglicus[3] was a Franciscan who flourished successively at Oxford, Paris (about 1220), and Magdeburg (after 1230). About 1240 he wrote a work well known in the thirteenth century, entitled *De proprietatibus rerum*. This is not only an encyclopædia of knowledge containing the most varied information, and a repertoire of new experimental, geographical, and ethnological material collected together by a careful observer and manifesting the scientific spirit then in process of formation at Oxford—it is also brimful of philosophical ideas, particularly in psychology and metaphysics. The general plan of the work is based on a philosophic scheme, for he refers the *proprietates rerum* to the substances of which they are the manifestation, and studies in turn God, angels, man, corporeal nature, and the *accidentia corporum*. The author adopts the seven definitions of the soul,[4] and devotes himself especially to anatomical and physiological data. His metaphysics studies matter and form, movement and time. He regards matter as a chaos of the four elements,[5] and by " element " he means the simple and indivisible particle of water, earth, air or fire. The form or determining principle, is looked upon as the sum of properties (p. 55). This applies to the soul, which accordingly is a substance complete in itself, independently of its union with the body. The form is the source of all determination. The author cannot make up his mind whether or not spiritual substances are composed of matter and form.

There is no question of a synthesis here. Bartholomew is a

[1] For some reason Haureau calls him an unusually frank realist. *Hist. phil. scol.* II, 64.

[2] " Inter auctores . . . non potest . . . numerari." *Comp. studii philos.*, c. 7., ed. Brewer, p. 457.

[3] T. Plasmann, *B. Anglicus* (*Arch. franc. hist.* 1919), p. 83, identifies him with Bartholomew of Glanville.

[4] Felder, *op. cit.* p. 252.

[5] In qua velut in quadam massa erant potentialiter quattuor elementa non distincta. Schneider, *Metaph. Begriffe d. B. A.*, p. 149.

collector, and thoroughly receptive, " but does not take into account the opposition between Aristotelian and Platonist or Augustinian elements."[1] Bartholomew is dependent upon Alexander Neckam ; he mentions Alexander of Hales, Albert the Great and other contemporaries. The work of the *Magister de Proprietatibus* was translated into French, English and Spanish. Berthold of Regensburg was influenced by it.[2]

219. Bibliography.—Ehrle, *San Domenico*, etc. R. Martin, *Quelques premiers maîtres dominicains de Paris et d'Oxford et la soi-disant école dominicaine augustinienne* (*R. Sc. phil. theol.*, 1920, pp. 556-580) ; Grabmann, *op. cit.* On Philip of Greve see Minges, *op. cit.* An early printed edition of the *S. Aurea* of William of Auxerre appeared in 1500 at Paris. Another at Paris, by Regnault, later and not so good (Minges, *Philos. Jahrb.*, 1914, p. 435). J. Strake, *Die Schol. Methode in d. Summa Aurea d. W. v. Auxerre* (Theol. u. Glaube, 1913, p. 549-557). Correns, *Die dem Boethius fälschlich zugeschriebene Abhandlung d. D. Gundisalvi de unitate* (*BGPM*, I, 1), text and short study ; Dr. G. Bulow, *Des D. Gundissalinus Schrift v. d. Unsterblichkeit d. Seele*, etc. (*ibid.*, II, 3), contains the *De Immortalitate Animæ* of William of Auvergne ; Endres, *Die Nachwirkung von Gundissalinus de immort. animæ* (*Philos. Jahrb.* XII, 4, 1899) ; Lowenthal, *pseudo-Aristotelisches über d. Seele* (Berlin, 1891), gives the *De Anima* ; Menendez y Pelayo, *Historia d. l. Heterod. espanoles*, I, 691-711, publishes the *De Processione Mundi ;* Baur, *D. Gundissalinus, de divisione philosophiæ, BGPM*, IV, 2 and 3, text and long study of doctrinal sources; Baeumker, *Les écrits philos. de D. Gundissalinus* (*R. Thomiste*, 1898, p. 727), short general study ; A. Levi, *op. cit.*, p. 357.

Critical and complete edition of the *De Motu Cordis* of Alfred of Sereshel by Baeumker, *BGPM*, XXIII, 1-2, replaces the defective edition by Barach (*Excerpta e libro A. Anglicus de motu cordis*, Innsbruck, 1878) ; Baeumker, *Die Stellung des Alfred von Sereshel (Alfredus Anglicus) und seine Schrift de motu cordis in der Wissenschaft des beginnenden XIII. Jahrh.* (Sitzungsberichte Bayerischen Akad. Wissensch. 1913, Munchen) ; A. Pelzer, *op. cit.* Alexander Neckam is published in *Rerum Britannic. medii ævi script.* A. Schneider, *Metaphys.*

---

[1] Schneider, *op. cit.*, p. 143.
[2] Ueberweg-Baumgartner, *op. cit.*, p. 430.

Begriffe d. B. Anglicus (Baeumker, Festg. 1913, pp. 139-181, and Th. Plasmann, *B. Anglicus* (Arch. franc. hist. 1919, pp. 68-109), biographical researches.

Art. III—The Older Scholasticism in the Thirteenth Century (Pre-Thomist Scholasticism)

§ 1—*Augustinism, or the Older Scholasticism.*

220. Augustine and the doctrinal system of Augustinism.— Since the publication of a study by Ehrle in 1889,[1] the term "Augustinism" has been applied to a certain tendency in scholastic philosophy which developed during the first half of the thirteenth century and later on came into conflict with the Thomist school of thought.

Taking as our basis a well-known text of John Peckham, contained in a letter to the Bishop of Lincoln (1285), opposing the Thomistic innovations in the name of traditional teaching, we may enumerate the following as the chief doctrinal characteristics of the Augustinian group : a certain pre-eminence of the good over the true, and a corresponding primacy of the will over intelligence in God and man ; the production of knowledge without the causal concourse of the external object ; the necessity of an immediate illuminative action on the part of God for the accomplishing of certain intellectual acts ; a constant tendency to identify being and light, and accordingly to call God the Uncreated Light ; a tendency to discover a luminous nature in spirits and created bodies ; the ascription of a low but still a positive degree of actuality to prime matter independently of any substantial information ; the presence in matter of active principles or " seminal reasons " ; the existence of matter and form in spiritual substances ; the multiplicity of forms in natural beings, especially in man ; the identification of the soul with its faculties ; and the impossibility of the creation of the world *ab æterno*. To these may be added a more or less pronounced tendency to accentuate the apologetic function of philosophy.

Should this group of doctrines be called "Augustinism" ? To reply to this question, we must determine in what measure

[1] Ehrle, *Der Augustinismus u. Aristotelismus in d. Scholastik gegen Ende d. XIII. Jahrh. (Arch. Litt. u. Kirchengesch. d. Mitt.* 1889, pp. 603–635). Cf. Mandonnet, *Siger*, Vol. II, pp. 43 *et seq.*

they are in harmony with the authentic teaching of St. Augustine. Now, these doctrines were not all taught by him. In the above enumeration, we can distinguish between different groups of theories :

(i) *Doctrines the Augustinian origin of which is not in doubt :* the identity of the soul with its faculties, the relations between willing and knowing, the substantial independence of the soul and body, the absence of causal activity on the part of the object in the act of representing an object, the theory of the " seminal reasons," the creation of the world in time, and the identity of being and light (60).

(ii) *Theories opposed to the real thought of St. Augustine,* for instance the doctrine that a special illumination is indispensable for the acquisition of certain truths. St. Augustine was not acquainted with this strange notion, and none of the texts concerning the foundations of knowledge is capable of such an interpretation. This theory is a consequence of the Arabian theory of the separated acting intellect.

(iii) *Theories foreign to Augustine, and of Jewish or Arabian origin,* such as the plurality of forms in one and the same being, and this other doctrine, inspired by Avencebrol, that spiritual substances are composed of matter and form.[1]

(iv) As for the tendency to attribute to philosophy only an auxiliary and apologetic function, this is undoubtedly Augustinian in spirit, but it comes directly from a group of theologians of the twelfth century, arising from a more or less pronounced mistrust for the philosophy of Aristotle, which certain people were inclined to consider responsible for the errors current in the schools.[2] These apprehensions are manifest in many documents of the University of Paris,[3] in treatises and letters of regulars and seculars (John of St. Giles, Eudes of Chateauroux, James of Vitry, William of St. Amour), in sermons, and in various Dominican and Franciscan constitutions.

It follows from this that if we call the doctrinal system

---

[1] Augustine speaks of a *quasi materia* in the angels, but this is not used in the sense of a spiritual matter.

[2] Mandonnet, *op. cit.*, VI, 156. St. Bonaventure attributes to Aristotle a " triplex error, scilicet occultatio exemplaritatis, divinae providentiae, dispositionis mundanæ ; " and a " triplex caecitas, de æternitate mundi, de unitate intellectus, et quod post hanc vitam non est felicitas nec poena." (*In Hexaemeron, collatio* VI, *Opera*, V. 360, Quarracchi). But it must not be forgotten that Bonaventure nevertheless borrowed from Aristotle numerous important theories, for example that of act and potency. See later on.

[3] See for instance the letter of Gregory IX. in 1228 (*Chart.*, I, 115).

characterizing the pre-Thomist scholasticism of the thirteenth century "Augustinism," we can only do so with certain definite reservations.

To these considerations, resulting from an examination of the doctrines in question, may be added others based upon historical circumstances. St. Augustine did not become the patron of a philosophical and theological party until later on, in point of fact after the appearance of Thomism. Then indeed his name was put forward, and the doctrinal system outlined above ascribed to his immediate authority, in order to counter-act the new philosophy.[1] Peckham wrote in 1284-6 ; he appealed to St. Augustine for controversial reasons, and his letters interpret vague or even categorical texts of the Bishop of Hippo in the sense of his own personal views. Ehrle admits that in the early writers of *Summæ* up to and including Robert Kilwardby, there is very little if any trace of a combat between Augustinism and Aristotelianism,[2] and Père Martin says the same of the Dominican theologians up to Peter of Tarentaise.[3] The designation "Augustinism," then, had mainly a polemical signification, and applies only from about 1270.

But if this is the case, it ill suits the group of doctrines already described which characterized an interesting group of scholastics prior to these discussions, namely, William of Auvergne, Alexander of Hales, and St. Bonaventure, to mention no others.

There are yet other points to consider in this distinction between the "Augustinian" scholastics and the later or Aris-totelian ones. These two groups cannot be contrasted with each other as if they respectively held Augustinian and Aris-totelian ideas exclusively.[4] Certain Augustinian doctrines, exemplarism for instance, form part of the common heritage of all scholastics, and enter into the systems of Thomas Aquinas the Aristotelian, and St. Bonaventure the Augustinian. On the other hand, the foundation upon which these so-called Augustinian ideas were superposed remained a peripatetic one (instances would be the doctrines of act and potency, matter and form). Again, Duns Scotus later on adopted

[1] It was because the pseudo-Augustinian work *De spiritu et anima* was invoked by his adversaries, that Thomas Aquinas mentioned it so frequently. This is pointed out by G. Théry (*op. cit.*, p. 374). See p. 185n.

[2] Ehrle, *San Domenico* etc., pp. 29 and 42.

[3] Martin, *Les premiers maîtres dominicains*, etc., p. 579.

[4] A similar opinion is held by Grabmann, *Die philos. u. theolog. Erken-ntnislehre des Kard. Mathaeus ab Aquasparta* etc., p. 19 (Wien, 1906) and by P. de Groot, *Het leven van den hl. Thomas* (Amsterdam, 1907), p. 313.

several of these ideas but no one would on this account number him among the Augustinians of the thirteenth century, nor question his peripateticism.

For all these reasons, we prefer in place of the designation "Augustinism" a more general term : " the older scholasticism of the thirteenth century, or pre-Thomist scholasticism."

221. The older scholasticism and the common synthesis.—In general we may say that the typical doctrines of the first great philosophers of the thirteenth century were additions, superposed with varying degrees of coherence and harmony, upon the great group of ideas which we have called the common synthesis. Theories like that of the excellence of the will, the special illumination, and the purely active nature of sensation, did not prevent those holding them from stressing the dependence of the will upon knowledge, and making abstraction the keystone of ideological spiritualism. Those who declared the soul to be independent of the body explained their union nevertheless by the theory of matter and form. The theories concerning light were additions which do not modify any organic thesis, and the group of doctrines concerning the plurality of forms and the actuality of matter was a development—possibly a parasitical one, but still a development—of hylomorphism. The edifice into which these various theories were built up was scholastic in style, and we easily recognize the important part played in it by the theories of act and potency, the distinction between sensation and thought, the Infinity of God, etc.

It is true that the heterogeneity of the influences giving rise to the doctrines peculiar to the older scholasticism had an adverse effect upon the coherence of the whole. But we shall see that this incoherence gradually disappeared. Alexander of Hales and above all St. Bonaventure succeeded in incorporating into a characteristic synthesis *sui generis*, doctrines simply juxtaposed in a William of Auvergne.

Moreover, the doctrinal basis of the earlier scholasticism was a somewhat variable quantity. Each doctor chose the doctrines which suited him and did not necessarily adopt all, and even the same doctrine was given varying shades of meaning. Hence it is impossible to draw up a uniform catalogue of ideas applicable to all. Thus Alexander of Hales rejected the identity of the soul and its faculties ; St. Bonaventure adopted it only with reservations ; while others considered this theory a fundamental one. Similarly, the theory of a special illumination was given the most varied interpretations, and was not held by all.

The historic succession of the representatives of pre-Thomist scholasticism displayed progressive steps towards co-ordination. The following is the classification which in the actual state of knowledge seems to us to correspond best with the results acquired : William of Auvergne and his contemporaries (§ 2), Robert Grosseteste and the Franciscan School of Oxford (§ 4), the anonymous author of the *Summa Philosophiæ* (§ 5), St. Bonaventure, the typical representative of the group (§ 6), his immediate disciples (§ 7), Peter Olivi, who occupies a place apart (§ 8), and a group of Franciscans and Dominicans who were not influenced by Thomas Aquinas (§ 9). From another point of view, we could distinguish two groups : that of Oxford, where mathematics and the experimental sciences were increasingly cultivated, and where philosophy was studied in the light of these sciences ; and the group of Paris, the masters of which paid more attention to pure speculation. For the Oxford teachers, as for those of Paris, questions of psychology and metaphysics were in the forefront of philosophy.

§ 2—*William of Auvergne and his Contemporaries.*

222. William of Auvergne was born at Aurillac. He studied arts and theology at Paris, and afterwards became one of the most prominent professors in the young University. From 1228 till his death in 1249 he held the episcopal see of Paris (hence he is known as William of Paris). He was contemporary with the beginnings of the Dominican and Franciscan schools, and must have known Albert the Great and Alexander of Hales.

His chief work is the *Magisterium divinale*, which comprises the following treatises : *De primo principio, De universo creaturarum ; De anima ; Cur Deus homo ; De fide et legibus ; De sacramentis ; De virtutibus et moribus.* We have in addition twenty other works by him, among them being the *De immortalitate animæ*, copied from D. Gundissalinus and written before 1228.[1] The *Magisterium* was composed between 1223 and 1240, and in particular the *De universo* dates from 1231 to 1236.[2]

[1] J. Kramp, in *Gregorianum*, 1921, p. 186.
[2] p. 78.

223.   Position in Philosophy.—Although in many places William states that his intentions are apologetical, and that he wishes to convert unbelievers to the faith and convince the Albigenses and Cathari of their errors, it is certain that he devotes a great deal of attention to pure philosophy. The *De universo* is a treatise on metaphysics ; the *De anima* a complete manual of psychology ; the *De immortalitate animæ* is similarly a purely philosophical work.

William of Auvergne was in point of fact the first great philosopher of the thirteenth century.[1] In the first place he knew and made use of the new works of Aristotle, and these had a powerful influence upon his mind. He laid under contribution the works of the Arabians, Alfarabi, Averrhoes, and above all Avencebrol, whom he thought to be a Christian, and held in high esteem (*unicus omnium philosophantium nobilissimus*). He was the first to endeavour to make a selection from this mass of doctrines, and he was aware of the difficulty of his task.[2] Moreover, he succeeded in building up these doctrines into a whole which aimed at being coherent, manifesting a great independence of mind and a well-informed eclecticism.[3] The metaphysics of Aristotle provided the keystone for his conception of the world. Hence his "Augustinism" is a modified and very weak form. Indeed, in more than one important question he is anti-Augustinian, and Thomist by anticipation.

Again, the title of "the first great scholastic" belongs to William of Auvergne because he revealed the true character of the most dangerous of the theories which the Latin anti-scholastics derived from the Arabians : in particular, the unity of the active intellect (Averrhoes) and the fatalistic emanation of the real from the Divinity. He was a clear thinker and a vigorous writer, and introduced logical discipline into his thoughts, although he was often obliged to interrupt the train of ideas in a work not intended for public teaching.

We may add that his writings abound in observations on the customs of the people, clergy, and the university, and furnish those who read him attentively with valuable data on the civilization of the beginning of the thirteenth century.[4]

---

[1] Kramp, *Gregorianum*, 1920, p. 538.
[2] Of emanation he writes : "pene nihil ab eis qui nos præcesserunt . . . devenit." *ibid.*, p. 44.
[3] This opinion is held also by Baumgartner, Bülow and Schindele, *op. cit.*
[4] p. 73 and p. 576. He describes as "rotten fishes" his University colleagues "qui in studio seu scholis scilicet theologiae senescunt et semper infulsi et insipidi remanent." Those who accumulate benefices are spiritual monsters,

224. Metaphysics.—God occupies a central place in the *De universo*. In order to prove His existence, William makes use of St. Augustine, the scholasticism of the early Middle Ages, and the Arabians. The peripatetic argument on the first mover is not mentioned, although William regards God as the one efficient cause of the world.[5] On the other hand, in an argument which reminds us of St. Anselm,[6] he reasons from the being existing by participation (*ens per participationem*) to the being existing of itself (*ens per assentiam*) ; and this he does, not by applying the principle of causality, but in virtue of the parallelism of the two concepts.

The Infinity of God is based upon the perfection of *esse*. God is pure existence. In all other beings, *esse* is limited and distinct from the essence.[7] This theory of the real distinction, which here appears for the first time, is taken from Avicenna.[8] It gives great coherence to the system, although the philosopher was not able, as Thomas Aquinas was later on, to establish its connection with the couple of act and potency. Compared to the *esse* of God, the existence of the creature is but an imitation, as false silver or an ape is real silver or a man only in appearance.[9]

Creatures are distinct from God. They pre-exist in the eternal truth (Augustine, Anselm), the light of which sustains the truth of contingent essences.[10] God knows all things in Himself (*non potuit intelligere in se nisi se*).[11]

In opposition to the compact group of Arabian philosophers who appealed to Aristotle, William defends the Augustinian thesis of the creation of the world in time. He rejects the neo-Platonist thesis of creation by intermediaries : *nullo enim modorum aliunde adjutus, per seipsum solum creavit universum.*[12]

"qui decanus est in una Ecclesia, praepositus in alia, cantor in' tertia, archi diaconus in quarta, quid est nisi monstrum spiritale in corpore universalis Ecclesiae ? " *De vitiis*, cap. 9, Vol. I, p. 284, G. 1 and G. 2.

[5] *De universo*, Paris Edn. 1674, I, 1. 26, p. 622.

[6] Schindele, *Beitr. z. Metaph. d. Wilhelm v. Auvergne* (Munich, 1900), pp. 45–56. Cf. Baeumker, *Witelo*, pp. 313–315 ; Grunwald, *op. cit.*, p. 92.

[7] "In omni igitur est aliud ipsum ens, aliud ejus esse seu entitas." II, 2, cap. 8, p. 852, a fine passage.

[8] Schindele, *op. cit.*, p. 23.

[9] Quoniam . . . esse quod prædicatur per hoc verbum esse, hoc est, esse quo unumquodque est, hoc inquam esse, de unoquoque aliorum dicitur accidentaliter, sive secundum participationem. De solo autem creatore dicitur essentialiter. Ab omni quippe alio est separabile actu, vel ratione vel intellectu. A creatore vero nullo modorum separabile est. *De universo*, I, 3, cap. 26, p. 794.

[10] Influentia a luminositate primæ veritatis descendens super omnia vera. *ibid.*, cap. 25, p. 794, col. 1.

[11] I, 1, cap. 24, Cf. II, 1. cap. 43. [12] I, 2, cap. 8, p. 692.

Accordingly Providence extends to all creatures.[1]   He will
have nothing to do with the theory of emanation which represents the coming forth of the contingent from the supreme
Being as the flowing of waters from a spring, for this would
make the world a part of God.[2]   That would destroy God's
Infinity.   Hence, when he says elsewhere that the *esse* of God
envelops all things, he is speaking only of efficient causality,[3]
which gives existence and conserves it.   The Bishop of Paris
is then a decided upholder of pluralism, and he criticizes those
who liken the unity of the world to the unity of the waters of
the Euphrates or the Nile.[4]

The *De universo* deals at length with the intelligences, and
its author was the first among the scholastics of the thirteenth
century to consider them as pure forms.   In view of the fact
that they have no spatial extension, there is no reason for
attributing to them prime matter ; they are *abstractissimæ a
materia ;* intellectual lights (*lux*) destined to contemplate
not some other creature immediately above them (neo-
Platonism) but the Creator Himself.[5]

On the other hand, corporeal substance, involving as it does
extension in space, is composed of prime matter and form.[6]
Furthermore, it has as many substantial forms as there are
distinct perfections.[7]

225. Psychology.—Man is composed of body and soul, and
the latter is defined with Aristotle as the substantial form of
the body.   But this does not prevent William from comparing
their union to that of a harpist and his instrument (Augustine).
He is an Augustinian in refusing to distinguish between the
soul and its faculties,[8] and a Peripatetic in denying the existence
of a plurality of souls in man, and affirming the impossibility
of a composition of matter and form in the spiritual soul.

---

[1] I, 3, cap. 2.
[2] I, 1, cap. 17, p. 612, a fine passage.   " Fuerunt qui dicerent cætera creata
omnia exire a creatore per modum emanationis ex fonte . . . Error . . . quoniam
id quod emanat ex fonte . . . erat in fonte pars ejus."
[3] The most striking passage is on p. 920.   " Amplitudine spirituali . . .
totum universum intra se continet."   There is nothing pantheistic in this
doctrine.   At the most there are some rather strong expressions which must
be interpreted in the light of other texts.
[4] I, 1, cap. II, p. 605.
[5] He generalizes for all intelligences, and hence for man : " intellectum
igitur idest virtutem intellectivam necesse est creatum esse propter intellectum solius creatoris," II, 1, c. 8.
[6] " Et hoc propter operationes suas corporales quas exercere non potest
nisi per dispositiones materiales . . . quae sunt quantitas . . ." II, 2, cap. 2
[7] *ibid.*
[8] *De anima*, cap. 3, 6.

The *De anima* deals at length with the problem of knowledge. William distinguishes three objects of knowledge : the external world, the soul, and the first principles of demonstration.[1]

(*a*) *The external world.* Two sources of knowledge which are essentially distinct, namely, the senses and intelligence, give us information on the external world. The senses receive a sensible form (Aristotle), which William like the Arabians reduces to a physical impression. As to the intelligible form, the possible intellect produces this within itself on the occasion of the sensible representations (Augustine). Hence there is no need for an active intellect : the intelligible form can be produced without it. Accordingly William excludes from his psychology this superfluous element.[2] In order to justify this mutilation of the Aristotelian ideology, we have a first group of arguments based upon the simplicity of the soul (Augustine) which is incompatible with this division of the intellectual faculty. Other arguments establish the unsatisfactory nature of the theories put forth by contemporaries concerning the active intellect. These criticisms by the Parisian philosopher show that he had a clear perception of the difficulties and problems of the theory of ideas. Among these theories of the active intellect which he declared to be insufficient, the first was the theory of the separated intellect (which he thought to be the authentic theory of Aristotle). William thus begins the line of scholastics rejecting Arabian monopsychism. He also refuses to allow with some contemporaries the theory of the " spiritualized phantasma," i.e., the sensible species transformed into an intelligible species under the purifying influence of the active intellect. It would be interesting to know more of these philosophers, who must have examined the complete text of the *De anima*, and who by adopting a false idea of the *species intentionales* (p. 293) were immediately led astray, as were certain Greek commentators on Aristotle. Their error was a common one in the thirteenth century.

By means of the intelligible forms, the intellect knows in the first place individual substances (contrary to Aristotle) ; and afterwards abstract and universal reality. Finally, by means of a third mode of knowledge (*modus per connexionem sive per colligationem*), to explain which William has appeals either to an infused *habitus* communicated by God (cf. *c*), or else one acquired

---

[1] Cf. Baumgartner, *Die Erkenntnisslehre des Wilhelm von Auvergne.*

[2] " Figmentum igitur est et vanissima positio intellectus agentis." *De Anima*, VII, 3.

by personal exercise, we judge, reason and freely recall to the sphere of consciousness our past knowledge.

(*b*) *The soul*. William stresses the value of the immediate evidence of the fact of consciousness (Augustine). Consciousness reveals directly, not only the existence of the soul, but also its essential properties, its immateriality, simplicity, and indivisibility. Nay more, consciousness discovers one category of rational knowledge, namely, the first principles.

(*c*) *The first principles of demonstration*, such as the principle of contradiction, have a value independently of the existence of the contingent world. William wrongly infers from this, against the real mind of Aristotle, that the consideration of the world cannot give rise to them. Whence do they come ? The intellect sees them directly in God, thanks to a special illumination.[1] The Bishop of Paris interprets in a Christian sense the Arabian theory of the illumination of the intelligence by a separated acting intellect, and at the same time considers he remains true to the exemplarism of St. Augustine. The Divine illumination in the state of ecstasy, the prophetic vision, and pathological hallucination directly recall certain neo-Platonist Ideas in the *De immortalitate animæ*, while the place assigned to the soul at the boundary of the two worlds suggests the Alexandrian theory of the descending emanation of things.

The clear distinction between essence and existence, the pluralistic interpretation of the neo-Platonist formula that God is the *esse* of all things, the absence of prime matter in spiritual beings, the plurality of forms in corporeal things, and the refusal to allow an active intellect in an intelligence which does not undergo any causal determination by sensations, constitute a group of remarkable theories, several of which are put forth for the first time by this vigorous thinker.

226. Bibliography.—Edition of William of Auvergne in 1591 (Venice), and a better one in 1674 (Aureliæ). N. Valois, *Guillaume d' Auvergne, evêque de Paris* (Paris, 1880), contains some works which are not authentic. See tables in Haureau, *Not. et extr. qqes. ms. lat.* Werner, *W's v. Auvergne Verhältniss z. d. Platonikern d. XIII Jahrh.* (Vienna, 1873), and *Die Psychologie des W. von Auvergne* (1873), difficult to follow. Schindele, *op. cit.*, studies only

[1] " Hoc igitur (speculum) divinum . . . conjunctissimum est et præsentissimum naturaliterque coram positum intellectibus humanis." *De Anima*, VII, 6.

the notion of being ; Guttmann, *G. d'A. et la littérature juive* (in *Revue des études juives, XVIII, pp. 243 et seq.*); Baumgartner, *BGPM*, II, 1, well done ; Bülow, *op. cit.*, Ziesché, *Die Sakramentenlehre d. W. v. Augergne* (Weidenauer Studien, Bd. IV, 1911); I. Kramp, *Des Wilhelm von Auvergne Magisterium Divinale* (*Gregorianum*, 1920 and 1921), a good study. J. Weser, *Das Absolute in seinem Verhältnisse zum Gewordenen nach W. v. Auvergne* (*Philos. Jahrb.*, 1917, pp. 302-312) ; *Die Naturphilosoph. Begriffe W. v. Auvergne* (*ibid.*, 1919, p. 24-27), contains nothing new.

§ 3—*Alexander of Hales and John de la Rochelle.*

227. Life and Works of Alexander.—This philosopher was born in Gloucestershire between 1170 and 1180. He studied arts at Paris, and afterwards theology. Roger Bacon tells us that at the time when he was a Master of Arts, the *Physics* and *Metaphysics* had not yet been translated ;[1] so this part of Alexander's life must be previous to 1210. He entered the Friars Minor about 1231, and was the first *magister regens* of the chair of theology held by his order in the University. He resigned his office several years before his death (1245), and was succeeded by John de la Rochelle. With these two men the intellectual party in the Franciscan order began to make its influence felt in favour of learning, against the "Spirituals," who were henceforth unsuccessful in opposing it.

Many works have been wrongly attributed to Alexander. His great, and perhaps his only, work is the *Summa Theologica*. It utilizes the *Summa* of Philip de Grève, that of William of Auxerre,[2] and a commentary by Thomas of Verceil. From this we infer that it was composed not long before 1231.[3] Death prevented its author from finishing it. A document of Alexander IV dated the 28th July, 1256, recommended William of Melito to complete it.[4] Accordingly, the latter made additions to the work, and others did the same after him. The *Summa de Virtutibus*, which fills up a great gap in the third part (qq. 27-69) is subsequent to St. Bonaventure, by whom it is manifestly

[1] *Opus Minus*, in Brewer's edition, p. 326.
[2] Minges, *Theol. Quartalsch.*, 1915, pp. 508–529.
[3] The Commentary "super Hierarchiam" is not earlier than 1224–1226. See Felder, *op. cit.*, p. 195. The *Compendium chronicarum fr. mirorum* by Marianus de Florentia ascribes to Alexander many other works (*Arch. francisc. histor.*, 1909, p. 307).
[4] *Chart.*, I, 328.

inspired.[1] A critical edition of Alexander's *Summa* is in preparation at the Franciscan College at Quaracchi. Until this
is completed, it is impossible to determine what portion of the
work published under Alexander's name really belongs to him.
This reservation must be borne in mind in summarizing his
doctrines.

Like all the similar productions of the thirteenth century,
the *Summa* is at once a theological and a philosophical work.
Alexander's contribution to the development of theology
consists in the formulation of new questions, but not in definitive solutions given to them. Even in his own order, he was
supplanted by St. Bonaventure, and later on by Duns Scotus.[2]
In the division of the subject-matter, he follows the arrangement of the *Sentences* of Peter Lombard.[3]

It is in this theological setting that the philosophy of Alexander of Hales must be sought. He utilizes almost all the
philosophical works of Aristotle, who began to come again into
favour about 1231. He also makes use of the Arabian commentators, and especially of Avicenna. At the same time he borrows
arguments and solutions from authorities of opposite tendencies,
and above all he gives a prominent position to many theories
of the older scholasticism. He is often confused and verbose,
lacking in assurance, and confines himself to detailing the
various solutions of which a problem admits.

228. Philosophy.—In the *Summa*, we find the method of
exposition in its definitive didactic form. Alexander first gives
the *pros* and *cons* of a question, after the manner of Abelard
and the composers of *Sentences*. He collects together arguments
not only from the sources utilized by his predecessors, but also
from Greek, Arabian and Jewish works. Then he develops the
systematic solution of the question at issue, and discusses the
value of the arguments advanced on either side. This threefold division of the questions studied was in use everywhere
in his time, and is found in all the scholastic works of the
thirteenth century.

[1] Bonaventure, *Opera*, Quaracchi edition, Vol. X, Dissertatio, p. 3. See
on this point Minges, *Philosophiegeschichtl. Bemerkungen über die dem A.
von H. zugeschriebene Summa de Virtutibus* (Baeumker, Festgabe, *BGPM*).
Roger Bacon denies that Alexander of Hales was the author of the *Summa :*
" Fratres adscripserunt ei magnam summam illam, quae est plus quam pondus
unius equi, quam ipse non fecit sed alii. Et tamen propter reverentiam ascripta
fuit, et vocatur Summa fratris Alexandri." *Opus minus*, p. 326.
[2] " Exemplar apud fratres putrescit et jacet intactam." Roger Bacon,
ibid p. 326.
[3] Four parts deal respectively with God, creatures, Christ, the Sacraments
and last things.

God is pure act, and infinite reality. His perfect knowledge embraces the plan of the world before creation (*rationem sempiternam qua Deus mundum fecit*), and this knowledge is not itself distinct from God (exemplarism). The human mind can prove the existence of God, by considering His works (the arguments of the Victorines) and by analysing the content of ideas (arguments of St. Augustine and St. Anselm).

All other beings are outside God, and are substantially distinct from Him. Furthermore, all things, whether spiritual or corporeal, are really composed not only of essence and existence,[1] but also of matter and form, that is to say, potency and act. This theory recalls that of Avencebrol (p. 229), although the name of the Jewish philosopher is not mentioned. Still, there are important differences between the scholastic and the Jew. In the first place Alexander bases himself on the doctrine of act and potency. Then the *materia universalis* is purified from any monistic character. Hence Alexander refuses to allow with the Arabians that the human soul is an emanation from an intelligence, or with David of Dinant (p. 194) that God is the prime matter of all things and of the human soul.[2] Furthermore, spiritual matter is not subject to local motion, and does not admit of substantial transformation (*nec est subjecta motui nec contrarietati*). In this it differs from terrestrial corporeal matter, which has both these characteristics, and also from celestial corporeal matter, which is subject only to the laws of motion.[3] The whole Franciscan school, with the exception of John de la Rochelle, adopted the thesis of the hylomorphic composition of all contingent substances. It went together with this other doctrine characterizing the pre-Thomist schools : the plurality of substantial forms. This plurality is found, according to Alexander, in compound bodies (*mixta*), whether living or inorganic.

[1] Alexander holds the real distinction between essence and existence. Certain commentaries on the *Metaphysics* which have been wrongly attributed to him, and are really the work of Alexander of Alexandria, combat the real distinction. Cf. Schindele, *Zur Geschichte d. Untersuchung von Wesenheit und Dasein in d. Scholastik* (Munchen, 1900), pp. 26 and 27. There were two Alexanders of Alexandria, both contemporaries of Alexander of Hales. One died in 1214. It is not known which was the author of the commentaries in question, and other Aristotelian commentaries.

[2] Alexander's doctrine is in no wise dependent upon that of Rhaban Maur on the corporeal character of all creatures, although the two theories present certain analogies (see p. 94).

[3] Guttmann, *op. cit.*, p. 39, denies that Alexander was inspired by Avencebrol inasmuch as the latter teaches the homogeneity of prime matter, which theory is rejected by Alexander.

In psychology[1] Alexander makes a bold but unsuccessful endeavour to combine the doctrines of Aristotle and Augustine. He mentions seven definitions of the soul, found for the most part in the *De spiritu et anima*, and endeavours to harmonize them with that of Aristotle.[2] In order to discover the nature of the soul, we must examine its ultimate causes : God is its efficient cause, and happiness its end. It is composed of matter and form, just as the body itself has its *forma corporalis.* The union (*unio nativa*) of the two takes place *ad modum formæ cum materia.* This multiplicity of real elements is in harmony with Alexander's metaphysics. It brings out the independence of the soul and body (Augustine), but weakens the unity of the compound.

In dealing with the activities of the soul, Alexander hesitatingly opposes the theory of the identity of the soul with its faculties (anti-Augustine). He regards the *vis naturalis* as the principle of life, with the heart as its organ, following in this the physiological teaching of the *De motu cordis* of Alfred of Sareshel. On the other hand, in the study of intellectual knowledge we find the Augustinian division of the *ratio, intellectus* and *intelligentia,* having as their respective objects the knowledge of the corporeal world and the judgments connected therewith, that of created spirits, and that of the *rationes æternæ* and the first principles. This Augustinian doctrine is combined in a curious way with the peripatetic theory of abstraction : only the intelligible forms of the *ratio* are abstract, and their origin is explained by the combined action of the acting and possible intellect—two spiritual faculties existing in us—with that of a third, the *intellectus materialis,* material and perishable in nature, and which seems to be identical with the *phantasia* or *vis cogitativa.*[3] The proper sphere of abstraction, then, is limited to the corporeal world ; the *rationes æternæ* or the deductive knowledge of creatures viewed in the Divine essence (exemplarism) and also the first principles, are innate, thanks to a special illumination on the part of God.

The expressions used by Alexander concerning the *illuminatio* have various meanings, as in the case of Augustine and other

[1] According to Endres. Minges (*Philos. Jahrb.* 1915, p. 143), points out that certain questions announced in the plan are not dealt with. The chapter on the body was possibly written by William of Melito.

[2] " Anima, non tantum ut forma substantialis, sed ut quod ens in se, præter hoc quod est actus corporis . . . est substantia præter substantiam corporis." (*S. Theol.,* q. 59, m. 2, § 1, res).

[3] Cf. Averrhoes, who gives the *intellectus materialis* another meaning.

scholastics. The reference is to the luminous nature of our intelligence when he calls this an *illuminatio*, and an *interioris oculi creatio*[1] ; but when he contrasts the intellectual knowledge arising out of sensation with that which is the fruit of a divine illumination he is thinking of the ideological process.[2]

As for the will, Alexander was one of the first to study the distinction between the synderesis and the conscientia from the psychological point of view.

The *Summa* of Alexander was mentioned and made use of by Berthold of Regensburg († 1272) and Vincent of Beauvais ; and Albert the Great was influenced by it.[3] St. Bonaventure gave it filial homage ;[4] Thomas Aquinas utilized it. But in no instance was there any question of plagiarism. Roger Bacon himself who abused it so roundly, bore witness to its fame, since he coupled its author's name with that of Albert the Great, describing them as *duo moderni gloriosi*.[5] The services which Alexander rendered to the progress of scholastic philosophy have for a long time been overlooked, the glory of his successors having eclipsed his merits.[6]

229. John de la Rochelle. H. Felder, the recent historian of the Franciscan order, in commenting on the *Chronica Fabrianensis*, shows that according to Alexander the Friars Minor occupying the chair held by the Franciscans in the University did so in the following order : John de la Rochelle ; Odo Rigaud, whose Commentaries on the *Sentences* were probably the first work of this kind by a member of the order ; William of Melito, who completed the *Summa* of Alexander and also wrote *Quæstiones* and *Quodlibet ;* and then St. Bonaventure.

Alexander's influence can be seen in GUIDO DE ELEMOSINA, the first Cistercian profesor at Paris (1254) ; for the Prologue to his *Summa* (*Summa Guidonis Abbatis*) presents close affinities to that of Alexander.[7]

Of the disciples of Alexander of Hales, JOHN DE LA ROCHELLE

---

[1] Pars III, q. 73, m. 1.

[2] *ibid.*, q. 69, m. 2, l. a.

[3] Minges, *Excerpte aus A. von Hales bei Vincenz von Beauvais.* (*Franc. Stud.*, 1914, p. 52); *Abhängigkeitsverhältn. zu A. von Hales u. A. dem Groszen,* (*ibid.*, 1915, p. 208); *Abhängigkeitsverhältniss zw. der Summa A. von Hales und d. hl. Thom. von Aquin,* (*ibid.*, 1916, p. 58).

[4] No. **240.**

[5] *Communia naturalium,* liber 1, c. 3, quoted by Charles, *R. Bacon,* p. 573. Cf. Felder, *op. cit.*, p. 187.

[6] The accusation of plagiarism directed against Thomas Aquinas in theological matters is without foundation. See Vacant, *Dict. théol. cath.,* 1900, *s.v.* Alexander.

[7] Minges, *Arch. franc. hist.*, 1913, pp. 13–22 and 433–438.

is so far the best known. He was born about 1200, and succeeded Alexander as *magister regens* about 1238. He died in
1254.[1]

His chief work was a *Summa de anima*. The large number of
manuscript copies in existence bears witness to its great
reputation. It borrows from Philip of Greve and from Alexander,[2] but also touches on subjects with which these did not
deal (*de vi vegetativa*, *de affectibus*, *de motibus*, etc.). John also
wrote a *Summa de vitiis*, a *Summa de virtutibus* based largely
on Philip of Greve, a *Summa de decem præceptis*, and a *Summa
de articulis fidei*. It is doubtful if he wrote a second *Tractatus
de anima* which some ascribe to him.

The disciple is more didactic than his master. He establishes
the real distinction between existence (*ens*, *quo est*) and essence
(*essentia*, *quod est*) with greater decision and clearness than any
other scholastic. This composition of real principles is found
in every created thing ; it is the foundation of its distinction
from God and the only composition found in spiritual substances. John de la Rochelle rejects his master's theory that
spirits are also composed of matter and form. He expounds in
turn the theories which affirm and deny the identity of the soul
with its faculties, and without definitely taking sides, declares
that the two may be harmonized if we take " identity " to mean
that the substance of the soul cannot exist without its faculties.

In psychology John remains faithful to the Augustinian
theories as found in Alcher of Clairvaux, and endeavours to
adapt Aristotelian formulæ and doctrines to these theories.
Thus the possible and active intellects explain the genesis of
our abstract ideas of the sensible world ; but contact with a
divine illumination is necessary in order that we may acquire
certain truths. This " illumination," however, is used in various senses : sometimes it means an action of grace, sometimes
the function of the active intellect or even of the senses. The
theory of ideas of the Franciscan scholar lacks homogeneity ;
" it juxtaposes the data of Aristotle, Augustine, Avicenna, and
John Damascene without succeeding in harmonizing them."[3]

[1] Felder, *op. cit.*, p. 297, and also his article in *Etudes franc.*, p. 612.
[2] Minges, *Die psycholog. Summa des Joh. v. Rupella u. Alexander v. Hales*,
(*Franc. Stud.* 1916, pp. 365–378). Is John alluding to Alexander or to others
of his predecessors when he writes as follows : " Non novitates adinventas,
sed magistrorum nostrorum non solum summas sed et verba sequentes " ?
See Minges, *Arch. franc. hist.*, p. 610.
[3] Minges, *Zur Erkenntnisslehre des Franziskaner J. v. R.* (*Philos. Jahrb.*
1914, p. 477).

230. Bibliography.—The best edition of the *Summa* of Alexander of Hales is that of Venice, 1576, in 4 vols. Other editions were published at Nuremberg in 1442, and Cologne in 1622. A critical edition is in preparation at Quaracchi, and the first volume appeared in 1924. Fr. Parthenius Minges, in his article, *De relatione inter prooemium Summæ Alexandri Halensis et prooemium Summæ Guidonis Abbatis* (*Archiv. franc. histor.* 1913), comes to the conclusion that while the prooemium of Guido Abbas presents striking resemblances with that of Alexander, it cannot have been written before the death of the latter. He suggests as its author Guido de Elemosina, *magister* about 1254, who in this view would have been inspired by Alexander. Cf. pp. 13-22, and *additamentum* (*ibid.*, p. 433) which confirms this conclusion. The best monograph is that of Endres, *Des Alexander v. Hales' Leben u. psychologische Lehre* (*Philos. Jahrb.*, 1888). On his relations with Avencebrol, see Guttmann, *op. cit.* (pp. 32-64), see 140 ; *A. de Hales et le judaisme* (*R. études juives*, 1890). Vacant, *Alexandre de Hales* (*Dict. Théol. Cath.*, 1900, Vol. 1, col. 775-785), superficial. Cf. Ehrle, Felder, and De Martigné (referred to on p. 267); Minges, *Zur Psychologie des A. von H.*, in *Philos. Jahrb.*, 1915, p. 143.

The *De Anima* of John de la Rochelle is edited by Domenichelli (Prato, 1882), a poor edition. Haureau (*Not. et extr. qqes. ms. lat.*, V. 45-48) compares with this work an anonymous treatise *De definitione multiplici potentiarum animæ*. Lucquet, *Essai d'analyse et de critique sur le texte inédit du traité de l'âme de J. de la Rochelle* (Paris, 1875) ; *J. a Rupella ... psychologicam doctrinam exprompsit* H. Lucquet (Lutetiæ Paris, 1875). A description of his works is given in Minges, *De scriptis quibusdam Fr. J. de Rupella* (*Arch. franc. hist.* 1913, pp. 597-622) ; G. Manser, *Die Realdistinctio von Wesenheit und Existenz bei Joh. von Rupella* (*Revue Thomiste*, 1911, pp. 89-92) ; *J. v. R., Ein Beitrag zu seiner Charakteristik mit besonderer Berucksichtigung seiner Erkenntnisslehre* (*Jahrb. f. Philos. u. spek. Theol.*, 1912, pp. 290-324), considers him to be an Augustinian Platonist, and a partisan of the special illumination theory in psychology. This is criticised by Minges.

§ 4—*Robert Grosseteste and the Franciscan School of Oxford.*

231.   Robert Grosseteste.—The organizer of philosophical studies at the *studium generale* of Oxford and the Franciscan *studium* in this city was Robert Grosseteste (*Grossum Caput*). He was born at Stradbroke about 1175, and became first a Master and then Chancellor of the University. It has not been established whether he studied at Paris, but he was certainly influenced by the Parisian programme, and his relations with Alexander of Hales and John de la Rochelle link him up with the intellectual movement having its centre at Paris. Besides translations of the commentaries on the *Posterior Analytics*, the *Physics*, the *Sophistical Reasonings*, and the works of pseudo-Dionysius,[1] Robert wrote numerous *opuscula*,[2] dealing chiefly with natural philosophy, metaphysics, and psychology.

His cosmological and astronomical teaching concerning the formation of the universe and the movements of the planets and comets, and his project for the reform of the calendar, together with his investigations on perspective, colours, the rainbow, tides, heat, sound, etc., constitute Robert Grosseteste one of the most prominent men of science of his time. The mathematical form of reasoning is the dialectic method *par excellence*. Robert holds that mathematics alone is able to provide an explanation of physical phenomena, and he himself applies geometry to optics. This predominance of the mathematical point of view was to become one of the distinctive characteristics of the Oxford masters. Roger Bacon, the disciple of the great Chancellor, who closely followed him on these points,

---

[1] Haureau, *Hist. phil. scol.*, II, 182.

[2] Baur, *BGPM*, IX, catalogues his works as follows : (1) Propedeutical : *De artibus liberalibus, De generatione stellarum ;* (2) Natural Philosophy : works concerning astronomy : *De sphæra, De generatione stellarum, De cometis.* Works concerning meteorology : *De impressionibus aeris sue de prognosticatione.* Works on cosmology : *De luce sue de inchoatione formarum, Quod homo sit minor mundus.* Works on optics : *De lineis angulis et figuris, seu de fractionibus et reflexionibus radiorum, De natura locorum, De iride, De colore.* Works on physics : *De calore solis, De differentiis localibus, De impressionibus elementorum, De motu corporali, De motu supercælestium, De finitate motus et temporis ;* (3) Metaphysics : *De unica forma omnium, De intelligentiis, De statu causarum, De potentia et actu, De veritate, De veritate propositionis, De scientia Dei, De ordine emanandi causatorum a Deo ;* (4) Psychology : *De libero arbitrio.* Under-the heading of non-authentic works he includes the commentary on the *De Consolatione philosophiæ* of Boethius, and the *Summa philosophiæ* (see § 5). The *De anima,* of doubtful authenticity, dates from the middle of the thirteenth century, and deals with the origin of the soul, its immortality, quantity, and union with the body, from a very pronounced Augustinian point of view, though the abstract character of thought is also appealed to in support of immortality. See *ibid.*, pp. 113 *et seq.* Grosseteste's translations are dealt with on p. 241.

recognized his merit and his priority : " præ aliis hominibus scivit scientias "[1]; " per potestatem mathematicæ sciverunt causas omnium explicare."[2]

In his natural philosophy, metaphysics, and psychology, Grosseteste builds up a characteristic combination of Augustinian, neo-Platonist, and Aristotelian theories, giving a very personal touch to his scholasticism.

He appeals constantly to Augustine and Anselm, mentions their names with great respect, and adopts many of their doctrines. It is from Augustine that he obtains his principal neo-Platonist theses, in particular the interpretation of natural and psychological phenomena in terms of light, which makes him, as Baeumker so well says, one of the chief representatives of the *Lichtmetaphysik*. The *Liber de Causis* is quoted but the doctrine of emanation by cascade is altogether absent. As for the Aristotelian elements in his system, such as the doctrine of act and potency, matter and form and causes, they constitute his system a form of pluralism and moderate dynamism, which at once links him up with the great metaphysical system of the thirteenth century.

232. Metaphysics and Natural Philosophy.—God, the Infinite Being, is known to us by our consciousness of His existence (Augustine), and also by reason, for the explanation of change necessarily implies the existence of the unchangeable being. Everything outside God is distinct from Him, created directly by Him in time (Augustine). This applies to the intelligence and the soul referred to by " the philosophers in the *Liber de Causis*."[3] With Augustine, we may call God the *forma omnium*, provided we exclude from this idea anything which would compromise the substantial distinction between God and creatures.[4] In other words, God is the *forma exemplaris :* he knows all things which can exist outside Him, and these *rationes æternæ* are His very essence.[5] This relation between God and everything other than Him constitutes the eternal truth of things, by which they are what they are. *Veritas rerum est earum esse prout debent esse.*[6] God's knowledge extends

---

[1] *Compendium studii*, Brewer's edition, p. 472.
[2] *Opus magus*, Bridges' edition, I, 108. Cf. Baur, *Die Philos. d. R. Grosseteste*, pp. 96 *et seq.*
[3] *De Ordine emanandi causatorum a Deo*, p. 149.
[4] " Non enim sic est earum forma velut pars earum substantialis completiva," Baur's edn. p. 109.
[5] p. 194.
[6] *De Veritate*, p. 135.

to individuals and to future contingent things ;[1] His will rules everything which exists. We recognize here the classical Augustinism.

God is the light *par excellence ;* other beings are participated lights. This applies not only to spirits, to whom the luminous character especially belongs, but also to bodies.

At this point Robert Grosseteste introduces a new and original fusion of metaphysical and scientific data : the *lux* serves to explain corporeal reality. The treatise *De luce seu de inchoatione formarum* establishes that " all corporeal beings are composed of matter and form," and that " the form of corporeity is light." " Formam primam corporalem quam quidam corporeitatem vocant, lucem esse arbitror."[2] The *quidam* here mentioned are the scholastics of Paris, such as Alexander of Hales, whose principal metaphysical theory is adopted by Grosseteste. Light is a substantial element (neo-Platonism), a subtle reality penetrating bodies which, by spreading itself *subito* in prime matter, confers upon it spatial extension.[3] It is also, as in the Aristotelian conception, the principle of all perfection in a body, i.e., its beauty, colour, and activity.

The multiplicity of bodies and their evolution is explained by the notions of act and potency and by the operation of causes ; but here again the theory of light plays an important part : the luminous form multiplies itself by its very nature ; it is *generativa sui ipsius,* and since it cannot be separated from prime matter, it involves the latter in its self-diffusion.[4] In other respects, this activity of self-diffusion, which Grosseteste calls a *species* (a term which Roger Bacon borrows from him), is itself luminous in nature, so that light signifies both the substantial principle of bodies (*lux*) with an organizing function, and also the energy of which it is the source (*lumen*).[5] The dynamic diffusion of light in the three directions of space engenders the *Quantum.*[6] Light becomes rarified towards the

[1] pp. 153, 160.
[2] Commencement of the *De luce,* p. 51.
[3] " Lux enim per se in omnem partem se ipsam diffundit, ita ut a puncto lucis sphera lucis quamvis magna generetur, nisi obsistat umbrosum. . . . Lucem esse proposui cujus per se est haec operatio : scilicet per seipsam multiplicare et in omnem partem subito diffundere," p. 51.
[4] " Lux ergo, quæ est prima forma in materia prima creata, seipsam per seipsam undique infinities multiplicans . . . materiam quam relinquere non potest, secum distrahens in tantam molem quanta est mundi machina, in principio temporis extendebat," p. 52.
[5] *Hexæmeron,* cf. Baur, *Die Phil. Werke,* etc., p.p 79, 80.
[6] " Infinities vero multiplicatum necesse est finitum quantum generare." Baur's edition, p. 52. Cf. p. 54.

periphery, but it then returns towards the centre and there gives rise to condensations. Thus in spite of the diversity of things, the universal presence of *lux* confers upon the material universe a wonderful unity.[1]

The degree of luminosity of a being determines its perfection and its specific character. This applies even to man, whose soul is a light of a superior kind to the body.

233. Psychology.—The psychology of Robert Grosseteste is Augustinian in inspiration. The soul is diffused throughout the body, just as God is present in the whole universe,[2] but it is in no way subject to the causal influence of the body.[3] Thus sensation and thought are pure activities of the soul. The soul is not other than its faculties,[4] and the bond which unites it to the body is itself a luminous body.

The phenomenon of knowledge is an operation which is luminous in character, and human knowledge consists in an effulgence of the increated light, in which we see the truth of things. *Omnis creata veritas non nisi in lumine veritatis summæ conspicitur.*[5] These formulæ, and many others which Grosseteste borrows from various works of St. Augustine, are explained either in the sense that God is the creator of participating luminous beings and of the human reason, or else that the supreme ontological foundation of created essences is God.

Even the *immundi*, i.e., those with impure souls, know the truth of things, but do not realize that it springs from the uncreated luminous Source. We have not found in the *De Veritate* the theory of illumination in the sense of William of Auvergne.

Human liberty is studied in a well-ordered treatise *De libero arbitrio* which is noteworthy for its clearness and its systematic arrangement. Human liberty is a fact which cannot be denied without destroying the notion of duty (*alioquin esset omne præceptum cassum*) and remorse (*remordet et accusat conscientia*).[6]

This faculty of willing does not exclude a *vertibilitas ad utrumque oppositorum*. A *vertibilitas* of this kind is even found in the Divine will.[7] It is only in the case of the creature that it involves the power to do evil. Grosseteste adds that the free decision is preceded by a judgment ; but the free act is nevertheless one, for knowing and willing are one and the same and

---

[1] De luce, p. 57. "In hoc sermone . . . est intentio dicentium ' omnia esse unum ab unius lucis perfectione ' et intentio dicentium ' ea quæ sunt multa, esse multa ab ipsius lucis diversa multiplicatione.' "
[2] *De intelligentiis*, p. 114.   [3] p. 119.   [4] *De libero arbitrio*, p. 228.
[5] p. 138.   [6] p. 213.   [7] p. 224.

emanate from one source (*idem esse in essentia et in radice apprehensivum et appetitivum*,)[1] just as heat and light have one identical source, the sun. The Divine foreknowledge, predestination, grace, fate, and the existence of sin are not incompatible with liberty.[2] Having established the *fact*, Grosseteste passes on to consider the *nature* of liberty. He first explains what it is not, and shows that the power to do evil does not form part of its essence.[3] Then he defines it with Anselm as *potestas servandi rectitudinem voluntatis propter ipsam rectitudinem*.[4]

234. The Oxford Masters. Thomas of York.—Grosseteste interrupted his lectures in 1235 on becoming Bishop of Lincoln, but continued to take an interest in the studies of his order. Thanks to his efforts, three secular clerics succeeded each other in the chair of the friars minors (a certain MAGISTER PETRUS, ROGER WESHAM, and THOMAS WALLENSIS). With ADAM MARSH or DE MARISCO begins a long series of Franciscan masters. His correspondence with Grosseteste shows that already in 1248 Adam was a master of theology at Oxford. He was succeeded by RALPH OF COLEBRUGE (about 1250), EUSTACHIUS OF NORMANVILLE, THOMAS OF YORK, and RICHARD CORNUBIENSIS.[5]

THOMAS OF YORK, master at Oxford about 1253 (he died 1260), was the author of a large work *Super Metaphysicam Aristotelis*. While others dealt with metaphysical questions in the form of commentaries on Aristotle, chapters in a *Summa*, monographs, *Quæstiones* or *De Quolibet*, Thomas of York adopted a plan personal to himself : after an introduction on the value of philosophy (*sapientia*) he gives us a treatise *De Creatore*, a complete summary of natural theology, and then another *De Creaturis*. It is here that Thomas brings in metaphysics, and introduces for the first time the distinction between general metaphysics (*de ente secundum quod est ens et de his quæ sunt entis per se*) and special (*de ente in speciali, de his quæ subsunt enti*).[6] The one studies being as such, the first principles,

---

[1] p. 228.   [2] pp. 152–210.
[3] Videamus quid non sit et quod posse peccare non est vere de essentia liberi arbitrii, p. 220.   [4] p. 222.
[5] Thomæ de Eccleston, *Tract. de adventu fratrum minorum in Angliam*, Little's edition, 1909, p. 63. Cf. Felder, *op. cit.*, pp. 284–301.
[6] According to Grabmann, the division adopted by Thomas would weaken the thesis that psychology and physics—here included under special metaphysics—were taught before general metaphysics. Grabmann, *Der metaphysic d. Th. v. York*, p. 192. The order adopted by Thomas is not a didactic order, as is shown by the section concerning God and creatures, which precedes his division into general and special metaphysics.

the transcendental attributes (unity, truth, etc.), and the categories of substance and accident. The other treatise, unfinished, contains dissertations on the world and the human soul. The work of Thomas of York is inspired throughout by the scholastic theory of the plurality of substances,[1] and constitutes the first attempt at metaphysical systemization produced in the thirteenth century. It was contemporary with the commentaries of Albert the Great and prior to the labours of Thomas Aquinas. Its publication will throw new light on the philosophical tendencies of the group of Franciscans who preceded St. Bonaventure and reacted against the exaggerations of the Spirituals.[2] It will also furnish us with equally important data concerning the influence of the great Arabian philosophers in metaphysics.

235. Bibliography. — Baur, critical edition of Robert Grosseteste, *BGPM*, IX, also a good study, *Die Philosophie des R. G.*, etc., *ibid.*, XVIII, 4-6. J. Felton, *R. G., Bischof v. Lincoln, ein Beitrag z. Kirchen und Kulturgesch. d. 13. Jahrh.* (Freiburg, i. B. 1887). F. S. Stevenson, *R. Gr. Bishop of Lincoln, a Contribution to the Religious, Political and Intellectual History of the 13th Century* (London, 1899) ; A. L. Smith, *Church and State in the Middle Ages* (1913), devoted to the personality of Robert Grosseteste. M. Grabmann, *Die Metaphysik d. Thomas von York* (Baeumker, Festch Festchrift, pp. 181-195), an analysis according to the Vatican MS. Baur, *Das licht in der Naturphilosophie d. Robert Grossetête* (Festgabe v. Hertling, Freiburg, 1913). On the *Sapientiale* of Thomas of York see Pelzer, *Les versions latines des ouvrages de morale*, etc., p. 403.

§ 5—*The anonymous author of the "Summa Philosophiæ."*

236. General characteristics.—The *Summa Philosophiæ*,[3] wrongly attributed to Robert Grosseteste, is one of the most remarkable philosophical syntheses of the middle of the thirteenth century.

(i) It is built up on the doctrinal system of the older or "Augustinian" scholasticism. Its two chief metaphysical

---

[1] In particular he subscribes to moderate realism. *ibid.*, p. 190.
[2] *ibid.*, p. 185.
[3] Edited by Baur, after the works of Robert Grosseteste, with a study of the manuscripts and their authenticity. See the two works by Baur mentioned in No. **235**.

theories are the plurality of forms and the presence of prime matter in all contingent things. Other characteristic doctrines concerning the non-eternity of the world and the foundations of truth bring out the Augustinian sympathies of the writer. On the other hand, his psychology breaks away from Augustine and approximates to peripateticism.

(ii) *Historical tendencies*. The author begins his treatise with a sort of history of scholastic philosophy—one of the few summaries which the thirteenth century produced—and he gives a historical review of theories in connection with the questions dealt with. His love of erudition is everywhere manifest. The development which he gives to certain discussions (for instance that concerning the plurality of forms), and the character of novelty he attributes to certain solutions in which it is not difficult to see the philosophy of St. Thomas (for instance, the controversies concerning the eternity of the world, and the multiplicity of angelical species), enable us to put its redaction between 1260 and 1270.

(iii) *Didactic qualities*. The *Summa* is a complete manual, in which the subjects are treated according to a strict and methodical plan. After the historical introduction, the author lays down the directive principles of his metaphysical interpretation of reality. Then, passing from the more perfect to the less perfect, he examines in turn the nature of God, the created universe as a whole, pure intelligences, the human soul, animals and plants. We may add that the work is written in a lively and picturesque style, full of bold and original expressions.

(iv) In connection with his views on the nature of the inorganic world he gives us scientific dissertations properly so called on optics, astronomy, meteorology and mineralogy. We have already seen that this predilection for the natural sciences characterized the traditions of the Oxford school.

237. Historical introduction.—The introduction with which the work begins embraces an account of Greek, Arabian, patristic and scholastic philosophy. The author expresses his surprise that up to the time of the Arabians, Plato was thought more of than Aristotle.[1] Contemporaries are cited as well as the ancients and the Arabians. In particular, he is full of praise for Alfred of Sereshel (*eximiæ philosophiæ viri*), and, coming nearer his own time (*moderniores*), Alexander of Hales

[1] p. 278.

and Albert the Great.[1] The author does not mention Thomas Aquinas, doubtless because his authority was not then sufficiently established. But it is surely Thomas Aquinas who is referred to in the text which says that one angel differs from another as one species differs from another—*et hoc ultimum est in quo famosi requiescunt moderni.*[2]

Augustine is included among the philosophers. In point of fact, the author is careful to distinguish the *philosophi* from *theosophi* or writers of revealed books, and *theologi*, who are the *theosophiæ declaratores seu expositores*, and who make use of philosophical reasoning for this purpose.[3] This distinction is worthy of note.

238. Philosophy.—(i) *God.* There exists a First Being, uncreated and necessary, *virtus absolute prima increata*, without which the efficient causality which we see in the world and which the author calls *vigor alicujus actionis vel passionis causalis*, would be inexplicable[4]—an *a posteriori* proof. Among the perfections which are to be attributed to God, *intellectualitas* or conscious thought belongs to Him in the first place. The author describes the properties of thought in these remarkable terms : *intellectualitas proprium est, etiam in creatura, considerare, distinguere, ordinare, componere, numerare, super se primo actualiter reflecti, actum volendi producere, sed mediante virtute volitiva.*[5]

It will be seen that the will also is given an intellectualist interpretation, and it is unnecessary to point out that these diverse forms of activity coincide in God with the unity of His essence. As for St. Augustine so for the author, God is *veritas æterna, substantia increata.*[6]

(ii) *God and the world.* Contingent things, created or possible, are distinct from God ; their truth is their limited being itself (*veritas incomplexa est ipsa rei cujusque entitas*) ;[7] it is distinct from the truth of our knowledge.

Like all scholastic treatises, the *Summa philosophiæ* is very careful to combat the various forms of monism. Although God may be called the *forma omnium esse naturale habentium* in the sense that He is the exemplary and efficient cause of all

---

[1] p. 280. He calls Hugh of St. Victor : " Hugo Hierarchicus "—p. 429.
[2] p. 425.
[3] " Moderni Theologi utiliter philosophiam theosophiæ . . . faciunt deservire," p. 288. The theologians are divided into three groups according to their reputation in the Church. The *Summarum confectores* comprise the third group.
[4] pp. 370–371.   [5] p. 381.   [6] p. 292.   [7] p. 292.

things (Augustine, cf. Robert Grosseteste, p. 353), it would be absurd to say that His essence forms any part of the composition of a creature (*in compositionem cujuscunque creaturæ*)[1] or that the existence of the world is the existence of God (*esse divinum*)[2]. Thomas Aquinas reasoned in the same way but with more force.

The pluralism of reality extends to the various creatures, each one of which is an independent substance. When people speak of the unity of the universe,[3] there can be no question either of the unity belonging to a particular individual (*hoc vel illud individuum substantiæ verum esse non potest*), nor of the artificial unity which belongs to a heap of stones, nor the functional unity of a group of singers, but the teleological unity conceived by the Supreme Intelligence.[4]

The world was created in time,[5] but the author is aware of the discussions of *nonnulli modernorum philosophantium* concerning the eternity of creation, originated by the Arabians.

(iii) *The metaphysics of contingent being.* God alone is absolutely simple. Every contingent being is a mixture of act and potency, and consequently of form and matter.

A cleavage is introduced into the hierarchical arrangements of substances, giving us corporeal and incorporeal things. This he calls the *binarium famosissimum*. Certainly in both series we find a similar prime matter[6] denoting passivity, and a form of substantiality, very poor in determinations; but this form, which belongs in the same way to all limited things, becomes enriched in a twofold way, and it is thus that we get pure spirits and corporeal substances.[7] The author rightly holds that the doctrine of the multiplicity of forms in one and the same contingent being is a necessary corollary to the theory just outlined.[8] To the *forma communissima* others are added, each one conferring a new perfection right up to the last, the individual form. It is worthy of note that the author does not

---

[1] p. 407.
[2] p. 430.
[3] Cap. 108. Quod universum de necessitate est unum et qua necessitate, pp. 406–407.
[4] A remarkable synthesis of the various ways of understanding unity.
[5] " Manifestum est ergo, tempus . . . et motum . . . incepisse," p. 408.
[6] p. 315.
[7] " Prima . . . contrarietas in linea prædicamentali substantiæ . . . partim ratione materiæ ad utrumque se habentis, partim a natura formæ communissimæ gradatim secundum proportionem receptivitatis materiæ ad particularitatem tendentis binario famosissimo continetur, i.e., corporeo et incorporeo," p. 361.
[8] p. 331.

regard the multiplication of forms as an *additio* or *superpositio* of one upon another, but as the perfecting of one by another, *ad complementum actuale perfectio*. This is the explanation which Robert Kilwardby, Richard of Middleton, and later still Duns Scotus developed in order not to compromise the unity of form while holding the plurality of its components.[1]

The author devotes an important treatise to pure intelligences, or angels. Their specific form is *nobilissima ;* and their prime matter—simple passivity—has no connection with extension and divisibility.[2] Hence each angel is unique in its species, but on the other hand each one is *individua substantia*.[3]

(iv) *Man.* Descending one step further, the author defines man in Aristotelian terms. The soul is the substantial form, and the body the prime matter of the human compound. Certainly the soul is an intrinsic complement of other forms, but from its union with the body arise the *accidentia nobilissima*, and particularly the intelligence, thanks to which man ranks with the spirits highest to dignity (*cum formis primæ dignitatis*).[4] The theories of abstraction, the formation of the *species*, the distinction between the passive and active intellects, and the *ratio inferior* and *superior* (Augustine) are interpreted in peripatetic terms.[5] The same is true of the notions of science, and the universal,[6] and the truth of judgment (*veritas incomplexa*) which he contrasts with the truth of things, and of which he gives this excellent definition : *est adequatio rei et intellectus, intentionem prædicati cum intentione subjecti copulantis vel hanc ab illa distinguentis*.[7] There is no trace of a special illumination as understood by William of Auvergne— and this is all the more remarkable because the author speaks at length of *lux*. The only concession to Augustinism seems to be the affirmation of the complete substantial nature (*in actu completo*) of the soul separated from the body—a point on which he differs from the *moderni philosophantes*.[8]

(v) *Living and inorganic beings.* After the study of man we get long dissertations on the souls of animals and plants, and their activities. This leads the author on to scientific

---

[1] A fine passage, p. 332.
[2] p. 424. Cf. p. 429.
[3] p. 427 : " nobilissima forma carente dimensione et contrarietate."
[4] pp. 458 and 459.
[5] pp. 472 and 475.
[6] Tract. II, and p. 347 and 348.
[7] p. 292.
[8] p. 463.

considerations, which are also found in his study of the inorganic kingdom. Light is studied at length, and this is a point which links up the *Summa* with Robert Grosseteste. But we must note this important difference : light is not a substantial element, but an accident of a body.[1] It is the activity thanks to which the body propagates itself and is multiplied without losing any of its substance.[2] It is clear from all this that the theory of the *lux* plays only a secondary part ; it is not the keystone of the arch of the system of nature as in Grosseteste ; it is a neo-Platonist and Augustinian theory which the *Summa* incorporates in a much wider conception.[3]

§ 6—*St. Bonaventure.*

239. Life and Works.—John of Fidenza, usually known as BONAVENTURE, was born in 1221 or 1222 at Bagnorea in Tuscany. About 1240 he took the Franciscan habit, and made his theological studies at Paris from 1243 to 1245. In the latter year he became a Bachelor, and followed the lectures of Alexander of Hales, whom he calls *pater et magister*. In 1248 he received he *licentia publice legendi*, and was appointed to the Franciscan chair. From this time dates the commencement of most of his theological works. In 1255 he was involved in the differences between the seculars and regulars, and made a bold defence of his position, in conjunction with Thomas Aquinas, for whom he had a great affection. It was not until the 23rd October, 1257, that the University, in obedience to Papal injunctions, conferred upon Bonaventure and Aquinas the title of *magister*. In February of the same year Bonaventure was appointed general of his order. From that time on his scientific activity was at an end, and his literary production consisted chiefly of ascetical works. In 1260 he drew up the new Constitutions of the Franciscans at the Chapter of Narbonne. He was created Cardinal on the 28th May, 1275, and took part in the Council of Lyons, but died in 1274 before its end. Posterity gave him the name of *doctor devotus*, and, since the time of Gerson, that of *doctor seraphicus*.

[1] " Solam formam de genere substantiæ eam ponere inconvenientissimum est," p. 134.
[2] " Splendor autem ejus est in continuo fieri sine deperditione substantiæ suæ," p. 535.
[3] Baur points this out, and hence the chief argument which he gives (p. 139) for attributing the *Summa* to the school of Robert Grosseteste seems of no value. These ideas were current in Paris as well as at Oxford. Again the natural sciences were studied at other places besides Oxford.

The chief works containing Bonaventure's philosophy and at the same time of certain authenticity, are :[1] (i) *Commentarii in IV. lib. Sententiarum*, begun about 1248, in which he bases himself on Alexander of Hales, but surpasses him in depth and doctrinal clarity. The passages from the *Summa* of Alexander which have been thought to constitute plagiarisms, are on the contrary interpolations in accordance with his teaching introduced after Bonaventure's time. (ii) *Quæstiones disputatæ* (especially *De paupertate*) ; (iii) *Breviloquium* (previous to 1257) ; (iv) *Itinerarium mentis in Deum* (1259) ; (v) *De reductione artium ad theologiam*, a classification of human knowledge. His principal mystical works are : *De triplici via*, and the *Soliloquium*, modelled on the writings of Hugh of St. Victor.

240. Personal characteristics.—Bonaventure possessed the complex personality of a philosopher, and a dogmatic and mystical theologian. In each of these departments he wishes only to carry on the tradition. In particular he writes in the *Prælocutio ad* II. *lib. Sentent. :* "At quemadmodum in primo libro sententiis adhæsi et communibus opinionibus magistrorum, et potissime magistri et patris nostri bonæ memoriæ fratris Alexandri, sic in consequentibus. . . . Non enim intendo novas opiniones adversare, sed communes et approbatas retexere. Nec quisquam æstimet quod novi scripti velim esse fabricator, etc." Hence it is not surprising that his philosophy is inspired by the older scholasticism. He not only retains its spirit, he gives it its most perfect form. Augustinism, with its neo-Platonist tendencies, is attached to a peripatetic basis and the whole is thought out and co-ordinated in an original manner. The passages in which he describes himself as a poor and insignificant compiler[2] must accordingly be ascribed to his humility. Bonaventure's conservatism does not make him a slave of the past. He points out the errors of Aristotle and the Arabians, and even of his master Peter Lombard, for he draws up a list of ten false theories taken from the *Sentences*, which are equally repudiated by Bonaventure's successors. Bonaventure was by temperament and tendency a placid and peaceful continuer of tradition. While he defended the organic doctrines of the older school right up to the end, there is no trace in his works of a direct opposition to the Thomistic

---

[1] According to the studies published in Vol. X of the Quaracchi edition.
[2] *II Senient. Praeloc. p.* 1 ; cf. " miseratus paupertatem scientiæ," *III Sent.*, p. 896.

innovations. He was a faithful friend of St. Thomas, and took no part in the attacks which other Augustinians directed against the Dominican master.

The philosophy of Bonaventure links him up with the great common synthesis of the thirteenth century. He is in agreement with the great scholastics on essential doctrines. Their opponents are his, and he lets no occasion pass without refuting Averrhoism and Pantheism (especially David of Dinant).

The study of God is the centre of Bonaventure's system, so that he is Augustinian by inclination as much as by tradition. We shall see that this study constitutes an ardent search for God, and not merely a cold and rational investigation.

241. Natural Theology.—The existence of God is evident : (i) it suffices for the soul to turn back upon itself in order to feel the presence of God : He is close to us, and it is not difficult for us to find Him.[1] He is in fact the being whose existence is most certain.

(ii) The unchangeable light of the judgments of our changing mind can only be God.[2] The Divine presence is implied in each one of our certitudes.[3]

(iii) To these arguments, Augustinian in tone but peculiar to him, Bonaventure adds a form of the argument of St. Anselm : if we consider the Divine essence in itself, or if we suppose an intelligence which has a proper idea of it and not merely a negative and analogical one, it is true to say that essence implies existence.[4]

(iv) He also maintains that nature as a whole declares the existence of God (*quod omnis creatura proclamat*), thus adding *a posteriori* arguments to those based on intuition and *a priori* analysis. But in any case it is clear from the foregoing that the examination of the sensible world is not indispensable for the demonstration of God's existence.[5]

Bonaventure dwells at length on the Divine attributes, being, life, and power. He calls God the uncreated light, and

---

[1] " Deus præsentissimus est ipsi animæ et eo ipso cognoscibilis ; ergo inserta est ipsi animæ notitia Dei sui." *De Myst. Trinitatis*, IV, L, 1.

[2] *Itinerarium mentis ad Deum*, c. 3, n. 3. Cf. Grunwald, *op. cit.*

[3] *De mysterio Trinitatis*, *Opera*, V. 45. " Ostenditur triplici via. Prima est ista : omne verum omnibus mentibus impressum est verum indubitabile. Secunda est ista : omne verum, quod omnis creatura proclamat, est verum indubitabile. Tertia est ista : omne verum in se ipso certissimum et evidentissimum est verum indubitabile."

[4] This is in the interpretation of the Quaracchi editors, Vol. I, pp. 155 and 156.

[5] " Deus enim non cognoscitur per similitudinem a sensu acceptam, immo Dei notitia est nobis naturaliter inserta." *II. Sent.*, p. 904.

truth ; he delights in the doctrine of the *rationes æternæ*
(Augustine). Creation provides the only possible explanation
of the origin of the world. It took place in time : creation
ab æterno implies a contradiction. In this question which was
the subject of such animated controversies in the thirteenth
century, Bonaventure boldly defended the older scholasticism,
not only against Aristotle and the Averrhoists, but also against
the moderate solutions of Thomism.

242. Metaphysics and Philosophy of Nature.—Finite beings
are distinct from God, and from each other (pluralism). They are
shadows, images, vestiges of the Divinity, and Bonaventure
unceasingly applies himself to discovering the relationship
which unites the creature to the creator. At no time is a limited
being studied for its own sake : the stress is always on the
Divine relation which completes and sustains its reality and
activity.

Every creature is composed not only of essence and existence
but also of matter and form. Act and potency, form and matter,
are convertible pairs of terms : hence the angels are not " subsistent forms."[1] Although matter cannot exist without a form,
it has its corresponding idea in the Divine intelligence, for it
constitutes an undetermined reality ; and if we abstract from
the forms which differentiate it, it must be declared homogeneous (as against Alexander of Hales) in material bodies and
spiritual beings. Both owe their finite character to the element
of undetermination which they possess. This theory of the
hylomorphic composition in the peripatetic sense of immaterial
substances is a legacy from Avencebrol. But Bonaventure
is apparently ignorant of its origin, and does not mention the
name of the Jewish philosopher. Indeed, he endeavours to
ascribe it to St. Augustine, and after his time the Franciscans
invoke more and more the authority of the Fathers rather than
that of Avencebrol.

The plurality of substantial forms is a second theory derived
from Alexander of Hales. Bonaventure does not indeed reject
the axiom : *unius perfectibilis una sola est perfectio*, but he
thinks that the *forma completiva* which gives to a being its
ultimate and specific perfection, is not incompatible with other
subordinate substantial forms which are principles of inferior
perfections. This applies not only to organic and inorganic
compounds (*mixta*), but also to the elements of nature. The

---

[1] See for instance *II. Sent.*, dist. III, p. 1. a. 1. q. 1.

plurality of substantial forms now becomes an accepted doctrine in the Franciscan schools.

When applied to corporeal things, the two theories of the plurality of forms and prime matter are complicated by the addition of new theories which give an original form to the philosophy of nature.

In the first place, prime matter is not pure passivity. It is not only a plastic aptitude for the forms to which it gives itself in order to constitute, in union with them, bodies of a particular nature, it also carries these very forms within itself as *rationes seminales*. The *ratio seminalis* is an incomplete but active germ, an interior energy which in every substantial transformation works together with external agents—*movet et operatur ad effectus productionen*.[1] Hence prime matter is endowed of itself with an *actus essendi* or reality of its own, an *actus appetendi* or permanent desire for the series of forms destined successively to complete it in conformity with the plan of nature, and an *actus efficiendi* which confers upon it a function of productive causality. Bonaventure revived this old Augustinian doctrine[2] in order to differentiate the transformation of natural substances from *creatio* and *annihilatio*. Those who react against Thomism at the end of the century appeal to his authority (Art. VI, § 1).

In the next place, Bonaventure considers that the fundamental and most noble form, that which confers corporeity itself, is light (*lux*). It is found everywhere. He defines it as *natura communis, reperta in omnibus corporibus tam cælestibus quam terrestribus*.[1] In terrestrial bodies it is present side by side with forms increasingly specialized accounting for the particular state of the body either as an element or a *mixtum*,[4] but it retains throughout a primordial function inasmuch as this luminous form, instead of being absorbed and completed by the subsequent forms, acts as a basis for them and makes it possible for them to fulfil their office. We have here again the Augustinian theories of the " Metaphysics of Light " (232), adapted to the exigencies of peripateticism : the *lux* is not a

---

[1] *II Sent.*, dist. 18, art. 1. q. 3, concl.

[2] " Hanc positionem credo esse tenendam non solum quia eamdem suadet ratio, sed etiam quia confirmat auctoritas Augustini." T. II, p. 198.

[3] *In II Sent.*, dist. 12, a. 2, q. 1. p. 302 b.

[4] " Duplex est informatio materiæ corporalis, quædam generalis, quædam specialis : generalis per formam communem omnibus corporibus, et hæc est forma lucis, specialis vero per alias formas sive elementares sive mixtionis," *II. Sent.*, d. 13, p. 310a.   Again : " lux cum sit forma nobilissima inter corporalia," p. 321a.

complete body in itself (Augustine), but an incomplete element, a form which cannot exist without matter (Aristotle).[1] Light multiplies itself (*lux de luce*) by an instantaneous self-diffusion (*generatio, diffusio, multiplicatio*). The activity of light, its accident (*fulgor, lumen*), fills all space, by the intermediary of the air which acts as a vehicle for it.[2] The terms which Bonaventure uses in describing this phenomenon are neo-Platonist, but one gets the impression that they are images covering a certain lack of precision.[3]

In any case, the doctrine that all bodies possess light in the inmost part of their being enabled Bonaventure to emphasize his optimistic interpretation of the world, to exalt its beauty and divine relationship, and to authorize the transports of Divine love which St. Francis of Assisi experienced for the humblest of creatures.

From another point of view, the luminous character of all things naturally plays a part in the phenomenon of knowledge, which is likewise of a luminous character, and one can easily understand that it facilitates the mystical transports of the soul.

243. Psychology.—(i) *The activities of the soul.* Although Bonaventure loves to repeat that the will is nobler than the intelligence (Augustine), he nevertheless confines the cognitive function to the latter alone, and hence the study of the intelligence occupies the same pre-eminent place in his system that it does in all other scholastics.

The Franciscan master holds the peripatetic ideology in all that concerns the origin and nature of sensation and our abstract knowledge (*ratio inferior*) of the corporeal world. On this important question he departs from the Occasionalism of Augustine.[4] From this interpretation of human knowledge he logically infers that the individual is not directly attained by the intelligence.[5] He sets forth the respective functions of the active and passive intellects in a somewhat personal way : the passive intellect is endowed with a sort of spontaneous activity inasmuch as it turns itself towards the sensible and

---

[1] " Si ergo lux formam dicit, non potest esse lux ipsum corpus, sed aliquid corporis," *ibid.*, a. 2, q. l. p. 317b.

[2] On this question see Baeumker, in *Witelo*, p. 394-114.

[3] " Lumen quamvis sit in aere, causatur a corpore luminoso et ab illo principaliter dependet ; nec est in aere sicut in sustinente, sed sicut in deferente," *ibid.*, p. 326 b. One wonders how the *lumen* can exist in the air without being an accidental determination of the particle of air.

[4] Cf. Luyckx, *Die Erkenntnisslehre B.*, p. x, 1-37.

[5] *II Sent.*, d. 3, p. 1. a. 1 (p. 107).

then receives from the active intellect the power to abstract. We learn elsewhere that there is no question here of two faculties really distinct from each other, which helps to account for some of the confusion to which the theory leads.

But when we come to the soul and to God—knowledge which belongs to the *ratio superior*—the intervention of the senses and of *species* abstracted from sensible data is useless.[1] The spiritual is not implied in the sensible, and no process of abstraction can discover it. But as soon as the soul turns back upon itself, it beholds itself in its existence and in its faculties, for it knows itself *per suam essentiam, per præsentiam*. If it regards itself, it will discover God in virtue of a *naturale judicatorium*. Hence it knows directly the spiritual being which is itself (*ad par*), and that which is above it (*ad supra*).

In many places in the Commentaries on the *Sentences*, in the *Itinerarium mentis in Deum*, and the *Hexæmeron*, and *ex professo* in a *Quæstio disputata de cognitionis humanæ suprema ratione*,[2] Bonaventure comments on the celebrated Augustinian texts which say that all knowledge is brought about *ratione lucis increatæ* or *rationibus æternis*, that God is light, and present by His truth to every intelligence. It is quite certain that he does not understand these texts in an ontologist sense;[3] on the other hand, his opposition to the Averrhoistic theory of the unity of the human intellect (*hic error destruit totum ordinem vivendi et agendi*) and his ideology show quite clearly that man is the efficient cause of his intellectual acts. What then does he mean? We may reply that in his writings, as in those of almost all the scholastics, these formulæ have not a uniform and homogeneous meaning, but are capable of all the interpretations which we find in the works of Augustine himself (p. 120).

Sometimes this illumination refers to the luminous resemblance which the creative act impresses upon our minds. God is the uncreated light, and the more perfect intellectual creatures are, the more they resemble Him. *Propriissime enim Deus lux*

---

[1] " Utrum omnis cognitio sit a sensu. Dicendum est quod non. Necessario enim oportet ponere quod anima novit Deum et se ipsam et quæ sunt in se ipsa sine adminiculo sensuum exteriorum. . . . Quod omnis cognitio habet ortum a sensu intelligendum est de illis quæ quidem habent esse in anima per similitudinem abstractam." *II Sent.*, d. 39, a. 1. q. 2, p. 904.

[2] Published in the *De humanæ cognitionis ratione anecdota quædam S. D. S. Bonaventuræ* etc. (Quaracchi. 1883). Reproduced, with a few additions, in *Quæstiones disputatæ de scientia Christi*, q. IV, (Vol. V. p. 17).

[3] See the *Scholion* which follows the edition of the *Itinerarium*, Vol. V. pp. 313–516.

est, et quæ ad ipsum magis accedunt, plus habent de luce.[1] The intelligent soul is a torch lit from the eternal flame. At other times the divine illumination has to do with the immediate *concursus* of the first cause in the exercise of thought. God is the *ratio motiva*, and acts with the *ratio creata* belonging to us. But generally Bonaventure is simply laying stress on the Augustinian theory of the Divine ideas as the objective foundation of truth and certitude. He does not subscribe to the theory of a special illumination which, according to certain representatives of the older scholasticism who were predecessors or contemporaries, is distinct from the general co-operation of God. On this important question of Augustinian exegesis, involving natural theology, metaphysics and the theory of ideas, there is hardly any divergence between Bonaventure, Thomas Aquinas and Duns Scotus : they differ only in their way of expressing themselves.[2]

[1] *ibid.*, p. 311 b.

[2] The Quaracchi editors have rightly insisted on this fundamental identity. See *Scholion* to d. 24, p. 1, in II. I. *Sent.*, Vol II, p. 570 ; also Vol. I, p. 70, and the *dissertatio ex professo* devoted to this doctrine at the beginning of the question just mentioned. Cf. also this other text in Vol. X (*Dissertatio de scriptis*, p. 31), which sums up the Bonaventurian ideology, and shows how Augustine combines Aristotle and Plato : " Licet anima secundum Augustinum connexa sit legibus æternis, quia aliquo modo illud lumen attingit secundum supremam aciem intellectus agentis et superiorem portionem rationis, indubitanter tamen verum est, secundum quod dicit Philosophus, cognitionem generari in nobis, via sensuum, memoriæ et experientiæ, ex quibus colligitur universale in nobis quod est principium artis et scientiæ. Unde quia Plato totam cognitionem certitudinalem convertit ad mundum intelligibilem, ideo merito reprehensus fuit ab Aristotele, Et hoc ponendo licet (Plato) videretur stabilire viam sapientiæ, quæ procedit secundum rationes aeternas, destruebat tamen viam scientiæ, quæ procedit secundum rationes creatas. Et ideo videtur, quod inter philosophos datus sit Platoni sermo sapientiæ, Aristoteli vero sermo scientiæ. Ille enim principaliter aspiciebat ad superiora, hic vero principaliter ad inferiora. Uterque autem sermo, scilicet sapientiæ et scientiæ, per Spiritum sanctum datus est Augustino tanquam præcipuo expositori totius Scripturæ satis excellenter, sicut ex ejus scriptis apparet." (*Sermo*, Vol. V. p. 572). Aristotle is a scholar, Plato a wise man, and Augustine unites both qualities in himself. Luyckx (*op. cit.*, p. 200-234, *et passim*) opposes Bonaventure to Thomas Aquinas on this matter, but has not convinced us. He does not distinguish between the many meanings of the contact of our minds with the *rationes æternæ* in Bonaventure, and he would reduce all of them to a uniform sense. Like Portalié (p. 120) ,he confines himself simply to the theory that God is the *ratio motiva* (*Berühren den Verstand*, p. 221). Cf. also his conclusion, p. 287. We still think that generally Bonaventure is thinking of something different, namely ,the objective foundations of certitude (" ad *certitudinalem* cognitionem requiritur ratio æterna," says Bonaventure, in a text which Luyckx himself quotes, p. 221). Now this has to do not with an intuition, but with an argument or form of reasoning, connected with several metaphysical doctrines, and leading us to seek in God the supreme foundation of our certitudes. Bonaventure and Thomas Aquinas are in agreement on this point. According to Gilson, the eternal reasons have a regulating and motive function ; they are implied in all knowledge, and in the case of the notion of being, they furnish our minds with the very idea of God. (*La Phil. de S. Bonaventure*, p. 379 *et seq.*).

In other places God is called the active intellect of the soul—an expression which we also find in Thomas Aquinas (see later on), but this is simply a variant of the Augustinian formula that God is the master of the soul. Moreover, the active and passive intellects, which serve to explain our abstract knowledge of the corporeal world, are proper to each thinking man.[1]

(ii) *The soul and its faculties.* The active and passive intellects are, moreover, only modes of mental activity, and the mind, like the will, reduces itself to the soul (*per reductionem*). On the delicate question of the kind of distinction to be placed between the soul and its faculties, Bonaventure hesitatingly[2] holds a somewhat obscure opinion, midway between the old Augustinian theory and the new Thomist theory. On the one hand he does not hold with Thomism that the three great faculties of the soul are realities distinct from the soul ; on the other hand he refuses to allow an identity of essence between the soul and the principles of action which flow from it : they are nevertheless consubstantial.

(iii) *Soul and body.* The soul unites itself with the body in order to penetrate the latter with its own life. But while Bonaventure subscribes to this common theory, he introduces complications similar to those which we have indicated in his metaphysics and philosophy of the corporeal world. In addition to the form of corporeity (*lux*), the human body possesses a multitude of forms explaining the perfections of its life. Moreover, the intellectual soul, which is spiritual in nature, is itself composed of matter and a form of spirituality. Hence the spiritual soul which informs the human body finds itself face to face with a being already more or less complete. Bonaventure endeavours to combine the advantages of unity in the human compound, and those of independence in the human soul. He endeavours to secure a close union between the two by conferring upon the soul as a whole a supreme determining function[3] perfecting an already constituted being. But above all he wishes to secure a semi-autonomy for the soul by attributing to it the principles of substantiality (matter and form). In

[1] *II Sent.*, d. 24, p. 1, a. 2, p. 568.
[2] *Scholion*, Vol. II, p. 78.
[3] Thus it determines all the interior forms, and also the *lux*. This enables one to say that *lux* is midway between the soul and matter. " Lux, quo mediante corpus unitur animæ," (*ibid.*, p. 379, b). The body (matter together with *lux* and other forms) is to the soul (matter with a spiritual form) as matter itself is to form.

this way the soul is freer to seek after God, and it is likewise easier to prove its spirituality and immortality.[1]   Hence his Augustinism is tinctured with peripateticism.

244.   Bonaventure as a dogmatic and mystical theologian.— When he comes to the question of the relations between theology and philosophy, St. Bonaventure maintains the common view. He looks upon theology as a practical science rather than a speculative one,[2] and stresses its affective side. This is an echo of the primacy of the will over knowledge.   The knowledge acquired by the reason is doubtless distinct from the teaching of the faith, but between pure faith and pure reason there is a delectable combination of the two.   Bonaventure prefers this apologetic point of view, and does not separate the sweetness of belief from that of understanding.   In this sense we may say that the conclusions of reason should be completed by the teachings of the faith.   We must believe in God in order to prove his existence ; we must interpret the universe with our eyes fixed on the doctrines of the Trinity, the Creation, and the Redemption.[3]

In addition to this apologetic form of theology, Bonaventure has a very well-developed system of mystical theology.   This does not extinguish philosophy,[4] as has so often been said, but it dominates it ; and it carries us on to regions with which philosophy has nothing whatever to do, just as in the mysticism of the Victorines.   Bonaventure's mysticism is above all interesting from the point of view adopted in this history inasmuch as it clearly enunciates the barriers which separate the mystical knowledge and love of God from those resulting from philosophy.   We have seen above that God is easy to

---

[1] Cf. Gilson, *Etudes de philos. médiévale*, pp. 106–107.

[2] The Quaracchi editors are nevertheless of the opinion that his formula differs little (*parum distat*) from that of Thomas Aquinas (*Opera*, Vol. I, p. 12).   According to Ziesché, *Verstand u. Wille beim Glaubensakt. Eine spekul. histor. Studie aus d. Scholastik im Anschlusse an Bonaventura* (Paderborn, 1909), Bonaventure agrees with St. Thomas in regarding the act of faith as a complex activity in which the intelligence and will intervene at the same time.   As to the *habit* of belief, Aquinas attributes this to the intellect alone, in conformity with his intellectualism and his doctrine of the real distinction between the faculties, while Bonaventure, a voluntarist, and less precise on the distinction of the soul and its faculties, attributes it equally to the two mental powers.

[3] E. Gilson, *La philosophie de S. Bonaventure*, last chapter, and note 1 on page 463.   In saying that Bonaventure always had in mind the apologetic function of philosophy, we arrive at Gilson's formula ; on the one hand theology and philosophy are distinct, on the other hand the results of philosophy are insufficient when isolated from theological data.

[4] The Quaracchi editors point out that out of nine volumes occupied by the complete works, only a part of one volume is devoted to the mystical works.

attain to, and that He is close to the soul (p. 364), but beyond this possession of the Divine resulting from our natural powers there is a supernatural possession, which is the work of grace, and which God gives as a bounty to whomsoever He wills.

To show that this is the true view it will suffice to examine the stages of man's progress towards God as outlined in the *Itinerarium Mentis* after the manner of the Victorines. Bonaventure first reminds us that besides the eye of the flesh (*oculum carnis*) and the eye of reason (*oculum rationis*) we possess the eye of contemplation (*oculum contemplationis*), and he then indicates seven stages in the knowledge and love of God. In the first three we attain to God either through corporeal nature (*vestigium*), in which (a) the external senses (*per vestigium*), (b) and the imagination (*in vestigio*) discover resemblances of God—or else through our soul, in which (c) memory, reason and will (Augustine) reveal to us a reflection of the Holy Trinity (*per imaginem*). The supernatural intervention of grace, although favourable to the advancement of the soul in the three first stages, is really required only in the fourth stage of the ascent, and particularly when (d) we see God in ourselves (*in imagine*) in the three theological virtues which He communicates to us.

But the ascent continues. After attaining a knowledge of God in His works, we rise to a direct knowledge. His grace reveals Him successively to us (e) in His being, (f) in His goodness, and in the mystery of the Holy Trinity. This seventh and last stage constitutes the unspeakable repose of ecstasy : we are ravished by the contemplation (*apex mentis*) of the Infinite, the supreme end of all knowledge. It goes without saying that this outpouring of love between the creature and the Creator in no way compromises the substantial distinction between them.

The *De reductione artium ad theologiam* ends with similar considerations. After establishing a classification of the profane sciences, fruits of an interior illumination, and showing that profane knowledge is a preparation for theology (*omnes istæ cognitiones ad cognitionem sacræ scripturæ ordinantur*),[1] Bonaventure establishes the symbolic value of profane knowledge and of nature, which are both reflections of the Divine wisdom, and a preparation for the supernatural union of the soul with

[1] Cf. Trimolé, *De reductione* etc. (*Franc. Stud.*, 1921, pp. 172–189).

God. Posterity has reverentially acknowledged the authority of this great master of contemplative mysticism.

245. The development of Augustinian scholasticism.— William of Auvergne, Alexander of Hales, and St. Bonaventure mark three stages in the evolution of Augustinian scholasticism.

The first mentioned collected together the materials for the system, but did not succeed in harmonizing them.

Alexander co-ordinates the specific doctrines of the system in metaphysics. The composition of matter and form is extended to all created things, and this doctrine, which in Avencebrol was essentially monistic in tendency, becomes a potent way of bringing out the contrast between the Infinite God and limited beings. It is the hall-mark of contingence. The *binarium famosissimum* (p. 360) establishes below God a double hierarchy in contingent reality, namely the corporeal and the spiritual. As for the plurality of forms, this not only provides us with the sufficient reason for the diversity of perfections in one and the same creature, it also enables us to understand how all beings, in spite of their individuality, occupy different positions on an ascending scale, and how higher beings (as for instance man) possess the determinations, such as life, found in lower things.

It was reserved for Bonaventure to enlist this metaphysic in the service of psychology. The doctrines of the hylomorphic composition and of the plurality of forms are after all an outgrowth of Aristotelianism. Bonaventure was able to harmonize them with the central idea of the Augustinian psychology, the substantial independence of the soul in relation to the body. If the soul is already composed of matter and form, it is self-sufficient, and if the lower functions of human life and the state of corporeity from which they arise result from the inferior forms, the soul can devote itself tranquilly to intellectual and moral activity and turn towards God. Philosophy agrees with mysticism in regarding God as the natural end of life. Augustine is consolidated by Aristotle.

246. Bibliography.—The critical edition of Quaracchi begun in 1882 and completed in 1902, is a model of its kind. Vols. One to Four contain the *Commentaries on the Four Books of the Sentences*. In each volume there are critical introductions, a critical apparatus for the text, and after the principal questions, *Scholia* which are veritable monographs on the history of the theories in question. Volume Five consists of eight theological or philo-

sophical *opuscula*. The last four volumes have no great interest
for philosophy. Many works, and especially the *Quæstiones
disputatæ* (except the *De paupertate*) are published for the first
time (Volume Five). The *Introduction* to Volume Three contains a table of the philosophical divergencies between Bonaventure and Thomas Aquinas in their *Commentaries on the
Sentences*. The tenth volume contains dissertations on Bonaventure's life and works, and also a list of the chief *Scholia*
in the four first volumes, and a study of a hundred and eight
apocryphal or doubtful works. Joannes a Rubino and
Antonius Maris a Vicetio, *Lexicon Bonaventurianum* (Venice,
1880).

Excellent biography by Lemmens, *Der hl. Bonaventura
Kardinal u. Kirchenlehrer aus d. Franziskanerorden*—1221-1274
(Kempten and Munich, 1909, Italian translation 1921). D.
Sparacio, *Vita di S. Bonaventure* (Rome, 1921) ; E. Clop,
S. Bonaventure (Paris, 1922), published on the occasion of the
seventh anniversary of the birth of Bonaventure. De Martigné,
op. cit., p. 253 ; Krause, *Die Lehre d. hl. B. über d. Natur. d.
körperl. u. geistigen Wesen u. ihr. Verhältniss z. Thomismus*
(Paderborn, 1888), a good exposition of a particular point.
By the same : *Comment. philos. quomodo S. B. mundum non
esse æternum sed tempore ortum demonstraverit* (Braunsberg,
1890). Henry, *Contribut. à l'hist. de la distinct. de l'essence et de
l'existence dans la scolast.* (R. Thom., 1911, 445). Grunwald,
op. cit., pp. 120-132. Menaisson, *La Connaissance de Dieu chez
S. B. (R. de Philos.*, 1910) ; Luyckx, *Die Erkenntnisslehre B.
(BGPM*, XXIII, 3-4), good but verbose. On exemplarism, see
De humanæ cognitionis ratione, etc. (see p. 368, n. 2) including
questions by Matthew of Aquasparta, John Peckham,
Eustachius, Roger the Englishman, and Richard of Middleton
on the foundations of certitude. Ziesché, *Die Lehre v. Materie
u. Form bei B. (Philos. Jahrb.*, 1900, p. 1). *Die Naturlehre
Bonaventura's (ibid.*, 1908), studies the theory of spiritual
matter and the rationes seminales ; cf. p. 371. n. 2 ; Lutz,
Die Psychologie B. (BGPM, VI, 4-5), a careful study of details,
shows that St. Bonaventure aims at solutions midway between
and conciliating Aristotelian and Augustinian ideas ; *Die
Æsthetik B.'s nach den Quellen dargestellt* (Baeumker, Festgabe),
p. 195 ; L. Baur, *Die Lehre von Nattur Naturrecht bei B. (ibid.*,
p. 217) ; E. Gilson, *Etudes phil. méd.*, p. 77 *et seq.* ; *S. B. et
l'évidence de l'existence de Dieu (R. Néo-Scol.*, 1923, p. 237),

and especially *La Philosophie de S. B.* (Paris, 1924), a complete study, bringing out the influence of theology on philosophical solutions. P. Ephrem Longpré, *La théologie mystique de S. B.* (*Arch. franc. hist.*, 1921, pp. 36-108) ; *Francisk. Stud.*, Festnummer, 1921, h. 2-3, contains *Der hl. B., seine Eigenart u. seine drei Lebensaufgaben*, by Fr. Ehrle, pp. 109-124 ; Trimolé, *Deutung u. Bedeutung der Schift De reductione artium ad theologiam des. hl. B.*, pp. 172-189 ; F. Andres, *Die Stufen der contemplatio in B.'s Itinerarium u. in Benjamin major de Richard von St. Victor*, pp. 189-200 ; R. Boving, note on the æsthetics of B., analysing above all the æsthetic sentiment.

§ 7—*Matthew of Aquasparta and John Peckham.*

247. Matthew of Aquasparta.—Of the immediate disciples of Bonaventure, Matthew of Aquasparta and John Peckham were the most important. MATTHÆUS AB AQUASPARTA (1235/40-1302), a master at Paris and at Bologna, was the second of his order to be called to Rome as Lector of the Sacred Palace (1281), in which Innocent IV had instituted a *studium generale.* He was elected General of his order in 1287, and created Cardinal in 1288. Shortly afterwards he became Bishop of Porto. He wrote commentaries on the *Sentences, Quodlibeta,* and *Quæstiones disputatæ,* the fruits of his teaching at Rome and Bologna. Himself imbued with the teaching at his master, from whom he borrowed liberally (see for instance his arguments against the eternity of creation, and the theory of the hylomophic composition of spiritual substances), Matthew imparted in turn to Duns Scotus not a few of his own ideas. We can form an estimate of Matthew from a collection of questions *De fide et de cognitione humana* taken from the *Quæstiones disputatæ.* These reveal him as a writer of talent, with a sober, clear, and precise style, and a depth of thought which makes him the equal of the most celebrated of his contemporaries.

The *De fide* expounds the foundations of faith and its relations with reason. In particular, Matthew repeats and refutes the arguments of Abelard, observing that the latter still had followers (*alii dixerunt et multi adhuc dicunt*).[1]

The *De cognitione* contains a complete psychology. We find

---

[1] Quaracchi edition, p. 63 : " In istum errorem lapsus fuit Petrus Baalardi." He also refers to the theory of Frederick II, who denied the existence of any positive law : " Istius erroris dicitur fuisse Fredericus, qui fuit imperator, qui omnes legislatores reputebat truffatores," p. 83.

first of all a discussion on the foundations of certitude and the
vision of truth in the " rationes æternæ." The author's sympathies for St. Augustine are manifest on every page. He sets
out his master's doctrine in clearer and more concise terms.
Knowledge begins from below, but ends in an influence coming
from above. Not only has God created the human intelligence,[1]
He also conserves it, and concurs in each of its operations.[2]
This immediate concourse which is necessary for the activity
of all created agents, is proportioned to the particular nature
of each one. Matthew emphasizes with Bonaventure the special
resemblance (imago, similitudo) between the intelligent creature
and the Creator. This resemblance results from the very power
of understanding, and it is in this sense that the Divine concourse, applied to the act of knowledge, is especially called an
illumination.[3] It is the ratio motiva (Bonaventure); we "attain
to " the Divine light and the eternal reasons, not as the object
of our knowledge, but as the motive principle which determines
in us the knowledge of other things, i.e., created things.[4] Since,
then, the rationes æternæ regarded as the object of knowledge
are known only by their relationship with the created essences
of which they reveal the ultimate real foundation,[5] we can
only regard the doctrine in question as a particular form of
the theory of the Divine foundation of the truth of things.

[1] He s ays that this interpretation of the doctrine of St. Augustine would
be inadequate.
[2] " Lumen ergo illud, movendo nostrum intellectum, influit quoddam
lumen menti nostræ, ita quod per lucem divinam videt objective et quasi
effective, sed per illud et in illo lumine videt formaliter ; quod quidem lumen
continuatur et conservatur in mentibus nostris ad præsentiam divinam.
Nec alicui subtrahitur cognoscenti, immo omnibus bonis et malis indifferenter
assistit secundum ordinationem et dispositionem immutabilem suæ sapientiæ,
quæ cooperatur in intellectuali operatione," p. 255.   " Ratio cognoscendi
materialis est ab exterioribus, unde ministrantur species rerum cognoscendarum
sed ratio formalis partim est ab intra, scilicet a lumine rationis, partim a
superiori, sed completive et consummative a regulis et rationibus æternis,"
p. 261.
[3] " Operatio intellectualis circa naturalia est.   Deus autem operatur et
cooperatur in operationibus creaturarum secundum modum et exigentiam
suæ naturæ, ut visum est.   Et quia creatura rationalis imago Dei est vel ad
imaginem, ipsa ratio imaginis exigit, ut in ejus operationibus cooperatur
secundum modum objecti moventi, eo quod mens nata est moveri et illuminari
illa luce,"—ad 1 (p. 262). Cf. ad 5, where he contrasts the influentia generalis
et communis with this illuminative influentia.
[4] " Attingit autem mens sive intellectus cognoscens lucem illam et rationes
ideales et cernit quodammodo eas non ut objectum quietans, terminans et in se
ducens, sed ut objectum movens et in aliud ducens " (p. 254). " Quidditas ipsa
concepta ab intellectu nostro, relata tamen ad artem sive exemplar æternum
in quantum tangens mentem nostram se habet in ratione moventis " (p. 233).
See also the whole of q. 1.
[5] Grabmann, (No. 249), sees in these texts doctrinal differences from
Thomism.   We find it difficult to discover them.

Matthew's ideology presents certain peculiarities :

(i) *Knowledge is an active phenomenon.* Although we are endowed from birth with a *judicatorium naturale*, no idea of the external world is really innate (Cf. Bonaventure, p. 368). All our ideas of corporeal reality come from without by means of the senses. Nevertheless, the sensible object does not act upon the soul. On the contrary, the latter forms for itself, on the occasion of a sensible impression, a corresponding sensation. The same is true of thought : the active intellect transforms the *species sensibilis* (" et illud vocat Philosophus abstrahere ") and determines the passive understanding, without any causal intervention on the part of the external object. This is pure Augustinism forcibly adapted to the Aristotelian theory of the active intellect.[1] Matthew thus returns to an Occasionalism which Bonaventure had found unsatisfactory.

(ii) *We know individual things by their proper species singulares.*[2] Matthew expressly examines the Thomist opinion according to which " intellectu singulare cognoscit per quandam reflexionem "[3] and declares it insufficient.

(iii) *The soul's direct knowledge of itself.* Although the soul is not the first object of its own knowledge (*nec primus actus cognitionis potest esse in semetipsam ; quantum ad cognitionis initium indiget . . . excitatione a corporis sensibus*), nevertheless, as soon as it is in possession of *species* abstracted from without, it can "*sua interiora . . . directo aspectu cernere et intueri, ita quod semetipsam et habitus existentes non cognoscit tamtum per arguitionem sed per intuitionem.*"[4] This thesis gives a definitely Augustinian sense to the author's refutation of the opinion of Thomas Aquinas that the soul perceives its existence and its habits only in the exercise of its acts (*percipit se esse et habitus sibi in esse per actus*).[5]

The Augustinian solutions of Matthew's theory of ideas do not prevent him from subscribing to the natural and substantial union of soul and body.[6] He is led to study the question in connection with the mystical states of the *raptus*, which, for him as for St. Bonaventure, belong to the super-

---

[1] " Sic igitur dico sine præjudicio, quod anima sive intellectus accipit sive capit species a rebus extra, non virtute rerum corporalium agentium in animam vel intellectum, sed intellectus sua virtute facit et format. Huic sententiæ Augustinus concordat in auctoritatibus adductis in opponendo ; concordat nihilominus Philosophus, et ideo huic positioni ad præsens adhæreo."—p. 291. Cf. p. 278 *et seq.*
[2] p. 309. [3] p. 307. [4] p. 239. [5] p. 326. [6] p. 142.

natural order, affect the intelligence, and are completed in the will.[1]

248. John Peckham, a pupil of St. Bonaventure at Paris, where he himself taught about 1269, became a Master at Oxford, a lector at the Roman Curia, and from 1279 to 1292 was Archbishop of Canterbury. Various *Quæstiones*, *Quodlibeta*, a commentary on the First Book of the *Sentences*, a *Tractatus Sphæræ*, treatises *De perspectiva*, *De numeris*, and *Super Ethicam*, are inscribed under his name in various manuscripts. The works so far published under the titles *Quæstiones de anima*, *De beatitudine corporis et animæ*, *Quæstiones selectæ et Comm. super. I. Sentent.*, confirm what we already know from his letters : Peckham is a fervent upholder of the scholastic tradition. We shall see later on that he defends them with animosity against the Thomastic innovations.

In the published texts, which are almost exclusivelyconcerned with psychology, we find no trace of the fiery temper and tendency to exaggerate manifested in his correspondence. His allusions to the Thomist theories are objective and impersonal, and there is no reference to his famous public discussion with Aquinas (Art. VI. § 1). As a good scholastic he reserves his invectives for Averrhoes (*perniciosus hæreticus*) and materialists (*vilissimi*). His style is diffuse, and not very attractive.

Peckham's psychology follows closely that of St. Bonaventure. The passive intelligence, which comprises both the *ratio inferior* and *superior*,[2] is illumined by God.[3] This must be understood in the many different senses which Bonaventure gives to the same formula. The intelligence knows the sensible world by abstraction, but attains directly to the existence of God, the existence and states of the soul, the notions of the suprasensible and the directing and unchangeable principles which underlie knowledge.[4] The will has a primacy over knowledge, and its self-determination does not admit of any causal action on the part of knowledge. The soul is spiritual

---

[1] p. 405.

[2] Spettmann's edition, p. 71 *et seq.*

[3] " Intellectus humanus videt quæcumque intellectualiter cognoscit, in ipso lumine increato," p. 67. God is called the *intellectus agens*, p. 73. In the same way, in the *De humanæ cognitionis ratione* etc., the *lumen increatum supersplendens* concurs with every act of intellectual knowledge with the *lumen intellectus creatum* and the *intellectus possibilis*, p. 181.

[4] " Res intelligibiles per se [seu] spirituales non intelliguntur per species abstractas," p. 86. Read the whole of the question. Cf. p. 215. Bonaventure says similarly : "simplices formæ non possunt introire per portas sensuum et sensibilium phantasias."—*Opera*, V. 303 b (2).

and immortal.[1] It is composed of matter and form, for *nulla creatura est pure simplex*,[2] and this form itself is complex inasmuch as there are at least three distinct perfections to which correspond three really distinct forms.[3] In order to harmonize this multiplicity with the unity of soul, Peckham sometimes refers to a disposition (*medium disponens*) resulting from the inferior form, and calling for the more elevated perfections. At other times he speaks of an intrinsic penetration of the inferior by the superior (*gradatim ordinatæ ad unam ultimam perfectionem*).[4] Add to this that the body for its own part also has prime matter and a *forma corporeitatis*, the latter being introduced to explain the supposed identity of the living body and the corpse ;[5] that this *forma corporeitatis* is completed by the *forma mixtionis* disposing this first compound towards a union with the soul ;[6] that the soul with its matter and its three formal parts possesses in its entirety the function of organizing the body attributed by scholasticism to the substantial form ;[7] and that lastly, to facilitate still more the union of soul and body, Peckham introduces certain *spiritus*[8]—and we get an idea of the complicated system of buttresses which the early scholastics found themselves obliged to employ in order to remain logical and self-consistent. Peckham is out to secure at any price a certain independence for the spiritual soul, without compromising the unity of the compound. He strives hard to remain an Augustinian without renouncing the advantages of the Aristotelian explanation.

The same complexity is found in the theory of the *potentiæ*, which Peckham does not hesitate to multiply since they are the very substance of the soul (Augustine). He distinguishes between these *potentiæ substantiales* and the *vires* or *potentiæ accidentales*[9] which are the *aptitudines variæ* or directions which our operative powers take when seeking for their objects. This distinction recalls the difficulties of Bonaventure on this point.

---

[1] See how well this is developed on p. 12 *et seq.*
[2] Quoted by Spettmann, *Die Psychol*, etc., p. 14.
[3] "Unam esse in homine animam, plene eum vivificantem, compositum ex triplici substantia et vita, scil. vegetativa, sensitiva et intellectiva," p. 37.
[4] The texts are collected together in Spettmann's study, pp. 38 and 39.
[5] "Quia vivum et mortuum nihil faciunt ad essentiam corporeitatis." Quoted in Spettmann, *Die Psychol*, etc., p. 28.
[6] *ibid.*, p. 39 : "non cujuscunque mixtionis, sed illus quæ est propria complexionis humanæ."
[7] p. 107 : "anima unitur corpori ut forma materiæ," cf. p. 187.
[8] Spettmann, *Die Psychol*, etc., p. 31.
[9] p. 203 : "in omni substantia creata pono substantialem potentiam et accidentalem."

To the first generation of the disciples of St. Bonaventure also belong : (a) WILLIAM DE LA MARE († 1298), a friend of Roger Bacon, and author of Commentaries on the first two books of the Sentences of St. Bonaventure, *Quæstiones Dispututæ* in which he follows equally closely the characteristic doctrines of Bonaventure's philosophical system,[1] *Quodlibeta sophistica* (unpublished) and above all a controversial work against Thomas Aquinas to which reference will be made later on.

(b) BROTHER EUSTACHIUS, of whom we possess *Quæstiones disputatæ*, and whom the Quaracchi editors are inclined to identify with Eustachius of Arras.[2]

(c) BROTHER SIMON, and

(d) WALTER OF BRUGES (Bishop of Poitiers, 1279-1307), author of *Quæst. disputatæ* and commentaries on the first and second book of the *Sentences*, a remarkable thinker. He analyses the immediate data of consciousness, and the way in which the soul is present to itself (Augustine). He also sketches out a Voluntarism to which Duns Scotus could add nothing. See E. Longpré, *Gauthier de Bruges et l'Augustinisme franciscain*, in *Miscellanea Ehrle, I*, pp. 190-218.

249. Bibliography. Ehrle, *Das Studium d. Handschriften*, etc. (p. 42) ; *Dissertatio de scriptis* of St. Bonaventure in Vol. X of the Quaracchi edition, and *De humanæ cognit. ratione*, etc., in the *Prolegomena* (see p. 368), Matthæus ab Aquasparta, *Quæstiones disputatæ selectæ*, Vol. I : Quæstiones de fide et de cognitione (Quaracchi, 1903), a critical edition ; Vol. II : Quæst. de Christo (theological). Long extracts from the first book of the *Sentences* in Daniels (*op. cit.*, p. 51, *et seq.*) ; Grabmann, *Die philosoph. und theolog. Erkenntnisslehre d. Kard. Matthæus von Aquasparta* (Wien, 1906, Theolog. Studien d. Leo-Gesellschaft de Ehrhard u. Schindler) ; Belmond, *A l'école de S. Augustin* (M. de Aquasparta, Thomas and Scotus on knowledge) ; *Etudes francisc.*, August, 1914. Daniels gives extracts from the first book of Peckham's *Sentences*. *Fr. J. Pecham tractatus tres de paupertate*, with bibliography, edited by Kingsford, Little, etc. (British Society of Franciscan Studies, Vol. II, 1910) ; Kingsford, article on Peckham in *Dictionary of National Biography*,

---

[1] On these two works see E. Longpré, *G. de la Mare*, in *France franciscaine*, 1921 and 1922.

[2] They publish a question of his on the foundations of knowledge (*op. cit.* p. 179 *et seq.*). The author gives a solution in the sense of Bonaventure and Thomas Aquinas.

Vol. 44, pp. 190-197 ; H. Spettmann, *J. Pechami quæstiones tractantes de anima* and *Die Psychologie d. J. Pecham* (*BGPM*, XIX, 5-6, and XX, 6) ; *Die Ethikkommentar des J. Peckam* (*BGPM*, Festgabe, 1923, pp. 222-242). The *Quæstiones* of Walter of Bruges are in preparation by E. Longpré in the series of Philosophes Belges (Louvain).

§ 8—*Peter John Olivi.*

250. Olivi was born at Sélignan (1248/49). We find him successively at the schools of Paris, Florence, Montpellier, and Norbonne, where he died (1298). He was a prominent personality, occupying a place apart in the group of early Franciscans after Bonaventure. He owes his fame to the disciplinary reforms which he promoted in his order, as much as to his philosophical and theological doctrines. It was he who put forward the question " de usu paupere " and who wanted to reduce evangelical poverty to the use of the minimum necessary for subsistence. The party of the " spirituals " who gathered around him came into conflict with the rest of the order.[1] In 1282 a reunion of the Chapter of the Order at Strasburg decided to censure Olivi's doctrines. In 1283, an assembly of doctors of the University condemned thirty-four propositions, almost all taken from his *Quæstiones*. The accused was not heard in his own defence, but addressed to his judges a long written justification of his position. The censure was at the same time applied to some of his philosophical doctrines, particularly his way of conceiving the relations between the intellectual soul and the body.

The *Quæstiones* of Olivi, discovered in 1878 and 1880,[2] and the publication of which has been begun by Jansen, contains a great number of dissertations of exclusively philosophical interest. They form an ordered whole, and relate to metaphysics, psychology and ethics.[3] Olivi here shows himself to be possessed of a mind of more than ordinary power. These dissertations, many of which are veritable treatises, show that their author was completely familiar with the philosophical

[1] This idealistic movement was continued in the fourteenth century by Ubertinus de Casale. See Callaey, *L'idéalisme franciscain au XIVe s., Etude sur Ubertin de Casale* (Louvain, 1911).
[2] Jansen, *Handschriftl.*, after the manuscript in the Borghese Collection, and above all, the Cod. Vatic. lat. 1116 (V) discovered by Ehrle. Cf. *Arch. Litter. u. Kirchgesch.* III, 470.
[3] Prologue to Jansen's edition.

systems of Aristotle, Augustine and the Arabians, and perfectly understood the meaning of contemporary discussions. He sets out the various solutions advanced, with their arguments, and hence his work constitutes a first-rate source for the study of the older scholasticism and its early relation with Thomism. His style is lively and personal, but lacking in elegance ; his method has the defect of excessive classification. Jansen ascribes a certain number of variations in doctrine to the author's prudent diplomacy.[1] But is not this going too far ? Generally Olivi is quite firm in his opinion, or else he explains why he hesitates. Above all, he sets forth a group of personal philosophical theories quite clearly, and at the same time expresses the common doctrines with originality.

251. Metaphysics and Physics.—After establishing that the creative act implies Divine perfection, and hence this power cannot be conferred upon any creature (against the neo-Platonists)[2] Olivi maintains " quod mundus non est æternus nec esse potuit ab æterno," [3] that God " non potest facere aliquid infinitum in actu," [4] and that every creature exists and acts in time.[5]

Individual substances alone exist ; the universal is a property of the concept (*iste modus dicendi solemnior est et communior et verior prout credo*).[6] Olivi tells us of interesting discussions as to whether all the accidental predicaments correspond to something really distinct from the substance of the concrete being, or whether some of them do not rather consist of aspects of things founded on other predicaments.[7] He hesitates to decide on this question, and again in face of the *silva opinionum* on the relations between the specific and the individual essences. At the same time he leans to the *solemnior et communior* solution according to which individuation adds nothing to the essence of the individual being.[8]

Created things—and therefore spiritual creatures also—are composed of matter and form. Among the many arguments which he sets out, Olivi gives one which endeavours to show that any form not received in an undetermined subject would

---

[1] *Die Erkenntnisslehre* etc., p. 17.
[2] Quaest. 1.   [3] p. 95.   [4] p. 35.
[5] "Alii vero non minus catholici dicunt quod esse omnium creatorum est successivum . . . et istis magis assentiendum judico," p. 165.
[6] p. 235.
[7] " Quæ prædicamenta secundum se dicant essentias distinctas ab aliis et quæ dicant solummodo rationes super essentias aliorum fundatas," p. 483.
[8] pp. 213, 226, 321.

be identical with the infinite simplicity of God.[1] Undetermined
matter, implying contingence, has already of itself a certain
actuality other than the actuality of the form,[2] but Olivi will
not go so far as to say that it can exist without the latter.[3]
He categorically refuses to introduce new distinctions in matter
itself, or differences (*differentiæ materiales*) which would
specify common matter.[4] Olivi defends no less energetically
this other thesis of the older scholasticism, that the richness of
perfection of a being must be explained by the presence of many
forms. These are in a sense independent of each other, but are
bound together by the common matter receiving them and
determined by them. Faithful to his pluralistic conception,
he does not regard matter as one numerically, but concep-
tually, and this unity is based upon the similarity between the
matter of various creatures, in which it is really multiplied.[5]
We also find in Olivi the idea underlying the *distinctio formalis
a parte rei*, which Duns Scotus adopted and made one of the
principal features of his metaphysics. (Longpré, *La philosophie
de Duns Scot*, p. 244).

Efficient causality and movement, which so few scholastics
studied in detail, is the subject of long and keen analyses.[6]
Lastly, after expounding at length the contemporary theories
concerning the distinction between essence and existence
(*tres modi dicendi hodie satis solemnes*), he refutes the arguments
which tend to identify them, and seems to lean towards the
real distinction.[7]

On more than one question in physics, Olivi differs from his
masters. He denies the existence of active germs or *rationes
seminales* in corporeal matter:[8] the little treatise which he
devotes to this question is an excellent exposition of this
delicate problem. On the other hand, he attributes a lesser
intensity to the forms of the corporeal elements when absorbed

---

[1] " Omnis enim forma quæ non est in alio a se recepta et participata . . .
est absolutissima, simplicissima, universalissima et infinitissima et breviter
est summum ens et ipsemet Deus," p. 320. The whole question should be read.
[2] " Materia secundum suam essentiam dicit aliquem actum et actualitatem
distinctam tamen sufficienter ab actu qui est idem cum forma," p. 306.
Cf. p. 308.
[3] " Aliorum judicio derelinquo," p. 370.   [4] p. 373.
[5] Q. XXI. " An materia sit una numero. Sicut enim entia sunt distincta
realiter, sic et principia eorum constitutiva," p. 385.
[6] Q. XXXIII *et seq.*   [7] Q. VIII.
[8] "Cum non solum sit magnorum sed etiam potissimorum magistrorum
meorum, quia tamen aliam melius meo judicio intelligo," p. 516, Q. XXXI.
Curiously enough, he thinks that his theory is in conformity with the doctrine
of Augustine, p. 517 and 543.

in a compound[1] and from this he infers that corporeal substance *suscipit magis et minus*.[2]

The most original element in his physics is undoubtedly his theory of corporeal movement. He rejects the commonly accepted distinction between the natural place towards which a body tends of its own nature (*motus naturalis*) and violent movement impressed by an external agent (*motus violentus*),[3] teaching that the *impulsus* of a projectile comes entirely from the projecting agent, and is continued under its influence.[4] This constitutes a departure from Aristotelian theory. Olivi is the first representative of the theory of the *impetus* which we find later on in Buridan and Albert of Saxony, and which prepare the way for modern mechanics.

252. Psychology.—In the matter of knowledge, liberty, and the union between the soul and body, Olivi has noteworthy theories : (i) Both in the case of sensation and thought, knowledge is a purely active phenomenon. The known object does not exercise any causal activity, but is called the *terminus*, *causa terminativa*,[5] *occasio*. Hence there can be no question of any *species*, or any causal action on the part of the object. Olivi lays stress on the contradictions and inconsistencies found in those of his contemporaries (Henry of Ghent for instance) who regard the *species* as a kind of material substitute for the object, engendered in the medium and intercepted by the organism : in this case we should not know the object, but its image.[6] Hence it is not necessary to wait till the fourteenth century for a refutation of this false theory of the *species impressa*.

But if the soul draws out from itself all its knowledge, is the latter truthful ? Olivi replies in a somewhat naïve manner : Yes, because the soul in knowing turns towards the exterior object (*aspectus*). Knowledge is modelled upon the object, just as a ray of light which passes through a spherical vase adapts itself to the contour of the sphere.[7]

---

[1] p. 394.
[2] Q. XXII.
[3] Cf. Thomas Aquinas, *Comment. in lib. III de cælo.*
[4] " Impulsus seu inclinationes datæ projectis a projectoribus movent ipsa projecta etiam in absentia projicientium," p. 563. Cf. Jansen, *Philos. Jahrb.* 1920.
[5] The word " causa " is used here in an improper sense.
[6] " Ergo sola species immediata gignens speciem, per quam fit visio, videbitur . . . proprie." Jansens refers to q. 73.
[7] Q. 72. " Sicut actualis irradiatio vasis sphærici . . . fit sphærica ex hoc quod lux generat illam . . . sic quia vis cognitiva generat actum cognitivum cum quadam informativa imbibitione actus ad objectum . . . fit ipsa similitudo." Quoted by Jansen, *Die Erkenntnisslehre*, etc., p. 62.

Although the sensible reality does not act in the production of our abstract knowledge, the latter starts from experience, even in the case of our knowledge of suprasensible realities and the nature of the soul. This enables Olivi to find a place for the theory of abstraction, and to combat the special illumination theory attributed by some to St. Augustine. Only the knowledge of the soul's existence and its substance (Augustine) in the fruit of an intuition.

(ii) The freedom and absolute self-determination of the will are established from psychological observation. Freedom constitutes the very essence of the will. Do we not sometimes will the objects which previously we detested? Do we not always retain the power to suspend our very acts of will, and to choose between two objects? Without freedom there can be no responsibility, and no distinction between good and evil.[1] In no case does the *ratio ex melioritate sumpta* necessitate our adhesion (against Aquinas; cf. Scotus).

(iii) The soul and its faculties. The faculties are *partes constitutivæ animæ;* they constitute the soul, but differ from it as the part differs from the whole. But inasmuch as they are all rooted in the *materia spiritualis*, or profound element of indetermination which underlies the soul, they are united together by a sort of sympathy. This leads us to a new theory : that of the *colligantia potentiarum*, or sympathetic repercussion between the faculties linked together in the same *materia spiritualis*. It is thus that the excitation of our senses is accompanied by the stimulation of the corresponding thought,[2] although this parallelism does not involve any real action of one faculty upon another.[3]

(iv) Soul and body. The body is of itself a natural being. Similarly, we find in the soul a spiritual matter and three forms, the principles respectively of the vegetative, sensible and intellectual life, and which by their union give rise to one human soul (*anima rationalis*). So far there is nothing peculiar. Neither the plurality of forms, nor the existence of spiritual matter were a novelty in the times of Olivi. The Dominican Kilwardby, and Richard of Middleton, a more

---

[1] Q. 57. See texts in Jansen, *Philos. Jahrb.*

[2] " Quia materia potentiarum animæ est eadem, idcirco actio unius est sicut quædam motio suæ materiæ communis utrique potentiæ," Q. 72.

[3] " Patiens non subicitur activæ virtuti agentis directe et immediate, sed solum oblique et mediate . . . ex hoc quod est alteri patienti firmiter et fortiter colligatum." *ibid.* Quoted by Jansen, *Die Erkenntnisslehre*, etc., p. 77 *et seq.*

2C

important person and one of the examiners of Olivi at Paris, subscribed to the same theories in almost identical terms. But Olivi grafted on to this Franciscan doctrine a new thesis : he maintained that the intellectual part of the soul (*pars intellectiva*) does not act as the informing principle of the body. If it did, he says, it ought to confer upon the body its own proper being, its spirituality and immortality.[1] How, then, is the union of the extended body with the spiritual part of the soul to be explained ? In a mediate and indirect way, namely, by the intermediary of the vegetative and sensitive parts. These determine the body as forms, and since they are found in one and the same spiritual matter together with the intellectual part, the latter can act through them upon the body without compenetrating it : the union of the intellectual part with the body is substantial, not formal.[2]

If we bear in mind the meaning of the expressions " substance " and " form," it is clear that the spiritual soul becomes something foreign, united to a body from without, and in no wise fashioning it.

Bitter complaints were made[3] by the other Franciscans against this doctrine, and they induced Clement V to take cognizance of the dispute. Protracted negotiations began in 1309, and ended at the Council of Vienne in 1311. One of the propositions condemned by the Council is concerned with the union of the soul and the body. It runs thus : " *Quisquis deinceps asserere . . . præsumpserit, quod anima rationalis seu intellectiva non sit forma corporis humani per se et essentialiter, tanquam hæreticus sit censendus.*"[4] The definition of the council takes up Olivi's terminology and establishes an intentional identity between *rationalis* and *intellectiva ;* it

---

[1] Questions 52 and 67 sum up all the arguments for the immortality of the soul. See Jansen, *Die Unsterblichkeitsbeweise*, etc.

[2] " Dico quod anima rationalis sic est forma corporis quod tamen non est per omnes partes suæ essentiæ, utpote non per materiam nec per partem. materialem, nec per partem intellectivam, sed solum per partem sensitivam. . . . Et ideo ponuntur sibi invicem unita [intellectiva anima et corpus] et sic verum [est] quod eorum unio est intima, non tamen immediata " Jansen, *Die Definit. d. Koncils von Vienne*, pp. 477–479, and *Gregorianum*, p. 87. The texts are contained in qq. 51, 54, 59.

[3] In the complaint drawn up against the Spirituals by the others, we read : " Item docuit, quod anima rationalis non est forma corpori humani per se ipsam, sed solummodo per partem sensitivam ; adjiciens, quod si esset forma corporis, sequeretur, quod aut communicaret corpori esse immortale aut ipsa non haberet esse immortale de se ; ex quo posset inferri quod Christus, qui veraciter nostram humanitatem assumpsit, non fuit in quantum homo ex anima rationali et humana carne compositus et subsistens, sicut fides docet catholica." (Ehrle, *Arch.*, etc., II. 369).

[4] Denzinger, *Enchiridion symbolorum*, 1908, p. 209.

leaves open the question of the number of forms in man, but implies that every substantial form informs the compound *of itself and essentially.*

In spite of his respect for Augustine, Olivi rejects his teaching on several points : hence he is not an Augustinian. He combats Thomas Aquinas without mentioning his name ; he opposes the neo-Platonist emanationism, and although he appeals to Alexander of Hales and to St. Bonaventure, he is after all an independent thinker.

253. Petrus de Trabibus was a French Franciscan who lived towards the end of the thirteenth century, and wrote a commentary on the first two books of the *Sentences*,[1] closely following Olivi. He adopted the latter's theories on the union of the soul and body, and defended the implied plurality of forms against the new Thomistic explanation, which was constantly growing in favour (see later on). He also adopted Olivi's views on the *colligantia*, the relations between the faculties and the soul, freedom, and the absence of the *rationes seminales*, which he calls a *vocabulum* invented by Augustine in order to designate the potentiality of matter. He maintains even more clearly than Olivi that the divine perfections are *rationes reales* which result in unity, and that their distinction does not rest solely upon mental aspects. Similarly in created things, *esse, vivere, intelligere*, or again *actio* and *passio* are one and the same reality *secundum rationes diversas*. And he adds : " Ergo non repugnat unitati essentiæ, etiam in creaturis, habere rationes reales ; multo minus ergo repugnat unitati et simplicitati essentiæ divinæ." (Comment. in I Sent. [unpublished]. Texts are given in Longpré, *La philosophie de Duns Scot*, 1924, pp. 244 and 245). Duns Scotus speaks in the same way. But Peter differs from Olivi on two important questions, in which he is very clear. First, existence and essence are identical in a concrete thing, so much so that the one adds nothing to the other.[2] In the second place, the active and passive intellects are an unnecessary mechanism which should be expunged

---

[1] Discovered by Ehrle in the cod. Florent. Bibl. Nation., 1149B5 (*op. cit.*, III, 459); cf. Jansen, *Die Erkenntnisslehre*, p. 84, and *Petrus de Trabibus* (BGPM, Supplt. Bd. Festg. Baeumker, 1923, p.p 243–255) which contains interesting extracts. Others are found in E. Longpré, *Pietro de Trabibus, un discepolo di P. G. Olivi*, in *Studi Francescani*, 1922.

[2] Omnis essentia de sua ratione et intellectu habet aliquod esse et aliquam actualitatem. Licet enim aliqua essentia, ut materia, de se non habeat aliquam actualitatem, necesse est tamen quod habeat aliquam, licet imperfectam quæ per formæ actualitatem habet perfici et compleri. Et ideo nec in materia esse addit ad essentiam. Jansen, *op. cit.*, p. 247.

from the theory of ideas. Thought is an active phenomenon which the soul produces in itself with the concourse[1] of God (*cooperatur intellectui ut illustrans*). Peter is a clear thinker, but not so shrewd as his master, and the questions with which he deals are treated according to the traditional plan of similar works.

The condemnation of 1311 helped to consign to oblivion this thinker, who deserves to rank with the great scholastics.

254. Bibliography.—Ehrle, *Olivi's Leben und Schriften* (*Arch. f. Litt. u. Kirchengesch. d. Mittelalt.*, III, 409, 1887) ; *Zur Vorgeschichte des Concils von Vienne* (*ibid.*, II, p. 353, 1886 ; III, p. 1, 1887) ; *Ein Bruchstück d. Acten Ueberlieferung des spekul. Schriften Olivis* (*Phil. Jahrb.*, 1918, pp. 141-146) ; B. Jansen, *Die häschriftl. Ueberlieferung der spekul. Schriften Olivis* (*Phil. Jahrb.*, 1918, pp. 141-146) ; Fr. P. Joh. Olivi, O.F.M., *Quæstiones in II lib. Sententiarum*, Vol. IV, *Bibl. francisc. schol.*, 1922, Quaracchi edition : Vol. I, Qq. 1-48 according to the cod. Vatic. lat. 1116 (V). With the exception of qq. 32-48, these deal with theological matters. Vol. II (V in Quaracchi edition, 1924) contains qq. 49-71. The psychological and ethical questions will appear in subsequent volumes. Long extracts are given in various articles by Jansen : *Olivi, der älteste scholast. Vertreter des heutigen Bewegungsbefriffs* (*Philos. Jahrb.*, 1920, p. 137-152) ; *Ein neuzeitlicher Anwalt d. menschl. Freiheit aus d. 13 Jahrh.* (*ibid.* pp. 230-238, 382-408), *Die Lehre Olivis u. das Verhaltniss v. Leib und Seele ; Francisk. Stud.*, 1918, pp. 153-175, 233-258 ; *Die Unsterblichkkeitsbeweise bei O. u. ihre philosophiegeschichtl. Bedeutung* (*ibid.*, 1922, pp. 49-69) ; *Quonam spectat definitio Concilii Viennensis de anima* (*Gregor.* 1920, pp. 78-90) ; *Die Erkenntnisslehre Olivis* (Berlin, 1921). In view of the publication of Jansen's work, the discussions between Palmieri and Zigliara are out of date. On Petrus de Trabibus, see note, p. 387. F. Delorme, *P. de Trabibus et la distinction formelle*, in *France francisc.*, 1924, p. 255. He quotes texts showing that Peter holds a formal distinction between the divine attributes.

[1] p. 248.

§ 9—*Other representatives of the older scholasticism.*

255. William of Ware.—To the second generation of Franciscan teachers who were followers of St. Bonaventure belong WILLIAM OF FALGAR, the third lector of the Sacred Palace and Bishop of Viviers from 1284, author of *Quæstiones Disputatæ*; NICHOLAS OCKAM, a lector at Oxford (Commentary on the *Sentences*),[1] JOHN OF PERSORA ; HUGO DE PETRAGORIS ; ROGER MARSTON, who is referred to elsewhere ; ALEXANDER OF ALEXANDRIA, general of the Order († 1314). The last-mentioned brought out the Commentaries of St. Bonaventure on the *Sentences* in the form of a compendium, and was perhaps also the author of *Quæst. disputatæ* and of commentaries on the *Metaphysics* published in 1572 under the name of Alexander of Hales.[2]

The Englishman, WILLIAM OF WARE (*Varro*)[3], who probably taught at Oxford, and whom Bartholomew of Pisa and a fourteenth century manuscript call *magister Scoti sive doctoris subtilis*, was the author of *Quæstiones in IV Lib. Sentent.*, which are unpublished.[4] In a fragment published by Daniels, the author protests against the special illumination theory as understood by several members of his Order and also by Henry of Ghent.[5] Accordingly, the Augustinian texts concerning the *regulæ æternæ*, and the *ratio inferior* and *superior* must not be understood in a psychological sense, but are concerned with the metaphysical foundations of reality and truth. This explanation henceforth meets with increasing acceptance.

On the other hand, William of Ware holds to the Anselmian argument for the existence of God, and maintains that the judgment " God exists " is *per se notum*, and evident, resulting from the analysis of the subject and predicate. At the same time this analysis requires a great effort,[6] whence he concludes that the proposition in question is *minus per se nota*.

---

[1] Daniels, *op. cit.*, gives short extracts, p. 82 ; Little, *The Grey Friars in Oxford*, p. 158.

[2] See p. 347.

[3] Biographical and bibliographical notes by E. Longpré, *G. de Ware*, in *France Francisc.*, 1922, I, and H. Klug, *Zur Biographie d. Minderbrüder J. D. Scotus u. Wilhelm von Ware* (*Fr. Stud.*, 1915, p. 377).

[4] A. Daniels, *Zu ben Beziehungen zw. Wilhelm von Ware und Joh. Duns Scotus* (*Franc. Stud.*, 1917, p. 221) points out certain theories of the author concerning the end and object of theology, the Infinity of God, and human knowledge, and compares them with similar texts in the *Opus oxoniense* of Duns Scotus. He also draws attention to William's dependence upon Henry of Ghent in the case of the last two doctrines mentioned above.

[5] A. Daniels, *Wilhelm von Ware über das Menschliches Erkennen* (*Suppl. BGPM*, Bd. 1913, p. 316).

[6] Daniels, *Quellenbeitrage*, etc.(*BGPM*, VIII, I. 2, p. 102), gives extracts.

Other masters in this compact army of Franciscan philosophers would deserve mention. At the end of the thirteenth
and in the fourteenth century, the Commentaries of St. Bonaventure on the *Sentences* were the subject of numerous exegetical
works in the various branches of the Franciscan Order. The
Quaracchi editors give the names of seven theologians and
philosophers whose exegetical works are so far unpublished,
and twenty-three others whose works have been printed.[1]
But the success of Scotism slowed down the Bonaventurian
movement, without however stopping it altogether.

A place apart belongs to Richard of Middleton, an original
thinker who ought to be detached from the Bonaventurian
group (see later on), and the same must be said of Gilbert of
Tournai, who devoted his time to dealing with questions which
few of his confreres touched on.

256. Gilbert of Tournai, a Franciscan Master of Theology,
composed towards the middle of the thirteenth century,
various treatises on pedagogy and political philosophy, dedicated
to the princely personages to whom he acted as counsellor
and perhaps as tutor.

The *Eruditio regum et principum* dates from 1259, and was
written at the request of Louis IX, King of France. It sets out
the qualities which a prince should possess. It does not contain
much in the way of philosophic doctrine, but consists rather
of moral considerations based to a great extent on the *Polycraticus* of John of Salisbury, together with interesting descriptions of the customs of the times.

The *De modo addiscendi*, written about 1250[2] for John, the
son of the Count of Flanders, constitutes the third part of a
much larger educational work, the *Erudimentum doctrinæ*, in
which the author examines the final, efficient, formal and
material causes of teaching. After a general introduction, the
De modo addiscendi elucidates the nature of teaching and
education (formal cause), by analysing the conditions which
their success require in master and pupil. The author is thus
led to study the mental faculties the training of which is in
question, and sets out from the principles of the Augustinian
ideology as found in Robert Grosseteste or Peter Olivi. The
impressions of the sensible world act upon the understanding

---

[1] Vol. X, p. 34.
[2] About 1262 according to Longpré, in the Preface to his edition of the
Tractatus de Pace (Quaracchi, 1925).

only as exciting conditions, and the mind subjects the content of sensations to a progressive purification (*major depuratio*) which is entirely its own work.

By turning back upon itself, the soul finds God and sees in the Uncreated Light the foundation of its own knowledge. The summit of learning consists of a mystical contact with God, which the author treats after the manner of the Victorines. Other doctrines touched upon show Gilbert's attachment to the older scholasticism.

Two other treatises by Gilbert must also be mentioned : *De pace et animi tranquillitate*, composed for Marie de Dampierre,[1] and a letter to Isabella, the sister of Louis IX, King of France.

257. Peter of Tarentaise.—We have seen above that the first Dominican teachers of Paris and Oxford carried on many of the traditions of the past ; and those whose theological works reflected the tendencies of the older scholasticism did not take part in the so-called conflict between Augustinism and Thomism.

The most important of the group was PETER OF TARENTAISE. Born the same year as St. Thomas (1225), he taught at Paris from 1259 to 1265 and from 1267 to 1269. Subsequently he became Archbishop of Lyons, Bishop of Ostia, and Pope under the name of Innocent V († 1276). He wrote commentaries on the *Sentences*, and four philosophical treatises *De Unitate Formæ, De materia cœli, De æternitate mundi, De intellectu et voluntate*. He stresses the practical side of theological science, combats the eternity of creation, but hesitates between the hylomorphic composition of immaterial substances and their simplicity, the former opinion being *planior, facilior*, and the latter *subtililior*.[2] He is also inclined to adopt the *rationales seminales*, but holds to the real distinction between the soul and its faculties.

At Oxford, RICHARD FITZACRE mentions in his commentaries on the *Sentences* the theory of the plurality of forms, opposing to it a quasi-Augustinian doctrine of unity : the soul is one unique form endowed with various activities. He died in 1248, before the birth of Thomism.[3]

---

[1] Published in *Bibliotheca Patrum*, Cologne, XV, 703. Cf. De Poorter, *Le traité Eruditio regum et principum*, p. VI, re-edited by Longpré in 1925.
[2] Edition of Bonaventure's works, Vol. II, p. 94, *Scholion*.
[3] Martin, *La question de l'unité de la forme substantielle dans le premier collège dominicain à Oxford* (*Revue Néo-Scolastique*, 1920, p. 107) gives extracts from Fitzacre. Cf. *op. cit.*, No. **235**.

258. Kilwardby.—The celebrated Dominican, Robert Kilwardby, taught at Paris and Oxford (1248-61), subsequently became the English Provincial of his Order (1261-72), Archbishop of Canterbury (1272-1278), and Cardinal († 1279). He commented on the *Sentences* of the Lombard (p. 327), the two *Analytics*, the *Sophistical Arguments*, the *Physics*, *Metaphysics*, and *De Anima* of Aristotle, and various works of Boethius. He also wrote two original treatises, *De unitate formarum*, and *De ortu et divisione philosophiæ*. The last-mentioned work is an improvement on the similar one by Gundisalvi, and is described by Baur as the most remarkable introduction to philosophy produced in the Middle Ages.[1] Kilwardby combines the classifications of the school of St. Victor with those of the Arabian School of Toledo. The work is distinguished not so much by the novelty of its ideas as by the author's efforts to show the peripatetic character of the scheme, and the careful way in which he makes a detailed study of the various branches of the subject and their reciprocal relations. The mechanical arts appear in practical philosophy side by side with ethics, while logic, described as *scientia rationalis* as opposed to the *scientia realis*, is incorporated in philosophy properly so called.[2]

We shall see later on that Kilwardby undertook the defence of several doctrines of the older scholasticism against the *novitates* of the Thomists. The letter which he wrote on this subject to Peter of Conflans[3] endeavours to justify the plurality of forms and the theory of the *rationes seminales*. He describes the latter as active germs with which prime matter is impregnated, and from which arise corporeal things.[4] In support

---

[1] *Op. cit.*, p. 368.

[2] Baur also thinks that Kilwardby was influenced by Thomas Aquinas. Judging by the systematic opposition of Kilwardby to Thomist ideas, we may well question this. The following is the scheme of philosophy according to Kilwardby: I. Philosophia rerum divinarum (naturalis, mathematica, metaphysica). II. Philosophia rerum humanarum : (1) Practica. (a) Ethica (solitaria, privata, publica); (b) Artes mechanicæ. (2) Logica, scientia rationalis. Here is Thomas Aquinas' scheme for purposes of comparison : I. Philosophia realis : (1) Theoretica vel speculativa (naturalis, mathematica, divina), (2) Practica (ethica vel monastica, œconomica, politica). II. Philosophia rationalis, logica.

[3] The greater part of the letter is published by Ehrle, *Der Augustinismus*, etc. in *Archiv. Litter. und Kirchengesch. Mittelalters*, V, 1889, p. 614–632, and the last portion by Birkenmajer, *Der Brief R. K.'s an P. von Conflans und die Streitschrift d. Agidius von Lessines*, in *BGPM*, XX, 5, pp. 60–64.

[4] " Evolutio illarum rationum et explicatio per res actuales fit per secula, materia naturalis prima . . . est quid dimensiones habens corporeas, impregnatum originalibus rationibus sive potentiis ex quibus producendi sunt actus omnium specificorum corporum." Ehrle, *op. cit.*, pp. 620, 623.

of the first thesis, so dear to all the upholders of tradition, he collects together arguments from the logical, physical, metaphysical, and theological orders. Kilwardby attributes to man three *formæ vitales*, all of them substantial, besides a form which gives to the body its plasticity.[1] He thinks it impossible without these complications to justify the superiority of the soul and the identity of the body of Christ during his life and the three days in the tomb. These various forms are hierarchically subordinated. We thus arrive at a sort of unity, but it is one which results from complex elements, and it is interesting to note that, adopting a controversial attitude, Kilwardby endeavours to give a suitable interpretation to the *positio de unitate formarum* which had already become a celebrated formula in his time.[2]

259. Bibliography.—A de Poorter, *Le traité Eruditio regum et principum de G. de Tournai* (*Les Philosophes Belges*, Vol. IX, 1914), text and study; *Un traité de Pédagogie médiévale, Le de modo addiscendi de G. de Tournai*, Notes and Extracts (*Revue Néo-Scol.*, 1922, pp. 195-229). The *Commentaries on the Sentences* by Peter of Tarentaise were published at Toulouse in 1469-1652. Baur gives a list of the questions treated in the *De ortu et divis. philos.* of Robert Kilwardby. Long extracts are given in Haureau, *Not. et extr. qqs. ms. lat.*, V, 116. On the works and Mss. of Robert Kilwardby, see Tocco, *op. cit.*, British Society of Franciscan Studies, pp. 94-96, and works by Ehrle and Birkenmajer.

Art. IV—Albert the Great

260. Life and Works.—Albert was born at Lauingen in Souabe, in 1195 according to some authorities, in 1206 or 1207

---

[1] *ibid.*, p. 635.

[2] " Positio de unitate formarum, nisi plus dicatur non satis est mihi. Scio tamen, quod unus homo unam habet formam, que non est una simplex, sed ex multis composita, ordinem ad invicem habentibus naturalem et sine quarum nulla perfectus homo esse potest, quarum ultima completiva et perfectiva totius aggregati est intellectus." (Birkenmajer's edition, p. 63) It is difficult to place another master of the older scholasticism, GERARD OF ABBEVILLE († 1271), who held an important position in the University of Paris (p. 260), and left eighteen *Quodlibeta* and twenty-two *Quæstiones de cogitatione* so far unpublished. These questions seem to contain little in the way of philosophy : " Si trova in essa non più quel po di Logica e di Dialettica," Ehrle, *S. Domenico* etc., p. 29, note. Pelzer has in preparation an edition of the *Quodlibeta* and the *Quæstiones de cogitatione*.

according to others.[1] He belonged to the family of the Counts of Bollstadt, and took the Dominican habit in 1223. A lengthy scientific education, combined with much travel, developed his natural talents. He tells us that he observed a comet in Saxony (1240), and went abroad to study the nature of the metals. From 1228 to 1245 he taught in turn at Cologne, Hildesheim, Freiburg, Ratisbon, Strasburg, and then again at Cologne, where in 1245 he had Thomas Aquinas for a pupil. It was at Paris, from 1245 to 1249, that he reached the height of his fame as a *magister theologiæ*. From this time dates the publication of his great scientific and philosophical works. They were for the most part completed in 1256, but he went on perfecting them till after the death of Thomas Aquinas.[2] When he returned to Cologne in 1248 to organize the *studium generale* there that had been decided upon by the General Chapter of the Order, Thomas Aquinas was again at his school. In 1252, Albert suggested to the *magister regens* of the Order at Paris that his eminent pupil should be promoted to the baccalaureate. From this moment his studies were distracted by his intervention as arbitrator in many affairs, and by the responsibilities of his position as Provincial of the German province from 1254 to 1257. In 1256 he resided at the Court of Anagni, and wrote his work against Averrhoism. In 1259 we find him at Valenciennes, where together with Thomas Aquinas and Peter of Tarentaise he drew up a new plan of studies for his Order. From 1260 to 1262 he was Bishop of Ratisbon ; next he undertook to preach a crusade in Bohemia, and fulfilled various other missions in Wurzburg and Strasburg. According to another hypothesis of Endres,[3] he declined in 1268 an offer of teaching again at Paris, preferring to retire to his convent at Cologne, where he taught, and which he made his habitual residence. In 1270 he was in correspondence with Giles of Lessines in connection with the theses condemned a few months later by Stephen Tempier (Art. VI, § 1), and when in 1277 the Archbishop of Paris condemned the doctrine of Thomas Aquinas, he set out for Paris in order to defend the

[1] According to E. Michel, Albert was born before 1200, and very probably in 1193, *Wann ist Albert der Grosse geboren* (*Zeitschr. f. Kathol. Theol.*, 1911, pp. 561–576). Endres gives about 1207 (*Das Geburtsjahr und die Chronologie in d. ersten Lebenshalfte Alberts d. Grossen* in Hist. *Jahrb.*, 1910, Vol. XXXXI, pp. 293–304).

[2] Mandonnet, *Siger*. Vol. VI of *Philosophes Belges*, p. 36, note. Endres puts the theological works about 1236 (Festgabe von Hertling). For chronological details, see Ueberweg-Baumgartner, *op. cit.*, p. 466.

[3] *Histor. polit. Blatter*, 1913, pp. 749–758.

teaching of his pupil. He died at Cologne on the 15th November, 1280. His contemporaries called him *Coloniensis*.

Even during his own lifetime, Albert acquired a universal reputation as a man of science, and had an immense influence on teaching.[1] Roger Bacon, who did not like him, bears witness to his fame (*primus magister de Philosophia*).[2] In Albert's case an exception was made to the general rule recognized in the thirteenth century, of not quoting living authors by name in scientific works (*allegare, pro auctoritatibus allegari*). He is named together with Aristotle, Avicenna, and Averrhoes.

The works of Albert form a library in themselves, as may be seen by consulting the catalogue of the Abbey of Stams.[3]

PHILOSOPHICAL WORKS.—Pangerl classifies these in three groups, in which the following are the most important works :

(i) Philosophia rationalis or Logica : *De Prædicabilibus, De Prædicamentis, De Sex Principiis, Perihermenias,* the two *Analytica, Topica, Libri Elenchorum.* The two treatises on syllogisms have not been published. To the above may be added a commentary on the *De divisione* of Boethius.[4]

(ii) Philosophia realis : *De Auditu Physico, De Cælo et Mundo, De Natura Locorum, De Proprietatibus Elementorum, De Generatione et Corruptione, De Meteoris, De Mineralibus, De Anima, De Sensu et Sensato, De Memoria et Reminiscentia, De Intellectu et Intelligibili, De Somno et Vigilia, De Spiritu et Respiratione, De Motibus Animalium, De Morte et Vita, De Vegetabilibus, De Animalibus,[5] De Unitate Intellectus contra Averroistas ; Metaphysica ; De Causis et Processu Universitatis.*

(iii) Philosophia moralis. Before writing the commentaries on the Nicomachean Ethics and the Politics which have been

---

[1] De Loë terminates his account of Albert's *regesta* with this well-deserved judgment : " Nullus eo tempore in tam diversis negotiis simul tantus exstitit." *De Vita et Scriptis,* etc.

[2] *Opus minus,* Brewer's edition, p. 327. " Nam sicut Aristoteles, Avicenna et Averroes allegantur in scholis, sic et ipse," *Opera inedita* (Brewer's edition) p. 30. In the same way, Giles of Lessines writes : " Hæc est positio multorum magnorum et præcise domni Alberti quodam Ratisponensis episcopi," *De unitate formæ,* edited by De Wulf, p. 36. Theoderic of Freiburg calls him : " Dominum Albertum illum famosum."

[3] Published by Denifle, *Quellen z. Gelehrtengesch. d. Predigerordens,* etc., No. **153,** § 3.

[4] Ed. princeps by De Loë, Bonn 1913.

[5] In 1258 Albert lectured at Cologne on the *De Animalibus,* in a series of questions collected by a student present, Conrad of Austria. For this unpublished account, see Pelzer, *Albert d. Grossen neu aufgefundene Quæstionem zu d. Aristotel. Schrift De animalibus (Zeitschrift für Kath. Theologie,* 1922, pp. 332–334).

printed, Albert lectured on the former treatise. St. Thomas collected these lectures and edited them when he was his pupil, probably at Cologne (1248-1252).[1]

To this list we may add the treatises *De Fato*, *De Forma Resultante in Speculo*, *De Passionibus Æris*, and *De Potentiis Animæ*.[2] On the other hand, the *Philosophia Pauperum*, attributed to Albert, and which for a long time served as a manual in Germany, was the work of a compiler, Albert von Orlamünde.[3]

The *theological works* contain many philosophical doctrines. Besides sermons and commentaries on the Old and New Testaments, Albert composed in particular a *Summa de Creaturis* in five parts (*Summa de Quattuor Coæquævis*, *De Homine*, *De Bono* or *De Virtutibus*, *De Sacramentis*, *De Resurrectione*)[4]; a Commentary on the *Sentences* of Peter Lombard (the second book was written about 1246 and the fourth in 1249) ; a *Summa Theologiæ* begun after 1270 and never completed.

Among his *mystical works* we must mention in the first place his Commentaries on all the works of pseudo-Dionysius (the Commentary on the *De Divinis Nominibus* is unpublished save an extract forming the *opusculum De Pulchro* (wrongly attributed to St. Thomas). Grabmann has restored to John of Kastl, a Benedictine of the Bavarian Abbey of this name, (about 1400), the *De Adhærendo Deo*, wrongly ascribed to Albert.[5]

Pelzer distinguishes three periods in Albert's literary work : the period of youth, marked by the *Summa de Creaturis* and the Commentaries on the *Sentences* ; the second, devoted to

---

[1] A *Tractatus de Natura Boni*, unfinished, prior to 1245, discovered by Pelzer (*Theolog. Quartalschrift*, 1920, pp. 64–90), is chiefly theological in character. As for the unpublished course of lectures which Pelzer has discovered (see *Revue néo-Scolastique*, 1922, Aug. and Nov.), this has the peculiarity not only of belonging at once to master and pupil in common, but also that of being the first commentary on the *Ethics* employing the double method of the *Expositio litteræ* and the *Disputatio* or *Quæstio*. Moreover, it makes use of the complete version by Robert Grosseteste, as well as the rich documentation accompanying this. The *Quæstiones* in this course (up to chapter 4 of Book III, in other editions chapter 2) are contained separately in MS. 1236 of the Municipal Library of Troyes.

[2] Pelzer, *Neue philosoph. Schriften A. des Grossen*. (*Philos. Jahrb.*, 1923, p. 150).

[3] Grabmann, *BGPM*, XX, 2.

[4] Only the first two parts have been printed. The others have been found by Grabmann, *Drei ungedruckte Teile der Summa de creaturis Alberts d. Grossen* (*Quellen u. Forschungen zur Geschichte d. Dominikanerordens in Deutschland*, Heft 13, Leipzig, 1919).

[5] *Der Benediktinermystiker Joannes von Kastl, de. Verfasser d. Buchleins De adhærendo Deo* (*Theolog. Quartalschrift*, 1920, pp. 186–235).

the Commentaries on philosophical works ; and the works of his old age, to which belongs the *Summa Theologica*.[1]

261. Albert's personality.—Albert the Great was a unique figure in the history of ideas in the thirteenth century. His was a universal mind, and he collected together a considerable mass of material of which others made use ; he opened up new paths which his successors or contemporaries explored. As a commentator on Aristotle, the Arabians and neo-Platonists, he rendered incomparable services to his age. As a man of science he was one of the creators of experimental science, and gave to it the great repute which it was henceforth to enjoy. This is perhaps his greatest title to fame. The whole of the thirteenth century profited by his work. Again, Albert endeavoured to inspire scientific curiosity in others. He laboured hard to introduce new traditions in his order, and resisted those antagonists to philosophy (cf. p. 261).

On the other hand, Albert's philosophical doctrines lack coherence ; and if systemization is the criterion of the value of a system of philosophy, we must say that he did not succeed in controlling his thought. For when he comments on Aristotle, he is an Aristotelian ;[2] when he comes to the neo-Platonists he rallies to the Alexandrine ideas. In addition, on many points he remains faithful to the older scholasticism. It would require a vigorous effort to fuse together and think out all these materials, and Albert was not capable of this. He preferred to gather together these heterogeneous elements without sacrificing any of them. His was the temperament of a compiler and a widely-read man.[3]

262. Albert as a man of science.—Like Roger Bacon, Albert loudly proclaimed in many places the rights of observation, experiment and induction, and in this way he taught his con-

[1] *op. cit.*, p. 164.

[2] G. Manser, *A.'s Stellung zur Autorität seiner Vorgänger* (*Divus Thomas und Ihr. Phil.*, 1914, h. 1. p. 75).

[3] We may apply to his philosophic synthesis as a whole that which Schneider says of his psychology : " Nothing is more erroneous than to regard it as a closed and unique system. Certainly Aristotle's influence is predominant, but the co-existence of traditional and Arabian elements render it impossible to speak of one Albertine psychology." *BGPM*, p. x and 1. " Albert's influence and glory consist not so much in the construction of an original system of philosophy as in the wisdom and effort he displayed in bringing to the knowledge of the lettered class of the Middle Ages a summary of the knowledge so far acquired, in the creation of a new and powerful intellectual movement in his century, and in definitely winning over to Aristotle the best minds of the Middle Ages." Mandonnet, *Dict. théol. cath.*, Vol. 1, col. 672. Baeumker speaks in the same sense (*Zeitschrift f. Psych.*, 1908, p. 440) in connection with Schneider's work.

temporaries to turn their attention to nature : " oportet experimentum non in uno modo, sed secundum omnes circumstantias probare."[1] He was familiar with geography, astronomy, mineralogy, alchemy, medicine, zoology, and botany. But his most remarkable contributions were made to the last two sciences. His treatises *De Animalibus* tell us when he has been able to observe things himself, and when he has been obliged to rely on others worthy of belief ; he is full of references to subjects in which philosophic considerations are prominent, as for instance the difference between reason and instinct, and between man and the ape (XXI, tr. 1, cap. 3).[2]

263. Albert as a commentator on the ancient Arabian and Jewish writers.—Albert conceived and carried out the project of " adapting Aristotle to the use of the Latin races."[3] In order to render him intelligible, he made an extensive paraphrase of all the treatises of the Stagirite in due order and under the titles of the original works. " He did not undertake to comment on the text itself of Aristotle, but he drew up a general scheme, borrowed from the latter, and carried it out very fully, incorporating material from Aristotle and his commentators as well as his own observations."[4] " The printed commentaries by Albert and St. Thomas," says Pelzer, " do not contain questions, but differ in their method of exposition. Albert has recourse to paraphrase by interpolating, so to speak, the Latin translation from the Arabic or Greek. The only exception is the Politics, in which he expounds Aristotle after the manner of St. Thomas, dividing and subdividing the text into its parties in order to discover throughout the thought and intention of the author."[5]

Albert succeeded in his task, for we may say that it was he who introduced the educated classes to the riches of the peripatetic and Arabian systems. To undertake such a task called for a certain amount of courage if we bear in mind the mistrust which certain ecclesiastics harboured in connection

[1] *Ethic.*, lib. 6, tr. 2, c. 25. Cf. : " Experimentum enim solum certificat in talibus," (*De Vegetabilibus*, Jessen's edition, p. 339). Cf. Michael, *Geschichte d. deutschen Volkes von XIII Jahrh.*, III, 446 *et seq.*

[2] Many special works have been written on the place occupied by Albert the Great in each of these sciences. A list will be found in Michael, *op. cit.* Cf. Ueberweg-Baumgartner.

[3] " Nostra intentio est omnes dictas partes (physicam, metaphysicam et mathematicam) facere Latinis intelligibiles. *Phys.* lib, I, tr. 1, cap. 1.

[4] Mandonnet, *Siger*, Vol. 11, p. 38.

[5] A. Pelzer, *Un cours inédit d'A. le Grand sur la morale à Nicom. recuilli et rédigé par S. Th. d'Aquin* (*Révue néo-Scol.*, 1922), p. 347. On the double method employed in this unpublished course, see later on.

with Aristotle, and the heretical nature of several peripatetic theories.

It is important to note that Albert subjected Aristotelianism to a doctrinal purification. With greater consistence than William of Auvergne, he corrected or completed Aristotle in the direction of scholasticism. Thus he clearly teaches personal immortality, and replaces the idea of the first mover by that of the Infinite Being. From another point of view, Albert tends to follow Alfarabi and Avicenna in their interpretations of Aristotle, while at the same time he rejects the anti-scholastic doctrines of Averrhoes and Avencebrol.

The method of extensive paraphrasing which he employs makes his exegesis difficult to follow, and does not make it easy to grasp his own ideas on any point. In some places his commentaries are clearly only the objective exposition of the author's thought. At other times he shows that he himself holds the theory he is explaining.[1] The value of the paraphrase varies from one passage to another, and could only be determined by a monograph on the subject.

His didactic methods present other imperfections. His glosses are too long ; though of course it must be remembered that the works reproduce an oral exposition, and that the master is aiming at popularizing his subject. Again, he allows himself to be involved in endless digressions (*et præter hoc digressiones faciemus* is a favourite formula), especially in the *De Anima* and the *Metaphysics*. His language is uncultivated, and often lacks precision.

In addition to Aristotle, the Arabians and the Jews, Albert knew Plato's *Timæus*. He quotes more Jewish and Arabian writers than any other scholastic, and does not confine himself to philosophical writers.[2] At the same time he makes unpardonable mistakes in connection with the history of ancient philosophy.

264. Albert as a neo-Platonist commentator.—In the treatise *De causis et processu universitatis* we find a compact group of neo-Platonist theories evidently inspired by the *Liber de causis*, and in which we see evidence of a possibly direct

---

[1] See Schneider's Introduction, *Die Psychol. A. d. Grossen.* In the *Summa de Homine* and the *Summa Theolog.* we find psychological ideas which are peculiar to Albert ; in the *De Anima, Libri Ethicorum, and De Intellectu et Intelligibili*, a choice has to be made. Schneider suggests this criterion : Albert allows all those theories which can be reconciled with dogma (pp. 3–7).

[2] Guttmann, *op. cit.*, No. **140**, pp. 47–120 : *Seine Kenntniss d. nicht-philosoph. jüdischen Litteratur.*

contact with the *Theological Elements* of Proclus. It is not a question of a few doctrines concerning light and goodness, as in the case of his predecessors, but of a whole system of beings arranged in a descending hierarchical order, the lower engendered by the higher, from the intelligences presiding over the motion of the spheres down to the world-soul and corporeal substances. Certainly Albert purifies all these doctrines from their original Pantheistic tendencies, but he adopts a great number of ideas[1] which cannot be harmonized with the scholastic system of the universe.

God, at the summit of the scale, is not, as in Plotinus, the One or the First, preceding self-consciousness, but the *Intellectus universaliter agens ;* the uncreated light " quæ nunquam cessat illuminare causatum suum."[2] His essence (*quod est*) is His existence.[3] By a creative act which Albert calls *fluxus, processio, emanatio formæ a primo fonte*, God produces the *intelligentia* or the *primum causatum*, which collaborates in the production of the intelligences or inferior lights. This is in accordance with the important process explained in the *Liber de causis* : the inferior exercises its influence in concourse and in dependence upon its immediate superior.[4]

It is important to note carefully here that the Divine *esse* does not spread itself out in the *intelligentia*. The latter exists by its own distinct existence—an existence which may be called an obscure light, and which is derived from the *intellectus purus universaliter agens*.[5] Albert takes care to point out that he has constantly opposed pantheism—*in multis locis*.

The *Intelligentia*, or the first *causatum*, already contains within itself the reason of diversity and finitude : *non ad plenum comprehendet causam*.[6] With the concourse of God and the *Intelligentia* the series of inferior intelligences united to spheres is produced, in descending stages which may be compared to the degradations of light. Sometimes the active intellect, the soul, and nature are included in this process. In this exposition of the *ordo in gradibus entium*,[7] Albert sets

---

[1] " Often enough he speaks in his own name " Baeumker, *Witelo*, p. 407, note. He gives a masterly treatment of Albert's neo-Platonism.

[2] Borgnet's edition, Vol. X. p. 275 b. Cf. *Liber de causis*.

[3] " Causa enim prima lumen purum est, super quod non est aliud lumen, propter quod in ipsa idem est esse et quod est," p. 419 b.

[4] " Si secundum in ultimum ulterius fluat vel influat, non fluit nisi in virtute primi," p. 413, a.

[5] " Quidam dixerunt omnia esse unum et quod diffusio primi in omnibus est esse eorum," p. 419 b.

[6] p. 507, a.   [7] p. 419, a.

forth two or three schemes more or less complicated, taken from different sources, and which he adopts in turn.[1] Corporeal substances come into being under the action of the solar light, which produces the forms in collaboration with the Intelligence immediately superior.[2] This explains why they are themselves luminous in nature : the *forma corporeitatis* is a light. Moreover, to explain the specific nature and individuality of bodies, this form must be combined in each case with a number of other forms, which takes us back to the mentality of the older scholasticism. Albert never clearly stated his mind on the unification of the many forms in a body.

As a neo-Platonist commentator, Albert evidently delighted in the metaphysical descriptions and metaphors of the *Liber de causis*. Just as he introduced Aristotle to the Latins, so also he put into circulation a goodly number of Arabian and neo-Platonist doctrines connected with the emanation of things which, when developed and accentuated by a group of his successors, became the starting-point of Latin neo-Platonism.

In another work, *De Intellectu et Intelligibili*, Albert sets forth with equal satisfaction the neo-Platonist theory of knowledge.

265. Albert and Augustinism.—Lastly, on a number of questions, Albert remains faithful to Augustinism. In particular he adopts the *rationes seminales*, and we shall see that in the theory of matter and form he makes doctrinal concessions which it is impossible to harmonize with peripateticism.

266. Some philosophic doctrines.—The series of works written by Albert show that he adopted the classification of philosophical sciences current in his time. He held to the doctrine of matter and form, and interpreted it in a peripatetic sense, but did not carry it out to its ultimate consequences. Without actually employing the term *materia*, Albert holds that separated substances (the angels) are composed of subtantial parts, and that a *fundamentum* is required for their form, although this foundation does not imply any relations with quantity.[3] This doctrine is similar to that of St. Bonaventure, and also links up Albert with the older scholasticism.[4] On the other hand, he did not exclude the plurality of forms from his meta-

---

[1] Baeumker, *op. cit.*, p. 412.

[2] Cf. Baeumker, *op. cit.*, p. 412.

[3] " Ergo necesse est ponere substantiam communem quæ sit in eis ; et hæc meo judicio non dicetur materia, sed fundamentum." *In II Sent.*, dist. 3, a. iv.

[4] This is the view held by the editors of St. Bonaventure, Vol. II, pp. 93–94.

physics, and hence his teaching on the unity of a being is not
the same as that of Thomas Aquinas. It has been well said[1]
that the synthetic solutions of the problem of universals were
formulated by Albert before Thomas Aquinas, with this peculiar
feature, that the constitution or essence of things is independent
of its realization, and anterior to the latter.[2]

The concept of infinity, completing the Aristotelian notion
of pure actuality, is the centre of his natural theology.[3] The
existence of God is proved by *a posteriori* arguments, not by
the mere analysis of concepts. God is an individual, a creative
Intelligence, who produces inferior beings with the concourse
of the superior intelligences (p. 401). Albert combats the doctrine that matter is necessarily eternal, but he thinks that
reason is incapable of demonstrating either the eternity or the
commencement of the world in time : *nec putamus demonstra-
bile esse unum vel alterum.*[4]

The study of corporeal movement and of the substantial
changes of bodies, which succeed one another in a rhythmic
evolution dominated by finality, are studied in a peripatetic
spirit.[5] But Albert remains faithful to the older scholasticism
on two questions : (i) he adopts the *rationes seminales*, and
thereby departs from the peripatetic notion of prime matter
as a simple potentiality ; (ii) he admits the permanence of
the elementary forms in a compound, and the consequent
plurality of forms.[6]   Similarly, he holds that the soul is
not the *forma corporeitatis* (see below).

According to one of the best historians,[7] the co-existence
of Augustinian and Arabian elements, badly combined with the

---

[1] Willmann, *Gesch. d. Idealismus*, II, 357.

[2] " Cum sit de aptitudine essentiæ quæ est ante materiam et compositum,
patet quod nullo existente homine particulari, adhuc est vera, homo est
animal." *De Intellectu et Intelligibili, tr.* II, cap. III.

[3] Guttmann, *op. cit.*, p. 83.

[4] Phys., VIII, tr. 1, c. 13, Vol. II, p. 332. Cf. A. Rohner, *BGPM*, XI,
5, p. 45–84.

[5] This finality, says Schneider, has a neo-Platonist sense in certain places
in the *Ethics* and the *Metaphysics*. " Everything tends towards the Divine,
that is to say, the Sovereign Good, which constitutes the supreme beatitude.
. . . This idea is developed by Albert in a neo-Platonist sense, although he does
not seem to be aware that he is departing from Aristotle." (*op. cit.*, p. 281).

[6] *De cœlo et mundo*, Lib. III, tr. 2, c. 1. In particular, he says : " Elementorum formae dupliciter sunt, scilicet primæ et secundæ.   Primæ quidem
sunt a quibus est *esse* elementi substantiale sine contrarietate et secundæ
sunt a quibus est esse elementi et *actio*. Et quoad primas formas, salvantur
meo judicio in compositio . . . et quoad secundas formas sive quoad secundum
esse non remanent in actu sed in potentia." Cf. *De generatione et corrupt.*,
I, tr. 6, c. 8. This is Avicenna's theory.

[7] Schneider, *op. cit.*, pp. 2 *et seq.*

fundamental ideas of Peripateticism, deprives Albert's psychology of all organic unity, and it is not unusual to find the philosopher defending opposite ideas in one and the same work.[1] The human soul is not composed of spiritual matter and a form ; it is the substantial form, that is, the first actuality of the body (Aristotle). There are not three souls in man, as held by those who were consistent in the doctrine of the plurality of forms, but one single vital principle. Still, Albert somewhat illogically refuses to attribute the state of corporeity to the determining influence of the soul, although we do not find in his works any mention of a *forma corporeitatis*.[2] The soul is substantial form by the totality of its being, and in particular all its intellectual faculties are immanent (against Averrhoes). On the question whether the union of the soul with the body is immediate, as Peripateticism demands, or is rather effected by intermediaries (*media*) as certain Augustinians hold, Albert subscribes alternately to two opposed opinions.[3] Considered in itself, the soul is really distinct from its faculties.[4] It is immaterial and immortal, chiefly by reason of the independence of its higher operations with regard to matter (Aristotelian proof).

Three groups of faculties correspond to the operations of the vegetative, sensitive (cognitive and appetitive) and intellectual life (knowledge and will). Vegetative life comprises the *potentiæ nutritiva, augmentativa, generativa*, the functions of which the learned Dominican studies at great length. In plants and animals, the vegetative and sensitive soul appears as a result of the unfolding of the *ratio seminalis;* but the human soul, which includes in itself the perfection of the lower vital principles, is created by God. The sensible faculties are in part external (*vires apprehensivæ de foris*), and among these Albert includes the *sensus communis;* others are internal (*vires apprehensivæ de intus, imaginatio, æstimatio, memoria, reminiscentia*). We are given long physiological dissertations on dreams, the states of sleeping and waking (*proprietates animæ sensibilis*), and the functions of the brain. As for the intellectual faculties, the active and passive intellects, Albert deals with these in the

---

[1] *op. cit.*, p. 8. The following are the sources for Albert's psychology : *Summa de Homine*, a systematic exposition, and passages in the *Summa Theologica*, to which must be added the Commentaries on the psychological works of Aristotle.

[2] *ibid.* p. 27.

[3] *op. cit.*, p. 36.

[4] In the *De Potentiis Animæ*, he described the theory of the real distinction as *solemnior et verior*. Pelzer, *Neue* etc., p. 165.

peripatetic manner.[1] Arabian monopsychism in its various
forms is the subject of repeated refutations. In a special
treatise (*De Unitate Intellectus contra Averroistas*), in the *De
Natura et Origine Animæ*, and indeed throughout his writings,
he protests against this " error animo absurdus et pessimus et
facile improbabilis."

On the appetitive faculties, and especially on the will, his
doctrine varies. Freedom is sometimes the fundamental
prerogative of the *intellectus adaptus* (i.e., the intelligence
endowed with knowledge), and sometimes that of the *libera
voluntas*. Here we have the intellectualist (Aristotle) and voluntarist (Augustine) points of view.

Albert's works contain a number of ethical doctrines insuffi-
ciently co-ordinated.[2] The *liberum arbitrium* decides between
the goods presented by the reason. The synderesis is called
" a permanent rectitude inclining us to judge in the proper
way," while the *conscientia*, the fruit of an actual judgment,
can err.[3]

267. The disciples of Albert.—John of Freiburg, John of
Lichtenberg, Giles of Lessines, Ulric of Strasburg, Thomas
Aquinas, and a great number of other Dominicans attended
Albert's lectures. In particular there was one who was a
faithful disciple, and who speaks of him in enthusiastic terms
(*nostri temporis stupor et miraculum*). This was HUGH RIPELIN
OF STRASBURG, author of a *Compendium Theologicæ Veritatis*
in which we find the Augustinian doctrines of his master. This
treatise enjoyed a certain reputation, and in the beginning of
the fourteenth century, the Franciscan JOHANNES RIGALDUS
incorporated numerous extracts from it into his *Compendium
Pauperis Fratris Minoris*.

Albert was a pioneer, but not the head of a school, for his
hearers and immediate successors split up the collection of
disparate doctrines found in the master's works : some retained
the group of neo-Platonist doctrines and inaugurated a movement of ideas which we shall speak of as the Latin neo-
Platonism. Others developed the Aristotelian elements which
Albert utilized, and these all depended upon Thomas Aquinas.

Thus we may say that Albert's speculations, manifesting as
they did such diverse philosophical tendencies, gave rise to two

---

[1] *op. cit.*, p. 233.

[2] Cf. H. Lauer, *Die Moraltheologie Albert's* etc. Fribourg, 1911.

[3] " Synderesis est rectitudo manens in singulis viribus concordans recti-
tudine primæ." *Summa de Creaturis*, Vol. XIX, p. 321.

principal currents of ideas differing in importance, which lasted throughout the thirteenth and fourteenth centuries.

268. Bibliography.—The edition of Albert's works undertaken by the Dominican Jammy, comprises 21 folio volumes (Lyons, 1651). Borgnet began to reprint it in 1890 (36 volumes). Neither of these editions is critical. M. Weiss, *Primordia novæ bibliographiæ B. Alberti Magni*, 2nd edn., Paris, 1905. Indicates the *incipit* of the authentic and doubtful works, manuscripts, and editions. Mandonnet points out that the three last parts of the *Summa Theologica* remain unpublished (*Siger*, Vol. VI of *Philos. Belges*, p. 37, which gives a complete bibliography). Jessen has edited the *De Vegetabilibus*, Berlin, 1867. A critical edition of the XXVI books of the *De Animalibus* by H. Stadler from the autograph manuscript of Cologne (*BGPM*, XV and XVI) gives valuable data, distinguishes between the text of Aristotle, Michael Scot's version and Albert's own commentaries by means of a typographical artifice. By the same : edition of the *Liber de Principiis Motus Progressivi* (Progr. Munich, 1909) ; De Loë has edited the commentary on the *De Divisione* of Boethius (Bonn, 1913) ; Mandonnet, *Siger*, gives the *De Quindecim Problematibus*. De Loë, *De Vita et Scriptis B. Alberti Magni*, in *Anal. Bollandiana*, Vol. 19, p. 257, and Vol. 20, p. 273, enumerates the early fourteenth to sixteenth century sources for Albert's life, and edits an unpublished life of 1483. Also gives a clear table of Albert's *regesta*. Making use of these materials, Michael, *Gesch. d. deutschen Volkes wahrend d. XIII. Jahrh.*, III (1903), gives a detailed biography of Albert. Pangerl, *Studien über A. den Grossen* (*Zeitschr. Kath. Theol.*, XXXVI, 2, 3 and 4, 1912) ; Pelster, *Kritische Studien z. Leben u. zu den Schriften A. d. G.* (*Stimmen d. Zeit*, Ergänzungsh (1920). This has been completed in : *Ergänzungen u. Berichtigungen* (*Zeitschr. f. Kath. Theol.*, 1923). G. von Hertling, *Alb. Magnus*, Festschrift Cologne, 1880. New edition in *BGPM*, XIV, 5-6. Van Weddingen, *A. le Grand, maître de Thomas d'Aquin* (Brussels, 1881), article by Mandonnet in *Dict. Théol. Cath.* ; Lauer, *Die Moral theologie A. d. Grossen nach d. Quellen dargestellt* (*BGPM*, IV, 5-6), an excellent monograph, studies the peripatetic, neo-Platonist, and Augustinian elements ; Mansion, *L'induction chez Albert le Grand* (*Revue néo-Scol.*, 1906) ; Pouchet, *Histoire des sciences naturelles au moyen âge, ou Albert le Grand et son époque* (Paris, 1853) : Pfeifer, *Harmonische Beziehungen* *zwischen Scholastik u. moderner Naturwissenschaft mit specieller Rucksicht auf Albertus Magnus u. Th. von Aquino* (Augsburg. 1881) ; Fellner, *A. Magnus als Botaniker* (Wien, 1881) : H. Stadler, *Alb. Magnus als selbständiger Naturforscher*, Forschungen zur Geschichte Baierns, Vol. 14, 1906, pp. 95-114.

Endres, *Chronologische Untersuchungen zu den philosp. Kommentaren A. d. G.* in *Festgabe v. Hertling*, 1913, pt. 96-108 ; Birkenmajer, *Zur Bibliographie Albert d. Grossen*, in Philos. Jahrb., 1925, pp. 270-272.

M. Grabmann, *Studien u. Ulrich von Strasburg*, 1 : Leben u. Personlichkeit (*Zeitsch. f. Kath. Theol.* 1905).

L. Pfleger, *Hugo v. Strasburg und das Compendium theologiæ veritatis* (*Zeitschr. Kath. Theol.* 1904) ; R. Klingseis, *Das Aristotelische Tugendprincip der richtigen Mitte in der Scholastik* (*Divus Thomas*, VIII, 2), study on Ulric of Strasburg and the 5th and 6th books of the *Summa*. Extracts from the *Summa* of Ulric are given in Baeumker, *Der Anteil des Elsass*, etc.

INDEX

The numbers indicate pages. Numbers in leaded type refer to pages on which the persons in question are specially dealt with.

BRISTOL : BURLEIGH LTD., AT THE BURLEIGH PRESS.

171